The Social History of
Crime and Punishment
in America

The Social History of Crime and Punishment in America

AN ENCYCLOPEDIA

Wilbur R. Miller ■ EDITOR

State University of New York at Stony Brook

$SAGE reference

Los Angeles | London | New Delhi
Singapore | Washington DC

Los Angeles | London | New Delhi
Singapore | Washington DC

FOR INFORMATION:

SAGE Publications, Inc.
2455 Teller Road
Thousand Oaks, California 91320
E-mail: order@sagepub.com

SAGE Publications India Pvt. Ltd.
B 1/I 1 Mohan Cooperative Industrial Area
Mathura Road, New Delhi 110 044
India

SAGE Publications Ltd.
1 Oliver's Yard
55 City Road
London EC1Y 1SP
United Kingdom

SAGE Publications Asia-Pacific Pte. Ltd.
3 Church Street
#10-04 Samsung Hub
Singapore 049483

Vice President and Publisher: Rolf A. Janke
Senior Editor: Jim Brace-Thompson
Project Editor: Tracy Buyan
Cover Designer: Bryan Fishman
Editorial Assistant: Michele Thompson
Reference Systems Manager: Leticia Gutierrez
Reference Systems Coordinators: Laura Notton,
    Anna Villasenor
Marketing Manager: Kristi Ward

Golson Media
President and Editor: J. Geoffrey Golson
Director, Author Management: Susan Moskowitz
Production Director: Mary Jo Scibetta
Layout Editors: Kenneth Heller, Stephanie Larson,
    Oona Patrick, Lois Rainwater
Copy Editors: Mary Le Rouge, Holli Fort
Proofreader: Barbara Paris
Indexer: J S Editorial

Copyright © 2012 by SAGE Publications, Inc.

All rights reserved. No part of this book may be reproduced or utilized in any form or by any means, electronic or mechanical, including photocopying, recording, or by any information storage and retrieval system, without permission in writing from the publisher.

Library of Congress Cataloging-in-Publication Data

The social history of crime and punishment in America : an encyclopedia /
Wilbur R. Miller, general editor.
    v. cm.
 Includes bibliographical references and index.
 ISBN 978-1-4129-8876-6 (cloth)
    1. Crime--United States--History--Encyclopedias. 2. Punishment--United
States--History--Encyclopedias. I. Miller, Wilbur R., 1944-
 HV6779.S63 2012
 364.97303--dc23
                            2012012418

12 13 14 15 16 10 9 8 7 6 5 4 3 2 1

Contents

Volume 1
List of Articles   *vii*
Reader's Guide   *xvii*
About the Editor   *xxvi*
List of Contributors   *xxvii*
Introduction   *xxxv*
Chronology   *xxxix*

Articles
A	*1*	C	*193*
B	*91*	D	*427*

Volume 2
List of Articles   *vii*

Articles
D (*cont.*)	*463*	H	*727*
E	*515*	I	*811*
F	*573*	J	*869*
G	*661*	K	*937*

Volume 3
List of Articles   *vii*

Articles
L	*975*	O	*1269*
M	*1053*	P	*1315*
N	*1175*	Q	*1475*

Volume 4
List of Articles *vii*

Articles

R	*1479*	W	*1899*
S	*1595*	X	*1979*
T	*1745*	Y	*1983*
U	*1835*	Z	*1987*
V	*1857*		

Volume 5
List of Primary Documents *vii*

Primary Documents

1600 to 1776	*1991*
1777 to 1800	*2029*
1801 to 1850	*2063*
1851 to 1900	*2097*
1901 to 1920	*2161*
1921 to 1940	*2201*
1941 to 1960	*2263*
1961 to 1980	*2337*
1981 to 2000	*2407*
2001 to 2012	*2443*

Glossary *2487*
Resource Guide *2499*
Index *2507*
Photo Credits *2606*

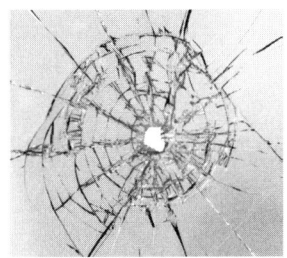

List of Articles

A
Ableman v. Booth
Abortion
Abrams v. United States
Adair v. United States
Adams, John (Administration of)
Adams, John Quincy (Administration of)
Adultery
Adversarial Justice
African Americans
Alabama
Alaska
Alcatraz Island Prison
Alien and Sedition Acts of 1798
American Bar Association
American Civil Liberties Union
American Law Institute
American Revolution and Criminal Justice
An American Tragedy
Anarchists
Anti-Federalist Papers
Antitrust Law
Appeals
Appellate Courts
Arizona
Arkansas
Arpaio, Joseph M.
Arraignment
Arthur, Chester (Administration of)
Articles of Confederation

Atlanta, Georgia
Attica
Auburn State Prison
Augustus, John
Autobiographies, Criminals'
Automobile and the Police
Aviation and Transportation Security Act of 2001

B
Bail and Bond
Bail Reform Act
Bailey, F. Lee
Bakker, Jim
Ballistics
Baltimore, Maryland
Barron v. Mayor of Baltimore
Beaumont, Gustave de
Bedford Hills Correctional Facility
Berkowitz, David
Bertillon System
Bible
Bigamy/Polygamy
Bill of Rights
Billy the Kid
Birmingham, Alabama
Black Panthers
Blackstone, William
Blood Sports
Blue Laws. *See* State Blue Laws
Bodie of Liberties

Bodine, Polly
Boles, Charles
Bonnie and Clyde
Book of the General Lawes & Libertyes
Booth, John Wilkes
Bootlegging
Borden, Lizzie
Border Patrol
Boston, Massachusetts
Bounty Hunters
Bowers v. Hardwick
Brandenburg v. Ohio
Brennan, William J., Jr.
Brocius, William
Brockway, Zebulon
Brown v. Board of Education
Brown v. Mississippi
Buchanan, James (Administration of)
Buck v. Bell
Bundy, Ted
Buntline, Ned
Bureau of Alcohol, Tobacco, Firearms and Explosives
Buren, Martin Van (Administration of)
Burger, Warren
Burglary, Contemporary
Burglary, History of
Burglary, Sociology of
Bush, George H. W. (Administration of)
Bush, George W. (Administration of)
Byrnes, Thomas

C
California
Camden, New Jersey
Caminetti v. United States
Capital Punishment
Capone, Al
Carter, Jimmy (Administration of)
Chain Gangs and Prison Labor
Chandler v. Florida
Chapman, Mark David
Chicago, Illinois
Chicago Seven/Democratic National Convention of 1968
Child Abuse, Contemporary
Child Abuse, History of
Child Abuse, Sociology of
Child Murderers, History of
Children, Abandoned

Children's Rights
Chillicothe Correctional Institution
Chinese Americans
Chinese Exclusion Act of 1882
Chisholm v. Georgia
Christie, Agatha
Cincinnati, Ohio
Citizen Participation on Juries
Civil Disobedience
Civil Rights Act of 1866
Civil Rights Act of 1875
Civil Rights Laws
Clayton Anti-Trust Act of 1914
Clemency
Cleveland, Grover (Administration of)
Cleveland, Ohio
Clinton, William (Administration of)
Clinton Correctional Facility
Code of Silence
Codification of Laws
Cohens v. Virginia
Coker v. Georgia
Colonial Charters and Grants
Colonial Courts
Colorado
Common Law Origins of Criminal Law
Community Policing and Relations
Community Service
Compton, California
Computer Crime
Comstock Law
Confession
Confidence Games and Frauds
Connecticut
Constitution of the United States of America
Convention on the Rights of the Child
Convict Lease System
Coolidge, Calvin (Administration of)
Corporal Punishment
Corrections
Corruption, Contemporary
Corruption, History of
Corruption, Sociology of
Counterfeiting
Court of Common Pleas
Court of Oyer and Terminer
Court of Quarter Sessions
Courts
Courts of Indian Offenses
Coverture, Doctrine of

Crabtree v. State
Crime and Arrest Statistics Analysis
Crime in America, Causes
Crime in America, Distribution
Crime in America, Types
Crime Prevention
Crime Rates
Crime Scene Investigation
Criminalization and Decriminalization
Criminology
Critical Legal Studies Movement
Cruel and Unusual Punishment
Cruelty to Animals
Cummings, Homer
Cunningham, Emma
Customs Service as Police
Czolgosz, Leon

D
Dahmer, Jeffrey
Darrow, Clarence
Davis v. State
Dayton, Ohio
Death Row
Declaration of Independence
Defendant's Rights
Delaware
Democratic National Convention of 1968. *See* Chicago Seven/Democratic National Convention of 1968
Dennis v. United States
Deportation
DeSalvo, Albert
Detection and Detectives
Deterrence, Theory of
Detroit, Michigan
Devery, William
Dewey, Thomas E.
Dillard v. the State of Georgia
Dillinger, John
Dime Novels, Pulps, Thrillers
Discretionary Decision Making
District Attorney
Domestic Violence, Contemporary
Domestic Violence, History of
Domestic Violence, Sociology of
Douglas, William O.
Dred Scott v. Sandford
Drinking and Crime
Drug Abuse and Addiction, Contemporary
Drug Abuse and Addiction, History of
Drug Abuse and Addiction, Sociology of
Drug Enforcement Administration
Due Process
Duren v. Missouri
Dyer Act

E
Earp, Wyatt
Eastern State Penitentiary
Eddy, Thomas
Eisenhower, Dwight D. (Administration of)
Eisenstadt v. Baird
Electric Chair, History of
Electronic Surveillance
Elkins Act of 1903
Elmira Prison
Embezzlement
Emergency Quota Act of 1921
Enforcement Acts of 1870–1871
English Charter of Liberties of 1100
Enron
Entrapment
Environmental Crimes
Equality, Concept of
Espionage
Espionage Act of 1917
Estes v. Texas
Ethics in Government Act of 1978
Everleigh Sisters
Executions

F
Famous Trials
Fear of Crime
Federal Bureau of Investigation
Federal Common Law of Crime
Federal Policing
Federal Prisons
Federal Rules of Criminal Procedure
Federalist Papers
Felonies
Ferguson, Colin
Fillmore, Millard (Administration of)
Film, Crime in
Film, Police in
Film, Punishment in
Fingerprinting
Fish and Game Laws
Fletcher v. Peck

Florida
Floyd, Charles Arthur
Ford, Gerald (Administration of)
Forensic Science
Fornication Laws
Fraud
Freedom of Information Act of 1966
Frontier Crime
Frontiero v. Richardson
Fugitive Slave Act of 1793
Fugitive Slave Act of 1850
Furman v. Georgia

G
Gacy, John Wayne
Gambling
Gangs, Contemporary
Gangs, History of
Gangs, Sociology of
Gardner, Erle Stanley
Garfield, James (Administration of)
Gates v. Collier
Gender and Criminal Law
Genovese, Vito
Georgia
German Americans
Gibbons v. Ogden
Gideon v. Wainwright
Giuliani, Rudolph
Glidewell v. State
Gotti, John
Grafton, Sue
Grant, Ulysses S. (Administration of)
Great Depression
Green, Anna K.
Gregg v. Georgia
Griffin v. California
Griswold v. Connecticut
Grutter v. Bollinger
Guiteau, Charles
Gun Control
Guns and Violent Crime

H
Habeas Corpus, Writ of
Habeas Corpus Act of 1679
Habeas Corpus Act of 1863
Hamilton, Alexander
Hammett, Dashiell
Hanging
Harding, Warren G. (Administration of)
Harris, Eric. *See* Klebold, Dylan and Eric Harris
Harrison, Benjamin (Administration of)
Harrison Act of 1914
Hauptmann, Bruno
Hawai'i
Hayes, Rutherford B. (Administration of)
Hays, Jacob
Hereditary Crime
Hillerman, Tony
Hispanic Americans
History of Crime and Punishment in America: Colonial
History of Crime and Punishment in America: 1783–1850
History of Crime and Punishment in America: 1850–1900
History of Crime and Punishment in America: 1900–1950
History of Crime and Punishment in America: 1950–1970
History of Crime and Punishment in America: 1970–Present
Holden v. Hardy
Holmes, Oliver Wendell, Jr.
Holt v. Sarver
Homeland Security
Homestead Act of 1862
Hoover, Herbert (Administration of)
Hoover, J. Edgar
Hurtado v. California

I
Idaho
Identity Theft
Illinois
Immigration Crimes
Incapacitation, Theory of
Incest
Indecent Exposure
Independent Treasury Act
Indian Civil Rights Act
Indian Removal Act
Indiana
Infanticide
Insanity Defense
Internal Revenue Service
Internal Security Act of 1950
International Association of Chiefs of Police
Internment

Interrogation Practices
Interstate Commerce Act of 1887
Intolerable Acts of 1774
Iowa
Irish Americans
Italian Americans

J

Jackson, Andrew (Administration of)
Jackson, Mississippi
James, Jesse
Japanese Americans
Jefferson, Thomas
Jefferson, Thomas (Administration of)
Jewish Americans
Johnson, Andrew (Administration of)
Johnson, Lyndon B. (Administration of)
Johnson v. Avery
Judges and Magistrates
Judiciary Act of 1789
Juries
Jurisdiction
Justice, Department of
Juvenile Corrections, Contemporary
Juvenile Corrections, History of
Juvenile Corrections, Sociology of
Juvenile Courts, Contemporary
Juvenile Courts, History of
Juvenile Delinquency, History of
Juvenile Delinquency, Sociology of
Juvenile Justice, History of
Juvenile Offenders, Prevention and Education
Juvenile Offenders in Adult Courts

K

Kaczynski, Ted
Kansas
Kansas City, Missouri
Katz v. United States
Katzenbach v. McClung
Kennedy, John F. (Administration of)
Kennedy, Robert F.
Kent State Massacre
Kentucky
Kevorkian, Jack
Kidnapping
King, Martin Luther, Jr.
King, Rodney
Klebold, Dylan, and Eric Harris
Knapp Commission

Korematsu v. United States
Ku Klux Klan
Kunstler, William

L

La Guardia, Fiorello
Landrum-Griffin Act of 1859
Larceny
Las Vegas, Nevada
Law Enforcement Assistance Act
Law Enforcement Assistance Administration
Lawrence v. Texas
Laws and Liberties of Massachusetts
Lawyers Guild
Leavenworth Federal Penitentiary
Legal Counsel
Leopold and Loeb
Libertarianism
Lincoln, Abraham (Administration of)
Lindbergh Law
Lindsey, Ben
Literature and Theater, Crime in
Literature and Theater, Police in
Literature and Theater, Punishment in
Livestock and Cattle Crimes
Livingston, Edward
Lochner v. New York
Los Angeles, California
Louisiana
Loving v. Virginia
Luciano, "Lucky"
Lynchings

M

Macdonald, Ross
Madison, James (Administration of)
Madoff, Bernard
Magna Carta
Maine
Malcolm X
Mandatory Minimum Sentencing
Mann Act
Manson, Charles
Mapp v. Ohio
Marbury v. Madison
Marshall, John
Martin v. Hunter's Lessee
Maryland
Maryland Toleration Act of 1649
Massachusetts

xii List of Articles

Matteawan State Hospital
Mayflower Compact
McCarthy, Joseph
McCleskey v. Kemp
McCulloch v. Maryland
McKinley, William (Administration of)
McNabb v. United States
McVeigh, Timothy
Memoirs, Police and Prosecutors
Memphis, Tennessee
Menendez, Lyle and Erik
Miami, Florida
Michigan
Military Courts
Military Police
Minnesota
Minor v. Happersett
Miranda v. Arizona
Miranda Warnings. *See Miranda v. Arizona*
Mississippi
Mississippi v. Johnson
Missouri
M'Naghten Test
Mollen Commission
Monroe, James (Administration of)
Montana
Moonshine
Morality
MOVE
Mudgett, Herman
Mug Shots
Muhammad, John Allen
Muller v. Oregon
Munn v. Illinois
Murder, Contemporary
Murder, History of
Murder, Sociology of
Murders, Unsolved
Music and Crime

N

Narcotics Laws
National Association for the Advancement of Colored People
National Commission on Law Observance and Enforcement
National Congress on Penitentiary and Reformatory Discipline
National Organization for Women
National Police Gazette

National Prison Association
National Security Act of 1947
Native American Tribal Police
Native Americans
Nebraska
Nelson, "Baby Face"
Ness, Eliot
Neutrality Enforcement in 1793–1794
Nevada
New Hampshire
New Jersey
New Mexico
New Orleans, Louisiana
"New Punitiveness"
New York
New York City
Newark, New Jersey
News Media, Crime in
News Media, Police in
News Media, Punishment in
Nitti, Frank
Nixon, Richard (Administration of)
North Carolina
North Dakota
Northwest Ordinance of 1787

O

Oakland, California
Obama, Barack (Administration of)
Obscenity
Obscenity Laws
Ohio
Oklahoma
Oklahoma City Bombing
Olmstead v. United States
Omnibus Crime Control and Safe Streets Act of 1968
Oregon
Organized Crime, Contemporary
Organized Crime, History of
Organized Crime, Sociology of
Oswald, Lee Harvey

P

Padilla v. Kentucky
Paine, Thomas
Paretsky, Sara
Parker, Isaac
Parker, William
Parole

Peltier, Leonard
Pendleton Act of 1883
Penitentiaries
Penitentiary Study Commission
Penn, William
Pennsylvania
Pennsylvania System of Reform
People v. Pinnell
People v. Superior Court of Santa Clara County
Percival, Robert V.
Peterson, Scott
Petty Courts
Philadelphia, Pennsylvania
Pickpockets
Pierce, Franklin (Administration of)
Pittsburgh, Pennsylvania
Plea
Plessy v. Ferguson
Poe, Edgar Allen
Police, Contemporary
Police, History of
Police, Sociology of
Police, Women as
Police Abuse
Political Crimes, Contemporary
Political Crimes, History of
Political Crimes, Sociology of
Political Dissidents
Political Policing
Polk, James K. (Administration of)
Pornography
Posses
Presidential Proclamations
President's Commission on Law Enforcement and the Administration of Justice
Prison Privatization
Prison Riots
Prisoner's Rights
Private Detectives
Private Police
Private Security Services
Probation
Proclamation for Suppressing Rebellion and Sedition of 1775
Procunier v. Martinez
Professionalization of Police
Prohibition
Prostitution, Contemporary
Prostitution, History of
Prostitution, Sociology of

Punishment of Crimes Act, 1790
Punishment Within Prison
Pure Food and Drug Act of 1906
Puritans

Q
Quakers

R
Race, Class, and Criminal Law
Race-Based Crimes
Racism
Rader, Dennis
Ragen, Joseph
Ramirez, Richard
Rape, Contemporary
Rape, History of
Rape, Sociology of
Ray, James Earl
Reagan, Ronald (Administration of)
Reform, Police and Enforcement
Reform Movements in Justice
Rehabilitation
Religion and Crime, Contemporary
Religion and Crime, History of
Religion and Crime, Sociology of
Reports on Prison Conditions
Retributivism
Reynolds v. United States
Rhode Island
Ricci v. DeStefano
Riots
Robbery, Contemporary
Robbery, History of
Robbery, Sociology of
Roberts v. Louisiana
Rockefeller, Nelson
Roe v. Wade
Romer v. Evans
Roosevelt, Franklin D. (Administration of)
Roosevelt, Theodore (Administration of)
Roth v. United States
Rothstein, Arnold
Ruby Ridge Standoff
Rule of Law
Rural Police

S
Sacco and Vanzetti
Salem Witch Trials

San Francisco, California
San Quentin State Prison
Santobello v. New York
Schenck v. United States
School Shootings
Schultz, "Dutch"
Scopes Monkey Trial
Scottsboro Boys Cases
Secret Service
Securities and Exchange Commission
Sedition Act of 1918
Segregation Laws
Selective Service Act of 1967
Sentencing
Sentencing: Indeterminate Versus Fixed
Serial and Mass Killers
Sex Offender Laws
Sex Offenders
Sexual Harassment
Shaming and Shunning
Sheppard, Sam
Sheppard v. Maxwell
Sheriffs
Sherman Anti-Trust Act of 1890
Simpson, O. J.
Sin
Sing Sing Correctional Facility
Sirhan Sirhan
Slave Patrols
Slavery
Slavery, Law of
Smith, Susan
Smith Act
Smuggling
Snyder, Ruth
Sodomy
South Carolina
South Dakota
Spillane, Mickey
St. Louis, Missouri
Stamp Act of 1765
Standard Oil Co. of New Jersey v. United States
State Blue Laws
State Police
State Slave Codes
State v. Heitman
Steenburgh, Sam
Strauder v. West Virginia
Strikes

Students for a Democratic Society and the Weathermen
Supermax Prisons
Supreme Court, U.S.
Suspect's Rights
Sutherland, Edwin

T

Taft, William Howard (Administration of)
Tax Crimes
Taylor, Zachary (Administration of)
Taylor v. State
Tea Act of 1773
Technology, Police
Television, Crime in
Television, Police in
Television, Punishment in
Tennessee
Terrorism
Terry v. Ohio
Texas
Texas Rangers
Texas v. White
Thaw, Harry K.
Theories of Crime
Thoreau, Henry David
Three Strikes Law
To Kill a Mockingbird
Tocqueville, Alexis de
Torrio, John
Torture
Townshend Acts of 1767
Traffic Crimes
Training Police
Trials
Truman, Harry S. (Administration of)
Twining v. New Jersey
Tyler, John (Administration of)

U

Uniform Crime Reporting Program
United States Attorneys
United States v. Ballard
United States v. E. C. Knight Company
United States v. Hudson and Goodwin
United States v. Nixon
United States v. One Book Called Ulysses
Urbanization
USA PATRIOT Act of 2001
Utah

V

Vagrancy
Vermont
Vice Commission
Vice Reformers
Victim Rights and Restitution
Victimless Crime
Victorian Compromise
Vigilantism
Violence Against Women Act of 1994
Violent Crimes
Virginia
Vollmer, August
Volstead Act

W

Waco Siege
Walling, George
Walnut Street Jail
Wambaugh, Joseph
Warren, Earl
Washington
Washington, D.C.
Washington, George (Administration of)
Watergate
Weathermen, The. *See* Students for a Democratic Society and the Weathermen
Webb v. United States
Weeks v. United States
West Virginia
White-Collar Crime, Contemporary
White-Collar Crime, History of
White-Collar Crime, Sociology of
Whitney v. California
Wickersham, George
Wickersham Commission
Wilson, James Q.
Wilson, O. W.
Wilson, Woodrow (Administration of)
Wisconsin
Witness Testimony
Wolf v. Colorado
Women Criminals, Contemporary
Women Criminals, History of
Women Criminals, Sociology of
Women in Prison
Wuornos, Aileen
Wyoming

X

Xenophobia

Y

Yates, Andrea
Yates v. United States

Z

Zeisel, Hans
Zodiac Killer

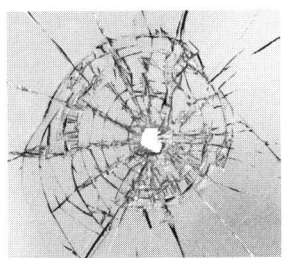

Reader's Guide

Biographies
Arpaio, Joseph M.
Augustus, John
Beaumont, Gustave de
Blackstone, William
Brennan, William J., Jr.
Brockway, Zebulon
Burger, Warren
Bush, George H. W. (Administration of)
Bush, George W. (Administration of)
Byrnes, Thomas
Cummings, Homer
Darrow, Clarence
Devery, William
Dewey, Thomas E.
Douglas, William O.
Garfield, James
Giuliani, Rudolph
Hamilton, Alexander
Holmes, Oliver Wendell, Jr.
Hoover, J. Edgar
Jefferson, Thomas
Kennedy, Robert F.
King, Martin Luther, Jr.
Kunstler, William
La Guardia, Fiorello
Leopold and Loeb
Livingston, Edward
Marshall, John
McCarthy, Joseph
Ness, Eliot
Paine, Thomas
Parker, William
Penn, William
Percival, Robert V.
Ragen, Joseph
Rockefeller, Nelson
Roosevelt, Theodore (Administration of)
Snyder, Ruth
Steenburgh, Sam
Sutherland, Edwin
Thaw, Harry K.
Thoreau, Henry David
Tocqueville, Alexis de
Vollmer, August
Walling, George
Warren, Earl
Wickersham, George
Wilson, James Q.
Wilson, O. W.
Zeisel, Hans

Courts, Corrections, Punishments
Adversarial Justice
Alcatraz Island Prison
American Law Institute
Antitrust Law
Appeals
Appellate Courts
Attica

Bail and Bond
Bedford Hills Correctional Facility
Capital Punishment
Chain Gangs and Prison Labor
Chillicothe Correctional Institution
Citizen Participation on Juries
Civil Rights Laws
Clemency
Clinton Correctional Facility
Codification of Laws
Colonial Courts
Common Law Origins of Criminal Law
Community Service
Comstock Law
Confession
Convict Lease System
Corporal Punishment
Corrections
Courts
Critical Legal Studies Movement
Cruel and Unusual Punishment
Death Row
Defendant's Rights
Deportation
Deterrence, Theory of
Discretionary Decision Making
District Attorney
Due Process
Eastern State Penitentiary
Electric Chair, History of
Electronic Surveillance
Elmira Prison
Executions
Famous Trials
Federal Prisons
Fingerprinting
Fish and Game Laws
Fornication Laws
Gender and Criminal Law
Habeas Corpus, Writ of
Hanging
Judges and Magistrates
Juries
Jurisdiction
Justice, Department of
Leavenworth Federal Penitentiary
Legal Counsel
Matteawan State Hospital
Military Courts
"New Punitiveness"

Parole
Penitentiaries
Petty Courts
Plea
Prison Privatization
Prison Riots
Prisoner's Rights
Probation
Punishment Within Prison
Race, Class, and Criminal Law
Reform Movements in Justice
Rehabilitation
Rule of Law
San Quentin State Prison
Segregation Laws
Sentencing
Sentencing: Indeterminate Versus Fixed
Sex Offender Laws
Shaming and Shunning
Sing Sing Correctional Facility
Slavery, Law of
Supreme Court, U.S.
Suspect's Rights
Torture
Trials
Victim Rights and Restitution
Witness Testimony
Women in Prison

Crime and Punishment in Media
An American Tragedy
Autobiographies, Criminals'
Buntline, Ned
Christie, Agatha
Dime Novels, Pulps, Thrillers
Film, Crime in
Film, Police in
Film, Punishment in
Grafton, Sue
Green, Anna K.
Hammett, Dashiell
Hillerman, Tony
Literature and Theater,
  Crime in
Literature and Theater,
  Police in
Literature and Theater,
  Punishment in
Memoirs, Police and Prosecutors
Music and Crime

News Media, Crime in
News Media, Police in
News Media, Punishment in
Paretzky, Sara
Poe, Edgar Allen
Spillane, Mickey
Television, Crime in
Television, Police in
Television, Punishment in
To Kill a Mockingbird
Wambaugh, Joseph

Crimes in America
Abortion
Adultery
Bigamy/Polygamy
Blood Sports
Bootlegging
Burglary, Contemporary
Burglary, History of
Burglary, Sociology of
Computer Crime
Confidence Games and Frauds
Corruption, Contemporary
Corruption, History of
Corruption, Sociology of
Counterfeiting
Crime and Arrest Statistics Analysis
Crime in America, Causes
Crime in America, Distribution
Crime in America, Types
Crime Rates
Criminology
Domestic Violence, Contemporary
Domestic Violence, History of
Domestic Violence, Sociology of
Drinking and Crime
Drug Abuse and Addiction, Contemporary
Drug Abuse and Addiction, History of
Drug Abuse and Addiction, Sociology of
Embezzlement
Environmental Crimes
Espionage
Felonies
Fornication Laws
Fraud
Frontier Crime

Gambling
Gangs, Contemporary
Gangs, History of
Gangs, Sociology of
Guns and Violent Crime
Hereditary Crime
Identity Theft
Immigration Crimes
Incest
Indecent Exposure
Infanticide
Kidnapping
Larceny
Livestock and Cattle Crimes
Lynchings
Moonshine
Murder, Contemporary
Murder, History of
Murder, Sociology of
Murders, Unsolved
Obscenity
Organized Crime, Contemporary
Organized Crime, History of
Organized Crime, Sociology of
Pickpockets
Political Crimes, Contemporary
Political Crimes, History of
Political Crimes, Sociology of
Pornography
Prostitution, Contemporary
Prostitution, History of
Prostitution, Sociology of
Race-Based Crimes
Rape, Contemporary
Rape, History of
Rape, Sociology of
Religion and Crime, Contemporary
Religion and Crime, History of
Religion and Crime, Sociology of
Riots
Robbery, Contemporary
Robbery, History of
Robbery, Sociology of
Serial and Mass Killers
Sex Offenders
Sexual Harassment
Smuggling
Sodomy
Tax Crimes
Terrorism

Theories of Crime
Traffic Crimes
Vagrancy
Victimless Crime
Violent Crimes
White-Collar Crime, Contemporary
White-Collar Crime, History of
White-Collar Crime, Sociology of
Women Criminals, Contemporary
Women Criminals, History of
Women Criminals, Sociology of

Criminals
Anarchists
Bakker, Jim
Berkowitz, David
Billy the Kid
Bodine, Polly
Boles, Charles
Bonnie and Clyde
Booth, John Wilkes
Borden, Lizzie
Brocius, William
Bundy, Ted
Capone, Al
Chapman, Mark David
Cunningham, Emma
Czolgosz, Leon
Dahmer, Jeffrey
DeSalvo, Albert
Dillinger, John
Everleigh Sisters
Ferguson, Colin
Floyd, Charles Arthur
Gacy, John Wayne
Genovese, Vito
Gotti, John
Guiteau, Charles
Hauptmann, Bruno
James, Jesse
Kaczynski, Ted
Kevorkian, Jack
Klebold, Dylan, and Eric Harris
Leopold and Loeb
Luciano, "Lucky"
Manson, Charles
McVeigh, Timothy
Menendez, Lyle and Erik
Mudgett, Herman
Muhammad, John Allen

Nelson, "Baby Face"
Nitti, Frank
Oswald, Lee Harvey
Peterson, Scott
Rader, Dennis
Ramirez, Richard
Ray, James Earl
Rothstein, Arnold
Sacco and Vanzetti
Schultz, "Dutch"
Sheppard, Sam
Simpson, O. J.
Sirhan Sirhan
Smith, Susan
Torrio, John
Wuornos, Aileen
Yates, Andrea
Zodiac Killer

Documents and Acts Shaping the American System of Criminal Justice
Alien and Sedition Acts of 1798
Anti-Federalist Papers
Articles of Confederation
Aviation and Transportation Security Act of 2001
Bail Reform Act
Bible
Bill of Rights
Bodie of Liberties
Book of the General Lawes & Libertyes
Chinese Exclusion Act of 1882
Civil Rights Act of 1866
Civil Rights Act of 1875
Clayton Anti-Trust Act of 1914
Colonial Charters and Grants
Constitution of the United States of America
Crimes Act
Declaration of Independence
Dyer Act
Elkins Act of 1903
Emergency Quota Act of 1921
Enforcement Acts of 1870–1871
English Charter of Liberties of 1100
Espionage Act of 1917
Ethics in Government Act of 1978
Federalist Papers
Federal Rules of Criminal Procedure
Freedom of Information Act of 1966
Fugitive Slave Act of 1793

Fugitive Slave Act of 1850
Habeas Corpus Act of 1679
Habeas Corpus Act of 1863
Harrison Act of 1914
Homestead Act of 1862
Independent Treasury Act
Indian Civil Rights Act
Indian Removal Act
Internal Security Act of 1950
Interstate Commerce Act of 1887
Intolerable Acts of 1774
Judiciary Act of 1789
Landrum-Griffin Act of 1859
Law Enforcement Assistance Act
Laws and Liberties of Massachusetts
Lindbergh Law
Magna Carta
Mann Act
Maryland Toleration Act of 1649
Mayflower Compact
National Security Act of 1947
Northwest Ordinance of 1787
Omnibus Crime Control and Safe Streets Act of 1968
Pendleton Act of 1883
Presidential Proclamations
Proclamation for Suppressing Rebellion and Sedition of 1775
Pure Food and Drug Act of 1906
Reports on Prison Conditions
Sedition Act of 1918
Selective Service Act of 1967
Sherman Anti-Trust Act of 1890
Smith Act
Stamp Act of 1765
State Blue Laws
State Slave Codes
Tea Act of 1773
Townshend Acts of 1767
USA PATRIOT Act of 2001
Vice Commission
Violence Against Women Act of 1994
Volstead Act

Historical Cities in Crime and Punishment
Boston, Massachussetts
Chicago, Illinois
Las Vegas, Nevada
Los Angeles, California
Miami, Florida
New York City
Newark, New Jersey
Pittsburgh, Pennsylvania
San Francisco, California

History of Crime and Punishment by State
Alabama
Alaska
Arizona
Arkansas
California
Colorado
Connecticut
Delaware
Florida
Georgia
Hawai'i
Idaho
Illinois
Indiana
Iowa
Kansas
Kentucky
Louisiana
Maine
Maryland
Massachusetts
Michigan
Minnesota
Mississippi
Missouri
Montana
Nebraska
Nevada
New Hampshire
New Jersey
New Mexico
New York
North Carolina
North Dakota
Ohio
Oklahoma
Oregon
Pennsylvania
Rhode Island
South Carolina
South Dakota
Tennessee
Texas
Utah

Vermont
Virginia
Washington
West Virginia
Wisconsin
Wyoming

History of the American Criminal Justice System
American Revolution and Criminal Justice
Court of Common Pleas
Court of Oyer and Terminer
Court of Quarter Sessions
Courts of Indian Offenses
Coverture, doctrine of
Equality, Concept of
Great Depression
History of Crime and Punishment in America: Colonial
History of Crime and Punishment in America: 1783–1850
History of Crime and Punishment in America: 1850–1900
History of Crime and Punishment in America: 1900–1950
History of Crime and Punishment in America: 1950–1970
History of Crime and Punishment in America: 1970–Present
Homeland Security
Prohibition
Puritans
Salem Witch Trials
Victorian Compromise

Juvenile Crime and Justice
Child Abuse, Contemporary
Child Abuse, History of
Child Abuse, Sociology of
Child Murderers, History of
Children, Abandoned
Children's Rights
Convention on Rights of the Child
Juvenile Corrections, Contemporary
Juvenile Corrections, History of
Juvenile Corrections, Sociology of
Juvenile Courts, Contemporary
Juvenile Courts, History of
Juvenile Delinquency, History of
Juvenile Delinquency, Sociology of
Juvenile Justice, History of
Juvenile Offenders, Prevention and Education
Juvenile Offenders in Adult Courts
School Shootings
Lindsey, Ben

Most Dangerous Cities
Atlanta, Georgia
Baltimore, Maryland
Birmingham, Alabama
Camden, New Jersey
Cincinnati, Ohio
Cleveland, Ohio
Compton, California
Dayton, Ohio
Detroit, Michigan
Jackson, Mississippi
Kansas City, Missouri
Memphis, Tennessee
New Orleans, Louisiana
Oakland, California
St. Louis, Missouri
Washington, D.C.

Organizations and Commissions
American Bar Association
American Civil Liberties Union
International Association of Chiefs of Police
Knapp Commission
Ku Klux Klan
Law Enforcement Assistance Administration
Lawyers Guild
National Association for the Advancement of Colored People
National Commission on Law Observance and Enforcement
National Congress on Penitentiary and Reformatory Discipline
National Organization for Women
National Prison Association
Penitentiary Study Commission
President's Commission on Law Enforcement and the Administration of Justice
Securities and Exchange Commission
Students for a Democratic Society and the Weathermen
Wickersham Commission

Police and Law Enforcement
Automobile and the Police
Ballistics
Bertillon System
Border Patrol
Bounty Hunters
Bureau of Alcohol, Tobacco, Firearms and Explosives
Code of Silence
Community Policing and Relations
Corruption, Contemporary
Corruption, History of
Corruption, Sociology of
Crime Prevention
Crime Scene Investigation
Customs Service as Police
Detection and Detectives
Drug Enforcement Administration
Federal Bureau of Investigation
Federal Policing
Forensic Science
Incapacitation, Theory of
Internal Revenue Service
Interrogation Practices
Military Police
Miranda v. Arizona
M'Naghten Test
Mug Shots
Narcotics Laws
National Police Gazette
Native American Tribal Police
Police, Women as
Police Abuse
Political Policing
Posses
Private Detectives
Private Police
Private Security Services
Professionalization of Police
Reform, Police and Enforcement
Rural Police
Secret Service
Sheriffs
State Police
Strikes
Technology, Police
Texas Rangers
Training Police
Uniform Crime Reporting Program
Vice Reformers
Vigilantism

Presidential Administrations and Crime and Punishment
Adams, John (Administration of)
Adams, John Quincy (Administration of)
Arthur, Chester (Administration of)
Buchanan, James (Administration of)
Buren, Martin Van (Administration of)
Bush, George H. W. (Administration of)
Bush, George W.(Administration of)
Carter, Jimmy (Administration of)
Cleveland, Grover (Administration of)
Clinton, William (Administration of)
Coolidge, Calvin (Administration of)
Eisenhower, Dwight D. (Administration of)
Fillmore, Millard (Administration of)
Ford, Gerald (Administration of)
Grant, Ulysses S. (Administration of)
Harding, Warren G. (Administration of)
Harrison, Benjamin (Administration of)
Hayes, Rutherford B. (Administration of)
Hoover, Herbert (Administration of)
Jackson, Andrew (Administration of)
Jefferson, Thomas (Administration of)
Johnson, Andrew (Administration of)
Johnson, Lyndon B. Administration of
Kennedy, John F. (Administration of)
Lincoln, Abraham (Administration of)
Madison, James (Administration of)
McKinley, William (Administration of)
Monroe, James (Administration of)
Nixon, Richard (Administration of)
Obama, Barack (Administration of)
Pierce, Franklin (Administration of)
Polk, James K. (Administration of)
Reagan, Ronald (Administration of)
Roosevelt, Franklin D. (Administration of)
Roosevelt, Theodore (Administration of)
Taft, William Howard (Administration of)
Taylor, Zachary (Administration of)
Truman, Harry S. (Administration of)
Tyler, John (Administration of)
Washington, George (Administration of)
Wilson, Woodrow (Administration of)

Socioeconomic, Political, and Religious Issues
African Americans
Chinese Americans

Civil Disobedience
Civil Rights Laws
Codification of Laws
Criminalization and Decriminalization
Fear of Crime
Gun Control
Hispanic Americans
Insanity Defense
Irish Americans
Italian Americans
Japanese Americans
Jewish Americans
Libertarianism
Morality
Native Americans
Obscenity Laws
Political Dissidents
Quakers
Racism
Sin
Slavery
Urbanization
Xenophobia

State and Federal Court Cases
Ableman v. Booth
Abrams v. United States
Adair v. United States
Barron v. Mayor of Baltimore
Bowers v. Hardwick
Brandenburg v. Ohio
Brown v. Board of Education
Brown v. Mississippi
Buck v. Bell
Caminetti v. United States
Chandler v. Florida
Chisholm v. Georgia
Cohens v. Virginia
Coker v. Georgia
Crabtree v. State
Davis v. State
Dennis v. United States
Dillard v. the State of Georgia
Dred Scott v. Sandford
Duren v. Missouri
Eisenstadt v. Baird
Estes v. Texas
Fletcher v. Peck
Frontiero v. Richardson
Furman v. Georgia

Gates v. Collier
Gibbons v. Ogden
Gideon v. Wainwright
Glidewell v. State
Gregg v. Georgia
Griffin v. California
Griswold v. Connecticut
Grutter v. Bollinger
Holden v. Hardy
Holt v. Sarver
Hurtado v. California
Johnson v. Avery
Korematsu v. United States
Lochner v. New York
Loving v. Virginia
Mapp v. Ohio
Marbury v. Madison
Martin v. Hunter's Lessee
McCleskey v. Kemp
McCulloch v. Maryland
McNabb v. United States
Minor v. Happersett
Miranda v. Arizona
Mississippi v. Johnson
Muller v. Oregon
Munn v. Illinois
Olmstead v. United States
Padilla v. Kentucky
People v. Pinnell
People v. Superior Court of Santa Clara County
Plessy v. Ferguson
Procunier v. Martinez
Reynolds v. United States
Ricci v. DeStefano
Roberts v. Louisiana
Roe v. Wade
Romer v. Evans
Roth v. United State
Santobello v. New York
Schenck v. United States
Sheppard v. Maxwell
Standard Oil Co. of New Jersey v. United States
State v. Heitman
Strauder v. West Virginia
Taylor v. State
Terry v. Ohio
Texas v. White
Twining v. New Jersey
United States v. Ballard
United States v. E. C. Knight Company

United States v. Hudson and Goodwin
United States v. Nixon
United States v. One Book Called Ulysses
Webb v. United States

Weeks v. United States
Whitney v. California
Wolf v. Colorado
Yates v. United States

About the Editor

Wilbur R. Miller is professor of history at the State University of New York at Stony Brook, where he has taught for 36 years. His interest in police history developed while he was an undergraduate at the University of California, Berkeley, during the Free Speech Movement years. He completed his dissertation at Columbia University, a comparison of the New York and London police 1830–1870. This became his first book, *Cops and Bobbies*. He then developed an interest in the post–Civil War reconstruction of the south, which in the face of determined southern resistance became a national policing problem. He soon learned that this topic was well covered, but realized that federal policing in the 19th century was a new realm of investigation.

Research led him to federal efforts to suppress moonshining in the mountain south in the later 19th century, a subject that had not been treated by historians in any depth. *Revenuers and Moonshiners*, his second book, was a result of this work. Since then he has been occupied with several administrative positions: department chair, adviser to the university's multidisciplinary program and faculty director of the Honors College. He is currently undergraduate program director.

During this period he has been developing an interest in the interdependence of public policing with private policing, the extent to which the state has openly or tacitly supported various private police and corrections, including vigilantes, antivice and antiradical groups, private detective agencies, and the more recent development of private security services and prisons. Miller has been developing this theme in papers presented at the Social Science History Association and European Social Science History Conference.

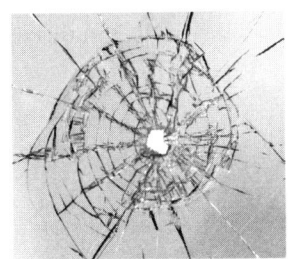

List of Contributors

Charles Frederick Abel
    Stephen F. Austin State University
John Felipe Acevedo
    University of Chicago
Janet Adamski
    University of Mary Hardin-Baylor
Mariah Adin
    State University of New York, Albany
Jeffrey S. Adler
    University of Florida
Celestina D. Agyekum
    Knox College
Michael A. Arntfield
    University of Western Ontario
Elyshia D. Aseltine
    Lycoming College
Nahel N. Asfour
    University of Vienna
Nick C. Athey
    Simon Fraser University
Ben Atkins
    Sam Houston State University
Mary Welek Atwell
    Radford University
Annessa A. Babic
    New York Institute of Technology
Frankie Y. Bailey
    State University of New York, Albany
Thomas E. Baker
    University of Scranton

Kyle Barbieri
    Georgia Perimeter College
John H. Barnhill
    Independent Scholar
Kathleen Barrett
    Georgia State University
Andrew Battle
    City University of New York Graduate Center
Marcel F. Beausoleil
    Fitchburg State University
Diana L. Beck
    Knox College
Tiffany Bergin
    University of Cambridge
Matthew H. Birkhold
    Princeton University, Columbia Law School
Nicola Davis Bivens
    Johnson C. Smith University
William D. Blake
    University of Texas
Curtis R. Blakely
    Truman State University
Anita Bledsoe-Gardner
    Johnson C. Smith University
Ethan Blue
    University of Western Australia
Eric Blumenson
    Suffolk University Law School
Sarah Boslaugh
    Kennesaw State University

J. Michael Botts
  Belmont Abbey College
Tina Fernandes Botts
  University of North Carolina, Charlotte
Suzanne Bouclin
  University of Ottawa
Samuel Brier
  Macalester College
Avi Brisman
  Emory University
Allen J. Brown
  Anna Maria College
Thomas F. Brown
  Virginia Wesleyan College
Kyle A. Burgason
  University of Arkansas at Little Rock
Michael Bush
  Northern Kentucky University
Christopher M. Campbell
  Washington State University
Jennifer D. Carlson
  University of California, Berkeley
Simone M. Caron
  Wake Forest University
Gabriel T. Cesar
  Arizona State University
John Martyn Chamberlain
  Loughborough University
Jacqueline Chavez
  Mississippi State University
Felix O. Chima
  Prairie View A&M University
Kimberly Chism
  Sam Houston State University
Tracey-Lynn Clough
  University of Texas at Arlington
Nigel J. Cohen
  Independent Scholar
Amy N. Cole
  Washington State University
Todd A. Collins
  Western Carolina University
Frank J. Colucci
  Purdue University Calumet
Sarah Combellick-Bidney
  Augsburg College
Hopi Costello
  Davis Polk & Wardwell LLP
Allison M. Cotton
  Metropolitan State College of Denver

Amanda K. Cox
  Pennsylvania State University, Altoona
Gordon A. Crews
  Marshall University
Cale T. Dahm
  Knox College
John Kelly Damico
  Georgia Perimeter College
Jacob Day
  Washington State University
Scott H. Decker
  Arizona State University
Antje Deckert
  AUT University
James I. Deutsch
  Smithsonian Institution
Daniel C. Dillard
  Florida State University
Christopher M. Donner
  University of South Florida
Amy S. Eggers
  University of South Florida
Helen Eigenberg
  University of Tennesse, Chattanooga
JoAnna Elmquist
  Butler Hospital and Brown University
Leslie Elrod
  University of Cincinnati
Theodore W. Eversole
  Independent Scholar
Katie A. Farina
  University of Delaware
Cary Federman
  Montclair State University
Melissa E. Fenwick
  Western Connecticut State University
Marianne Fisher-Giorlando
  Grambling State University
Robert W. Fleet
  University of Auckland
Jonathan R. Fletcher
  Knox College
Caroline Forsythe
  Truman State University
John F. Fox, Jr.
  Federal Bureau of Investigation
Henrgy F. Fradella
  California State University, Long Beach
Teresa I. Francis
  Central Washington University

Theodore O. Francis
  Independent Scholar
George R. Franks, Jr.
  Stephen F. Austin State University
Brian Frederick
  California State University, Long Beach
Jason Friedman
  Wasatch Academy
Gennifer Furst
  William Paterson University
Venessa Garcia
  Kean University
Susan Garneau
  Loyola University Chicago
Tony Gaskew
  University of Pittsburgh at Bradford
James Geistman
  Ohio Northern University
Tobias T. Gibson
  Westminster College
Wendy Perkins Gilbert
  Urbana University
Timothy J. Gilfoyle
  Loyola University Chicago
Trangdai Glassey-Tranguyen
  Stanford University
Daniel O. Gonshorek
  Knox College
Victoria Gonzalez
  Rutgers University
Laurie A. Gould
  Georgia Southern University
IndiAna Gowland
  Macalester College
Donna Cooper Graves
  University of Tennessee, Martin
Edward Green
  Eastern Kentucky University
Marie L. Griffin
  Arizona State University
Jennifer N. Grimes
  Indiana State University
Neil Guzy
  University of Pittsburgh at Greensburg
Hans J. Hacker
  Arkansas State University
Eric Ashley Hairston
  Elon University
Nicholas A. Hall
  University of Pittsburgh at Greensburg

Robin Annette Hanson
  St. Louis University
Tina P. Hanson
  Jefferson College
Katherine Harmer
  Lehigh University
Steven H. Hatting
  University of St. Thomas
Francis Frederick Hawley
  Western Carolina University
Erica Rhodes Hayden
  Vanderbilt University
M. Kristen Hefner
  University of Delaware
Theresa S. Hefner-Babb
  Lamar University
Jason A. Helfer
  Knox College
Brandy B. Henderson
  University of South Florida
Nicole Hendrix
  Radford University
Robin C. Henry
  Wichita State University
Armando Gustavo Hernandez
  Independent Scholar
Rhys Hester
  University of South Carolina
Sarah Higinbotham
  Georgia State University
Patty Hill
  University of Arkansas at Little Rock
Livia Holden
  Lahore University of Management Sciences
Jason J. Hopkins
  University of California, Santa Barbara
Julietta Hua
  San Francisco State University
Jennifer L. Huck
  Indiana University of Pennsylvania
Joshua Hyles
  Baylor University
Scott Ingram
  High Point University
Robin D. Jackson
  Sam Houston State University
Charles F. Jacobs
  St. Norbert College

Jennifer Lawrence Janofsky
  Villanova University
Jason R. Jolicoeur
  *Cincinnati State Technical and
  Community College*
William T. Jones
  State University of New York, Canton
Jerry Joplin
  Guilford College
Paul Kahan
  Montgomery County Community College
Chad M. Kahl
  Illinois State University
Thomas M. Kelley
  Wayne State University
Euijeung Kim
  California State University, Sacramento
Aaron J. Kivisto
  Massachusetts General Hospital
Thomas Daniel Knight
  University of Texas—Pan American
Helen J. Knowles
  Whitman College
Jeffrey Kraus
  Wagner College
Shane W. Kraus
  Bowling Green State University
Joseph Kremer
  Washington State University
Jonathan M. Kremser
  Kutztown University of Pennsylvania
Bill Kte'pi
  Independent Scholar
Francesca Laguardia
  New York University
Joseph Lalli
  Macalester College
Andrea G. Lange
  Washington College
Gavin Lee
  *University of Arkansas
  at Little Rock*
Keith Gregory Logan
  Kutztown University
Lucien X. Lombardo
  Old Dominion University
Kristina M. Lopez
  Texas State University
Arthur J. Lurigio
  Loyola University Chicago

Joan Luxenburg
  University of Central Oklahoma
Paul A. Magro
  Ball State University
Christian D. Mahone
  Knox College
Liz Marie Marciniak
  University of Pittsburgh at Greensburg
Susan Marcus-Mendoza
  University of Oklahoma
Alison Marganski
  Virginia Wesleyan College
Sanjay Marwah
  Guilford College
Jon Maskaly
  University of South Florida
M. Nathan Mason
  University of Nevada School of Medicine
Evan M. Massey
  Knox College
Jeremy Matuszak
  University of Nevada, Reno
Melissa J. Mauck
  Sam Houston State University
Michael Mazotti
  *California State University,
  Sacramento*
Logan M. McBride
  *City University of New York
  Graduate Center*
Heather McIntosh
  Boston College
Jerome McKean
  Ball State University
Robert J. Meadows
  California Lutheran University
Allen Mendenhall
  Auburn University
Kenneth W. Mentor
  University of North Carolina
Cedric Michel
  University of South Florida
Tiffany Middleton
  Independent Scholar
Stephen Mihm
  University of Georgia
Esmorie J. Miller
  Queen's University Belfast
J. Mitchell Miller
  University of Texas, San Antonio

Jennifer M. Miller
  University of Arkansas at Little Rock
Vivien Miller
  University of Nottingham
Wilbur R. Miller
  State University of New York, Stony Brook
William J. Miller
  Southeast Missouri State University
Todd Moore
  University of Tennessee, Knoxville
Weston Morrow
  Arizona State University
Alexander Moudrov
  Queens College, City University of New York
Barry D. Mowell
  Broward College
Lynn N. Mueller
  Knox College
Roslyn Muraskin
  Long Island University
Jennifer Murphy
  California State University, Sacramento
Tony Murphy
  University of Westminster
Stephen L. Muzzatti
  Ryerson University
Jonathan Nash
  State University of New York, Albany
Denise D. Nation
  Winston-Salem State University
Jamal A. Nelson
  Knox College
Samuel P. Newton
  Weber State University
Andrew Ninnemann
  Butler Hospital and Brown University
Christine A. Nix
  University of Mary Hardin-Baylor
M. Elaine Nugent-Borakove
  Justice Management Institute
Anne M. Nurse
  College of Wooster
Patrick O'Brien
  University of Colorado Boulder
Jules Odendahl-James
  Duke University
James C. Oleson
  University of Auckland
Mary Lou O'Neil
  Kadir Has University

Timothy J. O'Neill
  Southwestern University
Seong min Parks
  University of Tennessee at Chattanooga
Matthew Pate
  State University of New York, Albany
Justin Paulette
  Independent Scholar
Lee W. Payne
  Stephen F. Austin State University
Lynn Pazzani
  University of Arkansas at Little Rock
Anthony Petrosino
  WestEd
Mark N. Pettigrew
  University of Manchester
Elizabeth Rae Pierson
  California State University, Sacramento
Peter Constantine Pihos
  University of Pennsylvania
Wm. C. Plouffe, Jr.
  Independent Scholar
Sierra J. Powell
  University of California, Irvine
Cindy Pressley
  Stephen F. Austin State University
Karen S. Price
  Stephen F. Austin State University
Luca Prono
  Independent Scholar
Enrique S. Pumar
  Catholic University of America
Michael J. Puniskis
  Middlesex University
Elizabeth Rholetter Purdy
  Independent Scholar
Michael J. Reed
  Mississippi State University
Keramet Ann Reiter
  University of California, Berkeley
Bradford W. Reyns
  Weber State University
Kerry M. Richmond
  Lycoming College
Eric Walter Rise
  University of Delaware
Kathrin Ritter
  University of Tennessee, Knoxville
Pierre M. Rivolta
  Sam Houston State University

Gina M. Robertiello
Felician College

Augusta Rohrbach
Washington State University

Carl Root
University of South Florida

Jeffrey Ian Ross
University of Baltimore

Ashley T. Rubin
University of California, Berkeley

Janet Ruiz
California State University, Long Beach

Andrew Sargent
West Chester University of Pennsylvania

Robert A. Sarver, III
University of South Carolina, Upstate

Antoinette W. Satterfield
U.S. Naval Academy

Traci Schlesinger
DePaul University

Patrick Schmidt
Macalester College

Stephen T. Schroth
Knox College

Corina Schulze
University of South Alabama

David G. Schwartz
University of Nevada, Las Vegas

Jennifer Schwartz
Washington State University

Miriam D. Sealock
Towson University

Brian G. Sellers
University of South Florida

Rita Shah
University of California, Irvine

Derrick Shapley
Mississippi State University

Donn Short
Robson Hall Law School

Deborah A. Sibila
Sam Houston State University

Julie Ahmad Siddique
City University of New York Graduate Center

Dawinder "Dave" S. Sidhu
University of Baltimore School of Law

Marilyn Simon
University of Cincinnati, Blue Ash

Andrew Skotnicki
Manhattan College

Douglas M. Smith
University of Texas, San Antonio

Jesse M. Smith
University of Colorado Boulder

Marshall Smith
University of Colorado Boulder

Natalie J. Sokoloff
John Jay College of Criminal Justice

Peter Squires
University of Brighton

Amy Gilman Srebnick
Montclair State University

Carol A. Stabile
University of Oregon

Daniel Stageman
John Jay College of Criminal Justice

Rick M. Steinmann
Southern Illinois University

Victor B. Stolberg
Essex County College

Maya Strange
University of Nevada, Reno

Gregory L. Stuart
University of Tennessee, Knoxville

Megan Stubbendeck
University of Virginia

Jeanne Subjack
Sam Houston State University

Melinda Tasca
Arizona State University

Steven Tauber
University of South Florida

Josh Thompson
Ball State University

Matthew D. Thompson
Old Dominion University

Stephen E. Tillotson
Indiana University

Marcella Bush Trevino
Barry University

Mark Tunick
Florida Atlantic University

D. L. Turner
Arizona State University

Susan J. Tyburski
Women's College of the University of Denver

Mercedes Valadez
Arizona State University

Eric van der Vort
Ball State University

Michael S. Vaughn
Sam Houston State University

Samuel G. Vickovic
California State University, Long Beach

Carrie Wai
California School of Professional Psychology

John Walsh
Shinawatra University

Priscilla Warren
Western Carolina University

Andrew J. Waskey
Dalton State College

Robert W. Watkins
Florida State University

Travis F. Whalen
Virginia Polytechnic Institute and State University

Darren A. Wheeler
Ball State University

Mary Jo Wiatrak-Uhlenkott
University of Minnesota

Hettie V. Williams
Monmouth University

Meredith Conover Williams
Washington State University

Ryan K. Williams
University of Illinois, Springfield

Karie J. Wiltshire
U.S. Department of Agriculture Forest Service

David B. Wolcott
Independent Scholar

Kristina Wood
California School of Professional Psychology

William R. Wood
University of Auckland

Derek Worch
Ball State University

Kevin A. Wright
Arizona State University

Marvin Zalman
Wayne State University

Thomas Zawisza
University of Arkansas at Little Rock

Aharon W. Zorea
University of Wisconsin, Richland

Priscilla H. M. Zotti
United States Naval Academy

Introduction

The history of crime and criminal justice is almost by definition social history. It is the history of social and antisocial behavior and social institutions. However, social history is not only a matter of content but also of method or approach to history. The tumult of the 1960s was the background for development of "new social history," which went beyond the old method of describing interesting social details to analyze social trends in institutions and behavior.

The history of crime and criminal justice was part of this trend, heightened by the Presidential Commission reports on "Law Enforcement and the Administration of Justice" (1965–69) and "The Causes and Prevention of Violence" (1968). This was also the era of the Warren Supreme Court decisions protecting the rights of criminal suspects, defendants, and prisoners. The 1960s and 1970s were a period when crime and punishment were central to political debates about the direction of American society. Popular, legal, sociological, and historical writers explored many facets of crime, policing, punishment, and legal developments.

In academia social history's earlier form was "social science history," the use of social science methods and theories to elucidate events and institutions of the past. This approach was the first to treat the history of crime and criminal justice beyond description and chronology. There had been popular histories of criminals like Herbert Asbury's *The Gangs of New York* (1929) or celebratory histories of individual police forces going back to the 19th century (e.g., Augustine E. Costello's *Our Police Protectors,* 1885, about the New York City police). A pair of early works that brought the comparative perspective to bear was Raymond Fosdick's *European Police Systems* (1913) and *American Police Systems* (1920), written from the viewpoint of a Progressive Era reformer.

The modern analytical approach to policing was pioneered by Roger Lane, *Policing the City: Boston 1820–1865* (1967), and James D. Richardson, *The New York Police: Colonial Times to 1900* (1975). In addition to police, prisons, reformers, and other aspects of the criminal justice system received new attention during an era marked by sharply increasing crime rates, ghetto riots, and scrutiny of the entire spectrum of crime and punishment.

Historians could draw from the work of sociologists and criminologists who had long been interested in the motivations of crime and the operations of police, judicial, and correctional institutions. Criminal motivation was probably the earliest area of sociological investigation, pioneered by Richard Dugdale's *The Jukes* in 1877 and H. V. Redfield's *Homicide North and South* in 1880. Beginning in the 1870s, the Italian "criminal anthropologist"

Cesare Lombroso's investigation of convicts' physical indications of criminality was very influential in the later 19th century, although later researchers rejected his views. The fields of criminology and penology developed in this period, usually emphasizing social reform (unfortunately, including eugenics). In the 1920s and 1930s appeared the first systematic sociological studies of street gangs, pioneered by Frederick Thrasher in 1927. By the 1970s, when social histories of criminal justice institutions appeared, deviance and social control were well-established fields in social science.

Social science history took two paths: the use of sociological theory to place institutional development in context (e.g., W. R. Miller's *Cops and Bobbies*, 1977) and quantitative social science methodology, pioneered by Eric Monkkonen's *The Dangerous Class* (1975). In both theoretical and quantitative studies social control was the leading conceptual argument, influencing histories of prisons (David Rothman, *The Discovery of the Asylum*, 1971), moral reform movements (Anthony Platt, *The Child Savers*, 1969), hospitals, and public education.

History of the Inarticulate

Conceptual social science history was joined by another form of social history, a more empirical "history from the bottom up" or "history of the inarticulate." This approach, inspired by European historians E. P. Thompson and George Rude, encouraged historians to focus on criminals and ordinary people and their interactions with the criminal justice system. Although earlier work has often discussed responses of different groups of people to institutions, they were more focused on development of the institutions themselves.

Probably the first members of the underworld to attract attention were prostitutes (Ruth Rosen, *The Lost Sisterhood*, 1982). Drawing from and analyzing George Appo's autobiography, Timothy Gilfoyle traced this late-19th-century pickpocket's life and its meaning in *A Pickpocket's Tale* (2006). Allen Steinberg's *The Transformation of Criminal Justice* (1989) was an innovative study of how ordinary Philadelphians used local courts to resolve neighborhood disputes. People involved with institutions of criminal justice emerged from obscurity.

In the 1980s, cultural history, with its emphasis on interpretation of texts and the influence of French theorists, seemed on the way to dominating the study of American history generally. Michel Foucault's *Discipline and Punish* (first published in English in 1975) was a major influence in criminal justice history.

Focusing on prisons, Foucault used the change from corporal punishment to incarceration to argue that the whole society has become one in which the state can reach into all aspects of citizens' lives. Governmental power permeates all social activity, much of it indirect through self-policing of behavior. Historians have criticized Foucault as more a philosopher than an archival researcher. He tends to make power too far-reaching, not allowing for various forms of opposition, particularly passive resistance. Even before Americans embraced Foucault, social control theory was meeting similar criticisms.

Representations of crime and punishment were important in Foucault's work, and this aspect has encouraged many scholars to explore the social and cultural context of specific crimes. For example. there are Amy Gilman Srebnick (*The Mysterious Death of Mary Rogers*, 1995), Patricia Cline Cohen (*The Murder of Helen Jewett*, 1999), and Mary Ting Yi Lui (*The Chinatown Trunk Mystery*, 2005). These studies developed media representation of crime and criminal justice as an aspect of American culture, exploring not only the crime but its meanings to different groups.

The violent 1960s launched a long-continuing trend, the study of the history of homicide and other forms of violence. Historians have sought to answer the question of why the United States has the highest homicide rates in the Western world.

Highest Homicide Rates

The academic response included a documentary collection compiled by Richard Hofstadter and Michael Wallace, *American Violence* (1970). More recent studies are Richard M. Brown's *No Duty to Retreat: Violence and Values in American History and Society* (1991) and Roger Lane's *Murder in America: A History* (1997). These studies were narrative histories interwoven with arguments about the meaning of events and trends.

Within the last decade the study of violence has developed as a marriage of quantitative analysis and sociological argument. The old issue of the unreliability of crime statistics has been carefully addressed, as in Eric Monkkonen's *Homicide in New York City* (2001). Monkkonen, Andrew Roth, and others over many years compiled a violence database from scattered statistics. They have sought systematic methods to elucidate the causes of American murderous violence. This quantitative approach reveals fluctuating rates, important regional differences, and some unsuspected aspects of American homicide, such as its ups and downs over the years but overall a decline until the 1960s and the familar further decline in the late 1990s.

In a recent discussion, Roth and Douglas Ekberg point out that declines in homicide may well be due to modern medical techniques, much more efficient at saving lives than in the past, as well as possible cultural shifts. An assault is now less likely to result in death than 150 years ago, or even 50 years ago, because of developments in traumatic wound treatment. Roth points to a correlation between national homicide rates and perceptions of government legitimacy: murders are up when legitimacy is down. The databases have allowed historians to see trends much more clearly and to develop arguments that reflect the data.

Explanations for American violence remain disputed, the main disagreement being between Roth and European historians who emphasize Norbert Elias's theory of "the civilizing process" defined by Stephen Mennell as "changes in people's ordinary behavior ... [due] to the formation of states with relatively effective monopolies of violence and to changes in the balances of power between social groups within states."

In short, American homicide rates and violence generally remain higher than in Europe because of a number of physical, cultural, and ideological factors that have limited state power compared to Europe. Pieter Spierenburg, perhaps the leading champion of Elias, argues that in the United States democracy came before development of an effective state. In short, cultures of localism, small government, and gun toting developed in a context of a weak state whose authority continues to be contested not only by criminals but by respectable voters.

The social history of crime and criminal justice, inspired by the violence of an era of conflict in the 1960s, has continued to grow in our relatively less violent era. It has built on its earliest work to become a major contributor to understanding our nation's past and present.

The editors of *The Social History of Crime and Punishment in America: An Encyclopedia* have aimed for comprehensive coverage of the field from the colonial era to the present. Crime, policing, courts and law, imprisonment, theoretical and philosophical issues all have their place. Articles range from large conceptual approaches (e.g., "Murder, Sociology of") and thorough historical treatments (e.g., "Murder, History of") to smaller articles on individuals (police leaders, criminals, mystery writers, reformers, etc.) or specific crimes (e.g., the Lizzie Borden murder case).

Individual laws, official reports, calls for reform are among the documents important in history that are analyzed in articles. The role of media in representing crime and criminal justice receives full attention. Unique features are the history of crime and criminal justice in individual states (an area not fully researched for all states) and treatment of crime and criminal justice under different presidential administrations.

The fifth volume of the encyclopedia contains some 150 primary documents, along with introductory headnotes, and 10 chronological essays as background.

We seek a wide audience for *The Social History of Crime and Punishment in America: An Encyclopedia*. Historians, of course, and other social scientists, teachers at all levels developing courses, students writing papers, lawyers interested in famous cases and development of criminal law, and last but by no means least, the citizen seeking understanding of issues that have been of concern since the first colonists landed.

Wilbur R. Miller
Editor

Chronology

1275: The Statute of Westminster in England regulates the legal procedure of bail, a matter that had previously been left to the discretion of local authorities.

1619: Slavery begins in the geographical region that will become the United States as 20 captive slaves are sold at Jamestown, Virginia.

1627: The English parliament passes the Petition of Right, which specifies that people cannot be imprisoned without hearing the charges against them and must be allowed bail.

1640: John Punch, an African American servant, becomes the first person in the American colonies documented to be sentenced to a life of servitude. He receives this sentence as punishment for running away from his employer.

1641: Massachusetts prohibits imprisonment of an accused person before sentencing, other than in capital cases or cases where the defendant had shown disrespect for the court, if the person could provide a guarantee that they would appear for trial.

1646: Massachusetts passes the first law in the American colonies banning gambling in public houses.

1652: Rhode Island passes a law forbidding a person from being enslaved for more than 10 years.

1662: Virginia establishes that the children of slave mothers are slaves even if their father was a free white man, based on the legal principle of *partus sequitur ventrem*.

1679: In England, the Habeas Corpus Act specifies that a person must be brought before a judge within a specified number of days following a receipt of habeas corpus and must be released on bail within a specified number of days if the offense is bailable.

1692: Nineteen men and women are put to death during the Salem witch trials.

1705: Virginia passes a series of laws, many of which were adopted by other slaveholding colonies, legislating that all African, mulatto, and Native American servants brought to Virginia were slaves who could be held in permanent bondage, used in commercial trade, punished for infractions, and had no legal standing in the courts.

1740: South Carolina passes a comprehensive Negro Act legalizing execution of rebellious slaves and prohibiting slaves from, among other things, assembling in groups, raising food, earning money, and learning to read English.

1763: Cesare Beccaria publishes the pamphlet *On Crimes and Punishments*, which argues against the usefulness of the death penalty.

1765: William Blackstone begins publication of *Commentaries on the Laws of England*, an influential work in the development of both the English and American legal systems.

1786: Pennsylvania adopts the Wheelbarrow Law, which requires convicts to perform public labor while chained to a cannon ball (to prevent escape) and while wearing unattractive clothing, thus requiring them to work and also to be exposed to public ridicule. The experiment is copied by several other states but ultimately proves a failure as some convicts escape while others get into fights with each other or with passersby.

1789: In the United States, the Judiciary Act of 1789 specifies which crimes are bailable and sets guidelines for establishing bail.

1793: The Fugitive Slave Act makes it illegal to assist escaped slaves. It also authorizes agents to seize alleged slaves and petition for their removal to their alleged home state, encouraging the industry of "slave catching," which sometimes also captured free blacks and sold them into slavery.

1793: William Godwin publishes *Enquiry Concerning Political Justice and Its Influence on Modern Morals and Manners*, now seen as a fundamental text in the growth of anarchist thought.

1794: A Pennsylvania law creates the category of first-degree murder, meaning murder that was planned or particularly heinous, and makes it the only crime eligible for capital punishment (those convicted of second-degree murder would be sentenced to imprisonment).

1798: The Alien and Sedition Acts are passed by the U.S. Congress. These four acts permit the president to deport noncitizens, increase to 14 years the time of residence necessary for an immigrant to obtain citizenship, and criminalize the publication of writings that criticize the government or government officials.

1821: Connecticut becomes the first U.S. state to pass a law regulating abortion.

1821: With *Cohens v. Virginia*, the U.S. Supreme Court asserts its power of judicial review over state supreme court decisions.

1830: President Andrew Jackson signs the Indian Removal Act into law. This results in the migration (theoretically voluntary, but in fact often coerced or forced) of Native Americans from the southeastern United States to the so-called Indian Territory in what is now Oklahoma.

1831: Gustave de Beaumont and Alexis de Tocqueville travel to the United States to study the prison system.

1833: In *Barron v. Mayor of Baltimore*, the U.S. Supreme Court rules that the Bill of Rights only applied to actions of the federal government and did not limit the action of state governments. The case in question involves a wharf operator in Baltimore who sued the city for damages, claiming that they had redirected the natural course of several streams, which made the water near his wharf too shallow for use.

1835: In England, Henry Goddard is the first to successfully use ballistic characteristics to establish guilt in a court case. He is able to match a blemish on a bullet taken from a shooting victim with that found on an imperfect bullet mold found in the home of the suspected shooter.

1841: John Augustus, a shoemaker from Massachusetts, invents the system of probation by convincing a court to release an indigent man, charged with drunkenness, to be released into his care. Reportedly, by 1858 Augustus assists almost 2,000 men and women as well as about 30 children in this way.

1845: The *National Police Gazette*, a popular magazine specializing in lurid coverage (including illustrations) of crime, begins publication.

1850: The Fugitive Slave Act, passed by Congress as part of the Compromise of 1850, requires federal marshals to assist in the recovery of escaped slaves in free states (those that had abolished slavery) and establishes special commissioners to enforce the law.

1859: The case of *Ableman v. Booth* determines that the federal judiciary is the final authority, superior to state courts, on matters concerning the Constitution and laws of the United States.

1862: President Abraham Lincoln signs the Morrill Anti-Bigamy Act.

1864: The International Working Man's Association, a global cooperative sometimes called the First International, is founded by anarchists, trade union organizers, and members of left-wing political parties.

1865: President Abraham Lincoln is assassinated by John Wilkes Booth.

1865: The Thirteenth Amendment to the U.S. Constitution prohibits slavery and involuntary servitude.

1865: The Ku Klux Klan (KKK) is founded in Pulaski, Tennessee, as a vigilante organization with the goal of maintaining control over newly freed slaves (i.e., returning them to a state similar to slavery) through violence and intimidation. It also directs violence toward Union sympathizers and carpetbaggers.

1868: The Fourteenth Amendment to the U.S. Constitution overrules the 1857 *Dred Scott v. Sandford* decision and establishes that persons born or naturalized in the United States, regardless of race, are citizens and entitled to equal protection under the law.

1873: The federal Comstock Law prohibits the importation, mailing, or interstate transportation of information regarding contraception and abortion in the United States.

1875: San Francisco is the first city in the country to pass an ordinance prohibiting opium dens.

1876: The Jesse James/Cole Younger gang attempts to rob the First National Bank of Northfield, Minnesota, but the townspeople successfully resist and most of the gang members are killed or arrested (but both James brothers escape).

1878: Massachusetts creates a state system of probation with paid officers to supervise those released into the system.

1881: President James Garfield is shot by Charles Guiteau; Garfield dies 11 weeks later from infections related to his injuries.

1882: Congress passes the Chinese Exclusion Act that prohibits Chinese laborers from immigrating to the United States. Originally meant to be in place for 10 years, it was amended but remained largely in place until the 1943 Magnuson Act.

1886: A public rally in Chicago on May 4, organized to support trade unions and the eight-hour day, is disrupted by a bombing that injures a number of people. This becomes known as the Haymarket bombing (the rally was held at Haymarket Square) and Albert Parsons, head of the International Working Man's Association, is tried for conspiracy to commit murder alongside seven anarchists: August Spies, Samuel Fielden, George Engel, Adolph Fisher, Louis Lingg, Oscar Neebe, and Michael Schwab.

1887: Major Robert W. McClaughry, then warden of the Illinois State Penitentiary, adopts the Bertillon system of recordkeeping (developed in France) and advocates its adoption across North America.

1887: The Interstate Commerce Act is created in response to the 1886 Supreme Court decision in *Wabash, St. Louis & Pacific Railway Company v. Illinois*, which established that states have no authority to regulate interstate commerce.

1890: William Kemmler, a convicted murderer, becomes the first person to be executed using the electric chair.

1892: A strike at the Carnegie Steel Company in Homestead, Pennsylvania, becomes violent: After members of the Amalgamated Association of Iron and Steel Workers defeat 300 Pinkerton agents, the factory is retaken by 6,000 state militia troops and the union is broken.

1896: With the decision in *Plessy v. Ferguson,* the U.S. Supreme Court rules that segregation is legal in the United States and establishes the doctrine of "separate but equal."

1898: The Erdman Act prohibits railway companies from prohibiting employees from joining labor unions and provides for arbitration in the case of unions and railway companies.

1899: Cook County (Chicago), Illinois, passes the first juvenile justice law in the country, based on the principle that children and adolescents should be treated as children in need of help rather than hardened criminals.

1901: President William McKinley is shot by the anarchist Leon Czolgosz and dies eight days later. After McKinley's assassination, the Secret Service is charged with providing security protection for U.S. presidents.

1903: The New York State prison system begins the first systematic use of fingerprints to identify criminals.

1905: California becomes the first U.S. state to require registration of automobiles and, shortly thereafter, to require drivers to hold a license.

1907: The military fort on Alcatraz Island in San Francisco Bay ceases to operate as a fort and becomes a military prison.

1908: The Bureau of Investigation, the forerunner of the FBI (Federal Bureau of Investigation), is founded to investigate interstate crime.

1908: The U.S. Supreme Court, in *Adair v. United States,* rules that employers have the right to prohibit employees from joining labor unions, thus legalizing so-called yellow-dog contracts.

1909: The U.S. Congress passes the Opium Exclusion Act, the first federal law governing opiates, forbidding the importation, possession, or use of smoking opium.

1910: The Mann Act, or White Slave Traffic Act, intended to combat human trafficking and prostitution, forbids taking women across state lines for "immoral purposes."

1914: The U.S. Supreme Court rules in *Weeks v. United States* that items seized during search of a private residence without a search warrant have been illegally obtained and cannot be used as evidence in federal trials.

1914: The Harrison Narcotics Act, intended to curb the abuse of opiates, requires registration of all those who prescribe opiates, including physicians and pharmacists. This law is also the first to place cocaine in the same category as heroin.

1915: In *Coppage v. Kansas,* the U.S Supreme Court rules that yellow-dog contracts, which allow employers to prohibit their employees from joining unions, are legal, thus striking down 13 state statutes outlawing discrimination in hiring on the basis of union membership.

1917: The Espionage Act prohibits interference with military recruitment or operations, lending support to U.S. enemies during wartime, or promotion of insubordination in the armed forces.

1919: The Dyer Act (also known as the National Motor Vehicle Theft Act) makes it illegal to drive a stolen vehicle across state lines or to deal in stolen vehicles that had crossed state lines.

1920s: American police forces adopt the use of the automobile, increasing the area one man or team can patrol and also increasing the speed by which they can respond to calls for help.

1920: Crystal Eastman, Roger Baldwin, and Walter Nelles found the American Civil Liberties Union (ACLU), a private voluntary organization dedicated to defending the freedoms guaranteed in the Bill of Rights.

1922: The U.S. Congress passes the Narcotic Drugs Import and Export Act (the Jones-Miller

Act) providing stiff fines and prison sentences for those importing illegal narcotics.

1923: The American Law Institute is founded in response to dissatisfaction with the uncertainty and complexity of American law, with the goal of improving and clarifying the law and also supporting legal scholarship and education.

1923: In *Frye v. United States*, a court case involving the admissibility of the results of a polygraph test as evidence, the U.S. Supreme Court establishes rules for expert testimony in the courtroom.

1923: The United States bans all narcotics sales.

1924: J. Edgar Hoover becomes the head of the Bureau of Investigation and serves 48 years with the organization (later renamed the Department of Investigation and then the Federal Bureau of Investigation).

1925: The Bureau of Forensic Ballistics, a private firm, is established in New York to provide firearms identification services and remains in business until 1929.

1925: Theodore Dreiser publishes the novel *An American Tragedy*, whose plot is based on a much-publicized 1906 case in which Chester Gillette was convicted of murdering Grace Brown (he claimed her death was accidental) by drowning her in a lake.

1926: New York becomes the first state to make drunk driving a felony.

1927: Italian immigrants Ferdinando Nicola Sacco and Bartolomeo Vanzetti are executed following their conviction for murder; the case is controversial and many believe the men did not receive a fair trial due to their political views.

1928: Ruth Snyder, convicted of the murder of her husband, is executed; a photograph of her in the electric chair is published in the *New York Daily News*.

1928: The Straus totalisator is invented, a machine enabling rapid calculation of the odds that a bet will pay off, greatly speeding the adoption of pari-mutuel betting at horse tracks.

1929: Following riots, Clinton Prison in New York State institutes rehabilitation programs including mandatory educational instruction.

1930: The Federal Bureau of Prisons is created in the Department of Justice and has responsibility for managing and regulating federal prisons.

1930: The first UCR (Uniform Crime Report) is issued, reporting on the incidence of various types of crimes in the United States, aggregated at the city, state, and other levels.

1931: Casino gambling is legalized in Nevada.

1932: The Norris–La Guardia Act bans yellow-dog contracts (which allowed employers to stipulate that employees could not join unions), bars federal courts from interfering with nonviolent labor disputes, and states that employers may not interfere with the right of employees to consider joining a trade union.

1932: The infant child of aviator Charles Lindbergh is kidnapped. The case is highly publicized and Congress reacts by passing the Lindbergh Act, the first federal kidnapping law; the death penalty for kidnapping is added in 1934.

1933: The U.S. Bureau of Immigration merges with the Bureau of Naturalization to form the Immigration and Naturalization Service (INS).

1933–34: Clyde Barrow and Bonnie Parker commit a series of robberies in the midwest and south; they become nationally known and are immortalized in the popular media, most notably in Arthur Penn's film *Bonnie and Clyde* (1967).

1934: A high-profile federal prison is established on Alcatraz Island in San Francisco Bay, designed to house dangerous and notorious criminals or those who had escaped from other facilities. Among those who are housed at Alcatraz are the gangsters Al Capone and George Kelly Barnes ("Machine Gun" Kelly) and the murderer Robert Stroud, known as "the Birdman of Alcatraz."

Alcatraz is operated as a federal prison until 1963 and serves as a model for other high-security prisons across the United States. Since 1973 it is operated by the National Park Service as a wildlife sanctuary and museum.

1935: With *Norris v. Alabama,* the U.S. Supreme Court overturns the convictions of the Scottsboro Boys, nine African American teenagers, on the grounds that they had been denied equal protection under the law because African Americans had been systematically excluded from the juries that heard their cases.

1941: President Franklin Roosevelt establishes the Fair Employment Practices Commission with Executive Order 8802, banning discrimination in the defense industry on the basis of race, color, religion, or national origin.

1942: In response to the attack on Pearl Harbor by Japan, President Franklin Roosevelt authorizes the removal of over 100,000 Japanese and persons of Japanese descent from their homes in the western United States to internment camps. The constitutionality of the executive order authorizing this removal is upheld by the Supreme Court in 1944.

1948: President Harry S. Truman, with Executive Order 9981, orders that the U.S. armed forces become racially integrated.

1950: The FBI begins issuing a Ten Most Wanted Fugitives list.

1950: Ford produces the first custom police car.

1950: William Parker becomes chief of police for Los Angeles, taking charge of a notoriously corrupt department and implementing selection and training of officers using methods adapted from military peacekeeping. However, Parker is also charged with fostering animosity among nonwhite residents of Los Angeles and of creating a police force that was disconnected from the communities it patrolled.

1950–51: The Kefauver Committee (United States Special Committee to Investigate Crime in Interstate Commerce) conducts an investigation into the extent of organized crime in the country and the corruption of police forces across the nation.

1953: Julius and Ethel Rosenberg, convicted of espionage, are executed in New York.

1954: With the *Brown v. Board of Education* decision the U.S. Supreme Court overturns the "separate but equal" standard for schools and requires that they be integrated "with all deliberate speed."

1955: A 14-year-old African American, Emmett Till, is murdered in Mississippi, allegedly for flirting with a white woman; his mother insists on an open-casket funeral, and the image of his mutilated body is published in many newspapers and magazines, focusing intense scrutiny on the justice system in Mississippi.

1956: The Federal Bureau of Investigation begins a counterintelligence program, known as COINTELPRO, which is aimed at infiltrating and disrupting domestic social and political organizations, including many involved in the civil rights movement. COINTELPRO continues until 1971.

1958: The Planned Parenthood Federation of America requests that the American Law Institute draft a model abortion statute. The resulting statute supports abortion if the pregnancy resulted from rape or incest, if the baby is believed to have a severe physical or mental handicap, or if carrying the pregnancy to term is likely to cause the woman several physical or mental damage.

1960: The U.S. Supreme Court, in *Boynton v. Virginia*, rules that segregation in public interstate transportation facilities (such as bus or train stations) violates the Interstate Commerce Act.

1961: In *Mapp v. Ohio,* the U.S. Supreme Court rules that evidence seized from a person's home without a search warrant is inadmissible in state courts, thus extending the principles established in *Weeks v. United States* (1914) that prohibit the use of such evidence in federal courts.

1962: Television personality Sherri Finkbine is refused an abortion in her home state of Arizona despite the fact that she took thalidomide, a drug associated with severe birth defects, during pregnancy. This case galvanizes public support for abortion in specific circumstances.

1962–65: An epidemic of German measles (rubella) sweeps the United States. Because exposure to rubella during pregnancy is associated with a greatly increased rate of birth defects, this epidemic increases public support for abortion in specific circumstances.

1963: On September 15, the 16th Street Baptist Church in Birmingham, Alabama, is bombed, killing four girls and drawing attention to the need for increased legislation protecting civil rights in the United States.

1963: President John F. Kennedy is shot and killed by Lee Harvey Oswald. An investigation by the Warren Commission in 1963–64 concludes that Oswald acted alone, yet several conspiracy theories linger for decades.

1963: The U.S. Supreme Court establishes, in the case *Gideon v. Wainwright*, that indigent defendants are entitled to legal counsel, which must be provided by the state if the defendants cannot pay for it.

1964: The Civil Rights Act of 1964 is signed into law by U.S. president Lyndon Johnson. This act prohibits discrimination based on race, color, religion, sex, or national origin in employment and public accommodations and overrules all state and local laws mandating such discrimination.

1964: New Hampshire becomes the first state to offer a lottery; New York follows three years later and New Jersey begins a lottery in 1970.

1964: A student demonstration at the University of California, Berkeley explodes into violence that results in over 700 arrests.

1964: In *Cooper v. Pate* the U.S. Supreme Court rules that prison inmates may sue for grievances under the Civil Rights Act of 1871.

1964: In *Heart of Atlanta Motel v. United States* the U.S. Supreme Court rules that a motel owner did not have the right to refuse to allow African American guests because such a prohibition interfered with interstate commerce.

1965: African American activist Malcolm X is assassinated in New York City.

1965: A riot in Watts, an African American neighborhood in Los Angeles, requires over 16,000 policemen, highway patrolmen, and National Guard troops to restore order. This highlights problems of institutional racism and poor relations between the police and the local community.

1965: President Lyndon Johnson signs the Voting Rights Act of 1965 that prohibits impediments such as poll taxes and literacy tests, which had been used to prevent African Americans from voting.

1965: *Griswold v. Connecticut*, a U.S. Supreme Court decision, strikes down a Connecticut law prohibiting the use of contraceptives and establishes a "right to marital privacy."

1966: In *Miranda v. Arizona*, the U.S. Supreme Court rules that a defendant must be informed of his/her right to refrain from self-incrimination (the Miranda warning) and his/her right to legal counsel. The decision also states that a statement of self-incrimination is not admissible as evidence unless the defendant has been informed of these two rights before making the statement.

1966: The Black Panther Party is founded by Bobby Seale and Huey Newton, advocating economic and civic empowerment in the African American community as well as black nationalism.

1966: The Bail Reform Act of 1966 increases the access of accused persons to bail by providing a list of circumstances judges could consider and allows case review and resetting of bail for those individuals who could not make bail as originally specified.

1967: Richard Speck is convicted of the death of eight student nurses in Chicago; he is sentenced to death, but the sentence is later commuted to life in prison.

1967: California becomes the first U.S. state to legalize abortion in the case of a severely deformed fetus or to preserve the mother's mental health.

1968: Civil rights leader Martin Luther King, Jr., is assassinated in Memphis, Tennessee. James Earl Ray is convicted of the murder in 1969.

1968: U.S. senator and presidential candidate Robert F. Kennedy is shot and killed in California. Sirhan Sirhan is sentenced to death for the crime, a sentence later reduced to life imprisonment.

1968–69: The Zodiac Killer kills at least seven people in northern California; the killer, whose identity remains unknown, sends letters to the local media, signed "Zodiac," that contain non-public details about the crimes and sometimes cryptograms.

1970: The Controlled Substances Act is passed by the U.S. Congress. It creates five schedules or classifications of drugs based on factors such as potential for abuse and approved medical uses, with penalties and regulations based on the schedule of a given drug.

1971: The U.S. Supreme Court, in *United States v. Vuitch*, holds that abortion is a surgical procedure and physicians have the authority to determine if it is necessary to protect a woman's health.

1971: A highly publicized riot at the Attica Correctional Facility in New York State focuses attention on conditions within the prison as well as the civil rights of prisoners.

1972: In *Gates v. Collier*, the U.S. Fifth Circuit Court of Appeals places limits on the types of corporal punishment that can be administered in prisons. It also outlaws the "trusty system" in place at the state prison in Parchman, Mississippi, in which certain inmates were granted the power to control and punish other inmates.

1972: *Furman v. Georgia*, a decision of the U.S. Supreme Court, determines that the application of the death penalty in an arbitrary manner constitutes cruel and unusual punishment and is unconstitutional. Of particular concern was the perceived racial bias in many states, where African American prisoners were far more likely than white prisoners to be executed although their crimes might be quite similar.

1972: The National Crime Victimization Survey (NCVS), a method of determining the incidence of crime in the United States through sampling and surveys of crime victims, begins in response to dissatisfaction with the Uniform Crime Report (UCR).

1973: President Richard Nixon creates the Drug Enforcement Administration (DEA) to consolidate federal powers of drug enforcement within a single Justice Department agency.

1973: The U.S. Supreme Court, in *Roe v. Wade*, strikes down a restrictive Texas law regarding abortions and greatly expands access to abortions in the country, particularly during the first trimester (12 weeks).

1973: The Kansas City Preventative Patrol Experiment, by George Kelling and colleagues, challenges the conventional wisdom that motorized police patrols reduce crime. Kelling's conclusions were challenged on methodological and other grounds but also led to further research about the effectiveness of many other standard police tactics.

1973: *Doe v. Bolton*, a U.S. Supreme Court decision, strikes down a Georgia state law that requires approval of two consulting physicians and a hospital committee before an abortion can be legally performed.

1973: Governor Nelson Rockefeller of New York signs a bill containing a series of harsh penalties for those convicted of the possession and sale of narcotics, which come to be known as the Rockefeller Drug Laws.

1976: *Gregg v. Georgia* and several other cases end the unofficial moratorium on capital punishment in the United States, which began in 1972.

1976: The Hyde Amendment prohibits the use of federal funding, primarily that provided for Medicaid, to pay for abortions. This has the effect of restricting the ability of low-income women to obtain an abortion.

1976: New Jersey legalizes casino gambling in Atlantic City and two years later opens the first legal casino on the East Coast.

1976: In *Planned Parenthood of Central Missouri v. Danforth* the U.S. Supreme Court rules that a husband does not have veto power over his wife's choice to have an abortion but that a minor seeking an abortion could be required to have parental consent for the procedure.

1976–77: David Berkowitz, the Son of Sam killer, commits a series of murders in New York City.

1977–78: The Hillside Strangler, later revealed to be two men, Kenneth Bianchi and Angelo Buono, Jr., rapes, tortures, and kills at least 10 women in the hills surrounding Los Angeles.

1980: With the decision in *Harris v. McRae* the U.S. Supreme Court establishes that states are not required to provide funding for medically necessary abortions.

1981: President Ronald Reagan is shot by John Hinckley, Jr.; three others are wounded in the attack, most seriously Press Secretary James Brady, who is partially paralyzed as a result.

1982: Charles Brooks, convicted of murder in Texas, becomes the first person in the United States to be executed by lethal injection.

1982: James Q. Wilson and George L. Kelling publish an article introducing the "broken windows" theory, which claims that small social problems (e.g., litter allowed to accumulate on the street or graffiti on public buildings) create an environment that encourages more serious crime.

1984: The Bail Reform Act of 1984 addresses bail for immigration and material witness cases, provides a wide range of alternatives to financial bail, and prevents a judge from setting bail so high that a person cannot meet it (although detention is allowed if an accused person is considered a threat to the community).

1984: Serial killer Velma Barfield is executed in North Carolina; she is the first woman to be executed in the United States since 1962.

1986: The U.S. Congress passes the Immigration Reform and Control Act of 1986 that requires employers to ascertain that new employees have the legal right to work in the United States, while at the same time granting amnesty to illegal immigrants who had lived continuously in the country since January 1, 1982.

1987: With *McCleskey v. Kemp* the U.S. Supreme Court determines that the fact that the death penalty is disproportionately applied to African Americans, or to people who kill white versus African American victims, is not sufficient grounds to make capital punishment unconstitutional.

1990: Congress passes the Americans with Disabilities Act of 1990 that prohibits discrimination based on disability in several areas, including employment, public accommodation, and telecommunications.

1992: The U.S. Supreme Court affirms in *Parenthood of Southeastern Pennsylvania v. Casey* that medical clinics could require a 24-hour waiting period before performing an abortion and that states could require that women seeking abortions be informed of alternatives and fetal development.

1992: Congress passes the Professional and Amateur Sports Protection Act forbidding states from authorizing new sports betting, leaving Nevada the only state with legal betting on sporting events.

1993: Dr. David Gunn, an obstetrician/gynecologist who performed abortions, is killed in Pensacola, Florida, by Michael F. Griffin. This was the first known assassination in the United States of a physician by an antiabortion activist.

1994: New Jersey passes a law requiring local communities to be warned of sex offenders living in the area; the law is dubbed Megan's Law after Megan Kanka, a seven-year-old killed by a known child molester living on her block.

1994: The U.S. Supreme Court, in *National Organization for Women v. Scheidler*, rules that federal racketeering law may be used to prosecute violent antiabortion protesters.

1995: Former football star O. J. Simpson is acquitted in the murder of his wife Nicole Brown Simpson and companion Ronald Goldman, after a highly publicized trial broadcast on U.S. television.

1996: Theodore Kaczynski, known as the Unabomber, is arrested in Montana, after a lengthy FBI investigation. A former professor of mathematics, Kaczynski sent homemade bombs through the mail, many to university professors and graduate students.

1996: The U.S. Congress passes a law requiring every state to develop a procedure for notifying the public when a sex offender moves into a community, similar to the law enacted in New Jersey in 1994.

1996: Lyle and Erik Menendez are convicted of the murder of their parents after a highly publicized trial broadcast on Court TV.

1999: With *City of Chicago v. Morales*, the U.S. Supreme Court strikes down a Chicago ordinance against loitering, intended to prevent gang activity, as impossibly vague.

1999: During the Columbine High School massacre, two students, Eric Harris and Dylan Klebold, kill 12 students and a teacher before killing themselves. The case opens a national debate on school bullying, because Harris and Klebold had reportedly been bullied for years.

2000: Physician Joseph Michael Swango pleads guilty to poisoning three patients; the actual number of victims is believed to be much higher.

2001: On September 11, a series of coordinated attacks by Al Qaeda terrorists on the World Trade Center in New York City and the Pentagon in Arlington, Virginia, kill almost 3,000 people and result in heightened security measures for air travel as well as other legal changes.

2001: In November, the U.S. Congress passes the Airport Federalization Action and the Aviation and Transportation Security Act to standardize passenger and luggage screening for air travel and make them the responsibility of the federal government.

2002: Aileen Wuornos, a prostitute and serial killer, is executed for the murder of six men in 1989 and 1990.

2005: Dennis Rader is sentenced to 10 consecutive life terms for the murder of 10 children and adults in Wichita, Kansas. He is dubbed the BTK Killer (Bind, Torture, Kill) because he sent letters to news outlets and the police signed with those initials.

2006: Megan Meier, a teenager in Missouri, commits suicide after being subjected to cyberbullying by an adult neighbor. The case led Missouri to enlarge the scope of its harassment law to include text messages, e-mail, and other electronic communications.

2007: Michael Vick, a quarterback in the National Football League, is arrested and pleads guilty to federal felony charges relating to his participation in a dogfighting ring. This highly publicized case highlights differing attitudes regarding blood sports such as dogfighting, which is illegal but still practiced.

2007: Seung-Hui Cho, a student at Virginia Tech, shoots and kills 32 people on the Tech campus before killing himself. The case motivates many American universities to create explicit procedures to notify students on campus of the presence of immediate threats.

2008: The U.S. Supreme Court rules that execution by lethal injection, as practiced in Kentucky, is not unconstitutional.

2010: President Barack Obama signs the Fair Sentencing Act, which narrows the disparity in punishment for possession of crack versus powder cocaine, from 100-to-1 to 18-to-1. This addresses a long-observed phenomenon that African Americans are more likely to use crack rather than powder cocaine and that sentencing disparities contributed to a disproportionate share of African Americans jailed for drug use.

2010: Rodney Alcala, dubbed the Dating Game Killer because he appeared on the television game show *The Dating Game* in the 1970s, is convicted and sentenced to death for the murder of five girls and women.

2010: Arizona passes the Support Our Law Enforcement and Safe Neighborhoods Act, a law intended to prevent and punish illegal immigration. Among its measures are the requirement that aliens carry identification at all times, a provision that makes it a crime to aid illegal immigrants, and a prohibition against state or local officials restricting enforcement of federal immigration laws. A federal court issues an injunction against the law taking effect due to concerns about its constitutionality and violations of civil liberties.

2011: Conrad Murray, a physician who treated pop singer Michael Jackson, is convicted of manslaughter in the singer's death, which was caused by an overdose of the anaesthetic propofol.

2011: Oscar Ortega-Hernandez shoots at the White House, with two bullets actually striking the building; he is charged with attempted assassination of President Barack Obama, although Obama was in Hawai'i at the time.

2011: Representative Gabrielle Giffords is shot by Jared Lee Loughner during an outdoor public meeting near Tucson, Arizona; 18 other people are shot and six die.

2011: Former Illinois governor Rod Blagojevich is convicted on 17 federal corruption charges and is sentenced to 14 years in prison.

2011: Whitey Bulger, a noted organized crime figure from Boston who had been a fugitive for many years, is arrested in California.

2011: Ingmar Guandique is convicted of the murder of Chandra Levy, an intern working at the Federal Bureau of Prisons at the time of her disappearance in 2001.

2011: Brian David Mitchell is sentenced to life in prison for the kidnapping and rape of Elizabeth Smart, 14 years old, from her Salt Lake City home in 2002.

2012: In several U.S. states, including Alabama, Tennessee, South Carolina, and Georgia, a law takes effect requiring employers to use a federal program called e-Verify to confirm that their employees are eligible to work in the United States. In California, a state law takes effect that prohibits private employers from being required to use e-Verify unless its use is mandated by federal law.

2012: Laws in Delaware and Hawai'i allow same-sex couples to enter into civil unions, a status that carries the same rights and benefits enjoyed by married couples.

Sarah Boslaugh
Kennesaw State University

Ableman v. Booth

Resulting in a major ruling in which the U.S. Supreme Court determined that state courts cannot issue orders that contradict or circumvent the holdings of federal courts, *Ableman v. Booth*, 62 U.S. 506 (1859) stands as a landmark case that determined the supremacy of federal law. Although *Ableman* dealt with the authority of the Fugitive Slave Act, its holding set a precedent that state courts must recognize the supremacy of the U.S. Supreme Court in determining cases arising pursuant to the U.S. Constitution and laws of the United States. The *Ableman* holding has had significant ramifications for prosecutors, defense attorneys, and defendants.

The *Ableman* case involved a dispute that arose in Wisconsin in 1854 regarding the custody of a fugitive slave. At that time, Wisconsin was a center for abolitionism and its constitution had outlawed slavery. In 1850, however, the U.S. Congress had passed the Fugitive Slave Act as a part of the Compromise of 1850. The Compromise of 1850 had defused four years of controversy between slaveholding southern states and the free states of the North. The Fugitive Slave Act was intended to allay Southern concerns that abolitionists in the North were assisting escaped slaves. To remedy these concerns, the Fugitive Slave Act required federal marshals to assist slave catchers in capturing fugitive slaves present in states that had abolished slavery (free states).

The Fugitive Slave Act established special commissioners who had concurrent jurisdiction with the U.S. district courts in enforcing the law. The special commissioners were empowered to assist in the return of runaway slaves to their masters. Any federal marshal who refused to assist in the return of a slave was subject to a $1,000 fine, and rewards were provided to those who assisted in the apprehension of runaways. At an ex parte hearing before the special commissioner, a claimant's sworn testimony regarding ownership of a suspected runaway was sufficient to establish fugitive status, and suspected slaves could not request a jury trial or testify on their own behalf.

Sherman Booth, an abolitionist, was the editor of the *Milwaukee Free Democrat*. When Booth became aware that Joshua Glover, a runaway slave from Missouri, was being held in a jail in Milwaukee, he gathered a group of over 100 men, who attempted to have the U.S. marshal holding Glover arrested. When this attempt was unsuccessful, Booth led a raid on the jail, freeing Glover. Glover was able to escape to Canada, but Booth was arrested for violating the Fugitive Slave Act. Booth appealed to the Wisconsin Supreme Court, which granted him a writ of habeas corpus and declared the Fugitive Slave Act unconstitutional. Federal officials appealed the Wisconsin Supreme

Court ruling, and the U.S. Supreme Court ruled the supremacy of federal law meant that Booth must stand trial. After being tried and convicted in the U.S. District Court for Wisconsin, Booth again appealed to the Wisconsin Supreme Court, which again ruled the Fugitive Slave Act was unconstitutional and overturned his conviction. The case moved between state and federal court for four years, until in 1859 the U.S. Supreme Court ruled that the supremacy clause of the U.S. Constitution made the Constitution, federal laws passed in accordance thereof, and treaties the supreme law of the land. These bound state judges, regardless of state constitutions or statutes to the contrary. The Wisconsin legislature issued a Declaration of Defiance, but Booth returned to jail until he was pardoned by President James Buchanan shortly before he left office in 1861.

Ableman was significant because it held that the U.S. Constitution grants the federal judiciary final authority with regard to matters involving the Constitution and laws of the United States. Because of this, state courts are unable to review or interfere with judgments issued by federal courts in matters involving the U.S. Constitution or federal laws. The U.S. Constitution thus restricts and limits the powers of the states, depriving their courts of the authority to annul the judgments of federal courts or to hold federal laws unconstitutional because of inconsistencies with their state constitutions. The holding has prevented state authorities from interfering with federal authorities when the federal authorities are carrying out duties pursuant to U.S. law.

Stephen T. Schroth
Jason A. Helfer
Lynn N. Mueller
Knox College

See Also: Buchanan, James (Administration of); Constitution of the United States of America; *Dred Scott v. Sandford*; Fugitive Slave Act of 1850; Judiciary Act of 1789; Slave Patrols; Slavery, Law of; Supreme Court, U.S.

Further Readings

Maltz, E. M. *Slavery and the Supreme Court, 1825–1861.* Lawrence: University Press of Kansas, 2009.

Simon, J. F. *Lincoln and Chief Justice Taney: Slavery, Secession, and the President's War Powers.* New York: Simon & Schuster, 2007.

Waldstreicher, D. *Slavery's Constitution: From Revolution to Ratification.* New York: Hill & Wang, 2009.

Abortion

During the colonial period, control over reproduction, similar to most family matters, remained a private concern. No laws prohibited abortion or the use of contraception. Most Americans did not consider abortion legally or morally wrong as long as it occurred prior to quickening, or the mother's first perception of fetal movement.

States passed the first wave of abortion laws in the 1820s and 1830s. Connecticut was the first state to enact a law in 1821, followed by Missouri, Illinois, and New York. By 1840, 10 more states had passed statutes. These laws did not intend to ban abortion but to make it safer through regulation. Legislators were concerned that women sometimes faced death or serious injuries from poison potions or dangerous instruments. Legislation generally made abortion illegal only after quickening and punished the abortionist, not the woman seeking the abortion.

A second wave of state laws resulted from an active campaign to criminalize abortion. Numerous factors influenced this drive. First, antiabortion champions harked upon race suicide notions, pointing to a perceived imbalance in fertility rates between the "best" women—wealthy, white, Anglo-Saxon Protestants—and the "inferior stock"—Irish and later southeastern European immigrants who were primarily Catholic or Jewish. Banning abortion, according to these campaigners, would force the "best" women to cease visiting abortionists such as Madame Restell and to fulfill their maternal and patriotic duty to bear "proper" children. Second, the American Medical Association (AMA), founded in 1847, was desperate to monopolize medical services. To this point, women controlled abortion; female relatives or midwives provided abortion information and services. Male doctors endeavored to redefine

This cartoon from between 1900 and 1912 points out the potential effects of Theodore Roosevelt's fear of the idea of "race suicide." A character called "Father Knickerbocker," representing New York City, arrives with a crowd of babies in Roosevelt's office, where newspapers on the floor announce "race suicide a crime" and "126,000 new New Yorkers." The caption asks, "Will this do?"

abortion as a dangerous procedure only licensed physicians could perform. As nearly all medical schools only permitted men, abortion would be controlled by male doctors. Third, state legislators continued to be concerned with women's safety. Abortions, similar to other surgeries in the pre-antibiotic era, could endanger women's health. The much-publicized death of Mary Rogers from abortion in 1841 led New York to strengthen its abortion law. Fourth, medical advances by mid-century led many doctors to agree that quickening was not a magic moment at which the fetus came to life; instead, life began at conception.

Despite the anti-abortion movement organized by the AMA and spearheaded by Dr. Horatio Storer of Massachusetts in 1860, not all doctors agreed. Some remained sympathetic to the plight of women facing unwanted pregnancies and continued to perform abortions. Some physicians maintained the priority of the mother's health while others began to value the life of the fetus over that of women. Anti-abortion doctors gained allies from social purity crusaders concerned with sexual morality and moral corruption. Many feminists also opposed abortion because it allowed men to exploit women sexually: male demands for sex led to undesired reproduction.

Thus abortion was not necessarily a sign of autonomy for women but a procedure to which they resorted because of male sexual aggression both inside and outside marriage. The federal government joined the crusade with the Comstock Law of 1873, which was named after moral reformer Anthony Comstock. This act forbade the importation, mailing, and interstate transportation of articles and literature concerning contraception and abortion. By 1880, 40 states had antiabortion statutes; 13 were new laws while 27 broadened existing measures. The great majority of these laws allowed abortion only if performed by a physician to save a woman's life.

Abortion During Criminalization

Criminalizing abortion at the state and federal level did not lead to its disappearance. Veiled advertisements for abortifacients continued to appear in newspapers and magazines, leading to a flourishing black market trade. Midwives, unlicensed doctors, and laypeople performed abortions, usually for working-class or indigent women. Licensed sympathetic physicians could stretch the definition of "lifesaving" in the law to perform legal abortions, generally for women of economic means. Many cities had several trusted abortionists, and most towns had a least one. Numerous doctors who did not perform the procedure considered the abortionist an important colleague to whom they could refer their patients. Abortion rates held steady through the period of criminalization: approximately 20 percent of all pregnancies for single and married women alike ended in abortion. Some noted increases occurred during the dire straits of the Great Depression and during World War II, as the nation relied heavily on female labor to sustain the industrial war effort. Officials often accepted cash payments from abortion providers to look the other way.

Postwar reassertions of traditional maternal roles for women led to a clampdown on abortion. Hospitals formed committees of five to seven doctors to decide if abortion was necessary to save a woman's life, reducing the power of an individual sympathetic doctor to perform legal abortions. Despite this closing of the legal loophole, doctors willing to risk their license and face jail time performed about one-third of abortions in the 1950s. Wealthy women could fly to other countries for the procedure while middle- and working-class women could use numerous underground services that functioned in urban areas. Indigent women often faced self-induced or "back-alley" abortions.

Calls for abortion reform began in the 1950s. Psychiatrists were the first professional group to question restrictive abortion laws because they dealt with the psychological damage women experienced from unwanted pregnancies. The American Public Health Association also promoted change: Mary Calderon, medical director of Planned Parenthood Federation of America (PPFA), wrote articles and delivered speeches about the public health concerns posed by illegal abortions. Some medical doctors joined the appeal because abortion laws undermined medical authority; in 1958, they, along with PPFA, requested that the American Law Institute (ALI) investigate state laws and draft a model abortion statute. The ALI draft endorsed abortion in three instances: if pregnancy would likely cause the woman serious physical or mental damage, if birth would result in a physically or mentally handicapped baby, and if the pregnancy resulted from rape or incest.

Events in the 1960s brought public notice to the demand for reform. In 1962, television personality Sherri Finkbine took thalidomide, which was touted as a cure for morning sickness in Europe where her husband had obtained the drug, while pregnant. Dr. Helen Brooke Taussig of the Food and Drug Administration (FDA) found that thalidomide caused fetal malformations, and Finkbine subsequently petitioned to be allowed to have an abortion. Her home state of Arizona denied her request. The American public sympathized with this middle-class mother of four who loved her children but simply did not want to carry this specific pregnancy to term. Similarly, an epidemic of German measles swept the nation from 1962 until 1965. Pregnant women who contracted the disease faced a 50 percent chance of fetal deformity. Some doctors ignored laws and performed abortions; when the state prosecuted them, a public outcry erupted. Other aspects also led to increased public awareness of the abortion debate, including concern over the environment and population growth; an increased openness about sexual matters, marital problems, and contraception; and technological advancements in new, simple, and safe abortion procedures.

The Quest for Legality

States began to respond to the pressure for change. In 1967, California became the first state to pass a bill that allowed doctors to perform abortions for a severely deformed fetus or to protect the mental health of the woman. The latter aspect gave physicians much greater latitude to perform legal abortions than the earlier stipulation to save the mother's life. Governor Ronald Reagan signed the bill into law. The same year, Colorado passed a new statute based on the ALI model. Between 1967 and 1970, 12 states liberalized abortion. In 1970, New York, Alaska, Hawai'i, and Washington legalized abortion on demand. By 1973, 16 states had liberalized their abortion laws.

While feminists welcomed reform, their impact on legislators was minimal. Feminists remained relatively quiet on the issue until Betty Friedan linked women's ability to control their reproductive life to their ability to participate fully and equally in the economic and political realm. The National Organization for Women, cofounded by Friedan, was the first group to argue for abortion in feminist and civil libertarian terms: Women have the right to control their reproductive lives. These contributions were important but not pivotal to liberalizing laws. Feminists admit that they often downplayed their arguments for abortion because it alienated big donors who supported reform for different reasons such as population control, welfare savings, environmental concerns, and medical autonomy.

The issue came before the Supreme Court in the early 1970s. In *United States v. Vuitch* (1971), the court held that abortion was a surgical procedure; as such, physicians should determine when it was necessary to protect a woman's health. Two years later, *Roe v. Wade* (1973) confirmed this medical jurisdiction. The court struck down a Texas law that deemed abortion illegal unless performed by a physician to save the woman's life. Justice Harry Blackmun wrote for the majority: Medical autonomy was paramount, but he also included abortion in the privacy rights established in *Griswold v. Connecticut* (1965). *Doe v. Bolton* (1973), the companion case to *Roe*, invalidated a Georgia law that required the approval of a hospital staff committee and two consulting physicians to perform an abortion; the court found that the approval of the woman's physician was sufficient. *Doe* also rejected state residency requirements for women to obtain abortions. While these cases invalidated the state's traditional power to criminalize abortion, they did not remove all restrictions. After the first trimester, the state may regulate abortions to preserve the woman's health; after fetal viability, usually the end of the second trimester, the state may prohibit abortion unless the mother's life is at stake.

Abortion After *Roe*
These Supreme Court decisions galvanized groups on both sides of the issue. Before 1973, prochoice activists had devoted their time and effort to legalizing abortion. After *Roe*, they worked to keep abortion legal. They also expanded their agenda to guarantee access to all reproductive choices, including abortion, birth control, birthing healthy babies, and bringing up children in homes above the poverty line. The change in organizational title from the National Abortion Rights Action League to the National Abortion and Reproductive Rights Action League in 1994 reflected this inclusive agenda. Activists called on the government to devise programs that empower women to make the reproductive choice that is in their best interest.

The "pro-life" movement in the wake of *Roe* was a coalition of the Catholic Church, the New Right, and the Republican Party. They lobbied the government to ban abortion, sex education in schools, and teen access to contraceptives. By the 1980s and 1990s, they had been joined by a radical antiabortion fringe that used violence and shock tactics such as bombings, murders, shootings, obstruction of clinics, threats, and harassment.

Efforts to overturn *Roe* failed, but numerous limits have been placed on abortion. When abortion became legal, fiscal conservatives touted it as a cost-saving measure: Public funding of an abortion was much cheaper than funding childbirth and child rearing for recipients of Aids to Families with Dependent Children. Such arguments influenced state and federal governments to pay for abortions among indigent women until the pro-life lobby effectively eliminated federal money for the procedure with the Hyde Amendment of 1976. The Supreme Court upheld such funding restrictions: *Beal v. Doe* (1973) and *Maher v. Roe* (1973) asserted that the Fourteenth Amendment does not compel states to pay for abortions if they pay for childbirth; *Poelker v. Doe* (1973) sustained public hospitals' rights to refuse to perform abortions; and *Harris v. McRae* (1980) decided that neither the federal nor state government must pay for abortions because they paid for live births. With these decisions, the court asserted that the government cannot place obstacles to free choice but it is not required to remove those obstacles that are not of its own making, including poverty. The court also upheld the Hyde Amendment, barring states from using Medicaid funds for abortions unless the woman's life was at stake.

In addition to funding, the court heard cases dealing with third-party consent to abortion. *Planned Parenthood of Central Missouri v. Danforth* (1976) allowed a patient's informed consent to the procedure but rejected the husband's veto power over his wife's decision. The justices also asserted that parents did not have an absolute veto over a minor's decision to abort. *Belloti v. Baird* (1979) affirmed *Danforth*, clarifying that parental consent for minors was allowable if an alternative procedure such as a judge's approval was in place, and *H. L. Matheson* (1981) upheld a Utah law requiring doctors notify "if possible" parents of an immature dependent minor prior to performing an abortion.

Akron v. Akron Center for Reproductive Health (1983) affirmed that minors need not have parental permission if minors can demonstrate to the court that they are mature enough to make the decision themselves. *Hodgson v. Minnesota* (1990) allowed states to require pregnant minors to inform both parents, and *Ohio v. Akron Center for Reproductive Health* (1990) required the notification of one parent of a minor before obtaining an abortion if states allowed judicial bypass. *Planned Parenthood of Southeastern Pennsylvania v. Casey* (1992) again upheld parental consent with judicial exemption and rejected husband notification.

The court has also restricted aspects of abortion. *Webster v. Reproductive Health Services* (1989) allowed states to prohibit abortion in public hospitals and to prohibit publicly employed doctors from performing the procedure, as well as to mandate viability testing in women over 20 weeks pregnant. *Rust v. Sullivan* (1991) upheld the gag rule passed during the Reagan administration whereby clinics receiving federal funds under Title X of the Public Health Service Act could not discuss abortion with patients as a medical option. President Bill Clinton suspended the gag rule in 1993. *Planned Parenthood of Southeastern Pennsylvania v. Casey* (1992) upheld 24-hour waiting periods and state mandates that doctors inform women about fetal development and alternatives to abortion.

Yet justices protected abortion in other court cases. *Akron v. Akron Center for Reproductive Health* (1983) and *Planned Parenthood of Kansas City v. Ashcroft* (1983) invalidated state laws that required second-trimester abortions take place in hospitals rather than clinics. *National Organization for Women v. Scheidler* (1994) ruled that clinics can invoke the 1970 federal racketeering law to sue violent antiabortion protest groups for triple damages, and *Hill v. Colorado* (2000) upheld state laws that protect abortion patients and doctors by prohibiting protesters within 100 feet of clinics. *Stenberg v. Carhart* (2000) struck down bans on partial-birth abortions because they lacked exemptions to save the mother's life.

A crowd backing Planned Parenthood and NARAL gathers in the rain on the steps of the legislative building in Olympia, Washington, for a rally in support of abortion rights in 2009.

The most recent trend has been toward restriction. In 2007, the court decided in *Gonzales v. Carhart* that states could prohibit a rarely used late-term technique called intact dilation and evacuation (better known as partial-birth abortion), even though no exemption for the woman's life existed, but left intact the more common technique of regular dilation and evacuation (D&E). Justice Ruth Ginsburg, the only woman on the court, dissented, arguing that this decision undermined both women's health and physicians' discretion.

New abortion techniques provide women with more options. President Clinton in 1993 allowed FDA testing of RU-486, or mifepristone, which gained FDA approval in 2000. This pill blocks progesterone, causing a medical miscarriage in 98 percent of cases. This option is especially beneficial to women who live in rural areas where access to clinics is minimal: More than 80 percent of counties in the United States have no abortion services. Mifepristone is safer than many abortion procedures because it can be used early in pregnancy. Another pill, misoprostol, causes miscarriages in 85 percent of cases. While not as effective as mifepristone, it is easily accessible because its original use was to cure ulcers.

These abortion pills can be obtained from a doctor's office, thereby allowing women to avoid violent clinic blockades. Such blockades, launched by Randall Terry and Operation Rescue among others, attempt to isolate doctors who provide surgical abortions and to terrorize them and their families. Beginning in 1993 with the murder of Dr. David Gunn in Pensacola, Florida, avowed pro-life militants killed seven other physicians who provided this medical procedure.

Since 1990, abortion rates have been falling for all ages and races. In 1990, the overall abortion rate was 27.4 per 1000; it fell to 19.4 in 2005. Women of color have much higher rates of abortion. In 1990, the black rate was 63.9, the Hispanic rate was 35.1, and the white rate was 21.5. By 2005, these rates had fallen to 49.3, 26.5, and 13.6, respectively. Part of this decline can be attributed to effective contraceptives such as the birth control pill, increased use of condoms in the face of AIDS, and the indistinguishable nature of medical versus natural miscarriage. Violence at clinics also played a role in the decline: Fewer practitioners offered abortion services out of fear for their lives.

The isolation of abortion providers from mainstream medicine since *Roe v. Wade* led to changes in services. Eighty percent of abortions in 1973 took place in hospitals, but obstetrician/gynecologists (OB-GYNs) began to move away from the procedure due to the controversy surrounding it. By the mid-1990s, only 12 percent of OB-GYN residencies offered abortion training. Clinics run mostly by women stepped into the vacuum; 90 percent of abortions occurred there in 1996. While clinics were more cost efficient with a more specialized and highly trained medical staff, they were also more easily targeted by pro-life fanatics than hospitals or doctors' offices.

Ongoing Debate

The 21st century has witnessed efforts to reverse this trend. A new generation of doctors led by Jody Steinauer and Medical Students for Choice has worked to reintegrate abortion into normal medical care. By 2010, 50 percent of OB-GYN programs required abortion training and 40 percent offered it as an elective. Advances in first-trimester abortion allow the procedure to be completed in five minutes, making it very low risk and allowing doctors to incorporate it into their regular practice where they conduct other minor procedures.

At the state level, a flood of legislation to restrict abortion access passed in 2011. Driven partly by the centrality of abortion in the healthcare debates and by Republican gains at the polls in 2010, these laws introduced technological issues not present in 1973, such as mandating that women undergo an ultrasound and/or listen to fetal heartbeats. Anti-abortion activists hope these measures will reach the Supreme Court to overturn *Roe v. Wade*.

Simone M. Caron
Wake Forest University

See Also: 1851 to 1900 Primary Documents; Buntline, Ned; Comstock Law; Criminalization and Decriminalization; *Griswold v. Connecticut*; National Organization for Women; *Roe v. Wade*; Supreme Court, U.S.; Terrorism; *Wolf v. Colorado*.

Further Readings

Ginsburg, Faye D. *Contested Lives: The Abortion Debate in an American Community*. Berkeley: University of California Press [1989] Rev. ed., 1998.

Gordon, Linda. *Woman's Body, Woman's Right: A Social History of Birth Control in America*. New York: Viking, 1976.

Greenhouse, Linda and Reva B. Siegel. *Before* Roe v. Wade*: Voices That Shaped the Abortion Debate Before the Supreme Court's Ruling*. New York: Kaplan Publishing, 2010.

Reagan, Leslie J. *When Abortion Was a Crime: Women, Medicine and Law in the United States, 1867–1973*. Berkeley: University of California Press, 1997.

Abrams v. United States

In *Abrams v. United States*, the government prosecuted five people for violating the Espionage Act of 1917. The government claimed the people, including Jacob Abrams, distributed pamphlets in New York condemning the actions taken by the U.S. government in World War I. Having been found guilty at trial, the defendants appealed their case to the U.S. Supreme Court. Although their convictions were upheld by the Supreme Court, the case became a landmark Supreme Court decision because Justice Oliver Wendell Holmes wrote a dissenting opinion that eventually formed the basis for future First Amendment decisions.

During 1918 and 1919, the U.S. government found itself in the midst of World War I and the Red Scare. The U.S. entry in the war brought strong internal dissent. Socialists and anarchists were some of the most vocal opponents. Having seen these opposition groups overthrow the Russian czar, the United States feared a similar fate from socialists and anarchists in the country, particularly from those of Russian descent. This small but vocal group of supporters began printing pamphlets for distribution in New York City. In August 1918, a joint raid by the Justice Department, War Department, and New York police yielded Abrams, his codefendants, and hundreds of pamphlets. All five suspects were Russian by birth and had not become U.S. citizens despite having lived in the country for 10 years.

Following their arrest, the defendants were indicted for multiple violations of the Espionage Act. The violations involved publishing disloyal and abusive language about the form of the U.S. government, language that would bring the government of the United States into contempt, and language that would provoke resistance to the war. The final count was for being involved in a conspiracy to publish the allegedly disloyal and subversive documents. Each defendant admitted the facts but they collectively argued that the Espionage Act violated their free speech rights guaranteed by the First Amendment.

Clear and Present Danger

In the fall of 1919, the case was argued before the U.S. Supreme Court. Earlier that year, the Supreme Court had upheld the constitutionality of the Espionage Act. Justice Holmes had delivered the unanimous decision of the Supreme Court in those cases. In doing so, he articulated that the First Amendment did not protect speech that gave rise to a specific and imminent harm to the United States. Holmes used the term *clear and present danger* to define the limits of the First Amendment. The *Abrams* case was the first case to come before the court regarding the First Amendment since those initial rulings.

Three weeks after hearing arguments on *Abrams*, the Supreme Court announced its decision upholding the convictions and holding that the Espionage Act did not violate the First Amendment. While the outcome did not surprise, the dissenting opinion issued by Justice Holmes did. Holmes claimed that the Espionage Act, as applied to the defendants, violated their First Amendment rights because there was no clear and present danger that the harm promoted by the speech would come to fruition. Instead, he found the content of the speech to be so unworthy of consideration that it would not persuade anyone to do anything.

Holmes's dissent was the result of conversations he had with New York Federal Judge Learned Hand and Harvard law professor Zechariah Chafee. Both informed Holmes about the lack of guidance his initial enunciation of the clear and present danger test provided. They were concerned that he had adopted the common law of sedition as the limit of the First Amendment. If this was the case, they argued, the First Amendment would only extend to the right to publish and would not protect people from prosecution based on the content of their speech.

Women marching for peace on Fifth Avenue in New York City on August 29, 1914, in response to the recent start of World War I. Jacob Abrams and his codefendants, who opposed U.S. involvement in the war a few years later, were arrested in August 1918 and eventually appealed their case to the U.S. Supreme Court.

Holmes took these comments and incorporated them into his dissent by linking the intent of the publication with the likelihood of its occurrence. He stated that the defendants had no intent to jeopardize the war effort. They could not have believed their publication would actually impair the government's ability to produce munitions for the war or cause resistance to the draft.

While Holmes's dissent pleased those favoring greater freedom of expression, his approach was not adopted by the court for nearly 20 more years. Today, it serves as a key piece of the foundation for First Amendment jurisprudence.

Scott Ingram
High Point University

See Also: Bill of Rights; Espionage Act of 1917; Holmes, Oliver Wendell, Jr.; Political Dissidents; Sedition Act of 1918; Supreme Court, U.S.

Further Readings
Abrams, et al. v. United States. 250 U.S. 616 (1919).
Polenberg, Richard. *Fighting Faiths: The Abrams Case, the Supreme Court and Free Speech.* New York: Viking, 1987.
Ragan, Fred D. "Justice Oliver Wendell Holmes, Jr., Zechariah Chafee, Jr., and the Clear and Present Danger Test for Free Speech: The First Year, 1919." *Journal of American History,* v.58 (1971).

Adair v. United States

Adair v. United States, 208 U.S. 161 (1908), is one of four cases chronicling the saga of "yellow-dog contracts," so named by labor stalwarts depicting those who signed them as equivalent to the lowest breed of mongrel dog. These contracts were characterized by terms prohibiting current and potential employees from joining or retaining membership in labor unions and came into increasing use as labor unions began to expand their influence in the early 20th century.

Pressured by unions, Congress enacted the Erdman Act (1908), in part criminalizing the discrimination, dismissal, and blacklisting of current or potential railroad employees because of union membership. *Adair* struck down Erdman as violating the Fifth Amendment due process clause and as an improper exercise of the interstate commerce clause. Citing Adair as precedent, the court in *Coppage v. Kansas*, 236 U.S. 1 (1915), invalidated 13 state statutes criminalizing discrimination in hiring on the basis of union membership, grounding its decision in the Fourteenth Amendment freedom of contract doctrine.

Court support for yellow-dog contracts climaxed in *Hitchman Coal & Coke Co. v. Mitchell*, 245 U.S. 229 (1917), wherein the court upheld the constitutionality of injunctions barring union organizers from soliciting union memberships and initiating strikes, again invoking *Adair* and opining that employers enjoyed a property interest in their workers. The demise of yellow dog contracts came in response to the changing political climate following the Great Depression. The Norris–La Guardia Act (1932) banned yellow-dog contracts, barred federal courts from issuing injunctions against nonviolent labor disputes, and established the right of employees to be free of employer interference when considering trade union membership. The Supreme Court upheld Norris–La Guardia in *Lauf v. E. G. Shiner & Co.*, 303 U.S. 323 (1938).

Significance

Adair is significant in the social history of crime as it illustrates three fundamental social dynamics operative in the development of criminal justice policy. First, it illustrates how particular behaviors come to be taken as either criminal or anodyne in particular historical socioeconomic and sociopolitical contexts. Second, it illustrates how particularizing issues—for example, focusing narrowly on the particular parties' freedom to contract—neglects the impact of changing socioeconomic and sociopolitical structures on a society's code of conduct and criminal law. Finally, *Adair* illustrates how criminal acts are often protests against the social code and social structure as expressed in criminal law.

Many labor-oriented scholars, for example, concede that the decriminalization worked by *Adair* may be perceived as justifiable under the Fifth Amendment in the context of that amendment's enactment. Both slavery and involuntary servitude were socially, politically, and constitutionally sanctioned at that time, and the presumption of equal bargaining power between an employer and an employee could be considered fairly sound. Yellow-dog contracts in such a context might be considered commensurate with social, political, and economic norms and so not the proper subjects of criminalization.

Yellow-dog contracting combined with blacklisting in the context of ever increasing unemployment from the depression of 1920–23 through the Great Depression altered the socioeconomic context significantly. The increasing competition for jobs, in concert with the changes in social structure wrought by the Industrial Revolution, including the concentration of wealth and political power in corporations, banks, and the securities industry, also transformed the sociopolitical context. Freedom in general was now perceived as under threat by private economic power. Constraints on the freedom to contract that could not have been anticipated at the founding were taken as one important example, and these changed perceptions mobilized social movements, undermining the legitimacy of established norms.

These changes in perception, sociopolitical context, and socioeconomic structure generated spiraling violence, engaged in by labor and capital alike, closing factories, disrupting commerce, and posing escalating threats to life, liberty, and the rule of law. Governing entities at all levels became convinced that the costs of not criminalizing behaviors like those at issue in *Adair* outweighed the costs of criminalizing them and restricting the individual liberty to contract. The Supreme Court's failure to focus upon the changing structural and normative landscape frustrated the nation's capacity to deal positively with the very phenomena that courts and criminal policy are intended to control.

Finally, *Adair* illustrates the emotional attractions of crime, regardless of material benefit and the threat of punishment. Both sides of the dispute over criminal justice policy as reflected in *Adair* were focused not on the instrumental benefits of one policy over the other alone but on the moral righteousness of their positions. The criminal acts of each were in this sense laced with moral condemnation of extant policy.

Charles Frederick Abel
Stephen F. Austin State University

See Also: Criminalization and Decriminalization; Equality, Concept of; LaGuardia, Fiorello; Strikes.

Further Readings
Black, D. "Crime as Social Control." *American Sociological Review,* v.48 (1983).
Chamberlain, N. and J. Schilling. *The Impact of Strikes: Their Social and Economic Costs.* Westport, CT: Greenwood Press, 1954.
Forbath, W. E. *Law and the Shaping of the American Labor Movement.* Cambridge, MA: Harvard University Press, 1991.
Pope, J. "The Thirteenth Amendment Versus the Commerce Clause: Labor and the Shaping of American Constitutional Law, 1921–1957." *Columbia Law Review,* v.102/2 (2002).
Tomlins, C. L. *The State and the Unions: Labor Relations, the Law, and the Organized Labor Movement in America, 1880–1960.* New York: Cambridge University Press, 1985.

Adams, John (Administration of)

Although John Adams served a single term as president of the United States, as a lawyer, political theorist, and statesman, he played a major role in shaping American views of crime and punishment. Adams's career as an attorney made him a strong believer in the rights of criminal defendants and in the importance that any accused individual receive adequate counsel. As president, Adams's support for the Federalist legislation that became known as the Alien and Sedition Acts opened him to tremendous criticism by contemporaries, and later historians, as infringing on the constitutional rights of citizens opposed to government policies.

Born on October 30, 1735, Adams entered Harvard College at the age of 16, initially intending to become a minister. After graduating in 1755, Adams trained to become a lawyer after several years' service as a schoolteacher, gaining admittance to the bar in 1758. A prominent opponent of the Stamp Act of 1765, Adams drafted instructions that the residents of Braintree, Massachusetts, sent to their representatives in the legislature regarding objections to the Stamp Act, focusing partly on the rights of all English citizens to be tried only by a jury of one's peers. Adams also gained a reputation as a staunch advocate for legal representation for those accused of criminal charges. Adams agreed to represent eight British soldiers who were charged with killing five civilians during the events that became known as the Boston Massacre. Although the British soldiers had experienced difficulty finding legal representation, Adams worked as their defense counsel even though he feared this would harm his reputation. Although paid only a nominal amount for his work, Adams obtained acquittals for six of the soldiers tried, with the two who had fired shots being convicted of manslaughter rather than murder. As an elected member of the Massachusetts General Court, the colony's legislative body, Adams authored a pamphlet, *Thoughts on Government*, which advocated for the separation of powers between the executive, legislative, and judicial branches of government. This work was tremendously influential and later influenced many state constitutions, as well as James Madison when he wrote the U.S. Constitution.

A member of the committee charged with writing the Declaration of Independence, Adams and the rest of the group left this task primarily to Thomas Jefferson. Jefferson later credited Adams as the individual chiefly responsible for garnering the declaration's passage on the floor of the Continental Congress. Sent twice by Congress to Europe to negotiate with Britain and France, Adams also wrote the Massachusetts constitution of 1780, again emphasizing his strong belief in the value of independent executive, legislative, and judicial branches of government. Adams served two terms as George Washington's vice president, joining the Federalist Party, although uneasiness with that entity's leader, Alexander Hamilton, kept him from enjoying complete trust from that group's partisans. Despite this, Adams was elected to succeed Washington as the United States' second president in 1796, defeating Jefferson, who became his vice president.

As president, Adams maintained Washington's cabinet and sponsored little new legislation. Of the initiatives that dealt with criminal law that passed during his administration, perhaps the most controversial were four separate acts, popularly known as the Alien and Sedition Acts. Passed by Congress in 1798, the four acts were intended to suppress opposition to the Federalists from the Democratic-Republicans, led by Jefferson. Collectively, the Alien and Sedition Acts extended the period of residence necessary before an immigrant could obtain U.S. citizenship to 14 years, permitted the president to deport any noncitizens he deemed dangerous to the nation, and made it a crime to publish writings that criticized the government or its officials. The Alien and Sedition Acts were severely criticized by the Democratic-Republicans. Jefferson secretly wrote resolutions passed by the Kentucky and Virginia legislatures condemning the legislation as a violation of the First and Tenth Amendments of the U.S. Constitution, insofar that they abrogated rights of free speech and asserted powers not assigned to the federal government. Although the acts were never appealed to the U.S. Supreme Court, at least 10 individuals were convicted of violating them and others were alleged to have left the United States to avoid prosecution or deportation.

The Democratic-Republicans used opposition to the Alien and Sedition Acts to build support for Jefferson in the presidential election of 1800, where he defeated Adams by a narrow margin. Before leaving office, Adams signed the Judiciary Act of 1801, which enabled the Federalists to make a series of appointments to the bench, a group known collectively as the "Midnight Judges," before Jefferson assumed the presidency. Although many of these judges lost their positions when the Judiciary Act of 1802 reconfigured the courts, perhaps Adams's greatest accomplishment was the last-minute appointment of John Marshall as the chief justice of the U.S. Supreme Court. Marshall, who served until 1835, was influential in establishing the federal judiciary as a branch of government equal to that of the executive and legislative.

Stephen T. Schroth
Jason A. Helfer
Jonathan R. Fletcher
Knox College

See Also: Adams, John Quincy (Administration of); Articles of Confederation; Declaration of Independence; Jefferson, Thomas (Administration of); Washington, George (Administration of).

Further Readings
Cappon, L. J. *The Adams-Jefferson Letters: The Complete Correspondence Between Thomas Jefferson and Abigail and John Adams*. Chapel Hill: University of North Carolina Press, 1988.
McCullough, D. G. *John Adams*. New York: Simon & Schuster, 2001.

Adams, John Quincy (Administration of)

John Quincy Adams, the sixth president of the United States (1825–29), was also the eldest son of John Adams, the second president (1797–1801). His public service to his country was as a senator, diplomat, congressman, secretary of state, and president. John Quincy Adams was born in Braintree, now known as Quincy, Massachusetts, to John Adams and Abigail Adams. He was named after his mother's grandfather, John Quincy, who was a member of the Massachusetts legislature for many years.

Adams spent much of his youth in Europe, accompanying his father, who served as the U.S. minister to France (1778–79) and to the Netherlands (1780–82). In 1781, at the age of 14, he accompanied Francis Dana to St. Petersburg, Russia, as his private secretary on a mission to negotiate for the recognition of the new United States. Also in 1782, he went to Paris with his father as an additional secretary to the commissioners del-

An 1826 engraving of President John Quincy Adams, who opposed slavery in the United States and led a successful fight to force Congress to receive antislavery petitions.

egated to negotiate the peace treaty that formalized the conclusion of the American Revolution.

Adams studied law at Harvard College and graduated in 1787. Upon graduation, he apprenticed as a lawyer with Theophilus Parsons in Newburyport, Massachusetts (1787–89). In 1791, he was admitted to the Massachusetts bar and began the practice of law in Boston. In 1794, President Washington appointed him minister to the Netherlands, a post he filled until 1797, when he became minister to Prussia during his father's presidency. On a diplomatic mission to London in 1795, Adams met Louisa Catherine Johnson, and they married in 1797. The couple had three sons, George Washington Adams, John Adams, and Charles Francis Adams. They also had a daughter, Louisa, who died in infancy.

Political Career

Adams returned to the United States from his foreign service in 1801 and was elected to the Massachusetts state senate in 1802. In 1803, he was elected by the Federalist state legislature as one of the U.S. senators from Massachusetts. As an independent political thinker, he outraged the Federalist base when he supported Jeffersonian policies in the Louisiana Purchase and also in the embargo on American shipping, the Embargo Act of 1807.

Adams resigned from the senate in 1808 under removal threat from the Massachusetts Federalist legislature. President James Madison appointed Adams as the first U.S. minister to Russia, a position he held from 1809 to 1814. While there, he helped end the War of 1812 by serving as one of the five American commissioners and as the chief negotiator to draw up the Treaty of Ghent in 1814. Thereafter, he served as minister to Great Britain from 1815 until 1817, a position that his father previously first held. Adams served as the secretary of state in President James Monroe's administration from 1817 until 1825. He was regarded as one of America's greatest secretaries of state for his role in the peaceful acquisition of Florida from Spain and arranging with England to jointly occupy the Oregon Territory. He was instrumental in devising and developing the Monroe Doctrine, which was designed to limit European nations' involvement in the affairs of the Western Hemisphere.

During the 1824 presidential election, the candidacies of John Quincy Adams, Andrew Jackson, and Henry Clay all failed to receive a majority in the electoral college. Consequently, the election was decided in the House of Representatives in favor of Adams. Before his presidency, Adams was respected for his singular intelligence, enormous experience, indisputable integrity, and his love for his country. His administration (1825–29), nevertheless, was ineffective and ended without any major legislative, diplomatic, military, or administrative accomplishment, despite his efforts to establish a broad program of domestic improvements. The failure of his presidency is often chalked up to the venomous opposition of the Jacksonian Democrats and an uncooperative Congress.

Adams retired to Quincy after his presidency and was elected to the U.S. House of Representatives in 1830, a position he held for 17 years. As a leading opponent of slavery, one of his greatest accomplishments, perhaps, was to end the House gag rule on debate about slavery by leading the fight to force Congress to receive antislavery petitions. On February 21, 1848, Adams suffered a massive cerebral hemorrhage and collapsed on the House floor. He was carried to the Speaker's Room, where he died two days later, with his wife, Louisa, and son at his side.

Felix O. Chima
Prairie View A&M University

See Also: 1777 to 1800 Primary Documents; Adams, John (Administration of); Madison, James (Administration of); Massachusetts; Monroe, James (Administration of).

Further Readings
Mattie, Sean. "John Quincy Adams and American Conservatism." *Modern Age*, v.45/4 (Fall 2003).
Richard, Leonard L. *The Life and Times of Congressman John Quincy Adams*. Oxford: Oxford University Press, 1986.

Adultery

Adultery is often defined as any act of a sexual nature with another person while you are in a marital relationship. There are a wide variety of punishments for adultery based on the culture, religion, and power status of women in different regions. In most advanced democracies today, adultery is not a crime but the act may be used against the adulterer if he or she is going through a divorce. In the United States, there are still laws on the books against adultery but it is rarely prosecuted. However, adultery in the military is a potential court-martial offense.

In the Kinsey Reports, *Sexual Behavior in the Human Male* (1948) and *Sexual Behavior in the Human Female* (1953), it was estimated that as much as 50 percent of the population had committed adultery. Other studies have put the number at about 25 percent for males and 10 percent for females. In *The Monogamy Myth*, Peggy Vaughan puts the estimate between 50 percent and 65 percent for males and 40 percent to 55 percent for females. There are wide variations on the statistics for adultery. This may be because adultery is very underreported in surveys because of the stigma that is attached to it. While adultery is practiced frequently in the United States, most surveys show that Americans highly disapprove of adultery, with as much as 80 percent disapproving of the act of adultery itself. While the public highly disapproves of the act of adultery, most people feel that it should not become a crime, according to a CNN/*Time* poll conducted in 2008.

Many people who commit adultery tend to be younger, with younger women being as likely as younger men to engage in adulterous behavior. There is some evidence that adultery is more of a phenomenon among middle-class families than upper- or lower-class families. There seems to be very little to no variation between races as far as adulterous acts. People who have very little education or people with a master's degree or higher seem to commit adulterous acts at higher levels than other educational groups. Adultery is the cause or partial cause of 17 percent of all divorces in the United States; according to a study cited by David Buss in his book the *Evolution of Desire*, adultery is also the number one reason for spousal abuse or murder. Couples who rate their marriage as not too happy also have higher infidelity rates than those who are happy with their marriage.

History of Punishment
In ancient Greece and Rome, punishment for adultery was only prescribed against women. Under Napoleonic Code, a man could ask to divorce his wife if she committed adultery but a wife could not divorce her husband. In the code of Hammurabi, punishment for adultery was by drowning. Wealth and power have also freed many from the rules that govern the rest of society. Louis XIV was known to have many mistresses while ruling France. Many British monarchs also had numerous affairs outside their marriages, with little or no public rebuke for their actions. In the United States during colonization, adultery was punishable by death although there is no evidence that death was ever imposed. Severe punishments included fines, public whippings, floggings, or brandings.

Most religions widely condemn adultery but the punishments vary. In many Islamic countries such as Iran, Somalia, and Afghanistan under the Taliban, if a woman commits adultery, it is punishable by death via stoning. Some countries have had exemptions from punishments for so-called honor killings. These punishments are either partial exemptions or full exemptions in such countries as Argentina, Ecuador, Jordan, Syria, Egypt, Guatemala, Iran, Israel, Peru, and Venezuela. In many societies, because those of lower economic classes also tend to be more religious than those in upper classes (especially contemporarily), the punishment and rebuke may be larger toward the lower-class adulterer among his friends and colleagues than toward a person from an upper-class background.

Besides religion, another reason adultery is condemned so harshly is because family is often seen as a primary component of society. Many consider the family to be the most important institution in society. Therefore, anything that violates the institution of marriage could be punished harshly, according to the view of many within society. Before contraception was common, the practice of adultery often resulted in pregnancy. Therefore, a husband could raise a child not of his own genes or be forced to split time between two families. Before the advent of paternity testing, men could deny that a child was theirs, leaving the parenting to the mother's family.

Lawrence Friedman argues that punishment for adultery and other acts against god and religion started changing in the United States after the Revolutionary War. He notes that in Middlesex County, Massachusetts, in 1793, three divorces were granted on the grounds of adultery but the offenders were not criminally punished. After 1793, divorce for adultery was a regular occurrence but Friedman notes only one case in which the accused was criminally punished from 1793 to 1810. Similar patterns were also noted by William Edward Nelson in Georgia. While criminal prosecutions for adultery declined after the passage of the Constitution, they were still on the books in most states, and many states still prosecuted offenders.

In the United States, 25 states still have laws regarding adultery. However, these laws are rarely enforced. In 1969, California under the governorship of Ronald Reagan passed the Family Law Act. This law dramatically changed divorce in the United States. No longer did a person need to prove fault in divorce; the married couple could simply cite irreconcilable differences. This is what has become known as no-fault divorce. Through no-fault divorce there was no longer a need to prove adulterous acts. With the passage of a no-fault divorce measure in New York in 2010, all 50 states now offer a no-fault divorce option. While there has not been as of 2012 a constitutional challenge to adultery laws, *Griswold v. Connecticut* (1965) established a right to privacy in the United States and *Lawrence v. Texas* (2003) overturned sodomy laws on the books in many states.

The passage of the constitution in the 1790s and the liberalization of divorce laws in the late 1960s marked a decrease in the cases prosecuted for adultery and the punishment handed out to the offender. These events also reflected changes that were occurring in society with regard to the separation of church and state in the 1790s and the

Henry Ward Beecher, a prominent 19th-century preacher, became the subject of a national scandal and was tried for adultery in 1875 for an alleged affair with a friend's wife.

feminist and civil rights movements of the 1960s. Many feminists felt that the divorce laws were too burdensome and caused women to remain in bad marriages. Through no-fault divorce reform, a person no longer had to prove violence or adultery to get out of a marriage.

Reasons for Adultery
Many psychologists and sociologists argue that adultery results from other underlying problems within the marriage that can range from psychological or physical abuse to lack of companionship or time together. There are also some who argue that monogamy is not part of our instinctual makeup as human beings. In her book *Adultery*, Louise DeSalvo argues that adultery may make evolutionary sense as a way of guaranteeing the survival of the human species. Sigmund Freud argues that it is natural for humans to have sexual needs and desires. Some argue that the purpose of marriage is to control sexual partnering, but that humans are not wired to have these controls; therefore, adultery in many marriages may be inevitable.

Whether adultery is a biological or a social phenomenon is a matter of wide debate. Adultery, like most other human relations, is a complex phenomenon that cannot be easily explained. Reasons for adultery can be entirely different based on the individuals involved. In order to understand the reasons somebody commits adultery, one must first understand the relationships of the individuals who commit the acts.

Most marriages in which an adulterous relationship occurs end in divorce. However, divorce does not have to be the only option. If a couple works with counselors and the person who committed the adulterous act seeks to regain the trust of the other spouse, then it may be possible for the marriage to be saved. Underlying issues within the marriage must first be resolved in the relationship for the marriages to be reconciled. Contrary to popular belief, most people who have an adulterous affair and get divorced do not go on to marry their lover; in cases where this does happen, there is an extremely high divorce rate. According to Frank Pittman, this is often because of underlying issues from the affair such as distrust, guilt, distrust of marriage, and the intervention of reality. Affairs fall into three different types, according to A. Thompson: sexual only, emotional only, and sexual and emotional combined. There is some evidence, according to S. Glass and T. Wright, that men are more likely to have sexual-only affairs whereas women are more likely to have emotional-only affairs; however, the authors of this article caution that more research is needed.

Adultery in Cyberspace and the Workplace
With the creation and widespread use of the Internet, adultery has come to mean different things to different people. Is having an affair online considered adultery? Is looking at porn online considered adultery? These are questions that some families deal with each day. Adultery is not just about the physical act of sex but also the emotional acts of bonding that bind relationships. One reason online relationships and cybersex have become common is the ubiquity of online sexual chat rooms. There is some evidence of a correlation between people who engage in cyber affairs and those who engage in real affairs. The Internet is easy to access, and sexual Websites and chat rooms are easy to find. K. Young et al. define an online affair as a relationship that begins with online contact but continues with further contact through e-mails and chat rooms and possibly even meeting in person.

One of the most common places for adulterous relationships to occur is the workplace. Spouses often spend more time with coworkers than with each other. Therefore, the probability that a relationship will occur in the workplace is likely greater than anywhere else. Many companies have policies that strictly forbid workplace romances but the allure of the romance leads some people to take the risk. Similar to online affairs, affairs in the workplace are common because they are convenient and easy. There is some evidence they may be easier to hide than other affairs.

Conclusion
Adultery is a major issue in many families, and the punishments for adultery have varied across societies and history. While adultery is often viewed as a simple act, it has complex ramifications for the people involved. The individual emotions that are involved with adultery not only affect immediate family members but children and other relatives who learn about the affair. There may also be ramifications for the adulterer in the workplace, community, church, and other organizations. Adultery

is not merely a social phenomenon; it also can become a social stigma because the act itself violates the norms of a large segment of society.

Derrick Shapley
Mississippi State University

See Also: 1600 to 1776 Primary Documents; 1921 to 1940 Primary Documents; 1981 to 2000 Primary Documents; Fornication Laws; *Griswold v. Connecticut*; *Lawrence v. Texas*; Sin; Sodomy.

Further Readings
Atkins, D. C., N. S. Jacobson, and D. H. Baucom. "Understanding Infidelity: Correlates in a National Random Sample." *Journal of Family Psychology*, v.15 (2001).
Buss, D. M. *The Evolution of Desire*. New York: Basic Books, 1994.
Friedman, L. M. *American Law and Constitutional Order*. Cambridge, MA: Harvard University Press, 1988.
Glass, S. P. and T. L. Wright. "Sex Differences in Type of Extramarital Involvement and Marital Dissatisfaction." *Sex Roles*, v.12/9–10 (1985).
National Healthy Marriage Resource Center. "Infidelity." http://www.healthymarriageinfo.org/resource-detail/index.aspx?rid=2393 (Accessed September 2011).
Nelson, W. E. *Americanization of Common Law: Impact of Legal Change on Massachusetts Society*. Athens: University of Georgia Press, 1994.
Thompson, A. P. "Emotional and Sexual Components of Extramarital Relations." *Journal of Marriage and Family*, v.46/1 (1984).
Treas, J. and D. Giesen. "Sexual Infidelity Among Married and Cohabitating Americans." *Journal of Marriage and Family*, v.62 (2000).
Young, K. S., et al. "Online Infidelity: A New Dimension in Couple Relationships With Implications for Evaluation and Treatment." *Sexual Addiction and Compulsivity*, v.7 (2000).

Adversarial Justice

There are several different types of legal systems. The major types are adversarial system of justice, inquisitorial system of justice, political system of justice, and theological system of justice. The United States of America has an adversarial system of justice. However, for comparative purposes, a brief review of the other types of systems of justice will be presented.

Theological, Political, and Inquisitorial Systems of Justice

A theological system of justice is one based on religion. Such systems of justice are usually associated with a theocracy, which is a political system based on religion. A modern example of such a political system would be one based on Islamic law, or shari'a. Islam is most widely practiced in the Middle East, Africa, and Asia. Under a theological system of justice, the primary source of law is religion, divine texts, or revelation, with the primary purpose of the legal system being the advancement of the purposes of that religion. For example, if the worship and idolization of a particular god were the focus of the religion in question, then whether a person were actually guilty of a crime would not be paramount. If the acquittal of a person would bring discredit to that religion or god, then a finding of guilt would be the likely result of a trial. A historical example of a religious system of justice is the Inquisition of the Catholic Church in the Middle Ages. The purpose of the Inquisition was to extinguish heresy, and the guilt or innocence of the suspects was irrelevant to the accomplishment of this purpose. In a religious system of justice, the primary qualification of a judge is that judge's religiosity.

A political system of justice is based on the political goal of maintaining that particular political view. Under a truly political system of justice, the primary purpose of the legal system is not justice, per se, but to advance the political philosophy of that society. Although it would appear that all legal systems would necessarily be political systems of justice, this is not the case. For a historical example, under traditional communist or fascist political systems such as Italy in the 1930s through the 1940s and the Soviet Union for most of the 20th century, proving actual guilt or innocence was not the ultimate goal. Advancing the goals of communism or fascism was paramount. The courts were required to help educate the people and compel them to accept the values of the political system. Under such legal systems, a factually innocent person would likely be found guilty of a crime if an acquittal would damage the political standing of the state or its officials, or if a finding of guilt would help educate the general populace. In a political system of justice, the primary qualification of a judge is that judge's political ideology.

An inquisitorial system of justice is a system where the judge is an active participant in not only the trial of the suspect but even in the investigation of the crime. In an inquisitorial system of justice, the judge is not a neutral arbiter of the dispute. The judge will take part in the investigation and may even direct certain portions of it. But the judge's purpose is not to ensure a guilty finding but to gather all the facts, both inculpatory and exculpatory. An inquisitorial system of justice does not differ from adversarial systems of justice concerning the substantive law. The criminal laws of both systems are frequently quite similar. Murder in an inquisitorial system of justice is murder in an adversarial system of justice. Thus, the primary difference is procedural. A modern example of an inquisitorial system of justice is France. It could be argued, however, that the system in France is not purely inquisitorial because guilt or innocence is still determined by a jury for criminal charges.

History of the Adversarial System of Justice
The United States has an adversarial system of justice. The basic principles of the adversarial system of justice are that the fact finder, either a judge or a jury, is a neutral (at least in theory) arbiter of the dispute, with the prosecution and the defense presenting opposing testimony, evidence, and arguments as to the truth of what actually occurred. In many criminal trials, the judge is not the fact finder, which is a duty performed by the jury. The judge is merely an overseer to ensure that the proper procedures are followed during the course of the trial. The underlying philosophy of the adversarial system of justice is that the truth can best be determined when each side presents its perspective of what happened.

The American philosophy of justice has its roots in the English common law. When America was founded, the English settlers brought with them the English system of law. The adversarial system of justice began in England. There are no definable stages in its development. Rather, it developed slowly as a matter of custom.

In the Middle Ages, obtaining justice from feudal lords or from the king was problematic. The modern idea of a right to a fair trial with the right to present witnesses and evidence and to cross-examine witnesses simply did not exist. Frequently, justice was reserved for the more powerful party. However, justice did have a religious perspective, as God was considered the ultimate judge. From these two traditions of justice for the powerful and justice as a function of religion, the idea of trial by combat evolved. A person charged with a crime could demand trial by combat, where the accuser and the defendant would do battle, with the victor being found to be the just party, partly on the theory that God would not let evil prevail. On some occasions, parties to the dispute could select a champion to fight for them. As the era of knights began to wane, so did the practice of trial by combat. Thus, it can be argued that the adversarial system of justice started with the trial by combat. This was the beginning of the adversarial system of justice in Anglo-American law, although the concept was present in the ancient systems of law found in Rome and Greece.

Subsequently, courts were developed to hear cases, as the kings and the feudal lords did not have the time or inclination to sit in judgment over each and every case. As a general matter, until the late 1600s, trials were not very structured. The accused and the accuser would just engage in an ongoing back-and-forth argument. Further, criminal defendants were prohibited from having attorneys, from calling witnesses, and from cross-examination. Moreover, juries were frequently instructed by the judge concerning the evidence and the guilt or innocence of the defendant. At this point, the justice system was fully adversarial, but it was not fair and was heavily biased against the defendant.

Over the next 100 years, through the 1700s, significant changes happened. Defendants were allowed to have attorneys represent them, partially in response to the practice of the English Crown's use of attorneys to prosecute people. There was sharp division between the presentation of the accuser's testimony and the presentation of the defendant's testimony. A presumption of innocence was established. During this time period, defendants were allowed to remain silent. This right was not codified but was recognized in a few decisions, which eventually became universally recognized.

With the founding of the United States and the enactment of the Constitution and the Bill of Rights, which formalized and added many rights for criminal defendants, the adversarial system of justice began to take shape. This burgeoning system had certain protections built into the system to help ensure fairness.

The Modern Adversarial System of Justice

A U.S. criminal trial is highly structured, requiring a number of steps before a suspect can be found guilty of a crime. Although the process is adversarial, there are a number of protections built into the system to balance the overwhelming power of the state to help ensure fairness and ensure that the trial process is not one in which individual defendants are crushed by the resources of the state and the machinery of justice. These protections include being informed of the charges, having the right to an attorney, having the right to confront one's accusers, having the right to present witnesses and evidence, having the right to cross-examine witnesses, having the right to compel witnesses to attend trial, having the right to a trial by jury, having the right to an impartial and independent judge, being given the presumption of innocence, and having the right to appeal. These rights are frequently referred to as due process rights. With these protections, a criminal jury is, at least in theory, a fair contest between the state and the suspect. However, as any person in the criminal justice system knows, the state has an enormous advantage in resources, which all too often results in innocent people being convicted of crimes they did not commit.

Although most Americans would say that the American adversarial system of justice is the best in the world, it does have its flaws. There are numerous criticisms of the adversarial system of justice from both sides of the system: prosecution and defense. One of the most common criticisms is that of delay. The courts in the American criminal justice system have become crowded to the extent that it might take years before a matter comes to trial. Many people charge that the adversarial system of justice is to blame for this

Up to the late 1600s, trials were often unstructured and quite biased against defendants. Minister George Burroughs, above, was hanged in 1692 during the hysteria of the Salem witch trials.

delay, as the various steps in the process lengthen the time to try a suspect and that lawyers, who control the litigation, frequently file motions that serve no purpose except delay. The response to this criticism is that to limit the number of steps and to quicken trials would result in many more innocent people being convicted of crimes they did not commit.

The adversarial system of justice has also been criticized for being responsible for allowing otherwise guilty people to escape punishment by acquittal on technical points of law. However, this criticism fails to acknowledge the countervailing consideration that it is better to let five guilty people go free rather than to convict one innocent person. Indeed, without the procedural protections of the adversarial system, that system of law would quickly degenerate into a political system of justice, which would raise even more issues as to fairness and justice.

Another criticism of the adversary system of justice is that the search for truth is not valued and is subordinate to the idea of winning at all costs. This particular criticism is most potent against prosecutors who want to have a high conviction rate to help ensure reelection to office or promotion. The work of Project Innocence has highlighted the fact that many people in jail and on death row for crimes they did not commit are there because of prosecutorial misconduct and the hiding of exculpatory evidence. Too many prosecutors forget that they are ministers of justice whose job is to ensure that only guilty people are convicted, not to ensure that they convict and incarcerate as many people as possible.

This situation leads to a fourth criticism of the adversarial system: that it encourages people to lie. To operate properly as it is philosophically intended to function, the adversarial system requires that the lawyers and the parties tell the truth. Defendants, having the right to remain silent and the presumption of innocence, are protected from the need to lie. However, as is commonly accepted in the United States, a number of attorneys, both prosecution and defense, engage in some form of deceit or misrepresentation, at least on occasion, to prevail.

Despite the failings of the adversary system of justice, it has many supporters and is still the law of the land for resolving the issue of guilt or innocence in response to a criminal charge. When compared to the other types of legal systems, the criticisms of the adversarial system of justice seem to wither and fade.

Wm. C. Plouffe, Jr.
Independent Scholar

See Also: Bill of Rights; Colonial Courts; Constitution of the United States of America; Courts; Defendant's Rights; Due Process; Legal Counsel; Suspect's Rights; Trials.

Further Readings
Hale, Matthew. *History of the Common Law of England*. Chicago: University of Chicago Press, 1971.
Kagan, Robert A. *Adversarial Legalism: The American Way of Law*. Cambridge, MA: Harvard University Press, 2001.
Landsman, Stephan. *Readings on Adversarial Justice: The American Approach to Adjudication*. Eagan, MN: West, 1988.
Reichel, Philip L. *Comparative Criminal Justice Systems*, 5th ed. Upper Saddle River, NJ: Pearson Prentice Hall, 2008.

African Americans

Perhaps no other racial or ethnic group in history has had its human identity and social history so constructed and determined by legislation, judicial pronouncement, and assessments of criminality and punishment than Africans in America. The early operation of American law was aimed at protecting the human trafficking and enslavement of people of African descent. The United States also broadly criminalized a number of acts that aided African Americans, up to and including educating them. Moreover, the massive legal machinery of the United States worked nearly incessantly from the ratification of the Constitution until the middle of the 20th century, with a brief interruption during and after the Civil War, to curtail African American access to civil society, civil rights, and the protections of the law, while imprisoning and otherwise punishing African Americans who resisted.

The middle- and late-20th-century civil rights movements helped alter the legal environment for African Americans and others but also eventually increased the numbers of African Americans represented within the broader political process, including the law. Although late-20th- and early-21st-century American law and criminal justice can be said to have been tremendously altered from previous periods, scholars, activists, jurists, legislators, and the general public still decry remaining inequities in criminal prosecutions, civil judgments, jury selection, policing, constitutional protections, sentencing and incarceration rates, and state and federal legislation.

Early History
By the time the first African slaves landed in 1619 in the British colonial territory, slavery in the Americas was already well established in Spanish

colonies, including Florida. Yet these captives, like many others, black and white, entered into bondage under the established system of indentured servitude. This system contractually bound people in labor to others for a fixed period of time, was not race linked, was governed by British law, and dated in the British system at least back to the 13th century. However, by the 17th century, wealthy plantation owners desired a more steady and dependable workforce, and chattel slavery emerged in Virginia as an American signature institution.

In 1654, John Casor, an African born in Africa, ran away from his master Anthony Johnson (also African) when Johnson failed to release him at the end of his contract indenture. The Northampton County, Virginia, courts ruled against Casor, determining that he had contracted into life slavery. This case marked a historic turn in that it allowed other Christians to be enslaved. Also, Casor was not considered an English citizen and therefore had no protection under English common law. Other cases were more favorably adjudicated when Africans could prove they were British subjects. After a number of cases like that of Elizabeth Key, who proved her British citizenship through her white father, Virginia introduced the link to slavery through the mother. The 1662 law derived from civil law the doctrine of *partus sequitur ventrem*, the condition of a child would derive from that of the mother, regardless of mixed race and particularly the race of the father. This legal construct provided the foundation for perpetuating generational and race-linked chattel slavery and empowering white men to engage in the wholesale sexual exploitation of black women for economic and private purposes. In both cases, centuries of literature and scholarship have been devoted to calculating the immensity of the cataclysm.

In 1676, Bacon's Rebellion erupted, and a large number of indentured servants, both black and white, joined the rebellion. One of the causes of the rebellion was the desire of certain colonists to see Native Americans driven out beyond the frontier. When the ruling class in Virginia refused to take a hard line against the Native Americans, a substantial number of frontiersmen, indentured servants, and other aggrieved Virginians revolted. It is reasonable to imagine that the dangers of the indentured servants and slaves revolting alarmed Virginia's gentry and prompted tighter control of servant classes. In 1705, Virginia instituted slave codes that further solidified slavery as a race-based institution. These codes indicated that all servants brought to Virginia who were African, mulatto, or Native American were considered slaves or personal property. They could be held in permanent bondage, punished for infractions, and used in commercial trade. Moreover, they could travel away from plantations only with permission and had no legal standing in the courts. These codes became the model for the rest of the developing American slaveholding colonies.

By the time of the American Revolution, the slave population was substantial enough to be a military asset, and as rowdy colonists became rebels, the alarmed British offered liberty to any slaves of American revolutionaries who would join royal forces. General George Washington, allegedly after a long visit from African American poet Phillis Wheatley, changed his mind to accept blacks into the Continental army with the promise of freedom for service. At the close of the Revolutionary War, the retreating British resettled tens of thousands of African Americans in their remaining territories. However, American blacks fared much worse. Many blacks were returned to slavery, and with the advent of large-scale cotton production and with substantive legal support, chattel slavery expanded.

Early Legal Status

The U.S. Constitution emerged with the Three-Fifths Compromise intact, which counted slaves as three-fifths of a person for the purpose of determining legislative apportionment. This created an inflated political influence of southern states that persisted until the Civil War. The Constitution also established a timetable for ending the lawful importation of slaves. Notably, Article 4, Section 2 of the Constitution separately provided that those held as slaves in one state could not be freed in other states but had to be returned to lawful slaveholders. However, this section of the Constitution did not provide an enforcement mechanism. The Fugitive Slave Act of 1793 gave slaveholders a functioning mechanism for recovering slaves. The act criminalized assistance to escaped slaves and other fugitives. It also imposed a $500 fine for aiding an escaped slave and authorized agents and attorneys of the slaveholder to seize alleged slaves and petition the courts for removal to the home state. This act gave birth to the bustling industry of slave catching, and manhunters roamed the young nation, seizing fugitive blacks and reportedly dragging many free men and women into slavery. The case of Solomon Northup, an educated New York free man who was enticed to travel with men who drugged him and sold him into slavery in Louisiana, is very instructive. His attempt to sue the men who abducted him is a celebrated New York case.

The 19th century saw substantial legal activity affecting African Americans, almost entirely related to the conflict over slavery. Scholarly, legal, and literary works all indicate that the slave system reached maximum development in the 19th century, as did the mechanisms for legally managing the system. The Fugitive Slave Act was in full force, and on plantations, slaveholders had full authority to punish, imprison, and in most cases kill slaves. In South Carolina, aiding an escaped slave carried the death penalty. The Supreme Court case of *Prigg v. Pennsylvania* (1842) affirmed the supremacy of the act over state laws. Prigg had attempted to seize Margaret Morgan, a Maryland slave who had never been emancipated, and ran afoul of 1788 and 1826 Pennsylvania laws that protected escaped slaves and regulated the action of slave catchers. Although *Prigg* upheld the Fugitive Slave Act, it gave states a loophole through which they could leave enforcement of the act to federal officials. However, such small victories were largely overshadowed by the strengthened Fugitive Slave Act of 1850 and legal decisions like *Dred Scott v. Sandford* (1857), which rejected African American claims to relief in the courts and affirmed their role as property that could not be seized without due process. African Americans and white abolitionists were forced to resort to direct action to resist slave catchers, resulting in regular attempts to free blacks ensnared by the fugitive slave apparatus.

In the 1851 "Jerry Rescue," William "Jerry" Henry was arrested in Syracuse, New York, under the Fugitive Slave Act. Word of the arrest under the unpopular act spread to the Liberty Party convention, and hundreds of abolitionists converged on the city jail and released Henry. Joshua Glover,

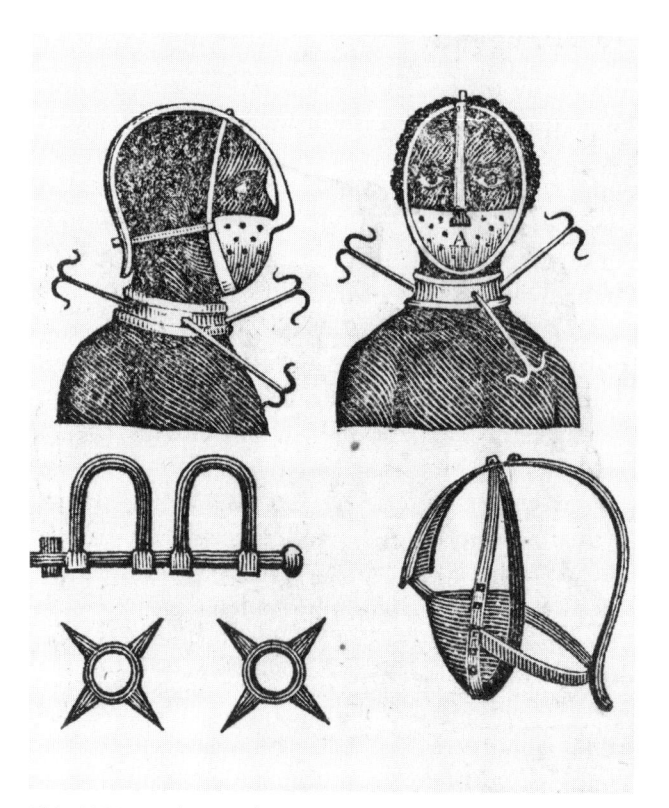

This 1807 woodcut made in New York shows an iron mask and collar, leg shackles, and spurs, which were all examples of instruments American slaveholders used to restrain slaves.

a slave from Missouri was similarly sprung from jail, after being arrested in Racine, Wisconsin. Glover escaped to Canada via the Underground Railroad, which grew in participants and strength with the outrage over the 1850 act. The failed Thomas Sims (1851) and Anthony Burns (1854) and the successful Shadrack Minkins rescue in 1851 were among many celebrated cases that illustrate the divisiveness of the Fugitive Slave Act.

The era of controversy produced a hardening of positions in the north and the south. Within the slave system proper, the regulation of slaves reached an unprecedented level of brutality. A notorious North Carolina Supreme Court case, *State v. Mann* (1830), which held that slaveholders could not be prosecuted for assaults on slaves, illustrated the logic of slavery perfectly: "[T]he power of the master must be absolute to render the submission of the slave perfect." With a free hand to control slaves as property, punishment was regular and varied and was carried out by slaveholders and their agents. The most celebrated tool of punishment was the whip, but accounts of escaped and freed slaves indicated a variety of methods to control slaves. Heavy cudgels, sticks of wood, switches and whips, iron collars and chains, yokes, suspension by limbs, hanging, tarring and feathering, commitment to stocks, burning, amputation, branding, castration, rape, starvation, separation from children and other family, sale to more brutal owners, and firearms were all reportedly in use. Solomon Northup, Harriet Jacobs, William Wells Brown, Frederick Douglass, and others recorded these methods of punishment, in addition to the sexual exploitation suffered by slave women.

Rape was a regular part of slavery, both as a matter of private lusts and as a cynical economic move. Reproduction via rape increased the property holdings of male slaveholders, even as it produced disruptions in family relationships. Solomon Northup reports being asked to carry out the murder of a slave by a slaveholder's jealous wife. In addition, a brisk trade in attractive women—mulatto, quadroon, octoroon—bustled in some southern cities like New Orleans, and many women were kept by men of means. Far more women were simply savaged by men, with no legal protections to rely upon. Slave marriages and lines of descent were also largely ignored at law in southern states.

Legal status in other areas was limited as well. Slaves for certain and even free blacks in most cases could not give evidence against white men, and contract protections were nonexistent in most cases in law or practice. In Virginia, Kentucky, Arkansas, and Louisiana, slaves existed as real estate for a time, but they were ultimately recognized as chattel and could be bought, sold, or leased, as well as inherited, used as collateral, or otherwise disposed of as property. They could legally be policed by slave patrols, which enforced pass requirements for blacks in transit anywhere outside the immediate control of a slaveholder. They also hunted and returned fugitive slaves with the protection of the law, and in some cases, laws compelled citizens to assist patrols.

The legal fiction of reducing a human to property did conflict with the fact of will and volition and other elements of humanity that could not conveniently be denied. Slaves could not be held responsible for their acts if they did not have free will, yet almost universally, state codes held that slaves could be punished by masters and at law for offenses. In *Ford v. Ford* (1846), Tennessee Supreme Court justice Nathan Green famously observed while ruling in favor of a slave's freedom via a will that "a slave is not in the condition of a horse or an ox." Similar concessions to conditional humanity were usually not so beneficial to slaves. The Georgia slave codes (1848) made insurrection or conspiracy, rape or attempted rape on a free white woman, murder of a free white person or free person of color, and poisoning of a human punishable by death when committed by a slave or a free person of color. Other offenses were punishable by death at the discretion of the court, including striking or maiming a free white person, burglary, and arson. Notably, slaves could be totally excused if the violence against a white person was at the command of a slaveholder or overseer or other person in charge of the slave. In that case, the white owner was held responsible.

Legal Complications

Additional complications arose from the general legal principle that slaves could not testify against whites. Evidentiary problems also arose when slave testimony was excluded in total because slaves could not testify as even the witnesses to crimes committed by other slaves, provided that slave defendant actually made it to trial alive. Holding a slave as fit to be sworn also presented a problem because a slave had to be presumed to have the conviction, understanding, and belief in the Christian God. By the 19th century, slaves could testify for the purposes of convicting other slaves, although evidence rarely came solely from slaves. Alleged free confessions of slaves were always admitted into evidence.

Criminal brutality against slaves presented a particularly difficult problem. In the 18th century, some colonies and states prosecuted slaveholders for excess brutality. The 1713–14 case of Frances Wilson, who allegedly beat to death one of her husband's slaves, caused a stir in Virginia. The long case included a ruling that a slave was at once the property of a master and the king's subject. The British Crown could bring to trial anyone who destroyed the life of a subject. However, the prevailing mood was that the public was unwilling to deal with killings or heavy abuses of slaves by white colonists or state citizens. Statutes existed in many states, including South Carolina and Louisiana, that barred punishments such as removing limbs or burning or removing tongues and eyes but left even deadly whipping largely untouched. But in *State v. Maner* (1834), a South Carolina court ruled that criminal assault and battery could not be committed at law against a slave. Driving many public and political decisions on punishment were fears of rebellion and resistance. Many states made unauthorized gatherings, leaving the plantation without permission, and a variety of infractions seen as insubordination or insolence grounds for punishment. This often included attending religious services or attempting to attain education. In addition, many states made educating slaves a serious offense. The threat of rebellion was not an imagined danger. More than 250 slave revolts of varying success occurred during the period of American slavery. Stono's Rebellion, Prosser's Rebellion, and Nat Turner's Rebellion are some of the more famous. John Brown's raid on Harper's Ferry, intended to inspire a slave revolt, stands on its own as a precursor to the Civil War.

In the early 19th century, a variety of laws governing African Americans came into being, generally classified as Black Codes. These Black Codes existed in the north as well as in the south, where they covered free blacks who remained outside the slave codes. As the abolitionist movement developed, some northern states sought to control black migration and settlement. Combined with antimiscegenation statutes, these rules formed the foundation for what would eventually become the more complex Jim Crow system. Indiana and Illinois instituted formidable Black Codes in their constitutions of the mid-19th century, and eventually both barred black settlement. Pennsylvania provides a unique example of African Americans within the context of criminal justice, both because of its abolitionist history and for figuring prominently in one of the earliest scholarly examinations of African American life in the north, including criminal activity, W. E. B. Du Bois's *The Philadelphia Negro*. African American crime in the north, as observed by Du Bois, manifested itself in purported rowdy conduct by slaves in the early to mid-18th century and was largely handled by local ordinances. Later in the 18th century and early 19th century, free men and immigrants produced a rash of reported petty thefts, assaults, and murders. Popular concern over the growing Negro population, particularly in the wake of the Nat Turner Rebellion, prompted the Pennsylvania legislature to disenfranchise blacks in 1837. The Eastern Penitentiary opened in 1829 in Pennsylvania, and between 1829 and 1834, 29 percent of prisoner commitments were African Americans. Between 1836 and 1845, the percentage of blacks in the prisoner population was 48.29 percent, decreasing to 32.01 percent from 1846 to 1855. As Du Bois noted in his study, the activities of the criminal class in Philadelphia caused African American churches and broader black society to band together against its own criminal element. While crime statistics stabilized in the 1860s, crime in Philadelphia and other urban areas of the north rose steadily among African Americans with the advent of postwar migration.

Civil War

The Civil War and its immediate aftermath brought revolutionary changes to African American legal circumstances, albeit briefly. The 1865 Thirteenth Amendment to the U.S. Constitution ended slavery and involuntary servitude, except as punishment for a crime. The Fourteenth Amendment (1868) contained a three-pronged remedy for African American civil exclusion. It dismantled the *Dred Scott* decision by extending citizenship to African Americans and extended due process protections, which eventually resulted in the Bill of Rights applying more broadly. It also extended equal protection guarantees, which became the foundation for the civil rights era rollback of Jim Crow rules generally described as segregation. Notably, the Three-Fifths Compromise met its end with the Fourteenth Amendment. The Fifteenth Amendment (1870) guaranteed the right to vote to citizens regardless of race, color, or having previously been a slave.

These amendments would seem to have introduced African Americans to full citizenship, except that the end of Reconstruction saw a massive retrenchment and tireless campaign of southern states and some northern states to intimidate and newly disenfranchise former slaves. The federal government did not abandon postwar gains immediately. Deploying Attorney General Amos

T. Akerman and Solicitor General Benjamin H. Bristow, President Ulysses S. Grant attempted to quell the violence against Republicans and African Americans in the south. Federal policy was to prosecute crimes vigorously. However, no modern federal investigative force existed, and limited funds were at hand in the postwar period. Administration of cases was difficult, with judges literally riding the circuit and expanding court dockets, producing numbers of untried cases in the thousands. Moreover, southern partisans mounted spirited defenses of accused Ku Klux Klan militants, often producing large sums for defense expenses and procuring top attorneys. At the local level, federal officials were under threat in their homes when living in the communities where crimes were committed or where sympathies ran with the mob. With militants often occupying respected positions in the white community, the situation was even more difficult. These problems, coupled with dwindling national support for Reconstruction, doomed government efforts.

Jim Crow Era

With the expiration of Reconstruction, a series of revived Black Codes or Jim Crow statutes emerged, with every southern state eventually enacting some barrier to black suffrage. The most well-known strategies were the poll tax, the grandfather clause, and literacy tests. A steady procession of states revised statutes to bar interracial marriage as well. West Virginia, for instance, invalidated the marriages and imposed a fine of $100 and imprisonment for up to one year on participants and a fine of as much as $200 for officiants. In addition, the Supreme Court invalidated the 1875 Civil Rights Act, which barred segregation in many public accommodations. Through the end of the 19th century, states around the country proceeded to separate blacks and whites in almost all public venues, including schools. In 1896, the Supreme Court validated segregation and Jim Crow rules in *Plessy v. Ferguson.*

In addition to the legislative and judicial retreat from civil rights, a process using the criminal justice system to return large portions of the black population to unpaid labor emerged in some southern states as the convict lease system. With blacks disenfranchised and removed from the roll of eligible voters, they were also in many jurisdictions no longer eligible for jury duty. In other jurisdictions, they were simply excluded. This created local and state judicial systems where blacks were excluded from political office, barred from voting, excluded from juries, and variously blocked from the practice of law. Within this system, all-white prosecutors, judges, and juries sentenced African Americans to long prison terms and then sold their labor to private contractors who maintained labor camps, complete with armed guards. The states pocketed part of the income from the unpaid prison workers and had ample reason to incarcerate African Americans at a disproportionate rate. Additionally, within the prison system, the state had broad ability to punish workers with brutality largely unseen by the public.

However, the south was not the exclusive theater for African American crime and punishment during this period. Monroe Work's pioneering study of African American crime in 1897 Chicago notes that blacks made up 29.49 percent of prisoners in the United States in 1890. Moreover, in

A portrait of an unidentified African American man from between 1860 and 1870. Jim Crow statutes such as the poll tax and literacy tests soon cut into many postwar advances.

proportion to their population, more blacks were in prison in the north than in the south. In Chicago, a full quarter of blacks inhabited slum areas, and this group committed a substantial number of crimes—largely of larceny, burglary, and robbery. Similar to what Du Bois found of Philadelphia, Chicago crime showed an increase over a 25-year period to 1897 correlating with migration from the south and with prisoners from southern states disproportionally represented in the population.

Where the law and incarceration were inefficient or simply insufficient to satisfy the mob, public violence and intimidation substituted for legal sanction. Lynching became a regular feature of African American life, especially in the American south, where it was a chilling method of social control—a reminder to surrender any remaining protected civil rights and submit to white hegemony. Lynching itself is not confined to hanging but refers to an entire class of brutality, including maiming, burning at the stake, castration, shooting, and various types of amputation or dismemberment. Reasons for lynching were suspected crimes of theft, attempting to register to vote, insolence or conflicts with whites, and insults to whites otherwise undefined. In truth, no substantive reason was actually necessary; lynching served as a tool of terror. One particular crime for which black men could be regularly accused was rooted in the white political assertion and social mythology of black men's insatiable urge to rape white women. Rape included a range of imagined offenses against white womanhood, and the rhetoric of rape and miscegenation punctuated the speech of white terror groups of the era as well as political discussions of "the Negro Question." Estimates of the number of African Americans lynched between 1882 and 1950 range from a conservative estimate of approximately 3,400 to some estimates of well over 5,000.

What have often been termed *race riots* of the 19th and early 20th centuries are more accurately described as mass murders, mass lynchings, or political coups. Unbearable conditions in the south, which included the Black Codes, lynchings, disenfranchisement, and economic re-enslavement in the penal or sharecropping systems led to large-scale black migration to the northeast and west. In addition, World War I produced a body of black veterans who were less inclined to accept the racism in America after having seen the more liberal operation of race in Europe. In the case of the Wilmington, North Carolina, Riots of 1898, the riot was sparked by white resistance to black political participation in the city and the resulting stolen election, which included a campaign of intimidation and violence. In 1919, similar "riots" resulted in large numbers of black deaths in more than 25 conflicts across the south, midwest, and Texas. The so-called riots were, in fact, acts of mob violence by disgruntled whites against black communities for some imagined slight, purported threat or evidence of blacks failing to submit to white authority, or evidence that blacks' civil rights were being honored. Riots in Memphis, Tennessee, in 1866; Wilmington, North Carolina, in 1898 (and spawning Charles Chesnutt's *The Marrow of Tradition*); Atlanta, Georgia, in 1906; Springfield, Illinois, in 1908; Tulsa, Oklahoma, in 1921; and Columbia, Tennessee, in 1946 are representative cases. The first modern race riot that characteristically involves destruction of property within African American communities is generally believed to have been the 1935 Harlem Riot, which occurred after a Puerto Rican youth was inaccurately reported to have been beaten to death in a Kress Five-and-Ten store.

Early to Mid-Twentieth Century

In the midst of the lynchings and massacres of this period, some Supreme Court decisions of note emerged. In *Powell v. Alabama* (1932), eight of nine African American men, the Scottsboro Boys, who had been accused of raping two white women, had been rapidly sentenced to death in one-day trials. They had seen their attorneys just before the trials and had no opportunity to construct an adequate defense and appealed on that basis. The Alabama Supreme Court rejected the appeal, but the U.S. Supreme Court ruled that in capital cases, to satisfy due process requirements, a defendant had to be given access to his attorney when requested. According to the court, the defendants had not received a fair and impartial trial, nor had they been adequately afforded the right to counsel. The court recognized that they had been tried by juries from which blacks had been excluded. In *Norris v. Alabama* (1935), Scottsboro convictions were overturned yet again because African Americans had been excluded from the jury pool.

The period of World War II had a marked effect on African Americans, partly because the dissatisfaction with stateside discrimination that had been feared from World War I veterans was greatly multiplied in returning World War II soldiers, who had seen the workings of race elsewhere, had fought bravely against white men, and had earned rank and accolades. African American soldiers had faced discrimination in the military, including the excessive use of "blue discharges," a dishonorable discharge from the military disproportionately used on blacks that also stripped them of many military benefits. Still, substantive desegregation in the United States came early in the armed forces, when a 1948 order by President Harry Truman integrated the military, including military posts and bases and living areas—base housing, schools, and amenities. This period also saw increasing attention to the causes of African American crime, especially in urban areas that would see a second wave of black migration to the northeast. In *Juvenile Delinquency and Urban Areas* (1942), C. R. Shaw and Henry McKay linked delinquency and crime to the health of communities and the effects of segregation and economic status. These observations recalled Du Bois's observations about immigration, slum-dwelling, and crime in Philadelphia and Chicago, and looked ahead to scholarly studies of unemployment, black family disintegration, and juvenile violence in the late 20th century.

Civil Rights Movement
The era of the American civil rights movement was characterized by grassroots nonviolent protests and civil disobedience involving students, activists, and a large contingent of participants in African American religious culture. These protests and acts of civil disobedience regularly targeted exemplary forms of racial discrimination. Sit-ins at segregated venues like the Greensboro, North Carolina, sit-ins (1960), and boycotts like the Montgomery, Alabama, Bus Boycott (1955–56) directly challenged legal segregation, bringing national and global attention to the civil inequities. This group faced substantive opposition from local and state law enforcement agencies in the American south, as well as political and judicial elements. Violence, murder, and intimidation, combined with prosecution and imprisonment, were deployed against the movement participants.

In 1954, the Supreme Court handed down its decision in *Brown v. Board of Education*, declaring segregated schools unconstitutional and later ordering the system of segregation dismantled "with all deliberate speed." Subsequent challenges to the Montgomery bus system (1955–56, ending with *Browder v. Gayle*), the segregated Central High School in Little Rock, Arkansas (1957–58, ending with *Cooper v. Aaron*), and others marked the progress of the movement. However, a campaign to take nonviolent action into the heart of the segregated south resulted in escalating violence. Freedom Rides in 1961 in South Carolina, Alabama, and Mississippi were particularly brutal. A bus was firebombed, and police allowed members of the Ku Klux Klan to attack another group. A substantial number of Freedom Riders were arrested and imprisoned, and still more were beaten by mobs. In addition to Freedom Rides, various organizations within the movement organized and advanced a voter registration project, harnessing the black voter strength long reduced by white intimidation. The response from the southern opponents was brutal and violent, including murder. The Civil Rights Act of 1964, given a burst of public support by shock over the murder of three civil rights activists in Mississippi, made the premier components of racial discrimination illegal, including barriers to voter registration and barriers to equal access to public accommodations. In addition, the Voting Rights Act of 1965 more finely combed the list of barriers to suffrage and also required states with a history of discrimination in voting rights to clear any proposed change to voting requirements with the federal government.

African Americans in the Law
Along with civil rights advances, the 20th century saw increasing numbers of African Americans in the ranks of law enforcement, legal practice, and the judiciary. As early as 1865, John Swett Rock became the first African American admitted to Supreme Court practice, and Jonathan J. Wright sat on the South Carolina Supreme Court until 1877. Robert H. Terrell served as the District of Columbia municipal judge from 1909 until 1925, and in 1911, William H. Lewis became the first black assistant attorney general at the Department of Justice. William Hastie became the first

black U.S. District Court judge in 1937, after being appointed by Franklin Roosevelt. Thurgood Marshall became the first African American justice of the U.S. Supreme Court in 1967. During the Carter administration, 28 African Americans were appointed to U.S. District Court judge positions. The Reagan and George H. W. Bush administrations continued a more limited appointment trend, and Clarence Thomas became the second black Supreme Court justice when he was confirmed to replace Thurgood Marshall in 1991.

The later 20th and 21st centuries saw continuing service by African Americans, including examples of judicial leadership like the ascension of Leah Ward Sears to chief justice of the Georgia Supreme Court in 2005. African American attorneys followed a similar course of growth and service, in public and private practice and in legal academe. However, progress in the profession is small in comparison to overall population, with African Americans making up only 3.9 percent of attorneys. Numbers of black law students fell to 6.6 percent by 2004, from 7.4 percent in 2002. In law enforcement, African Americans have become a more substantial part of police and other law enforcement arms in the nation, and organizations like the National Black Police Association (1972) have developed to support African Americans in law enforcement and improve relationships between minority communities and law enforcement. Interestingly, African American police officers have been entangled both in long-standing conflicts over policing of African Americans, especially in urban areas, and their own struggles for racial equity within law enforcement. K. Bolton and J. Feagin's *Black in Blue* (2004) chronicles this complex balancing act.

Part of the impetus for the increase in African Americans as regular participants in the judicial and law enforcement hierarchy was that the mid- to late 20th century saw critiques of substantive economic deprivation and direct challenges to the racial makeup of law enforcement and the application of criminal prosecution. The long-term effects of the educational, economic, and civil disenfranchisement revealed by earlier academic studies were increasingly visible to the large population, and especially in the urban spaces of America, African Americans acutely felt the impact of economic weakness, crime, and

Justice Thurgood Marshall's official Supreme Court portrait from January 1976. He became the first African American justice of the U.S. Supreme Court in 1967.

conflict with largely white representatives of law enforcement and the legal system. Civil unrest in the Watts section of Los Angeles in 1965 was one of many violent community reactions to violence and inequities in policing by white police officers, combined with structural changes in the U.S. economy that reduced industrial jobs and exacerbated existing economic stress. Regular civil unrest plagued major urban areas throughout the 1960s and 1970s and recurred in the 1980s and 1990s. Although urban police forces became more diverse in the latter part of the 20th century, concerns about policing and prosecution echoed concerns of African Americans in earlier eras. Notable events include the 1991 car pursuit and beating of Rodney King by Los Angeles Police Department officers, which was captured on videotape. The advent of widespread personal video recording made this case particularly volatile, and when the officers involved were acquitted of charges, public anger sparked the Los Angeles Riots of 1992. In 1997, Abner Louima was sexually assaulted with a broom handle by New York Police Department (NYPD) officers and left bleeding from the rectum. Two years later, Amadou Diallo was killed by NYPD officers who claimed the unarmed man had reached for a gun. Officers fired 41 rounds of ammunition at Diallo.

Into the Twenty-First Century

Concern about gang activity also sparked a series of city ordinances that were widely believed to target African Americans and other ethnic minorities in an attempt to deprive them of the ability to move about or congregate in urban spaces. In *City of Chicago v. Morales* (1999), the Supreme Court ruled that Chicago's Gang Congregation Ordinance was impermissibly vague and an unconstitutional restriction on personal liberties. Late-20th-century drug enforcement regimes also proved a flashpoint for racial concerns about crime and punishment. The Anti–Drug Abuse Acts of 1986 and 1988, tools in what was termed a federal war on drugs, helped create a 100 to 1 sentencing disparity for comparative convictions for the sale of crack versus powder cocaine. Crack, a smoked form of cocaine, was more prevalent in urban communities and among minority populations, especially African Americans. Combined with concerns about targeted policing and racial profiling, the sentencing disparities appear to have been a great contributor to the disproportionate number of African Americans in U.S. prisons for drug offenses, estimated at one point to have been 74 percent of all Americans sentenced to prison for drug offenses. In 2010, Congress passed the Fair Sentencing Act, which responded to growing concern that the sentencing disparity was intolerably high. The current act sets the disparity at 18:1.

The late 20th century and early 21st century have also been periods of introspection and scholarly debate about race, crime, and what scholars like Michael Tonry have termed *moral panics*, which drive periods of excessive public, law enforcement, and political, legislative, and judicial responses to imagined crises of crime. These moral panics disproportionately affect ethnic minorities, including African Americans, but they and the criminal hoax phenomenon may also entangle majority populations. High-profile hoaxes involving alleged African American perpetrators—carjackings, white child/white woman kidnappings, and rapes—punctuated the turn-of-the-century period, but hoaxes like the Tawanna Brawley episode and the Duke lacrosse team case illustrated the manipulations of race that made African Americans victims and perpetuators of race stereotypes and emphasized the complicated legacy of race in criminal justice.

Conclusion

The history of African American engagement with crime, punishment, and the legal system in the United States is one inextricably linked to the nation's long and tumultuous struggle to escape the legacy of slavery, racism, and exclusions from broad rights and legal protections. The contemporary landscape of African American engagement with the field is marked by an increased black presence within law enforcement, the judiciary, and the legal profession. The presence of African Americans among legislators is greater as well, and the broader expansion of civil rights and access to ethnic minorities and women has combined with long-standing African American strides toward equality to suggest a future marked by both resistance to lingering elements of discrimination in criminal law and punishment and substantive contributions to the construction and execution of the law.

Eric Ashley Hairston
Elon University

See Also: 1600 to 1776 Primary Documents; 1777 to 1800 Primary Documents; 1801 to 1850 Primary Documents; 1961 to 1980 Primary Documents; Black Panthers; *Brown v. Board of Education*; Civil Rights Act of 1866; Civil Rights Act of 1875; Civil Rights Laws; *Dred Scott v. Sandford*; Fugitive Slave Act of 1793; Fugitive Slave Act of 1850; King, Martin Luther, Jr.; King, Rodney; Ku Klux Klan; Lynchings; Malcolm X; *Plessy v. Ferguson*; Police Abuse; Racism; Riots; Segregation Laws; Slave Patrols; Slavery; Slavery, Law of.

Further Readings

Bolton, K. and J. Feagin. *Black in Blue: African-American Police Officers and Racism*. New York: Routledge, 2004.

Free, M. D., Jr. *African Americans and the Criminal Justice System*. New York: Garland, 1996.

Gabbidon, Shaun L. and Helen Taylor Green, eds. *Race, Crime and Justice: A Reader*. New York: Routledge, 2005.

Gabbidon, Shaun L., et al., eds. *African-American Classics in Criminology & Criminal Justice.* Thousand Oaks, CA: Sage, 2002.

Keyssar, Alexander. *The Right to Vote: The Contested History of Democracy in the United States*, Rev. ed. New York: Basic Books, 2009.

Morris, Thomas D. *Southern Slavery and the Law 1619–1860.* Chapel Hill: University of North Carolina Press, 1996.

Muhammad, Khalil Gibran. *The Condemnation of Blackness: Race, Crime and the Making of Modern Urban America.* Cambridge, MA: Harvard University Press, 2010.

Russell, John H. "Colored Freemen as Slave Owners in Virginia." *Journal of Negro History,* v.1 (June 1916).

Russell-Brown, Katheryn. *The Color of Crime*, 2nd ed. New York: New York University Press, 2009.

Tonry, Michael. *Thinking About Crime.* New York: Oxford University Press, 2004.

Tushnet, Mark V. *Slave Law in the American South: State v. Mann in History and Literature.* Lawrence: University Press of Kansas, 2003.

Wilson, William Julius. *The Truly Disadvantaged: The Inner City, the Underclass, and Public Policy.* Chicago: University of Chicago Press, 1987.

Alabama

Originally part of the Mississippi Territory, Alabama was admitted to the union as a separate state in 1819 and developed an economy around its large cotton plantations. At the time, the state lacked a prison system, and in fact the general public opposed one: Even the spartan prisons of the 19th century consumed more tax revenue than punishments like flogging, branding, and hanging. Further, without a state prison system, a greater share of punitive power rested at the county level, and in Alabama—still considered the frontier at the time—county officials like sheriffs were not perceived as bureaucrats or politicians in the same way as state officials. It took nearly a decade of effort by governors and legislators to finally begin a state prison system. Alabama's first state prison, Wetumpka State Penitentiary, was created in 1839 when the state legislature passed a criminal code authorizing it. Construction of the prison was completed in 1841, and the first prisoner arrived the following year. Though the public was promised that prison industries would pay for prison expenses, the revenue from those industries, like the manual manufacture of rope and shoes, fell far short of paying for prison expenses. Originally for both sexes, Wetumpka was reclassified as a women's prison in 1922, and closed 20 years later.

Alabama was one of the states to secede from the Union and form the Confederate States of America, and was subject to the changes of Reconstruction in the aftermath of the Civil War. The numerous Ku Klux Klan chapters that opened in Alabama in the mid- to late 19th century were a reaction against Alabama's loss of face and power after the war. Institutionalized white supremacy was restored with the passage of Jim Crow laws that limited the rights of blacks and established racial segregation in public facilities and the new public school system.

The right for a defendant to be provided with counsel as part of due process, which is today one of the important rights included under Miranda law, was established in the Supreme Court's 1932 decision of *Powell v. Alabama*. The Powell ruling led to an ongoing debate about whether court-appointed attorneys needed to be provided in non-capital cases—Powell had been accused of rape and faced a death sentence—which was ultimately decided by the 1963 *Gideon v. Wainwright* decision establishing that the Sixth Amendment requires defendants to be provided with attorneys if they cannot afford their own. To this day, Alabama does not have a statewide public defender system; court-appointed attorneys are hired by and compensated by the court, typically at a lower hourly rate than they would otherwise earn.

Moonshine was big business in Alabama both before and after Prohibition. While bootlegging—the smuggling of alcohol illegally—was a going concern throughout the nation under Prohibition, the moonshine business profited not only from subverting a ban on alcohol but also from an opportunity to make money from Alabama's agricultural resources. Grain, typically corn, could be mashed, fermented, distilled, and sold for a much greater profit than the corn would have been worth on its own. The principle legal issue with moonshine was that amateur distillers did not pay the tax collected from legal professional distillers—though in the course of a moonshine enterprise, many other laws may have also been broken, in order to keep the enterprise viable.

In 1935, the Alabama legislature attempted to pass a bill that would sterilize by surgical procedure or castration "those suffering from perversions, constitutional psychopathic personalities or marked departures from normal mentality," which included inmates of prisons and asylums who were considered "sexual perverts, sadists, masochists, homosexuals, or sodomists." Sodomy in Alabama included not only homosexual sex but also oral sex. The law was struck down by the Alabama Supreme Court as unconstitutional, and Governor Bibb Graves vetoed a subsequent bill modified to accommodate some of the court's objections. Alabama's sodomy laws, effectively criminalizing nonprocreational sexual acts, were ruled unconstitutional by the Alabama Supreme Court in 1973's *Horn v. State*—but the 1977 Alabama Criminal Code included a "sexual misconduct" law explicitly outlawing oral and anal sex between persons not married to each other. The sale, but not possession, of sex toys was outlawed in a 1998 law, which was upheld upon its challenge in federal court.

Alabama is a state that practices capital punishment. From 1927 to 2002, its executions were carried out by "Yellow Mama," the state's sole electric chair, built by a British inmate and installed at Kilby State Prison in Montgomery. It was retired—and is now stored in an attic at Holman Correctional Facility in Atmore—after legislation that allowed lethal injection as a means of execution. Yellow Mama was the means used to execute James Coburn (b. 1926) in 1964, the last defendant executed in the United States for a crime other than murder. Coburn had been sentenced to death for robbery. In 1972, the Supreme Court's ruling in the *Furman v. Georgia* case found that extant death penalty statutes were unconstitutional. When the subsequent Supreme Court case *Gregg v. Georgia* found death penalties feasibly constitutional in 1976, Alabama passed a new capital punishment law and resumed its executions. Prior to the new law, capital crimes included rape, arson, and robbery; most convicts executed for rape were black men. The death penalty system in Alabama, both pre- and post-*Furman*, has been criticized for providing insufficient legal support to defendants, for the racial imbalance of its convictions, and in some cases a lack of sufficient evidence to establish guilt. Black jazz musician Jeremiah Reeves, whose appeals were twice rejected by the Supreme Court, but who was seen by many civil rights workers as a victim of institutionalized racism, claimed that he was forced to sit in Yellow Mama overnight to encourage him to confess, before he was executed for rape in 1956.

Alabama was the site of much of the civil rights movement's activity, as activists worked to fight segregation laws and enroll black voters. A turning point for the civil rights movement nationwide was the 1963 bombing of the 16th Street Baptist Church, a black church in Birmingham. The church had been a prominent meeting place for activists and became the target of members of the United Klans of America, the most violent Ku Klux Klan group of its time. The explosion injured 22 people and killed four girls aged 11 and 14. The case remained unsolved until the late 1970s, when newly elected Attorney General Bill Baxley reopened the investigation, leading to the conviction of one bomber, Klansman Robert Chambliss. The remaining bombers—Herman Cash, Thomas Blanton, and Bobby Cherry—were not identified until 2000. All four bombers had been considered serious suspects by the Federal Bureau of Investigation (FBI) in 1965, but witnesses had been reluctant to talk. By 2000, Cash was dead, Blanton was tried and sentenced to life in prison, and Cherry was ruled mentally incompetent by a court-ordered psychiatric evaluation.

Crime

Since the 1960s, Alabama has been a home to the Dixie Mafia, an organized crime group based in nearby Biloxi, Mississippi. Dealing mostly in robbery, gambling, loan sharking, strip clubs, and prostitution, the Dixie Mafia was also known for its contract killings during its rise to power in the 1970s and 1980s. At one point, it had strong ties to the Chicago Outfit and the State Line Mob, the latter a group of criminals mainly from Phenix City, Alabama, but operating along the Mississippi–Tennessee state line. The mob was formed in response to the declaration of martial law in Phenix City in the 1950s, when the National Guard

Part of an exhibit on the Ku Klux Klan at the Birmingham Civil Rights Institute in Birmingham, Alabama, in March 2010. Alabama was the site of much activity during the civil rights movement and Birmingham was a target for the United Klans of America, the most violent Ku Klux Klan group of the time. The Birmingham Civil Rights Institute was dedicated in 1992.

was brought in to clean up the gambling dens, brothels, and moonshine joints.

The earliest police departments in Alabama were formed shortly after statehood, county sheriffs having been the primary law enforcement in the territorial years. The Montgomery Police Department was established in 1820, the year after Alabama was admitted as a state. As in many states, Alabama's state police agency—the Department of Public Safety—began with the need for an agency to enforce law on the highways, and the Alabama Highway Patrol was founded accordingly in 1935. It was funded with fees paid for driver's licenses, mandated in the state for the first time that year. In 1939, the Highway Patrol became the Department of Public Safety, and today includes a Bureau of Investigation as well as the highway troopers. Haleyville, Alabama, was the site of the first 911-call system in the United States. Congress had called for a universal emergency number in 1958, but implementation was long delayed over arguments about which institution (police, fire department, a local hospital, or others) should answer calls, as well as technical issues in establishing the emergency number. The Alabama Telephone Company was the first to implement a 911-system, converting equipment in Haleyville over to the new system in 1968, 10 years after the congressional decision, when many were still skeptical that the plan was practical. Emergency 911 calls were forwarded to a dispatcher at the Haleyville police station, who determined which personnel should respond on a case-by-case basis.

Later adoption of the modern touchtone system made implementation of 911 calls easier. In 1977, after a rise in violent crime, theft, and drug crime since World War II, Alabama passed the Habitual Felony Offender Law, one of the strictest in the country. Habitual offender laws, which assign enhanced penalties for those who repeatedly commit the same kind of crime, date back to at least the 19th century. Modern habitual offender laws, which are typically restricted to violent crimes or drug offenses, often enhance the penalty beyond the normal maximum sentence for the crime, essentially treating recidivism as an aggravating circumstance. Alabama's law, though, predates the wave of "three strikes" laws enacted in the 1990s and is more of a "one strike" law, mandating a longer sentence for any offender with a prior felony conviction—regardless of whether the crime is of the same type—and making no allowances for the amount of time between convictions.

In the over 30 years since the Habitual Felony Offender Law was enacted, such laws have been the focus of numerous studies by sociologists and criminologists, most of which have failed to show that habitual offender laws fail to reduce crime rates. Proponents of Alabama's law have countered that the correlation between high crime rates and habitual offender laws may be explained not by the failure of the latter to reduce the former, but rather from the presence of high crime rates motivating the enactment of the habitual offender law. In other words, without the law, the crime rate would be even worse. Others argue that when criminals know that the court will not be lenient, they become more desperate to avoid capture, which can turn robberies and assaults into homicides. Either claim is difficult to prove without coming to agreement about fair and useful ways to compare crime rates between different communities.

In 2003, the Supreme Court ruled in *Ewing v. California* that contrary to opponents' arguments, habitual offender laws do not violate the Eighth Amendment prohibition against cruel and unusual punishment.

As in other jurisdictions, the habitual offender law led to prison overcrowding. The courts were also busied by the number of convicts arguing in their appeals against the constitutionality of the habitual offender law. In 2000, the Alabama legislature passed a bill sponsored by Speaker Pro Tem Demetrius Newton to allow parole for four-time offenders whose fourth offense was a Class A felony, provided it was their first Class A, and in 2001 Newton introduced further legislation making that qualification retroactive for nonviolent offenders, which opened the door for many inmates to begin petitioning for parole. The provisions were slowly implemented, though, and in 2005, one-third of Alabama inmates had been convicted as habitual offenders.

Further bruising the claims of efficacy made by the law's advocates was the 2005 Brenda Kennedy case, in which a mother guilty of neglect successfully appealed her conviction under the habitual offender law because the Alabama criminal code did not set high enough penalties for child abuse and neglect for child abuse to be considered a serious enough crime to be relevant under the habitual offender act.

Violent crimes in Alabama climbed steadily in the 20th century. When the habitual offender law was passed in 1977, the state experienced 414.4 violent crimes per 100,000 inhabitants; this peaked in 1992 at a rate of 871.7 crimes per 100,000 inhabitants, more than doubling in 25 years. The crime rate then began to steadily fall, reaching 377.8 crimes per 100,000 inhabitants in 2010. Though posting one of the worst crime rates in the country in many years, the general trend followed that of most of the nation. Not all crimes fell or rose at equal rates; the murder rate actually began falling in 1977, and by 2010 was one-third of its 1977 level, while larceny peaked in the late 1990s and has fallen only about 10 percent since.

Recently, Alabama has made the news by enacting a historic abortion ban. Originally designed to ban all abortions, and then rewritten to ban all surgical and many chemical abortions, the bill as passed by the House of Representatives was the Pain-Capable Unborn Child Protection Act. Mirroring similar legislation in Idaho, Kansas, and Oklahoma, the bill banned abortions of any fetuses capable of feeling pain.

Bill Kte'pi
Independent Scholar

See Also: Abortion; African Americans; Birmingham, Alabama; Capital Punishment; Civil Rights Laws; Due Process; Electric Chair, History of; Ku Klux Klan; Lynchings; Moonshine; Sodomy.

Further Readings
Barnes, Margaret Anne. *The Tragedy and the Triumph of Phenix City, Alabama*. Macon, GA: Mercer University Press, 1999.

Rogers, William Warren, Leah Rawls Atkins, Robert D. Ward, and Wayne Flynt. *Alabama: The History of a Deep South State*. Birmingham: University of Alabama Press, 2010.

Stewart, Bruce. *Moonshiners and Prohibitionists*. Lexington: University Press of Kentucky, 2011.

Alaska

The largest state in the United States—its coastline is longer than the rest of the U.S. coastline combined, with more than twice as much land as Texas—Alaska was purchased from Russia in 1867 and remained a territory until 1959. It is the least densely populated state. Known for its remoteness, Alaska is far north and west of the rest of the country, with many of its settlements on islands accessed by ferry or plane; even the capital, Juneau, is not connected to the North American highway system.

Crime

Remote rural living is a defining feature of Alaskan life and of Alaskan crime. The state has the highest rate of sexual assault in the nation, thanks to a staggeringly high rate of acquaintance rape and nonconsensual incest: In about 80 percent of rape cases, the rapist is a relative or acquaintance. The average age of reported rape victims is 16. Domestic abuse and assault are both very high; though many rural communities in Alaska are dry, alcoholism is common and fuels violent crimes.

Alaska's alcohol laws have gone through many changes. Prior to the creation of the first civil government in Alaska in 1884, beer and wine were permitted by the Treasury Department (which had regulatory authority over the territory), but not spirits. The civil government banned alcohol entirely, except for medicinal, industrial, scientific, and sacramental purposes. But it did almost nothing to enforce this ban, and alcohol was widely available in the cities of Juneau and Sitka, where breweries openly operated saloons, and throughout much of the territory, pharmacies sold alcoholic beverages without a prescription. Liquor sales were legalized in 1899, but an expensive license and tax system (under which it is illegal to sell alcohol without a license and without paying a tax) led to the number of saloons decreasing by at least 80 percent. Liquor revenue helped to fund town governments at the turn of the century, as well as the state school system. Today, under the most recent (1979, amended in 1986) version of the state's alcohol laws, the permitting or banning of alcohol is left to local communities to decide, and there are both wet and dry communities throughout the state. Smuggling alcohol to dry towns, many of which are remote villages, is extremely profitable, often commanding a 1,500 percent markup.

The crime rate in Alaska has followed the general national trend of increasing gradually after World War II, peaking in the 1990s, and falling since then. Violent crimes peaked at 766.3 per 100,000 Alaskans in 1994, falling to 565.4 in 2002. Since 2002, crime rates have risen overall, though crime has been on the decline (638.8 in 2010) since the onset of the recession in 2008. Burglary has seen the greatest decline since the 1990s peak; rape rates remain high.

Police

Law enforcement in Alaska is principally handled by the state's Department of Public Safety, which consists of the divisions of Administrative Services, Alaska State Troopers, Fire and Life Safety, Statewide Services, and Alaska Wildlife Troopers, and which administers the state's Police Standards Council, Fire Standards Council, Alcohol Beverage Control Board, Council on Domestic Violence and Sexual Assault, and Scientific Crime Detection Laboratory. Many rural towns and villages lack local police departments and have to rely on public safety officers, who aren't issued firearms. Before the official organization of the Alaska State Troopers (AST) in 1941, most law enforcement in the state was handled by federal authorities; the AST subsequently assumed that role.

One reason for this unique arrangement is that Alaska's extremely low population density means that the state has no counties—and thus no county sheriff's departments. There is a borough system, but it lacks a real police force except in the North Slope Borough. Outside of that borough, jurisdictions in Alaska are state and local—and local jurisdictions more often than not lack the resources for effective law enforcement.

In Alaska's territorial days, the discovery of gold made the federal government's involvement in law enforcement necessary because gold rush towns had tremendous crime rates. The U.S. Marshals Service deployed a number of its deputy marshals to the territory in 1884 and maintained a presence until the middle of the 20th century. The AST began as the Alaska Highway Patrol (AHP), created by the territorial legislature. Originally commissioned to enforce traffic laws on the state's highways, officers were soon deputized as special U.S. marshals in order to alleviate the burden of law enforcement from the federal government. The legislature resisted making the change in the AHP's duties official until 1953, when additional personnel were hired directly from the ranks of the marshals and the new agency was renamed the Alaska Territorial Police, which became the Alaska State Police in 1959. The current name was adopted in 1967.

Five detachments of the AST—A, B, C, D, and E—are responsible for specific geographic areas of Alaska. Additionally, the AST includes the Highway Patrol Bureau; the Alaska Bureau of Investigation, which provides detectives and investigative support to areas without local police; the State Fire Marshal office; the Bureau of Judicial Services; and the Alaska Bureau of Alcohol and Drug Enforcement (ABADE). ABADE's duties are more wide-reaching than its name indicates, as it investigates an assortment of drug and vice offenses, including gambling, prostitution, human trafficking, and the sexual exploitation of children. ABADE typically coordinates with local and federal agencies and assigns task forces and undercover agents to cases throughout the state.

Initiated in the 1970s, the Village Public Safety Officer (PSO) program provides the public safety officers in towns and villages without their own police departments and without a local AST post. Public safety officers are trained by the state through an eight-week training course at the Department of Public Safety Academy but are not fully credentialed and do not carry firearms. AST troopers in the area supervise public safety officers in their region. PSOs are primarily first responders to emergencies and work to preserve crime scenes and issue citations for misdemeanors and violations. They are empowered to make misdemeanor arrests, but in the case of felonies, they merely detain suspects before turning them over to the AST.

During World War II, the Highway Patrol assisted federal authorities by patrolling Alaskan transportation infrastructure and watching for Japanese invaders (two of the outer Aleutian islands were invaded and occupied and became the only part of the United States to be occupied during the war). In the aftermath of September 11, these special duties have been revived, with the AST coordinating with the Department of Homeland Security to safeguard against terrorist activity. A 2009 joint project between the Alaska Bureau of Investigation (ABI) and Federal Bureau of Investigation (FBI) led to the arrest of two Islamic converts planning a terrorist attack.

Punishment

From 2009 to 2011, Alaska's prison population rose by 10 percent and was projected to increase by another 4 percent by 2012. Anticipating an overcrowding crisis, in February 2011, Governor Sean Parnell requested supplemental funding. The funding request for the prison system accounted for nearly a 20 percent of the supplemental funding request from the general fund for the year, causing some to call for prison reforms in order to reduce the incarceration rates and periods for inmates convicted of minor offenses, and to find other ways to deal with the mentally ill and with drug addicts who weren't convicted of violent crimes.

Bill Kte'pi
Independent Scholar

See Also: 1981 to 2000 Primary Documents; Bootlegging; Border Patrol; Frontier Crime; Rape, Contemporary.

Further Readings

Dellinger, A. B. "Processing Serious Crimes in Alaska: Do Differences Exist?" *Alaska Justice Forum*, v.10/1 (Spring 1993). http://justice.uaa.alaska.edu/forum/10/1spring1993/a_process.html (Accessed September 2011).

Justice Center, University of Alaska Anchorage. "Violent Deaths in Alaska and Nationwide." *Alaska Justice Forum*, v.25/4 (Winter 2009). http://justice.uaa.alaska.edu/forum/25/4winter2009/b_nvdrs.html (Accessed September 2009).

Rosay, Andre B., Greg Postle, Darryl S. Wood, and Katherine TePas. "Sexual Assaults Reported to Alaska State Troopers." *Alaska Justice Forum*, v.25/1–2 (Spring/Summer 2008). http://justice.uaa.alaska.edu/forum/25/1-2springsummer2008/d_ast.html (Accessed September 2011).

Alcatraz Island Prison

The U.S. penitentiary on Alcatraz Island is perhaps the most famous of all American prisons. Located on the 12-acre island in San Francisco Bay, California, it stands as a reminder of the public's desire to shield itself from dangerous offenders. Originally a military fort that protected the San Francisco seaport, it eventually evolved into a disciplinary barracks for military prisoners. In 1907, Alcatraz ceased operations as a fort and was designated a U.S. military prison. It operated as a military prison until 1933. The soaring costs associated with its upkeep eventually convinced military officials to close the facility and withdraw from the island.

Shortly after the military abandoned the island, the Department of Justice acquired it and turned it into a federal prison. Alcatraz operated under the auspices of the Federal Bureau of Prisons from August 1934 until 1963 and was one of only 11 federal prisons in existence during the early 20th century. The bureau intended for Alcatraz to serve as a high-profile prison that would deter rising crime rates. Prohibition, the Great Depression, and the advent of organized crime led citizens and politicians alike to demand a prison that could securely house dangerous and notorious crime figures.

Upon arriving at Alcatraz, inmates were housed in single-occupancy cells. It was initially operated as a silent institution, but this approach proved unpopular and was eventually abandoned. All movement within the facility was strictly controlled to ensure that horseplay, violent confrontation, and escape attempts were minimized. In addition to its housing units, Alcatraz also had a hospital, sanitation department, auditorium, kitchen, and library for recreational reading and legal research. The development and progressive use of inmate

A former Alcatraz prison guard stands by an empty cellblock. The last inmates were transferred in 1963, and 10 years later the island became a museum and wildlife sanctuary.

grievance procedures helped ensure that its prisoner population had an avenue available to resolve complaints without resorting to violence. Institutional and industrial work assignments were available to those inmates who wanted to earn a wage. Many of these industrial assignments were initially geared toward the war effort. At its highest capacity, Alcatraz housed more than 300 inmates, with its average population being closer to 200.

Over the course of its history, Alcatraz served as the prison of choice for those inmates who were particularly dangerous, disruptive, or skilled at escape. Most inmates were sent to Alcatraz directly from lower-security facilities. Alcatraz housed such infamous criminals as gangster Al "Scarface" Capone and George "Machine Gun Kelly" Barnes. Known as "The Rock" or "Devil's Island," Alcatraz became the prototype for maximum-security prisons in the decades following its closing.

Escape Attempts

Because Alcatraz was remote and physically isolated, it was billed as an inescapable institution. Therefore, all escape attempts were viewed with great public interest. Over the course of its history, there were 15 documented escape attempts involving a total of 30 inmates. Every inmate who attempted an escape is thought to have drowned in the frigid and turbulent waters of the San Francisco Bay, was shot by guards, or was recaptured. In one of these escape attempts that occurred in May 1946, a small number of inmates took six guards hostage and were able to gain control of their cellblock. When their escape attempt failed, they refused to surrender and unsuccessfully sought to enlist the support of other inmates in the ensuing insurrection. After nearly two days, officials entered the cellblock and confronted the six inmates—three of whom were immediately killed. Two guards also lost their lives. The remaining three inmates were captured, and two of them were later executed for their participation.

Perhaps the most celebrated escape attempt involved just three inmates, two of whom were brothers. Frank Morris and John and Frank Anglin were able to gain access to the rooftop of their cellblock in June 1962. Once outside, they attempted to float their way to the mainland onboard makeshift rafts. The papier-mâché heads used to dupe guards into believing that they were asleep in their bunks can be viewed today during the daily tours given at the prison. Evidence suggests that all three men drowned.

Conclusion

Alcatraz was plagued with ongoing deterioration caused by the harsh sea environment, and with the high costs associated with its upkeep, officials increasingly began to seek an alternative to the continued use of Alcatraz Island. A new prison was sought to serve as the nation's highest-security institution. Envisioned as the new Alcatraz, United States Penitentiary Marion, in Illinois, was specifically designed and built to house the most dangerous offenders in America. While Marion was still under construction, Alcatraz began to transfer inmates to facilities throughout the United States—eventually transferring the last of its inmates in March 1963. In 1973, the National Park Service acquired Alcatraz Island and turned it into a museum and wildlife sanctuary. Tourists to Alcatraz occasionally encounter former inmates and guards eager to speak about their unique experiences with this prison.

Curtis R. Blakely
Truman State University

See Also: Capone, Al; Federal Prisons; Film, Crime in; Film, Punishment in; Native Americans; Penitentiaries; Prison Riots; San Francisco, California.

Further Readings

Beacher, Milton. *Alcatraz Island: Memoirs of a Rock Doc.* Lebanon, NJ: Pelican Island Publishing, 2008.
Esslinger, Michael. *Alcatraz—A Definitive History of the Penitentiary Years.* Carmel, CA: Ocean View Publishing, 2003.
Presnall, Judith. *Life on Alcatraz.* San Diego, CA: Lucent Books, 2000.
Ward, David and Gene Kassebaum. *Alcatraz: The Gangster Years.* Berkeley: University of California Press, 2010.

Alien and Sedition Acts of 1798

The last half of the 18th century was a time of social upheaval in North America after the successful American Revolution, which lasted from 1775 to 1783, and the ratification of the Constitution in 1787. After a long and occasionally bitter debate, the Bill of Rights was adopted in 1791. The adoption of the Bill of Rights was problematic. There was a dispute between the Federalists, who did not want a Bill of Rights, and the Anti-Federalists, led by Thomas Jefferson, who wanted a Bill of Rights. The Constitution was adopted only after the Federalists agreed to enact the Bill of Rights. The founding of the United States of America was based on preserving individual rights and liberty that had been denied under the English Crown. However, it did not take long before these rights were forgotten.

After George Washington, John Adams was elected to the presidency. Adams was a Federalist and believed in a strong central government. The Democratic-Republican Party, led by Thomas Jefferson, opposed the Federalist Party. The Democratic-Republicans were considered the progeny of the Anti-Federalists, who were not organized into a political party. A number of people, including the Democratic-Republicans, were critical of the Adams presidency and applauded the French Revolution that began in 1789, which caused the Federalists much concern because it threatened to impose "mob rule" and depose men of property from political domination. A number of French immigrants had recently come to America. Adams was worried that these immigrants and the French Revolution might threaten the existing political and economic order.

In response to the French Revolution and the criticism of the Democratic-Republicans, Adams and the Federalist-controlled Congress enacted the Alien and Sedition Acts of 1798. There were four parts to the acts. The Naturalization Act increased the residency requirement to become a citizen and to vote from five to 14 years. The Alien Act gave the president the power to deport any alien that the president deemed to be dangerous to the security of the United States. The Alien Enemies Act gave the president the authority to restrict the freedom of enemy aliens or have them deported. The Sedition Act made it illegal for American citizens to oppose the laws of the federal government and made it illegal to publish criticism of the American government. The Sedition Act expired on the day before Adams's term as president ended, which only highlighted the political basis for the act.

The result was pandemonium. Thomas Jefferson, who was vice president at the time, denounced them as unconstitutional and claimed that they violated the First Amendment. Several states passed resolutions against them. The Democratic-Republicans accused the Federalists of creating a tyranny just like that of the English Crown, which the colonists had defeated. Petitions were presented to Adams to repeal the Alien and Sedition Acts, which Adams ignored. The Federalists were quick to enforce the new laws. A number of Democratic-Republican newspaper publishers were arrested, and 10 people were convicted of sedition before Federalist judges. One of the convictions highlights how ridiculous the enforcement of the law was. When a bystander stated that they were firing at Adams's ass when he was saluted by the firing of a cannon, another bystander was convicted for saying that he did not care if they fired through his ass. No appeals of the convictions were made to the U.S. Supreme Court, as the judges were Federalists. No Federalists were indicted for similar attacks against the Democratic-Republicans.

In the next election, the Democratic-Republicans lambasted the Federalists for the Alien and Sedition Acts. The election was an unparalleled success for the Democratic-Republicans, who defeated the Federalists in almost all of the elections. Upon assuming the presidency, Jefferson pardoned all of those persons who had been convicted under the Sedition Act. In 1832, the House Judiciary Committee authorized a refund of all fines under the Sedition Act. As Justice William O. Douglas stated in his concurring opinion in the decision of *Watts v. United States* (1969): "The Alien and Sedition Laws constituted one of our sorriest chapters; and I had thought we had done with them forever."

Wm. C. Plouffe, Jr.
Independent Scholar

See Also: Adams, John (Administration of); Anti-Federalist Papers; Bill of Rights; Civil Disobedience; Civil Rights Laws; Deportation; Federalist Papers; Immigration Crimes; Jefferson, Thomas (Administration of); Political Crimes, History of.

Further Readings
Martin, James P. "When Repression Is Democratic and Constitutional: The Federalist Theory of Representation and the Sedition Act of 1798." *University of Chicago Law Review*, v.66/117 (1999).
Miller, John C. *Crisis in Freedom: The Alien and Sedition Acts*. Boston: Little, Brown, 1951.
Smith, James Morton. *Freedom's Fetters: The Alien and Sedition Laws and American Civil Liberties*. Ithaca, NY: Cornell University, 1966.
Stone, Geoffrey. *Perilous Times: Free Speech in Wartime From the Sedition Act of 1798 to the War on Terrorism*. New York: Norton, 2005.

American Bar Association

The American Bar Association (ABA) was established in 1878. It is a voluntary professional association for legal professionals and law students unspecific to any jurisdiction, unlike state or local bar associations. It is the largest voluntary professional association in the world. With more than 400,000 members, the ABA provides law school accreditation, continuing legal education, information about the law, programs to assist lawyers and judges in their work, initiatives to improve the legal system for the public, and educational resources for teaching the public about the legal system and the role of law in society. The ABA is headquartered in Chicago, Illinois, maintains a second office in Washington, D.C., and manages rule-of-law initiatives around the world.

Mission and Activities

The mission of the ABA is "to serve equally our members, our profession, and the public by defending liberty and delivering justice as the national representative of the legal profession." To fulfill its mission, the association works toward four goals: serving members, serving the profession, eliminating bias and enhancing diversity, and advancing the rule of law. The ABA is governed, for the most part, by members who have actively served the public and the profession for many years. These members comprise the ABA House of Delegates and Board of Governors, the policy-making bodies of the association. Elected ABA officers include the president, whose term lasts for one year, the president-elect, the chair, the secretary, and the treasurer of the House of Delegates. The association's executive director is the chief operating officer of the organization. The association is comprised of more than 2,200 individual entities, which address specific legal areas and issues, provide continuing education opportunities for lawyers, publish materials, and educate the public about the law. The ABA maintains a code of ethical standards for lawyers, which has been adopted in 49 states and in the District of Columbia. The association also accredits law schools. In most U.S. jurisdictions, graduation from an ABA-accredited law school is expressly required to sit for that state's bar exam or for existing lawyers to be admitted to the bar of another state. Finally, the association acts as a voice for the legal profession by issuing policy resolutions regarding important issues relevant to the legal community or general rule of law. Resolutions have addressed such issues as civil rights, civic education in schools and communities, capital punishment, affirmative action, gun control, nuclear nonproliferation, and same-sex marriages.

The ABA has faced accusations of elitism, as critics claim membership favors white male corporate lawyers. Critics also suggest that the ABA's law school accreditation requirements are outdated and expensive. Others believe that ABA positions on public policy issues favor liberal attitudes and are beyond the organization's mission. Most recently, the ABA has faced criticism for failing to stop law schools from publishing misleading data regarding employment and salary prospects and the actual cost of law school.

Criminal Justice

The Criminal Justice Section of the ABA was founded in 1920 and is responsible for the association's work on issues related to criminal law, as well as criminal and juvenile justice. The section has been party to numerous resolutions related to many aspects of the criminal trial process and criminal justice system. In 1997 the section was party to an ABA resolution that called upon jurisdictions to impose a moratorium on capital punishment until they could ensure that all death penalty cases were administered fairly and impartially, thus minimizing the risk that an innocent person may be executed. More recently, the section has addressed issues such as microstamping technology in semiautomatic weapons, simplified Miranda rights for juveniles, communications between incarcerated parents and their children, and arrests of homeless persons for otherwise non-criminal acts. Since 1968, the section has issued Criminal Justice Standards, which guide policy makers and criminal justice practitioners. Then Chief Justice Warren Burger described the project as the "single most comprehensive and probably the most monumental undertaking in the field of criminal justice ever attempted by the American legal profession in our national history."

Tiffany Middleton
Independent Scholar

See Also: Capital Punishment; Chicago, Illinois; Lawyers Guild; Reform Movements in Justice; Washington, D.C.

Further Readings

Carson, Gerald. *A Good Day at Saratoga.* Chicago: American Bar Association, 1978.

Matzko, John A. "'The Best Men of the Bar': The Founding of the American Bar Association." In *The New High Priests: Lawyers in Post–Civil War America,* Gerard Gawalt, ed. Westport, CT: Greenwood Press, 1998.

American Civil Liberties Union

The history of the American Civil Liberties Union (ACLU) is the story of free speech and the protection of civil liberties in American life. Over the past 90 years, the ACLU has played a major role in the evolution and growth of modern constitutional law. The ACLU has been involved in more than 80 percent of court cases listed as proverbial "landmark" cases in any constitutional law textbook, and in several critical cases, the Supreme Court's opinion was drawn directly from the ACLU brief. The ACLU was founded in 1920 by Crystal Eastman, Roger Baldwin, and Walter Nelles and was the successor organization to the National Civil Liberties Bureau founded during World War I to defend free speech. The ACLU is essentially a private voluntary organization dedicated to defending the Bill of Rights.

For over 90 years, the ACLU has worked to defend rights such as freedom of speech, freedom of religion, and the right to privacy. According to the ACLU Website, its mission is to preserve and protect American constitutional rights and freedoms as set forth in the U.S. Constitution and its amendments. The ACLU works in three basic areas: freedom of expressions, conscience, and association; due process of law; and equality under the law. The ACLU also works to enhance and extend these rights to those U.S. citizens who have historically been denied their rights. Such groups include people of color, lesbians, homosexuals, bisexuals, transgendered people, women, mental health patients, prisoners, people with disabilities, and the poor.

The ACLU reported more than 500,000 members in 2010, and in addition to a national office in New York and large legislative office in Washington D.C., it maintains 54 locally based affiliate offices from which the majority of the ACLU's cases originate and are handled. The ACLU has staffed offices in all 50 states, Puerto Rico, and Washington, D.C. These affiliates or state organizations are the fundamental units of the ACLU framework and are constantly involved in litigation, lobbying, and public education. The ACLU often refers to itself as "the nation's largest law firm." The ACLU is involved in an estimated 6,000 court cases a year and appears before the Supreme Court more than any other organization aside from the federal government.

The fundamental, and most controversial, facet of the ACLU is its professed commitment to the nonpartisan defense of the Bill of Rights. The ACLU holds an absolutist approach to liberties and rights, and it defends all people whose rights have been violated, even if their behaviors and/or beliefs are wholly unpopular. This means defending the civil liberties of everyone, including the free speech rights of Communists, Nazis, NAMBLA (North American Man/Boy Love Association), and Ku Klux Klan members. It means defending the due process rights of even the most contemptible criminals. Defense of the detested has always been the ACLU's standard and the basis of the most virulent attacks on it. According to the ACLU, it is not a political organization, as its doctrines and ideology do not adhere to the manifesto of any political party. However, because of the ACLU's defense of the powerless and those on the fringes of mainstream society, most ACLU members have historically been liberals or people with leftist sympathies.

Key issues identified by the ACLU are firmly within the realm of crime and punishment. Such issues include a repeal of the death penalty through advocacy and education; drug law reform, especially in the realm of the decriminalization of all drugs; the protection of the rights of prisoners by fighting unconstitutional conditions of confinement; protection of the rights of immigrants and people of color; and

The ACLU of Southern California distributed these information sheets about torture as part of an event called Torture Awareness Day on June 25, 2010. The boxes represent the space needed to store some of the 150,000 pages of declassified documents on the U.S. government's use of torture during interrogations that the ACLU acquired through a Freedom of Information Act request.

ensuring that the United States complies with universal human rights principles. However, even with a strong emphasis in the field of crime and punishment, given the law and order mood that dominates U.S. politics and the Supreme Court, this area is where the ACLU has suffered its most consistent defeats. Historically, the Supreme Court has been unsympathetic to the rights of offenders, the war on drugs has eroded Fourth Amendment rights and sent incarceration rates soaring, and the public consistently supports the death penalty in the United States. The ACLU has faced consistent defeat in its call for the full and complete decriminalization of the use, possession, manufacture, and distribution of all drugs.

Landmark Cases

A brief list of landmark cases named by the ACLU in the realm of crime and punishment can be found below. A landmark case, according to the ACLU, is one that establishes a precedent that either substantially changes the interpretation of the law or that simply establishes new case law on a particular issue.

1. *Mapp v. Ohio* (1961): The Supreme Court ruled in this case that the Fourth Amendment's exclusionary rule, first applied to federal law enforcement officers in 1914, applied to state and local police as well.
2. *Gideon v. Wainwright* (1963): An indigent drifter from Florida made history when, in a handwritten petition, he persuaded the court that poor people had the right to a state-appointed lawyer in criminal cases.
3. *Escobedo v. Illinois* (1964): Invoking the Sixth Amendment right to counsel, the court threw out the confession of a man whose repeated requests to see his lawyer were ignored throughout many hours of police interrogation.

4. *Miranda v. Arizona* (1966): This famous decision established the Miranda warnings, a requirement that the police, before interrogating suspects, must inform them of their rights. The court embraced the ACLU's amicus argument that a suspect in custody has both a Sixth Amendment right to counsel and a Fifth Amendment right against self-incrimination.
5. *Indianapolis v. Edmond* (2001): Indianapolis's checkpoint programs violated the Fourth Amendment because their primary purpose was indistinguishable from general interest in crime control and did not fit into the established exceptions to individualized suspicion.
6. *Virginia v. Hicks* (2003): The Richmond Redevelopment and Housing Authority policy authorizing the police to serve notice or arrest any person lacking "a legitimate business or social purpose" in the low-income housing development was not overbroad and did not violate the First Amendment because it targeted all trespassers equally.

Patrick O'Brien
University of Colorado Boulder

See Also: Bill of Rights; Civil Rights Laws; Constitution of the United States of America; Defendant's Rights; Prisoner's Rights; Supreme Court, U.S.; Suspect's Rights.

Further Readings
Cottrell, Robert C. *Roger Nash Baldwin and the American Civil Liberties Union.* New York: Columbia University Press, 2000.
Donahue, William A. *Twilight of Liberty: A Legacy of the ACLU.* New Brunswick, NJ: Transaction Publishers, 1994.
Walker, Samuel. *In Defense of American Liberties: A History of the ACLU.* Carbondale: Southern Illinois University Press, 1999.

American Law Institute

The American Law Institute is the leading independent U.S. organization that is dedicated to clarifying and improving the law. The American Law Institute is influential not only with U.S. courts and legislatures but also internationally, as well as being a leader in the areas of legal scholarship and education. The American Law Institute is a 501(c)(3) nonprofit organization that is incorporated in Washington, D.C.

The American Law Institute was created in 1923 after a review by the Committee on the Establishment of a Permanent Organization determined that there was a general dissatisfaction with the administration of justice in America largely caused by the uncertainty and complexity of U.S. law. There was reportedly a lack of precision in the use of legal terms and a voluminous amount of recorded legal decisions, most of which did not benefit from systematic development. The founding members of the institute included Chief Justice of the Supreme Court and former President William Howard Taft, future Chief Justice Charles Evans Hughes, and former Secretary of State Elihu Root. These three individuals were the first to sign the certificate of incorporation of the American Law Institute on February 23, 1923. Since its inception, the institute has served as an instrument for the dissemination of new innovative perspectives in American jurisprudence.

Structure and Function
Membership in the American Law Institute is restricted to 3,000 elected members; after 25 years, elected members are eligible to become life members. New members must be nominated by a current member, who submits a letter of recommendation, and seconded by two other members. A membership committee reviews the prospective members and makes the final selection. Members are lawyers, judges, and legal educators with demonstrated professional achievement and interest in improving the law. Ex officio members include chief justices and associate justices of the U.S. Supreme Court, chief judges of each U.S. Court of Appeals, U.S. attorneys general, U.S. solicitors general, chief justices/judges of each state, deans of law schools, and presidents of the American Bar Association, among members of other prominent legal organizations.

The American Law Institute, in collaboration with the National Conference of Commissioners

William Howard Taft (left) and Elihu Root in 1904. On February 23, 1923, they helped found the American Law Institute along with Charles Evans Hughes.

on Uniform State Laws (now known as the Uniform Laws Commission), developed and monitors the Uniform Commercial Code (UCC). The UCC is a comprehensive code that covers most areas of U.S. commercial law applicable to every phase of any business transaction, including sales, bills of lading, commercial paper, vendor security, and so forth. Other model statutory projects have included the Federal Judicial Code Revision, the Federal Securities Code, the Model Code of Evidence, the Model Code of Pre-Arraignment Procedure, the Model Land Development Code, and the Model Penal Code. Another joint venture of the American Law Institute was with the International Institute for the Unification of Private Law, which collectively promulgated the Principles of Transnational Civil Procedure in 2004. The institute has helped transform jurisprudence through these types of initiatives.

The organization has a reputation for impartial and thoughtful analysis of legal issues. For instance, an early project of the institute was the drafting of its Statement of Essential Human Rights; this was used by the United Nations in the preparation of its Universal Declaration of Human Rights, which was adopted by the UN General Assembly on December 10, 1948. Publications of the institute are produced through a careful and deliberative process; active members of the institute are expected to submit comments on drafts of publications. These vehicles have helped the institute forge a modernist jurisprudence perspective.

The American Law Institute publishes an array of resources catalogued under topics such as restatements of the law, principles of law, and codifications and studies, as well as various special publications. In 1987, the third series of Restatements was begun with a new Restatement of the Foreign Relations Law of the United States; other Restatements Third include those on Agency, Apportionment of Liability, Property, Restitution and Unjust Enrichment, Torts, and Unfair Competition. Restatements of law describe law as it is; principles of law are directed to courts, legislatures, and governmental agencies and endeavor to express what the law should be. The organization also publishes several legal periodicals, including the *CLE Journal*, the *Practical Lawyer*, and the *Practical Litigator*.

The American Law Institute, in collaboration since 1947 with the American Bar Association, also offers an array of continuing professional education opportunities, including traditional classes on an array of legal topics, as well as course materials such as audio and videotapes, satellite broadcasts, and offerings in other media. The American Law Institute–American Bar Association Committee on Continuing Professional Education telecasts training seminars nationally via satellite on its American Law Network. The two organizations also jointly sponsor the American Institute for Law Training within the Office (AILTO).

Victor B. Stolberg
Essex County College

See Also: American Bar Association; Codification of Laws; Lawyers Guild; Reform Movements in Justice.

Further Readings
Hull, N. E. H. "Restatement and Reform: A New Perspective on the Origins of the American Law Institute." *Law and History Review,* v.8 (1990).
Macey, Jonathan R. "The Transformation of the American Law Institute." *George Washington Law Review,* v.61 (1983).
White, G. Edward. "The American Law Institute and the Triumph of Modernist Jurisprudence." *Law and History Review,* v.15 (1997).

American Revolution and Criminal Justice

The American Revolution greatly shaped the criminal justice system in what would become the United States. The criminal justice systems in place before this time had been imported from Europe. Each of the thirteen colonies, an independent entity with a separate charter from the monarch, had its own criminal justice system, traditions, and set of laws and precedents. While influences of the criminal justice systems of France, the Netherlands, and Spain could be found in the North American colonies, certainly the English common law system was the dominant model. Experiences that occurred during the American Revolution, as well as increasingly more cosmopolitan and interrelated interactions, created a need for revisions to traditional notions of criminal justice.

Virginia was the earliest of the colonies to adopt the English criminal justice system and practices, doing so in the early 17th century. Virginia established a system of county courts mirroring the English system, with Admiralty, General, and Chancery courts being established. Traditional English practices and procedures such as arrest, indictment, bail, trial, juries, judgment, and execution were adopted, although with some changes. Beginning in 1623, the House of Burgesses also established a five-member appellate court to hear appeals from lower courts, which was also known as the Quarter Court as it met four times per year. These practices and procedures spread to the other 12 colonies, so that by the eve of the American Revolution, all colonies had a judicial system. Certain English constitutional guarantees, such as the Charter of Liberties and the Magna Carta, were known and embraced by the colonists, as was the common law system of legal precedent. Certainly, the American system tended to be more democratic than that of England, with a wider spectrum of the population serving on juries, for example. Other differences existed as well. In the Massachusetts Bay Colony, for example, Puritan magistrates heard pleas, and if they were satisfied that charges were grounded, suspects were handed over to a superior court, which then called a grand jury.

Many colonies also moved toward a more liberal and humane imposition of punishments, as the number of capital crimes was reduced and defendants were provided with greater legal rights. In New Holland, for example, the Dutch West India Company had given certain stockholders, called "patroons," large tracts of land, as well as manorial rights and privileges that permitted them to set up civil and criminal courts and to appoint judges. Although New Holland, which existed from 1614 until 1674, permitted slavery, slaves were allowed to sign legal documents, could bring legal actions against whites, and were allowed to testify in court. Despite these changes, the criminal justice system was rudimentary and was tied strongly to the past. Trained peace officers did not exist, and if local authorities were faced with a serious emergency, they were forced to call in the militia to deal with it. No penitentiary system existed; prisoners were housed indiscriminately in local jails or other emergency settings. Indeed, it was not until the 1790s, when the Pennsylvania legislature ordered construction of a cell house in the yard of Philadelphia's Walnut Street Jail, that serious thought went into what was needed for a penitentiary system.

With War Comes Change
Certain actions that exacerbated the American Revolution also played a role in changing attitudes toward the criminal justice system. The Royal Proclamation of 1763, for example, sought to regulate trade, settlement, and land purchases on the then western frontier. This was unpopular with certain colonists who wished to settle in the areas covered by the Royal Proclamation and caused an increase in behaviors that disregarded the law. The Stamp Act of 1765, which imposed a

direct tax on many materials printed in the colonies, was hugely unpopular and caused a surge of opposition, law breaking, and civil disobedience. The Stamp Act provided jurisdiction for trying violators to the courts of admiralty, which further enraged colonists as these courts lacked a jury and were seen as a violation of natural and constitutional rights. Although the Stamp Act was repealed in 1766, it set the stage for later upheaval as well as an assertion of certain fundamental rights when dealing with taxation and the criminal justice system. Finally, the "Intolerable Acts" (e.g., the Tea Act of 1773, the Boston Port Act of 1774, the Massachusetts Government Act of 1774, the Administration of Justice Act of 1774, the Quartering Act of 1774, and the Quebec Act of 1774) were a series of laws that triggered outrage and resistance in the thirteen colonies. Collectively, the Intolerable Acts imposed penalties for resistance to the Tea Act, including closing the Port of Boston, bringing the Massachusetts government under the control of the Crown, allowed government officials to be tried in Great Britain rather than in the colonies and allowed British troops to be housed in private homes. This series of acts stoked sympathy for the radicals in Massachusetts and increased interest across the colonies in their constitutional and natural rights and their colonial charters. These acts were seen as a threat to the liberties of all and helped to spur the formation of the First Continental Congress.

John Adams, although a well-known patriot, greatly promoted the rights of defendants when he agreed to represent eight British soldiers charged with murder for deaths that arose out of what became known as the Boston Massacre. While devoted to the patriot cause, Adams believed that all criminal defendants deserved a fair trial, even though he knew his choice of clients might harm his future political aspirations. Adams mounted a vigorous defense, arguing that because the soldiers feared for their lives and had been threatened by the crowd, they had acted in self-defense. The jury that heard the case acquitted six of the defendants and gave the remaining two reduced sentences that resulted in their thumbs being branded. Adams's actions helped to solidify support for the rule of law, in Massachusetts and elsewhere.

The American Revolutionary War began in 1775. At that time, pursuant to the Proclamation

Bostonians forcing tea on a tarred-and-feathered British loyalist in a 1774 print. Loyalists, who were often subject to threats and persecution, made up about 15 to 20 percent of the population.

for Suppressing Rebellion and Sedition of 1775, George III of Great Britain had declared all members of the American armed forces to be traitors rather than prisoners of war (POWs). Pursuant to normal practices of the time, this would have meant that all captured American troops would have been tried and, if found guilty, executed. British officials declined to pursue these charges, however, in an attempt to preserve whatever public sympathy the British enjoyed in the colonies. While the patriots were critical of British practices regarding POWs, their treatment of Tories loyal to the Crown was also suspect. Tories, who are estimated to have represented 15 percent to 20 percent of the population, were subject to confiscation of their property by patriots and often threatened with physical harm, including being covered with tar and feathers.

Conclusion

American experiences throughout the Revolutionary War and the period immediately preceding it resulted in tremendous interest in the rights of those charged with criminal offenses. Such interests were memorialized in the Articles of Confederation, the U.S. Constitution, and the Bill of Rights. After American independence, and even before, citizens became much more ready to disregard English legal precedents and rules in an effort to improve the implementation of the criminal justice system. Improvements in the efficiency and equity of the judicial system, the perceived need for peace officers, and the growth of penitentiaries were all responses to these experiences.

Stephen T. Schroth
Jason A. Helfer
Cale T. Dahm
Knox College

See Also: Articles of Confederation; Bill of Rights; Colonial Courts; Common Law Origins of Criminal Law; Constitution of the United States of America; Declaration of Independence; Intolerable Acts of 1774; Proclamation for Suppressing Rebellion and Sedition of 1775; Stamp Act of 1765; Tea Act of 1773.

Further Readings
Benton, L. *A Search for Sovereignty: Law and Geography in European Empires, 1400–1900.* New York: Cambridge University Press, 2009.
Jensen, Merrill. *The Articles of Confederation: An Interpretation of the Social-Constitutional History of the American Revolution, 1774–1781.* Madison: University of Wisconsin Press, 1989.
Wilf, S. *Law's Imagined Republic: Popular Politics and Criminal Justice in Revolutionary America.* New York: Cambridge University Press, 2010.

An American Tragedy

Theodore Dreiser, often considered the foremost naturalist writer of his day, gave his readers descriptive tales of human survival and the abuses of forces beyond their control. One of his most famous works, *Sister Carrie* (1901), gives the grim tale of a young girl working in a Chicago shoe factory. She works for wages that do not cover the bills, she has a loveless marriage, and her body aches from the work, pain, and sorrow of her life. Her story, like Upton Sinclair's *The Jungle*, captured the laborer's life. Yet, Dreiser wrote about more than the sorrows of the working class in the factory. *An American Tragedy* (1925) also showcases the life of the poor, but this time Dreiser honed in on the rise of crime.

The plot of *An American Tragedy* rests on Clyde, a poor boy raised by religious parents in Kansas City. He dreams of better things, shiny cars and new clothes. Quickly, he takes a job as a bellboy where his coworkers appear more sophisticated than him. Their speech and dress are more refined, and when they introduce Clyde to prostitution and alcohol he has little power to resist. He sees these lures as part of higher society, mainly because he has the funds to obtain them. All the while, Clyde is desperately seeking the eye of Hortense Briggs. These attempts run short when Clyde accidentally kills a child while driving a stolen car. He flees, briefly stopping in Chicago and ending up in upstate New York with a distant uncle.

Secretly, Clyde views his uncle as the type of family he never had. He is wealthy, sophisticated, and established in society. Unfortunately, his uncle only provides him a job in his factory. He quickly promotes Clyde to a position of power. Still wounded and confused about the turn of events in Kansas City, and attempting to look strong and proud for his uncle's approval, Clyde begins his New York life eschewing women. Very quickly, this mindset changes when he catches the eye of Roberta Alden. Roberta, fitting the stereotype of the female factory worker, is a poor farm girl working for him at the plant. Clyde, evolving from the young and naïve poor boy in Kansas City love-struck by an unapproachable female, turns the tables with Roberta. She is desperately in love with him, and he convinces her to sleep with him. He thrives on the thrill of the forbidden relationship—as he is her boss—and he has no intention of marrying her. He clearly views himself above Roberta, even though they come from similar backgrounds.

While sleeping with Roberta, Clyde begins to court Sondra Finchley, the beautiful daughter of a wealthy businessman. Her father is also friends with his uncle, and as the months go by Clyde's uncle begins to introduce him to his society friends. Roberta finds herself pregnant and Clyde fails to procure an abortion for her. Instead, he is still making plans with Sondra. All the while, Clyde is making plans to kill Roberta in a way that looks accidental. He takes her for a canoe ride on Big Bittern Lake, and during a conversation about ending their relationship she moves toward him. He, seeming startled, strikes her in the face with his camera. The boat flips, and he swims ashore unwilling to save her. Even though no clear evidence shows that Clyde intended to kill the girl or that it was an accident, a sensational trial unfolds. His uncle's money cannot buy him an acquittal, and manufactured evidence helps convict him to death.

The story line of *An American Tragedy* showcases the working poor in America, and Clyde's hostile jury epitomizes middle and upper class loathing for the lower classes. More so, Clyde's ascension to a position of power in the plant and his dating a wealthy girl assaults domestic ideals of place and stature in society. Dreiser's tale also was based in reality. In July 1906, Grace Brown was found dead in Big Moose Lake in upstate New York. Her boyfriend, Chester Gillette, was convicted of killing her, even though he claimed it was an accident. His love letters to her were read in court, and he was electrocuted in 1908. The trial drew international attention, and Dreiser studied the case for years before writing his novel. Dreiser, basing his novels on remnants of reality and showcasing a well-covered trial, only reinforces the rise of crime dramas and fiction in popular culture during a time of rising gang violence, corporate espionage, and stressed legal divisions as law-like prohibition tested law enforcement's might.

Annessa A. Babic
New York Institute of Technology

See Also: 1600 to 1776 Primary Documents; 1777 to 1800 Primary Documents; Capital Punishment; Literature and Theater, Crime in; Murder, Sociology of.

Further Readings
Dreiser, Theodore. *An American Tragedy* [1925]. New York: Library of America, 2003.
Pizer, Donald. "Crime and Punishment in Dreiser's *An American Tragedy*: The Legal Debate." *Studies in the Novel* (Winter 2009).

Anarchists

Anarchists hold that hierarchical institutional authority is inherently detrimental to human beings. A key difference between what can be termed *classical* and *contemporary* anarchism is the latter's increasingly fractured nature, which arguably reflects the culturally and politically diverse nature of contemporary American society. Anarchists follow the political philosophy of anarchy. The term *anarchy* comes from the ancient Greek, meaning "without ruler." Anarchists hold that society should consist of a free association of its members. Anarchists argue that there should be no formal institutionalized state government enacting prescriptive laws to police human behavior and social interaction. This does not imply that there should be no ethics, rules, or social order. Rather, it should be interpreted as meaning the rejection of any hierarchical secular, religious, or cultural authority in favor of a more creative and spontaneous order of individuals living in autonomous like-minded communities on a voluntary basis.

Anarchists emphasize free will and self-determination, arguing that ethics are a highly personal and individual matter. They focus on personal responsibility rather than the blind following of laws imposed by a social, cultural, or religious authority. For anarchists, such authorities are paternalistic and dehumanize people by demanding conformity and making them compliant and overly reliant on other people when making personal decisions. However, this should not be taken to mean that the wants and needs of other people are to be ignored. Anarchists hold that personal action should be based upon concern for the welfare of other human beings. Forms of oppression based upon sex, gender, race, disability, or class are frowned upon and argued to be a direct consequence of inequalities fostered by economic, social, cultural, and religious elites. Likewise, nationalism and the promotion of patriotism are similarly seen to be bound up with the promotion of the interests of elites to the detriment of the poor and socially excluded, and therefore are held to perpetuate social inequality.

Although they share a rejection of the hierarchical state, anarchists disagree over some key aspects of their political philosophy. Some argue for the need to use violent action to enforce social change and create a more humane system, while others argue for the need to engage in peaceful protest and action. Additionally, anarchists disagree in their focus on the individual and the collective, particularly in relationship to the organization of the economic system in an anarchist society. Individualist anarchists value individual freedom above all else. Some individualist anarchists—sometimes called "free-market anarchists"—argue for changes to be made to the free-market capitalist systems that dominate contemporary Western democracies so that can they operate on a more voluntary basis without the involvement of states. In contrast, anarcho-communists and anarcho-syndicalists focus more on how the action of the individual can benefit the social group. The key difference between the former and the latter is that anarcho-communists wish to replace democracy with communism and common ownership, while anarcho-syndicalists tend to (but do not always) wish to establish a collectively oriented socioeconomic system that nevertheless respects some element of private property ownership. Both anarcho-communists and anarcho-syndicalists argue against free-market economics and hold that in the ideal anarchist society, the needs of the collective can be met without affecting an individual's creativity and sense of self-agency.

The photo shows anarchist writer Alexander Berkman addressing a large crowd in New York City's Union Square on July 11, 1914. Berkman was the author of Prison Memoirs of an Anarchist.

Early History

Anarchism emerged as a political philosophy in the late 18th century. It came into being during a time when far-reaching social change was occurring in Western civilizations as the Enlightenment, birth of modern science, growing industrialization, and rapid urbanization increasingly led to the free exchange of ideas and goods across national borders with the result that notions of personal freedom and self-determination based upon political and economic self-rule began to influence both creative intellectual thought and collective social action. This state of affairs led to the English Civil War, the French Revolution, and the American Revolutionary War. A key founding figure of what can be called classical anarchism was William Godwin. In his *Enquiry Concerning Political Justice and Its Influence on Modern Morals and Manners* (1793), Godwin engaged in a wide-ranging critique of elitism and organized government as he argued that property monopoly, marriage, and monarchy stopped human beings from achieving their full potential.

Godwin's ideas influenced a number of important 19th-century European intellectuals, including Karl Marx, Pierre-Joseph Proudhon, and Mikhail Bakunin. However, unlike Godwin, these intellectuals advocated a form of anarchism focused upon collective action, trade unionism, and community ownership rather than individualism and personal property rights; this resulted in the creation of anarcho-communism and anarcho-syndicalism. These ideas spread from Europe to the United States, influencing notable early American anarchists such as William Greene, Ezra Heywood, and Josiah Warren, who were all members of the International Working Man's Association (IWMA). The IWMA (sometimes called the First

International) was a global cooperative established in 1864. It focused on engaging in public protest and collective action to create socialist government. It was made up of anarchists, left-wing political parties, and trade union organizations engaged in class politics and worker rights. Tensions existed within the IWMA in regard to whether violent or nonviolent action should be used. Differences also existed in the emphasis placed on the collective over the individual by anarcho-communist and anarcho-syndicalist members, which contrasted with the views of writers such as Henry David Thoreau who advocated a more individualist form of anarchism. The IWMA in Europe played an important role in supporting the Russian Revolution of 1917. However, Russian anarchists were persecuted along with a number of other social groups, such as the mentally ill, after the Bolsheviks seized power. During the 1920s, the emergence of the nationalistic tendencies of fascism led to anarchists engaging in direct armed conflict with Spanish and Italian fascists.

Haymarket Riot

An important historical point in the American anarchist movement was the Haymarket bombing. This occurred on May 6, 1886. On May 1, a worker strike was organized by trade unions and the IWMA with the goal of reducing working hours to a maximum of eight hours per day. The city of Chicago played a central role in the organization of the strike. On May 4 at a public rally in Chicago organized to galvanize support for the strike, someone threw a bomb at a group of police officers. It killed eight people and wounded more than 60 others. In response, the police attacked the crowd, injuring more than 200 people. The anarchists August Spies, Samuel Fielden, George Engel, Adolph Fisher, Louis Lingg, Oscar Neebe, and Michael Schwab were put on trial for the bombing alongside Albert Parsons, who was the head of the IWMA in Chicago. Although a number of witnesses were presented to prove that none of the accused threw the bomb, the prosecution used speeches and articles written by Spies and Parsons in particular to charge the group with conspiracy to commit murder on the grounds that they had publicly argued for the need to engage in violent protest and therefore had incited the unknown person to throw the bomb. All of the men were found guilty. Spies, Parsons, Fisher, Lingg, and Engel were given the death penalty. Neebe, Fielden, and Schwab were sentenced to life imprisonment.

The Haymarket bombing had a far-reaching impact on the anarchist movement in America (and, indeed, worldwide). Although there was initial public sympathy for the aims of the trade union movement and the individuals convicted of the Haymarket bombing, union leaders nevertheless became reluctant to use mass strikes to achieve political ends. The bombing also helped propagate a populist image of anarchism as a violent political philosophy. Emma Goldman, a renowned feminist and anarchist, was inspired by the political aftermath of Haymarket bombing to write a defense of the movement in her classic work *Anarchism and Other Essays* (1910). Goldman believed that targeted violence could be effective in achieving a greater good, although in her later writings she was heavily critical of the violence used by the Bolsheviks during the Russian Revolution. In 1892, Goldman and the writer Alexander Berkman planned and failed to assassinate the industrialist and financier Henry Clay Frick, which they had hoped would be an act of "propaganda by the deed." Both Goldman and Berkman were imprisoned for their assassination attempt. In prison, Berkman wrote the key anarchist tract *Prison Memoirs of an Anarchist* (1910), in which he argued that it was the capitalist free-market system, not human nature, that created "man's inhumanity to man." On their release, Goldman and Berkman continued to be vocal members of the anarchist movement, with the result that they were subsequently deported from the United States to Russia in 1919.

Propaganda by deed promotes targeted physical violence against political enemies as a way of inspiring the masses and catalyzing revolution. It was first advocated Luigi Galleani, an Italian anarchist active in the United States in the early 20th century until his deportation in 1919. Leon Czolgosz, who assassinated President William McKinley in 1901, claimed to be to a member of the anarchist movement and to be inspired by the ideas of Goldman and Galleani. This was strongly denied by Goldman and other key members of the anarchist movement. Between 1914 and 1932, Galleani's followers (known as Galleanists) carried out

In the aftermath of the suspected anarchist Wall Street bombing of 1920, policemen and soldiers attempted to control a crowd in front of the Morgan Bank. Body bags in the foreground hold some of the bombing's 38 victims. "Propaganda by deed" promoted targeted physical violence against political enemies, but the bombing eventually led to mainstream rejection of anarchism.

a series of bombings and assassination attempts against institutions and persons. Notable Galleanists included Nicola Sacco and Bartolomeo Vanzetti, who were executed in 1927 for the murder of two men during an armed robbery. It is suspected that Galleanists were behind the Wall Street bombing of 1920, which resulted in the death of 38 people. The anarchist movement's alleged involvement with the Wall Street bombing was never proven but its continued advocacy of public disorder and targeted violence undoubtedly led to the gradual public rejection of anarchism from mainstream American politics during the first half of the 20th century.

Modern Anarchism

Anarchism reemerged in America as part of the 1960s counterculture and civil rights movements and continued to grow within modern punk, urban dance, modern art, and the alternative culture scenes. Anarchism's focus on free thought and individual agency chimes with the shared existentialist concern with personal freedom from traditional forms of familial, interpersonal, and sexual relationships of these diverse groups. Feminist and green movement forms of anarchism also emerged during the 1960s, reflecting a growing concern with promoting female equality and the impact of human behavior on the natural environment. Contemporary forms of anarchism argue against capitalism and free-market economics, although some do wish to maintain individual property rights and global trade. For example, anarcho-capitalism (which is sometimes called libertarian anarchy or free-market anarchism) argues that voluntary trade of private property and services is necessary to maximize personal liberty and prosperity. The varied nature of anarchism today arguably reflects the diverse nature of modern American society. Notable contemporary American anarchists include Noam Chomsky, Paul Goodman, Murray Bookchin, and John Zerzan.

John Martyn Chamberlain
Loughborough University

See Also: 1777 to 1800 Primary Documents; 1901 to 1920 Primary Documents; Czolgosz, Leon; Kaczynski, Ted; Libertarianism; Political Dissidents; Riots; Sacco and Vanzetti; Strikes; Terrorism; Xenophobia.

Further Readings
McLaughlin, Paul. *Anarchism and Authority*. Aldershot, UK: Ashgate, 2007.
Perlin, Terry Michael. *Contemporary Anarchism*. Piscataway, NJ: Transaction Publishers, 1979.
Purkis, Jonathan and James Bowen. *Changing Anarchism: Anarchist Theory and Practice in a Global Age*. Manchester, UK: Manchester University Press, 2004.
Slevin, Carl. "Anarchism." In *The Concise Oxford Dictionary of Politics*, Ian McLean and Alistair McMillan, eds. Oxford: Oxford University Press, 2003.

Anti-Federalist Papers

After the American Revolution, when the thirteen colonies revolted from the oppression of English rule, the founding fathers wrote the Constitution in an effort to create a more fair and equitable form of government than the monarchies that were prevalent in Europe. However, when the founding fathers wrote the Constitution, there was not unanimous agreement among the states as to whether it should be ratified. The primary opponents to the original Constitution were the Anti-Federalists.

At that time, there were two main factions among the founding fathers: the Federalists and the Anti-Federalists. Essentially, the Federalists advocated a strong central government and were led by Alexander Hamilton. The Anti-Federalists favored a less centralized government and were led by Patrick Henry and Thomas Jefferson. Jefferson generally favored a more agrarian type of society. The Anti-Federalists were concerned about the power vested in the president and the Congress and thought that the states would have to cede too much of their sovereignty. One of the other major differences between the Federalists and the Anti-Federalists was that the Anti-Federalists wanted a Bill of Rights added to the Constitution and the Federalists did not. The reason for this disagreement was that the Federalists thought that if a written document were created listing the rights of the people, then the government would likely recognize only those written rights, whereas the Anti-Federalists wanted a written list of rights, otherwise they thought that the government would not allow the people any rights. Given these differences, ratification of the Constitution was uncertain.

As a matter of philosophical perspective, the Anti-Federalists held a strong conception of justice that was centered on individual rights that would prevent a strong central government from oppressing citizens. It can be rationally argued that the ultimate evil for the Anti-Federalists was a strong, oppressive, and tyrannical government. Thus, a Bill of Rights that guaranteed and protected fundamental individual rights was an absolute necessity.

Constitutional Critiques

After the proposed Constitution was written at the Constitutional Convention, the Anti-Federalists began to publish a series of articles critical of the proposed Constitution in an attempt to defeat its ratification. Essentially, the Anti-Federalists wanted a federal government that was more akin to the defunct Articles of Confederation, which had a very weak central government. Regardless, many of the objections raised by the Anti-Federalist were valid, and the Federalists, in response, began their own organized campaign of publications to counter the Anti-Federalists.

The Anti-Federalists, at least initially, used pseudonyms when publishing their critiques of the proposed Constitution. Some of the more frequent pseudonyms used were the Federal Farmer, Cato, and Brutus. It is thought that the use of these names was to inspire the populace against the Constitution. For example, Brutus was well-known in history as opposing the tyranny of Caesar, who was a strong individual leader (i.e., dictator) of ancient Rome. Cato was a famed Roman soldier and statesman who was a man of agriculture. Interestingly, when the Federalists started to publish their responses to the Anti-Federalist critiques and their defenses of the proposed Constitution, now known as the Federalist Papers, they used the pseudonym Publius, likely in an effort to counter the public recognition and identification with Brutus as a resister to tyranny, given that the people had just successfully revolted from the tyranny of the English monarchy.

The Anti-Federalists were not as well organized as the Federalists. Accordingly, it was not until much later, many years after the adoption of the Constitution and the Bill of Rights, that the Anti-Federalist Papers were compiled into a single work. However, this does not detract from the influence that the Anti-Federalists had on the American criminal justice system.

Resistance to the proposed Constitution was strong. The opposition of the Anti-Federalists almost derailed the ratification of the Constitution. The ratification vote in a number of the states was close. Although the Anti-Federalists were not successful in defeating the ratification of the proposed Constitution, they were very successful in that their efforts forced the adoption of a written Bill of Rights shortly after the Constitution was ratified. It has been recognized that without the adoption of a Bill of Rights, the proposed Constitution might have very well failed and gone the way of the Articles of Confederation.

Conclusion

Historically, in the context of crime and punishment in the United States, it is relatively certain that the Anti-Federalists and their opposition to the Federalists through the Anti-Federalist Papers were the quintessential proponents in the ultimate adoption of the Bill of Rights, which had a profound effect on crime and punishment in America. This is especially true when considering that the Fourth, Fifth, Sixth, and Eighth Amendments, which provide a series of constitutional protections for persons accused of crimes, would likely not have otherwise been adopted or present in the American criminal justice system today.

Wm. C. Plouffe, Jr.
Independent Scholar

See Also: American Revolution and Criminal Justice; Federalist Papers; Jefferson, Thomas; Political Dissidents.

Further Readings
Cornell, Saul. *The Other Founders: Anti-Federalism and the Dissenting Tradition in America: 1788–1828*. Chapel Hill: University of North Carolina Press, 1999.
Ketcham, Ralph, ed. *Anti-Federalist Papers and the Constitutional Convention Debates*. New York: Signet, 1986.
Storing, Herbert J., ed. *The Anti-Federalist*. Chicago: University of Chicago Press, 1985.
Storing, Hebert J. *What the Anti-Federalists Were For: The Political Thought of the Opponents of the Constitution*. Chicago: University of Chicago Press, 1981.

Antitrust Law

Illegal trusts are formed by any practice that restrains trade or commerce unduly. During the late 1800s and early 1900s, a small number of corporations and individuals exploited their dominant position in the tobacco, railroad, and steel industries to fix prices, control output, eliminate competitors, and manipulate labor markets. Perceiving a threat to democracy and free trade from companies employing their great wealth and power in these ways, Congress outlawed conspiracies and monopolies that restrain interstate or foreign commerce unreasonably with the Sherman Antitrust Act. Generally speaking, in concert with subsequent legislation, Congress prohibited agreements among competitors to fix prices, restrict output, allocate markets, apportion customers, rig bids, interlock directorates, merge or engage in joint ventures, or engage in any other kind of conspiratorial or monopolistic behavior that interferes with the ordinary, usual, and competitive system of the open market.

History

The Sherman Antitrust Act favored the ideal of economic competition among small businesses and came into direct conflict with financial and

This cartoon from February 27, 1901, comments on the vast reach of John D. Rockefeller's business empire, depicting him as a king with a crown topped with railroad cars and oil tanks.

business pressures militating toward large-scale enterprise during the last decade of the 18th century and the first decade of the 19th century. During the 1890s, these competing forces resulted in a political policy of lackadaisical enforcement and inattention to the enlarging gap between the economic ideal and the corporate reality. As the gap grew ever wider in the 20th century, public pressure grew to employ the legislation more vigorously. Politically, the problem came to be viewed by the executive branch as one of employing the Sherman Antitrust Act to promote competition through adequate regulation without damaging the economies of scale attendant to large-scale corporate enterprises. The pursuit of policies by the executive branch calculated to these ends brought down the ire of all concerned, and calls for repeal or amendment of the act grew. However, as the interests advocating change were at odds themselves, no unified opposition resulted, and attempts by various groups to introduce and pass counterlegislation soon disintegrated.

In response to this failure, corporate interests merged, uniting into a single company rather than engaging in practices or agreements with a view to controlling prices, demand, and supply. These practices established the groundwork for the Clayton Act and the Federal Trade Commission Act of 1914, which together regulated mergers and created a federal agency with the power to oversee businesses' practices and halt mergers that threatened competition substantially or tended to create a monopoly.

A change in public attitudes during the 1920s, occasioned by the economic boom following World War I, encouraged cooperation among businesses as this seemed to create new wealth. This, in turn, resulted in less rigorous enforcement of antitrust legislation, a trend that continued following the stock market crash in 1929. Continued economic decline refocused attention on preventing monopolies and vigorous enforcement of antitrust legislation. Vigorous enforcement peaked and wavered sporadically thereafter until the 1980s, when significant cuts were made to the budgets of the Federal Trade Commission and the Justice Department, curtailing enforcement efforts. Thereupon, state efforts took up the slack. Recessions during the 1990s reinvigorated federal enforcement efforts.

Antitrust Law Today

Federal law is complemented in every state except Pennsylvania by state antitrust statutes. Some track the language of the Sherman Antitrust Act, while others prohibit specific violations, and still others contain broad language permitting considerable flexibility in their application. In most cases, both civil and criminal penalties are provided, and civil actions may be brought by private parties.

The federal statutes also provide both civil and criminal penalties, and certain organizations and practices are exempt. These include patent ownership, certain activities within the scope of the Securities and Exchange Act, public utilities, labor unions, hospitals, public transit systems, public water systems, and companies supplying military equipment. In addition, some state policies, state legislation, and state regulatory programs are exempt from federal antitrust liability provided they are clearly articulated as state policy and are actively supervised by the state.

Federal antitrust legislation is enforced primarily by the Antitrust Division of the U.S. Department of Justice and the Federal Trade Commission, though private parties may bring suit as well. Only the Department of Justice prosecutes violations criminally. Antitrust violations may be either "per se" or contrary to the rule of reason. "Per se" violations are practices considered inherently detrimental to free trade and so require no further inquiry into their actual effect (e.g., price fixing). Practices contrary to the rule of reason produce anticompetitive effects whose impact on trade can be evaluated only by considering the facts distinctive to the business in question, the historical impact of the restraint, and the motivation behind the practice.

Two theories of antitrust enforcement contend for dominance in American jurisprudence. Many argue that consumer welfare measured in narrowly economic terms should direct the courts in their case-by-case applications of the rule of reason. Others argue that economic impacts ought to be only one consideration in antitrust analysis. Deeply held social and political values ought to be considered as well, along with how antitrust policy might help solve serious social problems. The former theory dominates currently.

In criminal antitrust prosecutions, the government must establish that a conspiratorial or monopolistic combination or conspiracy occurred, that the agreement restrained trade or commerce unreasonably, that the defendant intended the restraint, and that the trade or commerce was interstate or international in nature. Conspiracy is established when at least two competitors have reached a meeting of the minds regardless of any subsequent actions they may take or whether the endeavor was successful ultimately. Restraint of trade or commerce may be established by a showing that an essential part of the challenged practice directly or indirectly restrains a substantial volume of trade or commerce as a practical matter.

A majority of courts require that the interstate or international nexus be established by a relationship between the challenged activity and interstate or international commerce, while a minority hold that the required nexus is established if the nature of the defendant's general business activities affects interstate or international commerce. Criminal intent is assumed whenever per se analysis is appropriate but is an essential element of proof in rule of reason cases.

From a sociological perspective, given the difficulties in detecting trusts, antitrust legislation stresses control and deterrence theory, the reinforcing convictions that legal sanctions and social barriers to criminal behavior may be made sufficiently rigorous to dissuade potential wrongdoers and to regulate human behavior to conformity and compliance. Accordingly, the penalties of the Sherman and Clayton Acts were supplemented, under congressional pressure in the 1950s and 1980s, by voluntary corporate compliance programs establishing written procedures and codes of ethical conduct, including obligations to report misconduct to government authorities and to ensure public accountability for implementation and enforcement of their principles. These requirements, addressed to altering the corporate culture and engaging the general public, take notice of social ecology theories, subcultural theories, and structured action theories, all grounded in the idea that the desire for positive social, political, and economic relationships will moderate inducements to criminal behavior.

Conclusion

Historically and empirically, there is at best modest support for the effectiveness of these policies. The culture of any organization is remarkably difficult to change or to direct from outside. Acceptable behavior by and within companies is gleaned by corporate decision makers from the established social structure of opportunities available for attaining professional success within a company and from ingrained attitudes, values, and beliefs communicated from influential others and reinforced tacitly. Arguably, deviance may develop as executives share problems that require solutions not permitted by law or societal norms, or when anticipated failure to achieve valued goals is frustrated. Junior executives may learn sharp tactics and strategies from their seniors, among which may be the expectation that ethical guidelines and legal requirements must be bent on occasion (strain theory). Alternatively, when norms internal and external to the organization are confused or unclear, deviance may result as a resolution to the conflict (anomie theory).

Charles Frederick Abel
Stephen F. Austin State University

See Also: Clayton Anti-Trust Act of 1914; Sherman Anti-Trust Act of 1890; *Standard Oil Company of New Jersey v. United States*; White-Collar Crime, Sociology of.

Further Readings
Comegys, W. B. *Antitrust Compliance Manual: A Guide for Counsel and Executives of Businesses and Professions*. New York: Practicing Law Institute, 1992.
Gerla, H. S. "A Micro-Microeconomic Approach to Antitrust Law: Games Managers Play." *Michigan Law Review*, v.86 (1988).
Hester, S. and P. Eglin. *A Sociology of Crime*. London: Routledge, 1992.
Hill, T. J. and S. B. Lezell. "Antitrust Violations." *American Criminal Law Review*, v.47 (2010).
Miller, E. H. "Recent Developments: Federal Sentencing Guidelines for Organizational Defendants." *Vanderbilt Law Review*, v.46 (1993).
Pitt, H. L. and K. A. Groskaufmanis. "Minimizing Corporate Civil and Criminal Liability: A Second Look at Corporate Codes of Conduct." *Georgetown Law Journal*, v.78 (1990).
Simpson, S. S. "The Decomposition of Antitrust: Testing a Multi-Level, Longitudinal Model of Profit-Squeeze." *American Sociological Review*, v.51/6 (1986).
Young, J. *The Exclusive Society*. London: Sage, 1999.

Appeals

In general parlance, an appeal is a solicitation, plea, or petition earnestly seeking something; but in the criminal justice system, the term has a much narrower and more precise meaning and refers to a review of a decision or a verdict by a tribunal such as a court other than the one that rendered it. While the right to appellate review is not one of constitutional dimension, once a review system is put into place, considerations of due process require that it be fair, so, for example, an indigent seeking to perfect an appeal is entitled to the assistance of effective appointed counsel paid for by the state. All 50 states and the federal government provide for the appellate review of criminal convictions. In the federal courts, a two-tiered system is in place allowing first for a person convicted of a crime in a federal district court to appeal to the circuit court of appeals in the district of his or her conviction; and thereafter, with the permission of the U.S. Supreme Court via a writ of certiorari, which is a command to a lower court to send up the record, or in some cases, via an appeal if the constitutionality of a statute is involved, though the court tends to dismiss such appeals for want of a substantial federal question.

Two-Tiered Appellate Process
Many of the more populated states have a similar two-tiered review process. Thus, in New York, felony convictions are appealed to an intermediate appellate court called the Appellate Division, which is divided into four departments around the state to hear appeals by panels of four judges (a fifth is brought in in case of a tie vote) within their respective department. The court is allowed to consider both the law and the facts, though legal principles and statutes may limit the subject matter to be reviewed. Thereafter, an appeal may be taken to the state's highest court, the court of appeals that sits in Albany, New York, but only with the permission of either a judge of the court of appeals or the appellate division. If federal constitutional questions are involved, the appellant, after a decision by the New York Court of Appeals, as with its federal counterpart, may seek review in the U.S. Supreme Court. In neighboring Vermont, however, there are no intermediate appellate courts, and appeals go directly from their district court to the Vermont Supreme Court.

In addition to appeals from judgments of conviction, criminal defendants also make collateral attacks to their convictions and also bring claims with regard to the quality and quantity of their incarceration, if they are imprisoned, in what is

New York's two-tiered review process means that felony convictions are appealed to an intermediate appellate court called the Appellate Division, after which an appeal may be taken to the court of appeals in Albany, New York, shown above. If federal constitutional questions are involved, the appellant may eventually seek review in the U.S. Supreme Court.

usually known as writs of habeas corpus, which are subject to appellate review, though such review is usually with permission rather than a right, requiring a certificate of appealability to bring an appeal to a circuit court of appeals from the denial of habeas corpus relief. In many jurisdictions, cases tried in local courts are reviewed by their district court and then sent to the appellate court of the state. In some jurisdictions, there are specialized criminal courts of appeal, such as in Texas.

In most cases, criminal or civil, an appeal is started by serving one's adversary, the prosecutor in a criminal case, a notice of appeal and filing the same in the court where the conviction occurred. While the specific content may vary by jurisdiction, the notice usually names the court of conviction and its date and what court the appeal is being taken to along with what the defendant was convicted of. Some notices list the errors for review by the appellate court, but this is usually not required because many issues do not become patent until an examination of the record and transcript of the proceedings at the trial court. As for the timing of the service and filing of the notice, failure to serve and file it within the statutory period—which varies from jurisdiction to jurisdiction (i.e., 10 days in federal courts); for criminal appeals, collateral attacks are governed by civil rules; 30 days in New York—may lead to a dismissal of the appeal unless there was good cause or excusable neglect for the failure, which will allow for an extension of the time. The appeal must be presented to the appellate court in a timely fashion, though the exact amount of time varies from location to location and can usually be extended for good cause shown.

Role of the Attorney

Though there is a right of self-representation, criminal appeals are generally perfected by an attorney, who ensures that the record at the trial court, including the transcription of the minutes of the proceedings, is sent to the appellate court. Since most criminal appellants are indigents, due process requires that a lawyer be appointed to represent the individual without a fee and that there is access to a transcript of the minutes or other proceedings without charge. This is especially important for obtaining transcripts and copying them. Records can easily run into thousands of dollars without even considering the lawyer's fee. The appointment of the lawyer, however, is a matter for the courts so that the right of an indigent to counsel at the expense of the government does not include the right to select the lawyer, who is usually chosen from a panel of lawyers. These appointed lawyers agree to take such cases, usually at fees far less than would be charged to a private client, or by organized agencies such as a public defender or Legal Aid Society.

As part of the process of perfecting the appeal, the attorney, whether he or she be assigned or retained, writes a "brief," which is a written statement and account of what took place at the trial court followed by the legal arguments that may be submitted and or orally argued to the appellate court to support the claimed errors that took place to justify and convince the appellate court of the need for a reversal or modification of the verdict or order at the trial court. The appellate counsel's submission is responded to by the prosecutor with his or her written brief, which may be argued or submitted as well, and defense counsel may thereafter respond to it with a reply, which ends the written submissions.

Proceedings of the Appellate Court
As the appeal is not a "de novo" or new trial, the appellate court is bound by the record before it and cannot consider extraneous matter not presented at the trial court. Thus, in a most extreme case, if during the preparation and argument of the appeal defense counsel should discover new evidence that would exonerate the appellant, the particular appeal would not be the place to present such new material. This is not to suggest that other procedures to obtain relief were not available, but only that the appeal was not the place to obtain it.

In addition to not considering matters *dehors*, or outside the record, what and how appellate courts review the proceedings at the trial court level are subject to certain other limitations. In order to raise a legal issue at the appellate court, the issue must be preserved for review at the trial court with an objection or other protest with regard to the claimed error so that the trial court would have had an opportunity to review and correct its own mistake. Thus, in order to raise on appeal, as a matter of law, that the trial judge did not charge the jury that manslaughter was a lesser included crime of murder, trial counsel would have had to protest or object to the court's failure to so charge in order to preserve the claim for appellate review. Exceptions, of course, exist where the issue is so significant and fundamental such as where a court improperly delegates responsibility to nonjudicial personnel, depriving a defendant of his right to a trial by jury, an integral component of which is the supervision of the proceedings by a judge. A similar exception exists in the federal court under the doctrine known as "plain error" where the appellate court can correct an error not raised at trial where the mistake is clear and obvious and affects fundamental rights such as the outcome of the case and seriously impacts on the fairness, integrity, and reputation of the judicial proceedings. Another exception exists in those jurisdictions where the appellate court has the power to reverse in the interests of justice despite the absence of objection or protest or on the facts where the conviction is against the weight of the evidence.

In conducting a weight of the evidence review, the New York Court of Appeals indicated that the appellate court sits as a 13th juror, which must first determine that an acquittal would not have been unreasonable and thereafter weigh the conflicting testimony at the trial and review any rational inferences that may be drawn from the evidence and then evaluate the strength of the conclusions to determine whether the jury was warranted in its finding that the defendant was guilty of the crime beyond a reasonable doubt. This review by the intermediate appellate court is especially important in New York because it is a factual determination of the state's highest court, which considers only questions of law and cannot review the correctness of that determination.

The Verdict
A weight of the evidence review, however, does not mean that the appellate court sits as a super jury, substituting its view for that of the trial jury

or trier of the facts, and gives great deference to the determination at the trial court and does not move to set aside a jury verdict merely because if the appellate court were sitting as the jury it would have come to a different albeit reasonable conclusion. One reason for this is that the appellate court has only a cold record before it while the jurors below had an opportunity to both actually hear a witness and observe his or her demeanor.

However, the fact that an error, even one preserved for review, was made at the trial court does not always guarantee that a conviction will be reversed or modified because the error may be deemed harmless in that it had no impact on the verdict. The harmless error analysis, though, is not available in cases where the error is considered structural because it affects the framework in which the trial proceeds, such as the violation of the Sixth Amendment right to retained counsel of choice. While the scope of appellate review is expansive, it can also be short-circuited by a defendant's plea of guilty and/or a waiver of the right to appeal at the trial court, both of which require that they be made knowingly, voluntarily, and intelligently. And, of course, the question of whether the standard for the waiver in either or both situations has been met is itself susceptible to appellate review.

A plea of guilty, which is the equivalent of a conviction after a trial, waives objections to many rulings at the trial court. Thus, in the federal courts, the unconditional plea of guilty waives appellate review. Decisions of the trial court denying an application, even after a hearing, to suppress a confession or evidence on grounds that they were illegally obtained because the claim is considered nonjurisdictional include *United States v. Byrd* (2006), though New York, for example, allows for such review after a guilty plea. Though the appellate process provides for review of criminal convictions, what with a lack of uniformity for both rules of substance and procedure, its use is a complicated matter best left to those with the experience and training to wade through what might be a minefield to get the appellate court to both hear and decide the substantive issue brought before it.

Roslyn Muraskin
Long Island University

See Also: 1941 to 1960 Primary Documents; Appellate Courts; Courts; Defendant's Rights; Judges and Magistrates; Trials.

Further Readings
Abney v. United States, 431 U.S. 651 (1977).
Caperton v. A T Massey Coal Co., 120 S. Ct. 2252 (2009).
Gamach v. California, 131 S. Ct. 591 (2010).
Griffin v. Illinois, 351 U.S. 12 (1956).
Hammock v. State, 211 S.W. 3d. 874, Texas App. (2006).
Martinez v. Court of Appeals, California, 528 U.W. 152 (2000).
Muraskin, Roslyn. "The Right of the Indigent Defendant to Appeal: *Griffin v. Illinois* 351 U.S. 12 (1956)." Masters thesis. New York: New York University, 1962.
People v. Danielson, 9 N.Y. 3d. 342, (2007).
People v. Kelly, 11 A.D. 3d 133, New York 1st Dept. (2004).
People v. Stultz, 2 N.Y. 3d., 277 (2004).
State v. Blakney, 361 N.E. 2d. 567, Ohio Mun. 1975.
State v. Maloney, 709 N.W. 2d, 436, Wis. 2006).
United States v. Byrd, 166 Fed. Appx. 460, 11th cir. (2006).
United States v. Gonzalez-Lopez, 548 U.S. 140 (2006).
United States v. Marcus, 130 S. Ct. 2159 (2010).
Vermont Law Review, Vol. 22 p. 711 ft. note 210 (1998).
Washington v. Recuenco, 548 U.S. 212 (2006).
Williams v. Johnson, 169 F. Supp. 2d 594, Texas (2001).

Appellate Courts

Courts that receive cases from lower courts for examination of the constitutionality and legality of the lower court's actions, procedures, and decisions are appellate courts. The courts of first instance are usually the courts that try cases and then make decisions of fact about guilt or innocence. The idea of appellate courts can be found in the ancient Mesopotamian courts of the Sumerians, Babylonians, and Persians. It can also be found in the courts of the ancient Egyptians where Maat was the goddess of justice. Appellate courts were instituted by Moses at the insistence of the father-in-law, Jethro (Exodus 18:13–22). The system of appeals in the American system was influenced in part by its English legal heritage, by the Bible, and by the system developed by the Romans, which allowed Saint Paul to "appeal (his case) to Caesar."

The idea of appellate courts has not been universally accepted. In many of the tribal systems of the world there was no appeal from the chief. In modern times, there have been those who would prefer greater swiftness in meting out justice to prevent defendants, escaping on a technicality. At stake in a system of appellate courts is the knowledge that a second chance is very important for the establishment of justice. Trials may occur in conditions of passion and prejudice that may harm the fairness for a criminal defendant. Trial judges and juries are humans seeking to establish justice. They can and do err over questions of fact or the law. Granting appeals allows for a dispassionate review and examination of questions of law raised in the heat of a trial, questions that can argue that the law was fairly or unfairly interpreted or applied.

The American System
In a unified system of justice with appellate courts, there is a division of judicial labor organized through the granting of jurisdiction to each court. Trial courts have original jurisdiction, that is, the right to hear a case first. The courts that examine trials are appellate courts with appellate jurisdiction; they have the right to hear a case on appeal. In the American dual court system of one federal court system and 50 state court systems, there are trial courts and almost always two levels of appeals courts. The first level is the intermediate appellate level and the court of last resort is the supreme appellate court.

The federal intermediate appellate courts are the courts of appeal. Above them is the Supreme Court of the United States. The Supreme Court has both original and appellate jurisdiction. Its original jurisdiction is defined in the Constitution and was the subject of a landmark case, *Marbury v. Madison* (1803), early in American history. The case involved the granting of an expanded original jurisdiction to the Supreme Court by Section Thirteen of the Judiciary Act of 1789. Section Thirteen of the act, the primary author of which was Oliver Ellsworth (third chief justice of the Supreme Court), was declared (in its first exercise of judicial review) to be an unconstitutional expansion of the original jurisdiction of the Supreme Court. In effect, the Supreme Court has found itself to be a poor trial court and will almost always appoint a master to hear cases that come to it as original jurisdiction cases, the main body of which involve disputes between the states. The effect is to allow the Supreme Court to hear the decision of the case as decided before the master as an appellate case.

The appellate jurisdiction of the Supreme Court has been defined by Congress by legislative action. Overall, it is a very broad jurisdiction; however, from time to time Congress has limited the Supreme Court's appellate jurisdiction. In addition, the Eleventh Amendment to the U.S. Constitution was adopted following the case of *Chisholm v. Georgia* (1793) and in effect limited the appellate jurisdiction of the Supreme Court to prevent it from hearing cases brought by citizens against states. The federal courts of appeal today were originally the circuit courts of appeal. Historically, these courts met when a Supreme Court justice joined with federal district court judges to form the circuit court of appeals. It would hear appeals from the federal district courts of that region. The judges in the late 18th and all of the 19th century would literally travel in a circuit to hear cases.

Some cases in the 19th century involved criminal actions from the Wild West, such as the case of *In Re Neagle* (1890). The case was a story of romance, betrayal, and violent death out of the Old West. It involved Supreme Court Justice Stephen J. Field, U.S. Marshal David Neagle, and onetime California Supreme Court Justice David S. Terry. The Supreme Court held that a U.S. marshal (Neagle) was immune from state criminal prosecution when, acting as a U.S. marshal, he killed Terry in defense of Justice Field.

Federal cases are brought to the appellate courts through a writ of certiorari, which orders the lower court to send up the record for review. State cases can be appealed directly to the U.S. Supreme Court because of a provision in the Judiciary Act of 1793. The provision allows cases to be appealed from the highest state court to hear that type of case directly to the Supreme Court. The opinions of the appellate courts are recorded in bound volumes and housed in law libraries from the county to the state or federal level. These legal opinions form a special body of literature that has developed from a tradition of legal rhetoric that seeks truth and justice. The attorneys in their briefs use the best persuasive tool of legal reasoning to sharpen the issues to persuade the judges or justices to their views of law. The legal opinions often continue the common law tradition of judges making law on a case-by-case basis, so that justice can be brought out of the workings of humans in human courts.

Prior to the late 1940s, almost all American criminal law was state law, so only a few cases involving criminal issues made it to the Supreme Court. Almost all criminal cases were decided by state appellate courts. However, throughout the 20th century, the Supreme Court increased the jurisdiction of the federal courts by applying the Bill of Rights to the states through the due process and equal protection clauses of the Fourteenth Amendment. Several of these cases were major landmark civil liberties cases that involved limits on the power of the federal and state governments to jail people for objectionable speech, printing, or assembly whether the speech was pornographic, political, or religio-political, such as the refusal of Jehovah's Witness children to salute the American flag (*West Virginia State Board of Education v. Barnette, 1943*) in school rooms.

Many cases have involved defining specifically the meaning of "unreasonable search and seizure" as found in the Fourth Amendment. Others, such as the issue of double jeopardy (*Palko v. Connecticut*, 1937), right to counsel for indigents (*Gideon v. Wainwright*, 1963), or the Miranda Warning (*Miranda v. Arizona*, 1966), pushed law enforcement into more expensive forensic investigations of crimes rather than relying on confessions,

Courtroom One in the James R. Browning U.S. Court of Appeals Building in San Francisco, California, which was completed in 1905 and survived the San Francisco earthquake of 1906. Granting appeals allows for a dispassionate review and examination of questions of law raised in the heat of a trial, questions that can argue that the law was fairly or unfairly interpreted or applied.

which at times were found to be coercive. The case of *Rochin v. California* (1952) was the stomach pumping case that established the "shocks-the-conscience" rule. The case involved the constitutionality of forcibly pumping the stomach of a suspect in order to retrieve narcotics.

The 50 state court systems also have intermediate courts of appeal with one court serving as its state supreme court. The names of these courts vary among the states, but most use the terms *court of appeals* and *state supreme court* for the names of their appellate courts. New York, for example, uses *court of appeals* as the name of its supreme court. Usually, *judge* is the title in lower courts and *justice* is used as the title of judges in federal and state supreme courts. There are special courts such as military courts and the bankruptcy courts in the federal system and special courts such as traffic court in the state systems. Some of these courts hear criminal accusations, usually misdemeanor charges. The appellate courts hear these kinds of cases.

Andrew J. Waskey
Dalton State College

See Also: 1941 to 1960 Primary Documents; Appeals; Courts; Defendant's Rights; Judges and Magistrates; Supreme Court, U.S.; Trials.

Further Readings
Chemerinsky, Erwin. *Federal Jurisdiction*. New York: Aspen Publishers, 2003.
Coffin, Frank M. *On Appeal: Courts, Lawyering, and Judging*. New York: W. W. Norton, 1994.
Cross, Frank B. *Decision Making in the U.S. Courts of Appeals*. Palo Alto, CA: Stanford University Press, 2007.
Frederick, David C. *Rugged Justice: The Ninth Circuit Court of Appeals and the American West, 1891–1941*. Berkeley: University of California Press, 1994.
Hornstein, Alan D. *Appellate Advocacy in a Nutshell*. St. Paul, MN: Thomson West, 1998.
Klein, David E. *Making Law in the United States Courts of Appeals*. Cambridge: Cambridge University Press, 2002.
Lurie, Jonathan. *Military Justice in America: The U.S. Court of Appeals for the Armed Forces, 1775–1980*. Lawrence: University Press of Kansas, 2001.

Arizona

In popular culture, early Arizona is often portrayed as a lawless frontier where disputes were settled with guns. One example of this is the infamous gunfight at the O.K. Corral. This 1881 shoot-out took place in Tombstone, Arizona, and involved noted gunfighter and lawman Wyatt Earp. The state's actual history, however, is considerably more complex and varied in terms of crime and punishment.

Territorial Era
In 1863, the federal Arizona Organic Act established a provisional government for the newly formed Arizona Territory that included a U.S. marshal to maintain law and order. Later, a civilian policing system of county sheriffs, constables, and town marshals was established. Early criminal concerns focused on murder and property loss that resulted from Native American incursions. Because of this, the majority of early police duties fell to the U.S. Army. Conflicts involving Apaches proved so brutal during this era that more than 100 years later, some police districts experiencing violent cycles of crime nicknamed their stations "Fort Apache." Arizona's criminal history includes violent episodes of labor unrest within its mining districts, such as the Bisbee Deportation (1917), and feuds or range wars between the territory's cattlemen and sheepherders—the most infamous among these being the Pleasant Valley War. This running battle between the Tewksbury and the Graham families lasted nearly 10 years and ended in 1892. From 1901 to 1909, a small mounted police force known as the Arizona Rangers operated within the rural regions of the territory. Patterned after the Texas Rangers, this agency experienced a great deal of success in eliminating cattle rustling. It also received criticism for its role in the suppression of a 1906 copper strike in Cananea, Mexico.

Arizona's penal system developed slowly during its territorial years. Initially, county jails served as territorial penitentiaries, with sheriffs overseeing legal executions by hanging. The first territorial prison opened in Yuma in 1875. This facility quickly developed a reputation as a hellhole and was moved to Florence in 1909. During this time, adult men and women were housed at the same

These mounted police were taking part in a parade in the city of Scottsdale, Arizona, in 2009. Arizona's Uniform Crime Reporting Program showed that the state suffered an increase in violent crime from 8.7 percent in 2002 to 9.5 percent in 2010. That year, the legislature passed a controversial bill designed to curtail chronic illegal immigration and smuggling along the border.

compound. Juvenile offenders not sentenced to the penitentiary were placed in custodial care or were sent to a reform school beginning in 1902.

Statehood

Increasing growth and industrialization led to statehood in 1912. With these developments came an increased use of automobiles, necessitating the formation of the Arizona Highway Patrol in 1931. Still largely rural in nature, Arizona's remote regions and proximity to the Mexican border encouraged outside criminal organizations to enter the state in increasing numbers at the turn of the 20th century. Following the end of Prohibition, the enforcement of state liquor laws fell to the Temperance Enforcement Commission, followed by the Department of Liquor Licenses and Control in 1939. Arizona later combined this department, the Highway Patrol, and the Narcotics Division of the Department of Law to create a Department of Public Safety in 1969. The state also formed the Department of Corrections (DOC) in 1968 as the administrative agency of its various correctional facilities. Evolving from a weak and ineffective penal system, today this agency employs approximately 9,750 correctional professionals.

Over the years, Arizona has experimented with a number of reform efforts, including pardons, paroles, commutations, convict labor/leasing, the honor system, and indeterminate sentencing. Progressive Era reformers succeeded in abolishing the death sentence in 1916. Though vigilante activity continues along the border, Arizona's last vigilante hanging (1917) instigated the return of the death penalty in 1918. Arizona adopted poison gas in 1933 as its legal method of execution but has utilized lethal injection since 1993.

Contemporary Challenges

Criminal events in Arizona during the 20th century have had a marked influence on national crime and policing practices. The conviction of Ernesto Miranda for the 1963 rape and kidnapping of a young Phoenix woman eventually led to the well-known Supreme Court decision concerning Miranda rights and the mandate that police advise criminal suspects of their right to remain silent and to the presence of an attorney during questioning. In 1967, a Supreme Court case concerning Arizona juvenile Gerald Gault's obscene telephone calls led to expanded rights for due process for juveniles. Lastly, the organized crime–related fatal car bombing of an investigative reporter from the *Arizona Republic* newspaper in 1976 created such an intense backlash within the national news community that it resulted in a massive wave of investigative reports exposing the extent to which political and financial corruption operated within the state.

Today, Arizona continues to produce colorful law enforcement figures like Maricopa County Sheriff Joe Arpaio. Its criminal justice system also remains turbulent. Statistics gathered from Arizona's Uniform Crime Reporting Program indicate that violent crime has increased from 8.7 percent in 2002 to 9.5 percent in 2010. In its attempt to fight this increase, Arizona's legislature keeps the state in political hot water. In October 2010, it passed SB 1070, a crime-fighting measure designed to curtail chronic illegal immigration and smuggling along the border. This bill quickly became politically divisive and was widely attacked as a racist measure. Within months of its passage, a gun battle between five bandits and a U.S. Border Patrol agent resulted in the officer's death near Nogales, further promoting the perception that Arizona remains a lawless region where criminals operate openly and without impunity.

D. L. Turner
Scott H. Decker
Arizona State University

See Also: Arpaio, Joseph M.; Border Patrol; Earp, Wyatt; *Miranda v. Arizona*; Native American Tribal Police; Rural Police; Television, Crime in; Texas Rangers; Urbanization; Vigilantism.

Further Readings
Arizona Department of Corrections. "Arizona Death Penalty History." http://www.azcorrections.gov/ Prisca_Datasearch_DeathPenalty.aspx (Accessed September 2011).
Murphy, James M. *Laws, Courts, and Lawyers Through the Years in Arizona*. Tucson: University of Arizona Press, 1970.
Stuart, Gary L. *Miranda. The Story of America's Right to Remain Silent*. Tucson: University of Arizona Press, 2004.

Arkansas

Arkansas was granted statehood on June 15, 1836; it was the 25th U.S. state. Arkansas was admitted to the Union as the 13th slave state because of its plentiful cotton cultivation. By the start of the Civil War, slaves comprised more than 25 percent of the state's population. Arkansas seceded along with other slave states to form the Confederate States of America at the outbreak of war. An examination of the state's history has much to offer in terms of understanding crime, police, and punishment in the United States.

Crime
Arkansas was riddled with criminals and outlaws before it gained statehood. Families moving west to settle land were prime targets on the Arkansas frontier because they were carrying their possessions with them. The lack of communication and centralized law enforcement units made it difficult to apprehend these thieves. It was not unusual for these families to be killed if they refused to give up their valuables to the thieves. One outlaw who was known throughout the country was Henry Starr, who came from a family of thieves and outlaw, and took over the family business in the 1890s. Starr was known for robbing banks on horseback with other thieves. A warrant for his arrest was issued after he killed U.S. marshal Floyd Wilson in 1892. He was sentenced to death by hanging by Judge Parker in Fort Smith in 1893. Starr managed to escape his death sentence after a courageous negotiation in which he convinced fellow outlaw Cherokee Bill to give up his gun during a shooting rampage. Starr was issued a pardon after this incident. Starr continued to have various run-ins with the police in Arkansas

and what is now Oklahoma. In 1921, Starr met his end when he was shot by the president of a bank he was robbing. Starr died four days later in the Boone County Jail.

Several other accounts of violence during the mid-1800s can be attributed to the fact that carrying weapons such as knives and guns was a common practice during this time. One account describes two friends who quarreled over a race and ended with both drawing their guns and shooting each other. Increased taxes on alcohol during the Civil War led moonshiners to produce and sell illegal alcohol in Arkansas. In 1898, John Burris, a local tax collector, went on a seven-day trip from Hot Springs to Scott County, where he destroyed several stills, poured out gallons of beer and whiskey, and arrested 23 men for the illegal production of alcohol. These men were transported to Fort Smith for trial, and they received sentences that ranged from 30 days in the local jail to two years in a U.S. penitentiary.

Racial crime and vigilante justice was also very common throughout Arkansas history. Lynching was the most common form of punishment imposed by vigilante groups in the early 1900s. Among those who were lynched was John Carter, an African American man accused of assaulting a white woman. Carter was hanged, shot, lynched, and burned in the center of Little Rock's African American community. Lynchings occurred even after a police force and penal system had been established in Arkansas.

Police

In order to combat the violent crime that plagued early Arkansas, Governor Carl Bailey created the first state-run police department in 1937 under Act 166. Prior to this decision, law enforcement was largely left to local entities and individual citizens. Many of these local forces feared the transition to a state-run police department because it was believed the police would become a force of oppression and gain too much power. The shift in attitudes for members of the legislature came from the fear of crime and from the increasing number of automobiles in Arkansas. Statistics show that in 1934, the fatality rate from automobiles in Arkansas was about 24 deaths for every 100 million miles traveled. Translated to today's rates, that would be equivalent to about 7,000 deaths for every 100 million miles traveled. The fear of crime came from the ineptitude of local law enforcement to arrest nonlocal criminals. Hot Springs saw many mobsters during this time, and law enforcement officials in the city were easily manipulated. The first police force had 13 members. Today, there are more than 1,000 officers and employees within the Arkansas State Police Department.

Punishment

Before he served as governor, Carl Bailey was the prosecuting attorney for the state of Arkansas. During his time in this position, Bailey was responsible for the extradition of Charles "Lucky" Luciano to New York. Luciano fled to Hot Springs, which had become a haven for mobsters. After Luciano was arrested, Bailey was bribed to not follow through with the extradition. Bailey stated that Arkansas would not be bought and publicly denied the bribe. Luciano was returned to New York, where he was convicted of running multiple prostitution rings.

The first state penitentiary in Arkansas was established in 1839 by Governor James Conway. This penitentiary was built where the Arkansas State Capitol now stands. In 1902, land for the Cummins prison was purchased; Cummins is still in operation today. A permanent death chamber was established and housed at the Cummins prison. The first man to be executed at Cummins was Lee Sims, who was convicted of rape, in 1902. Today, there are 20 facilities controlled by the Arkansas Department of Corrections. These range from work-release programs to supermax facilities. The state's death row is housed in the Varner Unit's supermax facility in Lincoln County. Executions are carried out adjacent to Varner at Cummins Unit.

Major changes were made to the Arkansas penal system after the landmark case *Holt v. Sarver* (1969). Judge J. Smith Henley presided over this case, which was brought by prison inmates who alleged physical abuses and torture. A device known as the "Tucker telephone" was used by prison officials to discipline inmates. This device used an old-fashioned crank telephone to issue electrical shocks through wires connected to an inmate's genitals. These complaints came from Cummins Farm Unit and

Prison inmates and guards at work, likely in the Cummins State Farm Unit in Gould, Arkansas, around 1934. This prison farm unit was the site of torture and abuse that led to statewide prison reform in Arkansas more than 30 years later in the landmark case Holt v. Sarver *(1969). The Cummins prison is still in use today and houses the state's execution chamber.*

Tucker Reformatory. During this time, guards were simply armed inmates called trusties. Judge Henley sided with the inmate petition and declared the prison practices unconstitutional. Statewide prison reform followed this decision to ensure all prisons met state and constitutional regulations.

Patty Hill
University of Arkansas at Little Rock

See Also: *Holt v. Sarver*; Luciano, "Lucky;" Lynchings; Moonshine; Parker, Isaac; Penitentiary Study Commission; Prisoner's Rights.

Further Readings
Moneyhon, Carl H. *Arkansas and the New South, 1874–1929.* Fayetteville: University of Arkansas Press, 1997.
Whayne, Jeannie M., et al. *Arkansas: A Narrative History.* Fayetteville: University of Arkansas Press, 2002.
Williams, C. Fred and S. Charles Bolton. *A Documentary History of Arkansas.* Fayetteville: University of Arkansas Press, 1984.

Arpaio, Joseph M.

Joseph M. Arpaio was born on June 14, 1932, in Springfield, Massachusetts. He is the sheriff of Maricopa County, Arizona, which includes Phoenix and the surrounding area. Joe Arpaio was first elected to the office in 1992 and has been reelected every four years since. He proudly promotes himself as "America's Toughest Sheriff." As sheriff, he is responsible for managing the county jail and it is in this role that he has garnered the most attention. Arpaio is a controversial figure who has been described as seeking publicity and has been accused of abusing his power and of committing civil rights violations.

Arpaio's mother died giving birth to him. He served in the U.S. Army from 1950 to 1953 as a military police officer. After being discharged, Arpaio lived in Washington, D.C., where he became a police officer, and later moved to Las Vegas, Nevada. In 1957, he was appointed as a special agent with what was then the Federal Bureau of Narcotics (now the Drug Enforcement Administration [DEA]). He married his wife Ava in 1958 and has two children. Arpaio spent 25 years with the DEA, where he served overseas in Turkey and other Middle Eastern countries as well as Mexico and other Central and South American countries. After 32 years as a federal law enforcement officer, he retired as the special agent in charge of the DEA's Phoenix Division.

As sheriff, Arpaio oversees over 10,000 inmates in the county jail system. In August 1993, he created the country's largest "tent city," where 2,000 convicted men and women live, eat, and sleep in a canvas-covered field on the jail grounds and where, he is fond of saying, the vacancy sign is always on. Arpaio has created "get tough" conditions by instituting rules that forbid coffee, all but G-rated movies, and TVs that air anything but the Disney and Weather Channels. He also banned pornographic material; the United States Court of Appeals for the Ninth Circuit upheld the ban, deciding that the policy was not a violation of the First Amendment. In 2007, Arpaio created KJOE, a radio station that airs classical music, opera, patriotic music, and educational programming throughout the jail.

He reduced meals to twice each day, feeds inmates surplus food (such as serving corn dogs for both meals for days on end), and removed salt and pepper from dining areas; the average cost of a meal in his jail system is under 20 cents. He is also well known for issuing all male inmates pink underwear. In fact, he ordered most items inmates wear to be pink, including the towels they use and the sheets on their beds. All inmates wear the traditional black and white striped jumpsuits. Also harking back to an earlier era, he reinstated chain gangs as a way of providing the county with free labor. Men, women, and juveniles remove graffiti, sweep streets, and bury unclaimed bodies in the county cemetery. Arpaio also started a program in which the nearly 300 people arrested each day can be viewed as they are processed into the jail

Sheriff Joe Arpaio during an appearance at a Tea Party Patriots event in Phoenix, Arizona, in February 2011. Arpaio has been reelected every four years since 1992.

on live streaming video over the Internet on the Maricopa County Sheriff's Department Web page.

In contrast to the tent city, Arpaio relocated the county animal shelter to climate-controlled buildings on the jail compound that formerly housed inmates. Inmates who are chosen for the coveted work assignment at the no-kill shelter are trained in animal behavior and nutrition. The jail's hog farm, worked by inmates, provides fertilizer for the Christmas tree farm, also cultivated by inmates, where trees are sold for less than $10 each during the holiday season. He also established Hard Knocks High, the only accredited high school in the United States with a sheriff serving as principal.

In federal court, the Maricopa County jails have been found to violate the constitutional rights of inmates in areas including medical care.

Most recently, Arpaio has been sued by the U.S. Justice Department for refusing to answer to federal authorities who are investigating allegations of discrimination stemming from racial profiling as well as conducting illegal searches and seizures. Arpaio does not hide that his law enforcement officers, as well as a posse of nearly 3,000 volunteer community members, regularly pursue undocumented people in predominantly Latino communities in anti-immigration efforts. Some question whether, at the local law enforcement level, he has the power to arrest noncriminal undocumented people and turn them over to Immigration and Customs Enforcement (ICE), the agency responsible for deportation.

Gennifer Furst
William Paterson University

See Also: Arizona; Immigration Crimes; Posses; Sheriffs.

Further Readings
Arpaio, J. and L. Sherman. *Joe's Law: America's Toughest Sheriff Takes on Illegal Immigration, Drugs and Everything Else That Threatens America*. New York: AMACON, 2008.
Maricopa County Sheriff's Office. http://www.mcso.org (Accessed November 2011).

Arraignment

According to the Sixth Amendment arraignment clause, arraignment is a pretrial procedure in which a defendant is "informed of the nature and cause of the accusation." In other words, he/she is told specifically with which crime or crimes he/she is charged. The first mention of the concept of arraignment is found in the Assize of Clarendon (1166). It is also found in the Magna Carta (1215).

The right to notification of charges was important to the early British colonists in America. Many were religious dissenters. Some of them had been arrested, tried, and sentenced because of their religious beliefs without being informed of the charges against them. Perhaps for this reason, many colonies built the concept of arraignment into their laws. By the time the Constitution was written, most states had included the concept of arraignment in their own constitutions.

Arraignment Process
In some states, arraignments occur at the same time as a defendant's initial appearance before a magistrate or judge. This usually takes place within 24 to 48 hours of arrest. In *County of Riverside v. McLaughlin* (1991), however, the Supreme Court found that there may be circumstances under which a person who is subject to a warrantless arrest may be held longer than 48 hours. At an initial appearance, the defendant is informed of the charges and of his/her right to an attorney. Bail is then set or the defendant is released on his/her own recognizance, that is, the defendant is freed as long as he/she agrees to return to court voluntarily when ordered to do so. If bail is set but the defendant cannot afford it, he/she will spend the time until his/her next court appearance in jail.

In other states, arraignments occur at some time after the initial appearance. Arraignments are conducted for both misdemeanors and felonies. In the case of misdemeanors, the initial appearance and arraignment occur simultaneously. The person is asked to enter a plea. If he/she pleads guilty, a sentence is handed down immediately. If the plea is not guilty, the person is either given a chance to post bond or is released on his/her own recognizance.

If the charge is a felony, the arraignment takes place after probable cause has been established. Probable cause is established in one of two ways: the information (which is a formal charging document filed with the court by the prosecutor that names the specific charge or charges of the accused) or the indictment (which is a charging document issued by a grand jury that names the specific charge or charges against the accused). One of these documents is presented to the court. The specificity of the charges is required in order to make the defendant aware of what he/she is accused of so that he/she can prepare a knowledgeable defense. It also helps ensure that the defendant is not being charged twice for the same crime.

After the charges are read, the defendant is required to enter a plea. According to *Hamilton v. Alabama* (1961), arraignment is a considered a "critical stage" under the Sixth Amendment. A defendant is required to have counsel (unless he/she has knowingly and willingly waived that right) during a critical stage because of the chance of losing his/her freedom. The defendant may plead one of three ways: guilty, not guilty, or nolo contendere. If a defendant pleads guilty, the judge must determine that the defendant understands the rights being waived, that the plea was made voluntarily, and that the plea has a basis in fact. If the judge is satisfied as to these facts, the defendant is either sentenced on the spot or a sentencing date is set. If a defendant pleads not guilty, a trial date is set, and he/she either returns to jail (if he/she has not been able to make bail), remains free on bail, or continues release on his/her own recognizance. If a defendant refuses to enter a plea or stands mute, the court enters a not guilty plea for him/her.

A defendant may also plead nolo contendere (literally, "I will not contest it"). This means that while the defendant is not admitting to being guilty of the charges, neither is he/she refuting them. Essentially, he/she is willing to accept punishment. This plea is often entered in cases where the defendant also faces civil action for his/her criminal actions. Since the defendant has not admitted guilt, the plea cannot be used against him/her in a civil case. A defendant who pleads nolo contendere, like the defendant who pleads guilty, is sentenced immediately or given a sentencing date.

Because the defendant knows exactly what he/she is charged with, arraignment often marks the beginning of plea bargaining, which may continue until the trial, or, in some states, until just before a verdict has been reached. In a plea bargain, the defendant agrees to plead guilty in exchange for some benefit from the prosecution. There are three types of plea bargains: charge, count, and sentence bargaining. In charge bargaining, the defendant pleads guilty to a charge that is less serious than the one with which he/she was originally charged (e.g., simple assault instead of aggravated assault). In count bargaining, the defendant agrees to plead guilty if the number of counts against him/her is reduced. In sentence bargaining, the defendant agrees to plead guilty in exchange for a shorter sentence. If the judge determines that the defendant understands his/her rights, that he/she voluntarily waived them, and that there is a factual basis to the charges, he/she will accept the plea agreement.

James Geistman
Ohio Northern University

See Also: Bail and Bond; Defendant's Rights; Magna Carta; Plea; Trials.

Further Readings
Carp, Robert A. and Ronald Stidham. *Judicial Process in America,* 8th ed. Washington, DC: CQ Press, 2010.
del Carmen, Rolando V. *Criminal Procedure: Law and Practice,* 8th ed. Belmont, CA: Wadsworth, 2009.
Harr, J. Scott and Kären M. Hess. *Constitutional Law and the Criminal Justice System,* 4th ed. Belmont, CA: Wadsworth, 2008.
Neubauer, David W. *America's Courts and the Criminal Justice System,* 8th ed. Belmont, CA: Wadsworth, 2005.

Arthur, Chester (Administration of)

Chester A. Arthur (1829–86) was born in Vermont, though his opponents claimed his "real" birthplace was across the nearby border in Canada. He was a lawyer, a Republican, an advocate for black rights, and a firm believer in the spoils system. He received a patronage job as collector of customs in New York City under the Grant administration and rose to become a power in state Republican circles. He had to resign his position in 1879 after an investigation revealed widespread corruption even though it did not implicate him. In 1880, Arthur was chosen as running mate to James A. Garfield to unify the party. When Garfield died after being shot in 1881, Arthur, the spoilsman, became president. He later refused to intervene when the man convicted of Garfield's assassination, Charles Guiteau, sought a stay of execution. Arthur's focus was reform, including, to the surprise of many, hiring based on merit. The Pendleton Act was the first act to require a merit examination for would-be federal employees. Although the Pendleton Act covered only 10 percent of federal jobs, it was the beginning of a long, slow process of replacing spoils with merit. He improved the navy, reduced government waste, and outlawed polygamy. The Chinese Exclusion Act, the first-ever general immigration law, came into effect during his administration; initially, Arthur vetoed it but he signed it after Congress shortened its duration.

Arthur called for expansion of the court system to handle the increased volume in the federal courts but requested no specific change, noting that Congress was already dealing with the situation. The system's increased workload was initially thought to be a consequence of the dislocation of Reconstruction, but Arthur recognized that the increase was permanent, coincident to the industrialization of the United States.

Cowboys and Indians

More bothersome was the ongoing lawlessness in the Arizona Territory and into Mexico, where a gang of 50–100 cowboys was engaging in lawless and brutal acts. Arthur was unsure if the territorial government was adequate to the task and believed that, given its reach into Mexico, the situation might better be served by a national government effort under the antifilibuster laws. Arthur interpreted the law to preclude federal assistance to a territory suffering "domestic violence." Only states were entitled to call on the federal government because the revision to the federal statutes dropped the provision covering territories.

Chester Arthur's presidential party crossing the Snake River on horseback during an excursion into Yellowstone National Park and northwestern Wyoming in 1883. Arthur struggled throughout his presidency to impose order on western and southwestern territories, especially in underpopulated areas with an insufficient nearby civilian population to form posses.

In the territories, there were areas with insufficient nearby civilian population to form posses. The army from nearby posts had manpower to fill the void in order to control the cowboys. As Reconstruction began to falter, however, federal law barred the army from participating in a posse comitatus. Arthur speculated that perhaps army assistance to a territory in enforcing its laws was not contrary to the intent of the Posse Comitatus Act. Before sending troops to enforce the law in Wyoming for a 17-month period, Arthur sought reassurance that he was authorized to do so. A report by the Senate Judiciary Committee in 1882 indicated that the law restricted marshals only; the president still had the authority to call out troops.

In addition to cowboys, Arthur had to deal with Indians. He found fault with the ongoing treatment of Indian tribes individually and with the continual renegotiation of agreements that allowed the Indians to live in traditional ways on land that was no longer limitlessly abundant. Reservation Indians often clashed with whites covetous of their land. After wasting thousands of lives and millions of dollars, a new approach was implemented—acculturation and absorption into the general population after making state and territorial law applicable to reservations, including fair access to courts, adequate Indian schools, and allotment in severalty. The belief was that Indians, aware that the hunting life was history, when given the opportunity to own their own land would break away from their tribes and become farmers.

Polygamy and Other Issues
The most significant crime Arthur sought to stop was polygamy in Utah and other territories. The Morrill Anti-Bigamy Law of 1862 outlawed polygamy, but it was hard to prove a case, so there were few arrests. Brigham Young was arrested but was released without standing trial. The law was on the books but mostly unenforced, and Mormons expanded into Idaho, Arizona, and other territories in relatively large numbers, causing worry and an apparent need for new antipolygamy measures. Because polygamous marriages were performed secretly and thus were hard to prove, Arthur wanted a law allowing a wife to testify against her husband and a law mandating that the person performing the ceremony had to file a document in territorial court.

He got the Edmunds Act in 1882. Probably ex post facto and thus unconstitutional, Edmunds banned cohabitation with more than one woman. Under the law, Arthur disenfranchised all practicing polygamists and put more than 1,300 men in jail. In 1885, Idaho began requiring all citizens to swear their opposition to polygamy and any organization supporting it or lose their right to vote. In 1887, Congress disincorporated the Mormon church under the Edmunds-Tucker Act and seized its property. The law also mandated loyalty oaths for officeholders, barring even nonpolygamous Mormons from office. Thousands of Mormons left for Canada and Mexico. The Mormons abandoned polygamy in 1890 after a new church president had a revelation.

Arthur made other efforts to maintain order. The Foran Act outlawed contract labor, a source of abuse of immigrants as well as a tool for weakening unions and driving down wages. The Star Route scandal involved postal service employees, but two trials failed to win convictions (the second trial was ordered after the foreman claimed a bribe attempt by the federal government during the first). Arthur also issued a warning to Sooners to keep out of Indian Territory; it was not open for settlement.

Arthur sought a second term in 1884 to avoid lame duck status. He recognized that his health was fading because he had Bright's disease, a kidney disorder. He was denied the nomination after he alienated both sides of his party. Arthur's administration was noted for his efforts to reduce abuses of the law and to combat scandals.

John H. Barnhill
Independent Scholar

See Also: Bigamy/Polygamy; Frontier Crime; Garfield, James; Guiteau, Charles; Pendleton Act of 1883; Posses; *Reynolds v. United States*.

Further Readings
American Presidency Project. "Chester A. Arthur: First Annual Message." http://www.presidency.ucsb.edu/ws/index.php?pid=29522#ixzz1NHQe46FS (Accessed September 2011).

Felicetti, Gary and John Luce. "The Posse Comitatus Act: Liberation From the Lawyers." http://www.carlisle.army.mil/usawc/parameters/Articles/04autumn/felicett.pdf (Accessed September 2011).

History.com. "Chester A. Arthur." http://www.history.com/topics/chester-a-arthur (Accessed September 2011).

Miller Center. "American President: Chester A. Arthur (1829–1886)." http://millercenter.org/president/arthur (Accessed September 2011).

Mormonwiki.com. "Post–Civil War Persecution and the End of Polygamy." http://www.mormonwiki.com/Post-Civil_War_Persecution (Accessed September 2011).

Articles of Confederation

The Articles of Confederation were created under the Second Continental Congress in 1777, though the states did not fully approve the document until 1781. Since the colonies declared themselves independent in 1776, they were technically under their own rule until the articles took effect in 1781. Yet the Articles of Confederation were not a binding document for the newly independent colonies. Instead, the articles acted as a loose organizing document giving the new states comrades and the support of one another but little more.

Originally, plans for the articles looked toward a loose confederation of states. John Dickenson headed the committee to form the articles, and he foresaw a strong central government. Unfortunately for him, when he presented his plan to the Continental Congress in July 1776, hostilities immediately arose. His plan placed the western territories under the control of Congress, even though much of the territory was claimed by various states. He also called for equal representation among all states. States like Virginia and Massachusetts held the largest populations, and accordingly they argued for more representation. Additionally, and most volatile, was Dickenson's proposal that African Americans and whites be equally counted for the population so that taxes could be determined. Clearly, the south opposed taxing on population the most.

Congress set out to redraft the articles and those adopted in November 1777 barely resembled Dickenson's strong central government plan. The articles were drafted by revolutionary leaders who shared the philosophy that a central government, removed from the people, would breed corruption and tyranny. These were the same arguments used throughout the Revolutionary period to ignite the colonists to rise up against English rule.

Provisions

The Articles of Confederation made Congress the dominant force, with no executive branch of government or federal courts. The articles called for a president, but he was a figurehead at best as everything had to pass through Congress. There were no federal courts because there was no united nation at this time. Furthermore, the Articles of Confederation crippled itself with its own binding rules. The five basic foundations of the articles stated that all bills before Congress required two-thirds vote for passage, any amendment to the articles needed a unanimous vote, Congress had no power to regulate commerce, and Congress could not enforce taxes as the states would pay them voluntarily. Also, it loosely set the boundaries of states and territories along natural boundaries, like the Great Lakes, the Mississippi River, and the Appalachian Mountains.

Since the writers of the adopted articles feared a central government, and the legacy of perceived unfair taxation still lingered in the minds of many colonists, no earnest attempts were made to force states to pay taxes. Congress had no means to support itself or the fledging confederation, and most states refused to pay taxes on the grounds that they needed the monies for their own upkeep. The continual battlefront also played a key role in states' refusing to pay taxes, as the general populace remained largely divided on its support of the war. In spite of these obstacles, Congress did pass the Land Ordinance of 1785 and the Northwest Ordinance of 1787.

The two ordinances came to be seen as a way for Congress to secure funds, since it had no means of enforcing taxes. The Land Ordinance of 1785 said that the Northwest Territory would be sold to pay off debt, particularly as France loaned the colonies money to support the Revolutionary War. In addition to selling off this land, the ordinance mandated the land be divided into townships of six miles square with 36 sections of one square mile each. Farms were to be 640 acres, to secure family units, and one section of each township must be secured for a public school. An attempt to outlaw slavery in the territory failed by one vote, but the issue quickly resurfaced with the ordinance's revisions in 1787. In 1787, the ordinance stayed the same, except slavery was forbidden and a clause enabled territories to become states of equal status with the original 13 once obtaining 60,000 inhabitants.

The Articles of Confederation stood as a loosely binding document for the states, making them a confederation but not a nation. Sometimes the short-lived nature of the articles gets them dubbed as a failure, but they were not. They did what was intended: to give the newly independent colonies a guide through the war to discover what they wanted and needed for a government. Yet growing foreign and domestic problems forced the states to reexamine the articles in 1787 when Britain refused to send an ambassador, France demanded repayments of funds, Spain seized lands along the Mississippi River, inflation crippled the economy, interstate squabbles roared about boundaries and taxes, and uprisings like Shays's Rebellion threatened the confederacy and the states. These were the issues intended to be dealt with by Congress and the articles, but practice verses theory proved to be difficult.

At the Annapolis Convention, Congress met to deal with interstate commerce disputes but quickly decided to disband and remeet in Philadelphia to reform the articles. In May 1787, 55 delegates from 12 states (Rhode Island boycotted) assembled, and almost immediately they began drafting the Constitution versus reforming the Articles of Confederation.

Annessa A. Babic
New York Institute of Technology

See Also: American Revolution and Criminal Justice; Colonial Courts; Constitution of the United States of America.

Further Readings
Jensen, Merrill. *The Articles of Confederation: An Interpretation of the Social-Constitutional History of the American Revolution, 1774–1781.* Madison: University of Wisconsin Press, 1989.
Our Documents Initiative. "The Articles of Confederation." http://www.ourdocuments.gov/doc.php?flash=true&doc=3 (Accessed September 2011).
Sobel, Russell S. "In Defense of the Articles of Confederation and the Contribution Mechanism as a Means of Government Finance: A General Comment on the Literature." *Public Choice*, v.99/3–4 (1999).

Atlanta, Georgia

Atlanta is the capital of Georgia and the state's most populous city at more than 540,000 (the population of the metropolitan Atlanta area is more than 5 million). The Atlanta area was settled by Native American tribes before the arrival of the first white settlers in the 1820s. Atlanta suffered severe damage during the Civil War but was rebuilt on the model of the "new South" with a diversified economy. Today, Atlanta is a center of business and commerce (among the companies with headquarters in Atlanta are UPS, Coca-Cola, Home Depot, and Turner Broadcasting) and boasts a transportation hub that includes the busiest airport in the United States (Hartsfield-Jackson Atlanta International Airport).

The Atlanta Police Department
The history of the city of Atlanta dates back to 1837 when the site of what was then called Terminus was marked by railroad surveyors. The organization of police services developed gradually: Originally, the town was patrolled by a marshal (first appointed in 1844) and then by an elected policeman (starting in 1853). By 1858, the number of policemen increased to 20, and in 1873, the first Board of Police Commissioners met; among their official acts was appointing Thomas Jones as the first chief of police of Atlanta. In 1896, the detective bureau was reorganized under Bradley Slaughter and began using the Bertillon system of identification through anthropometric measurements. In 1918, the first two female police officers joined the force (although women were not

assigned to regular beat patrols until 1957), and in 1924, the Women's Bureau was established. In 1947, the police union, dominated by members of the Ku Klux Klan, was abolished, and the following year, the first black officers joined the force. These black officers had limited authority, however: They were not authorized to arrest white criminals until 1962 and were not assigned to regular patrols until 1966.

In 1955, Howard Baugh and Ernest Lyons became the first black detectives on the force, which by this time included 15 black officers. Baugh became the first black superior officer in 1961, and in that same year, the police department was recognized by the U.S. Civil Rights Commission for the role it played in the peaceful integration of public high schools in Atlanta. In 1974, Maynard Jackson became the first black mayor of Atlanta and made improving race relations in the city, including reforming the police department and increasing the number of black officers on the force, a priority (Atlanta at this time was about 60 percent black while the police department was only 23 percent black). Jackson created the new post of public safety commissioner and appointed A. Reginald Eaves to this position while relegating the white chief of police, John Inman (who had resisted court orders to increase the number of black officers), to a figurehead position. Eaves implemented a team policing program that is credited with reducing homicides from 248 in 1974 to 185 in 1975. By 1981, he also increased the proportion of black officers to 35 percent, second only to Washington, D.C., among U.S. city police forces. In 1991, the first woman achieved the rank of major, and in 1994, Beverly J. Harvard became chief of police, the first black woman to achieve this rank in a major U.S. city.

Crime in Atlanta has declined sharply in the first decade of the 21st century. In 2002, Atlanta ranked as the third most dangerous city in America, according to the CQ Press Index, while in 2009 it was ranked 16th, and in 2010 it was ranked 25th. The city's crime rate fell from 11.2 percent to 8.2 percent between 2002 and 2009, and the rate of violent crime dropped by about 40 percent during that period. Among Georgia metropolitan areas with more than 100,000 inhabitants, Atlanta often has the most crimes because

The city of Atlanta was the first major city in the United States to have a black female chief of police. Above, a black policewoman at work in Atlanta in July 2008.

of its large population, but it has a lower rate per 100,000 population than many other cities. For instance, 323 murders were reported in Atlanta in 2009, for a rate of 5.9 per 100,000; although that is the largest number of murders reported, several metropolitan areas had a higher rate, including Brunswick with a murder rate of 15.5 per 100,000 and Macon with 23 per 100,000. Similarly, Atlanta had 9,578 reported robberies in 2009 for a rate of 174.3 per 100,000; although that is the largest number of robberies reported for any metropolitan area, more than 100,000 inhabitants, several cities had higher rates of robbery, including Savannah, Columbus, and Brunswick. In 2009, Atlanta also had 1,156 reported forcible rapes (21 per 100,000), 12,838 cases of aggravated assault (233.7 per 100,000), 53,867 burglaries (980.4 per 100,000), and 21,944 motor vehicle thefts (399.4 per 100,000).

The 1906 Race Riot

In the early 20th century, Atlanta was a growing city beset, as was much of the American south, with racial and economic tensions. The two factors were intertwined, as white capitalists considered the black population a cheap labor pool to be exploited while blacks naturally wanted to improve their status. Many had already done so: Atlanta at this time had the largest black middle class in America, as well as the world's largest concentration of black colleges. Some whites did not agree that blacks should enjoy equal rights, and in the 1906 campaign for governor of Georgia, two candidates, Clark Howell and Hoke Smith, explicitly highlighted racial issues, including their desire to prevent black men from voting (a right granted in 1870 by the Fifteenth Amendment to the U.S. Constitution). Atlanta newspapers fanned the flames of racial hatred by carrying stories of lynchings and calling for a renewed Ku Klux Klan to "control" blacks. A series of sensationalistic stories alleging attacks on white women by blacks provided the final spark that set off the riot on September 12, 1906.

The riot began in downtown Atlanta (the Five Points area) as a mob of white citizens attacked blacks. The riot continued for days (some felt the Atlanta Police Department, then an all-white organization, did not respond sufficiently), and the official death count was 12 blacks and two whites but many historians think the death toll for blacks was much higher, in the range of 20–40 dead. Black businesses and homes were also destroyed. In the aftermath of the riot, black and white community leaders began meeting to try to address the city's racial problems, marking the beginning of the interracial civil rights movement.

Leo Frank

In 1913, Leo Frank, the Jewish American superintendent of the National Pencil Company in Atlanta, was convicted of the murder of Mary Phagan, a 13-year-old girl who worked in the factory. Frank was sentenced to death but his sentence was commuted to life imprisonment. In August 1915, he was kidnapped from the Midgeville State Penitentiary and lynched in the town of Frey's Mill, near Marietta, Georgia. As was common in the lynching of black men, photographs of his body, including clear images of the lynch mob, were taken and sold in local stores. Many felt that Frank had been accused and convicted because of his religion (in 1986, he was granted a posthumous pardon from the Georgia Board of Pardons and Paroles); this motivated the founding of the Anti-Defamation League by the Jewish service organization B'nai B'rith.

The Atlanta Youth Murders

Atlanta was rocked in 1979–81 by the murders of 28 children and young adults, all of them black. The first victim was Edward Smith, age 14, who disappeared on July 21, 1979; the last was Timothy Hill, 13, who disappeared on March 13, 1981. The murders received wide publicity, and the Federal Bureau of Investigation (FBI) was called in to assist in the investigation. In May 1981, Wayne Williams (a black man) became a suspect in the case, and in 1982, he was convicted of several of the murders, based largely on physical evidence (hairs and other fibers from Williams's home were found on the victims); the others were also attributed to him by the Atlanta Police Department.

The 1996 Olympics Bombing

The Summer Olympics were held in Atlanta in 1996, and a large public park, Centennial Olympic Park, was constructed in downtown Atlanta as a gathering location for visitors. On July 27, 1966, a bomb exploded in this park, injuring more than 100 people and killing one and indirectly causing another death as a journalist suffered a heart attack while covering the bombing. This incident received worldwide coverage as it occurred during the Olympics (President Bill Clinton denounced it as a terrorist incident).

Security guard Richard Jewell, an initial suspect in the bombing, was eventually cleared and filed several lawsuits claiming he had been slandered by news organizations. Eric Rudolph, who was also suspected of involvement in three other bombings (of abortion clinics and a bar), was formally named a suspect in October 1998 but evaded capture for several years. Rudolph was arrested in 2003, pled guilty to all four bombings, and is currently serving four life terms without parole in a maximum security federal prison.

Sarah Boslaugh
Kennesaw State University

See Also: African Americans; Georgia; Jewish Americans; Lynchings; Racism; Terrorism.

Further Readings
Atlanta Police Department. "History of the APD." http://www.atlantapd.org/apdhistory.aspx (Accessed June 2011).
Dulaney, W. Marvin. *Black Police in America*. Bloomington: Indiana University Press, 1996.
Headley, Bernard D. *The Atlanta Youth Murders and the Politics of Race*. Carbondale: Southern Illinois University Press, 1998.
Lohr, Kathy. "Century-Old Race Riot Still Resonates in Atlanta." National Public Radio. http://www.npr.org/templates/story/story.php?storyId=6106285 (Accessed June 2011).
Schuster, Henry with Charles Stone. *Hunting Eric Rudolph*. New York: Berkley Books, 2005.

Attica

From September 9 to 13, 1971, prisoners in New York State's Attica correctional facility held control of this maximum-security prison. During the revolt, 43 people died, most when the authorities retook control. State police and correctional officers killed 29 prisoners and 10 correctional staff members and wounded 80 people during the quarter of an hour that it took officials to retake the prison.

The McKay Commission, which investigated Attica, called it the "bloodiest one-day encounter between Americans since the Civil War." When these events occurred, nearly 60 percent of Attica's population was African American and 100 percent of the correctional officers were white. While the prisoner revolt at Attica took place over five days, the event is best understood within three contexts that span decades both before and after the Attica revolt.

Attica Over Time

Ironically, Attica prison opened in 1931 as a response to a wave of prison riots in New York and elsewhere in the late 1920s. Attica was to be "a convict's paradise," with spring beds and radios in each cell. From the time it was opened until the late 1960s, Attica experienced occasional prisoner uprisings, as did many maximum-security prisons. However, the 1960s provided a different political context. This was a decade of protest—and of government use of force to suppress protests. The period included the civil rights movement (including prisoner's rights), anti–Vietnam War protests, violent disturbances in America's urban centers, and prison riots in New York and other states. These events saw government repression of protest and activist organizations, including the Black Panthers and Black Muslims. These events provided a model of violence for both prisoners and the state. The assassinations of Malcolm X, Martin Luther King, Jr., Robert Kennedy, Fred Hampton (a Black Panther leader in Chicago), and George Jackson that occurred in the decade before the five-day revolt at Attica also provided a political context for violence.

In addition, during the 1960s, a new emphasis on research on all aspects of criminal justice from arrest to parole was raising questions about the legitimacy of criminal justice processes and was finding race to be an important factor throughout. Through these events and this research, the understanding of the politics of criminal justice was enhanced. In this environment, prisoners were redefining themselves as political prisoners, and the criminal justice process was seen as an exercise in political power to control the underclass of society (especially African Americans). This allowed prisoners to transform their criminal/deviant/prisoner status into a more empowered political status befitting men.

In New York, prisoner disturbances in New York City's House of Detention (Tombs) in August 1970 and Auburn Correctional Facility in November 1970 preceded the events at Attica. Prisoners from Auburn were transferred to Attica and were placed in segregation. This was contrary to promises from correctional officials that there would be no reprisals for those involved in the Auburn protest over the handling of a Black Solidarity Day event.

The Attica Revolt

On September 8, 1971, confusion over the handling of an inmate interaction (whether it was a fight or horseplay) provided the spark for what was to come on September 9. On September 9, when a lieutenant involved in the September 8 incident asked a group of prisoners to return to their cells after breakfast, he was attacked. From the chaotic violence that followed, prisoners eventually gained control of the institution after a failed weld on a gate allowed them access to a central control area called Times Square. The McKay Commission that investigated the events at Attica reported that the inmates had control of all four cellblocks and all of the tunnels and yards in the Attica complex and that more than 1,200 inmates had gathered in "D" yard with more than 40 hostages.

New York Governor Nelson Rockefeller, shown here in February 1975, gave the order for the National Guard and state police to retake control of Attica prison on September 13, 1971.

While the prison revolt at Attica was part of a larger pattern of prison disturbances and protests during the late 1960s and early 1970s, for a number of reasons, the negotiations that occurred in an attempt to obtain a peaceful settlement made the event much more significant and visible. That the negotiations took place at all was unique because negotiating with prisoners was not common practice. Further, an "observers committee" containing prominent African American and Hispanic political leaders from New York, activist lawyers, journalists, activists form the Black Panthers and Young Lords, and others representing more conservative perspectives gave some celebrity to the negotiations.

Members of the committee were used to mediate the negotiations and served to provide diverse perspectives and advice to Commissioner Russell Oswald. The decision to allow television reporters to enter the prison and film negotiations and comments of prisoners and hostages brought the events inside the prison to national attention. During the five days of negotiations, tensions within groups of correctional personnel and their families, prisoners and their families, and state police officials continued to build. On the evening of September 12, 1971, negotiations finally ended.

September 13, 1971

On the morning of September 13, 1971, after a final ultimatum from Commissioner Oswald was read to prisoners, the prisoners took eight hostages to catwalks and held knives to their throats or bodies. Fifteen minutes after inmates rejected Commissioner Oswald's ultimatum, a helicopter dropped tear gas into the yard and shotgun and rifle fire from state police and correctional officers commenced. When the firing stopped, 10 hostages and 29 inmates were dead or dying. From a state police helicopter, inmates were told to place their hands on their heads and surrender. They were told to sit or lie down and that they would not be harmed.

Within an hour, the prison had been secured. State police and correctional officers then started the process of dealing with the dead and wounded correctional personnel and prisoners, and with having the surrendered prisoners stripped, searched, and moved back to the cellblocks. In December 1971, a U.S. Court of

Appeals found that the harassment and reprisals directed at prisoners by correctional officers in the days after the riot entitled prisoners to protections against any recurrence.

One of the most infamous incidents of the revolt at Attica occurred shortly after the main yard had been secured. Gerald Houlihan, public information officer for the Department of Corrections, told the press that several hostages died as a result of inmates having slashed the throats of officers. This comment and interviews with state police officers who reported being eyewitnesses to such inmate brutality generated sensational headlines in the media. Less than 24 hours later, however, autopsy reports of the dead hostages found that all had died from gunshot wounds inflicted by representatives of the state.

Aftermath
Throughout the years since the events at Attica, criminal prosecutions of inmates, court hearings, and lawsuits seeking to hold prison and government officials in New York responsible for the deaths continued. In all, 62 inmates were indicted for more than 1,200 criminal acts. By contrast, one trooper was charged for a single crime in relation to the revolt. In 1974, New York Governor Hugh Carey sought to end inquiries into the Attica uprising when he pardoned seven inmates and commuted the sentence of a prisoner convicted of killing a correctional officer. In addition, Governor Carey ruled that no disciplinary action should be taken against 19 police officers and one civilian who investigators had suggested should be disciplined for their actions in the retaking and aftermath of the disturbance.

While criminal prosecutions had ended, civil suits by prisoners seeking monetary damages for the use of excessive force continued for years. It was not until 2000, nearly 30 years after the Attica riot, that the state of New York settled a civil suit brought by inmates for $12 million. In 2005, New York Governor George Pataki created a $12 million fund as a settlement with the Forgotten Victims of Attica, families of hostages and other correctional officers killed and injured during the retaking of the prison.

Lucien X. Lombardo
Old Dominion University

See Also: Auburn State Prison; New York; Penitentiaries; Political Crimes, Contemporary; President's Commission on Law Enforcement and the Administration of Justice; Prison Riots; Prisoner's Rights; Rockefeller, Nelson; San Quentin State Prison.

Further Readings
Bell, Malcolm. *Turkey Shoot: Tracking the Attica Cover-Up*. New York: Grove, 1985.
Oswald, Russell. *Attica: My Story*. Garden City, NY: Doubleday, 1972.
Wicker, Tom. *Attica: A Time to Die*. New York: Quadrangle/New York Times Books, 1975.

Auburn State Prison

Opened in 1817 on the fringes of Auburn village in western New York, Auburn prison was among the first modern penitentiaries in the United States. The prison quickly rose to national and international prominence for its renowned "silent system" that combined congregate labor during the day with cellular isolation at night, all in complete silence and enforced under threat of corporal punishment. Boasting this novel approach to penology that promised to discipline and reform criminals, Auburn drew visitors from across the country and around the world and served as the model for hundreds of prisons built at home and abroad. The Auburn correctional facility still houses inmates today, making it the oldest continually operating prison in the United States.

Building a Silent System
The New York legislature approved a second state prison in 1816 to alleviate overcrowding at New York City's Newgate Prison (est. 1797), and the first 53 inmates arrived in 1817 to accelerate construction. The original south wing of the new prison consisted largely of congregate cells, but as conditions at Newgate became increasingly violent and riotous, reformers, politicians, and prison officials questioned the wisdom of housing inmates together. Influenced by the Quaker system of solitary confinement pioneered in Pennsylvania, Auburn's first warden, William Brittin, oversaw the construction of a north wing made

up of individual cells in two rows, back to back, stacked five tiers high. Completed in 1821, the cells in this wing measured less than 4 feet wide, 7 feet deep and 7.5 feet high. The only windows were along the outside wall of the narrow corridor onto which the cells opened.

Housing prisoners individually helped to prevent communication that might lead to riots or escapes and also prevented the corruption of young offenders by hardened criminals. In 1821, at the recommendation of the legislature, Auburn graded its prisoners, keeping 80 of those deemed most dangerous in solitary confinement. After 18 months, prison officials determined that the physical and psychological damage of solitary confinement was too great, citing grave illness, insanity, self-mutilation, and suicide. In 1823, the governor pardoned 26 of these men, marking an end to the experiment with total isolation and this system of classification.

The hallmark of the Auburn system was its use of congregate labor during the day. Heads shaven and clothed in black-and-white-striped uniforms, prisoners lock-stepped every morning from their cells to the bucket room to dispose of their waste, then to the prison workshops. Considered important for both remaking the criminal and defraying the costs of the prison, inmate labor was contracted to the highest bidder. Prisoners worked in silence six days a week building furniture, weaving cloth, and making shoes, tools, brooms, and other goods. Silence in the workshops and on the cellblock was enforced under threat of brutal physical punishment. Prisoners were also isolated from the outside world; visits and correspondence were strictly forbidden.

Auburn first received female convicts in 1825 and housed them together in a large attic room. Although women escaped the hard labor of the men, visitors and prison officials remarked at the horrid conditions in which they were housed, receiving little exercise or fresh air and left to their own devices. In 1828, Governor DeWitt Clinton proposed a separate women's prison, but the legislature refused, citing the immense savings at Auburn from the sewing, ironing, and washing the female inmates did.

In 1857, the legislature approved funds for the New York State Asylum for the Criminally Insane, and Auburn became the first prison to house men-

This 19th-century photograph taken inside the Auburn prison shows long rows of metal doors on the small individual cells in which prisoners were segregated at night.

tally ill inmates separate from the general prison population. The asylum was converted into the State Prison for Women in 1893 and remained open until the operation was moved to Bedford Hills in 1933. Auburn was also the first prison to use electricity as a method of execution in 1890. In total, 55 men and one woman were put to death in Auburn's electric chair.

Penal Reform
By the turn of the century, Auburn's silent system was unraveling: Contract labor was eliminated in favor of a state-use system, leaving many inmates idle, and silence proved unenforceable as the prison population swelled. But once again, Auburn was at the forefront of penal reform. The highly publicized experience of local businessman and reformer

Thomas Mott Osborne in 1913 brought prisons to the center of public and political debate. Osborne had entered Auburn as inmate "Tom Brown" for a voluntary stay of one week to glean insight into the conditions and life of a prisoner. Osborne was the driving force behind the establishment of the Mutual Welfare League (MWL), an inmate self-governing organization that, under the motto "Do Good, Make Good," sought to replace the stick with a carrot. The MWL organized inmate activities and helped to run the "honor" work camps where inmates labored outside the prison walls on public works projects such as road building. In the wake of two bloody riots in 1929, the MWL was disbanded.

Extreme overcrowding led to the riots on July 28 and December 11, 1929. Several inmates and guards were killed and injured during these uprisings, and the fires set to the prison workshops during the riots left the prison complex in shambles on the eve of the Great Depression. With little funding in the 1930s, and later resources directed to the war effort, reconstruction of the prison lasted more than a decade. New cellblocks eventually replaced old ones, with cells, still in use today, that are slightly larger and now include a sink and toilet.

The heated struggle for civil rights could be found behind Auburn's walls. Following a peaceful inmate work stoppage in observance of Black Solidarity Day in November 1970, prison administrators identified and punished 14 inmate leaders. When administrators failed to discuss or drop these reprisals, a riot broke out. Using makeshift weapons, inmates took 43 hostages and issued demands for better conditions and greater educational opportunities. Several hours later, the inmates were persuaded to surrender peacefully.

Auburn continues to operate today as one of New York State's maximum-security prisons, housing approximately 1,800 male inmates.

Logan M. McBride
City University of New York Graduate Center

See Also: Attica; New York; Penitentiaries; Prison Riots; Prisoner's Rights.

Further Readings
McHugh, Eileen. *Auburn Correctional Facility*. Charleston, SC: Arcadia Publishing, 2010.

McLennan, Rebecca M. *The Crisis of Imprisonment: Protest, Politics, and the Making of the American Penal State*. New York: Cambridge University Press, 2008.

Rothman, David. *The Discovery of the Asylum: Social Order and Disorder in the New Republic*. Glenview, IL: Scott, Foresman, 1971.

Augustus, John

John Augustus (1785–1859), a Massachusetts shoemaker, is credited with being the "father of probation." Although much of his work pertained to pretrial supervision, it nonetheless contributed greatly to the origin of the American probation system. Augustus coined the term *probation*, which he derived from the Latin word *probare* meaning to be tested or proven.

Born in Woburn, Massachusetts, in 1785, he moved to Lexington at the age of 21 and began making shoes. (Augustus was married twice, fathering two daughters and two sons.) In 1827, Augustus again moved, but this time to Boston, where he continued his work as a cobbler. Shortly after his arrival, he noticed that the criminal justice system was failing to reform offenders. He commented on seeing drunkards, prostitutes, and petty thieves being sentenced to jail, only to return to the streets unprepared to lead law-abiding lives. Many unprepared ex-offenders would then commit additional crimes for which they would again be sentenced and imprisoned. For many offenders, this formed a reccurring cycle. This convinced Augustus that when possible, the criminal justice system should rehabilitate offenders.

Consistent with this observation and his convictions, Augustus joined the Washington Total Abstinence Society, a group devoted to the humane treatment and rehabilitation of offenders. This group believed that alcohol consumption was the root cause of criminality, destroying both the moral and economic core of America. Augustus first entered a Boston courtroom in 1841. While there, he asked that an indigent man being arraigned on a charge of drunkenness be temporarily released into his care. The judge complied. Under his supervision, the man found a job

John Augustus's influential work led to the creation of probation systems throughout the United States for both adults and juveniles. By 1910, 32 states had followed the lead of Massachusetts and established juvenile probation. Among this group of newsboys and gum sellers photographed by Lewis Hine in Washington, D.C., in 1912 was at least one young boy on probation.

and swore to quit drinking. After three weeks, the man reappeared in court and surprised the judge with his improved appearance and penitent demeanor. Spared a term of incarceration, the judge levied a fine of one cent plus court costs, which totaled $3.76. Subsequent requests were met with resistance from local police officials, whose pay was based upon the number of offenders sentenced to jail. Nevertheless, Augustus continued in his work. He soon expanded his efforts to include the supervision of children. By 1846, he had supervised approximately 30 children ranging in age from 9 to 16. By 1858, he had helped 1,152 men and 794 women. Of that number, it is reported that only four failed, requiring Augustus to forfeit bail.

When selecting individuals to supervise, Augustus paid particular attention to the extent of their criminal record as well as their character, always looking for signs of remorse and an interest in redemption. Augustus was a volunteer, never being paid for his effort. Furthermore, he personally paid the bail of those he supervised. Although he received funding from several well-known philanthropists like Horace Mann, Theodore Parker, and Wendell Phillips, he eventually exhausted his financial resources. Augustus retired from both his probation work and his cobbler shop in 1858. He died in 1859 at the age of 75.

Although Augustus did not live to see the influence that his efforts would have on the American correctional system, they have nonetheless served as the cornerstone for all forms of community-based supervision. He is also credited with helping establish the use of the presentence investigation. Because of his work and its success, in 1878 Massachusetts created a state probation system with paid officers. Other states soon followed. By 1900, Illinois, Minnesota, New Jersey, New York, Rhode Island, and Vermont also created similar systems. By 1910, 32 states had also passed legislation establishing juvenile probation. Today, adult and juvenile probation exists in every state and plays a significant role in the justice system.

Caroline Forsythe
Curtis R. Blakely
Truman State University

See Also: Drinking and Crime; Massachusetts Probation.

Further Readings
Augustus, John. *A Report of the Labors of John Augustus.* (1852). Lexington, KY: American Probation and Parole Association, 1984.
Jones, Mark. *Criminal Justice Pioneers in U.S. History.* Boston: Pearson Allyn & Bacon, 2005.
Klein, Andrew. *Alternative Sentencing, Intermediate Sanctions and Probation.* Cincinnati, OH: Anderson Publishing, 1997.
New York State Division of Criminal Justice Services, Office of Probation and Correctional Alternatives. "Meet John Augustus." http://www.dpca.state.ny.us/augustus.htm (Accessed December 2010).

Autobiographies, Criminals'

Autobiographical narratives written by criminals have provided both information for social scientists who study crime and entertainment for the general public. These works share narrative space with other works about the lives of criminals, such as gallows confessions, broadsheets, pamphlets, and fiction, including novels and films. In the United States, criminal autobiographies first began to be published in the 18th century. In these autobiographies, men and women who were accused and/or convicted of a crime not only recount the events of their lives but often offer an explanation. These explanations often take the form of a mea culpa (an admission of fault). However, often the criminal also will blame people, events, or society for contributing to his or her downfall. This is particularly the case with post–Civil War western outlaws and the "political prisoners" of the 1960s. Autobiographical narratives reflect the perspectives and beliefs of the subject, who may wish to present him/herself in the best possible light. As with all such narratives, there is the issue of memory. The story is told retrospectively, and the teller may forget or distort the events that he or she is recalling. But even with these caveats, criminal autobiographies provide the researcher or general reader with insight into the time period and the world inhabited by the criminal.

Early Autobiographies
Perhaps the earliest American criminal autobiography, *The Memoirs of Stephen Burroughs* was published in 1798. In the memoir, Burroughs, a notorious 18th-century New England rogue, recounted his path from preacher's son to confidence man. Burroughs recounts the struggle of wills with his father that began in his childhood when he played pranks and engaged in petty theft. Although he attended Dartmouth College, Burroughs dropped out. Aside from assuming the guise of a minister and then a schoolteacher, Burroughs became a counterfeiter, thief, and seducer. He escaped from prison on several occasions. His exploits became so well known that crimes he had not committed were attributed to him. In his memoirs, Burroughs deals with his perception of self, a perception that allowed for shifting identities. Burroughs's *Memoirs* has been described as bearing similarities to the memoirs of a notorious British thief, James Dalton (1728), and to have been influenced by Henry Fielding's novel *Tom Jones* (1749).

In the 19th century, dime novels about western outlaws became popular among eastern readers. These pulp novels were often written by eastern writers, some of whom had never gone west. These books contributed to the mythology of the western frontier, particularly to the legend of western gunslingers and outlaws in the "Wild West." The image of the outlaw as hero, of the "good bad man," was constructed in the pages of these novels. A few western gunmen took part in their own legend building by writing accounts of their lives. Cole Younger was one of four brothers, who with Jesse James and James's brother Frank led the James-Younger Gang in the years after the Civil War. In *Confessions of a Missouri Guerrilla: The Autobiography of Cole Younger* (1903), he opens the first chapter with an account of his boyhood in Missouri from 1856 to 1860. During the war, Younger joins Quantrill's Raiders, the pro-Confederate guerrillas led by William Quantrill. That he should fight on the side of the Confederacy is preordained, Younger explains, by the "political hatreds" that existed along the Missouri and Kansas border. Although he is the seventh of 14 children, the family is well to do and is politically prominent. But then his father was brutally murdered and three of his sisters and two cousins are imprisoned by Missouri militia. His mother is forced to burn her own house to the ground and walk through the snow for help with a faithful servant. These events before and during the war, and the government's failure to provide postwar amnesty in Missouri to Confederates, Younger writes, paves the way to his career as an outlaw. In the afterword to the book, he explains that he has written the book because of the libelous stories told about him and his dead brothers. Younger asserts that the worst offenders in this regard are the New York publishers of "five-cent-dreadfuls."

In 1896, *The Life of John Wesley Hardin as Written by Himself* was published. As had Younger, Hardin had made a reputation for himself as a gunman. He was killed in 1895, shot in the back of the head, while in a saloon. The manuscript he had written was found and turned over to his children. Although his daughters objected, his son decided to publish it. The book was withdrawn from circulation soon after publication, but copies remained in a warehouse. These copies of the book became collector's items. One of the debates about the book from the time of publication was whether Hardin had been literate enough to write the manuscript. The evidence suggests that he was. He had been the son of a Methodist preacher and had attended school. When he killed a man at age 15, he became a fugitive. Later, after serving time in prison, he had studied law, passed the bar exam, and even set up a law practice. But he began drinking and gambling again and was killed at age 42. Although he was only 9 when the Civil War began, Hardin, as did Younger, experienced the war as a southern sympathizer and grew up rebellious.

In an example of the use of oral history, Willis and Joe Newton recounted their lives to two interviewers in *The Newton Boys: Portrait of an Outlaw Gang* (1994). The book was based on audiotapes made in 1976. The brothers were also the subject of a documentary and a popular film. One aspect of the gang activities in Texas from 1919 to 1924 was what has been described as the use of technology to avoid violence. The bank robberies were carefully planned, and the gang was not captured until after a $3 million Illinois train robbery. In their joint narrative, the brothers discuss their perception of themselves as businessmen and their belief in the corruption of business and government institutions.

Twentieth Century

During the early 20th century, social scientists were interested in the careers of professional criminals. One of the more famous of these professional criminals was Joseph "Yellow Kid" Weil, whose book about his life is now subtitled *The Autobiography of America's Master Swindler* (1948). Weil (1875–1976) was a Chicago confidence man who began his career as an assistant to a patent medicine salesman. He asserts that he was able to succeed as a con man because of human nature; the people he cheated were greedy and wanted something for nothing. Weil's criminal career inspired the film *The Sting* (1973), starring Paul Newman.

In 1924, two young Chicago college men of wealthy families became notorious for their attempt to commit the perfect crime with the "thrill killing" of 14-year-old Bobby Franks. The prosecution focused on the "deviant" sexual relationship between the two young men, Nathan Leopold and Richard Loeb. The defense turned to alienists (psychiatrists) to do a psychological evaluation of the two, who, inspired by their reading of Frederich Nietzsche, had believed themselves above the law. Defense attorney Clarence Darrow admitted their guilt but offered a classic argument against the death penalty. The two were sentenced to Stateville Penitentiary, where Loeb was killed by another inmate, who claimed Loeb tried to sexually assault him. The year before his parole from prison, Leopold published his autobiographical *Life Plus Ninety-Nine Years* (1957). The title came from the sentence that he and Loeb were given by the judge for Bobby Franks's murder. In the book, Leopold addresses the issue of his motive for the murder. He says it "was to please Dick" [Loeb]. He recounts his confused thoughts after the murder when there was no turning back. Looking back at his crime from the vantage point of the 32 years he has spent in prison, he wonders how his mind worked. He admits that he felt no remorse until several years later. Leopold also comments on his reaction to *Compulsion* (1957), the novel by Meyer Levin based on the case. Leopold recalls that as he read he felt nauseated and exposed and knew that he was not the same person described in the book.

The book by Leopold is one of many works written by American prisoners while and after serving time in prison. This genre of "prison literature" has a long tradition, dating to the inmates of early European dungeons, gaols, and prisons. In 20th-century America, African American writer Chester Himes recalled his seven years in prison in *The Quality of Hurt* (1972). When he was growing up in the south, Himes's father was a faculty member at a historically black college. The lab accident that blinded his brother, his own suspension from college, and a fall down an elevator shaft while working in a hotel were all prologue to the armed robbery that sent Himes to the Ohio Penitentiary. Himes described his fits of rage that kept bigger and tougher inmates from harming him. In prison, he became aware of his own capacity for violence. Himes began to write short stories that he submitted and had accepted by magazines, including *Esquire*. After his release, Himes tried to make a living as a novelist, writing what has been described as "protest novels." His success came after he moved to Europe and began to write his "Harlem domestic" series featuring two black police detectives (one of whom was prone to blind fits of rage after being permanently disfigured by the acid thrown in his face).

Chester Himes, who spent seven years in prison and later wrote A Rage in Harlem, The Quality of Hurt, *and other works, is shown here in a 1946 photograph by Carl Van Vechten.*

"Political" Prisoners

In *The Autobiography of Malcolm X* (1965), the man who had been born Malcolm Little, but who became a Muslim while in prison, told the story of his life and his spiritual and political transformation. The product of a collaboration between Malcolm X and journalist Alex Haley, the book was named by *Time* magazine as one of the 10 most influential nonfiction books of the 20th century. Malcolm X recounts the events that led to his conviction for robbery. He had spent time as a sleeping car porter, one of the better jobs that an educated young black man could expect to find. He had dressed in Zoot suits and conked his hair. He had been involved with white women in a society that punished black men for such relationships. When he reached prison, he was angry and defiant, but under the tutelage of a prisoner, he began to read and think and eventually experienced a conversion to the Muslim faith. After prison, Malcolm X became a controversial figure during the civil rights era. As he was reevaluating his world view in the aftermath of a visit to Mecca, Malcolm X was assassinated.

A number of other prisoners during this era wrote about their experiences, describing themselves as "political" prisoners. Several of the women who were members of the revolutionary group or associated with the Black Panthers have written about their experiences. These books include Angela Davis's *Angela Davis: An Autobiography* (1989) and Elaine Brown's *A Taste of Power: A Black Woman's Story* (1993).

In 2001, a book by Assata Shakur was published in the United States. In *Assata: An Autobiography*, Shakur, who escaped from prison after being convicted for her role in the death of a New Jersey state trooper, tells her side of the story. Badly injured during the confrontation, Shakur alleges that she was brutally treated by the police who responded to the scene and the medical staff at the hospital. Having survived, she was confined as the only woman in a men's prison. She challenges the fairness of her trial and the testimony of the other police officer who took part in the shoot-out. After escaping from prison, she fled to Cuba, where the government has refused to extradite her back to the United States. Shakur presents her story in the context of the Federal Bureau of Investigation (FBI) COINTELPRO (surveillance program) that involved an effort to destroy the Black Panthers and other groups. Angela Davis, now a University of California professor, provided a foreword to Shakur's book in which she discusses prisons, racial profiling, and the images of offenders.

Contemporary Accounts

Members of organized crime also have provided accounts of their encounters with the criminal justice system. These books include the bestseller, first published in 1973 as *Killer*, by "Joey the Hitman." The present title of the book is *Joey the Hitman: The Autobiography of a Mafia Killer* (2002). David Fisher, the writer who collaborated with Joey on the book, recounts in his introduction that he was approached by Joey for help in telling his story, but that he never knew his real name or where he lived. Joey's authenticity was confirmed by reliable sources, and Fisher agreed to work with him. In his autobiography, Joey offered an account of the day-to-day operation of the mob as seen from the perspective of a mob hitman. Joey achieved notoriety for both his book and his appearance on *The David Susskind Show* for an interview with a paper bag over his head to protect his identity. In Joey's account, he led an ordinary life, but he was able to quietly enjoy the money that he earned as a killer. He accepted death as an occupational risk. In *A Man of Honor: The Autobiography of Joseph Bonanno* (1983), another mobster offered an inside look at organized crime. Bonanno had immigrated to the United States from Sicily during Prohibition. He eventually became the boss of one of the five New York Mafia families. Bonanno is said to have been a likely model for Don Corleone in the book and the film *The Godfather* (1972).

One of the more usual "as told to" books is *Final Truth: The Autobiography of Mass Murderer/Serial Killer Donald "Pee Wee" Gaskins*. In a series of interviews with journalist Wilton Earle, over a 15-month period, Gaskins provided a graphic account of his life and crimes. Born in the backwoods of South Carolina and small in stature, Gaskins claimed to have been abused by his mother's live-in lovers and then later bullied in school. He committed his first sexual assault as an adolescent when he and two friends raped the 11-year-old sister of one of the friends. He himself was gang-raped while in reform school. Later, in adult prison, Gaskins claimed to have realized that the only way he could survive was by becoming a "powerman." He killed another violent prisoner to establish his reputation. On his release from prison, Gaskins began his career as a sadistic rapist who eventually killed his victims. He died on death row in 1983. The foreword to his autobiography is written by Colin Wilson, the well-known British crime writer.

In her autobiography *Stranger in Two Worlds* (1986), Jean Harris, who became notorious for only one murder—that of her lover Herman Tarnower, "the Scarsdale Diet doctor"—wrote from prison. Harris, who was the headmistress of an exclusive school, maintains as she did during her trial that she had intended to kill herself, and that Tarnower's death was an accident. She also asserts that she was a victim of a media trial and the misinterpretation of forensic evidence as well as false testimony by witnesses.

Other autobiographies include those of former gang members, such as Luis J. Rodriguez's

Always Running: La Vida Loca: Gang Days in L.A. (1994) and *Monster: The Autobiography of an L.A. Gang Member* (2004) by Sanyika Shakur. These books recount the life-and-death struggle for status and survival and the ritual encounters with fellow gang members, rival gangs, and the police. These books are sometimes referred to as "gangbanger autobiographies."

In a twist on the criminal autobiography, historian Timothy J. Gilfoyle's *A Pickpocket's Tale: The Underworld of Nineteenth Century New York* (2006) uses an unpublished memoir by George Appo as the foundation for an exploration of crime and justice. The son of a Chinese father and Irish mother, Appo was a newsboy turned pickpocket and con man.

Frankie Y. Bailey
State University of New York, Albany

See Also: Darrow, Clarence; History of Crime and Punishment in America, 1970–Present; Leopold and Loeb; Literature and Theater, Crime in; Literature and Theater, Punishment in; Organized Crime, History of.

Further Readings
Brumble, H. David. "The Gangbanger Autobiography of Monster Kody (aka Sanyika Shakur) and Warrior Literature." *American Literary History*, v.12/1–2 (2000).
Cebula, Larry. "A Counterfeit Identity: The Notorious Life of Stephen Burroughs." *Historian*, v.64/2 (2002).

Automobile and the Police

It is difficult to separate the institution of policing from the tools and technology officers use to accomplish their assigned tasks. Just the term *police officer* conjures a mental image of a person in a particular type of uniform with predictable markings and equipment. For over 100 years, this constellation of police symbols has also included the distinct automobiles that they use. Variously called "squad cars," "patrol cars," "prowl cars," "marked units," or "black-and-whites," these vehicles are an important part of police culture and identity. The adoption of automobiles by police transformed both how police did their job and what the public expected in terms of appropriate police response.

Early Use of Automobiles
In the late 19th century, law enforcement agencies began to use motor vehicles. These early forays into motorized policing did not resemble modern automobile patrol. Rather, they were usually limited to "paddy wagon"–type large conveyances for prisoners or the police. If police used a motorized vehicle for individual patrol or transportation, more often it took the form of a motorcycle. As the early 20th century unfolded, offenders began to use automobiles more frequently, so the police followed suit. Beginning with the 1920s, American policing was transformed through the use of automobiles.

The benefit of officers in automobiles was seen as twofold. First, it represented an economy of service. A police officer traveling in a car could patrol a larger area, thus obviating the need to position more officers across a given territory. Second, motorized officers could more quickly respond to increasingly distant calls for service. During the first few decades of motorized policing, the cars used by law enforcement were typically the same as any other retail automobile. They would then be modified by the agency to suit their particular needs. In these early years, the modifications were mostly basic: distinct paint and markings and additions of lights and sirens.

After World War II, American automakers recognized the growing market for specially modified fleet vehicles for law enforcement. This was the dawn of custom police packages that contained many of the popular options as regularly ordered by law enforcement agencies. Starting with Ford in 1950, a succession of automakers debuted these special police-equipped cars. Chevrolet began offering a package in 1955, Dodge in 1956, and Plymouth in 1957. Typical police package enhancements of the 1950s included more powerful engines, improved cooling systems, and heavier-duty transmissions and brakes. In addition to high performance suspension systems and "crash" bumpers, more current package offerings often include alternators and batteries capable of supporting the array of computers, radios, and other electronics (light bars, deck, grill, and other emergency lights) found in the typical patrol vehicle. Many custom vehicle packages include special inserts designed for improved prisoner transport. These inserts typically replace some or all of the stock backseat in favor of a more secure and easier-to-clean transport unit. Likewise, many aftermarket vendors provide agencies with customized weapon and equipment storage mechanisms for use inside the cabin or trunk of the vehicle.

Popular Models and Equipment
Since the 1950s, certain models have proven especially popular with law enforcement. The Chrysler Enforcer, Dodge Polara, and Chevrolet Biscayne were common in the 1960s. Models such as the Mercury Monterey, Dodge Monaco, Ford Torino, Plymouth Fury, and Chevrolet Nova were popular in the 1970s. Many of these models retained popularity across several decades and design generations. Of particular note in this category are the Chevrolet Caprice and Ford LTD Crown Victoria. The third and fourth generations of Chevrolet Caprice (1986–96) were widely adopted by agencies all over the United States, but it is the Ford LTD Crown Victoria (1978–present) that has enjoyed even longer and greater market dominance.

In 1996, Chevrolet discontinued production of the popular Caprice. This left a wide opening for Ford. The Police Interceptor version of the Crown Victoria had many of the attributes desirable for law enforcement. Also given the model designation P71 (and later P72), this automobile came with rear-wheel drive, a large V8 engine, and body-on-frame construction. As one of the few available cars built using a body-on-frame design, relatively inexpensive repairs could be accomplished (after minor collisions) without the need to straighten the chassis. These features, combined with the paucity of other large, rear-

A long row of Fords reserved for use as police cars waits at the Robey Motor Company in Washington, D.C., in the early 1920s. In the early years of police automobiles, law enforcement cars were usually the same models as those offered to the general public. Custom police cars became more prevalent after 1950, when Ford and other automakers created special models for the police.

wheel drive models, positioned Ford for near market monopoly.

In recognition of the now aging Crown Victoria, other companies have again entered the fray. In 2006, Dodge introduced a Police Package version of its popular Charger model. The exterior styling of the vehicle is reminiscent of muscle cars from the 1960s and 1970s. The police version Charger features a 340 Hp Hemi V8 engine, heavy-duty brakes, a severe-duty cooling system, police-performance Electronic Stability Program, police performance-tuned steering, and a gear shift mounted on the steering column instead of the center console. In place of the center console, the police Charger has an aluminum plate for mounting radio equipment, computers, and controllers for lights and sirens. The vehicle's electrical system is specially designed for integration of siren and light controls and other common accessories. Perhaps owing in part to its overtly masculine styling and powerful drivetrain, the Charger has proven instantly popular with law enforcement agencies. Even so, other automakers have continued to develop contenders to challenge the Crown Victoria's market share. These include the newly released Chevrolet Caprice PPV, Carbon Motor Company's E7 prototype car, as well as Ford's own police edition of the Taurus model. Apart from four-door sedans, many agencies have also adopted SUVs and other truck-framed vehicles as part of their patrol fleet, although these vehicles have tended to be more commonly purposed in non-pursuit capacities. Many highway patrols have adopted high-performance models such as the Ford Mustang, Chevrolet Camaro, and Dodge Magnum for highway pursuit purposes.

Motorized Versus Walking Patrol

Whatever model a given agency has adopted, the impact of motorized patrol has been great. Going back to the initial postwar proliferation of "radio cars" (police cars equipped with two-way radio units), policing was transformed by virtue of its greater mobility, speed of response, and expanded coverage area. Many advocates of community-oriented policing suggest that the move away from walking a patrol beat had negative consequences for police–community relations. Supporters of this position argue that patrol cars create a barrier between the police and citizens. They argue that officers in cars are less likely to directly engage with the community. As this reasoning goes, with modern conveniences such as air conditioning and computers, police are more likely to drive along with the windows up and the public shut out. Scholars who study police and police tactics have devoted a great deal of effort to better understanding the way motorized patrol influences police practice. Policing scholar David Bayley observes that 60 to 65 percent of all police personnel in America are assigned to motorized patrol. As such, studies of this type explore an important dimension of police practice.

One of the most influential patrol studies is commonly referred to as the Kansas City Preventive Patrol Experiment. In this 1973 study, George Kelling and his coauthors sought to empirically test the validity of one of the major strategies of modern policing: routine, visible, motorized, random patrol. In other words, they wanted to know whether the regular presence of police officers in cars changed crime in the officers' patrol areas. The conclusions reached by Kelling and his coauthors in Kansas City challenged the conventional wisdom that random patrol had a significant effect on crime and fear of crime. This conclusion was quite controversial and not without its detractors. Critics argued that the patrol areas in Kansas City were not representative of the wide-ranging urban environments across the country. Other scholars contended the study did not contain enough beats, that the samples of citizens surveyed were too small, and that the statistical power of the tests was too weak to use as the basis for broader inference. Even so, by calling into question basic assumptions of police strategy, the study led to a wave of empirical research challenging many of the core assumptions of police strategy and tactics.

In the wake of Kansas City, many researchers took a position articulated by Carl Klockars, who discounted the value of random police patrol. In a now famous statement, Klockars likened random police patrol to firefighters roaming around looking for fires. Echoing this sentiment, police departments across the United States shifted focus from a traditional law enforcement mandate to one targeting public order and service. James Wilson, who would later partner with Kansas City author George Kelling, interpreted the results differently. Wilson argues that the Kansas City study shows that only random patrol is of questionable value. He contends that other types of patrol, such as foot patrols or patrols in unmarked cars, might work to reduce crime. Out of this controversy, there is one strong consensus: Simply increasing the number of police doesn't reduce crime. In this, most experts agree that the number of police is not as important as what the police are doing.

The patrol car itself can form a barrier between the police officers and the public. This has also prompted a return to strategies like foot patrol, bicycle patrol, and even horse-mounted patrol. These techniques have been adopted to break down the perceived barrier and better integrate the officers into the communities they serve. However, placing officers on foot, bicycle, or horse may come with certain functional trade-offs. Whatever benefits these alternative conveyances provide in terms of improved community access, they also sacrifice certain capabilities in terms of response speed, ability to confine or transport suspects, and protection (or comfort) for the officer. The ability to quickly answer calls, cover larger areas, and do all that now typifies modern policing would be almost impossible without some motorized capabilities. Moreover, with the addition of computers and other means to transmit and receive electronic information, the patrol car is as much mobile office as it is officer transport.

Matthew Pate
State University of New York, Albany

See Also: Community Policing and Relations; Dyer Act; Police, History of; Professionalization of Police; Technology, Police.

Further Readings
Bayley, David. *Police for the Future*. New York: Oxford University Press, 1994.
Kelling, George L., Tony Pate, Duane Dieckman, and Charles E. Brown. *The Kansas City Preventive Patrol Experiment: A Technical Report*. Washington, DC: Police Foundation, 1974.
Klockars, Carl and Steven Mastrofski. *The Police and Serious Crime*. New York: McGraw-Hill, 1990.
McCord, Monty. *Police Cars: A Photographic History*. Iola, WI: Krause Publications, 1991.
Sanow, Edwin J. *Encyclopedia of American Police Cars*. Minneapolis, MN: Motorbooks International, 1999.

Aviation and Transportation Security Act of 2001

Following the terrorist attacks in the United States on September 11, 2001, airport and aviation security became a key area of reform in the international effort against terrorism. Although some passenger and luggage screening methods had been utilized prior to 2001, a standardized international protocol was lacking. Following the attacks, concern about the future threat of airplane hijackings initiated widespread reform of airport security and screening practices, both in the United States and abroad; both the Airport Federalization Act (AFA) and the Aviation and Transportation Security Act (ATSA) were passed by the U.S. Congress in November 2001. By federalizing security services, these acts were designed to standardize passenger and luggage screening procedures.

The Aviation and Transportation Security Act also established the Federal Transportation Security Administration (TSA) as part of the Department of Transportation and charged it with monitoring all sea and air transportation security operations. In addition, the TSA was placed in charge of hiring and training airport screeners to screen all passengers and luggage prior to travel. Furthermore, these employees were required to be American citizens. Although the TSA's reach only extends within the United States, many of its standards and protocols have since been adopted internationally.

Beyond the federalization of security services and security personnel, the ATSA also called for significant changes in how screenings of persons and luggage were performed. For example, devices designed to detect residue of explosive materials and increased hand searches of baggage were among the proposed reforms. Passenger screenings also became more comprehensive, and in addition to the continued use of metal detectors already standard in most U.S. airports, more thorough checks of cellular phones, laptops, and carry-on luggage became routine. Furthermore, items previously permitted in carry-on baggage such as scissors and razors were prohibited, and

Inspectors with U.S. Customs and Border Protection examining business equipment and computers brought into the United States by a passenger on an international flight. Hand searches of suspicious luggage have become increasingly common, and there has been controversy over profiling techniques that are thought to unfairly select certain passengers and luggage for further screening.

the quantity of liquid substances was significantly limited. The ATSA also supervised the implementation of increased security measures within aircraft. Most notably, it required fortified cockpit doors in all aircraft, which are to remain closed throughout the duration of the flight. In addition, aircraft crew can monitor passenger activity via onboard video equipment. Emergency communication systems able to notify airport personnel, 911 operators, and federal authorities in the event of hostile activity were also required by the Department of Transportation to be installed in all aircraft. Changes were also made within airports, which the ATSA declared as secured areas to be surrounded by monitored fences. Private vehicles were no longer permitted to be parked within 300 yards of an airport and the number of airport security personnel was significantly increased. In addition, access to airport arrival and departure gates became restricted to only ticketed and pre-screened passengers.

Given ATSA's primary goal of reforming standard passenger and baggage screening practices, standardized protocols for conducting such screenings were developed. As declared by the ATSA, confirming the identity of passengers is the first step of the screening process. To that end, passengers are now required to present a valid form of identification with names matching the itinerary. International travelers are further screened by the newly developed Advance Passenger Information System (APIS), an international database of security information on travelers.

Upon check-in, both individuals and their luggage undergo thorough physical screening and passengers' identities are checked for a second time. Travelers are also checked by pulse induction metal detectors that send high-voltage pulses to detect hidden metal objects, or wand metal detectors, while baggage is screened by X-ray machines. Hand searches of suspicious luggage have also become commonplace. At the gate of departure, passengers are required to answer detailed questions regarding their travel plans while security personnel conduct additional random searches of any carry-on bags. During the boarding process, passengers are often required to provide identification for a third time while computers compile a complete passenger list to be forwarded to federal and local agencies. Luggage surrendered to the cargo hold is first matched to its owner, and should that individual not board the flight, the luggage is automatically prevented from being placed into the airplane. CT scanners are also vital for the screening process and have the ability to calculate the density of items within a bag and compare the density to that of known chemicals and explosives.

Despite the general acceptance of these heightened security measures, some programs remain controversial. Mainly, some fear that profiling techniques have overwhelmed the screening process and unfairly select passengers and luggage for further screening. Random hand searchers have received recent criticisms given the claim that profiling, primarily racial and ethnic profiling, are the leading reasons for choosing passengers to be screened. Critics have also claimed that these searches can instill fear in other passengers since most are done in plain sight of other travelers.

This controversy escalated when the Department of Homeland Security and the Department of Defense suggested the use of the total information awareness (TIA) system, which is a database of private information and includes medical and financial documents. Although the TIA system was proposed for the use of gathering information and locating terrorist groups, Congress significantly restricted the program in 2003 by banning its use for domestic security purposes and the TIA was renamed the Terrorist Information Awareness system.

The Transportation Security Administration in charge of reforming aviation and transportation security was integrated into the Department of Homeland Security (DHS) in 2002, which has combined existing and new anti-terrorism measures. The development of the Early Alert System, a warning system designed to indicate the possibility of a terrorist attack, marks the most recent change in security measures. Although the TSA is now a subsidiary of the DHS, the Department of Transportation and the Federal Aviation Administration continue to assist in reforming United States and international aviation security policies through recommendations and review of current transportation practices.

Kathrin Ritter
Todd Moore
University of Tennessee, Knoxville

See Also: 2001 to 2012 Primary Documents; Border Patrol; Bush, George W. (Administration of); Customs Service as Police; Homeland Security; New York City; Obama, Barack (Administration of); Terrorism; USA PATRIOT Act of 2001.

Further Readings

Hoffman, Bruce. *Inside Terrorism.* New York: Columbia University Press, 2006.

Implementation of the Aviation and Transportation Security ACT: Hearing Before the Committee on Commerce, Science, and Transportation, United States Senate. Washington, DC: Government Printing Office, 2005.

Pious, Richard M. *The War on Terrorism and the Rule of Law.* Los Angeles: Roxbury, 2006.

Bail and Bond

Bail regulations in the United States were originally based on English laws that developed in reaction to the misuse of bail. Laws since the Eighth Amendment provision against "excessive bail" have incorporated both provisions for nonfinancial bail that will ensure more people are able to be released and a concern for community safety that will prevent some people from being released. The idea of releasing a person on bail is based on the belief that people are innocent until proven guilty and should not be punished until they are convicted of a crime. As the Supreme Court noted in *Stack v. Boyle*, it is also important for a person to remain free during the pretrial stage to assist in the preparation of his or her defense. Bail reform continues to be debated in Congress around concerns about the equality of the bail process.

The primary purpose of bail is to ensure that the accused appears at trial. Whether a person accused of a crime is eligible for bail is determined by a judge, who also sets a financial amount or conditions that must be met to guarantee appearance at trial. Once the bail has been posted, the accused is released from detention. If the accessed fails to appear, the amount is forfeited to the court. If the accused does appear, the amount is reimbursed. Bail can be imposed in the pretrial and appeal stages of criminal and deportation cases. Material witnesses are also subject to bail. Since not everyone can afford to provide the amount of bail, people have the alternative of providing a bond. A bond is a surety, or promise, by a third party to meet the bail obligation of the accused. Bonds can be posted by a commercial bondsman, who usually charges the accused a nonrefundable amount of 10 percent or more of the court-determined bail.

History of Bail

Bail can be traced back to England, with the first legal regulation of bail appearing in the 1200s. Laws concerning bail have evolved more in reaction to misuse of bail than to changes in society. The first law to include bail was the Statute of Westminster in 1275. Prior to this, local sheriffs, who were the king's agents, had sole discretion of whether to release an accused prior to trial. They were also able to set the amount of bail at their discretion. Reacting to the frequent misuse of this power, the Statute of Westminster lists those offenses that were and were not bailable, thus limiting the sheriff's discretion.

The legal guarantees provided in the Statute of Westminster remained in effect until the 1600s, when several changes occurred in reaction to the king's misuse of power. When King Charles I needed money, he forced his noblemen to issue him loans; those who did not were jailed and not allowed bail. A case was brought to court, known as Darnel's case, arguing that the men should be allowed freedom since they were accused but not convicted. The court felt that they should not question the king's judgment and therefore denied the request. In reaction, Parliament passed the Petition of Right in 1627, which specifically references Darnel's case. This requests the king to prohibit detention without due process of law, including presentation of charges and trial. Consequently, people could no longer be imprisoned without having charges presented against them, being allowed bail, and having a judgment against them. The Petition of Right also gave people the right to challenge their imprisonments. Although there was concern at the time that this might impair the Statute of Westminster, the Petition of Right was intended to be read in conjunction with the statute and therefore ensured that people would be charged and released on bail if the charge was listed as a bailable offense.

Although the king respected the request, thus providing legal guarantees that arbitrary detention would no longer occur, three loopholes were quickly found. First, the king could not arrest people without cause but there were no provisions preventing others in positions of power from doing so. Second, anyone arrested outside the jurisdiction of the court did not fall under the provisions of the Petition of Right. Finally, procedural delays in the presentation of charges and assignment of bail could keep people detained indefinitely.

This last loophole was illustrated in the Jenkes case of 1676. When Jenkes was arrested on sedition charges for a speech calling for Parliament to be assembled, he challenged his imprisonment. After several delays, the court refused to hear his case. To eliminate these loopholes, Parliament passed the Habeas Corpus Act of 1679. The introduction of this act specifically mentions Parliament's concern with the continued imprisonment of people charged with bailable offenses but not convicted. The act states the number of days from receipt of a writ of habeas corpus until the person is to be brought before a judge. The number of days between the time the accused is brought before the judge and the judge releases the prisoner on bail, if the charge is bailable, is also established.

Although the Habeas Corpus Act blocked the use of procedural methods to detain people, judges still found that they could continue to detain people by setting high bail amounts. This was one of the issues Parliament stated in the introduction to the English Bill of Rights of 1689. Among the rights stated is a prohibition of excessive bail, excessive fines, and cruel and unusual punishment. Consequently, by 1689, reaction to misuse of bail resulted in the legal statement of bailable offenses, a prohibition against arbitrary imprisonment, the right to habeas corpus, procedural requirements for bail, and prohibition of excessive bail.

Bail in America

Learning from the experiences in England, the American colonists were also concerned with the misuse of bail and, therefore, included bail provisions in some of their earliest documents. The Massachusetts Bodie of Liberties of 1641 prohibited imprisonment before sentencing if the accused was able to provide a guarantee that he would appear at trial. Only capital cases and cases in which the accused had shown contempt for the court were exempted. The Massachusetts law also required the accused to post either a bail or surety and imposed a condition of "good behavior."

Two other colonies adopted similar bail provisions in their laws, although there were subtle differences and the "good behavior" condition was not imposed. The Frame of Government of Pennsylvania 1682 allowed bail in all but capital offense cases where there was either a clear indication or presumption of guilt. In the 1683 New York Charter of Liberties and Privileges, bail was allowed in all cases except treason and felony.

As constitutions were drafted for the states, the wording from the English Bill of Rights started appearing. The North Carolina Constitution of 1776 contained the statement from the English Bill of Rights with only two words changed: North Carolina stated that excessive bail "should not" rather than "ought not" be imposed and used the phrase *cruel nor unusual punishment* as opposed to the English phrasing of "cruel and unusual punishment." Georgia's Constitution of 1777 was more limited and included only provisions against excessive fines and bail. Reverting back to earlier phrasing, the Constitution of Vermont of 1786 stated that all prisoners were bailable unless there was clear evidence that the prisoner had committed a capital offense and that excessive bail could not be required. The Northwest Ordinance of 1787 also combined provisions from several of the English laws by guaranteeing habeas corpus and trial by jury, stating that bail is allowed in all cases except capital offenses where there is clear evidence of guilt, instructing that fines are to be moderate, and prohibiting "cruel or unusual" punishments. Although Virginia did not include a provision against the misuse of bail in its constitution, the state legislature passed revisions to Virginia's laws in 1785 that included restrictions on judicial discretion in the application of bail.

Consequently, leading up to the drafting of the Constitution of the United States, there were several perspectives on the legal restrictions necessary to prevent the misuse of bail. Some of the new states were concerned enough with bail to include it in their constitutions and others were not. Some wanted to ensure restrictions on judicial discretion at several points in the process while others focused on the most recent abuse, the setting of the amount of bail.

At the time that the Constitution was being debated in Congress, the Judiciary Act of 1789

A bail agent's office in California in 2006. The value of bail agents and bounty hunters was seen in the early days of the United States when the law enforcement system was just establishing itself and the vast frontier afforded the opportunity to easily escape prosecution. The role of the bounty hunter established by the judiciary in the 1800s remains in effect today.

was also being debated. While the bail provisions in the Constitution were simply put, bail provisions in the Judiciary Act were more extensive. The Judiciary Act allows bail in all cases except those subject to the death penalty. When the death penalty is associated with a charge, the Judiciary Act allows only judges of the supreme, circuit, or district courts to grant bail upon consideration of the "nature and circumstances" associated with the charge. The Judiciary Act also provides for cases where bail is raised but a local judge is not available to take the bail by allowing judges of higher courts to take the bail.

Based on the history of abuse of bail leading up to the drafting of these two bills and the variance of bail laws between the states, it is interesting to note that records of Congress at the time do not record any debate on the bail provisions in either document. The only recorded comment expressed concern about the ambiguous wording of the Eighth Amendment.

Bail Reform

It was not until the Bail Reform Act of 1966 that another change occurred. This act enhanced the ability of people to be released on bail by increasing the options to financial bail, providing a list of circumstances that judges could consider in assigning bail, and allowing people who could not arrange bail to have their cases reviewed by a judge with the possibility of resetting bail. This law was passed in response to an increase in the number of people who were unable to arrange for financial bail. It also recognized the efforts of organizations such as the Vera Institute to provide background information to judges on people being considered for bail.

Up to this point, bail laws had been a reaction to abuse by those who awarded bail at their discretion and an effort to ensure those who had not been sentenced were not imprisoned. By the late 1960s, civil and criminal law had been revolutionized by the Warren Court. Americans were, therefore, concerned with rising crime rates and the belief that officials were "soft" on criminals.

A 1969 congressional hearing on the Bail Reform Act of 1966 was held in part because of the crime perpetrated by people released on nonfinancial bail, particularly in the District of Columbia. In response, Congress passed a law for the District of Columbia that allowed judges to consider whether or not the accused would pose a danger to the community in determining whether to grant bail. The law also provides a list of criteria that the judge may use in this determination and requires that a written statement explaining the decision be provided. This signaled a legal shift in the determination of bail from being based solely on the determination of whether the person will appear at trial to a balance between appearance at trial and other considerations.

Judges were given an even larger role in protecting the community through the Bail Reform Act of 1984. Although the act provides a wide range of alternatives to financial bail and prevents the judge from setting financial bail at an amount that would result in the detention of the person, it does allow detention if the judge finds the person to be a danger to the community. This bill also addresses bail for immigration and material witness cases.

Reforms to correct the problems created by the Bail Reform Act of 1984, including the forfeiture of bail for failing to meet additional conditions associated with bail even though the person appeared at trial, have been proposed but have yet to be approved by Congress.

Throughout the evolution of bail, the U.S. Supreme Court has remained all but silent, issuing only three notable opinions on the subject, none of which provides definitive insight into the meaning of "excessive bail." The first, *Stack v. Boyle*, occurred in 1951. This was a challenge that bail was set at an excessive amount and that there is a statutory right to bail. The Supreme Court decided bail that exceeded the amount necessary to ensure the accused appeared at trial was excessive but fell short of finding a right to bail in the Constitution.

In 1951, the court ruled in *Carlson v. Landon*, which dealt with bail in connection with a pending deportation, that the Eighth Amendment does not provide a right to bail. The decision also fails to say that all arrests are bailable. Finally, in 1987, *United States v. Salerno et al.* challenged the Bail Reform Act of 1984. The Supreme Court not only upheld the act, but it also failed to find a substantive right to bail and determined that "excessive bail" was no more than a limit on the discretion of the judiciary. The only clear directive from these cases is that there is no right to bail.

As Congress has moved to increase both nonfinancial options to bail and the ability of judges to deny bail, the Supreme Court has moved toward a more restrictive interpretation of the "excessive bail" clause of the Eighth Amendment. Concerns about the current bail structure include the impact of racial and income disparities in both the assigning of bail and the ability to meet bail requirements.

Bail Agents and Bounty Hunters

The bail system in the United States functions through the private efforts of both bail agents and bounty hunters (also known as bail enforcement agents). These functions are viewed as beneficial but controversial. Since the relationship between the bail agent, bounty hunter, and defendant is based on a contract, they are constrained by constitutional protections of rights, as are their counterparts in law enforcement.

Bail agents arrange bail for the defendant. Because they are seen as serving a clerical function, bail agents are not viewed as part of the law enforcement system. However, they are in a position to provide their clients legal advice, names of attorneys, and information on the legal process. Conversely, law enforcement officers, lawyers, and court personnel are in a position to refer defendants to bail agents. Therefore, it is important that the bail agent have a good reputation among the professionals of the legal system. The symbiotic relationship between bail agents and legal system professionals allows the system to work smoothly and efficiently but also provides opportunities for bribery and corruption.

The most important part of a bail agent's reputation is that clients appear in court as scheduled. When the client disappears, a bail agent may employ a bounty hunter to locate and return the defendant. Because their role is to capture a defendant who has fled prosecution, bounty hunters are frequently seen as playing a role similar to law enforcement. Their status as private individuals affords them both the necessary freedom to find and apprehend defendants as well as opportunities to use excessive violence and act without due process.

The value of bail agents and bounty hunters was seen in the early days of the United States when the law enforcement system was just establishing itself and the vast frontier afforded opportunity to easily escape prosecution. The role of the bounty hunter established by the judiciary in the 1800s remains in effect today. In *Nicolls v. Ingersoll*, the New York Supreme Court ruled that bail agents could appoint another party to retrieve a defendant. They also established that the appointed party could break into a house to capture a defendant and transfer the defendant to another state. These provisions were supported and extended by the U.S. Supreme Court in *Taylor v. Taintor*. The court upheld the right of the bounty hunter to enter a defendant's dwelling as necessary, pursue defendants across state lines, capture a defendant without a warrant, and imprison the defendant.

Both bail agents and bounty hunters are seen as increasing the efficiency of the legal system while decreasing costs associated with pretrial incarceration. The need for both bail agents and bounty hunters increases as the use of bail increases. However, this also means that the potential for corruption and abuse of these functions increases.

Kathleen Barrett
Georgia State University

See Also: Arraignment; Bail Reform Act; Bill of Rights; Bodie of Liberties; Bounty Hunters; Courts; Defendant's Rights; Due Process; Habeas Corpus, Writ of; Habeas Corpus Act of 1679; Habeas Corpus Act of 1863; Judiciary Act of 1789.

Further Readings

Foote, Caleb. "The Coming Constitutional Crisis in Bail: I." *University of Pennsylvania Law Review*, v.113/7 (1965).

Foote, Caleb. "The Coming Constitutional Crisis in Bail: II." *University of Pennsylvania Law Review*, v.113/8 (1965).

Harr, J. Scott and Kären M. Hess. *Constitutional Law and the Criminal Justice System*, 4th ed. Belmont, CA: Wadsworth, 2008.

Neubauer, David W. *America's Courts and the Criminal Justice System*, 8th ed. Belmont, CA: Wadsworth, 2005.

Bail Reform Act

Federal bail procedures have been set by two statutes, the Bail Reform Act of 1966 and the Bail Reform Act of 1984. The differences between the two acts—one designed to protect criminal defendants and the other designed to allow for preventive detention—may be seen as representing the broader changes that the criminal justice system underwent over the course of the late 1960s into early 1980s. Bail reform in the United States began with the bail reform movement of the 1960s. Studies suggested that the cash bail system was overly harsh and discriminatory. Poor defendants were held in jail prior to trial where more affluent defendants in similar cases would have been released; conditions in pretrial detention facilities were so poor as to be worse than the prisons in which convicts were held; defendants would be held in these jails while awaiting trial, only to be acquitted later, after seemingly unnecessary suffering.

In addition to these practical concerns, reformers questioned the constitutionality of the system. Critics believed that the only constitutionally acceptable reason to set bail was to ensure a defendant's presence at trial. From this perspective, the Eighth Amendment's prohibition on excessive bail created a constitutional right to bail, which was further supported in the 1951 case *Stack v. Boyle*, which stated the following:

> Federal law has unequivocally provided that a person arrested for a noncapital offense shall be admitted to bail ... conditioned upon the accused's giving adequate assurance that he will stand trial and submit to sentence if found guilty.

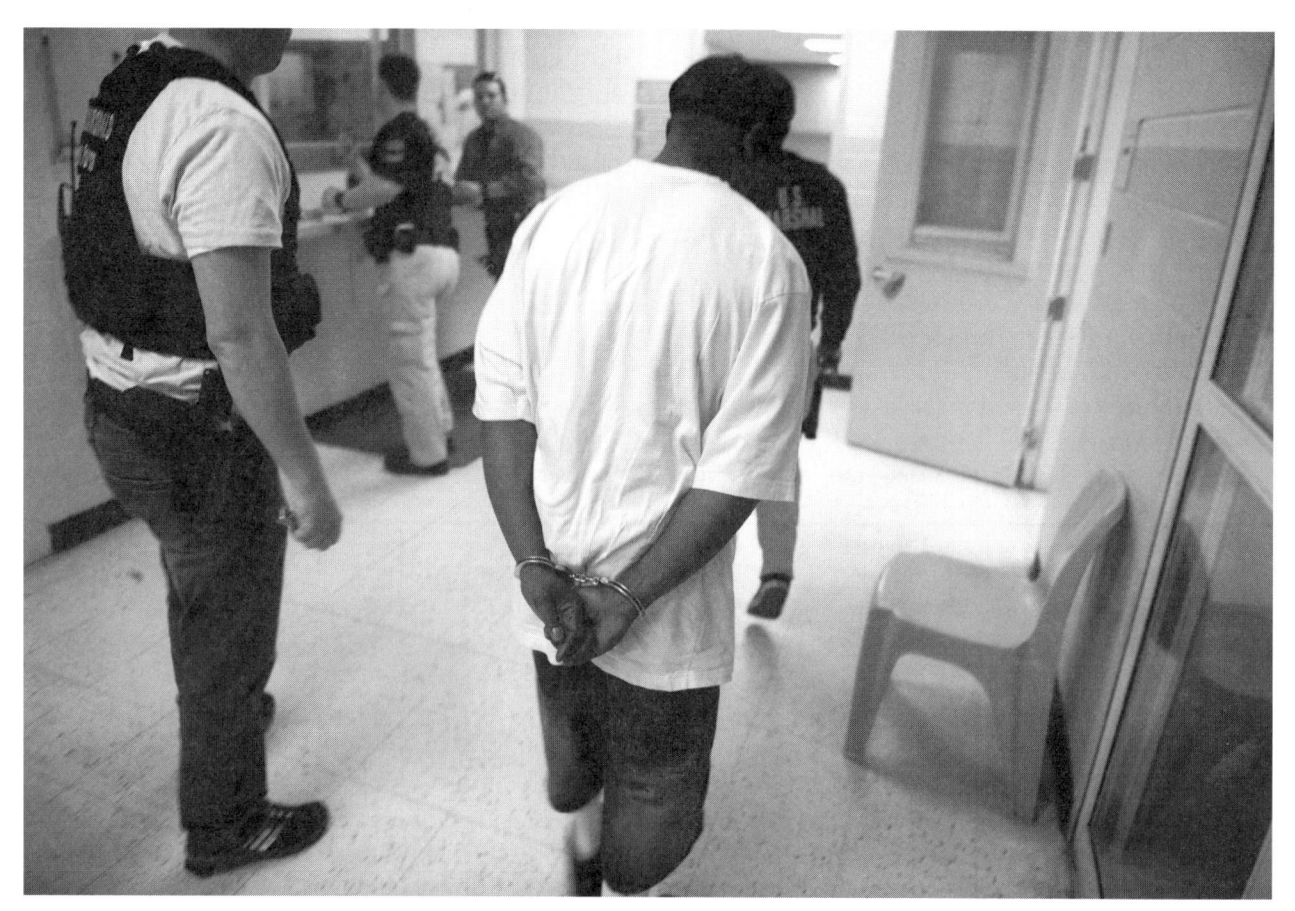

A prisoner being processed in May 2011 after a sweep of drug-related gangs in Tulsa, Oklahoma, that resulted in 129 arrests. The Bail Reform Act of 1984 allows for pretrial detention of dangerous defendants if there is a serious risk that they will flee, obstruct justice, or threaten or harm a witness or juror. Others subject to pretrial detention include those charged with serious drug offenses.

The right to bail was necessary in order to allow a defendant to adequately prepare for his own defense. Additionally, constitutional critics questioned the procedural sufficiency of bail proceedings. Aside from the fact that bail hearings offer lesser procedural protections than a full trial, critics argued that, in practice, judges gave high bail based on evaluations of dangerousness without ever mentioning the issue, thereby without allowing the defendant to respond. The ability to set high bail and thereby incarcerate defendants prior to trial was seen as de facto preventive detention and punishment without trial.

Bail Reform Act of 1966
The Bail Reform Act of 1966 was passed to rectify these complaints. Under the 1966 act, defendants were entitled to be released prior to trial under conditions that were only as harsh as might be required to ensure that the defendant return to face trial. Rather than relying on cash bail, the defendant's presence could be assured with personal assurances, travel restrictions, the use of unsecured bonds, or by placing the defendant in the custody of a third party. These conditions would be determined based the defendant's "risk of flight," that is, the likelihood that he would not return to court if he were allowed to leave. Only in cases that might result in the death penalty was a judge allowed to consider the defendant's dangerousness in determining bail prior to trial.

The first Bail Reform Act came at a peak of emphasis on reform and rehabilitation in the criminal justice system. This emphasis was soon abandoned in the face of the fundamental social changes and shocking increase in crime that the United States experienced in the late 1960s. This change was reflected in debates about bail reform after the first act had passed. Negative reactions to the act were apparent almost immediately, based on the fear that dangerous defendants would commit harmful acts while awaiting trial, including acts of violence and witness tampering.

In 1969, President Richard Nixon asserted that the act had contributed to an increase in crime rates. The following 15 years saw state legislation allowing for pretrial bail and the successful passage of a federal preventive detention statute for the District of Columbia (D.C. Code Ann. §§23-1321 to 1332, 1981). Supreme Court decisions also clearly favored preventive detention, such as *Schall v. Martin*, 467 U.S. 253 (1984), which found preventive detention of juveniles was regulatory rather than punitive and offered sufficient procedural protections to satisfy constitutional requirements.

Bail Reform Act of 1984
The Bail Reform Act of 1984, codified at 18 U.S.C. §§3141–3150, specifically allows for pretrial detention of dangerous defendants in order to protect society from their continued dangerous behavior. Defendants may be eligible for preventive detention if there is a serious risk that they will flee, obstruct justice, or threaten or harm a witness or juror. Additionally, they may be eligible for preventive detention if they are (1) charged for a crime that may result in the death penalty or life imprisonment, (2) charged with certain violent crimes (in 1996 this was amended to include the list of crimes defined as federal crimes of terrorism), (3) charged with nonviolent crimes involving minors, firearms, or destructive devices, (4) charged with certain drug offenses that may result in a sentence of 10 years or more, or (5) charged with a felony and have a history of convictions for the types of offenses listed above.

Defendants who have been convicted of committing any of the above types of offenses while awaiting trial also may be subject to a rebuttable presumption that they should be detained; this means that the burden is on the defendant to prove that there are conditions by which he can be safely released while awaiting trial. Although scholars argued that accurate predictions of dangerousness were impossible, the act was conclusively found to be constitutional in the 1987 Supreme Court case *United States v. Salerno*, 481 U.S. 739 (1987).

Conclusion
In focusing on public safety, the Bail Reform Act of 1984 has been cited as a primary example of the general shift toward preventive criminal justice noted since the 1970s. Outside of the above types of cases, the presumption that a defendant should be released under the least restrictive conditions possible still applies. Still, since 1984, pretrial detention has steadily increased, and the act and Supreme Court cases supporting it have opened the door to preventive detention in other areas,

including civil commitment of sexual predators and detention of enemy combatants. It remains subject to criticisms of discrimination, lack of due process, and undue difficulties placed on defendants who must try to prepare for trial from jail.

Francesca Laguardia
New York University

See Also: Bail and Bond; Fear of Crime; History of Crime and Punishment in America: 1950–1970; History of Crime and Punishment in America: 1970–Present; Incapacitation, Theory of; Violent Crimes.

Further Readings
Corrado, M. L. "Sex Offenders, Unlawful Combatants, and Preventive Detention." *North Carolina Law Review*, v.84 (2005).
Goldkamp, John. "Danger and Detention: A Second Generation of Bail Reform." *Journal of Criminal Law and Criminology*, v.76 (1985).
Harcourt, Bernard. *Against Prediction: Profiling, Policing and Punishing in an Actuarial Age.* Chicago: University of Chicago Press, 2007.
Stack v. Boyle, 342 U.S. 1 (1951).
Wiseman, Samuel. "Discrimination, Coercion and the Bail Reform Act of 1984: The Loss of the Core Constitutional Protections of the Excessive Bail Clause." *Fordham Urban Law Journal*, v.36 (2009).

Bailey, F. Lee

F. Lee Bailey (1933–) was a prominent American defense lawyer who helped establish the role of the modern celebrity attorney. Bailey was recognized as one of the most effective and successful criminal defense lawyers practicing in the United States in the second half of the 20th century. He was noted for his careful selection of jury members and his thorough pretrial preparation. He is also well known for the exorbitant fees that he demanded and received.

Francis Lee Bailey was the eldest of three children; the family lived in Waltham, Massachusetts. His father was a newspaper salesman and his mother, Grace L. Mitchell, was a teacher and nursery school director who died on January 27, 2000. Bailey attended Cardigan Mountain School in Canaan, New Hampshire, and in 1950, he graduated from Kimball Union Academy, also in New Hampshire; then he entered Harvard University. After completing two years at Harvard, he dropped out and enlisted in the U.S. Navy Flight Corps. After joining the U.S. Marine Corps as a fighter pilot, he served as defense counsel in more than 200 court-martial cases. In 1960, Bailey graduated first in his class at Boston University Law School and in the same year was admitted to the Massachusetts bar.

Notable Cases
Bailey was involved in several prominent cases. In 1966, he successfully argued before the U.S. Supreme Court and obtained a retrial for Dr. Samuel H. Sheppard, who had been found guilty of the murder of his wife; Sheppard was found not guilty in the retrial. Other cases included the defense of Albert DeSalvo (the so-called Boston Strangler), of Dr. Carl A. Coppolino for the murder of his wife, of U.S. Army captain Ernest Medina for the My Lai incident, of Patty Hearst for armed bank robberies while kidnapped by the Symbionese Liberation Army, and of O. J. Simpson for the murders of Nicole Brown Simpson and Ronald Goldman.

The innovative use of tactics engineered by Bailey for the legal defense of some of his clients have made him a major legal pioneer. His public grandstanding as an attorney, now widely taken for granted, was considered quite radical when he introduced it. His bold approach to legal defense made him somewhat controversial, but many of his strategies have since become rather common in legal practice. He paid very close attention to the process of jury selection and devised techniques to increase the odds for his clients. For instance, he hired a purported expert on reading body language as a consultant. Bailey was trained as a polygrapher and drew upon his intimate familiarity with the technique to cross-examine expert testimony from witnesses for the prosecution. He astutely used mass media in attempts to sway public attitudes in hope of generating a more sympathetic jury pool. His adroit use of such techniques and strategies helped transform modern approaches to legal defense.

Controversy

Bailey ran afoul of the legal establishment on several occasions. In 1970, he was censured by a Massachusetts judge for breach of legal ethics for being critical of the conviction of one of his clients on the *Tonight Show With Johnny Carson*. In 1971, his license to practice law in New Jersey was suspended for one year after he accused a prosecutor of attempting to bribe witnesses. In 1973, Bailey was indicted in Florida for mail fraud, but the charges were never brought to trial. In 1982, he was arrested for drunk driving in California, but was successfully defended by Robert Shapiro.

On January 25, 1996, U.S. District Judge Maurice Paul, in a Tallahassee, Florida, court, ordered Bailey to surrender stocks that he claimed had been given to him as part of the payment for his legal fees and expenses in his defense of Claude DuBoc. DuBoc was a French Canadian drug trafficker who had been a client of Bailey's and was awaiting sentencing after pleading guilty on May 17, 1994. In question were 602,000 shares of Biochem Pharm, Inc., a Canadian-based pharmaceutical company; the value of the stocks when given to him as payment was estimated to be about $6 million, but by April 1996, the value had risen to about $27 million. Bailey had converted some of the stock to make a down payment on his estate in Florida and to purchase two airplanes, and he spent another $1.9 million to purchase a 74-foot-long yacht, the *Spellbound*.

He at first refused to hand over the remaining stocks, so Judge Paul had Bailey placed in jail for contempt until he turned over the stocks. On March 1, 1996, he surrendered to the U.S. marshal in Gainesville, Florida. After 44 days in federal prison, he turned over about 400,000 shares of stock worth about $16 million that Judge Paul insisted had been forfeited by DuBoc and could not be claimed by Bailey.

On January 14, 2000, he was cited for contempt of court in an unrelated case in Orlando, Florida, for failing to turn over $2 million in assets forfeited by William McCorkle, who was convicted of fraud and money laundering in 1998; Bailey was found guilty of contempt in August 2000 for this case. Finally, on November 21, 2001, he was disbarred by the Florida Supreme Court; he was found guilty of seven counts of misconduct, including misappropriating funds while defending DuBoc, giving false testimony, and disclosure of confidential client information. He was also ordered to pay $24,400 for court costs. On April 11, 2003, Bailey received reciprocal disbarment in Massachusetts.

Writings

Bailey is also an accomplished author. He has written 17 books. In one of his early books, *The Defense Never Rests*, published with coauthor Harvey Aronson in 1971, he asserted that the competency of an individual's lawyer, which he admitted was directly related to how much money he or she could spend on his or her defense, was more important in gaining an acquittal than the individual's actual innocence or guilt.

In 1971, Bailey, with coauthor Henry Rothblatt, published *Successful Techniques for Criminal Trials*, a manual for use by defense attorneys; it emphasizes strategy and tactics and presents the basic mechanics of the role of defense counsel. In 1975, he published *For the Defense*, which describes his bold and innovative style of legal defense. In 1977, with coauthor John Greenya, he published *Cleared for the Approach: F. Lee Bailey in Defense of Flying*. In 2008, he published *When the Husband Is the Suspect*, which provides an overview of some of the most notorious cases of spousal homicide in the United States, including profiles of Sam Sheppard, Robert Blake, Claus von Bulow, and O. J. Simpson.

Victor B. Stolberg
Essex County College

See Also: DeSalvo, Albert; Famous Trials; Legal Counsel; Sheppard, Sam; Simpson, O. J.; Trials.

Further Readings
Bailey, F. Lee and Harvey Aronson. *The Defense Never Rests*. New York: Signet, 1972.
Robinson, Kenneth Michael. *The Great American Mail-Fraud Trial: United States of America v. Glenn W. Turner, F. Lee Bailey, Dare to Be Great, Koscot Interplanetary Incorporated et al*. New York: Nash Publishers, 1976.
Whitten, Les. *F. Lee Bailey*. New York: Avon, 1971.

Bakker, Jim

Jim Bakker is a television evangelist who had a spectacular and very public fall from grace. Sex scandals led to his resigning as chairman of the Praise the Lord (PTL) ministry. He was convicted on 24 counts of mail and wire fraud and conspiracy. Jim Bakker was born James Orsen Bakker on January 2, 1940, in Muskegon, Michigan. He graduated from Muskegon High School in 1959. Jim Bakker met his future wife, Tammy Faye, at North Central Bible College in Minneapolis, Minnesota. In 1961, they left the school and got married.

In 1966, Jim and Tammy Faye debuted their first evangelical television show on Pat Robertson's Christian Broadcast Network (CBN). Jim Bakker was the original star of the popular *700 Club* on the CBN. Jim Bakker was known for weeping on air while encouraging his viewers to send money to save him and Christianity. Jim and Tammy Faye Bakker split from CBN in 1972 and cofounded the Trinity Broadcast Network, where, with Paul and Jan Crouch, they created their *Praise the Lord* (PTL) television show. In 1974, Jim and Tammy Faye created their own *PTL Club* television show and associated PTL ministry; by 1978, it included a satellite network on 1,200 cable systems with 13.5 million viewers. As part of PTL, they started building Heritage USA in Fort Mill, South Carolina, which was to be a 2,300-acre Christian-themed retreat, gospel park, and condominium resort project. While only 250 rooms were available at Heritage USA, Bakker sold over 68,000 partnerships, which were supposed to provide three nights of lodging each year at the resort. It was estimated that contributions requested from PTL viewers exceeded $1 million a week.

On January 3, 1987, Jessica Hahn, a former PTL secretary, admitted to reporters that she had a sexual encounter with Jim Bakker at a motel in

The pyramid-shaped headquarters of Jim and Tammy Faye Bakker's PTL ministries in Pineville, North Carolina, as it looked in 1988. Jim Bakker was found guilty of one count of conspiracy, eight counts of mail fraud, 15 counts of wire fraud, and tax evasion the next year. While Bakker was sentenced to 45 years in a minimum-security penitentiary and fined $500,000, he ended up serving only four-and-a-half years in prison after successful appeals that resulted in two separate sentence reductions.

Florida on December 6, 1980. She claimed that John Wesley Fletcher, a PTL preacher, arranged the assignation and that she was then paid to keep silent. It was later learned that PTL executive vice president Richard Dortch had paid Hahn $265,000 with funds reportedly obtained from Roe Messner, a contractor, for nonexistent work done at the Heritage USA passion play amphitheater.

Other allegations of sexual misconduct surfaced from those within PTL, including Fletcher, who claimed that he and Bakker had homosexual relations and that Fletcher had obtained young men for homosexual acts with Bakker. On March 19, 1987, Jim Bakker resigned as PTL chairman. Jerry Falwell, cofounder of Moral Majority, was selected by Bakker to be his successor. However, Falwell found that there had been considerable misappropriation of PTL funds. In May 1987, the Assemblies of God Church revoked Jim Bakker's ministerial credentials. PTL filed for bankruptcy on June 12, 1987. Falwell resigned as PTL chairman in October 1987. In August 1989, the Heritage USA assets were sold for $65 million to Stephen Mernick, a Toronto-based real estate developer.

On October 5, 1989, Jim Bakker was found guilty on all counts, including one count of conspiracy, eight counts of mail fraud, 15 counts of wire fraud, and tax evasion. He was sentenced to 45 years in a minimum-security penitentiary and fined $500,000 by Judge Robert D. Potter at the federal courthouse in Charlotte, North Carolina. Bakker was immediately taken to the Federal Correctional Institution in Talladega, Alabama, to begin serving his sentence; he was later transferred to the Federal Medical Center in Rochester, Minnesota. In August 1991, on appeal, the sentence was reduced to 18 years. On March 13, 1992, Jim and Tammy Faye Bakker were divorced. A sentence reduction hearing was held on November, 16, 1992, and his sentence was reduced to eight years. He was transferred to a minimum-security federal prison in Jesup, Georgia, in August 1993. Jim Bakker was moved to a halfway house on July 1, 1994, and he was released from the Federal Bureau of Prison's custody on December 1, 1994, after serving four and a half years.

A North Carolina jury threw out a class action suit filed on behalf of the over 160,000 previous supporters who in the 1980s contributed up to $7,000 each to PTL coffers. In 1998, Bakker married his second wife, Lori Graham Bakker, and they started a new ministry called Covenant House. They then moved to Branson, Missouri, where they established a new church, television show, and condominium project called Morningside.

Victor B. Stolberg
Essex County College

See Also: Fraud; Religion and Crime, Contemporary; Religion and Crime, History of; Religion and Crime, Sociology of.

Further Readings
Bakker, Jim, with Ken Abraham. *I Was Wrong: The Untold Story of the Shocking Journey From PTL Power to Prison and Beyond*. Nashville, TN: Thomas Nelson, 1996.
Shepard, Charles E. *Forgiven: The Rise and Fall of Jim Bakker and the PTL Ministry*. New York: Atlantic Monthly Press, 1989.

Ballistics

Ballistics is the science of how a projectile travels in flight. Ballistics has been used for more than 150 years by police to match guns to crime scenes. Most people think of crime dramas such as *CSI* when they hear the term *ballistics* and only consider the comparison of bullets in the labs of those dramas. Ballistics, however, is much more than that. It includes the bullet exiting from the gun (internal ballistics), the bullet traveling through the air (external ballistics), and the bullet traveling into and/or through the target (terminal ballistics).

History of Ballistics
The extensive use of firearms in the United States, especially in the west, meant guns were often used in the commission of crimes. Police, therefore, often needed to be able to match a gun to a particular crime. This occurred somewhat by accident in the beginning, but before long, ballistics became

an accepted practice of police investigations. The first successful attempt at matching ballistic characteristics occurred in 1835 by Henry Goddard. He was an English "thief taker" (what would now be called a bounty hunter). During one case, he noticed an unusual marking on a bullet removed from a shooting victim. He was able to match that blemish to an imperfect bullet mold found in the suspect's home.

For many years, bullet comparison was crude, and only entailed looking at bullets with the naked eye. It was not until 1898 that microscopic comparisons were made. This process was introduced by a German chemist, Paul Jeserich, when he fired a test bullet from a suspect's gun and compared that fired bullet under a microscope to a bullet pulled from a shooting victim. Using the microscope, Jeserich was able to better examine and compare the tiny markings on the bullet. In 1922, an attorney and researcher of bullet identification, A. J. Eddy, testified in a murder case regarding his own experiments with the suspected murder weapon. This was the first testimony related to guns' leaving individualized marks and led to the conviction of the suspect. The conviction was later upheld by the Arizona Supreme Court. In 1925, the Bureau of Forensic Ballistics was created by Charles E. Waite, Calvin H. Goddard, Philip O. Gravelle, and John H. Fisher as a private firm that sought to provide firearms identification services to the police. Goddard and Gravelle developed comparison microscopy, where two bullets could be compared under the same microscope. This allowed easier identification of matching striations on fired bullets. The company went out of business in 1929 because the Federal Bureau of Investigation (FBI) developed a lab of its own to help police investigations.

The chief forensics firearms examiner with the Multi-National Corps–Iraq Provost Marshal's Office Law Enforcement Forensics Lab fires a Dragunob sniper rifle into a machine that catches the round. The test round can then be compared with other rounds fired from the same weapon in order to determine whether it was used in a particular crime.

For many years, there was no national database of ballistics. The FBI had a ballistics lab, but most ballistics work was done by local law enforcement, and the investigations were essentially on a case-by-case basis. This only allowed bullets to be compared on a localized level. In the early 1990s, the FBI and the Bureau of Alcohol, Tobacco, and Firearms (ATF) both attempted to develop a national-level database where bullets from across the United States would be cataloged and ballistics matches could be made on a national level. The FBI database was called DRUGFIRE, and the ATF database was called the Integrated Ballistics Identification System (IBIS).

In the beginning, IBIS only recorded bullet markings, while DRUGFIRE only documented cartridge casing marks. These two programs were combined in 1997 with the development of the NIBIN (National Integrated Ballistic Information Network Program) system. In this system, each agency contributed its part of the identification process. NIBIN was transferred completely to the ATF in 2003. The database does not match the markings but holds the images for a firearms examiner to match them. The database will find a batch of similarly marked entries, but a human must do the final comparison for an admissible match. Nearly 100,000 pieces of evidence have been entered into NIBIN to date, with approximately 10,000 positive matches made by experts.

Over the years, ballistics has been used in several high-profile criminal investigations. In 1963, ballistics was used to identify the gun used by Lee Harvey Oswald in the assassination of President John F. Kennedy. In that case, FBI firearms examiners linked three bullet fragments and three cartridge casings to Oswald's rifle. In 1976, New York was captivated by the murders of the serial killer David Berkowitz (the Son of Sam). The New York Police Department was able to determine what type of gun was used in the killings from distinctive markings on the bullets.

Ballistics has not always been accepted as evidence in court. There have been frequent attempts to exclude firearms examiner testimony or to discredit ballistics as a science altogether. In a 1997 case that reached the U.S. Supreme Court, Anthony David Smith appealed his conviction for the murder of his wife, challenging the ballistics used in the case. In that case, the court ruled that the testimony should have been excluded because the expert witness had no formal training in ballistics but was a recreational hunter. This established that courts would only accept the testimony of trained ballistics experts if the bullet comparisons were to be admissible in court.

After many years of inconsistency in admitting ballistic evidence, the U.S. Supreme Court in *United States v. Jose Santiago* (2002) was asked to determine if ballistics experts qualified as experts the same as other scientists, and if the testimony of ballistics experts would assist the jury in understanding evidence (a key requirement for scientific evidence to be admitted into court). The court found that his testimony would clearly assist the jury in answering the question of a match between bullets and shell casings from the crime scene and the gun recovered from the defendant. The court disagreed that forensic ballistics is a pseudo-science and allowed the testimony based on the expert's background in ballistic science.

The ruling in *Jose Santiago* was strengthened in 2003 in *United States v. Michael J. O'Driscoll*. In this case, the court ruled that ballistics meets evidentiary rule requirements necessary for it to be admitted in court and that ballistics is a proper form of expert testimony. In 2004, the court in *United States v. Richard Hicks* also upheld expert testimony in ballistics. The expert in this case had received FBI training in firearms comparisons testing and had completed examinations for more than 20 years. These cases show that ballistics has become an accepted part of criminal investigations and court cases.

Science of Ballistics

A fundamental element of ballistics is examining rifling marks. This is what is referred to as internal ballistics. This includes comparing a bullet against one known to have been fired from a particular gun, comparing two bullets, and other comparisons. The goal is to establish which gun fired a particular bullet. This type of comparison is possible because of the way guns are made and because of rifling inside the barrel of a gun. A gun barrel is rifled, or imprinted with the spirals that help stabilize the projectile when in flight. As the bullet moves through the barrel, it leaves striations (markings). Each gun leaves a different pattern of striations, enabling a bullet to be matched to the correct gun.

There are other marks left by a gun. One mark is made by the firing pin striking the primer of the bullet. Markings are also made on the casing by firing the gun. The casing of a bullet moves slightly within the barrel when the gun is fired. This leaves markings on the casing that can link the casing to the gun that fired it. For semiautomatic weapons, markings are also left on the casing by the extractor and ejector of the gun. The extractor removes the spent casing from the firing chamber of the firearm and removes the casing from the gun. These marks are found on the rim of the expelled casing.

The basic goal of ballistics is matching a bullet to a gun using the distinctive markings on the bullet or on the casing. There is actually much more to ballistics than just matching, however. The science of ballistics involves how the bullet exits from the gun (internal ballistics), how the bullet travels through the air (external ballistics), and what happens when the bullet hits the target (terminal ballistics). All of these elements combine to make a distinctive set of marks that can place a fired round from a gun with that gun. Police and other investigators use these markings to solve crimes.

Also important to ballistics use in criminal investigations is what happens to the bullet once it makes impact and what happens to the object impacted. This is called external ballistics. Several types of external ballistics are important to solving crimes. These are penetration within the target, the damage done to the target (called a permanent cavity and a temporary cavity), and fragmentation of the bullet itself. Penetration is how deep into the target the bullet travels. Bullets are typically not made to pass through a target. They are made to stop 6–12 inches into the target. This creates the most damage and allows a complete transfer of energy from the bullet to the target (whereas a bullet that exits the target takes most of the energy with it). Penetration is important to criminal investigations because rifle bullets will often penetrate deeper than pistol bullets.

Two things happen to the target when a bullet penetrates it. A permanent cavity is caused by the path of the bullet—in other words, the bullet hole. A temporary cavity is caused by stretching the inside tissues around the path of the bullet caused by the continued transfer of energy into the tissues surrounding the entry point. The permanent and temporary cavities can tell police such things as how far away the gun was fired from the target, what type of gun was used, and the angle from which the gun was fired.

Fragmentation is caused by pieces of the bullet splintering off and entering other areas of tissue from the permanent cavity. For example, a shot to the abdomen could result in fragments causing damage to parts of the rib cage. Fragmentation can also cause collateral bleeding such as when a fragment breaks off and cuts an artery in another part of the body beyond the permanent cavity. Fragmentation can also tell investigators about the angles, proximity, and type of gun used and aids in identifying markings of the bullet.

Ballistics Investigations

Typically, for ballistics to be compared between a crime scene and a gun in the possession of police, bullets must be fired from the gun. The bullets must be fired under similar circumstances, however, for accurate comparisons to be made. For example, firing a bullet against a brick wall would produce a different bullet for comparison than one recovered from a body or from the wall of a house. To mimic a bullet fired into a person, or to get a "clean" bullet for comparison, ballistic gelatin and ballistic soap are often used. Ballistic gelatin can be mixed to compare to human tissues, while ballistic soap is meant to be denser than tissue (for example, in comparing a bullet recovered from a wall).

Obtaining "clean" bullets for comparison and understanding internal, external, and terminal ballistics allows police to understand how guns are used in crimes and to compare guns used in crimes to those discovered through investigations. The science of ballistics has helped police solve crimes for more than 150 years, and as the science continues to advance, it is likely even more cases will be able to be solved with ballistics.

Jennifer M. Miller
University of Arkansas at Little Rock

See Also: Berkowitz, David; Crime Scene Investigation; Forensic Science.

Further Readings

Haag, Lucien C. *Shooting Incident Reconstruction*. Maryland Heights, MO: Academic Press, 2006.

Joyce, Jaime. *Bullet Proof! The Evidence That Guns Leave Behind*. New York: Scholastic, 2007.

Nickell, Joe and John F. Fischer. *Crime Science: Methods of Forensic Detection*. Lexington: University Press of Kentucky, 1999.

Song, J. and T. Vorburger. *Development of NIST Standard Bullets and Casings Status Reports*. Rockville, MD: National Institute of Justice, 2000.

University of Utah Spencer S. Eccles Heath Sciences Library. "Firearms Tutorial." http://library.med.utah.edu/WebPath/TUTORIAL/GUNS/GUNBLST.html (Accessed December 2010).

Baltimore, Maryland

Baltimore, Maryland, a major American city, the 21st most populous in the nation, is located on an upper tributary of the Chesapeake Bay, roughly 40 miles from Washington, D.C., and 100 miles from Philadelphia, Pennsylvania. It is home to the Inner Harbor, Baltimore Ravens, and Baltimore Orioles. An industrial city, Baltimore played a critical role in the historical development of the United States. More recently, Baltimore has been beset by violence, stemming to a large degree from the drug trade that has plagued—if not defined—the city for the better part of the modern era, particularly in the 21st century. Baltimore's struggles with drugs and related crime have been chronicled and embedded in critically acclaimed elements of popular culture, have led to critical assessments of the city's approach with respect to crime and drugs, and have contributed to reconsiderations as to the effectiveness and propriety of the "war on drugs" more broadly.

Historical Background

In 1752, Baltimore, a port city, had a modest population of about 200. By this time, other east coast port cities, such as Boston, New York, and Philadelphia, were thriving. Baltimore's location—as the farthest west of these existing cities and as an inland port—began to give it competitive advantages and resulted in Baltimore's establishment as a hub of industry and trade. Growth was such that, by the late 1700s, the city was home to around 20,000 residents. Baltimore briefly served as the nation's capital from December 1776 to February 1777, as the leaders of the nascent nation left Philadelphia to avoid hostilities with the British.

Following the War of 1812, in which the American forces withstood a British naval attack on Baltimore's Fort McHenry, the Baltimore and Ohio (B&O) railroad was built, connecting Baltimore with cities in the midwest and significantly enhancing Baltimore's position as a hotbed of manufacturing and commerce. Rail between Baltimore and Washington was also built by 1834. As travelers from the north and west went through Baltimore in order to reach Washington, Baltimore served as a central link in the nation.

In the mid-19th century, riots related to labor or politics were not uncommon in Baltimore. In the 1830s and 1840s, disputes between rival volunteer fire companies regularly escalated into violent "collisions." In 1836, in the wake of frequent rioting, the *Baltimore Sun* asked,

> When shall we be able to pass a Sabbath day without being called upon to record some act of disgraceful violation of the peace, some daring outrage amounting almost to bloodshed?

Election day riots provoked by nativists in the 1850s also helped contribute to its reputation. Baltimore came to be known as "Mob City."

One particular episode of unrest was of great historical and constitutional significance. Responding to Abraham Lincoln's call for troops on the heels of the Civil War, in 1861, a group of hundreds of volunteers from Massachusetts, traveling south toward Washington, were greeted by a mob of 20,000. Baltimore, in a border state, was home to southern sympathizers. In the ensuing melee, several people were killed, with both sides suffering losses. Rail bridges were burned north of the city in order to prevent federal troops from going through Baltimore again. The riots and burning of bridges led President Lincoln to authorize the suspension of habeas corpus—the time-honored writ used by an individual to challenge the legality of his detention—"at any point on or in the vicinity of any military line which is

Baltimore had become known as "Mob City" by the mid-19th century for its frequent riots. The engraving shows a violent confrontation between troops of the Sixth Maryland Regiment and striking workers during the Great Railway Strike of 1877.

now or which shall be used between the city of Philadelphia and the city of Washington."

John Merryman, accused of having taken part in these disruptive activities, was arrested by a general pursuant to the president's order suspending habeas rights. In the landmark ruling of *Ex Parte Merryman* (1861), the Supreme Court was asked whether President Lincoln could lawfully suspend the writ of the habeas corpus. The court answered in the negative, ruling that Congress, not the executive, possesses the power to suspend the writ and held that Lincoln's unilateral suspension of the writ was unconstitutional as a result.

Baltimore bore witness to an economic depression in the 1870s and the effects of postwar migration by freed blacks into the city. Riots, strikes, and general unrest related to class and race accompanied these precarious times. For example, in the Great Railway Strike of 1877, B&O railway workers objected to wage cuts by striking and attempting to impede the progress of railcars along the route. The workers clashed violently with federal troops charged with protecting the railways and restoring order. That said, Baltimore experienced urban development and economic growth as a result of its industrial capabilities.

Contemporary Era

In another wartime setting—World War II—Baltimore's contribution in manufacturing to meet military needs resulted in further economic and population expansion. In particular, white migrants moved to Baltimore in search of industrial work, helping the city reach about 1 million residents by 1950—its largest population on record. In the postwar period, however, a confluence of factors led to population decreases, including the loss of manufacturing jobs, the desirability of more open suburban living, and "white flight" brought on by the desegregation of schools, riots in response to the assassination of Dr. Martin Luther King Jr. and the presence of blacks in the city proper. In addition to the movement of whites away from the city, some middle-class blacks similarly migrated into the suburbs. Accordingly, whereas about 35 percent of Baltimore was black in 1950, by 1990 this number had increased significantly to 59 percent.

In the 1950s and 1960s, a heroin epidemic began to take hold in Baltimore. Accompanying this drug activity were significant violence, health problems among addicted residents, increased allocation of city resources to combat the existence and effects of the drug trade, and a general diminution in the quality of life of segments of the city. The state of the city was perceived to improve under the leadership of Governor William Donald Schaefer (1971–86). For example, the city's Inner Harbor was well developed and other parts of the city were revitalized.

Baltimore was not viewed as favorably under the administration of Mayor Kurt L. Schmoke (1988–99). Believing in the futility of the "war on drugs" and that drugs were more of a healthcare issue than a criminal problem, Schmoke advocated the decriminalization of drugs, particularly marijuana. During his tenure, violent crime associated with drugs, particularly heroin and cocaine, reached very high levels. In 1990, for instance, half of all felony prosecutions were drug offenses and 55 percent of all murders were drug related. In 1998, the city's murder rate was over seven times the national average, and the murder rate for blacks was six times higher than for whites. The city ranked second nationwide in violent crime and second in murders among large cities. Due in large part to this violence, Baltimore's population in the 1990s fell 11.5 percent. Baltimore was one of only four large American cities in which its population declined in the 1990s. These and similar statistics contributed to a nationwide reputation for Baltimore's struggles with drugs and crime. Indeed, the city has been referred to as "Bodymore, Murdaland."

These struggles continued in the 2000s, which further solidified the city's link to drugs and related violence. In 2002, more than half of all defendants charged for felony crimes were charged with narcotics violations. In 2003, it was reported that approximately 90 percent of homicides in Baltimore are drug related. A front-page story in the *New York Times* declared that Baltimore's 2004 homicide rate was five times that of New York. In 2007, 650 nonfatal shootings took place in the city, which amounts to nearly two per day.

Indicating how serious the heroin epidemic has been in the city for decades, *USA Today* proclaimed, "Baltimore is the heroin capital of the United States," with one in 10 residents—60,000—addicted to the substance. A report found that Baltimore has the highest concentration of heroin use in the country and that of people arrested, about 40 percent of males and 50 percent of females test positive for the drug.

Violent crimes, particularly homicides, have been a central part of Baltimore's identity. In 1985, Baltimore witnessed 213 murders, which, based on a population of more than 761,000, works to a 27.98 murder rate. In 1993, however, there were 353 murders in the city, a 48.77 murder rate. In each of the years in the 1990s, Baltimore had a murder rate greater than 41. By the 2000s, Baltimore had been ranked as the most dangerous city in the nation and the "murder capital" of the United States.

Such crime has led to a disproportionately greater police force as compared to the general population. For example, a 2011 report issued by the Department of Justice's Bureau of Justice Statistics identified the Baltimore Police Department as the 10th-largest local law police department in the nation, consisting of 2,990 sworn officers, even though it is only the 21st-largest city. Baltimore's police force is greater than some state law enforcement agencies, such as Massachusetts (2,310 officers) and Illinois (2,105).

The Baltimore Police Department, formally established in 1853, has had its share of difficulties. A frequent criticism, made perhaps most strongly in the 1990s, has been the department's inability to quell the violent crime associated with the drug trade. Some have objected to the police arrests for petty crimes, seen as insignificant and superficial in comparison to systemic problems in the city, including those tied to drugs. Calls for reform and reorganization were particularly acute in the 1960s and 1990s in large part

A member of a Baltimore Police Department motorcycle unit in 2010. The department is the 10th-largest local law police department in the country, with 2,990 officers.

because drugs and related violent crime continued to outpace police efforts.

Broader Points

The factual situation in Baltimore concerning drugs and violent crime spawned multiple television series that have etched the Baltimore experience with drugs and violence into the nation's social consciousness. *Homicide: Life on the Street* (1993–99) and *The Wire* (2002–08) are perhaps the two most prominent series that have made Baltimore, especially its history with drugs and criminal behavior, part of popular culture. These series depict not only the situation on the ground but also systemic problems that permit drugs, violence, and decaying conditions to persist over many years.

These include a police department's focus on street-level drug arrests. While these arrests may increase statistics that political figures may point to in arguing that safety has been enhanced, apprehending low-level drug dealers leaves the core of the drug operations—the mid- and senior-level drug operatives—untouched and able to continue their activities. The low-level dealers are not only easily replaced by individuals attracted by the allure and financial gains of the drug trade but are generally insulated from the actual decision making of the higher-level people in the drug rings. Thus, they make for modestly informative criminals for police purposes. These arrests, however, do provide some measure of statistical evidence for political statements that the police and political powers are focusing on drugs and related crime. The police and politicians may claim an improved quality of life in certain areas of the city, but skeptics may counter that such arrests only displace—rather than eliminate—drug and violent crime.

Politics aside, there is a question as to whether the police forces, given budgetary constraints, are able to conduct the sophisticated investigations necessary to nab the higher-level drug operatives. Moreover, the school system, also affected by limited budgets, appeared in *The Wire* to be unable to effectively reach students and to provide an attractive alternative to the streets and corners of the city. The media was infected by those more interested in personal accolades and quick stories than in the complex, nuanced reporting on the city's systemic social and criminal problems, which would require serious investigations that may lie beyond the interest or capabilities of the journalists on staff. There is ample factual information supporting these portrayals of Baltimore, though one point of these series is to suggest that other major cities may be contending with similar problems that enable drugs and crime to carry on relatively unabated.

Dawinder "Dave" S. Sidhu
University of Baltimore School of Law

See Also: *Barron v. Mayor of Baltimore*; Drug Abuse and Addiction, Contemporary; Habeas Corpus Act of 1863; Maryland; Poe, Edgar Allen; Riots; Television, Crime in; Television, Police in.

Further Readings

Bar Association of Baltimore City. "The Drug Crisis and Underfunding of the Justice System in Baltimore City." Report of the Russell Committee 9, 1990.

La Vigne, Nancy G., et al. *A Portrait of Prison Reentry in Maryland*. Washington, DC: Urban Institute, Justice Policy Center, 2003.

Rehnquist, William H. *All the Laws But One: Civil Liberties in Wartime*. New York: Random House, 1998.

Taylor, Ralph B. *Breaking Away From Broken Windows: Baltimore Neighborhoods and the Nationwide Fight Against Crime, Grime, Fear, and Decline*. Boulder, CO: Westview Press, 2001.

Barron v. Mayor of Baltimore

The Bill of Rights, the first 10 amendments to the U.S. Constitution, lists the most valued freedoms held by Americans and states that the government may not legally violate these freedoms. The decision in *Barron v. Mayor of Baltimore* held that the Bill of Rights only limited the actions of the federal government and did not apply to state or local governments. Although this decision has not been overruled, in the 20th century its legacy and impact were limited by a series of

U.S. Supreme Court decisions holding that some amendments do restrict the actions of all governments—a process known as the incorporation of the Bill of Rights.

In order to undertake a series of city developments, Baltimore redirected the natural course of several streams. This had the effect of washing deposits of earth and sand into some of the city's wharfs. *Barron* came to the U.S. Supreme Court on appeal from the Court of Appeals for the Western Shore of Maryland when one wharf owner sought compensation for the loss of business that resulted from the reduction of the water level in his wharf. The court was asked to decide whether the takings clause of the Fifth Amendment—which says "nor shall private property be taken for public use without just compensation"—required Baltimore to pay compensation. The larger question was whether provisions of the Bill of Rights restricted state and local governments. Writing for a unanimous court, Chief Justice John Marshall held that it did not and that, as a result, Baltimore had not engaged in a taking of property for which there was a legal remedy under the U.S. Constitution.

The counsel for Barron, the wharf owner, contended that Article I, Section 10 of the Constitution supports the interpretation that the Fifth Amendment places specific limits on the powers of state governments. This argument could not withstand judicial scrutiny, argued Marshall, when one examined Section 9 of the same article, which places restrictions on governmental power using broad language. While these restrictions might be read to limit any government, they also appear in Section 10 but this time as specific limits on the actions of state governments. Consequently, when the Constitution limits the states, it does so expressly, and only "on subjects entrusted to the general government, or in which the people of all the states feel an interest."

Marshall explained that this conclusion was supported by the fact that the Constitution was a document created by the people of the nation for themselves and their *national government*, just as the constitution of each state was established by that state's citizens for themselves and their *state government*. Any limit that a citizenry wished to place upon its government had, therefore, to be expressed using specific language—and there was no such language in the Bill of Rights to indicate that it restricts the state governments. This was consistent with the theme of national unity present in many of the decisions during Marshall's tenure as chief justice (1801–35).

Marshall interpreted the Constitution and the Bill of Rights as two documents underpinned by the same principles. This understanding of the relationship of the Bill of Rights to the Constitution was generally consistent with the way in which Americans thought of individual rights in the late 18th century. However, after the decision in *Barron*, many people sought instead to highlight the differences between the Bill of Rights and the Constitution. For example, they emphasized that discussions of individual rights were conspicuously absent from the language of the Constitution.

Debates about the relationship between the Constitution and the Bill of Rights played a role in the framing of the Fourteenth Amendment, which was ratified in 1868. Through a series of 20th-century decisions, the Supreme Court has used the due process clause of this amendment—"nor shall any State deprive any person of life, liberty, or property, without due process of law"—to hold that provisions of the Bill of Rights can restrict the actions of state governments. This process intensified during the 1960s under the leadership of Chief Justice Earl Warren. To date, most of the provisions of the Bill of Rights have been incorporated. However, because of *Barron*, some provisions still only limit the federal government.

Helen J. Knowles
Whitman College

See Also: Bill of Rights; Constitution of the United States of America; Marshall, John; Supreme Court, U.S.; Warren, Earl.

Further Readings
Amar, Akhil Reed. *The Bill of Rights: Creation and Reconstruction.* New Haven, CT: Yale University Press, 1998.
Hall, Kermit L., Paul Finkelman, and James W. Ely, Jr. *American Legal History: Cases and Materials.* New York: Oxford University Press, 2010.
Newmyer, R. Kent. *The Supreme Court Under Marshall and Taney.* Arlington Heights, IL: Harlan Davidson, 1968.

Beaumont, Gustave de

French magistrate, aristocrat, and prison reformer Gustave de Beaumont was born February 6, 1802. In 1831–32, he investigated the penitentiaries of the United States with his lifelong friend Alexis de Tocqueville (1805–59). Upon their return to France, they coauthored *On the Penitentiary System in the United States and Its Application in France* (1833), which academics still consider a classic work in the fields of penology and the history of Jacksonian America. Beaumont also published a novel, *Marie; or, Slavery in the United States* (1835), and the sociological study, *Ireland: Social, Political, and Religious* (1839). In the late 1830s, he became a member of the French parliament and served in the National Assembly after the French revolution of 1848. Following a brief imprisonment for opposing Louis Napoleon's coup d'état in 1751, Beaumont retired from public life. He died 15 years later on February 22, 1866, in Paris.

In 1831, Beaumont and Tocqueville received a commission from France's July Monarchy to investigate the United States' two competing penitentiary systems: the New York system of daytime congregate labor and nighttime solitary confinement at the state's Auburn and Sing Sing prisons, and the Pennsylvania system of completely separate confinement at hard labor at Philadelphia's Eastern State Penitentiary. The two men traversed the United States for nine months, visiting prisons, almshouses, and houses of refuge throughout the nation. In 1833, they published their report, which compared and contrasted the penitentiary systems of the United States and made recommendations for the reform of France's penal code and penitentiaries.

Beaumont and Tocqueville's *On the Penitentiary System* offers insightful observations on the workings of prison discipline in Jacksonian America. The men visited New York's Auburn and Sing Sing prisons, where during the day, prisoners worked together in silence, in factory-like workshops. At night, the prisoners of New York's state prisons retired to solitary cells. Beaumont and Tocqueville reported that guards enforced the prisons' regulations through the ferocious snap of the whip. In Pennsylvania's Eastern State Penitentiary, on the other hand, prisoners spent their entire confinement isolated from one another inside solitary cells where they read the Bible and worked as shoemakers and weavers and at other crafts suited to solitary labor. Beaumont and Tocqueville claimed wrongly that prisoners at the Eastern State Penitentiary were subjected to a "wholly mental punishment." An 1835 investigation would bring the guards' physical torture of inmates to the public's attention.

Gustave de Beaumont, shown here in an 1848 portrait, traveled the United States with Alexis de Tocqueville and made a detailed comparison of the New York and Pennsylvania systems of prison labor and confinement for potential use in France.

They augmented their personal observations with interviews with guards, wardens, prisoners, and prison reformers, and self-compiled statistics on recidivism. Toward the conclusion of their 1833 report, Beaumont and Tocqueville reflected on the applicability of the penitentiary systems of the United States to France. Both the New York and the Pennsylvania systems rested upon the isolation of convicts from one another and hard labor. In the systems the men observed, silence, isolation, forced labor, and compulsory religious instruction punished all prisoners and maybe even reformed some. Theoretically, they preferred the Pennsylvania system, but the high cost of building prisons along this plan led the men to recommend the New York system as a more economical alternative. The men, however, stopped short of advocating the direct implementation of the New York system in France. Instead, they called for a measured, systematic reform of France's prisons, which contemporaries considered cesspits of immorality, disease, and criminality.

On August 20, 1849, after over a decade of debate in which Beaumont and Tocqueville participated, the government of France's Second Republic issued an executive order to construct cellular penitentiaries modeled upon the Pennsylvania system. In 1853, before the new penitentiaries were built, Napoleon III overturned the order, and a year later, France began the transportation of convicted criminals to its penal colony on Devil's Island in French Guiana.

The recommendations of Beaumont and Tocqueville's *On the Penitentiary System in the United States and Its Application in France* were never fulfilled during their lifetimes. Nonetheless, the book distinguishes Beaumont and Tocqueville as astute observers of penitentiary discipline and of the intersection of punishment and society.

Jonathan Nash
State University of New York, Albany

See Also: Auburn State Prison; Corrections; Eastern State Penitentiary; History of Crime and Punishment in America: 1783–1850; New York; Penitentiaries; Pennsylvania; Punishment Within Prison; Sing Sing Correctional Facility; Tocqueville, Alexis de.

Further Readings
Beaumont, Gustave de. *Ireland: Social, Political, and Religious*, W. C. Taylor, ed. and trans. Cambridge, MA: Belknap Press of Harvard University Press, 2006.
Beaumont, Gustave de. *Marie; or, Slavery in the United States*, Barbara Chapman, trans. Baltimore, MD: Johns Hopkins University Press, 1999.
Beaumont, Gustave de and Alexis de Tocqueville. *On the Penitentiary System in the United States and Its Application in France*. Carbondale: Southern Illinois Press, 1964.
Brogan, Hugh. *Alexis de Tocqueville: A Life*. New Haven, CT: Yale University Press, 2006.
Pierson, G. W. *Tocqueville in America*. Baltimore, MD: Johns Hopkins University Press, 1996.

Bedford Hills Correctional Facility

Bedford Hills Correctional Facility, located in Westchester County, New York, is the state's sole maximum-security prison for women as well as the reception center for all women committed to the New York State Department of Corrections. Bedford's history as a female penal institution dates back to the turn of the 20th century. From its earliest years as a reformatory, Bedford Hills has been on the forefront of penology and has served as a model for other prisons.

In the late 19th century, the women's reformatory movement and the flurry of concern over prostitution and "white slavery" led to a focus on the moral uplift of fallen women. In this context, reformers such as Josephine Shaw Lowell and Abby Hopper Gibbons successfully persuaded New York state officials to establish a female reformatory at Bedford Hills in 1892. The State Reformatory for Women at Bedford was the third such facility in New York when it finally opened in 1901 to receive women between ages 16 and 30 convicted of misdemeanors who were considered reformable. These women were given indeterminate sentences, the length of which would be determined by their behavior and progress at Bedford.

Initial Success
Unlike male prisons that held convicts behind metal bars in massive stone and concrete buildings set behind high walls, women's reformatories tended to house small groups of inmates in cottages in rural pastoral settings. It was believed that in a familial setting under the guidance of morally exemplary matrons, fallen women could

be redeemed. Moreover, it was believed that exposure to the outdoors and fresh air was healthy for these women. As such, Bedford was constructed on 200 acres of rural land and included, in addition to administrative buildings, four cottages among which women were classified by age and behavior. Named for the reformatory's founders, the cottages each had a kitchen, flower garden, china and linens, and 28 individual rooms.

Katherine Bement Davis, a Vassar graduate with a Ph.D. from the University of Chicago, was tapped as Bedford's first superintendent. An educated and professional woman, Davis was not as concerned as some of her forerunners at other institutions with strict gender roles. Thus, although inmates at Bedford did learn domestic arts such as needlework and sewing, Davis sought to diversify the training women received to also include academic and industrial skills. And it was not uncommon to find women at Bedford draining swamps, engaged in masonry, cobbling shoes, building furniture, harvesting ice in winter, and even building a road. Upon release or parole, however, most women still found work only in domestic service.

Davis also embraced the "new penology" of the day that promoted good behavior through rewards. Bedford had an honor cottage for especially well-behaved inmates who had the privilege of electing their own officers and determining discipline for those among them who broke the rules.

The reformatory under Davis ushered in a medical approach to crime control. Looking for a scientific explanation for criminality, Davis received funding in 1910 from the New York Foundation to conduct psychological testing of Bedford's inmates. John D. Rockefeller, Jr., who abhorred prostitution and associated it with feeblemindedness, was impressed with a pamphlet written by Davis on the use of such testing and invited her to join the board of his newly founded Bureau of Social Hygiene in 1911. Funded by Rockefeller, the bureau purchased 71 acres of land adjacent to the reformatory and established the Laboratory of Social Hygiene at Bedford Hills. In an agreement with the state that included a five-year lease of the facility for a nominal fee, the laboratory evaluated inmates to determine their proper sentences and collected data to better understand the causes of crime and prostitution. As studies revealed that many defiant inmates were psychopathic or psychotic, Rockefeller's Bureau of Social Hygiene funded a psychopathic hospital that opened on the grounds of the laboratory in 1916. In 1920, the legislature ordered mentally defective female prisoners sent to the Division for Mentally Defective Women (DMDW) at Bedford, where they would serve indefinite sentences with parole or release to be determined by the superintendent.

Decline

The strains of overcrowding and underfunding at Bedford Hills were somewhat mitigated by Davis's leadership and the presence of additional staff through the Bureau of Social Hygiene. In 1914, however, Davis left Bedford to become the first female commissioner of corrections for New York City. Following her departure, and with

As the first superintendent of Bedford Hills, Katherine Bement Davis helped make it a model for other prisons. Shown here in the early 1910s, she became the first female Commissioner of Corrections for New York City in 1914.

increased overcrowding, the reformatory had disciplinary problems, mismanagement, inmate abuse, escapes, and rebellions over the tenure of four different superintendents. When a 1915 investigation revealed interracial homosexual relations at Bedford Hills, critics blamed Davis's policy of integration, and by 1916, the institution opened two new cottages specifically for African American women. On July 24, 1920, a riot broke out between black and white inmates as they were preparing for a visit from the governor. Local police and state troopers were called in to quell the fighting among nearly 150 women wielding knives, stones, clubs, and irons from the laundry room. In the aftermath, it was announced that psychologist Amos Baker would be brought in to serve as the first male superintendent at Bedford.

Bedford, which had been under the administration of the State Board of Charities, in 1926 came under the authority of the Department of Corrections. In 1932, the DMDW was transferred to Albion, the Bedford reformatory was renamed the Westfield State Farm, and a new prison was built on the grounds. In 1933, the State Prison for Women at Auburn was closed, and felons were sent to the new prison at Bedford. Only in 1970 did the entire complex come to be named Bedford Hills Correctional Facility.

Although Bedford Hills is now a maximum-security prison, there are vestiges of its reformatory past. Although most of the inmates are housed in large cellblocks, there is still an honor cottage on the campus where, as under Davis, the women are subject to fewer restrictions and engage in a form of self-governance. Since opening in 1901, Bedford has maintained a nursery, which is now part of a larger children's center that runs parenting programs, has a playroom for visiting children, and, in coordination with volunteers in the neighboring community, hosts weekend and summer visiting programs for children with mothers incarcerated there. The prison runs a number of tutoring and counseling programs, and inmates have established their own programs, including ACE, and human immunodeficiency virus and acquired immune deficiency syndrome (HIV/AIDS) counseling and education programs.

Logan M. McBride
City University of New York Graduate Center

See Also: Auburn State Prison; Corrections; New York; Prostitution, History of; Women Criminals, History of; Women in Prison.

Further Readings
Freedman, Estelle B. *Their Sisters' Keepers: Women's Prison Reform in America, 1830–1930*. Ann Arbor: University of Michigan Press, 1981.
New York State Archives. "Bedford Hills Correctional Facility." http://www.archives.nysed.gov/a/research/res_topics_legal_corrections_inst_bedford.shtml (Accessed September 2010).
Rafter, Nicole Hahn. *Partial Justice: Women, Prisons, and Social Control*, 2nd ed. New Brunswick, NJ: Transaction Publishers, 1990.

Berkowitz, David

At the age of 24, serial murderer David Berkowitz terrorized New York City residents for more than a year until his apprehension in 1977. His rambling letters to police and to the media added to the public's fear of the bizarre motives and unpredictability of someone claiming to be acting on the orders of a demonically possessed dog. Calling himself the Son of Sam, this seemingly mentally disordered individual prowled the streets, randomly darting out of the darkness and shooting unsuspecting strangers. The public's fear did not end with the arrest, since Berkowitz cautioned from his prison cell that there were others in a satanic conspiracy who would continue the killings. Although only six deaths and seven other injuries resulted from the Son of Sam shootings, the nature of the crimes made this one of the city's most notorious cases.

Berkowitz was born December 1, 1953, in Brooklyn to Betty Falco (a Jewish waitress) whose husband had left her and their daughter several years prior. Because the biological father, Joseph Kleinman (a married, Jewish businessman) insisted, Betty gave up the newborn. He was adopted by Nat and Pearl Berkowitz, a childless Jewish couple. The Berkowitzes told young Berkowitz of his adoption but chose to tell him that his biological mother had died during the birth. Consequently, Berkowitz grew up believing that he had contributed to his mother's death and that his biological father hated him for it. Pearl died of breast cancer when Berkowitz was 14 years old, leaving him devastated by the loss. Nat, the owner of a hardware store, remarried, but Berkowitz did not care for his new stepmother or stepsister. When Nat retired and moved to Florida, Berkowitz enlisted in the service at age 18. He was stationed in Korea, as well as Kentucky, received a marksman rating, and was honorably discharged. During his time in Kentucky, in 1974, he converted from Judaism to the Baptist faith, but soon lost interest in his newfound religion.

After the service, Berkowitz located his biological mother and his older half-sister, Roslyn. He maintained a relationship with them, but that contact started to dissipate around the time he appeared to experience a self-imposed isolation and possibly a decline into mental illness. During this time, Berkowitz held a series of jobs as a security guard, air conditioning duct worker, taxi driver, and postal sorter. He also enrolled in the spring of 1975 at Bronx Community College.

Before his killing spree began, Berkowitz had engaged in fire-setting and would keep journals of dates, times, locations, and call box numbers for the fires. Although police did not find a journal for 1976, from the very detailed accounts Berkowitz kept for 1974, 1975, and 1977, it appears that he set over 1,400 fires. After reportedly hearing voices telling him to kill, he began his attacks, with botched stabbings of one unidentified female and 15-year-old Michelle Forman, minutes apart from each other in the Bronx on Christmas Eve 1975. They survived.

After acquiring a Charter Arms .44-caliber Bulldog revolver on a visit to Houston, Berkowitz used it in the following eight shootings: July 29, 1976 (Bronx), Donna Lauria (18) dead, with Jody Valenti (19) wounded; October 23, 1976 (Queens), Carl Denaro (20) wounded, with Rosemary Keenan escaping harm; November 27, 1976 (Queens), Donna DeMasi (16) wounded, with Joanne Lomino (18) paralyzed; January 30, 1977 (Queens), Christine Freund (26) dead, with John Diel (30) escaping harm; March 8, 1977 (Queens), Virginia Voskerichian (19) dead; April 17, 1977 (Bronx), Valentina Suriani (18) dead, with Alexander Esau (20) dead; July 26, 1977 (Queens), Judy Placido (17) wounded, with Salvatore Lupo (20) wounded; and July 31, 1977 (Brooklyn), Stacy Moskowitz (20) dead, with Robert Violante (20) blinded. Initially, the press dubbed the assailant the .44-Caliber Killer, but after he signed a letter as Son of Sam, that became his label.

Berkowitz's capture took place in his car (containing guns and ammunition) outside his Yonkers apartment building after a six-hour stakeout on August 10, 1977. Police found him through a series of discoveries, such as a parking ticket received by him near the Moskowitz/Violante shooting, a witness coming forward who saw him in the vicinity remove the ticket from his car that night, and reports by neighbors to Yonkers police about odd contacts they had from him. Although Berkowitz claimed to have received commands to kill from the dog belonging to his neighbor, Sam Carr, he pled guilty to all the shootings and received a 365-year prison sentence.

At a 1979 Attica prison press conference, Berkowitz recanted his previous stories about demons and dogs ordering him to kill. In later televised interviews, he said that he was not the shooter in all of the incidents. He implicated Sam Carr's sons (John and Michael), claiming that he and the Carr brothers were members of a satanic cult (the Process Church of the Final Judgment). According to Berkowitz, the Son of Sam shootings were part of a satanic conspiracy and he was chosen to take the fall for all of the murders, even though he participated in only some of them.

Whether Berkowitz suffered from schizophrenia, experiencing delusions (of a demon conspiracy) and auditory hallucinations (of voices telling him to kill), or whether he was malingering may never be known. However, the .44-caliber killings stopped after his arrest. In 2010, for the fifth time, he was denied parole from Sullivan Correctional Facility, where he is a Jew for Jesus and prefers to be called the Son of Hope.

Joan Luxenburg
University of Central Oklahoma

See Also: Attica; New York; Serial and Mass Killers.

Further Readings
Klausner, Lawrence D. *Son of Sam: Based on the Authorized Transcription of the Tapes, Official Documents and Diaries of David Berkowitz.* New York: McGraw-Hill, 1981.

Levin, Jack and James Alan Fox. *Mass Murder: America's Growing Menace*. New York: Plenum Press, 1985.

Terry, Maury. *The Ultimate Evil: An Investigation Into America's Most Dangerous Satanic Cult*. Garden City, NY: Doubleday, 1987.

Bertillon System

Toward the close of the 19th century, police agencies worldwide developed innovative scientific methods to help combat crime. Chief among these techniques were classification systems designed to measure and catalog physical, psychological, and social characteristics collected from criminal offenders. Of the many early forays into biometric data analysis, the Bertillon system is perhaps the best-known and most widespread.

The Bertillon system derives its name from its inventor, Alphonse Bertillon (April 24, 1853–February 13, 1914). While working for the police department in his native Paris, Bertillon developed a system to measure, photograph, and categorize offenders. The system Bertillon devised relied on what was then known as anthropometrics, a set of very precise anatomical measurements intended to uniquely identify an individual. Modern incarnations of this same approach are commonly referred to as biometrics.

As print technology evolved in the late 19th century, police departments began to keep photographic records of suspects and convicted offenders (mug shots). These so-called rogues' galleries

This class was learning the Bertillon method of criminal identification in Paris, France, between 1910 and 1915. The photographs on the wall were called portrait parles, *now known as mug shots. Two of French criminologist Alphonse Bertillon's great contributions to the field were the standardization of criminal mug shots and the development of systematic crime scene photography; his general approach to systematic recordkeeping continues to influence law enforcement practices to this day.*

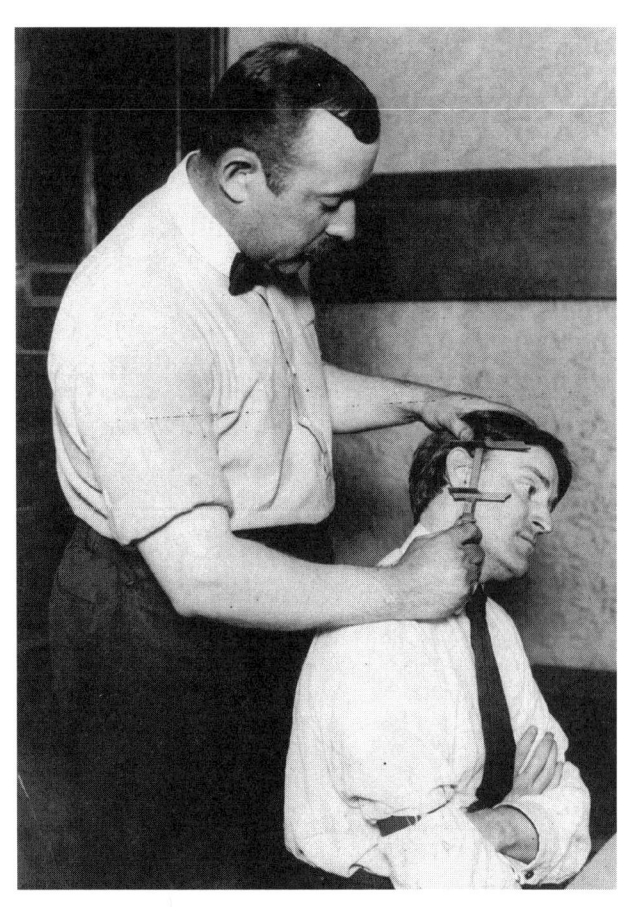

A New York City police officer practicing taking Bertillon measurements of a subject's ear around 1908. There were 15 pages of instructions on ear measurement in the first English translation of Bertillon's original work.

were often little more than disorganized collections of known ruffians with little probative or investigatory value. What the Bertillon system did was to augment and organize these collections along structured and orderly principles. Two especially lasting contributions made by Bertillon were standardization of criminal mug shots (dimensioned front and profile views) as well as systematic crime scene photography. In the latter instance, Bertillon devised a process of "metric photography" for the purpose of reconstructing the dimensions of a particular space and the placement of objects in it.

Measurement and Classification

Bertillon's anthropometrical system was divided into three interrelated spheres: bodily measurements taken with extreme precision and under carefully prescribed conditions, mostly based on a series of dimensions of bony parts of the human anatomy; morphological description of the offender's body; and a detailed description of any peculiar or distinguishing marks and scars such as those left by disease, injury, moles, warts, or tattoos.

The Bertillon method combined these detailed measurements and the classification of unique features with frontal and profile mug shots of suspects. This information was recorded on standardized photo cards in a systematic filing structure. Bertillon's system was based on five primary measurements: head length, head breadth, the length of the middle finger, the length of the left foot, and the length of the cubit (the forearm from the elbow to the extremity of the middle finger). Each heading was then subdivided into three size classifications. Many other less-central metrics were also recorded. These included the length of the little finger, eye color, and the size and shape of the ears. Taken together, the indicia included in the system led Bertillon to calculate an interesting probability: Bertillon stated that the odds of finding any two individuals with identical measurements were 286,435,456 to 1.

A particularly remarkable aspect of the Bertillon system was his focus on dimensions and characteristics associated with human ears. While stopping short of a blanket decree of individual uniqueness, Bertillon suggested that ears are sufficiently distinct as to be a good general marker. In Bertillon's exhaustive directions for ear measurement, one sees the complicated nature of the larger anthropometric process. Bertillon directed that the following aspects of the ear had to be described and measured: three portions of the border of the ear (helix) and its degree of openness; the contour, degree of adherence to the cheek, and dimension of the ear lobe; the inclination from horizontal, the profile, and the degree of reversion forward of the antitragus; and the measurement and windings of both the ascending and the median anthelix (i.e., the fold). Additionally, Bertillon required a description of the general form of the ear; its separation from the body at the head; any peculiarities that are noted with the border, the lobe, the tragus, the antitragus, the concha, the superior fold, and the various depressions; and Darwinian characteristics, as well as other elements. In all, the directives for ear specification and measurement fill 15 pages in the first English translation of Bertillon's original work.

Inherent Difficulties
As a general construct, the system devised by Bertillon was so complex that its application was extremely difficult. As above, the aspects of the system requiring precise measurement were sufficiently cumbersome as to yield different measures of the same individual if performed by multiple observers. While high precision was one of the system's greatest attributes, complications in its uniform application ultimately gave cause for its abandonment.

Even with its incumbent difficulties, for a period in the late 19th century, the Bertillon system was very popular in both Europe and America. The broad adoption of the Bertillon system in the United States is largely attributable to the efforts of one man, Major Robert W. McClaughry. In 1887, while serving as warden of the Illinois State Penitentiary, Joliet, McClaughry and his records clerk, Gallus Muller, adopted the system for recordkeeping at the institution. As an active member of the Wardens Association of the United States and Canada, McClaughry effectively advocated use of the system by correctional administrations all over North America. As a relevant aside, when McClaughry was eventually obliged to face the inherent limitations of the Bertillon system, he became an equally staunch advocate for a more reliable and individually discrete biometric: fingerprints.

The Bertillon system was dealt another lethal blow when it was discovered that more than one person might have identical (or nearly so) measurements. Perhaps the most prominent case of mistaken identity involving the Bertillon system was that of Will West. Upon his arrival at the federal penitentiary at Leavenworth in 1903, West denied any previous incarceration there. When the record clerk took his Bertillon measurements, they matched those on file for an inmate named William West. Additionally, the photographs of William West looked identical to Will West. When the clerk turned over the card, it showed that William West was currently imprisoned in Leavenworth. The mistaken identity was only confirmed after the fingerprints of the two men were compared. Even from this one example, there was little doubt that the Bertillon system would give way to fingerprinting.

Apart from its place in the annals of criminal justice practice, the Bertillon system also holds a particular fascination for authors of crime-related fiction. Reference to Bertillon is made by Sir Arthur Conan Doyle in his Sherlock Holmes series. Likewise, mention of Bertillon and his methodology also appear in works by novelists Maurice Leblanc and Caleb Carr.

While the Bertillon system was quickly abandoned with the advance of fingerprint technology, Bertillon's basic ideas about individual distinctiveness and the use of precise measurement to capture it were among the most prescient and lasting developments in criminal justice history. Furthermore, that his general approach to systematic recordkeeping continues to inform police practice today suggests the importance of his legacy.

Matthew Pate
State University of New York, Albany

See Also: Crime Scene Investigation; Detection and Detectives; Fingerprinting; Forensic Science; Mug Shots; Technology, Police.

Further Readings
Kind, S. and M. Overman. *Science Against Crime*. London: Aldus Books, 1972.
McClaughry, M. W. "History of the Introduction of the Bertillon System Into the United States." *Finger Print Magazine*, v.3/10 (April 1992).
Tomellini, L. *Metric Photography, Bertillon System: New Apparatus for the Criminal Department; Directions for Use and Consideration of the Applications to Forensic Medicine and Anthropology.* Charleston, SC: Nabu Press, 2010.
Wagner, E. J. *The Science of Sherlock Holmes: From Baskerville Hall to the Valley of Fear, the Real Forensics Behind the Great Detective's Greatest Cases.* Hoboken, NJ: John Wiley & Sons, 2007.

Bible

The Bible is the foundational text of Jews and Christians, containing what adherents believe to be the revealed word of God. Although it begins with an account of the creation of the world, ends with a startling account of the world's demise, and roughly catalogs a series of events from the Fall in the Garden of Eden to the life and teachings of Jesus and his early followers, it is not rightly understood as a unified narrative. Rather, it is a series of stories, poems, aphorisms, prophetic soliloquies, and historical accounts meant to convey the central belief of Jews and Christians that all of creation is made, sustained, and guided by God to a glorious conclusion in which God will be revealed as ruler of the nations.

Biblical theology and ethics have had a great deal of relevance for the subsequent history of criminal justice, including the early development of the American penal system. This short essay discusses in general terms what the Hebrew Scriptures and the New Testament reveal about criminal justice and concludes with some of the ways these teachings were at the core of the penal experiments in the United States.

Crime and Punishment in Hebrew Scriptures

Judaism is a legal religion. It has a fully transcendent understanding of the deity who, in all things, lies infinitely beyond anything humans can think, do, or imagine. Thus, the very first commandment given to Moses on Mount Sinai is that there be no alien gods among the chosen people. It is strictly forbidden to create any image of the Creator, as this would suggest that humans have some conception of God's own essence. The only way one can show proper reverence to God and live righteously is to obey the laws (Torah) that God provides in the first five books of the Bible (the Pentateuch). As the Book of Deuteronomy states often, to follow the law is to live, to disobey is to die.

That same sense of urgency and seriousness is revealed in the consequences for flagrant violations of the Torah, among them the prohibition against murder found in the Ten Commandments. Capital punishment is required for a wide range of offenses, normally by way of stoning to death, although there are instances of hanging, decapitation, and burning.

Imprisonment in a formal judicial sense was unheard of until after the Babylonian exile. Prior to that period, one only sees ad hoc cases of punitive incarceration, as when the prophet Jeremiah is placed under restraint on several occasions, and of custodial confinement, as in the case of a person who blasphemed in the midst of an argument. After the exile, the Israelites, under the influence of King Artaxerxes II of Persia, began to place some types of offenders under formal detention. There is no indication, however, that the practice was widespread. In fact, the experience of exile led to a decrease in the severity of punishment for legal infractions, including a near-total rejection of the use of capital punishment.

Such moderation has ample precedent in biblical literature. Accompanying the stern warnings and punishments for failure to attend to the law, there is a rich genre of texts speaking of redemption and release of the captive, starting with Isaiah 42:7 and 61:1. God releases those imprisoned in the nether world in Psalms 30:4 and 40:3, brings the exile home in Ezekiel 39:27–28, and has mercy upon those bound in chains in Psalms 107:16.

Another of the traditions mitigating the practice of judicial violence was the establishment of cities of refuge. For those guilty of negligent homicide, certain localities were designated by divine command wherein the culpable could seek asylum and be assured protection from those intent on avenging the death of their kin.

Overall, then, the centrality of the law and punishments for its violation are predominant themes in the Hebrew scriptures. There is also a parallel commitment to free the captive and exiled after they have experienced punishment, and to quell the vendetta with its thirst for blood vengeance by providing safe havens for those who committed homicides under mitigating circumstances.

Crime and Punishment in the New Testament

The section of the Bible presenting the life and teachings of Jesus and those of some of his early followers leaves the reader with two strong impressions regarding criminal justice. The first is an overall wariness of law; the second is a strong theological position not only that Jesus was executed by the machinery of one of the world's most advanced legal systems but that he also identified with every prisoner, regardless of his or her crime.

As a Jew, Jesus had the utmost respect for the Mosaic law and its relevance to the lives and ethos of his people. He, however, took a position toward law that was diametrically opposed to that taken by the Temple aristocracy and most legal scholars of his time. Rather than a literal approach, Jesus insisted that every legal directive is explained, fulfilled, and hence should be evaluated in terms of the one true commandment: unconditional love of God and neighbor. His repeated clashes with the Sadducees and Pharisees would surface this tension, one that would lead him to heal on the Sabbath, pick grain on the Sabbath, and touch both lepers and the dead in violation of what were perceived to be sacred and inviolable commands. Such decisions were contributing factors in his condemnation.

This contextualizing of the value of law and of the punishments it prescribes within the ambit of charity is also revealed in the strong emphasis Jesus placed upon forgiveness. He stressed to his followers repeatedly that this virtue must be unconditional regardless of the degree of fault.

Jesus also offers concrete advice to avoid lawsuits, oaths, and going to court and provides the format for adjudication of conflict that was instrumental in the development of Western criminal justice: The aggrieved party must first confront the offender in person; if the matter is not settled, a group intervention is called for; a continued lack of consensus should then involve the entire community; finally, continued obstinacy by the offender is to be followed by expulsion from the fellowship.

St. Paul also emphasizes the correctional format as presented by Jesus. Even at his most contentious, as when a Christian married his stepmother in 1 Corinthians 5:1–5, Paul insists that expulsion from the community is for the purpose of creating a sense of shame and repentance that is to be followed by forgiveness and reincorporation. Of course, his own frequent imprisonment surfaces often in his letters and colors his sense that righteousness is not a matter of legal attentiveness but a matter of faith.

Despite the ambiguity concerning law and punishment in certain passages, particularly in Paul's famous assertion in Romans 13:1–4 that Christians must obey all secular authority, the dominant ethos of the New Testament is in the direction of legal minimalism and a recognition of the sacredness of those who are confined, as when Paul urges a slave owner not only to forgive his runaway slave, who stole from him, but to accept him as an equal, and in Paul's own evocative comment in Colossians 4:18: "Remember that I am a prisoner."

The Bible in Early American Correctional Experience

The Puritans who arrived in New England in the 17th century represented the radical wing of the English Reformation. Their strict demeanor bore testimony to their Calvinist-inspired interpretation of holy scripture. They instituted a strict biblical basis for punishment, corresponding to their belief that crime was tantamount to sin. While the corporal nature of correction was maintained, including the death penalty, their literal use of the biblical text reduced significantly the number of capital crimes that were then current in English law.

A similar adherence to scriptural guidelines was clearly in evidence when, in the 1820s, two penitentiaries were constructed in Pennsylvania and New York that became the centerpiece of a worldwide debate on the meaning and form of criminal punishment. The Eastern State Penitentiary in Philadelphia was founded by the Quakers

This 1842 print shows a Catholic priest confronting a reluctant New York City prison warden with a letter from the governor giving him permission to visit a murderer sentenced to death. The prisoner is shown kneeling in prayer with a Bible beside him.

and reflected their focus on the indwelling spirit of God within the person and on the nonviolent passages in the New Testament. The penitentiary at Auburn, New York, mirrored Calvinist biblical theology, including the belief in the inherent sinfulness of the individual. The urgency of the debate between the two systems was certainly fueled by economic questions centering on the most fiscally sound way to address the issue of crime, but the implications of the competing biblical theologies cannot be underestimated.

Another factor that made the matter so intensely argued was that the penitentiaries themselves grew out of the Second Great Awakening, arguably the most thoroughgoing religious movement in American history. The country was in the throes of a missionary crusade to bring each person to conversion, and the message of the leaders of the movement emphasized that the reformation of the social and moral environment and the building of remedial institutions, among them prisons, were the essential factors in creating the conditions for the lost to be found.

The penitentiaries initially allowed only one book for the inmate to read, the Bible. The salvation of the inmate and the fate of the nation depended on the power of its message. Chaplains saw it as their ministerial duty to have prisoners memorize as many scriptural verses as possible. Ministers read the Bible in the cellblocks each evening to the silent captives and, regardless of the misanthropy of some wardens, such as Elam Lynds in New York, the facilities were largely viewed as symbols of the belief that America was winning the war against evil and witnessing to the world that it was the New Israel.

The Auburn model, with common labor during the day and silence at all other times, came to dominate the philosophy of corrections, and its triumph was due in large part to the Reverend Louis Dwight. He was an employee of the American Bible Society whose job it was to travel to the different penitentiaries delivering Bibles to the inmates. He was so moved by the combination of labor, silence, and daily biblical preaching at Auburn and its sister institutions that he resigned his post and founded the Boston Prison Discipline Society, which did more than any other organization to spread that penal philosophy as the greatest tool in the conversion of the errant.

The history of American corrections took on a more scientific and therapeutic tone with the development of the social sciences in the late 19th century, exemplified in figures such as Lombroso and Ferri, but it was biblical religion that provided the instigation and structure of the prison systems in America and, through the efforts of its proponents, many prison systems elsewhere.

Andrew Skotnicki
Manhattan College

See Also: Auburn State Prison; Corrections; Morality; Penitentiaries; Punishment Within Prison; Puritans; Quakers; Religion and Crime, History of.

Further Readings
De Vaux, Roland. *Ancient Israel: Its Life and Institutions.* New York: McGraw-Hill, 1961.
Jenks, William. *A Memoir of the Reverend Louis Dwight.* Boston: T. R. Marvin, 1856.
Lewis, Orlando F. *The Development of American Prisons and Prison Customs.* Montclair, NJ: Patterson Smith, 1967.
Sanders, E. P. *Paul, the Law, and the Jewish People.* Philadelphia: Fortress, 1983.
Senior, Donald. *Jesus: A Gospel Portrait.* New York: Paulist, 1992.
Skotnicki, Andrew. *Religion and the Development of the American Penal System.* Lanham, MD: University Press of America, 2000.

Bigamy/Polygamy

Polygamy intended as plural marriage or polygyny, that is, a marriage in which the man has more than one wife at the same time, has been a widespread practice throughout history, including in the Judeo-Christian tradition. Bigamy is the criminal act of marrying another person when one is still married to someone else in countries with laws against multiple marriage. In such countries, the resulting second marriage becomes void if discovered.

The Old Testament mentions Abraham and David having multiple wives and King Solomon having as many as 700 wives. In the 16th century John of Leyden, leader of a group of Anabaptists, took control of the city of Munster in Germany and, after expelling all non-Christians from the town, declared that polygamy would be law under his jurisdiction. The government of the Anabaptists lasted barely one year, but during that time polygamy was considered to be the ideal form of marriage.

However, historical sources suggest that the Anabaptists' lifestyle did not attract a consensus among the other Christian sects. Although their leader laid down a strict code of conduct that would not allow sex outside marriage, the Republic of the Saints founded by the Anabaptists was met with widespread disdain, and it would not be until the 19th century that another Christian sect, the Mormons, would embrace polygamy again.

In 1830 Joseph Smith, Jr., founded the Church of Jesus Christ of Latter-day Saints. Since then the Mormons have had a difficult relationship with the government of the United States, probably not only because of their polygamous practices but also, and more importantly, because of their radical autarchy that included an autonomous system of dispute settlement and an independent militia. Furthermore, polygamy was the target of criticism and pressure from American society at large. In 1862 Congress prohibited polygamy in the United States, and in 1890 the Mormon Church banned the practice among its followers. There seems to be no evidence of church punishment for polygamous marriages, however, and some conclude that nothing had changed in reality. In 1888, new territories claiming statehood were required by Congress to pass antipolygamy amendments, and when in 1896 Utah entered the United States, its constitution included a formal ban of polygamy.

American legal precedents on polygamy date back to 1878 with the case *Reynolds v. United States*. Reynolds's arguments for the legitimacy of his plural marriage rested upon the First Amendment that protected religious freedom, but his claim was rejected based on the harm that polygamy would cause to American society, namely, patriarchy and despotism. This decision was followed by similar case law successfully arguing that polygamy was a criminal offense. In 1946, in the case of *Cleveland v. United States*, for the first time a justice of the Supreme Court engaged the court with arguments in favor of polygyny, defining it as a cultural institution and as a form of marriage ruled by a set of moral and social principles. However, all the other justices dissented and declared polygamy to be a return to barbarism. As with fornication and sodomy laws, it has been argued that the ban of polygamy is challenging religious freedom as well as the right to privacy. Subsequent case law dating to the late 1970s shows a greater level of tolerance toward polygamous practices.

Although polygamy remains illegal, it is not declared barbaric any longer. In spite of its still being considered outside the law, Salt Lake City in Utah has remained the center of polygamist marriages. Besides Mormons, the Biblical Patriarchal Christian Fellowship of God's Free Men

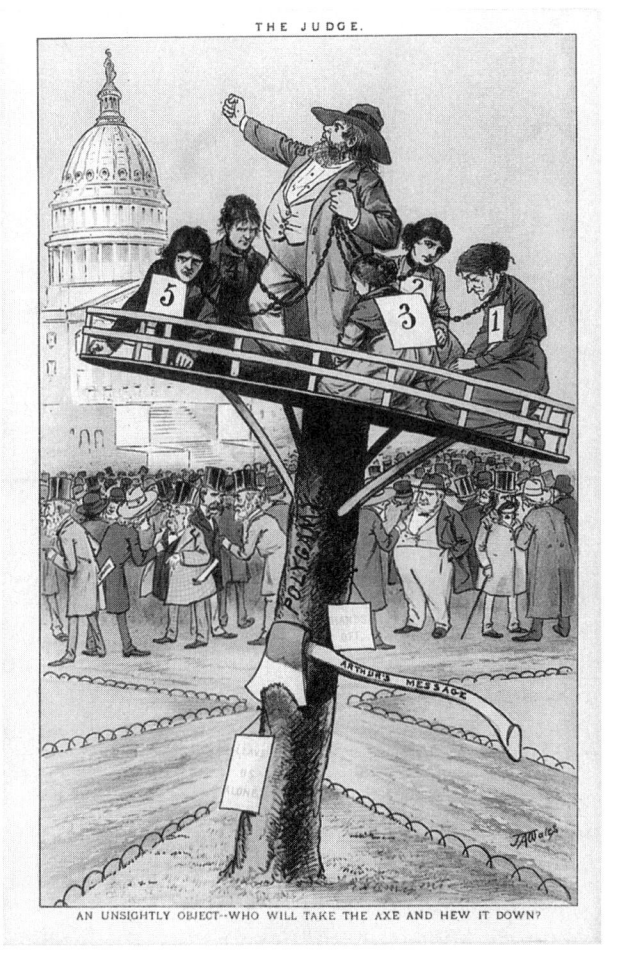

This 1882 cartoon depicts a polygamist holding five wives in chains atop a precarious tree and asks, "Who will take the axe and hew it down?" That year, President Chester Arthur used the Edmunds Act to help imprison 1,300 polygamists.

and Women, the Fundamentalist Church of Jesus Christ of Latter-Day Saints, the Latter-day Church of Christ, and the Apostolic United Brethren practice plural marriages, even if only in secret. Occasionally these communities attract the attention of activists, social services, and police in relation to child-bride practices, women's rights abuses, slavery, and domestic violence. However, it is proving hard to prosecute polygamists for polygamy because they engage in informal matrimonial arrangements. Nowadays, religious polygamists often marry only once in a civil ceremony. Hence, subsequent polygamous marriages lacking civil ceremonies are nonexistent in the eyes of the law, unless authorities were to conduct investigations into the private lives of families, including sexual habits and finances. Although it has been argued that the religious practice of polygamy is a fundamental right according to the free exercise clause and the right to privacy, polygamy is still formally banned in the United States.

Polygamy is not only secretly practiced and moderately tolerated among some Christian communities in the United States, but it is also evident among other sociocultural groups. Case law shows that Native Americans belonging to tribes recognized by the government for allowing polygamy have a right to plural marriages. In spite of this legal recognition, however, there is almost no trace of modern polygamy among Native Americans. Islam allows a man to marry multiple wives if he can treat them all with equal fairness. However, the leading interpretations of Islamic polygamy mitigate this male prerogative to a maximum of four wives, and most importantly, it requires the consent of the existent wife or wives. Some Islamic legal scholars go as far as to say that polygamy is not appropriate to modern times. Yet, even if practiced rarely, evidence of Islamic polygamy emerges from recent Euro-American case law, especially in relation to inheritance, alimony, social benefits, divorce, and immigration laws. Some socio-legal scholars in the field of immigration law argue that objecting to the immigration of second wives makes Euro-American law particularly harsh toward Muslim communities because it denies them the enjoyment of family unity and deprives Muslim women and children of the legal protection deriving from marriage.

In contrast to polygamists, bigamists often try to keep their relationships secret from each other and do not create openly plural marriages. Bigamy may be committed for different reasons than polygamy, often does not have a religious basis, and may be done for financial gain or even by accident when a spouse is believed to be dead. In the United States, various state laws provide for fines and/or imprisonment for those convicted of bigamy. Section 230.1 of the Model Penal Code makes bigamy a misdemeanor as opposed to polygamy, or "purported exercise of a plural marriage," which is a felony.

Livia Holden
Lahore University of Management Sciences

See Also: 1801 to 1850 Primary Documents; Adultery; Arizona; Arthur, Chester (Administration of); Children's Rights; Criminalization and Decriminalization; Fornication Laws; Religion and Crime, Contemporary; *Reynolds v. United States*; Utah; Victimless Crimes.

Further Readings
Barringer, Gordon Sara. *The Mormon Question: Polygamy and Constitutional Conflict in Nineteenth Century America*. Chapel Hill: University of North Carolina Press, 2002.
Shah, Prakash. "Attitudes to Polygamy in English Law." *International and Comparative Law Quarterly* (2003).
Zeiten, Miriam Koktvedgaard. *Polygamy: A Cross-Cultural Analysis*. Oxford: Berg Publishers, 2008.

Bill of Rights

The Bill of Rights—the first 10 amendments to the U.S. Constitution, ratified in 1791—are designed to protect individual civil liberties from government oppression and arbitrary prosecution. They include 28 specific rights, of which 16 concern criminal justice. The framers understood that procedural limits on the state's power to enforce criminal law are necessary to protect the "Blessings of Liberty." The Bill of Rights was grounded in British liberties that had evolved since the 12th century, including trial by a local jury, the writ of habeas corpus, and the principle that the government could deprive no one of life, liberty, or property without due process of law, drawn from the Magna Carta (1215). From English common law came the privilege against self-incrimination and the rule that a previous conviction or acquittal barred reconviction.

Parliamentary and judicial reactions to oppression by 17th-century Stuart kings cemented the view that rights and institutions, like the self-incrimination prohibition and the grand jury, were essential to liberty. The Glorious Revolution (1688), overthrowing James II, was confirmed in law by the English Bill of Rights of 1689, which prohibited excessive bail, excessive fines, and cruel and unusual punishments and guaranteed arms to Protestants for their defense. In the 1770s English courts held that officers who broke into houses searching for evidence of political crimes, on orders of high government officers but without search warrants, violated citizens' privacy rights and were liable for damages in civil lawsuits.

British liberties were included in the charters of England's American colonies; the new American states included many in their constitutions. The U.S. Constitution, drafted in 1787, guaranteed federal jury trials and federal and state habeas corpus but had no Bill of Rights. The Constitution's opponents, known as Anti-Federalists, feared a strong central government with taxation powers. They attacked the Constitution in ratification conventions because it lacked a Bill of Rights. The Constitution's narrow ratification impelled James Madison, a key Constitutional drafter and representative from Virginia, to draft a Bill of Rights for the First Congress. The need to do so was urgent, as Anti-Federalists planned to amend the Constitution by calling a second constitutional convention to unravel the government that went into effect in 1789. Madison's proposed amendments were debated, modified, and approved by two-thirds of the House and Senate. Ten were ratified by three-quarters of the states and became part of the Constitution in 1791.

The criminal justice provisions include the Fourth Amendment, which prohibits unreasonable searches and seizures of "persons, houses, papers, and effects" and generally requires search warrants, although the Supreme Court recognizes search warrant exceptions. The Fifth Amendment includes four criminal justice provisions: federal trials must be preceded by a grand jury indictment; double jeopardy is prohibited; no person can lose life, liberty, or property by government action "without due process of law"; and the privilege against self-incrimination is protected. The Sixth Amendment guarantees rights to an accused in a "criminal prosecution": a speedy and public jury trial, an impartial jury drawn from the crime's vicinity, notice of the criminal charges that will be brought against the defendant, the right to subpoena favorable witnesses, and the right to a defense lawyer. The Eighth Amendment offers three additional rights: "Excessive bail shall not be required, nor excessive fines imposed, nor cruel and unusual punishments inflicted."

Effect on Criminal Justice

The Bill of Rights had little effect on criminal justice before the 20th century and did not apply to state or local governments. After the Civil War, defendants tried to apply the Bill of Rights to state and local governments by "incorporating" them into the Fourteenth Amendment due process clause, which was ratified in 1868. This process was finally successful in the 1960s when the Supreme Court expanded defendants' rights by holding that the criminal provisions in the Bill of Rights applied to local justice. The incorporation cases, collectively known as the "due process revolution," brought American criminal justice closer to the ideals of the rule of law.

The history of incorporation begins with *Barron v. Mayor of Baltimore* (1835), which held that the Bill of Rights limited only the federal government and did not apply to state or local governments. The opportunity to revise *Barron*'s constitutional ruling arose with the ratification of the Fourteenth Amendment. It established the civil rights of former slaves after the Thirteenth Amendment (1865) abolished slavery. The Fourteenth Amendment declared that all naturalized or born citizens were citizens both of their state and the United States; it guaranteed the privileges or immunities of citizens and decreed that states could not deprive persons of life, liberty, or property without due process of law, or deprive any person of the equal protection of the laws.

The U.S. government's official parchment copy of the Bill of Rights. Articles 3 to 12, ratified December 15, 1791, by three-fourths of the state legislatures, constitute the first 10 amendments of the U.S. Constitution.

To many, the criminal procedure provisions of the Bill of Rights were expressions of due process—the principle that criminal trials and criminal justice must be fundamentally fair. Defendants' attorneys appealed state convictions to the Supreme Court, seeking incorporation because federal procedural rules under the Bill of Rights were more favorable to defendants' rights than state rules of criminal procedure. In cases from 1884 to 1961, the Supreme Court declined to incorporate criminal provisions of the Bill of Rights.

In *Hurtado v. California* (1884), the Supreme Court refused to incorporate the grand jury clause. However, Justice John Marshall Harlan's impassioned dissent forced the majority to agree that if a state law or procedure violated "fundamental principles of liberty and justice" included in a Bill of Rights provision, the Supreme Court would find that a state had to abide by the constitutional provision, via the Fourteenth Amendment's due process clause. The majority, however, did not believe that state laws allowing prosecutors to charge by their own "information" rather than by grand jury indictments violated fundamental rights. Likewise, *Twining v. New Jersey* (1908) held that state judges' comments on defendants not testifying did not violate a fundamental right, although in federal prosecutions such comments violated the Fifth Amendment privilege against self-incrimination. The strongest reason for the court's refusal to apply the Bill of Rights to the states was Federalism—the idea that criminal justice should be left entirely to the states.

After *Twining*, the Supreme Court began to find some state criminal justice practices unconstitutional, vacating state defendants' convictions. These cases did not apply the Bill of Rights to state procedures but ruled that the practices simply violated the Fourteenth Amendment's due process clause. The first cases targeted the worst injustices against African Americans under Jim Crow racial practices. Trials held under lynch-mob threats, rushing defendants incapable of defending themselves to trial without an opportunity to consult with attorneys, indictment by all-white grand juries, and confessions secured through torture all violated due process. After 1940, the Supreme Court ruled more frequently on criminal cases from all parts of the nation under the due process clause.

A Uniform Standard
The Due Process Revolution was hastened by the incorporation of the First Amendment in the 1930s and 1940s, the weakening of states' rights, growing civil liberties awareness, and the rights-affirming goals of the Warren Court. In 1961, the Supreme Court held that the federal Fourth Amendment exclusionary rule applied to the states in *Mapp v. Ohio*. In 1962, the Eighth Amendment cruel and unusual punishment clause was incorporated. By 1969, the court incorporated the Fifth Amendment double jeopardy and self-incrimination clauses, paving the way for *Miranda v. Arizona*. The Sixth Amendment's counsel guarantee was applied in *Gideon v. Wainwright* (1963), followed by the confrontation, subpoena, and the speedy, impartial, and public jury trial provisions. By the end of the 1960s, these rights were considered fundamental. Piecemeal application of the Bill of Rights to the states was known as "selective incorporation," as opposed to the "total incorporation" of the entire Bill of Rights.

The incorporation of the Bill of Rights was accomplished by a "liberal" Supreme Court under

Chief Justice Earl Warren in the 1960s. Since that time, the more conservative Burger, Rehnquist, and Roberts courts have been more favorable to claims by police and prosecutors and more hostile to claims under the Bill of Rights by criminal suspects and defendants. In general, the court has strengthened defendants' rights under the confrontation clause and has supported procedures for the selection of race-neutral juries.

On the other hand, the court opened the door to preventive detention for jailed suspects and has created exceptions to the *Miranda* rule that excludes unwarned confessions from evidence. For example, an officer need not warn a suspect of his or her rights before interrogation if an immediate threat to public safety is present. The court has also created many exceptions to Fourth Amendment protections that give police a freer hand in conducting searches and seizures.

Incorporation made the Bill of Rights a reality in state and local criminal justice, where most police, prosecution, and judicial processes occur. It advanced police professionalization and injected greater legality into American criminal justice. Supreme Court interpretations in the last 40 years have generally favored the state rather than defendants' rights, but nationalizing the Bill of Rights has made America a more just nation.

Marvin Zalman
Wayne State University

See Also: *Barron v. Mayor of Baltimore*; Brennan, William J., Jr.; *Brown v. Mississippi*; Constitution of the United States of America; Defendant's Rights; Due Process; Habeas Corpus, Writ of; Interrogation Practices; *Mapp v. Ohio*; *Marbury v. Madison*; *Miranda v. Arizona*; Rule of Law; Supreme Court, U.S.; *Twining v. New Jersey*; Warren, Earl; *Weeks v. United States*; *Whitney v. California*; *Wolf v. Colorado*.

Further Readings
Amar, Akhil Reed. *The Bill of Rights: Creation and Reconstruction*. New Haven, CT: Yale University Press, 1998.
Cortner, Richard C. *The Supreme Court and the Second Bill of Rights: The Fourteenth Amendment and the Nationalization of Civil Liberties*. Madison: University of Wisconsin Press, 1981.
Labunski, Richard. *James Madison and the Struggle for the Bill of Rights*. Oxford: Oxford University Press, 2006.
Rutland, Robert Allen. *The Birth of the Bill of Rights, 1776–1791*. Lebanon, NH: Northeastern University Press, 1991.
Schwartz, Bernard. *The Great Rights of Mankind: A History of the American Bill of Rights*. New York: Oxford University Press, 1977.

Billy the Kid

Billy the Kid (1859–81) was born William Henry McCarty. The exact date and place of his birth are not known but are believed to have been sometime in 1859 in New York City, perhaps on the Lower East Side of Manhattan. The family's location and living arrangements between 1865 and 1873 also remain unknown. However, in 1873, the family moved to Santa Fe, New Mexico. Shortly thereafter, the family moved again, this time to Silver City, New Mexico, where, upon his mother's death, McCarty was uprooted and sent to live with a foster family. He worked odd jobs in a butcher shop and a hotel but was soon arrested and jailed for petty theft. Not wanting to be in jail, he orchestrated an escape. He then returned to his foster family, who promptly put him on a train to Arizona, where his stepfather lived. Upon arrival, his stepfather refused to allow McCarty to stay because of his status as a fugitive. With no home and with little money, he was forced to accept a low-paying position as a ranch hand.

Beginnings
McCarty committed his first murder around the age of 16 during a fight at a saloon in Camp Grand, Arizona. The victim, Frank "Windy" Cahill, had bullied McCarty in the past. During this encounter, the older, physically stronger, and more experienced Cahill gained the advantage. However, during the struggle, McCarty was able to reach his gun and mortally shoot Cahill. After this incident, McCarty returned to New Mexico, where he was given the nickname "Kid" because of his young age and youthful appearance. Unable to find work, he soon joined a gang called

the Boys. The Boys, operating in Lincoln County, New Mexico, were hired by rancher James Dolan. Dolan was embroiled in a bitter dispute with rival rancher John Tunstall. Eventually, this dispute became known as the Lincoln County War.

The Boys, under Dolan's direction and as a form of harassment, began to steal livestock from the Tunstall ranch. The sheriff arrested some of the gang's members, including Billy the Kid, and jailed them. When Tunstall realized that Billy the Kid was not a hard-core rustler but just a boy, he offered Billy the Kid a choice—if he would testify against the other rustlers, Tunstall would hire him to work on his ranch. Billy the Kid gladly accepted. Hopeful for a better future, Billy the Kid changed his name to William H. Bonney. His employment, however, did not last long, since Tunstall was soon murdered by members of the Boys.

An Outlaw

To avenge Tunstall's murder, Bonney and other Tunstall ranch hands banded together, creating the Regulators. Initially, the Regulators sought to use the law to their advantage but soon found it impossible to work through the existing court system. Increasingly, they took matters into their own hands, seeking vigilante justice. Eventually, they killed Bill Morton (leader of the group that had killed Tunstall), Frank Baker, and William McCloskey (a Regulator suspected of working for both sides). They also killed the sheriff and his deputy. These murders resulted in arrest warrants being issued for members of the Regulators.

Once warrants were issued, Dolan intensified his efforts to eliminate the Regulators. Soon, Dolan and his men surrounded a known Regulator hideout, trapping numerous members inside. The siege lasted for five days before Dolan ordered the house to be burned. Once the house was ablaze, Bonney took charge and had the men form two groups so that an escape could be attempted. As Bonney and the other members of the Regulators emerged, four were shot and killed. Their deaths effectively broke up the Regulators and ended the war. Once the Regulators disbanded, Billy the Kid was a fugitive on the run once again.

Eventually, when Bonney learned that a new governor had assumed office in New Mexico, he sought a pardon on his murder charges. In exchange, he offered to testify against Dolan, his ranch hands, and the Boys. The governor agreed. Bonney soon surrendered himself to the proper officials and testified; yet his testimony had little effect—each person who was tried was acquitted. Since Bonney was already in custody, prosecuting attorney William Rynerson put him on trial for murder, effectively making it impossible for the governor to follow through with his promise to issue a pardon. Not trusting the authorities or the court system, Bonney again escaped custody.

The only known photograph of Billy the Kid is this tintype taken around 1879 or 1880 in Fort Sumner, New Mexico, not long before the outlaw's death there on July 14, 1881.

Over the next two years, Bonney spent most of his time in and near Fort Sumner, New Mexico. During this time, Pat Garrett was elected sheriff of Lincoln County and accepted the task of bringing Billy the Kid to justice. Garrett was familiar with Bonney's usual hideouts and arrested him on December 23, 1880, in Stinking Springs, New Mexico. Bonney was put on trial for murder, found guilty, and sentenced to hang. After sentencing, Bonney was transported to Lincoln County to await execution. On April 28, 1881, he escaped custody yet again, killing two jail guards in the process. He then left Lincoln County and headed to Fort Sumner. Accounts of what happened next vary greatly and are difficult to confirm. Yet most accounts agree that Garrett, while searching for Bonney on July 14, 1881, stopped to ask a citizen of Fort Sumner about Bonney's whereabouts. At just that moment an unaware Bonney approached. Garrett recognized Bonney and fatally shot him in the chest. Other accounts tell of Garrett waiting in ambush style, killing Bonney as he entered a darkened room. Billy the Kid is buried at the Fort Sumner cemetery.

Caroline Forsythe
Curtis R. Blakely
Truman State University

See Also: Arizona; Frontier Crime; History of Crime and Punishment in America: 1850–1900; New Mexico; Posses; Rural Police; Sheriffs.

Further Readings
Brothers, M. "Summary on the Life of Billy the Kid." http://www.aboutbillythekid.com/index.html (Accessed September 2011).
Gardner, M. *To Hell on a Fast Horse: Billy the Kid, Pat Garrett, and the Epic Chase to Justice in the Old West*. New York: William Morrow, 2010.
Garrett, P. *The Authentic Life of Billy the Kid*. New York: Skyhorse Publishing, 2011.
New Mexico Tourism Department. "Billy the Kid Territory." http://www.newmexico.org/billythekid/index.php (Accessed September 2011).

Birmingham, Alabama

Birmingham is the largest city in Alabama (2010 population 212,237, a 12.6 percent drop since 2000); the Birmingham-Hoover metropolitan area had a 2009 population of more than 1.2 million. Birmingham was founded in 1871 during the Reconstruction period following the Civil War as an industrial center. It was a leader in iron and steel production (the city was named after the industrial city of Birmingham, England) through the 1960s as well as a railroad hub for the American south. Today, the economy of Birmingham is much more diversified and includes white-collar industries such as insurance, healthcare, and banking as well as higher education. Birmingham played an important role in the American civil rights movement, and events in Birmingham helped provide the momentum for passage of the 1964 federal Civil Rights Act.

Along with the rapid growth of industry and related enterprises such as coal mining, the city experienced recurring conflict between workers and owners of these businesses. The most notable incident was the Birmingham District coal strike of 1908, which lasted two months and was often marked by violence. Initially, the union seemed to hold the upper hand, but mine owners recruited strikebreakers from as far away as Ellis Island, New York, and leased convict laborers from the state in order to keep the mines operating; eventually, Alabama Governor Braxton Bragg Comer declared martial law and sent state troops into the coal fields. The strike ended in a crushing defeat for District 20 of the United Mine Workers, one of the few racially integrated labor unions in the American south at the time (about half the mining labor force in the Birmingham area was African American at the turn of the century).

Segregation and Civil Rights
As was typical in the American south in the 1950s, Birmingham was segregated by law, and although the city was about 40 percent black, only a small fraction of the black population was registered to vote. Blacks were extremely limited in the jobs they could hold in both city government (for instance, there were no black firefighters or police officers) and private businesses. Black unemployment was also substantially higher than white unemployment, and black income was substantially lower, partly by design as a steady supply of cheap labor served the interests of the city's industrialists. Birmingham became a focus of the American civil rights movement when in 1958, the Alabama Christian Movement for Human

Rights challenged the city's segregation laws. The city earned the nickname "Bombingham" in these years because of the number of bomb attacks on black churches and homes, perhaps the most famous of which was the September 1963 bombing of the 16th Street Baptist Church. In 1962, a series of boycotts of Birmingham businesses, modeled on the Montgomery Bus Boycott of 1955, drew attention to the growing power of the civil rights movement.

In 1963, the Southern Christian Leadership Conference (SLCC), led by Martin Luther King, Jr., began a campaign in Birmingham focused on changing hiring practices and desegregating Birmingham's downtown business district. The SLCC employed a variety of methods, including sit-ins at segregated restaurants, "kneel-ins" at white churches, marches, and voter registration drives. These efforts were opposed by the city's commissioner of public safety, Eugene Connor, better known as Bull Connor. Connor became nationally known as a symbol of segregation, proclaiming that the civil rights movement was inspired by Communism and refusing to cooperate with Federal Bureau of Investigation (FBI) investigations into police misconduct. He also obtained a court injunction against the desegregation protests and quadrupled the amount of bail required to free those arrested. On Good Friday, April 12, 1963, Martin Luther King was arrested in Birmingham, and was denied bail and access to a lawyer. This event drew widespread publicity, particularly after the release of King's "Letter from Birmingham Jail," a response to eight white clergymen who accused him of being an outside agitator. In the letter, King articulated his belief that forceful nonviolent action was necessary in order to bring about social change and that civil disobedience was justifiable if the laws were unjust.

The so-called Children's Crusade began in May 1963 as more than 1,000 students, some as young as 8, marched to the downtown area of Birmingham, where they were arrested. As this pushed the Birmingham jails far over capacity, it forced Connor to change tactics and attempt to keep protesters out of the downtown area. This was accomplished by turning high-pressure fire hoses and dogs on the students, a tactic that backfired when images of these acts were widely publicized in the news media and played a key role in turning national sentiment against the Birmingham police force and in favor of the protesters. Most private businesses agreed to desegregate shortly thereafter, and the city government followed within a few months, although the reality of integration was slower in coming than the legal recognition of the principle: For instance, the first black police officer, Leroy Stover, was not hired until March 1966. The Birmingham public schools were integrated beginning in September 1963 despite the efforts of Governor George Wallace to use the U.S. National Guard to keep black students from enrolling in formerly white schools. The events in Birmingham were instrumental in leading to passage of the Civil Rights Act of 1964, which prohibited segregation in public accommodations, including schools, as well as discriminatory voter registration requirements.

Police

In Birmingham's early years, police officers and the chief of police were selected by alderman and the mayor, and these positions were an important source of political patronage. This system persisted even after passage of an 1892 state law that gave the county probate judge the power to appoint a police commission; the appointed commission had no actual power, and the mayor also appointed his own force, thus retaining control over city policing. The Birmingham Police Department was entirely white into the 1960s, one of many issues addressed by civil rights protesters. Even after the department integrated, this history meant that police–community relations were often strained, and the department has taken a number of measures to address this. In the mid-1990s, Birmingham founded a Citizens' Police Academy (along the lines of the model established in Devon and Cornwall, England) to familiarize private citizens with the operations of the police department and to build bridges between the police and the community. The department also has a Volunteers in Police Services program (founded in 2002), a senior citizen paid volunteer program, and offers internships to high school and college students considering a career in law enforcement.

The FBI had agents working in the Birmingham area from its earliest years: For instance, they pursued cases of peonage (coerced labor) in a sawmill near Birmingham in 1909. The Birmingham FBI office was closed in 1925, with responsibilities shifted to the Atlanta Division, but was reopened in 1930 because of increasing casework in the Birmingham area (it remains open today). The FBI Birmingham office played a key role in the apprehension of George "Machine Gun" Kelly, protected army bases and industrial installations from sabotage during World War II, and participated in investigations into some of the key crimes (for instance, the 16th Street Baptist Church bombing) during the civil rights era.

Crime

Today, Birmingham is widely considered to have a high crime rate: CQ Press ranked it the 10th most dangerous city in America, with a crime index (based on FBI statistics from 2009) of 244.83 (0 would indicate average crime while a positive number indicates higher than average crime). Among 234 cities with a population of 100,000 to 499,000, Birmingham had the sixth highest crime rate ranking according to the CQ Press methodology. In 2009, 2,812 violent crimes were reported in Birmingham, including 65 incidents of murder or nonnegligent manslaughter, 198 incidents of forcible rape, 1,150 robberies, and 1,399 aggravated assaults. Further, 18,159 property crimes were reported in 2009, including 5,019 burglaries, 11,546 cases of larceny-theft, 1,594 cases of motor vehicle theft, and 135 cases of arson.

Sarah Boslaugh
Kennesaw State University

See Also: African Americans; Alabama; Civil Rights Laws; King, Martin Luther, Jr.; Ku Klux Klan; Racism; Segregation Laws; Terrorism.

Further Readings

Bass, S. Jonathan. *Blessed Are the Peacemakers: Martin Luther King, Jr., Eight White Religious Leaders, and the "Letter From Birmingham Jail."* Baton Rouge: Louisiana State University Press, 2001.

Birmingham Civil Rights Institute. http://www.bcri.org (Accessed June 2011).

"City Crime Rankings 2010–2011." CQ Press. http://os.cqpress.com/citycrime/2010/citycrime2010-2011.htm (Accessed June 2011).

McWhorter, Diane. *Carry Me Home. Birmingham, Alabama: The Climactic Battle of the Civil Rights Revolution.* New York: Simon & Schuster, 2001.

U.S. Department of Justice, Federal Bureau of Investigation. "Crime in the United States 2009." http://www2.fbi.gov/ucr/cius2009/data/table_78_al.html (Accessed June 2011).

Black Panthers

Also known as the Black Panther Party for Self-Defense, the Black Panther Party is an African American organization founded in 1966 by group members Bobby Seale and Huey Newton, advocating a platform of black nationalism and economic and civic empowerment within the African American community. Some of the more prominent members included civil rights activists Eldridge Cleaver, Stokely Carmichael, David Hilliard, and Fred Hampton.

Platform

On October 15, 1966, in Oakland, California, during one of the most turbulent times regarding civil rights in the United States, Huey Newton and Bobby Seale founded the Black Panther Party for Self-Defense, better known as the Black Panther Party. The Panthers quickly drew the attention of several of the most prominent African American activists of the era, who became vital members and leaders of the party: Eldridge Cleaver, Stokely Carmichael, David Hilliard, and Fred Hampton. The membership practiced a philosophy grounded in the theoretical foundations and practices of civil rights activist Malcolm X and the tenets of Maoism. The Panthers promoted a strong sense of communal self-respect, dignity, and responsibility while demanding economic and educational equality along with political and social justice from the United States government for African Americans and other oppressed communities. In fact, the Panthers developed an organizational plan of action, often referred to as the Ten-Point Program:

> We want freedom. We want power to determine the destiny of our Black and oppressed communities.

We want full employment for our people.

We want an end to the robbery by the capitalists of our Black and oppressed communities.

We want decent housing, fit for the shelter of human beings.

We want decent education for our people that exposes the true nature of this decadent American society. We want education that teaches us our true history and our roles in the present-day society.

We want completely free health care for all Black and oppressed people.

We want an immediate end to police brutality and murder of Black people, other people of color, and all oppressed people inside the United States.

We want an immediate end to all wars of aggression.

We want freedom for all Black and oppressed people now held in U.S. federal, state, county, city, and military prisons and jails. We want trials by a jury of peers for all persons charged with so-called crimes under the laws of this country.

We want land, bread, housing, education, clothing, justice, peace, and people's community control of modern technology.

Protest and Outreach
The Black Panther Party envisioned itself as the vanguard movement for equality and social justice for people of color and/or the oppressed masses, holding the U.S. government responsible for their well-being. On April 25, 1967, the Panthers published the first issue of *The Black Panther*, the organization's official newsletter, and shortly afterward marched on the California State Capitol fully armed to protest the state's attempt to outlaw carrying weapons in public. Although more than 30 members were arrested by police, this event set the tone for the Black Panthers as a true resistance movement in America, creating

A participant in a June 1970 Black Panther Convention in Washington, D.C., stands on the steps of the Lincoln Memorial holding a banner promoting the "Revolutionary People's Constitutional Convention."

new chapters around the country. At its height, the Panthers had charters all over the country, with membership of more than 10,000. In 1969, Panthers started the Free Breakfast for School Children Program, in which they set up kitchens in cities across the nation, feeding more than 10,000 children every day before they went to school.

As the Black Panther Party gained national prominence, it quickly drew the attention of various law enforcement agencies, specifically the Federal Bureau of Investigation (FBI). Huey Newton was arrested in 1967 and was charged with killing an Oakland, California, police officer. After this incident, the Black Panthers became a primary target of FBI director J. Edgar Hoover and his counterintelligence program, commonly known as COINTELPRO. Spearheaded by the FBI, COINTELPRO was a covert and often illegal operation that ran from 1956 to 1971 and designed to infiltrate, discredit, disrupt, and neutralize various domestic social and political organizations in the United States, including those supporting the massive civil rights movement. Hoover publicly stated that the Black Panther Party was the "greatest threat to the internal security of the country."

Schism

Internal strife within the Black Panther Party began to surface in the summer of 1969. Stokely Carmichael, the prime minister of the Black Panthers and chairman of the Student Nonviolent Coordinating Committee (SNCC), a nationally known proponent of black power, urged Panther members to completely separate themselves from white Americans and other civil rights organizations that included white members. Carmichael openly stated that white Americans cannot relate to the black experience and have a detrimental effect on black communities. Carmichael publicly declared:

> Whites who come into the black community with ideas of change seem to want to absolve the power structure of its responsibility for what it is doing, and say that change can only come through black unity, which is the worst kind of paternalism ... if we are to proceed toward true liberation, we must cut ourselves off from white people ... otherwise we will find ourselves entwined in the tentacles of the white power complex that controls this country.

Several Panther leaders disagreed with Carmichael's assessment, advocating the inclusion of all people, regardless of race, as long as they supported the Black Panther ideology. However, this issue created an interminable split among members, culminating in an open gunfight between sparring factions on the campus of the University of California, Los Angeles, resulting in the death of two Panthers, and giving the impression of the Black Panthers as a radical, dangerous, and violent anti-American organization.

From 1968 to 1971, numerous Black Panther Party members were arrested and/or killed in police-related shootings, including 17-year-old member Bobby Hutton and the party's charismatic Chicago leader, Fred Hampton. The Black Panthers were in disarray. Eldridge Cleaver fled the United States, and the remaining members were either jailed or disillusioned with the struggle, leaving the party leaderless. By the early 1980s, the Black Panther Party of Self-Defense was dissolved.

Tony Gaskew
University of Pittsburgh at Bradford

See Also: African Americans; Attica; Autobiographies, Criminals; Chicago, Illinois; Chicago Seven/Democratic National Convention of 1968; Hoover, J. Edgar; Racism.

Further Readings
BlackPanther.org. "Ten Points." http://www.blackpanther.org/TenPoint.html (Accessed April 2011).
Hilliard, David. *The Black Panther*. New York: Atria Publishing, 2007.
Hilliard, David and Cornell West. *The Black Panther Party: Service to the People Programs*. Albuquerque: University of New Mexico Press, 2008.
Joseph, Peniel, ed. *The Black Power Movement: Rethinking the Civil Rights–Black Power Era*. New York: Routledge, 2006.
Newton, Huey P. *Revolutionary Suicide*. New York: Penguin, 1995.
Seale, Bobby. *Seize the Time: The Story of the Black Panther Party and Huey P. Newton*. Baltimore, MD: Black Classic Press, 1996.

Blackstone, William

William Blackstone (1723–80) was one of the most famous legal philosophers of the Western world. He was a British judge, professor, author, and politician. He is best known for his four-volume treatise *Commentaries on the Laws of England*, which is a classic work on the common law.

William Blackstone was born in London to Charles Blackstone, a silk merchant, and Mary Blackstone nee Bigg, the sister of a surgeon, five months after the death of his father. Blackstone had three brothers, one who died before reaching adulthood; the other two attended Oxford and joined the church. Before the death of Blackstone's father, the family was considered to be prosperous, but the family's position declined after the father's death. Despite the decline in the family fortunes, Blackstone was sent to Charterhouse School, where he excelled. After the death of his mother in 1736, with the family wealth gone, Blackstone was able to obtain an appointment at the Charterhouse School as a poor scholar, which he held until 1738. At that time, Blackstone qualified for a scholarship and went to Pembroke College at Oxford University.

While at Oxford University, Blackstone studied the liberal arts but after a little more than a year, he switched to studying the civil law. In 1741, Blackstone was admitted to the Middle Temple, which permitted him to begin preparation for a career as a lawyer. While at Oxford University, Blackstone published several books on poetry and architecture, which won him some academic fame. He was subsequently elected a Fellow at All Souls College of Oxford University in 1743. In 1746, Blackstone was appointed an administrator at All Souls College. Blackstone continued his studies in law and was called to the bar in the Middle Temple in 1746.

Developing Legal Expertise
After his call to the bar, Blackstone began to divide his time between Oxford University and London so that he could practice law. The court records show that he had very few cases. However, he apparently acted as counsel for Oxford University. In 1750, Blackstone was awarded his Doctor of Civil Law from Oxford University, which allowed him to be appointed to the Convocation at Oxford University. In 1750, Blackstone's first legal publication was completed. It was titled "An Essay on Collateral Consanguinity." In 1753, Blackstone announced that he would no longer practice law but intended to lecture on the common law. The same year, Blackstone applied for a vacant professorship but was passed over for another person.

From 1753 to 1755, Blackstone gave a series of lectures on the common law, which were very well received. Blackstone was not noted as a good speaker, but the content of his lectures compensated for his lack of oratory skill. As a result of his success, Blackstone's prominence at Oxford University grew and he was appointed to be the assessor for the Chancellor's Court. As assessor, he adjudicated minor cases involving the faculty and the students.

In 1756, Blackstone published his first legal textbook, *An Analysis of the Laws of England*. The textbook was a huge success, resulting in the publication of six editions. He continued to publish various legal treatises over the succeeding years. By 1758, Blackstone was a widely accepted expert in English law and was appointed to be the first Vinerian Professor of English Law at Oxford University. Despite his recognition as a legal scholar, Blackstone was not popular within the university, due in large part to his personality. He had made a number of enemies, and he failed to be elected to the post of vice-warden of the university.

Despite his unpopularity within the university, Blackstone had an excellent reputation outside. The Prince of Wales sponsored Blackstone, and he obtained chambers in the Inner Temple and began to practice law as a barrister. He continued to successfully publish legal treatises. In 1761, Blackstone married Sarah Clitherow. He had a number of children, some of whom died during childhood, which was not uncommon during that period. In 1761, Blackstone was appointed to Parliament. He remained a member of Parliament until 1768. In Great Britain, at that time, service in Parliament was considered helpful in obtaining an appointment as a judge.

Commentaries on the Laws of England
Over the succeeding years, Blackstone made numerous attempts to obtain an appointment as a judge, without success. In 1766, Blackstone resigned from Oxford University. In 1766, Blackstone began publishing his magnum opus: *Commentaries on the Laws of England*. The work consisted of four volumes, the final volume being published in 1770. It was a huge success and was republished five more times until his death.

The *Commentaries* were, for the times, a vast compendium not only of the common law but of the philosophy of law. The first volume of the *Commentaries* contained a section that recognized and explained the nature of law as an expression of both natural law and the Creator. Blackstone is perhaps best known for his recognition of the absolute natural rights of individual persons, otherwise known as civil or political liberties. The first absolute right was the right of personal security in a person's life, limbs, body, health, and reputation. It is here that the basis for modern tort law can be found. The second absolute right was the right of personal liberty, which included the right of locomotion, changing one's situation, or removing oneself to another place. The right of personal liberty could not be ever abridged without sufficient cause and due course of law. It is here that the basis for the modern concept of due process of law can be found. The third absolute right was the inherent right to property, which included the free use, enjoyment, and disposal of all of a person's acquisitions.

This right could only be regulated by the law of the land and the judgment of a person's peers, under what is now known as due process of law. Not even the government could take private property for public use. Each of these three absolute natural rights is found throughout the Declaration of Independence, the Constitution, and the Bill of Rights. Ancillary to these three absolute rights, Blackstone presented five auxiliary rights to help protect the three absolute rights. These five auxiliary rights were a legislature separate from the executive branch of government so that the making and enforcing of the laws are not vested in a single person, a limitation of the sovereign to act within the bounds of the law, the right to apply to the courts for the redress of injuries, the right to petition the sovereign or the legislature for the redress of grievances not addressed by the courts, and the right to keep and bear arms for self-defense and opposition to tyranny.

In 1770, Blackstone was appointed to the Court of the King's Bench. After a few months, Blackstone was transferred to the Court of Common Pleas, where he handled primarily civil matters. Blackstone was considered an excellent jurist and remained on the Court of Common Pleas until his death on February 14, 1780, in Wallingford. After his death, the Fellows of All Souls College arranged to have a statue erected in his honor.

Blackstone's greatest legacy is the *Commentaries on the Laws of England*. It is considered the seminal work of English common law and has been considered to be the first systematic formulation of English law. Some authorities rank Blackstone with other figures of the Enlightenment, to include Montesquieu and Voltaire. There is little doubt that Blackstone was a significant legal philosopher who contributed much to the development of Western legal thought. Blackstone's influence on the founding fathers and the development of the civil and criminal law in America was significant. Until the last part of the 19th century the *Commentaries* were and remained the seminal legal reference for legal proceedings in America. Even today, the *Commentaries* continue to exert their influence on American law.

A copy of a portrait of William Blackstone from 1755, just before the publication of his very successful first legal textbook, An Analysis of the Laws of England. *By 1758, Blackstone was considered an important expert in English law.*

Wm. C. Plouffe, Jr.
Independent Scholar

See Also: Bill of Rights; Common Law Origins of Criminal Law; Constitution of the United States of America; Declaration of Independence.

Further Readings

Bader, William D. "Some Thoughts on Blackstone: Precedent and Originalism." *Vermont Law Review*, v.19/5 (1995).

Blackstone, Sir William. *Commentaries on the Laws of England*. Oxford: Clarendon Press, 1770.

Doolittle, Ian. *William Blackstone: A Biography*. Leeds, UK: Maney Publishing, 2001.

Prest, Wilfred. *William Blackstone: Law and Letters in the Eighteenth Century*. Oxford: Oxford University Press, 2008.

Blood Sports

Traditionally, the term *bloodsport*, or commonly, "blood sports," refers to sporting activities that involve humans inflicting pain on animals through their own agency or through the actions of other animals in the context of a game or agonistic contest. Such activities include cockfighting, dog fighting, bear baiting, hare or deer coursing, gander pulling, and eel pulling. Traditional activities such as fox hunting and hunting, per se, besides being complex subjects in their own right, are usually only considered blood sports by animal advocates and lobbyists.

Blood sports, though often viewed as coarse and faintly disreputable, enjoyed popularity among all classes of people worldwide until the 1600s. The Tudor monarchs, in particular, were patrons of cockpits and enjoyed bear baiting and other more outré forms of agonistic sport. Other bizarre variations included setting dogs on monkeys that were riding on ponies, and similarly baiting asses with dogs.

Rat catching, in which specially trained terriers would kill a large number of rats within an enclosure (typically a cockpit), was popular among the poor and within bachelor culture in urban areas into the late 1800s. However, beginning in the 1600s and 1700s, royalty, nobility, and the upper classes, as a whole, moved toward fox hunting and horse racing and away from the more common, rural pastimes such as cockfighting and folk activities where familiar farm animals were featured in highly ritualized spectacles. By the 1820s, animal cruelty legislation in England criminalized most forms of agonistic sport involving animals.

However, in premodern Europe, pitting animals against other animals of the same or different species, or sport in which humans contested to kill an animal, frequently occurred on religious feast days and had a faintly pagan veneer. That is, such pastimes were akin to animal sacrifice in many respects and at one time had enjoyed a religious or teleological significance. Although poorly understood today, it seems that the subject animal symbolized certain values or embodied qualities held in high esteem by rural folk. Its sacrifice afforded the participants and observers some linkage to ultimate causes and nature itself. The fact that agonistic sports events involving animals frequently occurred on religious feast days certainly suggests that many of these events were survivals from the pagan past.

Gander pulling, in which the greased neck of a live goose that was suspended upside down from a gallows-like structure was grasped at by riders moving at a high speed, fell from favor in the Low Countries and New Netherlands in the 1700s. It was also popular in frontier days in the United States. Eel pulling, an aquatic sport in which boatloads of intoxicated Amsterdammers jousted for a chance at tugging a greased or soaped eel that was suspended on a rope over a canal, was a Dutch variation on this theme.

Police officers attempting to stop an illegal eel tug in 1886 set off a riot that lasted days and caused more than 20 deaths. The Eel Uprising pointed to the fact that these activities were highly significant to the common people. Acadian people in southern Louisiana continue to enjoy a Mardi Gras (Shrove Tuesday) ritual of having often intoxicated, masked, mounted men collect live chickens from farmers to put in a collective stew or gumbo. The connection with old European days of pagan religious celebration where drunken, riotous sacrifice precedes ceremonial gluttony, followed by ritual abnegation, is scarcely coincidental or accidental and reflects ancient practices and belief systems.

Reduction Efforts

It is precisely this potentially uncontrolled riotousness that early reformers wanted to channel and limit when laws were passed banning blood

A Mexican American man holding two fighting cocks in Crystal City, Texas, in 1939. Cockfighting is now illegal in the United States but is still practiced in rural areas of the south and southwest by both Anglo and Hispanic Americans.

sports. Many laws that emerged in the 17th and 18th centuries were specifically sabbatarian and intended to halt any sort of amusement that might detract from an austere observance of the day of Christian worship. Feast day intoxication and drunkenness were anathema to Puritan Protestants in England and the Americas, and it was said in jest that they banned such sports not for the sake of the animal but to prevent humans from enjoying the sport. In their defense, they did, in fact, provide other protections for domesticated animals in a more general sense. Contemporary animal protectionism is supposedly based on more humane and ethical motivations, rather than proceeding from a fanatical adherence to theological observance, but issues of culturally-based abuse are emergent and manifest. That is, urban elites impose their mores and the pastimes of rural folk with an adherence to the program of "progress" used as a rationale. The suffering of animals used for food or for the sports of the rich, for example, horse racing, is almost never discussed by anti–blood sport activists.

Most blood sports are extinct in the United States. Survivors include dog fighting, brought into relief by the Michael Vick case, and cockfighting. Both are now illegal throughout the United States but enjoy large underground followings. Cockfighting, in particular, has a large rural audience of both Hispanic and Anglo Americans. Until recently, the activity was legal or minimally proscribed in Louisiana, Oklahoma, and Arizona, but well-funded efforts by lobbyists have succeeded in criminalizing the activity. Federal prosecutions of those who engage in interstate transport of fighting cocks or paraphernalia have increased, and stiff sentences have added a larger element of risk to the activity. Certainly, some participants and potential spectators have been deterred.

The distinction between the sport of pitting brute animals against each other for the amusement of humans and the spectacle of humans fighting for the enjoyment of other humans may seem obvious to some but nevertheless can be seen as artificial or at least highly paradoxical.

Although dog fighting has undergone a renaissance in recent years, it is still held in disrepute by society at large and fetches harsh penalties for those convicted of involvement. Cockfighting, more or less ignored by prosecutors, is now being vigorously prosecuted both at the federal and the state levels. Sentences of one year in federal prisons have been imposed.

That notwithstanding, cockfighting has been an occult pastime for the past 50 years and will continue in that vein. It will probably grow as a diversion because of the recent infusion of Hispanic participants.

Francis Frederick Hawley
Western Carolina University

See Also: Cruelty to Animals; Fish and Game Laws; Gambling; Livestock and Cattle Crimes; Puritans.

Further Readings

Hawley, F. Frederick. "Cockfight in the Cotton: A Moral Crusade in Microcosm." *Contemporary Crises*, v.13 (1989).

Hawley, F. Frederick. "Cockfighting in the Pine Woods: Gameness in the New South." *Sport Place*, v.1/2 (1987).

Huizinga, J. *Homo Ludens: A Study of the Play Element of Culture*. Boston: Beacon Press, 1950.

Mitchell, Timothy. *Blood Sport: A Social History of Spanish Bullfighting*. Philadelphia: University of Pennsylvania Press, 1991.

Blue Laws

See State Blue Laws.

Bodie of Liberties

One of the first legal codes established in British America, the Massachusetts Bodie of Liberties was composed by the Puritan minister Nathaniel Ward and adopted by the General Court in December 1641. It reflected the Puritans' vision of their mission to create a theocracy in the New World while at the same time pioneering some politically progressive ideas. Combining elements of the English common law and Mosaic principles, the code dealt with civil and ecclesiastical matters. The Bodie of Liberties was adopted during a trying period of New England history.

In the very first decade after the Puritans started to arrive in New England, the king nearly revoked the charter of their colony twice. In the late 1630s, the region was ravaged by the Pequot War. Furthermore, the settlers were torn in disagreements on a wide range of issues from religion to governance. Many Puritans envisioned their colony as a theocracy; they opposed any initiative to formalize laws because it could undermine the power of magistrates. Others insisted that laws should be codified to prevent arbitrariness in legal matters and hoped for a more representative government with well-defined functions.

Ward's legal code took into account the colony's precarious situation. Its provisions were called "liberties" rather than "laws," even though everyone was expected to "consider them as laws" (Sec. 96). It clarified punishments for various crimes, thus offering some protection against arbitrary judgment of magistrates. Furthermore, Ward's code appealed to different factions in the colony; it reflected Puritans' religious fundamentalism, while embracing some politically progressive ideas.

The progressive streak in the Bodie of Liberties is apparent in several areas. Everyone was declared equal in the face of law and had access to courts. Regardless of "whether Inhabitant or foreigner, free or not free," one had "liberty to come to any public Court, Counsel, or Town meeting, and ... to move any lawful, seasonable, and material question, or to present any necessary motion, complaint, petition, Bill or information" (Secs. 2 and 12). Furthermore, the code guaranteed trials "without partiality or delay" (Sec. 2), outlawed "imhumane Barborous or cruel" punishments (Sec. 46), and limited the use of torture to exceptional cases (Sec. 45). For the sake of economic fairness, the Bodie of Liberties prohibited monopolies, making exceptions only for "new Inventions that are profitable to the Country, and [only] for a short time" (Sec. 9). The code protected the rights of women, children, foreigners, and even farm animals. It specifically condemned domestic violence, allowing women to bring complaints against abusive husbands. It also protected indentured servants from mistreatment.

Although the majority of the Puritans nominally believed in the separation of church and state, the code dealt not only with civil but also with religious matters. It defined the functions of churches and created venues to resolve religious tensions. Most importantly, the code affirmed congregational principles—the notion that people can form congregations without much interference from the central government. This innovation reflected the Puritans' antipathy toward overly centralized religions such as Catholicism and Anglicanism. The Bodie of Liberties gave "all the people of god" the freedom to "gather themselves into a Church Estate" (Sec. 95.1). Furthermore, every congregation was guaranteed "free libertie of Election and ordination of all their officers" (Sec. 95.3). To underscore the importance of religion in legal matters, all capital laws in the Bodie of Liberties were adopted directly from the Bible. Capital punishment was reserved for such crimes as idolatry, blasphemy, perjury, adultery, murder, bestiality, homosexuality, and witchcraft (Sec. 94).

The code was meant to promote religious orthodoxy in Massachusetts by imposing several restrictions on religious freedom. The right to form congregations was given only to people "Orthodox in Judgment" (Sec. 91.1). Officers of any church were expected to be "pious and orthodox" (Sec. 91.3). Puritan appreciation of religious homogeneity was also apparent in the clause on immigration; the colony was open to refugees from "the Tyranny or oppression of their persecutors, or from famine, wares, or the like," as long as they professed "the true Christian religion" (Sec. 89). This clause was probably intentionally vague. In the decades that followed, the authorities in New England not only barred but also persecuted such religious minorities as Anabaptists and Quakers. The Bodie of Liberties served as a basis for the more extensive Laws and Liberties of Massachusetts, which was adopted in 1647. The new legal code echoed the principles established in the Bodie of Liberties, but was far better defined as a set of laws.

Alexander Moudrov
Queens College, City University of New York

See Also: Colonial Courts; History of Crime and Punishment in America: Colonial; Mayflower Compact; Puritans.

Further Readings
McManus, Edgar J. *Law and Liberty in Early New England*. Amherst: University of Massachusetts Press, 1993.
Wall, Robert E. *Massachusetts Bay: The Crucial Decade, 1640–1650*. New Haven, CT: Yale University Press, 1973.

Bodine, Polly

Born Mary Polly Housman (ca. 1808–92), Polly Bodine was dubbed the "Witch of Staten Island" after she was accused of murdering her sister-in-law and infant niece at their Staten Island home in 1843. The Housman home was ablaze that Christmas night, and after the fire had been extinguished, investigators discovered Emeline Van Pelt Housman and her daughter, Ann Eliza, under a mattress that had been set up in the kitchen to keep them close to the wood-burning stove during the cold winter months. Murder was suspected when investigators found that Emeline had been bound and that her limbs had been broken. Furthermore, both Emeline and the baby had suffered crushing blows to their skulls.

It was determined that Emeline and Ann had died on Christmas Eve, the night before the blaze, during a time that Polly Bodine had been at the house. Bodine, who was in her 30s and widowed at the time, lived with her teenage children, William Albert and Eliza Ann, in her father's home very near to the Housman home. Bodine admitted that she had spent Christmas Eve with her sister-in-law, who was often afraid to be left alone when her husband traveled. Emeline's husband and Bodine's brother, Captain George W. Housman, was away from home on a trip to Virginia at the time of the murders. He returned three days later to find his home burned, his wife and daughter dead, and his sister accused of the heinous crime.

Police, who first surmised that the murders might have followed a robbery committed by a band of thieves, quickly changed course and concluded that Bodine and her alleged lover, George Waite, had committed the crimes in order to take and sell the Housmans' belongings, and the pair was arrested within days on the circumstantial evidence that investigators had gathered in the intervening period.

Trials
Bodine's first trial began in Richmondtown in the summer of 1844. The prosecution provided accounts of Emeline's and Bodine's movements on Christmas Eve and Christmas Day, providing a timeline that established not only that Bodine had the opportunity, but that she might also have been responsible for selling some items that were taken from the Housman home before the fire. Against the mounting circumstantial evidence, defense attorneys presented witnesses who testified that Housman was alive on Christmas Day and

therefore could not have been murdered by Bodine the previous evening. That didn't satisfy prosecutors, who could not establish Bodine's whereabouts on the following evening either—she had not stayed with a friend, as she had told her son. Defense attorneys later contended that it had been an innocent lie; Bodine had not wanted to tell her son that she was staying with Waite. When the first trial ended, jurors took two days before declaring that they could not reach a verdict in the case. It was later reported that 11 of the jurors had been convinced of Bodine's guilt and were prepared to deliver a verdict of guilty against her. The holdout juror declared that he could not deliver a verdict, either an acquittal or a judgment of guilt, based on the circumstantial evidence provided.

A second trial for Bodine in Richmond County was aborted when attempts to convene a jury failed. The trial was moved to New York City in 1845. During the three-week proceedings, some of the witnesses who initially claimed to have seen Bodine at the pawn shop could no longer identify her as the woman who sold the items belonging to the Housmans. Despite the changed testimony and timeline, the jury quickly delivered a guilty verdict.

However, Bodine's defense attorneys submitted a petition to set aside the verdict, noting 29 exceptions, and the New York Supreme Court, in agreeing to 27 of those submitted, set aside the verdict before the end of 1845 and ordered a retrial. Bodine's trial had attracted so much public attention that attempts to find an impartial jury from among the thousands of possible jurors interviewed in Manhattan failed to seat the necessary 12-member panel. The third trial was moved to Orange County, New York. The jurors in the April 1846 trial found Bodine not guilty.

After two years in jail and three highly publicized trials, the charges against Bodine were dropped and she was freed. She returned to her family on Staten Island, moving with her children to a home in Port Richmond. She died on July 27, 1892. The Housman murders were never solved, and no one else stood trial for the crimes.

Tracey-Lynn Clough
University of Texas at Arlington

See Also: New York; Women Criminals, History of; Women Criminals, Sociology of.

Further Readings
Clinton, Henry L. *Extraordinary Cases*. Freeport, NY: For Libraries, 1972.
Lundrigan, Margaret. *Staten Island: Isle of the Bay*. Charleston, SC: Arcadia, 2004.
Van, Every Edward. *Sins of New York as "Exposed" by the Police Gazette*. New York: Frederick A. Stokes, 1930.

Boles, Charles

Charles E. Boles used several aliases, including Charles E. Bolton and T. Z. Spaulding, but he is best known as the infamous stagecoach robber Black Bart. He was born Charles E. Bowles in 1829 in Norfolk County, England. In 1831, when he was 2 years old, his family migrated to Alexandria, New York. At some point, he changed his name to Charles E. Boles. He made a couple of trips to California to try his luck at gold mining. In 1854, he married Mary Elizabeth Johnson in Plessis, New York. They had four children. He and his family moved to Decatur, Illinois, just prior to the outbreak of the Civil War. Charles E. Boles enlisted in the Union Army on August 13, 1862, at Decatur. During the war, he served as a sergeant with Company B, 116th Illinois Volunteer Infantry. After the war, Charles Boles returned to the west. He tried his hand at several odd jobs, including gold mining, but then he turned to robbing stagecoaches, particularly those affiliated with Wells, Fargo & Company. There is a story that he was forced to abandon a gold mine he was working in Montana by Wells Fargo men.

Charles Boles established a consistent modus operandi: he operated as a lone bandit, usually on foot. He typically selected a spot on a curve along a winding mountain road where, out of necessity, the stagecoach had to slow down. Boles generally wore a long duster coat over his clothing and covered his head; he carried a 12-gauge, double-barrel shotgun and often an ax to smash open the strongbox. His first stagecoach robbery was on July 26, 1875, in Calaveras County, California, about four miles outside Copperopolis, California. He usually got away with the Wells Fargo strongbox and mail sacks. For instance, Wells Fargo reported that the strongbox that Charles Boles got away with from his first heist contained $160. On his fourth and fifth stagecoach robberies, he gave each respective stagecoach driver a scrawled poem, both of which were signed "Black Bart, the P o 8." Black Bart, it turned out, was the name of a dime novel character from a story Charles Boles had read. He appropriated the name but created his own legendary exploits. He often waited several months between heists. He was always a gentlemanly bandit, particularly courteous to female stagecoach passengers. Boles is believed to have struck 28 times and to have garnered a total of about $18,000 from Wells Fargo & Co. strongboxes.

At the site of his last stagecoach robbery, on November 3, 1883, at Funk Hill in Calaveras County, Charles Boles left behind a handkerchief. Sheriff Tom Cunningham of San Joaquin County noticed a laundry mark on that critical piece of evidence. Eventually, Harry Morse, who ran the Morse Patrol and Detective Agency of San Francisco, found other laundry with the same markings, which led him to the subsequent apprehension of Charles Boles with the assistance of Detective James Hume of the Pinkerton Detective Agency. After he was caught, Charles E. Boles admitted to committing some of the stagecoach robberies attributed to him. He was convicted and sent to serve six years in San Quentin Prison, which he began doing on November 21, 1883. He was released on January 21, 1888, after serving about four years. He had not aged well during this incarceration, and although there continued to be unsubstantiated reports for some time that he had returned to robbing stagecoaches, he is believed to have died around 1917.

Victor B. Stolberg
Essex County College

See Also: California; Frontier Crime; Robbery, History of; San Quentin State Prison; Sheriffs.

Further Readings
Hoeper, George. *Black Bart: Boulevardier Bandit*. Fresno, CA: Word Dancer Press, 1995.
Hume, James B. and John N. Thacker. *Wells Fargo & Co. Stagecoach and Train Robberies, 1870–1884: The Corporate Report of 1885 With Additional Facts About the Crimes and Their Perspectives*. Jefferson, NC: McFarland & Company, 2010.
Wilson, R. Michael. *Great Stagecoach Robberies of the Old West*. Guilford, CT: Globe Pequot Press, 2007.

Bonnie and Clyde

During the Great Depression, in the beleaguered state of Texas, an outlaw couple made a name for themselves through robbery, kidnapping, and murder. Clyde Chestnut Barrow was born in Teleco, Texas, on March 24, 1909, to Henry and Cumie Barrow. Clyde's girlfriend, Bonnie Parker, was born in Rowena, Texas, on October 1, 1910, to J. T. and Emma Parker. Originally married to Roy Thornton, Bonnie became Clyde's girlfriend when Roy was imprisoned. Together, Bonnie and

Bonnie Parker and Clyde Barrow just before they died in May 1934. That month, Clyde Barrow had been indicted for theft of U.S. government property for stealing his weapons from National Guard armories.

Clyde ran the Barrow gang, also known as the Bloody Barrows, which was an assortment of small-time thieves who robbed small banks, grocery stores, and gas stations across the American midwest and southwest. Although responsible for murdering at least a dozen men between 1932 and 1934, Bonnie and Clyde's criminal exploits rarely caught the attention of northern journalists. Even other legendary gangsters of the era gave no respect to Bonnie and Clyde, who were seen as small-time bandits clashing with sheriffs in the backwoods of America.

While they were often romantically glamorized as a man-and-woman bandit team living for the moment in a chaotic world, Bonnie and Clyde were actually not imposing in stature and were considered to have childlike appearances. In fact, Bonnie weighed less than 100 pounds. Regardless of their looks, the heavy Browning automatic rifles used in the commission of their crimes gave them the edge they needed. These powerful firearms were stolen by the Barrow gang from National Guard armories around Texas and Oklahoma. Later, in May 1934, a federal grand jury indicted Clyde Barrow for the theft of U.S. government property in response to these weapon seizures.

Bonnie and Clyde would often kidnap a hostage to quicken their escape from whatever bank branch or grocery store they decided to rob. These hostages were often later released unharmed; however, in June 1933, the Barrow gang wrecked their car and, because of severe burns that Bonnie sustained, they were forced to take a farm family hostage, which resulted in an innocent woman having her hand shot. The debacle ended when the kidnapping of two law officers enabled the Barrow gang to escape to Erick, Oklahoma, where the officers were subsequently released. Other encounters with the authorities resulted in murder. For instance, in January 1934, Bonnie, Clyde, and James Mullen raided the Eastham Prison Farm in Texas to free Raymond Hamilton and four others, but they killed one guard and wounded another during the escape. In April 1934, the Barrow gang killed two highway patrolmen around Grapevine, Texas, and later killed Constable Cal Campbell near Commerce, Oklahoma.

After these three murders, Bonnie, Clyde, and Henry Methvin fled into Kansas. Soon, Bonnie and Clyde returned to Texas to visit their families. Despite the pleas from their family members, Bonnie and Clyde refused to go to Mexico to evade capture. Instead, Bonnie, Clyde, and Henry found refuge in the abandoned John Cole house near Gibsland and Sailes, Louisiana, which was close to where Henry's parents lived.

Concerned for his son's life, Ivy Methvin sent his neighbor, John Joyner, to negotiate a deal with Sheriff Henderson Jordan that would guarantee Henry Methvin's pardon in exchange for the lives of Bonnie and Clyde. Fearful of reprisals from Bonnie and Clyde, Ivy Methvin ardently argued for the death of the two bandits instead of their lawful capture. Frank Hamer, the legendary former Texas Ranger, agreed to Methvin's deal and planned the perfect ambush while using a posse of only three Texans along with Ivy Methvin, Sheriff Jordan, and his deputy. The seven men hid on a brush-covered embankment on the road that led to the Cole house. Methvin was instructed to stand by his car, which had the left tire off and was up on a jack. On May 23, 1934, when Clyde and Bonnie returned, they stopped to offer Methvin help, but they were shot 167 times by high-powered rifles from the men hiding on the other side of the road. Their bullet-riddled bodies were left inside Clyde's V-8 Ford as it was towed to Arcadia, where roughly 16,000 onlookers came to see their corpses. Their bodies were returned to Texas for burial.

Brian G. Sellers
University of South Florida

See Also: 1921 to 1940 Primary Documents; Great Depression; Guns and Violent Crime; Murder, History of; Robbery, History of; Texas.

Further Readings
Burrough, Bryan. *Public Enemies: America's Greatest Crime Wave and the Birth of the FBI, 1933–1934.* New York: Penguin Press, 2004.
Helmer, William and Rick Mattix. *Public Enemies: America's Criminal Past, 1919–1940.* New York: Facts on File, 1998.
Milner, E. R. *The Lives and Times of Bonnie and Clyde.* Carbondale: Southern Illinois University Press, 1996.
Phillips, John Neal. *Running With Bonnie and Clyde: The Ten Fast Years of Ralph Fults.* Norman: University of Oklahoma, 1996.

Book of the General Lawes and Libertyes

The first law code printed in colonial America, the *Book of the General Lawes and Libertyes of the Massachusetts Bay Colony* was a codification of rights, duties, and criminal penalties. The General Lawes were a revision of the 1641 Bodie of Liberties, a compilation of rights assembled by the Massachusetts General Court. The General Lawes reflected a strong reliance on Puritanical morality and individual liberty, expressing fundamental principles that served as the basis for later legal codes and constitutions.

As early as 1635, Massachusetts' legislature, the General Court, had sought a review of existing laws in order to establish a revised and unified legal code. Towns were requested to compile their fundamental laws so the court might draft a compendious abridgement. The effort languished until the utility of a uniform jurisprudence became apparent and the distraction of domestic and foreign hostilities subsided. Nathaniel Ward and John Cotton, Puritan ministers who emigrated from England to escape religious persecution, drafted the requested compilations in 1641. These drafts were sent to towns for further consideration and then revised and amended by the General Court before being presented as the Bodie of Liberties.

This precursor to General Lawes consisted of 100 provisions respecting rights and privileges, crimes and punishments, and the propriety of civil and ecclesial governance. The principal contributors were English-educated barristers and ministers, and the Bodie of Liberties clearly incorporated secular and religious as well as foreign and regional traditions. The influence of the Magna Carta, Bill of Rights, and English common law were evident in the code's persistent invocation of individual liberties and procedural due process. The democratic sentiment of the American colonists was reflected in the exclusive authorities granted to the General Court. As Massachusetts' economy thrived upon commercial ventures, as opposed to the agricultural system of the south, the code focused upon laws affecting trade and commerce. The entire code was grounded in a biblical foundation of morality and religion.

Yet the Bodie of Liberties was a general statement of rights intended to guide the legislature. An effort to refine this declaration into a formal code of statutes culminated in the *Book of the General Lawes and Libertyes* in 1648. The General Lawes remained faithful to the nature and objectives of the earlier code while expanding and clarifying its content. Massachusetts thereby established an unprecedented system of government—founded upon democracy, committed unto religion, and devoted to individual liberty.

Attesting that the protection of liberty is essential to the safeguarding of civil and religious order, the General Lawes introduced a variety of fundamental rights into the colonial legal system. In order to establish a just and equitable rule of law, the General Lawes incorporated rights to counsel, trials by jury, notices and hearings prior to trial, and appeals. Double jeopardy and cruel punishment were prohibited. Personal property was secured and fair compensation was mandated in cases of eminent domain. Slavery was banned and protections were extended to women, children, servants, and even animals. Public records were open to inspection. Authority over laws of a criminal nature was withheld from local jurisdictions.

While criminal offenses were broad and punishments severe, care was taken to ensure fairness and justice. Burglary incurred branding, whipping, and death, whereas theft earned fines, whipping, and stocks. Fornication unconsummated by marriage resulted in fines or corporal punishment. Gamblers were subject to fines, as were bartenders and customers in the event of drunkenness. Fraudsters faced fines and lashings. Anabaptists and Catholics faced banishment or death. Witchcraft, blasphemy, murder, sodomy, adultery, kidnapping, perjury, treason, rebellion, and rape brought about death. Servants, laborers, strangers, and the poor were all subject to criminal regulations. These measures were considered by contemporaries as practical legislation in keeping with traditions of liberty.

The General Lawes were revoked, along with colonial charters, by Charles II in 1684 and only temporarily restored upon the deposition of James II before being abrogated by William and Mary's 1691 provincial charter creating the Province of Massachusetts Bay. Nevertheless, the General Lawes' principles of individual liberty and procedural due process founded upon the authority of divine revelation provided the foundation of civil and criminal colonial law until the American Revolution. Thereafter, the fundamental ideas of the General Lawes would be incorporated into state constitutions and the Constitution of the United States of America.

Justin Paulette
Independent Scholar

See Also: 1600 to 1776 Primary Documents; Bodie of Liberties; Colonial Charters and Grants; History of Crime and Punishment in America: Colonial; Magna Carta; Massachusetts.

Further Readings
McManus, Edgar J. *Law and Liberty in Early New England.* Amherst: University of Massachusetts Press, 1993.

Shurtleff, Nathaniel B., ed. *Records of the Governor and Company of the Massachusetts Bay in New England: Printed by Order of the Legislature.* Boston: William White, 1853–54.

Booth, John Wilkes

American stage actor and Civil War southern sympathizer, John Wilkes Booth was born in Bel Air, Maryland. On April 14, 1865, he shot President Abraham Lincoln at Ford's Theater in Washington, D.C. Lincoln died the next morning. Booth was killed 12 days later, on April 26, when he and fellow conspirators were surrounded by pursuers while hiding in a barn. Booth was the ninth of 10 children of Junius Brutus Booth and Mary Ann Holmes. Booth's father was a renowned Shakespearean actor and his older brothers, Edwin and Junius Brutus Jr., followed in their father's footsteps. Booth also had theatrical ambitions. In 1855, at the age of 17, he made his stage debut. Because his early performances revealed his inexperience and he did not want to be compared to his father and brothers, Booth used a pseudonym, "J. B. Wilkes."

In 1858 Booth performed in *Hamlet* with his brother, Edwin, playing Horatio to Edwin's

A photograph of John Wilkes Booth taken in Washington, D.C., in 1865. The scheme to assassinate Abraham Lincoln was originally part of a larger plan to destabilize the government by also killing the vice president and the secretary of state.

Hamlet. By 1860 Booth had progressed from novice actor to leading man. He performed both in the south and north of the Mason-Dixie Line. In January 1861, Booth was performing in Albany, New York, on the same night that Abraham Lincoln stopped there en route to his inauguration as president of the United States. Having injured himself during an earlier performance, Booth was returning to the stage that night and did his performance with his injured arm strapped to his body. There is no record that Booth and Lincoln encountered each other that evening in Albany. As the war continued, Booth was estranged from his brother, Edwin, who supported the Union. Booth was arrested in St. Louis in 1863 when he made treasonous remarks about Lincoln and his administration, but released when he took an oath of allegiance to the Union. With a small group of conspirators, Booth began plotting to kidnap President Lincoln and turn him over to the Confederate administration in Richmond, Virginia. Booth thought that Lincoln could be exchanged for Southern prisoners of war held by the Yankees.

When the kidnapping scheme planned for March 1865 failed because Lincoln did not appear at the expected place, Booth began to think of assassinating Lincoln. According to the plan, Booth was to assassinate Lincoln. At the same time, the vice president, Andrew Johnson, and the secretary of state, William Seward, were to be killed. This would leave the federal government in disarray. However, Booth's conspirators, George Atzerodt and Lewis Powell, failed to successfully carry out their assignments. Powell seriously wounded but did not kill Seward. Atzerodt lost his nerve and did not try to kill Johnson.

On April 14, only Booth accomplished his part of the plan. He shot Lincoln as his wife, Mary Todd Lincoln, and Major Henry Rathbone and his fiancée, Clara Harris, sat in their box watching the performance of the play *Our American Cousin*. Rathbone was stabbed and seriously injured when he struggled with Booth. Then jumping to the stage below, Booth shouted out the motto of the state of Virginia, *Sic simper tyrannis* ("Thus always to tyrants") and then, "The South shall be free" (witnesses disagree about the wording of his second declaration).

Booth managed to escape, but had fractured a bone in his leg either when he jumped to the stage or later. He sought medical attention from Dr. Samuel Mudd (who would be arrested as one of the conspirators). After several days, Booth and the man accompanying him were able to cross the Potomac into Virginia. But they were tracked to the farm of Richard Garrett by a detachment of Union soldiers. When the barn was set on fire, Booth appeared and was shot.

According to the report of Lieutenant Colonel Everton Conger, the commander of the detachment, Booth was killed by Sergeant Boston Corbett, a hat maker from Troy, New York. Corbett had disobeyed the order that Booth be taken alive. Corbett claimed that he had fired because Booth raised his pistol to shoot. Booth's body was taken back to Washington for identification. The body was buried at the Washington Arsenal on October 1, 1867. In 1869, Booth's remains were turned over to his family for burial in the family plot in Baltimore. Eight people accused of conspiring with Booth were tried before a military tribunal. One of the accused conspirators was a woman, Mary Surratt. She and three men, including Powell and Atzerodt, were hanged on July 7, 1865. The other accused men, including Dr. Mudd, were sentenced to prison, but three (one died of yellow fever) were eventually pardoned.

Frankie Y. Bailey
State University of New York, Albany

See Also: 1851 to 1900 Primary Documents; 1961 to 1980 Primary Documents; Czolgosz, Leon; Guiteau, Charles; Lincoln, Abraham (Administration of); Political Dissidents.

Further Readings
Kauffman, Michael W. *American Brutus: John Wilkes Booth and the Lincoln Conspiracies*. New York: Random House Trade, 2005.
Shinsel, Ruth. "John Wilkes Booth: Man to Murderer." *Mankind: The Magazine of Popular History*, v.1/8 (1968).
Smith, Gene. *American Gothic: The Story of America's Legendary Theatrical Family—Junius, Edwin, and John Wilkes Booth*. New York: Simon & Schuster, 1992.

Bootlegging

While the term *bootlegging* likely entered the lexicon of American slang many decades earlier, it is chiefly associated with the illegal production, distribution, and sale of alcohol during Prohibition (1920–33). The precise origins of the term are somewhat vague. Many sources suggest the term dates to the 19th-century American west. Others extend the provenance of the term as far back as the 17th century. Most concur that the term derives from the practice of secreting contraband (or other items) in the top of a tall boot leg. While predominantly a reference to illegal alcohol trafficking, it now enjoys popularity as a way to describe many forms of illegal trading in copyrighted, trademarked, or otherwise protected forms of merchandise.

Prohibition began with passage of the Eighteenth Amendment to the U.S. Constitution. Section 1 of the amendment states, "After one year from the ratification of this article the manufacture, sale, or transportation of intoxicating liquors within, the importation thereof into, or the exportation thereof from the United States and all territory subject to the jurisdiction thereof for beverage purposes is hereby prohibited." With this one sentence, the impetus was given to establish a vast underground network of alcohol sales and distribution. Far from quelling the American appetite for intoxicants, Prohibition merely drove underground and arguably solidified alcohol consumption as a part of national culture.

In its original sense, the enterprise of bootlegging alcohol in America extends back to the beginnings of the nation itself. The right of rural settlers to manufacture alcohol and the power of the government to collect taxes on production fueled violent clashes throughout the hills and backwoods of early America. The inevitable conflict between individual enterprise and governmental "intrusion" via taxation was something the Scotch and British immigrants to America knew all too well. Whiskey had been taxed by European governments as far back as the mid-1600s. By 1700, the British had coined the term *moonlighters* for the brandy smugglers on the coast of England. In the American colonies, the illegal distiller came to be called a "moonshiner" or "bootlegger." The United States collected an excise tax on alcohol from 1791 to 1802 and then again from 1813 to 1817. Alcohol production was untaxed for the next 45 years, but in the midst of the Civil War, Congress again passed a whiskey tax. By 1865, the tax on whiskey was $2 per gallon. This rate of taxation amounted to as much as 12 times the actual cost of making a gallon of liquor.

Illegal production and distribution of alcohol was not a strictly rural phenomenon. Individuals in urban centers likewise developed their own culture of organized crime and violence revolving around the illegal importation and sale of untaxed or prohibited alcohol. In the cities and along the national borders (including coastlines), illegal alcohol trade centered on methods of undetected importation and promulgation of venues for sales (i.e., underground clubs or "speakeasies"). Competition between rival factions seeking to dominate or monopolize particular territorial interests eventually fomented the formation of what would become long-enduring organized crime syndicates. In contrast, rural areas tended to support a yeoman culture of covert production (i.e., "moonshiners") and overland distribution (i.e., "running") to cities and other distribution points.

The height of bootlegging activity in America came at the confluence of several important national trends. On the one hand, the enactment of Prohibition made scarce a once-plentiful resource. This drove up both price and demand. On the other hand, Prohibition became law less than a

Posing with a seized whiskey still during Prohibition. Trafficking in the illegal alcohol production of moonshiners became a widespread and lucrative activity during Prohibition and was often eased by the complicity of law enforcement.

decade before the onset of the Great Depression. During the economic cataclysm of the Depression, many suffering people turned to acts heretofore unthinkable as otherwise legitimate employment opportunities grew increasingly rare. Concomitantly, people in rural America, for whom the Depression was just another bump in the larger travail of subsistence living, saw the newfound demand for illegal alcohol as a uniquely fitted economic opportunity. Given that this era was a little more than a generation removed from the pioneer mythos and manifest destiny that opened the western frontier, the appeal of bootlegging as a means to exist (or perhaps become wealthy) is understandable. Trafficking in illegal alcohol became a widespread and lucrative empire, often with the complicity of law enforcement. Many sources recount systematic payoffs, bribery, and extortion involving those tasked with bringing bootleggers to justice. In particular, corruption among federal agents was so rampant, President Warren Harding remarked on it in his 1922 State of the Union address.

Many lasting and important cultural themes emerged out of Prohibition. The crime associated with bootlegging thrust underworld figures such as Al Capone and "Lucky" Luciano into peculiar antihero celebrity. The era also cemented the American fascination with crime dramas such as *The Untouchables*. In bootlegging, one sees the lasting imprint of dynamic individualism juxtaposed against the perception of draconian government. Both the urban gangster and the hillbilly moonshiner are celebrated, not for what they do, but for what they oppose.

Matthew Pate
State University of New York, Albany

See Also: Capone, Al; Drinking and Crime; Great Depression; Luciano, "Lucky"; Moonshine; Organized Crime, History of; Prohibition; Smuggling; Volstead Act; Wickersham Commission.

Further Readings
Behr, Edward. *Prohibition: Thirteen Years That Changed America*. New York: Arcade, 1996.
Coffey, Thomas M. *The Long Thirst: Prohibition in America, 1920–1933*. New York: W. W. Norton, 1975.
Kobler, John. *Ardent Spirits: The Rise and Fall of Prohibition*. New York: Putnam, 1973.
Pegram, Thomas R. *Battling Demon Rum: The Struggle for a Dry America, 1800–1933*. Chicago: Ivan R. Dee, 1998.
Rumbarger, John. *Profits, Power and Prohibition: Alcohol Reform and the Industrializing of America, 1800–1930*. Albany: State University of New York Press, 1989.

Borden, Lizzie

Lizzie Andrew Borden (1860–1927) was the daughter of Andrew Jackson Borden and Sarah Anthony Morse. The Bordens had three daughters: Emma Lenora, Alice Esther, and Lizzie, the youngest. The Bordens were wealthy members of aristocratic society living in a quiet neighborhood located near the business district of Fall River. The mystery surrounding Lizzie Borden began on August 4, 1892, at the Borden family home on 92 Second Street, Fall River, Massachusetts. Upon entering the parlor of her home, 32-year-old Lizzie Borden discovered the body of her 70-year-old father.

Abby Borden, the stepmother of Lizzie Borden, was discovered by Adelaide Churchill, a neighbor, in an upstairs guest bedroom in the Borden home, face down in a pool of congealed blood. An autopsy report revealed that she had been struck 19 times with a sharp object presumed to have been an axe. Her husband, Andrew, had been struck 11 times with a heavy sharp object, presumably the same weapon.

The Mystery Begins
The list of suspects was short. Those who had immediate access to the Bordens included Emma Borden; live-in maid Bridget "Maggie" Sullivan; and a visitor named John Vinnicum Morse, who was Lizzie's maternal uncle. However, police focused their investigation on Lizzie Andrew Borden.

As the murder investigation got under way, it became very clear that the local police department was not trained or prepared to handle a double murder of this magnitude. Police investigators determined that there were four significant events that took place on August 3, the day before the murders occurred. First, Abby Borden went to visit Dr. Bowen, claiming that she and Andrew Borden were being poisoned because they had become very ill during the night; the autopsy, however, showed no evidence of poison in either of the bodies. Second, Lizzie Borden went to a local drugstore and asked for the poison prussic acid, which she said she was going to use to rid her sealskin cape of bugs; however, she left without purchasing the drug because she did not have a prescription for it. Third, John Morse visited the Borden home unannounced, without luggage, and spent the night. It was reported that Lizzie Borden heard her parents and Morse arguing about money. Finally, Lizzie Borden visited her friend Alice Russell, who told police that Borden had seemed out of sorts and confided her worry that something bad would happen to her father.

As the police investigation continued, a timeline of events began to emerge. On the day of the murders, August 4, 1892, according to Churchill, Andrew Borden left his house around 9 A.M. to visit some of his business ventures. Workmen at one location stated that at approximately 9:40 A.M., Borden said he was returning home. Meanwhile, back at the Borden home, the maid, Bridget "Maggie" Sullivan, stated that between 9 and 10 A.M., Abby Borden said she was going to go upstairs to straighten up the guest room that Morse had occupied. Sullivan also stated that Andrew Borden returned home sometime after 10:40 A.M. At approximately 10:55 A.M., Sullivan went to her room to take a nap, and Andrew Borden went to lie down on the sofa in the parlor. During this time, Lizzie Borden testified that she had gone out to the barn loft to find some fishing sinkers to use during a planned fishing expedition with her sister Emma. At approximately 11 A.M., Lizzie Borden discovered her father's body, and shortly thereafter, Churchill discovered Abby Borden's body.

Given the nature of the wounds, police assumed the perpetrator of these crimes must have been a male and used an axe. A total of four axes were collected at the Borden home, and one with a recently broken handle was submitted as evidence. The most damaging statement came from Russell, who told police that on Sunday, August 7, she observed Borden burning a dress in the kitchen stove. Russell told police that when she asked Borden why she was burning the dress, Borden replied that the dress was stained with paint. Russell's testimony to these events at the inquest prompted Judge Josiah Blaisdell of the Second District Court to charge Lizzie Borden with the murders of her parents.

Trial

Lizzie Borden's trial began June 5, 1893, and lasted 14 days. An all-male jury was selected, consisting of local and area residents. Hosea M. Knowlton was selected as the lead prosecutor. It has been documented that Knowlton was reluctant to assume this role but was told by Attorney General Arthur Pillsbury to prosecute the case. Attorney

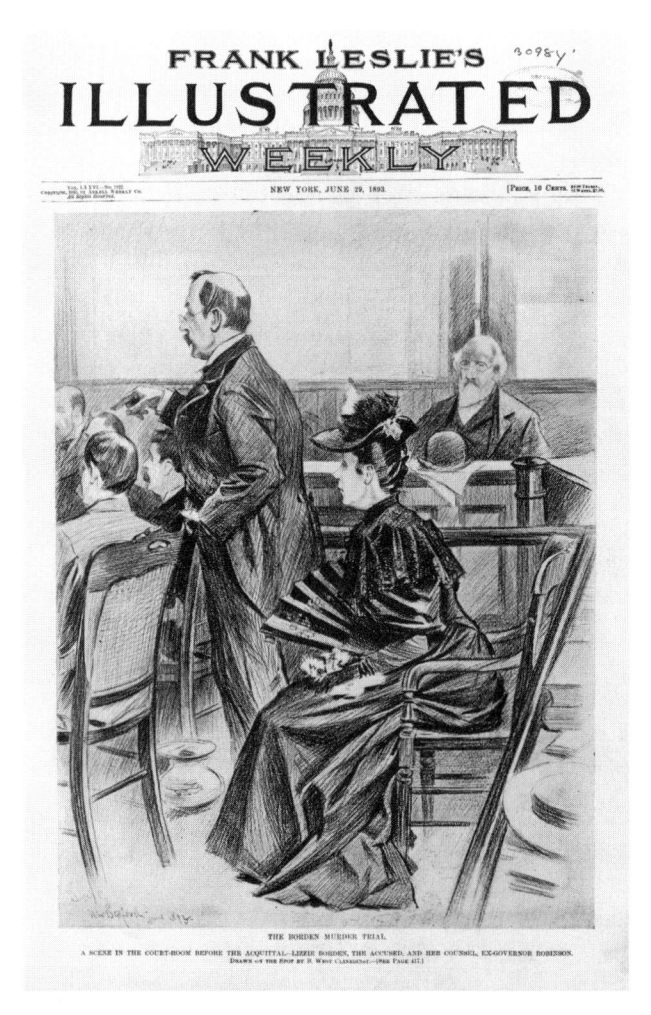

An 1893 newspaper illustration based on a courtroom drawing of accused murderer Lizzie Borden and her counsel just before her acquittal after jury deliberation of little more than an hour.

Knowlton appointed William Moody, who was the acting district attorney for Essex County, to assist him in the prosecution of Lizzie Borden.

Moody, during his opening statement to the jury, put forth three plausible arguments: (1) that Borden had planned the murders of her father and stepmother for some time, (2) that Borden committed the murders, and (3) that Borden's behavior and testimony were not those of an innocent person. The prosecution faced an uphill battle with no witnesses, a murder weapon that was suspect at best, and a basketful of circumstantial evidence.

Moody called witnesses to establish a motive for each murder, asserting that the motive was money: Andrew Borden was going to write a new will that would leave only small sums to Lizzie and Emma Borden with the remaining portion of his estate going to his wife, Abby. Defense attorneys Andrew J. Jennings, Melvin O. Adams, and George D. Robinson worked tirelessly at breaking down damaging testimony set forth by the prosecution. During closing arguments, Borden was asked if she would like to address the court. Borden's statement was brief: "I am innocent. I leave my counsel to speak for me." Justice Justin Dewey gave final instructions—which by today's standards would be considered extremely biased for the defense—to the jury. It took the jury just over an hour to return a not guilty verdict on all charges. Borden died on June 1, 1927, at the age of 67, from a long illness brought on by an earlier gall bladder surgery. Emma Borden died nine days later from a fall that occurred in her Newmarket, New Hampshire, home. The murders of Andrew and Abby Borden were never solved.

William T. Jones
State University of New York, Canton

See Also: Massachusetts; Women Criminals, History of; Women Criminals, Sociology of.

Further Readings
Encyclopedia Britannica. "Lizzie Borden." http://www.britannica.com/EBchecked/topic/73917/Lizzie-Borden (Accessed September 2011).
Kent, D. and R. A. Flynn. *The Lizzie Borden Sourcebook*. Boston: Branden Publishing, 1992.
Rehak, D. *Did Lizzie Borden Axe for It?* Charleston, SC: CreateSpace, 2010.

Border Patrol

The U.S. Border Patrol is a civilian federal agency, bound by federal laws and the Constitution, and is responsible for the security of the U.S. borders. Border Patrol agents, who are now part of the Department of Homeland Security (DHS), Customs and Border Protection (CBP), had very humble beginnings as inspectors with the Bureau of Immigration. As early as 1904, these mounted guards patrolled the southern border from El Paso, Texas, to southern California and the Pacific Ocean to stem the flow of illegal aliens. However, the illegal aliens who were of concern at the time were from China, not Mexico.

Establishing the Patrol

The United States borders two countries, Mexico to the south and Canada to the north; these borders span 6,000 miles of land, about 2,000 miles of coastal waters, and the island of Puerto Rico. But it is the border with Mexico that presents the biggest challenge. In the early 1900s, the U.S. Bureau of Immigration was responsible for controlling who crossed the border into the United States, and the Customs Service was responsible for controlling what entered into the United States. At the time, allotments had been established for the number of individuals of a particular nationality who were permitted to immigrate.

By 1915, inspectors were patrolling the southern border, attempting to control illegal immigration. There were also Texas Rangers and U.S. military personnel involved in these early border patrols, but they did not have the same legal authority as the inspectors. Supervising Inspector Frank Berkshire wrote to the commissioner-general of immigration in 1918 about the "lack of a coordinated, adequate effort to enforce immigration and customs laws along the border with Mexico"; this is a comment that is still relevant today. The Immigration Reform and Control Act of 1986 was intended to set the stage for amnesty, citizenship, and rigid enforcement of immigration laws and border security, yet the problem is still without resolution in 2011, along with a new element: national security.

Prohibition and two amendments to the Constitution briefly added a new focus to border activities, particularly in the north, but activity was targeted to illegal border crossings. The passage of the Labor Appropriations Act of 1924 officially established the U.S. Border Patrol. In 1933, the Bureau of Immigration merged with the Bureau of Naturalization to form the Immigration and Naturalization Service (INS). It remained the INS until the massive government reorganization in 2003 after the terrorist attacks on the World Trade Center and the Pentagon. As a result, today's Border Patrol focuses more on national security than it ever has.

Homeland Security

During the early years of the Border Patrol, the concern was stemming the flow of illegal aliens across the U.S. border. But there were also business owners and politicians who wanted open borders to ensure the flow of cheap labor and high profits. Up to 1 million people could illegally cross the border each year. Law enforcement efforts were usually directed at stopping the individuals and returning them to Mexico; little attention was paid to the businesses that provided the job incentives that would lure the workers across the border.

In reaction to the attacks of September 11, 2001, there were significant adjustments in federal law enforcement, especially regarding border security. On November 25, 2002, President George W. Bush signed the Homeland Security Act of 2002 (Public Law 107-296) into law. The mission of the new department included preventing terrorist attacks, reducing the vulnerability of the United States to terrorism, and carrying out all of the functions of the 23 agencies transferred to the department. Although the act abolished the INS, its immigration and border security responsibilities (including the Border Patrol) were brought into DHS.

The new law became effective in 2003. The functions of the INS and the U.S. Customs Service were moved into the Border and Transportation Security Directorate, reporting to an undersecretary of DHS. However, there have been several reorganizations within DHS. As of 2011, law enforcement functions of the INS and U.S. Customs come under the auspices of the Immigration and Customs Enforcement (ICE). The border control functions of the INS and Customs are located within Customs and Border Protection (CBP).

What started as an organization designed to stop illegal immigration has seen its mission grow extensively since 2001. Clearly, the Border Patrol is no longer a few mounted guards patrolling the southern U.S. border. Border Patrol agents are assigned around the world. Currently, there are CBP attachés in 20 different nations: Belgium, Brazil, Canada, China, Dominican Republic, Egypt, Germany, Hong Kong, India, Italy, Japan, Kenya, Korea, Mexico, Panama, Singapore, South Africa, Thailand, the Netherlands, and the United Kingdom. In 2011, the mission of the patrol has become more sophisticated and challenging. The patrol works with other federal, state, local, and tribal law enforcement elements to control access to the United States and is a key organization in the battle against terrorism and drug smuggling. The Border Patrol is a mobile uniformed law enforcement service that operates as an integral part of national and homeland security. From an initial 450 officers, the Border Patrol has grown to more than 20,000 agents. One of the most important activities of the Border Patrol is the

> ... detection, prevention and apprehension of terrorists, undocumented aliens and smugglers of aliens at or near the land border by maintaining surveillance from a covert position, following up leads, responding to electronic sensor television systems, aircraft sightings, and interpreting and following tracks, marks and other physical evidence.

The CBP has grown to include an Office of Air and Marine (OAM), which is the world's largest aviation and maritime law enforcement organization. It has a significant role in protecting the nation's critical infrastructure and key resources from terrorism and the smuggling of any form of contraband into the United States. CBP also has a key role, along with the U.S. Coast Guard (another part of DHS) for port security.

Training the Green Machine

The first Border Patrol Academy opened in 1934. With the establishment of the Federal Law Enforcement Training Center (FLETC), in Glynco, Georgia, in 1970, the Border Patrol joined with other federal agencies to provide basic training at a centralized location. FLETC now provides training to more than 80 federal agencies, as well law, border patrol operations, antiterrorism training, Spanish, firearms, ethics and conduct, report writing, fingerprinting, computers, vehicle operations, and physical training. Recruits for the patrol must be citizens of the United States under the age of 40; have a state driver's license; pass written, oral, and medical/drug exams; and have a favorable background investigation that includes criminal background checks. In each area, failure to perform to the high standards set for Border Patrol agents will result in the release of the recruit from his or her law enforcement position.

EPIC

The El Paso Intelligence Center (EPIC) was established in 1974 to ensure that information was collected and shared among federal, state, local, and tribal agencies that were involved in law enforcement along the southern U.S. border. It was the first among the many fusion centers that have developed since the terrorist attacks to enhance communications among law enforcement organizations. At the time of its creation, the INS and the Border Patrol were key participants. At the present time, DHS, CBP (Border Patrol), ICE, Alcohol, Tobacco, Firearms & Explosives, Drug Enforcement Administration, U.S. Marshals Service, Internal Revenue Service, El Paso County Sheriff's Office, and other domestic and foreign agencies staff the center.

Nonmilitary Border Security

Another key aspect of border security in the United States is that this function does not rest with the military; this reflects the very limited domestic role that the military has in this democracy. In Italy, the border police are part of the Italian Army; India's border patrol agency is part of a paramilitary force. In Russia, Soviet troops have relinquished primary border control duties to the new Federal Security Service. Egypt's Border Guards are part of the Ministry of Defense and are seen as a paramilitary organization.

Clearly, the responsibility of border security rests with the federal government, not the states. Over the years, immigration and border security agencies have been moved among various cabinet-level departments that were responsible for the oversight of these organizations. Most recently,

A Customs and Border Protection Blackhawk helicopter swoops down on vehicles in an isolated area of the southwest in June 2008. The agency's Office of Air and Marine is now the world's largest aviation and maritime law enforcement organization.

as state, local, tribal, and foreign enforcement personnel. The Border Patrol training is considered some of the toughest training at the center. Before the opening of the Border Patrol Academy at FLETC in Artesia, New Mexico, it was easy to tell when agents were moving about the site; they marched and jogged in formation. They were referred to as the Green Machine, a reference to the green uniforms worn by Border Patrol agents; while in basic training, many recruits also wore green T-shirts bearing the Green Machine logo.

In 2011, new agents receive 19 weeks of basic training at the Border Patrol Academy in Artesia, New Mexico. Border Patrol agents also receive training in Charleston, South Carolina, and Cheltenham, Maryland. The basic training of Border Patrol agents includes the following:

these entities have been part of the Department of Justice, Department of the Treasury, and the Department of Transportation. After September 11, 2001, 23 agencies (or parts thereof) were brought into the new Department of Homeland Security. There was a clear recognition of the need for a more secure border and not just to control illegal drugs or aliens.

Border Patrol Activities

A key responsibility of the Border Patrol is the apprehension of illegal aliens. Starting in fiscal year 2000, with the apprehensions of 1.7 million individuals, the apprehension numbers varied: 1.27 million in 2001, 0.96 million in 2002, 0.93 million in 2003, 1.16 million in 2004, 1.19 million in 2005, 1.09 million in 2006, 0.87 million in 2007, 0.72 million in 2008, and 0.57 million in 2009, with the vast majority of those apprehensions on the southern border. It is important to remember that there is a significant element of human trafficking crimes for labor and sex with the entry of illegal aliens. To emphasize this, CBP reports that there are at least 12.3 million enslaved adults and children in the world; 1.39 million are involved with sexual servitude; and more than 56 percent are female.

To help prevent this criminal activity, the Border Patrol has a Tactical Infrastructure Program (TIP). This involves the construction and maintenance of physical structures to reduce illegal border crossings. This includes fences, checkpoints, towers, sensors, screening facilities, lights, roads, and barriers. However, the primary goal for the Border Patrol, as part of DHS, is to "prevent terrorists and terrorist weapons, including weapons of mass destruction, from entering the United States." The TIP is intended to support national security by establishing a substantial probability of apprehending terrorists seeking entry into the United States, disrupting and restricting the smuggling of narcotics and humans, preventing violence against border residents and illegal immigrants, and restricting potentially harmful diseases (both human and agricultural) from crossing the border.

Conclusion

Some may only see the Border Patrol as an impediment to their entry into and employment within the United States; however, its role is far greater. The Border Patrol is an integral part of homeland security. It is the first line of defense in preventing drugs, terrorists, and criminals from entering the United States and is a key resource in fighting transnational crime at the border.

Keith Gregory Logan
Kutztown University

See Also: Bootlegging; Customs Service as Police; Drug Enforcement Administration; Immigration Crimes; Smuggling; Texas Rangers; USA PATRIOT Act of 2001.

Further Readings

Broyles, Bill and Mark Haynes. *Desert Duty: On the Line With the U.S. Border Patrol*. Austin: University of Texas Press, 2010.

Congressional Research Service. *Border Security: The Role of the U.S. Border Patrol*, RL32562. Washington, DC: Congressional Research Service, 2006.

Pacheco, Alex and Erich Krauss. *On the Line: Inside the U.S. Border Patrol*. New York: Citadel Press, 2005.

U.S. Department of Homeland Security. "Customs and Border Protection, Border Patrol." http://www.cbp.gov/xp/cgov/border_security/border_patrol/border_patrol_ohs/history.xml (Accessed January 2011).

Boston, Massachusetts

Boston, like most cities in the United States, has seen a reduction in crime rates since the 1990s. The Boston Police Department has played an essential role in these efforts, working with neighborhood and church groups as well as the federal government to steer young people away from gangs and toward more productive activities. Those efforts have been so successful that they have collectively been labeled the Boston Miracle, and Boston has served as a crime-reduction model for other cities. The success of the Boston Miracle was documented by a 58.7 percent drop in homicide rates between 1990 and 1996. Historically, however,

Boston has been one of the most crime-ridden cities in the United States. Members of Boston's Irish mob were major players in organized crime throughout much of the 19th and 20th centuries.

Throughout the 1980s, many large American cities experienced outbreaks of gun violence as a result of the crack cocaine epidemic that took place on urban streets. Boston was no exception, but the violence was generally limited to particular areas. Between 1980 and 1988, an average of 40 incidents of gun violence were reported each year. Such crimes peaked in 1990, with 86 crimes reported. A subsequent decline reached a low of 19 incidents in 1999. Gun violence began to increase again in the early 21st century, reaching 55 incidents in 2001. Again, a gradual decline followed. In modern-day Boston, approximately 75 percent of all serious gun assaults continue to take place in sections comprising only 5 percent of the city. Traditionally, Boston's Police District D-4, which includes Back Bay, Fenway, South End, and Lower Roxbury, has contained the highest concentrations of violent crime. Gang activity is responsible for much of that activity, particularly on Lenox Street, Villa Victoria, and in the Castle Square housing projects. Around half of all homicides are perpetrated by Boston youths, who commit 70 percent of all shootings. Hot spots such as high schools, housing projects, subway stations, and public parks report that crime rates have remained fairly constant over time.

Notorious Crimes and Criminals
Dominated by the Irish mob, organized crime was a major problem in South Boston for much of the 19th and 20th centuries. The most notorious figure associated with the latter part of that period was James "Whitey" Bulger, whose brother Billy served as president of the Massachusetts State Senate before becoming the head of the University of Massachusetts. Whitey Bulger was the leader of the Winter Hill Gang, which was heavily involved in drug dealing, loan sharking, extortion, and other forms of racketeering. Bulger was also an Federal Bureau of Investigation (FBI) informant, and he counted FBI agents among his cronies. Bulger was known for his savagery, which was in evidence when, with his bare hands, he killed 26-year-old Debra Davis, the girlfriend of his partner in crime, Steve Flemmi. After murdering Davis, he pulled out all of her teeth with pliers to prevent her identification by dental records.

More than 50 of Bulger's associates were indicted in 1990, and Bulger was wanted on charges of murdering 19 people. Following a tip-off that he was due to be arrested, Bulger went into hiding on December 23, 1994. Both Flemmi and Kevin Weeks, Bulger's former right-hand man, began cooperating with the police in 1999. It was not until the summer of 2011 that Bulger, then 81 years old, was finally discovered in Santa Monica, California, where he was living as Charlie Gasko. His girlfriend, Catherine Grieg, was arrested and charged with harboring a fugitive. Ironically, Bulger had killed two of Grieg's brothers-in-law. Law enforcement officers discovered 30 guns and $800,000 in cash in Bulger's apartment. In response to pressure from the families of victims, the U.S. attorney dropped all racketeering charges in order to focus on murder charges. John Connolly, the FBI agent who informed Whitey Bulger of his imminent arrest, was subsequently convicted of racketeering and obstruction of justice.

Boston was also home to one of the most notorious serial murderers in American history. The Boston Strangler's first victims were all older women, and the police developed a tentative profile identifying him as an 18-to-40-year-old white male who hated his mother. The theory was discarded when the strangler chose a 20-year-old as his next victim. He continued his modus operandi of raping his victim before strangling and "decorating" her with a bow made up of the item used to strangle her. He killed his last victim on January 4, 1964. During the same period, Albert DeSalvo raped at least 300 women in Massachusetts, Connecticut, Rhode Island, and New Hampshire. DeSalvo had become known as the Green Man because of his habit of masquerading as a handyman wearing green clothing. When arrested, he claimed to be the Boston Strangler. Although he admitted to murder, he was convicted solely on rape charges. DeSalvo was stabbed in prison in 1973. Serious doubts remain about his being the Boston Strangler.

Developing Law Enforcement Capabilities
In the American colonies, law enforcement tended to model itself after systems that had already

developed in England. The first American efforts involved the creation of a night watch in 1636. In 1824, Boston became the first city in the United States to create a professional police force, with 260 patrolling officers who answered to the first police chief. The department was separated into divisions under a captain and two lieutenants. The rank of sergeant was added in 1857. Patrol officers carried a blue-and-white six-foot pole and used a "rattle" to summon assistance. By 1838, Boston had created a day patrol. The night patrol continued to exist as a separate entity. The Boston Police Department (BPD) was established in 1854 in compliance with the model established in London by Sir Robert Peele (1788–1850). BPD endured one of its greatest ordeals in November 1872 when a patrolman chasing recalcitrant boys along Lincoln Street discovered a major fire in progress. The Great Boston Fire, as it became known, was the most disastrous fire in Boston's history, destroying 65 acres of valuable downtown property. At least 960 establishments were burned out and 776 buildings were destroyed. The total cost was estimated at $75 million.

Leaving City Hall behind, the department relocated to Pemberton Square in 1883. In September 1919, the safety of Bostonians was compromised when 1,117 police officers went on strike for increased benefits. With three-fourths of the force on strike, rioting and looting went virtually unchecked. Governor Calvin Coolidge replaced strikers with World War I veterans and rewarded the veterans by raising their salaries, instituting a shorter work week, and providing them with free uniforms. In 1925, BPD moved from Pemberton Square to 154 Berkeley Street. Resources were again overtaxed during the Cocoanut Grove nightclub fire of 1942, which resulted in 490 deaths and 166 injuries. The notorious Brinks robbery of 1950 focused the limelight on the BPD. The crime had occurred on January 17 when a group of men wearing Halloween masks absconded with $1.2 million in cash and $1.5 million in checks, money orders, and other securities. Because of the magnitude of the crime, the FBI took over the case, eventually arresting Anthony "Fats" Pino and his gang.

In 1997, BPD moved to its current headquarters at One Schroeder Plaza. Employing modern technology is instrumental to a modern police force, and BPD began using advanced identification imaging and ballistics identification. An in-house DNA laboratory became essential in reducing the time involved in crime investigations and in improving accuracy of criminal charges.

Criticism and Innovation

In the 1980s and early 1990s, the Boston Police Department came under heavy fire for its use of overly aggressive tactics, and officers were accused of prejudice against minorities. In response, the BPD began to reinvent itself, and was ultimately successful in repairing its tarnished image. Since that time, BPD has partnered with local neighborhoods to enforce a policy of zero tolerance in dealing with minor offenses that occur in neighborhoods with high crime rates. This practice has sent a message to would-be criminals that they will be apprehended and forced to pay for their crimes. Many of those efforts have involved working with minority communities. African American clergy played a major role in crime-reduction efforts following a gang-related attack at a funeral for an African American victim of a drive-by shooting.

During the violent 1980s and a nationwide crack cocaine epidemic, turf wars broke out in Boston. However, politicians and the BPD maintained a policy of denying that the city had a problem with gangs. Nevertheless, in 1988, the City-Wide Anti-Crime Unit (CWACU) was ordered to provide support in areas where violence was well established. Over the course of the next year, gangs became a major target of the CWACU. Simultaneously, two separate scandals besieged the department. Investigators were attacked for unquestioningly accepting the word of Charles Stuart, a white Bostonian, when he assured them that an African American had murdered his wife. In fact, Charles Stuart had killed Carol Stuart. A "stop and frisk" campaign directed at gang-related violence backfired on the BPD because of complaints that it targeted only African American males, leading to dismissed evidence because it was deemed illegal search and seizure. The CWACU was disbanded as a result of the latter scandal. The *Boston Globe* added fuel to the fire in 1991 by publishing a four-part series, "Bungling the Basics," in which it accused the BPD of repeatedly mishandling investigations and compromising its authority.

By 1993, following the resignation of the mayor, William Bratton was back in Boston, replacing Mickey Roache as police commissioner. Bratton had first came to public attention as a rookie police sergeant in 1975 when he faced down an armed bank robber holding a hostage, convincing him to lay down his gun. As police chief, Bratton's initiatives typically focused on increasing the number of patrol officers on city streets and dispatching them to areas where crimes were predicted to occur. He also created an environment in which police officers were held accountable for what occurred in their assigned neighborhoods and made the BPD more accessible to citizens with complaints.

Combining his knowledge of Boston with experience gained in New York City, Bratton reorganized the BPD, transforming the Anti-Gang Violence Unit into the Youth Violence Strike Force and implementing a philosophy of community policing. Under his leadership, the probation department became more proactive, and Operation Night Light was instituted to allow probation officers to work directly with patrol officers to monitor the activities of their charges. Cooperation among agencies was encouraged, and the BPD worked closely with a team of policy researchers at Harvard's John F. Kennedy School of Government.

In 1994, Boston implemented Operation Scrap Iron to target anyone illegally transporting guns into Boston. The following year, the city established the Boston Gun Project, a three-year program designed to bring city agencies together to address the issue of youth violence. In 1996, Operation Cease-Fire finalized the collaborative effort to fight crime in Boston. Two years later, the Bloods and Crips Initiative was established to

Policemen keeping order on a streetcar during a trolley strike in the city in June 1912. A few years later, the safety of Bostonians was seriously compromised when the police went on strike in September 1919. With 1,117 police officers comprising three-fourths of the entire force, on strike, rioters and looters swarmed the city from September 9 to 11.

bring interested parties together to fight the city's two largest and most well-established gangs.

Various private groups also work with law enforcement to reduce gang activity in Boston. For instance, the Boston Foundation provides grants to community groups that institute programs designed to steer gang members toward education, jobs, and services that provide them with opportunities to become more productive and to adopt law-abiding lifestyles. One of the guiding lights of the foundation is Robert Lewis, Jr., an African American city employee who grew up in an impoverished area of Boston. He had previously established the Streetworkers Program to get young people working with gang members in areas well known for their gang activity. Since 2008, through StreetSafe Boston, the foundation has monitored the 1.5-square-mile area of the city in which 78 percent of all shootings and homicides occur. An evaluation of the StreetSafe program by a Harvard professor revealed that crime rates in the targeted area had begun to decline at the same time that crimes in other areas of Boston were climbing.

Elizabeth Rholetter Purdy
Independent Scholar

See Also: 1600 to 1776 Primary Documents; DeSalvo, Albert; Los Angeles, California; Massachusetts; New York City; Organized Crime, Contemporary; Police, Contemporary; Sacco and Vanzetti; Violent Crimes.

Further Readings
Berrien, Jimmy and Christopher Winship. "Lessons Learned From Boston's Police-Community Collaboration." *Federal Probation,* v.63/2 (December 1999).
Braga, Anthony, et al. "The Concentration and Stability of Gun Violence at Micro Places in Boston, 1980–2008." *Journal of Quantitative Criminology,* v.26/1 (March 2010).
Carr, Howie. *The Brothers Bulger: How They Terrorized and Corrupted Boston for a Quarter of a Century.* New York: Warner Books, 2006.
City of Boston. "History of the B.P.D." http://www.cityofboston.gov/police/about/history.asp (Accessed October 2011).
Ferdinand, Theodore N. "Criminal Patterns of Boston Since 1849." *American Journal of Sociology,* v.73/1 (July 1967).

Lane, Roger. *Policing the City: Boston, 1822–1885.* Boston: Harvard University Press, 1967.
McCabe, Scott. "Crime History: 'Boston Strangler' Kills His Final Victim." http://washingtonexaminer.com/local/crime-punishment/2011/01/crime-history-boston-strangler-kills-his-final-victim (Accessed October 2011).
Shea, John "Red." *Rat Bastards: The Life and Times of South Boston's Most Honorable Irish Mobster.* New York: William Morrow, 2006.
Vanderwarker, Peter. *Boston Then and Now.* Boston: Courier Dove, 1982.

Bounty Hunters

The Eighth Amendment protects against excessive bail, but there is no constitutional right to bail. A judge may refuse to set bail for risky offenders, or those accused of serious crimes such as murder. Most offenders are able to post bond while awaiting trial or disposition of their case. The amount of bail depends on the crime; the more serious the crime, the higher the bail amount. Not everyone accused of a crime can afford bail money, which can run into the hundreds of thousands (if not millions) of dollars. In those cases, a bail bondsman will post a bond for an offender. The bond is given to the court until the case is disposed. In other words, the bail bond acts as insurance guaranteeing that the accused will show up for his or her scheduled court appearance. In essence, a bond is a guarantee to the court that the offender will appear for trial and remain in the jurisdiction.

What happens if an offender on bond decides to flee the jurisdiction, or jump bail? In such cases, bail jumping, or unlawfully skipping future court appearances (which about 20 percent of people do), results in the forfeiture of a bond. However, the bail bond must still be paid. Because bondsmen are liable for the bail bond amount, and the police cannot always track offenders across state lines, many bondsmen hire bail enforcement agents, or bounty hunters, to track the offenders (unless the state outlaws bounty hunting). In payment for their services, bail enforcement agents typically receive 10 to 20 percent of the total bail bond. If a bondsman cannot enforce bail by apprehending the fugitive, the bondsman, in cases where he works with a surety company, must pay the surety company the forfeited bail. If the bondsman is a professional bondsman (he uses his own capital for the bail), he forfeits his capital. Bounty hunters claim to catch 31,500 bail jumpers per year, about 90 percent of people who jump bail in the United States.

Evolution

The art of bounty hunting originated in England more than 100 years ago. In the 13th century, bail was a person, not an amount of money. An individual such as a friend or family member was designated custodian of the accused, and if the accused did not return to face his penalty, the custodian could be hanged in his place. During colonial times, America relied upon the bail system set up by the government of England. In 1679, the British parliament passed the Habeas Corpus Act, which guaranteed that an accused person could be released from prison on monetary bail. However, if the accused jumped bail, bounty hunters were sent after him.

In the Old West, bounty hunters were hired by local sheriffs or marshals to pursue wanted offenders who often fled hundreds of miles across desolate territory. They were hired because of the difficulty in locating fugitives and the limited resources of local jurisdictions. These bounty hunters were paid according to the seriousness of the offender's crimes: An escaped murderer and bank robber netted more than a common horse thief. To assist in capturing these offenders, the U.S. Supreme Court case *Taylor v. Taintor* (1872) gave bail enforcement agents nearly limitless power and authority when hunting down a subject. This decision remains in effect.

Modern Regulation

Many early bounty hunters were greedy and didn't care if they brought the fugitives in dead or alive, as long as they collected the posted reward. There were no regulations. Today, the rules have changed. Bail enforcement agents are regular citizens and operate under the same state and federal laws as everyone else who is not in law enforcement. This means that they are not bound by the Fourth Amendment search and seizure laws like law enforcement officers.

However, there are procedures that bail enforcement agents must follow. A bail enforcement agent cannot harm a defendant or any innocent bystanders but may use reasonable force to enter the residence or place where the defendant is hiding, although some states do not allow a bounty hunter to "break and enter" a place that does not belong to the defendant. The agent must be sure that the fugitive is in the place to be entered.

Bail enforcement agents cannot arrest anyone without a warrant authorized by the jurisdiction from which the offender fled. Bail enforcement agents are expected to use all possible legal methods to capture a defendant, including trickery or deceit. Bail enforcement agents may or may not carry a weapon, depending on the state laws. Agents can cross state lines to apprehend a defendant. An extradition treaty is not needed. While agents have more freedom than police officers, they may not break any laws in the apprehension of a defendant.

Bounty hunting is illegal in nearly every nation in the world. Only the United States and the Republic of the Philippines allow the occupation. There are a handful of states that have banned it completely, such as Florida. In that state, bail enforcement is the responsibility of the bondsman and local police authorities. The Florida bondsman must do a skip trace or hire a skip-tracing agency to try to find the fugitive. Once the bondsman finds the person, he can call the arresting agency to alert it to the possible location of the fugitive. It is hoped that the arresting agency will find the fugitive at that location when officers arrive.

For those states that allow bounty hunting, several require licenses for bail enforcement agents. Most licenses are available through a state's department of insurance, and each state sets its own prerequisites for licensure. There are many training programs available online and elsewhere, but not all of these fulfill the requirements to get a license. Some states, like California, require training and/or licensure, while other states require no formal training or licenses. In California, bounty hunters must be at least 18 years old and have no felonies on their criminal record. Agents must pass the Bureau of Security and Investigative Services class on using the power to arrest a citizen and a 40-hour course on "power of arrest" by the Commission on Peace Officer Standards and Training.

Job Skills

Becoming a bail enforcement agent requires other skills. An agent must have knowledge of how the bail bonds industry works and be proficient in other skills such as detecting deceit, surveillance, skip tracing, and negotiation. A bail enforcement agent must also know how to research and investigate missing persons. He must be able to access and analyze phone records of the fugitive's friends and family. He will have to know how to dig into the fugitive's past and find all past residences. He will need to learn the fugitive's habits, vices, friends, enemies, and hangouts. In other words, a bounty hunter must have good investigative skills, which include skip tracing, negotiating, interviewing and deception, and apprehension techniques. The bounty hunter's principal motivator is the reward for a successful hunt, while the skip tracer's reward is the predetermined fee that is earned.

One of the most famous bail enforcement agents is Duane "Dog" Chapman. Chapman gained notoriety in 2003 when he captured Max Factor cosmetics heir Andrew Luster, who jumped bail and fled to Mexico during his rape trial in California. Chapman made news with his capture of Luster, who was later returned to California; however, Chapman was arrested in Mexico because bounty hunting is illegal in that country. Chapman returned to the United States but faced extradition to Mexico. Because of political pressure, Mexico dropped its extradition order for Chapman. Chapman and his family have a successful business and a reality television series on bounty hunting.

Bail enforcement is a challenging and potentially dangerous business, and there are reports of agents being assaulted and killed, as well as reports of agents using excessive force and injuring innocent persons. A number of schools provide training for bail enforcement agents; getting established in bail enforcement usually requires working with experienced agents and officers. The job of a bail enforcement agent is challenging, but a career that needs more regulation as to jurisdiction and personnel. Regulation is especially needed since these agents may carry weapons and use force to apprehend others.

Robert J. Meadows
California Lutheran University

See Also: Bail and Bond; Bail Reform Act; Frontier Crime; Posses; Sheriffs; Vigilantism.

Further Readings

Foer, Franklin. "Bounty Hunters." *Slate*. http://www.slate.com/id/1072 (Accessed December 2010).

Harrell, L. Scott "The Business of Finding and Taking Bond Forfeiture Defendants Into Custody." http://www.bondforfeitures.com (Accessed December 2010).

Kinkade, Patrick and Leone Matthews. "Bounty Hunters: A Look Behind the Hype." *Policing: An International Journal of Policing Strategies and Management*, v.28/1 (November 2005).

Parenti, Christian. "I Hunt Men." *Progressive*, v.61/11 (1997).

Taylor v. Taintor, 83 U.S. 366, 21L Ed 287 (1873).

Bowers v. Hardwick

Beginning in the 1980s, the National Gay Task Force (NGTF) began a campaign to erase sodomy statutes from American law. By the mid-1980s, however, the U.S. Supreme Court had only heard two gay rights cases, *Doe v. Commonwealth's Attorney* (1976) and *National Gay Task Force v. Board of Education of Oklahoma City* (1984), both of which were summary affirmances that did not result in written opinions. The NGTF, along with the American Civil Liberties Union (ACLU), believed that if they could get the right case in front of the court, they would have a good chance of victory. With *Bowers v. Hardwick* (1986), many in the NGTF believe that it was the right case at the right time.

In July 1982, Michael Hardwick threw a beer bottle into a trash can outside the gay bar where he worked. Atlanta Police Officer Torick wrote him a citation for public drinking, and when Hardwick failed to appear in court, Torick issued a warrant for his arrest. When he went to Hardwick's apartment to serve the warrant, Hardwick was not at home. When Hardwick arrived home and found the warrant, he went to the courthouse and paid the ticket. A few weeks later, on August 3, 1982, Torick returned to Hardwick's apartment to serve the now-recalled arrest warrant. A houseguest opened the door and let Torick enter the apartment. Torick observed Hardwick's bedroom door slightly ajar, and entered Hardwick's bedroom. There, Torick found Hardwick and a male companion engaged in consensual, mutual oral sex.

Torick placed both men under arrest for sodomy. In Georgia, sodomy was defined as oral and anal sex between members of the same or opposite sex. The local district attorney decided not to present the case for further review by a grand jury. However, Michael Hardwick sued the attorney general of Georgia, Michael Bowers, in federal court, declaring that the state's sodomy law was invalid because under the law, he could be arrested for simply being a sexually active gay man.

After some consideration, Hardwick accepted the ACLU's offer to represent him in his court battles. Hardwick's attorney, Kathy Wilde, filed the case first in the U.S. District Court for the Northern District of Georgia, where it was dismissed. Hardwick appealed and the U.S. Court of Appeals for the 11th Circuit reversed the lower court's decision, finding that the state's sodomy law infringed on Hardwick's constitutional rights. The state of Georgia appealed to the U.S. Supreme Court, which decided to review the case in 1985.

The right of privacy was the central issue in the *Bowers* case; a right first recognized in *Griswold v. Connecticut* (1965) as an implicit right in the due process clause of the Fourteenth Amendment. However, in *Bowers*, the court maintained that the right to privacy did not extend to private, consensual homosexual sexual acts. Writing the opinion for the 5–4 decision, Justice Byron White framed the question as whether the Constitution confers "a fundamental right upon homosexuals to engage in sodomy." White believed it did not.

Marchers in a gay rights rally during the Democratic National Convention in New York City in 1976. While Bowers v. Hardwick *in 1986 was a major setback in the drive for gay rights in the United States, it did galvanize efforts to increase awareness of the issues and to continue a legal campaign that was eventually successful in overturning sodomy laws for adults in all states.*

In addition to White's opinion, Justices Warren Burger and Lewis Powell wrote concurring opinions that addressed and eliminated any possible future cases brought against state sodomy laws claiming a conviction for acts of sodomy to be a cruel and unusual punishment and thus in violation of the Eighth Amendment.

In the aftermath of the decision, gay activists and legal supporters were stunned. *Bowers v. Hardwick* produced three legal holdings. First, homosexual sodomy is not a fundamental right. Second, a state legislature only needs to demonstrate a rational basis for criminalizing homosexual sodomy. Third, public morality is a sufficient reason to criminalize homosexual sodomy. In essence, the U.S. Supreme Court declared that homosexuals did not have the same constitutionally protected right to privacy, even in their own bedrooms with consenting partners. Though activists referred to *Bowers* as the gay community's *Dred Scott*, *Bowers* did place gay rights into the public sphere and helped to ignite a serious legal rights campaign that attempted to align gay and straight Americans on the issue of equal rights.

In the years after *Bowers*, several state legislatures repealed their sodomy laws. In addition, state judiciaries invalidated sodomy laws, including the Georgia Supreme Court, which struck down the state sodomy law in the 1998 case *Powell v. State*. In 1996, the U.S. Supreme Court's *Romer v. Evans* decision overturned Colorado's Amendment 2, a law that allowed discrimination based on sexual orientation, and, according to Justice Antonin Scalia, placed the court in contradiction with its ruling in *Bowers*, paving the way for future cases. Finally, in 2003, the court's *Lawrence v. Texas* decision overturned *Bowers* and invalidated sodomy laws for consenting adults throughout the nation.

Robin C. Henry
Wichita State University

See Also: American Civil Liberties Union; Burger, Warren; Georgia; *Griswold v. Connecticut*; *Lawrence v. Texas*; *Romer v. Evans*; Sodomy.

Further Readings
Cain, Patricia A. *Rainbow Rights: The Role of Lawyers and Courts in the Lesbian and Gay Civil Rights Movement*. Jackson, TN: Westview Press, 2000.
Richards, David A. J. *The Case for Gay Rights: From* Bowers *to* Lawrence *and Beyond*. Lawrence: University Press of Kansas, 2005.
Richards, David A. J. *The Sodomy Cases*: Bowers v. Hardwick *and* Lawrence v. Texas. Lawrence: University Press of Kansas, 2009.

Brandenburg v. Ohio

The First Amendment to the U.S. Constitution says, "Congress shall make no law abridging the freedom of speech." This language can be interpreted as offering broad protection to expressive freedom. However, the U.S. Supreme Court did not adopt an expansive interpretation of this provision of the Bill of Rights until the last half of the 20th century. In *Brandenburg v. Ohio*, widely considered to be a landmark decision, the court wrote an opinion laying out a test for judging the constitutionality of speech advocating illegal actions. Still an important component of First Amendment law, the *Brandenburg* test offers a considerable degree of protection for free speech and demonstrates the way in which the Warren Court of the 1960s explicitly rejected earlier, more restrictive standards.

The Case
Clarence Brandenburg was convicted of violating the 1919 Ohio criminal syndicalism statute. This law prohibited the advocacy of criminal action "as a means of accomplishing industrial or political reform" and voluntarily assembling for the purpose of teaching or advocating such syndicalism (Brandenburg did not, himself, advocate the doctrine of syndicalism). Ohio was one of 20 states that adopted such laws between 1917 and 1920, a period immediately following World War I when there was widespread enactment of laws restricting many civil liberties, including free speech across the United States.

Brandenburg was arrested after films of a Ku Klux Klan rally that he organized and participated in were broadcast on television. The only people present at the rally were the Klan rally

This Ku Klux Klan rally and cross burning held sometime between 1921 and 1922 was likely similar to the ones that instigated the Brandenburg v. Ohio case. The decision in that case remains intact and continues to stand for the importance of affording the greatest protection to speech that can be classified as political, which is an important principle of modern First Amendment jurisprudence. It brought to an end the era of free speech opinions that used versions of the "clear and present danger" test.

participants and a television camera crew invited by Brandenburg. The film showed groups of hooded figures, some of whom were armed and some of whom assembled around a burning cross. Although most of their speeches were inaudible, at one point, a group of members could be heard saying that if the government continued to "suppress the white, Caucasian race," there was a possibility "that there might have to be some revengeance [sic] taken." The film included a speech given by Brandenburg containing racial slurs but saying nothing about potential "revengeance."

A unanimous Supreme Court overturned Brandenburg's conviction. The short *per curiam* opinion—an opinion that is issued by the court as a whole rather than being authored by a specific justice—struck down the Ohio law and overturned the decision in *Whitney v. California* (1927). In *Whitney*, the court upheld an almost identical law, but in *Brandenburg*, the court held that in the intervening years, *Whitney* had been "thoroughly discredited by later decisions." The court wrote that together, these subsequent decisions emphasized principles that created the following test. Under the First Amendment, a government may not

> ... forbid or proscribe advocacy of the use of force or of law violation except where such advocacy is directed to inciting or producing imminent lawless action and is likely to incite or produce such action.

This language has come to be known as the *Brandenburg* test.

Lasting Impact

The *Brandenburg* requirement that actual imminent harm be proven makes it very difficult for the government to convict anyone of criminal advocacy. In recent years, some Supreme Court decisions have revisited elements of the 1969 legacy. For example, in *Virginia v. Black* (2003), a divided court struggled to identify an appropriate standard for judging expressive actions, such as cross burning, that are done with a specific intent to intimidate and that might constitute a true threat. And the ability of *Brandenburg* to guide criminal advocacy rulings in the Internet age remains uncertain. However, the decision remains intact and continues to stand for an important principle of modern First Amendment jurisprudence—the importance of affording the greatest protection to speech that can be classified as political.

In overturning *Whitney*, the decision in *Brandenburg v. Ohio* brought to a decisive end the era of free speech opinions that used versions of the "clear and present danger" test. As a result, since 1969, it has been much more difficult for the government to limit free expression by seeking to remove from the societal dialogue speech that expresses particular points of view, even if the point of view in question is the advocacy of illegal action.

Helen J. Knowles
Whitman College

See Also: Ku Klux Klan; Supreme Court, U.S.; *Whitney v. California*.

Further Readings

Gey, Steven G. "The *Brandenburg* Paradigm and Other First Amendments." *University of Pennsylvania Journal of Constitutional Law,* v.12 (2010).

Gilles, Susan M. "*Brandenburg* v. *State of Ohio*: An 'Accidental,' 'Too Easy,' and 'Incomplete' Landmark Case." *Capital University Law Review,* v.38 (2010).

Smolla, Rodney A. *Free Speech in an Open Society.* New York: Vintage Press, 1992.

Virginia v. Black, 538 U.S. 343 (2003).

Brennan, William J., Jr.

William J. Brennan, Jr., was a U.S. Supreme Court justice from 1956 to 1990. During his time on the Supreme Court, Justice Brennan played a major role in the understanding of rights for criminals and the accused. William J. Brennan, Jr., was born in Newark, New Jersey, in 1906, into an Irish Roman Catholic family. Brennan received an Ivy League education, having attended college at the University of Pennsylvania and law school at Harvard University. Brennan was a colonel in the army during World War II. Prior to attaining a seat on the U.S. Supreme Court, Brennan was a judge on the New Jersey Supreme Court and lower state courts.

William Brennan was nominated by President Dwight Eisenhower in 1956, at the age of 50, but he was not confirmed by the Senate until 1957. Justice Brennan served on the court until

Justice William J. Brennan in 1976. Brennan served one of the longest terms ever on the Supreme Court and had a notable impact on protecting the rights of those accused of crimes.

he retired in 1990. His tenure on the court was one of the longest in U.S. history. According to several studies, Justice Brennan was one of the great Supreme Court justices. During his tenure on the court, Justice Brennan had a major impact on several areas of the law, notably the rights of the criminally accused and convicted. Brennan was in the majority twice in decisions, *Spano v. New York* (1959) and *Escobedo v. Illinois* (1964), which increased defendants' access to attorneys to prevent self-incrimination. Protections against self-incrimination became fully supported by the court in *Miranda v. Arizona*, the case that required suspects' rights to be read to them. Brennan again voted in the majority in this case. Justice Brennan was also vehemently opposed to the death penalty. In *Furman v. Georgia* (1972), a case in the Supreme Court that led to a nationwide moratorium on the death penalty, Brennan wrote that in his view, the death penalty was always unconstitutional. Brennan continued to support this view in his dissent in *Gregg v. Georgia* (1976), in which the Supreme Court reopened the use of the death penalty.

Justice Brennan had his largest impact in the area of search and seizure. In this area of criminal law, like those described above, Justice Brennan consistently voted to respect the rights of the accused. Brennan wrote the majority opinion in *Warden v. Hayden* (1967), a case that allowed a police force to search a house without a warrant if speed is necessary to apprehend a suspect or if there is reason to suspect that the officers might be in danger. However, Brennan also wrote the majority opinion in *Welsh v. Wisconsin* (1984), a case involving an alleged drunk driver who had already arrived home, that the police overstepped their bounds because speed was no longer of the essence and the public safety was not threatened. Justice Brennan was also an ardent supporter of the exclusionary rule. He voted in the majority for the incorporation of the exclusionary rule to the states in *Mapp v. Ohio* (1961). He continued to support this rule, even as it was contracted in subsequent opinions, including *United States v. Leon* (1984).

Although he was nominated to the Supreme Court by President Eisenhower, a Republican, Justice Brennan was one of the most important members of the Warren Court's efforts to expand protections to the accused and convicted. Brennan was a close confidant of Chief Justice Earl Warren and would meet regularly with Warren to discuss the court's cases. Moreover, Chief Justice Warren assigned Brennan to write some of the most important opinions of the Warren Court era. After Earl Warren's retirement, Brennan became the leader of the liberal voting bloc on the Supreme Court during Warren Burger's term. When Chief Justice Burger retired, William Rehnquist was elevated to chief justice, becoming the third and most conservative chief justice under whom Brennan had served. Although always a liberal lion on the court, Brennan and Rehnquist reportedly had a very cordial and respectful relationship.

Tobias T. Gibson
Westminster College

See Also: Douglas, William O.; *Furman v. Georgia*; *Gregg v. Georgia*; *Mapp v. Ohio*; *Miranda v. Arizona*; Suspect's Rights; Warren, Earl.

Further Readings
Epstein, Lee, Jeffrey A. Segal, Harold J. Spaeth, and Thomas G. Walker, eds. *The Supreme Court Compendium: Data, Decisions & Developments*, 3rd ed. Washington, DC: CQ Press, 2003.
Epstein, Lee and Thomas G. Walker. *Constitutional Law for a Changing America: Rights, Liberties, and Justice*, 5th ed. Washington, DC: CQ Press, 2004.
Schwartz, Bernard. *A History of the Supreme Court*. New York: Oxford University Press, 1993.

Brocius, William

William Brocius (ca. 1845–82) was an infamous outlaw in the American West of the 1880s. He used various aliases, including William Bresnaham and William Graham, but he is best known by his nickname "Curly Bill" (also spelled in newspapers of the day as "Curley Bill") Brocius. Cattle rustling, robberies, and several murders are attributed to the gunslinger William Brocius.

William Brocius is thought to have been born around 1845, but his actual origins are somewhat murky. He is reported to have stood six feet tall, with curly black hair, dark complexion, and blue eyes. Brocius had allegedly been involved in an attempted robbery of a U.S. Army stagecoach on May 20, 1878. During the failed holdup, a couple of enlisted men were wounded. After being apprehended, Brocius was sentenced to five years in the Texas Penitentiary. However, on November 2, 1878, William Brocius and two accomplices escaped from the Ysleta, Texas, jailhouse by digging under the adobe walls. He rapidly departed Texas, and a warrant was issued for his arrest.

William Brocius reportedly arrived in the Arizona Territory around 1878 after completing a cattle drive from either Missouri or Texas. He soon was serving as the head wrangler at the McLowery Ranch located outside Tombstone, Arizona, next to the Clanton Ranch. He also became a member of the Clanton-McLowery gang, which was involved in rustling cattle, robbing stagecoaches, and other associated criminal activities. The Clanton-McLowery gang, known locally as the Cowboys, was headed by Nathan Haynes Clanton, known as "Old Man" Clanton. Clanton apparently recognized the leadership ability and ruthlessness of Brocius and is said to have touted him as his successor. After "Old Man" Clanton's death, William Brocius, in fact, became one of the leaders of the Cowboys. It has been estimated that there were more than 400 outlaws working both sides of the Mexican border under Brocius as part of the largest rustling organization of the Old West.

William Brocius was reputed to have been quick to quarrel, including a tendency to shoot at his opponents, and he had a reputation for frequently being inebriated. Brocius reportedly sported two gun belts with holsters tied down, one normally worn on his right side and the other facing backward on the left hip.

Trouble With Lawmen
On October 28, 1880, William Brocius shot Deputy Marshal Fred White of Tombstone, Arizona, in the stomach while the marshal was attempting to arrest him. Brocius was intoxicated, and White, who died two days after the incident from his wounds, stated that he thought it had been an accidental shooting. Wyatt Earp, a Pima County law officer, had been with Marshal White while he was attempting the arrest of Brocius, and Earp clubbed Brocius hard on the head with his pistol, knocking him unconscious. Wyatt Earp testified at the trial of Brocius that he also thought the shooting of Marshal White was unintentional. William Brocius was thereafter acquitted of the shooting. Virgil Earp, Wyatt's brother, was appointed marshal of Tombstone by the mayor and city council to serve out the rest of Marshal White's term. Virgil Earp had already become a deputy U.S. marshal on November 27, 1879.

On May 25, 1881, William Brocius got into an argument in Galeyville, Arizona, with Deputy Sheriff William Breckenridge, a tough lawman, who shot Brocius in the mouth. Brocius recovered from this horrible wound and, according to some reports, settled in Texas using the name William Graham. Other reports claim that William Brocius continued his life of violent crime. In July 1881, Brocius and Johnny Ringo, another known gunman and assassin, are said to have killed Isaac and William Haslett in Hachita, New Mexico, as revenge for their earlier killing of two members of the Clanton gang who had tried to rob the Haslett brothers' general store.

After the famous shootout in October 1881 at the O.K. Corral, William Brocius may have been involved in the attempted killing of Virgil Earp and the assassination of Morgan Earp. However, there were no eyewitnesses to either crime, and thus Brocius was not charged. In December 1881, Pima County indicted William Brocius for rustling 19 head of cattle. However, in March 1882, Brocius was deputized by Sheriff Johnny Behan of Cochise County, Arizona, and given a warrant for the arrest of Wyatt Earp after his vendetta following the death of his brother Morgan. On March 24, 1882, Wyatt Earp and Brocius came upon each other at Iron Springs, Arizona. Earp allegedly shot and killed Brocius with a double shotgun blast to the chest.

Victor B. Stolberg
Essex County College

See Also: Arizona; Earp, Wyatt; Frontier Crime; History of Crime and Punishment in America: 1850–1900; Livestock and Cattle Crimes.

Further Readings
Marsh, Carole. *Arizona State Greats!* Peachtree, GA: Gallopade International, 1990.

Metz, Leon Claire. *The Encyclopedia of Lawmen, Outlaws, and Gunfighters*. New York: Facts on File, 2003.

O'Neal, Bill. *Encyclopedia of Western Gunfighters*. Norman: University of Oklahoma Press, 1979.

Yadon, Laurence J. and Dan Anderson. *Arizona Gunfighters*. Gretna, LA: Pelican, 2010.

Brockway, Zebulon

Following the Civil War, collective violence, personal crime, and crimes against persons rose precipitously. Immigrants and the urban poor were seen by elites as lacking in control and in need of training to aid their assimilation. The criminal justice process was insufficient to deal with the problem of crime in the urban milieu. Since the goal of the justice system was to maximize efficiency of the capitalist system, and criminals were *lumpenproletariat*, it would follow that these potential workers should and could be converted into dependable lower-class workers. The goal of prisons in the 1870s then, according to most contemporary experts, was to mold obedient citizen-workers. The foremost instigator in this process was Zebulon Reed Brockway (1827–1920), the founder and superintendent of Elmira Reformatory.

As a young man, Brockway started his career in the correctional field as a guard in a Connecticut jail. He moved to New York and became warden of the Monroe County Penitentiary in Rochester by 1854. Next, he became warden of a Detroit, Michigan, house of correction, where he tried to introduce a rudimentary version of indeterminate sentences. However, this nascent effort was nullified by state courts. A signal event in his career occurred when he became an enthusiastic penal reformer at the Cincinnati meeting of the National Prison Association in 1870. As a consequence of his activism and experience, he was appointed warden of the new Elmira Prison, taking office in 1876.

Reform and Rehabilitation

In 1880, Brockway was finally able to initiate a reform regime. The first attempts began with male first-time offenders between the ages of 16 and 25. It was widely felt that this age group would be more trainable, easier to educate, and more vulnerable to efforts at reform. The training focused on repetitive molding of fine motor skills and rote learning of mathematical principles and tables. Various prison industries such as a farm, a foundry, and prison maintenance were tasked to prisoners. Brockway had prisoners drilling with dummy rifles for hours during the day, primarily to keep them busy and to build discipline and obedience. If prisoners adjusted well, they were raised a grade and given a parole hearing after a period of time. If prisoners did not respond, they could be demoted a grade and not be eligible for a parole hearing. If they were obdurately recalcitrant, they could be beaten with a strap, have ice-cold water dumped on them while strapped to a chair, be placed in solitary confinement for months, or even be slapped in the face by the warden himself.

Brockway was a master of self-promotion and wrote numerous essays and several books expounding his philosophy and justifying his sometimes bizarre and seemingly brutal methods. That being said, it is only fair to point out that he popularized and basically originated the humane concept of indeterminate sentence and parole in the United States. Under indeterminate sentencing, a prisoner was held in a reformatory until he made a good institutional adjustment and qualified for parole. Parole was a strategy of managing prisoners and preparing them for reentry into the outside community. Prisoners who behaved while in prison and progressed according to a three-part system of grades earned a parole hearing. Paroled inmates remained under state jurisdiction for a period of six months on the outside. It was Brockway's notion that a longer probationary period was counterproductive.

In addition, the parolee had to report to a volunteer guardian once a month and give a full account of his situation during that period. Later, the guardian role evolved into the familiar parole officers employed by the state. This was the foundation of modern parole, which even today retains many of these characteristics. The hope was that the parolee, having made a satisfactory institutional adjustment and working his way through the grade system, would find a good job and become a good, conformist American worker.

The parolee would leave his criminal milieu, associations, and subcultures behind in the process. However, this seldom occurred.

After a long service in the correctional field, Brockway ran afoul of the prison's correctional supervisors because of his seemingly tireless self-promotion and resistance to change. He was forced out as superintendent in 1900. Brockway toured the lecture circuit for many years, and he wrote *Fifty Years of Prison Service* in 1912, when he was 85. His contributions include classification systems, indeterminate sentencing, parole, and creating the first modern reformatory-style prison.

Francis Frederick Hawley
Western Carolina University

See Also: Corrections; Elmira Prison; National Congress on Penitentiary and Reformatory Discipline; Parole; Penitentiaries; Rehabilitation.

Further Readings
Abadinsky, H. *Probation and Parole: Theory and Practice*. Upper Saddle River, NJ: Prentice Hall, 1997.
Pisciotta, A. W. *Benevolent Repression: Social Control and the American Reformatory-Prison Movement*. New York: New York University Press, 1994.
Putney, S. and G. Putney. "Origins of the Reformatory." *Journal of Criminal Law, Criminology, and Police Science*, v. 53/4 (December 1962).

Brown v. Board of Education

In *Brown v. Board of Education* (1954), the Supreme Court overturned its earlier decision in *Plessy v. Ferguson* (1896) in which the court had ruled that state-sponsored racial segregation was constitutional on the basis of "separate but equal." Prior to *Brown*, racial segregation was typical in public education and, in fact, many states had laws that either required or permitted segregation in public schools. In effect, African American children were restricted to African American schools and were often denied access to comparable educational resources and opportunities available to their white counterparts attending white schools.

Many plaintiffs from across the United States challenged racial segregation in public education; however, based on the precedent set by *Plessy*, state courts repeatedly held that racial segregation in education was acceptable on the basis of "separate but equal." Equality was measured by "objective" factors such as buildings, curricula, teacher salaries, and similar measures. In *Brown*, the court considered whether other "intangible" factors undermined the "separate but equal" doctrine set in *Plessy*.

In *Brown*, the court specifically confronted the question of whether racial segregation in public education failed to provide minority children equal protection under the Fourteenth Amendment. During arguments, the court heard testimony from social scientists about research findings on the effects of racial segregation on African American children. The court decided that "intangible" factors, such as the psychological effects of racial segregation on African American children, promoted and preserved inequality. The court determined that racial segregation had a detrimental effect on African American children because it established a sense of inferiority that was not conducive to education; therefore, "separate but equal" was an impossible standard in public education.

The court's unanimous ruling in *Brown* is considered a landmark decision that served as the first step toward eliminating racial segregation in American public schools. By finding racial segregation in public education to be unconstitutional, the *Brown* decision paved the way for further integration efforts and for the civil rights movement.

Case History
Linda Brown, a third-grade student in Topeka, Kansas, had to walk one mile through a railroad switchyard to a bus stop in order to be bused to her African American elementary school, even though there was a white elementary school only seven blocks away from her home. In 1950, Linda's father, Oliver Brown, attempted to enroll her in the neighborhood school, but the principal refused on the basis of racial segregation. Similarly, 12 other parents attempted to enroll their

The former Monroe Elementary School in Topeka, Kansas, seen here in 2010, is now the home of the Brown v. Board of Education *National Historic Site, which was established in October 1992. As the school that Linda Brown was bused to, it was one of four segregated elementary schools in Topeka that were central to the Kansas cases included in* Brown v. Board of Education.

children in neighborhood schools and were also denied on the basis of racial segregation.

Oliver Brown approached the Topeka branch of the National Association for the Advancement of Colored People (NAACP) and asked for help. The NAACP was prepared to help the Browns and the other families as it had long wanted to challenge racial segregation in public schools. The NAACP hired lawyers and, in 1951, filed a class action lawsuit against the Board of Education of the City of Topeka in the U.S. District Court for the District of Kansas. The NAACP asked the court for an injunction that would prohibit the segregation of Topeka's public schools.

The U.S. District Court heard Brown's case in June 1951. During the trial, the NAACP lawyers argued that racially segregated schools created a sense of inferiority in African American children. Expert witnesses testified that denying African American children contact and experience with white children created inherent inequality in education. The Board of Education's defense was that segregated schools prepared African American children for other kinds of segregation that they would later experience in adulthood. The board also denied that segregated schools were necessarily harmful to African American children and alluded to famous African Americans who were able to achieve success despite segregation.

The NAACP's request for an injunction put the court in a difficult situation. On the one hand, the judges agreed with the expert witnesses about the detrimental effect of racially segregated schools on African American children. On the other hand, the precedent set by *Plessy* allowed "separate but equal" school systems for blacks and whites, and no Supreme Court ruling had overturned the *Plessy* decision. Because of the precedent set by *Plessy*, the court felt "compelled" to rule in favor of the Board of Education.

The Supreme Court Decision

On behalf of Brown and the other plaintiffs, the NAACP lawyers appealed to the Supreme Court on October 1, 1951, and their case was combined with other cases that challenged racial segregation in public education in South Carolina, Virginia, and Delaware. The court first heard the case in December 1952, but failed to reach a decision. The case was reargued in December 1953 and finally decided on May 17, 1954. Chief Justice Earl Warren read the decision of the unanimous court:

> We come then to the question presented: Does segregation of children in public schools solely on the basis of race, even though the physical facilities and other "tangible" factors may be equal, deprive the children of the minority group of equal educational opportunities? We believe that it does ... We conclude that in the field of public education the doctrine of "separate but equal" has no place. Separate educational facilities are inherently unequal. Therefore, we hold that the plaintiffs and others similarly situated for whom the actions have been brought are, by reason of the segregation complained of, deprived of the equal protection of the laws guaranteed by the Fourteenth Amendment.

The *Brown* decision overturned the "separate but equal" doctrine of *Plessy* for public education, ruled in favor of the plaintiffs, and required the desegregation of schools across the United States. The decision, however, did not abolish segregation in other public areas, such as restaurants nor did it require desegregation of public schools within a specific time period. It did, however, declare that state laws requiring or permitting racial segregation in public schools were unconstitutional. As such, the *Brown* decision was instrumental in paving the way for further integration efforts and for the civil rights movement.

Julie Ahmad Siddique
City University of New York Graduate Center

See Also: African Americans; Civil Rights Laws; National Association for the Advancement of Colored People; *Plessy v. Ferguson*; Segregation Laws.

Further Readings

Friedman, Leon. *Brown v. Board: The Landmark Oral Argument Before the Supreme Court.* New York: The New Press, 2004.

Patterson, James T. *Brown v. Board of Education: A Civil Rights Milestone and Its Troubled Legacy.* New York: Oxford University Press, 2002.

U.S. Supreme Court. *Brown v. Board of Education, 347 U.S. 483 (1954): The Originals.* Raleigh, NC: Hayes Barton Press, 2006.

Brown v. Mississippi

The *Brown v. Mississippi* case involved the murder of a white farmer on March 30, 1934. Three black tenant farmers were accused of the murder: Arthur Ellington, Ed Brown, and Henry Shields. Anyone would confess to avoid horrific beatings with a metal-studded belt, simulated hangings, and additional consequences of brutality and police torture. The *Brown* case put a spotlight on some disturbing police interrogation practices. The constitutional legal issues concerned confessions that were introduced into the court proceedings. The trial lasted one day, with illegally obtained and forced confessions serving as the main case against the defendants, which resulted in guilty verdicts. The defendants were sentenced to be hanged, and the sentence was affirmed by the Mississippi Supreme Court on appeal. During the trial, the prosecution witnesses made statements that the defendants confessed after being severely beaten.

In *Brown v. Mississippi*, 279 U.S. 278 (1936), the Supreme Court held that such behavior was unconstitutional. In a unanimous decision, the

U.S. Supreme Court remanded the conviction to retrial. The court cited that the defendants' confessions obtained through the use of police violence would not be tolerated. The court cited the due process clause of the Fourteenth Amendment as grounds for excluding these involuntary confessions.

Involuntary statements from the defendants concern the right to not engage in self-incrimination. When self-incrimination violates the spirit of the Fourteenth Amendment's due process clause, the evidence must be suppressed. These constitutional issues are important when the state's case is based only on the defendant's confession. The protection of the court requires the elimination of contaminated evidence from reaching the jury. The self-incrimination clause prohibits the element of coercion; the clause provides that no person shall be compelled to give evidence against him- or herself in a criminal case. Therefore, cases involving statements that are solicited with harsh pressures that overcome a suspect's insistence on innocence do not meet these constitutional requirements.

The *Brown v. Mississippi* case is a classic example of police violence and torture. In addition, there are lesser forms of coercion, such as prolonged isolation from family or friends in a hostile setting, as in *Gallegos v. Colorado*, 370 U.S. 49 (1962). Moreover, officers conducting interrogations with physically or mentally exhausted suspects in long hours of interrogation is unconstitutional, as in *Watts v. Indiana*, 338 U.S. 49 (1949). The positive outcome is that the case focused on the need to protect the constitutional rights of citizens. Eventually, the famous Supreme Court case of an accused rapist in *Miranda v. Arizona*, 384 U.S. 346 (1966) decided that the defendant had the right to counsel and the right to remain silent during custodial interrogation. In addition, anything he said could and would be used against him in court of law.

The Supreme Court remanded the *Brown* case for retrial; rather than risk a retrial, the three defendants' pled nolo contendere to manslaughter. The sentences ranged from six months to seven years. The cases that followed *Brown* refined the process to represent the intent of the Constitution, Bill of Rights, and the protection from self-incrimination. Confessions that are not voluntary and that are illegally coerced undermine the Fourteenth Amendment and the due process clause.

Thomas E. Baker
University of Scranton

See Also: Appeals; Bill of Rights; Confession; Due Process; Interrogation Practices; *Mapp v. Ohio*; Police Abuse; Torture.

Further Readings
Brown v. Mississippi, 279 U.S. 278 (1936).
Chemerinsky, Erwin. *Constitutional Law: Principles and Policies*. Frederick, MD: Aspen Publishers, 2006.
Cortner, Richard C. *A Scottsboro Case in Mississippi: The Supreme Court and* Brown v. Mississippi. Jackson: University of Mississippi Press, 1986.

Buchanan, James (Administration of)

James Buchanan was the 15th president of the United States. Buchanan's administration is perhaps best known as the one that was in control when the southern states began to secede from the Union.

James Buchanan ran his 1856 campaign for the presidency on, ironically, a "Save the Union" theme. The slavery crisis had been forging a rift between sections of the country for some time. This issue led to the emergence of the Republican Party, which absorbed many northern Whigs and many of those who had helped form the nativist American Know-Nothing Party. The 1856 Republican candidate was John Charles Fremont, a well-known explorer and army officer. James Buchanan became the Democratic candidate, in large part because he had been serving for three years as minister to England and had thus been able to avoid taking a public stand on the festering Kansas-Nebraska issue as to whether new states admitted to the United States would be free or slave. Buchanan won the election, receiving 174 electoral votes and 1,838,169 popular votes to his Republican opponent Freemont's 114 electoral

President James Buchanan's administration has been criticized for not being able to maintain unity as the country moved closer to civil war. As a result, he is often ranked among the least popular presidents in U.S. history.

votes and 1,341,264 popular votes; the remaining eight electoral votes went to Millard Fillmore, the Whig candidate.

Attempts to Save the Union

After the election, Buchanan wrote that the main purpose of his administration would be to stop the unrest associated with the slavery question. To this end, he did not appoint any extreme sectionalists to his cabinet but selected more conservative ones. For instance, Buchanan chose Jeremiah S. Black to serve as his attorney general; Black functioned as the chief architect and the primary administration spokesman on the issues of slavery and secession. Black became Buchanan's secretary of state on December 17, 1860. Other members of Buchanan's cabinet included Secretary of War John Buchanan Floyd of Virginia; Secretary of the Treasury Philip Francis Thomas of Maryland, who was followed by John Adams Dix of New York, who assumed his duties on January 15, 1861; Secretary of the Interior Jacob Thompson of Mississippi; and Secretary of the Navy Isaac Toucey of Connecticut.

The U.S. Supreme Court handed down the famous *Dred Scott* decision in March 1857, two days after Buchanan's inauguration. This ruling declared the Missouri Compromise of 1820 unconstitutional, stating that Congress could not ban slavery from the territorial acquisitions; it further meant that slaves had virtually no rights and that even free blacks were not citizens. Buchanan intended to calm the volatile situation by enforcing the Fugitive Slave Law under the premise that citizens should not be deprived of their property without due process of law. It was naively hoped that this move would placate the southern slave-holding states and help prevent their impending secession. However, the vigorous enforcement of the Fugitive Slave Act kept attention on the slavery issue, and a few highly publicized attempts to rescue slaves in violation of the act fueled southern resentment against northern abolitionists.

Buchanan also declared that his administration would adhere to the principle of popular sovereignty at least with respect to the situation in Kansas. Two opposing governments were attempting to operate in Kansas. One was the antislavery Topeka faction, which Buchanan outlawed, and the other was the Lecompton faction that was proslavery and had been legalized by Franklin Pierce, the preceding president—a stance that Buchanan and his administration supported.

Buchanan selected Robert J. Walker, an antislavery advocate, to serve as governor of the Kansas Territory with clear instructions to hold impartial elections, at which time there would also be a vote for or against slavery as stipulated in the 1854 Kansas-Nebraska Act. However, the antislavery populace refused to register to vote for this referendum, forfeiting their right to decide. The proslavery convention presented the question to the electorate and, of course, won the vote; but that vote was condemned by the majority of the people of Kansas, who had refused to participate. Buchanan asked Congress to accept the Lecompton Constitution that would make

Kansas a slave state. William English offered a compromise bill that reduced the federal land grant to Kansas.

Buchanan accepted the English compromise, and thus Kansans rejected the Lecompton Constitution and in 1861, Buchanan signed off on the admission of Kansas as a free state.

Other Issues

The slave-free discussion was a national topic. The Lincoln-Douglas debates focused on this issue. Perhaps to divert attention, Buchanan proposed the annexation of Cuba, which he saw as a move to expand the boundaries of the country, as well as a way to help unite the fractured Democratic Party. Democrats in Congress heavily supported the proposal, but Republicans defeated the plan, feeling it might be a way to add another slave state.

Several other important events took place during Buchanan's administration. On May 11, 1858, Minnesota was admitted as the 32nd state. Oregon was admitted on February 14, 1859, as the 33rd state. On October 16, 1859, John Brown raided the federal arsenal at Harper's Ferry, Virginia, in a failed attempt to initiate a slave revolt. South Carolina then seceded from the Union on December 20, 1860. It was followed from January to February 1861 by the secession of Mississippi, Florida, Alabama, Georgia, Louisiana, and Texas. On January 29, 1861, Kansas was admitted as the 34th state. On February 8, 1861, the Confederate States of America was organized.

Buchanan's administration ruled the country at a time when it was rending itself apart. Historical critics have been harsh toward Buchanan and his administration. James Buchanan, and by extension his administration, is frequently ranked at or near the bottom of presidential popularity lists. However, given the deep-seated divisions that the issue of slavery had within regions of the nation at that time, it is unclear if any presidential administration could have prevented the crisis from erupting. Buchanan ended his administration on March 4, 1861, handing the presidency over to Abraham Lincoln.

Victor B. Stolberg
Essex County College

See Also: *Dred Scott v. Sandford*; Fugitive Slave Act of 1850; Kansas; Pierce, Franklin (Administration of); Slavery; Slavery, Law of.

Further Readings

Birkner, Michael J. *James Buchanan and the Political Crisis of the 1850s*. Selinsgrove, PA: Susquehanna University Press, 1996.

Klein, Philip S. *President James Buchanan: A Biography*. University Park: Pennsylvania State University Press, 1962.

Smith, Elbert B. *The Presidency of James Buchanan*. Lawrence: University Press of Kansas, 1975.

Weatherman, Donald V. "James Buchanan on Slavery and Secession." *Presidential Studies Quarterly*, v.15/4 (1985).

Buck v. Bell

The Supreme Court decision in *Buck v. Bell* (1927) was the culmination of a national movement to improve the quality of the population by implementing eugenic notions of heredity and racial improvement at the expense of individual rights. It serves as an example of how government decisions can affect the most intimate and private aspects of American lives.

Advocates of negative eugenics pushed for state laws to sterilize the "unfit," a word loosely defined to include imbeciles, "morons," the "feebleminded," and in some cases, alcoholics and prostitutes. A first wave of laws began with Indiana in 1907; by 1913, 16 states had laws that allowed a board of experts to sterilize state-institutionalized patients deemed unfit. Eugenic rhetoric swayed state legislators more than judges; the latter demanded proof that the procedure benefited the individual, not society. By 1918, the courts had struck down each of the seven civil laws that had been contested as violations of due process or equal protection of the law. A second wave of legislation passed in the 1920s, based on the model sterilization law drafted by Harry Laughlin, which attempted to address early court concerns.

Proponents of these new laws chose the Carrie Buck case in Virginia as a constitutional test.

Justice Oliver Wendell Holmes, Jr., rendered the Supreme Court's decision in May 1927. Holmes upheld the basic tenets of the eugenics movement: Mental defects and criminality are inherited; and mental defectives' fertility could overrun society with incompetence. Influenced by evolutionary science and social Darwinism, he accepted without question the three-generation theory that Emma Buck, her daughter Carrie, and Carrie's daughter Vivian were "feebleminded." He used the judicial precedent set in *Jacobson v. Massachusetts* (1905) that allowed for compulsory vaccination to protect society. In his view, Carrie was a potential parent of "socially inadequate offspring" who could be "sexually sterilized without detriment to her general health and ... her welfare and that of society [would] be promoted by her sterilization." Arguing that society had the right to "call upon those who already sap the strength of the State ... in order to prevent our being swamped with incompetence," he concluded that "three generations of imbeciles are enough." Dissenting without opinion was Justice Pierce Butler, presumably due to his Catholic opposition to sterilization.

In this case, the court accepted public welfare over individual rights, legitimating the government's right to control who could reproduce. The case lent the mantle of respectability to eugenic sterilization. It legitimized societal scrutiny of women's extramarital sexual behavior, allowing women with illegitimate births to be labeled "feebleminded," institutionalized, and then sterilized, thus "saving" society from the continuation of "socially unfit" offspring. Nuremberg attorneys used *Buck* to defend Nazi doctors' actions.

The case, however, disregarded important evidence. Holmes ignored increasing warnings among scientists and geneticists that eugenic assertions of hereditary social characteristics such as prostitution were baseless. Holmes also gave cursory consideration at best to the equal protection issue that had gained attention at state and lower federal court levels: The law in question mandated sterilization of feebleminded persons only in state, not private, institutions. He did not probe the labeling of these three females as "feebleminded," when in fact they were not. Emma had given birth to three illegitimate children and had sometimes supported them through prostitution. Carrie, born in 1906, had at age 3 been placed in foster care with the Dobbs family. Carrie progressed normally in school until the Dobbses removed her at age 16 to help out at home. The following year, the Dobbs's nephew raped Carrie. To avoid familial shame, Mr. Dobbs, the town peace officer, petitioned to have Carrie labeled feebleminded and thus institutionalized. Under pressure, a nurse testified that Carrie's 7-month-old daughter, Vivian, was feebleminded. Vivian later succeeded in school, achieving honor roll before dying at age 8 from complications of measles. Carrie's sister Dora Buck was also sterilized, although officials told her the procedure was an appendectomy.

In sum, *Buck* relied upon unsound scientific data, intervened in the personal liberty of citizens to reproduce, and legitimated an involuntary program of eugenics in an attempt to "protect" society from the "unfit." Officials wrongly deemed Carrie Buck and her daughter to be unfit. Although Virginia Governor Mark Wagner apologized in 2003 for using state power to enforce eugenic ideals, the case has yet to be overturned.

Simone M. Caron
Wake Forest University

See Also: Holmes, Oliver Wendell, Jr.; Supreme Court, U.S.; Virginia.

Further Readings
Berry, Roberta M. "From Involuntary Sterilization to Genetic Enhancement: The Unsettled Legacy of *Buck v. Bell*." *Notre Dame Journal of Law, Ethics and Public Policy*, v.12 (1998).
Lombardo, Paul A. *Three Generations, No Imbeciles: Eugenics, the Supreme Court and* Buck v. Bell. Baltimore, MD: Johns Hopkins University Press, 2008.
Siegel, Stephen A. "Justice Holmes, *Buck v. Bell*, and the History of Equal Protection." *Minnesota Law Review*, v.90 (2005).

Bundy, Ted

While the precise number of victims he murdered will never be known, Ted Bundy remains one of the United States' most infamous and prolific serial killers of all time. His true motives also remain a mystery. Nearing his execution, he blamed the violent pornography he viewed as a teen as well as the man he believed was his father, who he said tortured animals and was racist and anti-Semitic. Bundy was known to kidnap young women, knock them unconscious, violently sexually assault them, and strangle them to death.

On November 24, 1946, Theodore Robert Cowell was born in Burlington, Vermont, where his mother was living in a home for unwed mothers. Eleanor Cowell told her family she had an affair with a World War II veteran, but they suspected she was impregnated by her abusive father. Nonetheless, Bundy believed his maternal grandparents were his parents and his mother was his older sister. After living for a few years in Philadelphia, Pennsylvania, in 1950, she and Ted were sent to Tacoma, Washington, to live with relatives; one year later, she married Johnny Culpepper Bundy. Bundy's future behavior was only hinted at while he was a teenager. He was a withdrawn high school student, spending time in the library reading novels that included tales of victims of sexual violence and looking through magazines for pictures of dead bodies. To fund his hobby of skiing, he engaged in shoplifting and counterfeited ski passes to gain access to the slopes.

Bundy went to college at the University of Puget Sound and studied psychology. During these years, he drifted from one part-time job to another, suspected of stealing from his employers but never caught. After transferring to the University of Washington (UW) in Seattle, he met the woman who he believed was the love of his life. When she ended their relationship, Bundy became despondent, dropped out of school, and traveled to Vermont where he discovered the truth about his mother. He returned to college and graduated with honors. He met up with his former love from college in the summer of 1973. Impressed with the new Bundy, who was then enrolled in law school, she accepted his marriage proposal, but in January 1974, he abruptly ended the engagement. Shortly after, Bundy dropped out of law school and young women began to disappear in the Washington State area.

There is no consensus about when Bundy began killing or the identity of his first victim. Just before his execution, Bundy told his lawyer his

Notorious serial killer Ted Bundy's Volkswagen Beetle, which he used in his crimes, can be seen among the exhibits at the National Museum of Crime and Punishment in Washington, D.C.

first murder was in 1972; while being examined by a psychiatrist, Bundy said he killed two women during his brief time in Philadelphia. Bundy's first confirmed victim was in January 1974—a student at UW who survived the vicious sexual assault. His first substantiated murder was of another UW student in February 1974, whom he kidnapped from her room. Over the next several months, seven young women, mostly college students, disappeared. The victims were often last seen helping a man with an arm or leg in a cast struggling to load items such as books or a briefcase into his Volkswagen Beetle. Bundy moved to Salt Lake City in the fall of 1974 to attend law school at the University of Utah. He brutally raped and murdered at least five women in the Salt Lake City area. Another victim escaped his attack while in his car as he posed as a police officer. At the end of 1974, Bundy's girlfriend at the time called Salt Lake City police, reporting him as a match to the profile being publicized. He was quickly dismissed as a suspect, though, due to his charming personality and handsome appearance.

While still living in Utah, Bundy began committing crimes in Colorado, murdering at least six women and young girls. It was here that he was first arrested during a traffic stop. Although they found a ski mask, crowbar, handcuffs, and rope, the police thought they caught a burglar. He was placed in a line-up and two of his victims who had survived picked him out. He was convicted of aggravated kidnapping in Utah in February 1976.

He was extradited to Colorado, where law enforcement was certain they could obtain a murder conviction. He served as his own lawyer and was able to escape custody while doing research in the law library in June 1976; he was caught nine days later. He escaped again in December 1977 and was able to board a plane to Tallahassee, Florida. He went on a rampage, raping four women in a sorority house, killing two. The same night, he killed another college student in her bed; weeks later, he kidnapped, raped, and murdered a 12-year-old girl. Days later, he was arrested during another traffic stop.

One of the sorority house survivors gave convincing evidence during his second trial, in which he also served as his own counsel, and he was sentenced to death. Bundy was put on trial once more in Florida, for the murder of the young girl. His lawyer entered a plea of not guilty by reason of insanity, but he was again sentenced to death. Bundy maintained his innocence throughout the trials and several appeals. Over the next 10 years, he confessed to a number of other crimes, hoping to escape the electric chair. He was executed in Florida on January 24, 1989.

Gennifer Furst
William Paterson University

See Also: 1961 to 1980 Primary Documents; Rape, History of; Serial and Mass Killers; Sex Offenders.

Further Readings
Anderson, H. and R. W. Larsen. *The Deliberate Stranger*. DVD. Directed by Marvin J. Chomsky. Burbank, CA: Warner Home Video, 1986.
Rule, Ann. *The Stranger Beside Me*. New York: Signet, 2001.

Buntline, Ned

The author and entertainment entrepreneur known as Ned Buntline was born Edward Zane Carrol Judson in 1823 in Stamford, New York, a small rural farming community in the northern Catskill Mountains. He was the son of a Masonic schoolmaster who was also the author of moral and patriotic pamphlets. Beyond this, it is difficult to know what parts of Judson's past are authentic and what he invented in order to develop his popular persona and alter ego, Ned Buntline. The main source of biographical information about Judson is from his autobiography, *Ned Buntline's Life Yarn*, published in 1849. According to Buntline, he was a self-made and fiercely independent young man who sought adventure and success in the rough-and-tumble world of Jacksonian America. Rejecting his father's patriarchal authority, he proclaimed: "Resurgam is my motto—independence my character! Farewell, Sir; you might have made me all you could have wished—now I will make myself." This kind of bravado led Buntline to fit into the emerging, ruggedly masculine, and individualistic culture of mid-19th-century America.

Between 1838 and 1842, Buntline went to sea, holding a midshipman's commission in the navy and seeing some action in the Second Seminole War in Florida (1835–42). He commenced his literary career shortly thereafter, editing a journal called *Ned Buntline's Magazine* in 1844. He spent several years as a bounty hunter and brawler in Kentucky and Tennessee, arriving in New York City in time to emerge as a self-proclaimed leader of the nativist mob action that took place around the Astor Place Theatre Riot of 1849. His participation in this event, in defense of American actor Edwin Forrest, resulted in an arrest and jail sentence. In New York, he received the attention of sensational newspaper editor James Gordon Bennet, married Bennet's daughter, and became an active member of the Know-Nothing Party that endorsed anti-immigrant and anti-Catholic policies. In 1862, he enlisted in the Union army, only to be discharged two years later with a dishonorable record.

Dime Novels
Buntline is best known as a writer of sensational urban melodramas, and later as the promoter of

Ned Buntline wrote hundreds of stories that influenced popular views of crime and cities in the 19th century. One of his novels even helped lead to the criminalization of abortion in New York.

William Cody (popularly known as Buffalo Bill, an army scout who supplied buffalo meat to the railroad crews). He was central to the construction of a prolific and culturally significant mid-19th-century popular culture. His most famous dime novel, *The Mysteries and Miseries of New York* (1848), which drew upon the form of the French writer Eugene Sue's *Mysteries and Miseries of Paris*, was an attempt to create a panorama of the underside of New York's new urban polyglot culture. One of its principal subplots was configured around a fictionalized version of Mary Rogers (known as the "Beautiful Cigar Girl"), whose mysterious disappearance and death became a cause célèbre and the rhetorical inspiration for the New York City Police Reform Act and the New York State act criminalizing abortion, both passed in 1845. *Mysteries* was followed by *The B'hoys of New York* (1850), *The G'hals of New York* (1850), and *Three Years After* (1849). These works featured a group of white, working-class characters and a series of interconnected subplots that told the sagas of gamblers and rakes, prostitutes and brawlers, and the poor and the wealthy. As cultural critic Michael Denning and others have pointed out, these novels, which purported to introduce a middle-class audience to the perils of urban life, were probably more popular with the working class than with their wealthier neighbors, despite their very ambivalent portrayal of working-class characters.

Buntline's novels were instrumental in portraying a particularly problematic construction of the mid-19th-century city. For him, it was a dark and dangerous space, a place of social and sexual danger whose chaotic landscape threatened to undermine the entire social order. In *Mysteries and Miseries*, the author's xenophobic politics are supported by a set of appendixes, including a lexicon of urban slang, statistics on New York City crime, and official documents and reports relating to poverty, prostitution, and city asylums. The book also included a reprint of the 1845 Police Act. Throughout the later 1840s and 1850s, Buntline wrote dime novels set in exotic places: Peru, Mexico, Florida, and the Gulf Islands. His literary production was prolific, with his stories and tales numbering in the hundreds.

Buffalo Bill
In the late 1860s, he met William Cody (then a Pony Express messenger, soldier in the Civil War and several wars against the American Indians, hunter, and army scout), the man he would turn into the western adventurer, Buffalo Bill. The popular novel *Buffalo Bill, the King of the Border* inspired the production of many sequels by Buntline and others and eventually led to the creation of Buffalo Bill's "Wild West Show," a traveling extravaganza that critics have seen as instrumental in promulgating not only the myth of the frontier as an iconic feature of American culture but also the even larger dream of American imperial supremacy and power. Although Cody would eventually reject Buntline and replace him with another dime novelist as his chronicler and publicist, Buntline has endured as the primary creator of the legend of Buffalo Bill. In 1871, Buntline

returned to his birthplace of Stamford, New York, married his fourth wife, Anna Fuller, also of Stamford, and lived comfortably there until his death in 1886.

Amy Gilman Srebnick
Montclair State University

See Also: Abortion; Dime Novels, Pulps, Thrillers; Fear of Crime; Literature and Theater, Crime in; News Media, Crime in.

Further Readings
Buckley, Peter. "The Case Against Ned Buntline: The 'Words, Sigs, and Gestures' of Popular Authorship." *Prospects*, v.13 (1988).
Denning, Michael. *Mechanics Accents: Dime Novels and Working-Class Culture in America*. New York: Verso, 1988.
Gilman Srebnick, Amy. *The Mysterious Death of Mary Rogers: Sex and Culture in Nineteenth-Century New York*. New York: Oxford University Press, 1995.
Monahan, Jay. *The Great Rascal: The Life and Adventures of Ned Buntline*. New York: Bonzana, 1951.
Reynolds, David. *Beneath the American Renaissance: The Subversive Imagination in the Age of Emerson and Melville*. Cambridge: Harvard University Press, 1988.
Streeby, Shelley. *American Sensations: Class, Empire, and the Production of Popular Culture*. Berkeley: University of California Press, 2002.

Bureau of Alcohol, Tobacco, Firearms and Explosives

The Bureau of Alcohol, Tobacco, Firearms and Explosives (ATF) is a federal law enforcement agency within the U.S. Department of Justice (DOJ) charged with administering and enforcing federal laws related to the manufacture, importation, and distribution of firearms and explosives. It is also responsible for investigating arson cases with a federal nexus, as well as criminal violations of federal laws governing the manufacture, importation, and distribution of alcohol and tobacco.

Evolution of the ATF
ATF's roots as a law enforcement agency can be traced back to July 1862, when Congress created an Office of Internal Revenue (OIR) within the Treasury Department charged with the collection of taxes on distilled spirits and tobacco products. The following year, Congress authorized the OIR commissioner to hire detectives to facilitate the apprehension, punishment, and deterrence of tax evaders. The role of these detectives known as "revenoors" expanded significantly in 1919 when the Eighteenth Amendment to the U.S. Constitution, along with the Volstead Act, established Prohibition. These laws made illegal the manufacture, sale, transportation, and exportation of intoxicating liquors from or to the United States or its territories. In order to enforce the new statutes, a Prohibition Unit was established within the Bureau of Internal Revenue. Revenue agents assigned to the unit were tasked with investigating violations of internal revenue law, including the illicit manufacture of liquors. On April 1, 1927, the unit was elevated to bureau status and was transferred from the Department of the Treasury to the DOJ. The unit had jurisdiction over alcohol, as well as federal narcotics statutes, until 1930, when the Federal Bureau of Narcotics, a forerunner of the Drug Enforcement Administration, was established.

The Bureau of Prohibition was returned to the Treasury in 1934 at the end of Prohibition and was renamed the Alcohol Tax Unit (ATU). In addition to collecting liquor excise taxes, agents assigned to the unit were tasked with stopping the illegal manufacturing of untaxed liquor. ATU's list of responsibilities was later expanded to include the collection of firearm manufacturing and transfer excise taxes following the enactment of the National Firearms Act (NFA). In 1952, the ATU's title was changed to the Alcohol and Tobacco Tax Division (ATTD) and its list of responsibilities was again expanded to include the enforcement of tobacco tax laws.

In 1968, Congress passed two major pieces of legislation that significantly expanded the role of the ATTD. These were the Omnibus Crime

Control and Safe Streets Act and the Gun Control Act. The laws placed new restrictions on the ownership, manufacture, and transfer of firearms and implemented strict government regulation and control over bombs and other explosives. The ATTD was renamed the Alcohol, Tobacco, and Firearms Division (ATFD) and was given jurisdiction to enforce the firearm and explosives provisions of the new laws. In 1970, it was given the added responsibility of enforcing the Organized Crime Control Act and the Explosives Control Act. These laws provided for close regulation of the explosives industry and designated certain arsons and bombings as federal crimes.

Modern ATF

On July 1, 1972, the ATFD was given full bureau status and renamed the Bureau of Alcohol, Tobacco, and Firearms (ATF). The new agency was tasked with an eclectic array of enforcement and regulatory responsibilities, including the collection of federal taxes on alcohol and tobacco and federal regulation of firearms and explosives. Subsequent laws expanded ATF's jurisdiction. The 1976 Arms Export Control Act focused the bureau's attention on international gun smuggling. The 1982 Anti-Arson Act granted ATF authority to investigate the destruction of property by fire as well as by explosives. Regulatory measures such as the 1978 Contraband Cigarette Act enhanced the agency's ability to collect mandated government taxes from cigarette and liquor manufacturers.

Two incidents in the early 1990s focused national attention on the ATF and led to widespread condemnation of the newly formed agency. The first incident was the standoff at Ruby Ridge, Idaho, that occurred in March 1991. Even though ATF agents were not directly involved in the standoff that led to the death of a federal agent and the antigovernment extremist Randy Weaver's juvenile son and wife, the agency was nevertheless criticized for alleged malfeasance of its agents in the investigation that led to the standoff. The second incident began on February 28, 1993, when ATF agents unsuccessfully attempted to execute a federal search warrant at the Branch Davidian ranch at Mount Carmel near Waco, Texas. An intense gun battle took place, resulting in the deaths of four agents and six Branch Davidians. The Federal Bureau of Investigation subsequently assumed control of the standoff and initiated a siege of the Branch Davidian compound. This led to a fire that destroyed the compound and killed 76 people, including 24 children. Major changes were made in the ATF hierarchy as well as systemic changes in the agency hiring, recruiting, and training procedures following government investigations into the two controversial incidents.

As part of the Homeland Security Act signed by President George W. Bush after the terrorist attack on the World Trade Center on September 11, 2001, ATF's regulatory and enforcement functions for firearms and explosives were transferred from the Treasury to DOJ. The agency's title was also changed to the Bureau of Alcohol, Tobacco, Firearms and Explosives. Despite the name change, the agency is still referred to as ATF. The agency's regulatory responsibilities for alcohol and tobacco were given to a newly formed Treasury entity, the Alcohol and Tobacco Tax and Trade Bureau.

In recent years, the established link between firearms and drug trafficking has resulted in a significant portion of ATF's resources being dedicated to counternarcotics activities and the reduction of firearms-related violence. The agency is considered a major repository for gang-related information and intelligence incidents. ATF continues to dedicate significant resources to ensure that federally licensed gun dealers comply with federal firearm statutes. ATF is responsible for the National Integrated Ballistic Information Network, a state-of-the-art computerized program that enables law enforcement officers to rapidly determine if a piece of recovered ballistic evidence came from a firearm that was previously used in a crime. The agency has also been recognized for its investigative expertise in responding to both arson and explosives incidents. Specially trained ATF agents with postblast and cause-and-origin expertise assist federal, state, and local investigators with significant arson and explosives events. ATF agents also provide foreign governments with technical and forensic assistance in arson, explosives, and firearm smuggling investigations.

Deborah A. Sibila
Sam Houston State University

See Also: 1941 to 1960 Primary Documents; Drug Enforcement Administration; Federal Bureau of Investigation; Omnibus Crime Control and Safe Streets Act of 1968; Prohibition; Ruby Ridge Standoff; Volstead Act; Waco Siege.

Further Readings

Bock, Alan W. *Ambush at Ruby Ridge.* Irvine, CA: Dickens Press, 1995.

Bureau of Alcohol, Tobacco, Firearms and Explosives. http://www.atf.gov (Accessed September 2011).

Vizzard, William J. *In the Cross Fire: A Political History of the Bureau of Alcohol, Tobacco and Firearms.* Boulder, CO: Lynne Rienner Publishers, 1977.

Buren, Martin Van (Administration of)

Historians and political theorists often relate the name of Martin Van Buren with the establishment and consolidation of the Second Party System and with the collapse of the American credit system leading to the country's first harsh economic depression. Yet, his professional training as a lawyer and his position as New York State attorney general made him particularly sensitive to issues relating to crime and punishment. His pronouncements, however, were not entirely consistent, particularly when concerned with slavery. Although he stood firmly against the annexation of Texas during his administration to prevent the addition of slave territory to the United States and run for president for the abolitionist Free Soil Party in 1848, his presidency was marked by the judicial controversy of the Spanish slaveship *Amistad*. During the case, Van Buren acted against the defendants, using his influence to urge returning the ship to Spain.

Van Buren's career embodies the American myth of social mobility. Born into a humble family on December 5, 1782, he went on to become one of the most influential politicians of his era and was eventually elected the eighth American president, the first to be born a citizen of the United States. In 1796, when he was only 14, Van Buren managed to enter one of the most respected legal offices in his native town of Kinderhook, which gave him the opportunity to receive seven years of legal training. Van Buren was admitted to the bar in 1803, and the legal office that he established in Kinderhook with his half-brother James Van Alen quickly acquired fame beyond local borders. He particularly made a name for himself as a defendant of land renters and tenants who claimed the land tenure of the Hudson Valley to be based on imprecise colonial grants and sought to limit the power of the big landowners. His fame as a lawyer, together with his networking skills, quickly paved the way for a career in party politics, making Van Buren one of the first American professional politicians. In New York, Van Buren organized the Jacksonian Democrats building the Albany Regency, a shrewd political machine that aimed to maximize party loyalty and discipline. Van Buren actively engaged in fighting political corruption. Yet, his Albany Regency was a first example of a spoils system, as party allegiance was increased by giving government jobs to faithful voters.

In the 1810s and 1820s, Van Buren held important positions in the state of New York, first as senator, then as the state attorney general and, finally, as governor. After only three months in office, Van Buren resigned from governorship in March 1829 to join President Andrew Jackson's cabinet as secretary of state. One of his first legal initiatives as a senator was to fight for the abolition of debtors' prisons, arguing that imprisonment for people who were too poor to pay their debts was an inhumane measure. Once on the national scene, Van Buren was a loyal supporter of Jackson, becoming his vice president in the 1832 election and his successor as president of the United States in 1836. As a national politician, Van Buren affirmed his belief in a legal framework that asserted the primacy of states' rights over those of the federal government as long as these respected the Constitution. Van Buren applied this conviction to the contentious issue of slavery: Although he considered it morally wrong, as a president, he declared himself against its abolition.

The case of the Spanish slave ship *Amistad* forced Van Buren out of his noncommittal strategy as far as slavery was concerned. When the Africans aboard the *Amistad* seized control of the ship that had sailed off from Cuba, they brought

A modern replica of the Spanish ship Amistad *sailing off the coast of Connecticut in 2005. The 1841* Amistad *case became a defining event of Martin Van Buren's presidency.*

it into the port of New London in Connecticut. As they disembarked onto American soil, they immediately became a case for the federal judiciary. Against the abolitionists' claims that the Africans should be freed, Van Buren adopted a legalistic stance, ordering that, in compliance with international treaties, the slaves should instead be handed back to Cuba. Yet, the president maintained that it was the court's responsibility to decide the fate of the slaves. The final decision to return the Africans to their homeland rather than Cuba represented an apparent challenge to the president's wishes.

Luca Prono
Independent Scholar

See Also: African Americans; Jackson, Andrew (Administration of); Slavery; Slavery, Law of.

Further Reading
Mushkat, Jerome and Joseph G. Rayback. *Martin Van Buren: Law, Politics, and the Shaping of Republican Ideology.* DeKalb: Northern Illinois University Press, 1997.
Silbey, Joel H. *Martin Van Buren and the Emergence of American Popular Politics.* Lanham, MD: Rowman & Littlefield, 2002.

Burger, Warren

Warren Burger was the 15th chief justice of the United States (1969 to 1986). Regarded as a conservative court, the Burger Court did not reverse the decisions of the Warren Court. It did, in some instances, limit those decisions, especially as they related to the rights of the accused.

Warren Burger was born in St. Paul, Minnesota, on September 17, 1907, the fourth of seven children. His parents were Charles J. Burger and Katharine Schnittger. He grew up on the family farm and attended John A. Johnson High School, from which he graduated in 1925. Burger then worked his way through the University of Minnesota (1925–27) and the St. Paul College of Law while selling insurance. He received his law degree magna cum laude in 1931. He then took a job at the firm of Boyensen, Otis and Faricy. He also taught law at the St. Paul College of Law (1931–48). Burger married Elvera Stromberg (1907–94), whom he met while they were both students at the University of Minnesota, on November 8, 1933. They had two children, Wade Allen Burger and Margaret Elizabeth Burger.

Burger was active in Republican politics in Minnesota. He managed Harold Stassen's campaigns for governor in 1938, 1940, and 1942 and managed his unsuccessful bids for the Republican nomination for president in 1948 and 1952. From 1942 to 1947, Burger served on Minnesota's Emergency War Labor Board. In 1952, he played a key role in Dwight D. Eisenhower's nomination by delivering the Minnesota delegation (after Stassen's withdrawal) to the general at the GOP Convention, ensuring a first ballot victory. In 1953, Eisenhower then appointed Burger assistant attorney general for the Civil Division of the Justice Department. In 1956, he became a judge on the U.S. Court of Appeals for the District of Columbia Circuit, a position he held for the next 13 years. As an appellate court judge, he gave a number of speeches and wrote articles critical of the Warren Court's decisions concerning the rights of the accused.

President Richard M. Nixon nominated Burger to be chief justice of the Supreme Court to replace Earl Warren in 1969. The Senate confirmed Burger, and he took office on June 22, 1969.

When Burger was nominated for the chief justiceship, conservatives in the Nixon administration expected that the Burger Court would overturn controversial Warren Court–era precedents. By the early 1970s, however, it became apparent that the Burger Court was not going to reverse the rulings of the Warren Court and in fact might extend some Warren Court doctrines.

In 1972, the Burger Court issued a unanimous ruling against the Nixon administration's desire to invalidate the need for a search warrant and the requirements of the Fourth Amendment in cases of domestic surveillance with *United States v. U.S. District Court*. That same year, in *Furman v. Georgia*, the court invalidated all death penalty laws then in force in a 5–4 decision in which Burger dissented. In *Roe v. Wade* (1973), Burger voted with the majority to recognize a broad right to privacy that prohibited states from banning abortions. Burger later abandoned *Roe v. Wade* with the 1986 case *Thornburgh v. American College of Obstetricians and Gynecologists*.

Burger led the court in a unanimous 8–0 decision in *United States v. Nixon* on July 24, 1974. President Nixon was trying to keep several memos and tapes relating to the Watergate Affair private based on a claim of executive privilege. In the opinion, authored by Burger, the court held that the judicial branch alone would have the power to determine whether something qualifies to be shielded under executive privilege.

Burger wrote a concurring opinion in the court's 1986 decision upholding a Georgia law criminalizing sodomy (*Bowers v. Hardwick*). He referred to long-standing laws criminalizing homosexuality in his arguments against gay rights.

On the court, Burger rarely showed sympathy for criminal defendants or their asserted rights. In *Harris v. New York* (1971), he announced that a statement obtained without reading a suspect his or her rights as required by *Miranda v. Arizona* (1966) could be used in court cases. He voted with the court majority and helped bring back the death penalty in *Gregg v. Georgia* (1976). In a seemingly extreme example, in 1983 he even dissented from the court's holding in *Solem v. Helm*, which found that a life sentence for writing a $100 bad check was indeed cruel and unusual punishment.

Burger took seriously the chief justice's responsibility for administering the nation's legal system. He founded the Institute for Court Management (1970) and the National Center for State Courts (1971). In a December 1971 speech at the National Conference on Corrections, Burger called for the creation of a national training academy for corrections. This led to the establishment of the National Institute of Corrections in 1977. He began the tradition of the annual State of the Judiciary speech by the chief justice at the American Bar Association in 1970. He was both the founder of the Supreme Court Historical Society and, as chief justice, acted as chancellor of the Smithsonian Institution.

Burger retired on September 26, 1986, becoming the chair of the Commission on the Bicentennial of the U.S. Constitution. He had served longer than any other chief justice appointed in the 20th century. Burger led the national celebrations of the Constitution's 200th anniversary in 1987 and the Bill of Rights' 200th anniversary in 1989. He remained chair until the commission ceased to exist in 1991. He was also chancellor of the College of William and Mary from 1986 to 1993. He received the Presidential Medal of Freedom in 1988.

Burger died of congestive heart failure in Washington, D.C., in 1995. He was 87. After lying in state in the Great Hall of the U.S. Supreme Court Building, Justice Burger was buried at the Arlington National Cemetery.

Jeffrey Kraus
Wagner College

See Also: Abortion; *Bowers v. Hardwick*; Brennan, William J. Jr.; Capital Punishment; *Furman v. Georgia*; Nixon, Richard (Administration of); Obscenity; Pornography; *Roe v. Wade*; Sodomy; Suspect's Rights; *United States v. Nixon*; Warren, Earl; Watergate.

Further Readings

Blasi, Vincent. *The Burger Court: The Counter-Revolution That Wasn't*, 3rd ed. New Haven, CT: Yale University Press, 1983.

Funston, Richard Y. *Constitutional Counter-revolution? The Warren Court and the Burger Court: Judicial Policy Making in Modern America.* Cambridge, MA: Schenkman, 1977.

Halpern, Stephen C. and Charles M. Lamb, eds. *The Burger Court: Political and Judicial Profiles.* Urbana: University of Illinois Press, 1991.

Maltz, Earl M. *The Chief Justiceship of Warren Burger, 1969–1986.* Columbia: University of South Carolina Press, 2000.

Schwartz, Bernard, ed. *The Burger Court: Counter-Revolution or Confirmation?* New York: Oxford University Press, 1998.

Woodward, Robert and Scott Armstrong. *The Brethren: Inside the Supreme Court.* New York: Simon & Schuster, 2005.

Burglary, Contemporary

Burglary is an ancient common law crime against a dwelling, which was sometimes punishable by death. The felony crime of burglary is defined as the nocturnal breaking and entering into the dwelling house of another to commit a felony. Burglary is a felony crime against a habitat, as opposed to robbery, which is a crime against a person. Traditionally, burglary is a crime of stealth committed while the structure is unoccupied.

The Federal Bureau of Investigation (FBI's) Uniform Crime Reporting (UCR) program defines burglary as the unlawful entry into a structure to commit a felony or theft. To classify an offense as a burglary, the use of force to gain entry need not have occurred. The UCR program has three subclassifications for burglary: forcible entry, unlawful entry where no force is used, and attempted forcible entry. The UCR definition of a "structure" includes apartments, barns, house trailers, or houseboats, when used as permanent dwellings; offices; railroad cars (but not automobiles); stables; and vessels (i.e., ships).

Burglaries are among the most frequently committed crimes and the most difficult to investigate. This crime is committed approximately every 15 minutes. The average citizen thinks that burglaries only involve homes and business; however, many recent state statutes cover recreational vehicles, railroad cars, houseboats, airplanes, and other vehicles. A few states have included coin-operated machines—typically vending machines located outside businesses.

Automatic teller machines (ATMs) have attracted burglars in recent years because of their availability in businesses and convenience stores. These lucrative targets entice determined burglars to drive trucks through the windows of business establishments to gain access to ATMs. Smash-and-grab strategies require little skill, simply an unrestrained criminal impulse. Generally, after burglars gain entrance, they break into the ATM or try to move it to another location within two to seven minutes.

Burglary frequency and related economic consequences negatively impact the lives of hardworking citizens. Burglaries predispose spin-off crimes because stolen credit cards and checks provide additional criminal opportunities. The second and third burglary offenses may result when the profits are high. In addition, hot targets like laptop computers or jewelry are vulnerable items. When homeowners are the victims of serial burglaries, within 30 days of each other, trauma multiplies and heightens.

Burglary Statistics

According to the FBI, in 2009 there were an estimated 2,199,125 burglaries—a decrease of 1.3 percent when compared with 2008 data. There was an increase of 2 percent in the number of burglaries in 2009 when compared with the 2005 estimate, and an increase of 7.2 percent when compared with the 2000 estimate. Burglary accounted for 23.6 percent of the estimated number of property crimes committed in 2009. Of all burglaries, 61 percent involved forcible entry, 32.6 percent were unlawful entries (without force), and the remainder (6.4 percent) were forcible entry attempts. Victims of burglary offenses suffered an estimated $4.6 billion in lost property in 2009; overall, the average loss per burglary offense was $2,096. Burglaries of residential properties accounted for 72.6 percent of all burglary offenses.

Burglaries, which are defined as unlawful entry into a structure to commit a felony or theft, are among the most common crimes, with one occurring about every 15 minutes.

The FBI UCR program cannot offer a full picture of the burglary problem because some citizens do not report offenses; moreover, there are a multitude of UCR research reporting problems. For example, according to FBI statistics, the percentages of burglaries cleared by arrest are low: (1) forcible entry 11.7 percent; (2) unlawful entry, 13.7 percent; and (3) attempt forcible entry, 10.8 percent. The national arrest clearance rates have been consistently reported at fewer than 15 percent for decades.

The National Crime Victimization Survey (NCVS) measures the property crimes of household burglary, motor vehicle theft, and property theft. Since the survey information is obtained from a sample of households, it does not include property crimes affecting businesses or other commercial establishments. If these crimes are reported to the police, they are included in the UCR. NCVS includes property crimes affecting victims and household members that were not reported to the police.

Summary Findings

In 2009, members of U.S. households experienced about 15.6 million property crimes. Property crimes were experienced at a rate of 127.4 per 1,000 households in the United States during 2009. Rates of household burglary remained unchanged between 2008 and 2009. Property theft rates declined between 2008 and 2009.

Property theft is the most frequently occurring property crime. About 11.7 million property thefts occurred in 2009. About 95.7 per 1,000 households experienced property thefts during this period.

In 2009, about 40 percent of property crimes were reported to police. Motor vehicle theft (85 percent) was the property crime most frequently reported to police. About 32 percent of property thefts were reported. More than half of household burglaries (57 percent) were reported.

Burglary Typologies

High-security burglary targets require the skills of the professional burglar. For example, a former U.S. Army Airborne soldier earned the nickname "Spiderman" after a crime spree of burglarizing and terrorizing high-rise apartment owners in Florida. He stole $6 million in cash, jewelry, and credit cards. His unique abilities for rappelling the exterior walls of 30-story buildings placed him in a high-level expertise category. "Spiderman" was prosecuted for burglarizing and breaking into a total of 132 high-rise condominiums.

Unconventional jewel thieves and cat burglars like Jack "The Smurf" Murphy and John Henry "The Lizard" Coulthurst scaled balconies with a hook, breaking and entering to glean their targeted bounties. Professional burglary specialists like these often enjoy their criminal reputations, notoriety, and media attention. Their unique skills, method of operation (MO), and trademark behaviors may serve as the clues that lead to their arrest and conviction.

However, most burglary typologies are the result of low-level criminals or burglars create and search for further uncomplicated opportunities; they have mediocre breaking-and-entering skills. They engage in surveillance and develop contacts for stolen goods. Low-level amateur (novice) burglars tend to prey close to home, where they target unwitting neighbors because of prior knowledge and opportunities. Juvenile first-time offenders and repeat offenders are generally in the novice typology; however, they may graduate to the journeyperson or professional levels.

Burglaries always have the potential to turn violent when the lawful property owner returns unexpectedly. Burglary that evolves into a robbery/home invasion where victims are present can lead to violent homicides. Cases where drug addicts are seeking the means to feed their addiction multiply the violence equation. In most cases, the burglar wants to break and enter, seize the money and hot products that can be converted to drug money, and get out.

Burglary Rings

Most burglars are male, with less than 10 percent female offenders, and operate as lone wolves. There are, however, burglary gangs that operate in an organized fashion. These burglary rings may apply coordination strategies that involve cell phones; texting or police countersurveillance strategies are frequently applied. Gang operations may conduct specific targeting behaviors for potential victims and products like jewelry. Some of these gangs have operated successfully for decades without suffering arrests and prosecutions. For example, a Colombian burglary ring, the Code-wise Crew, committed up 12 daily burglaries. This burglary ring operated in groups of approximately three members, identifying structures for breaking and entering when the residents were absent.

Conclusion

Burglary is a crime that affects many citizens and violates the safety and security sentiments of millions of Americans. There is sense of psychological violation and emotional consequences for burglary victims. Lost cherished possessions and family heirlooms represent the theft of the owner's heritage. This kind of psychological loss should not be underestimated. Police agencies have the opportunity to win the support of victims when their personal property is returned. The crime of burglary is difficult to solve because prior contact between offender and victim is rare. Law enforcement agencies need to improve the burglary clearance arrest rate.

Thomas E. Baker
University of Scranton

See Also: Burglary, History of; Burglary, Sociology of; Crime in America, Types; Crime Prevention; Felonies; Larceny; Robbery, Contemporary.

Further Readings
Baker, Thomas, E. *Introductory Criminal Analysis: Crime Prevention and Intervention Strategies*. Upper Saddle River, NJ: Pearson Prentice Hall, 2005.
Federal Bureau of Investigation. *Uniform Crime Reporting (UCR) Program, Crime in the United States*. Washington, DC: U.S. Department of Justice, 2010.
Swanson, Charles R., Neil Chameleon, Terri Leonard, and Robert Taylor. *Criminal Investigation*, 10th ed. New York: McGraw-Hill, 2010.

Burglary, History of

While the historical underpinning of the law of burglary as developed by the common law judges in England starting in the reign of King Henry II in 1154 was the protection of the right of habitation, present-day statutes broadly apply to any building, not just a dwelling, though the focus remains on protecting occupancy and or possession. Under the common law as carried over to the American colonies and incorporated into the various state penal laws, burglary is defined as the breaking and entry of the dwelling house of another, in the nighttime, with the intent of committing a felony therein.

Although the various jurisdictions in this country have both expanded and contracted the scope of the crime and have divided it into degrees of culpability, the common law definition still survives as the core basis of the present-day burglary statutes.

Evolution of Burglary Statutes

The essential element of the common law burglary was the requirement that there be something literally broken, which was no doubt envisioned by Henry II's judges as the forcible invasion of a place of habitation such as the smashing in of a door to someone's home, but since the right to be protected was one of habitation as well as property, a constructive or symbolic break soon developed to satisfy the statute. Thus, opening an unlocked door was sufficient but passing through an open doorway was not. Indeed, by the middle of the 20th century, many states, including California, had eliminated the break requirement altogether, but other states such as New York had not. In the 1960s, New York's law was updated so that the basic definition of burglary was expanded to apply to a person who knowingly enters or remains unlawfully in a building with the intent to commit a crime therein. This definition is now accepted by the majority of the states.

Thus, in 1990, 11 men with copied keys unlocked a closed door and entered the Brinks Bank building with the intent of committing a robbery therein in Boston, Massachusetts—a state that still required breaking as well as entry but no longer limited the law to a dwelling house to constitute a burglary. The men overpowered the guards in the money-counting room and made off with $1.2 million in cash and another $1.5 million in checks and securities. All were eventually caught and were sentenced to long prison terms.

In the common law, an essential element of burglary was that it be committed in the nighttime; the intent of this provision was to protect a person sleeping in his house from an intruder who forcibly enters and with the intent to cause damage to persons or property. Common law determined that night was the period of time when a man's face could not be discerned by the light of the sun. The determination of when night began and ended was not a trivialization of the law because, as a felony, the crime of burglary was punished by death. Thus, the time that the crime was committed was of extreme importance.

At the present time some states, including New York, have eliminated the nighttime requirement in the definition of burglary, though most others retain night as an element of an aggravated form or higher degree of burglary, with some changing the common law definition to the period from sunset to sunrise.

As the common law protected habitation, a break and entry into a structure that was not a person's dwelling house such as a barn or mill did not meet the definition of the crime. By statute in just about every jurisdiction, the definition of burglary was expanded to include property crime. Thus, statutes include any type of structure or building or offices therein, including trains, cars, airplanes, and boats, though a burglary of another person's home is still considered more serious; in New York, for example, a burglary where a dwelling is involved raises the crime from third-degree burglary to second-degree burglary.

Case Study: Watergate

On June 17, 1972, a security guard at an apartment and office complex in Washington, D.C., noticed that a door leading from the building garage to the interior had been taped opened and later resealed. The guard called the police, who reported to the scene and discovered five men in the offices of the Democratic National Committee taking pictures and repairing a wiretap. This break-in at the Watergate, which has been referred to as a "third-rate burglary," was the beginning of one of the greatest political scandals of the 20th century, which ultimately led to the resignation of President Richard M. Nixon. While King Henry II's judges may have found the Watergate break-in to be a criminal act, they would never have found it to be a burglary because the offices where the men were apprehended were not a dwelling house of another person.

In discussing whether the acts of the Watergate perpetrators amounted to a burglary, no consideration would be given either in the common law or in today's statutes as to whether the individuals involved were armed with weapons or explosives because such fact is not an element of the basic crime; but such possession, if illegal, would not preclude prosecution for same as a separate crime. However, under the modern view, if burglars are in possession of weapons or explosives at the time of the crime, even if they are not used, it raises the risk and danger of harm to persons and property, so that the degree of burglary is enhanced, resulting in the possibility of greater punishment.

Breaking and Entering

As a shorthand, burglary is many times referred to as breaking and entering. While the breaking element may no longer be necessary under the law, entry remains an essential element of the crime even where the entry is only of a foot or hand of the perpetrator because of the tresspassory nature of the offense. In categorizing the type of entry, many states require that it be an illegal or unauthorized one with the intent to commit a crime. However, at least two states, California and New York, require only that there be an entry with an intent to commit a crime without consideration of whether the entry is authorized.

The New York approach would seem to be more preferable since without a special statute, it covers what the common law of burglary did not: the situation, for example, of a person who knowingly enters a department store lawfully and then unlawfully remains there after closing with the intent formed at the time of the entry to commit a crime such as the stealing of merchandise after the store closes.

In the common law as well as modern law, a burglary had to be of someone else's house or structure unless the possessory interest is split from legal title; for example, a landlord who owns a building could be guilty of burglarizing the apartment of a tenant therein, and in a matrimonial matter, a spouse who obtained a court order for exclusive use and occupancy of the marital home owned by both the husband and wife could have the spouse who was ordered out of the house charged with burglary if that spouse entered or broke and entered the house with the intent of committing a crime inside, such as assaulting the spouse who had the court order.

Intent

Though many elements of the crime of burglary have changed in both nature and scope since the 12th century, one element has remained constant: the intent to commit a crime once inside the dwelling. Thus, a person who breaks and enters and/or enters and remains unlawfully may be guilty of some tresspassory crime such as unlawful entry; but without an intent formed at the time of the entry, it is not a burglary. For proof purposes, intent can be inferred from the circumstances of the entry and conduct thereafter despite any disavowals from the perpetrator. However, once the unlawful entry is made with the requisite intent, the crime is complete regardless of whether the perpetrators then change their minds.

Therefore, if the Brinks or Watergate burglars, after entering the bank building or the Democratic National Committee headquarters, changed their minds and left, taking no money or documents, they could still have been prosecuted for burglary.

Conversely, if an individual were to unlawfully enter a dwelling with the intent to get out of the cold and take a nap, the person may be guilty of some tresspassory offense, but it would not be a burglary. Indeed, even if the individual were to awaken and then decide to steal something from the dwelling, it still would not be a burglary because the intent was not formed at the time of entry. It is also clear that the intent is to commit a criminal act but not necessarily any specific one. Thus, if the perpetrator unlawfully entered the dwelling house of another with the intent to steal jewelry therein, but then rapes the homeowner instead, burglary charges would still apply.

Under present law, most jurisdictions have expanded the intent requirement to include any criminal conduct. Thus, the intent can be for a larceny as at common law, but it also can be for an assault, arson, robbery, or rape. It may not, however, be for antisocial behavior, which does not amount to a crime; therefore, a person who unlawfully enters the dwelling of another with the intent to harass, annoy, or alarm another person is not guilty of burglary.

In the common law definition of burglary, the perpetrator had to have the specific intent to commit larceny, which was at the time defined as the felonious taking of the property of another and against his will with intent to convert it to the use of the taker. It is not unreasonable to assume that since the punishment for burglary and larceny was death, the legal community deliberately narrowed the definition of burglary to avoid the extreme penalty.

Under both common and modern law, the intended crime is not merged into the burglary, so that the perpetrator can be prosecuted for both the burglary and for the crime committed (e.g., larceny, rape, or assault).

A New York City policeman and dog with a man they captured carrying suspected stolen goods in 1912. New York's law was updated in the 1960s so that the basic definition of burglary was expanded to apply to a person who knowingly enters or remains unlawfully in a building with the intent to commit a crime therein, and this definition is now accepted by the majority of states.

Conclusion

The crime of burglary has changed over hundreds of years because of case law and wide interpretation by the courts. In reviewing the development of burglary cases, we understand the need to reshape our system. Burglary as represented here is as serious a crime as ever, and close attention must be paid to the way laws change.

Roslyn Muraskin
Long Island University

See Also: Burglary, Contemporary; Burglary, Sociology of; Common Law Origins of Criminal Law; Felonies; Larceny; Robbery, Contemporary; Robbery, History of; Watergate.

Further Readings

Boba, Rachel. "Burglary at Single-Family Home Construction Sites." U.S. Department of Justice. http://www.cops.usdoj.gov/files/ric/Publications/e08064509.pdf (Accessed September 2011).

Lamm Weisel, Deborah. "Burglary of Single-Family Homes." U.S. Department of Justice. http://www.cops.usdoj.gov/pdf/e07021611.pdf (Accessed September 2011).

Muraskin, Roslyn and Albert Roberts. *Visions for Change: Crime and Justice in the Twenty-First Century*, 5th ed. Upper Saddle River, NJ: Prentice Hall, 2008.

U.S. Department of Justice. "Crime in the United States 2009." http://www2.fbi.gov/ucr/cius2009/index.html (Accessed September 2011).

Burglary, Sociology of

Burglary as a concept is often thought of in terms of the crime it entails, which involves the breaking and entering of another's home or temporarily unoccupied dwelling with the intent of stealing. Yet this simple definition can be limiting, as there are many burglaries that do not involve "breaking," such as those on home construction sites; one-third of all burglaries have taken place when the offender entered through an open door or window in a house, basement, or garage. As a problem, burglary is no more prevalent now than it has been throughout history. In the United States, the number and the rate, respectively, were reported for 2009 as being 2,199,125 and 732.1 per 100,000 people—lower than the previous year. However, additional understanding of the people who commit and are affected by burglary has established the need for a sociology of burglary.

Burglars

The imperative to commit this type of crime is often the money that can be earned from such endeavors. Most burglars are directly inspired by their surroundings and thus often steal from those within their social or business networks. As a society, America has a very low success rate of catching burglars: only 13 percent. This has been attributed as giving established and potential burglars a sense of confidence in their actions and the belief that they will not be caught.

Typically, those who commit burglary are male and young, with most being under 25 and predominantly Caucasian. Evidence suggests that among this population of burglars there is a striking difference socially and skill-wise between those who get caught and those who have been successful and remain undetected, a group set apart from the general description. A burglar puts him/herself in situations that are often premeditated and knows that they are socially unacceptable. Many criminologists have determined that there is a specific type of personality associated with such antisocial behavior; this is referred to as a criminal personality type. Burglars often lack certain deterrence mechanisms that alert them to standard social norms.

Often, a burglar will not restrict him/herself to crimes of burglary but will also commit robberies and varying drug-related crimes. In fact, burglary in some cases has been utilized as a means to fund additional crime or drug/alcohol habits. It has been found that in the United States, crackdowns in heroin trafficking and on abusers also leads to decreases in burglaries. Studies have shown that an increase in the level of crack trafficking and use correlates with lower burglary levels but higher robbery levels. According to the U.S. Department of Justice, burglars have a tendency to be "recidivists: once arrested and convicted, they have the highest rate of further arrests and convictions of all property offenders."

Expertise and Specialization

Burglars can be classified as novice, middle-range, and professional. The novice is generally familiar with the target and has taken into account the visibility, accessibility, and vulnerability to spontaneously make attempts that most often yield minimal gains. The middle-range burglar may be more familiar with certain techniques and use strategizing as a way to guarantee the most successful gains. Professionals will take on more complicated jobs farther from areas they are familiar with.

There are several classifications of burglars, one of which is the home construction site burglar. People who decide to steal from these areas often enjoy a higher success rate as the flow of people, tools, and supplies on these sites is not often strictly regulated. Additionally, the groups of people who are affected by the thievery in these instances are larger and more dispersed as they are housing associations, insurance companies, and house buyers. As a unit, they have less agency and interest in retrieving stolen items, particularly with low-level burglary. The U.S. Department of Justice breaks home construction site burglars into three groups: amateur opportunists, insiders, and professional thieves. Amateur opportunists generally steal less valuable items that require less skill to move; professional thieves do the most damage financially as there is more planning and experience involved.

Victims

Home-site burglary results in little to no psychological damage to the victims as the housing associations, insurance companies, and house buyers usually have little personal attachment with what has been stolen. This is not the case with single- and multifamily homes where becoming a victim of burglary can be psychologically damaging and, depending upon the extent of the burglary, can be a label that carries throughout the life of the victim. Many victims of burglary are often repeat victims, with subsequent offenses occurring within a short time frame after the first.

Single-family homes may be more at risk of burglary than multifamily homes because of their physical separation from others. Another factor is that many homes are unoccupied during the daytime. This is the result of the larger societal transition of women en masse entering the workforce and thus leaving the home for a large portion of the day. In fact, the U.S. Department of Justice reported "in 1961, about 16 percent of residential burglaries occurred in the daytime; by 1995, the proportion of daytime burglaries had risen to 40 percent." This is in contrast to the general assumption that most burglaries occur late at night.

However, there are also those burglaries that occur while there is a member of the household present at the residence. The standard definition of burglary only alludes to the potential for property crime. This is true in 72.4 percent of the cases. Yet 27.6 percent occur while a household member is present, which often leads to additional violent crime. There are three basic scenarios in this situation: (1) the offender intended to harm a specific victim; (2) the offender mistakenly believed that the home was empty; (3) the homeowner returns to find the burglary in progress. It is reported that households of married couples who have no children are the least likely to experience this type of burglary—while single households, both male and female—with children are most likely to experience this, a fact attributed to a balancing of risk assessment and greed because families with children often occupy larger, more appealing dwellings. Furthermore, households that have higher incomes and heads of households that are older than 19 are least likely to experience a home invasion.

The pattern that seems to result when burglaries are committed in more suburban regions is that neighborhoods suddenly hit by a burglary will experience periods of hypervigilance where additional burglar alarms are installed, targets are hardened or entryways in homes are secured, property is marked to make it difficult for a burglar to sell any stolen goods, occupancy indicators are increased to give the impression that someone is present in a home, and initial police response and follow-up investigations are improved. This is less the case in large cities where burglaries are more commonplace.

Despite the fact that certain dynamics of burglary have shifted over time, the burglary rate has remained consistent like that of many other crimes. Therefore, the antisocial personality dynamic that leads to crime generally is a consistent factor within our society irrespective of law enforcement efforts.

Victoria Gonzalez
Rutgers University

See Also: Burglary, Contemporary; Burglary, History of; Crime in America, Types; Felonies; Larceny; Robbery, Sociology of.

Further Readings
Baumer, Eric, Janet L. Lauritsen, Richard Rosenfeld, and Richard Wright. "The Influence of Crack Cocaine on Robbery, Burglary, and Homicide Rates: A Cross-City, Longitudinal Analysis." *Journal of Research in Crime and Delinquency*, v.35/3 (1998).
Harmening, William M. *The Criminal Triad: Psychosocial Development of the Criminal Personality Type*. Springfield, IL: Charles C. Thomas, 2010.
U.S. Department of Justice. "Crime in the United States 2009." http://www2.fbi.gov/ucr/cius2009/index.html (Accessed September 2011).

Bush, George H. W. (Administration of)

George Herbert Walker Bush (1924–) was elected president of the United States in 1988 and served one term in office (1989–93). Before that, he served as vice president under Ronald Reagan from 1981 to 1989. His administration's focus on criminal justice policy largely revolved around advancing the war on drugs that was escalated during the Reagan administration. Like Reagan, Bush viewed drugs as synonymous with crime. While vice president, Bush led a task force on international drug smuggling in an effort to better coordinate federal efforts to reduce the importation of drugs into the country. As president, he escalated the war on drugs, following in Reagan's footsteps. He was the first president to appoint a "drug czar," as mandated by the 1988 Anti-Drug Abuse Act. He also signed into law several significant pieces of crime legislation, including the 1990 Crime Control Act and the Hate Crime Statistics Act.

Bush successfully used the crime issue to defeat Democrat Michael Dukakis in the 1988 general election. Bush was able to paint Dukakis, a former governor of Massachusetts, as soft on crime because of his opposition to the death penalty and a controversial weekend prisoner furlough program that Dukakis oversaw as governor. The furlough program, which allowed approximately 53,000 Massachusetts prisoners to leave prison for a short time in 1987 (mostly for the purpose of beginning to reintegrate into the community before release), was generally successful, with few inmates committing crimes while released. However, Bush highlighted one high-profile case: William Horton, a convicted murderer, raped a woman and stabbed her fiancé while on a weekend furlough. Bush's campaign bombarded viewers with television ads showing "Willie" Horton's picture and describing the crime made possible by Dukakis's furlough program. As a result, Bush was able to exploit this weak spot in the Dukakis campaign and make crime a central issue for voters.

The War on Drugs
As president, Bush was able to successfully raise public concern over the war on drugs. In a televised speech that aired on September 5, 1989, Bush rolled out his campaign to get even "tougher" in the war on drugs. In that speech, he famously held up a bag of crack cocaine that had allegedly been purchased by undercover agents in the park across the street from the White House. He told Americans, "Our most serious problem today is cocaine, and in particular, crack." Because of this speech, as well as a dramatic increase in television coverage of the "drug problem," the Gallup Poll showed a surge in public concern over drugs, with a record 30 percent of Americans naming drugs as the most important problem facing the United States. Even though a *Washington Post* reporter revealed several weeks later that the drug "bust" in front of the White House was staged by federal agents who lured the dealer into the park, the war on drugs proceeded rapidly forward.

Bush appointed William Bennett to be the director of the Office of the National Drug Control Policy; in effect, Bennett became the country's first "drug czar." Bennett, who had been Reagan's secretary of education, was outspoken and embraced media attention. Many of his stances and comments were controversial, including a statement he made on the *Larry King Live* show, saying that a viewer's suggestion of beheading drug dealers was "morally plausible." Bush's drug policy focused more on law enforcement than treatment. His first drug control budget provided more funds for police forces and jail space, in addition to funds to states for developing alternatives to incarceration such as boot camps for nonviolent drug offenders. Bush also expanded border interdiction systems, approving use of the National Guard to help local law enforcement officials in multiple states. Bush's drug policy drew criticism for not focusing enough money on drug treatment and prevention. Bush's administration defended its strategy by claiming that there was not enough money to expand the drug war on all fronts. Bennett left the Bush administration in 1990 and was replaced by former Florida Governor Bob Martinez. Bush's subsequent drug control strategy attempted to increase funding for health initiatives, but the appropriation was taken out of the final drug control budget. Overall, arrests and incarceration rates for drug offenses climbed considerably during Bush's administration.

Other Presidential Achievements
In addition to escalating the war on drugs, Bush focused on several other crime-related initiatives. In 1990, he signed into law the Crime Control Act. This legislation established the Crime Victims' Bill of Rights in the federal judicial system and provided $900 million to assist states with the functioning of their criminal justice systems. Among other things, the bill also enhanced penalties for child pornography. During the same year,

he also signed into law the Gun-Free School Zones Act, which forbade "any individual knowingly to possess a firearm at a place that [he] knows ... is a school zone." The law was eventually declared unconstitutional by the Supreme Court and was therefore voided. An amended version was signed into law in 1995. Another piece of legislation Bush signed into law in 1990 was the Hate Crime Statistics Act, which required the Justice Department to collect and publish data on crimes that "manifest prejudice based on race, religion, sexual orientation, or ethnicity."

Bush appointed two new Supreme Court justices during his administration—David Souter and Clarence Thomas. Thomas proved to be a highly controversial nominee when he was accused of sexual harassment by a former coworker. The Senate ultimately confirmed his appointment in a 52–48 vote. Significant Supreme Court decisions during Bush's administration related to crime and criminal justice include *Texas v. Johnson* (1989), in which the Supreme Court ruled that flag burning was protected under the First Amendment and therefore was not a criminal offense. The decision in *Hudson v. McMillan* (1992) reversed a lower court's ruling that the beating of a prisoner by guards only constitutes "cruel and unusual punishment" if the prisoner is "significantly" injured. The court decided that any "wanton and unnecessary infliction of pain" was cruel and unusual punishment. Thomas, who was one of two dissenters in the ruling (the other was Antonin Scalia) argued that prisoners who are beaten by guards are not protected under the Eighth Amendment.

Bush lost his reelection bid to Arkansas Governor Bill Clinton. While Bush was able to effectively use crime as an issue in his first election, he downplayed it in the 1992 election, possibly because he did not have the powerful crime symbol (Willie Horton) that he had before. As a result, Clinton was able to gain the upper hand in the crime issue, along with many other issues that voters felt were important.

Jennifer Murphy
Elizabeth Rae Pierson
California State University, Sacramento

See Also: Drug Abuse and Addiction, History of; Prisoner's Rights; Sentencing.

Further Readings
Greene, John Robert. *The Presidency of George Bush*. Lawrence: University Press of Kansas, 2000.
Oliver, Willard M. *The Law and Order Presidency*. Upper Saddle River, NJ: Prentice Hall, 2003.
Simon, Jonathan. *Governing Through Crime*. New York: Oxford University Press, 2007.

Bush, George W. (Administration of)

George W. Bush was the 43rd president of the United States, serving from 2001 to 2009. Bush defeated Al Gore in the closely contested 2000 presidential election, which was highlighted by the controversy surrounding the Electoral College votes in the state of Florida. As president, Bush was able to appoint many conservative judges to the federal bench, including John Roberts as the chief justice of the U.S. Supreme Court. However, the terrorist attacks of September 11, 2001, and the subsequent war on terror largely defined his presidency.

September 11 and the War on Terror

On September 11, 2001, 19 members of Al Qaeda crashed three civilian airliners into the Twin Towers of the World Trade Center in New York City and the Pentagon in Washington, D.C., killing almost 3,000 civilians. President Bush immediately announced that the United States was engaged in a "war on terror." His administration immediately took several steps designed to secure the United States from further attacks and to retaliate against Al Qaeda. Putting the United States on a war footing was an important part of the Bush administration's response to the attacks. Historically, wartime presidents have enjoyed a considerable degree to freedom when exercising their Article II commander in chief powers. By couching the government's responses to the September 11 attacks in terms of it being a "war," the administration hoped to receive substantial deference to its preferred antiterrorism policies. Some of President Bush's legal advisers, such as Office of Legal Counsel official John Yoo, were of the

President George W. Bush and Texas Governor Rick Perry face the media at a news conference in the aftermath of Hurricanes Katrina and Rita in Port Arthur, Texas, on September 27, 2005. That same year, Bush appointed the conservative Supreme Court Chief Justice John Roberts; this was followed by the appointment of Justice Samuel Alito in January 2006.

opinion that there were few, if any, limits on how the president could respond to the ongoing terrorist threat. This stance became highly controversial when it became clear that the Bush administration had used it as legal justification for many of its secret and most controversial programs.

On September 14, 2001, Congress passed the Authorization to Use Military Force (AUMF). The AUMF, which remains in effect, even after the death of Osama nin Laden, is a vague, open-ended grant of power articulating congressional support for the president's efforts to pursue those who helped commit the September 11 attacks. The president was also given the power to use military force to prevent future terrorist acts against the United States if/when needed. Later that fall, the United States launched attacks against Taliban and Al Qaeda forces in Afghanistan. The military effort in Afghanistan against these groups continued into the presidency of Barack Obama and remain ongoing as of 2011. In the spring of 2003, the Bush administration also launched a military campaign against Iraq premised on the argument that Saddam Hussein possessed weapons of mass destruction that could be used against the United States. The initial conflict was brief, and the United States and its coalition allies occupied Iraq and captured Saddam Hussein. However, no weapons of mass destruction were ever found. The continued occupation of Iraq and attempts to transition it to a functioning democracy occupied much of President Bush's second term in office. It was a difficult process marked by uneven progress and divisions among the various political factions in Iraq.

On October 26, 2001, Congress passed the USA PATRIOT Act, legislation designed to provide President Bush with enhanced tools to fight terrorists. The act made it easier for government to access e-mail, telephone, and financial records of suspected terrorists. It also expanded government surveillance powers and allowed government agencies to more readily share information. Although it easily passed both chambers of Congress, the PATRIOT Act soon became a focal point of Bush administration critics who argued that the act went too far and that it infringed on the constitutional rights of Americans. Despite these criticisms, the act—even its more controversial provisions—has been reauthorized several times, most recently by President Barack Obama in May 2011.

The Bush administration also unilaterally enacted a number of controversial antiterrorism policies. Some of these policies were public, but others were less so. As the fighting began in Afghanistan, the administration recognized that it would need a place to detain those captured by U.S. forces. As a result, the administration designated the American naval base at Guantanamo Bay, Cuba, as a primary detention facility for suspected terrorists. The use of the Guantanamo facility and the questionable treatment of many detainees there sparked harsh domestic and international criticism from those who believed that the United States was violating international law by engaging in torture. It later came to light that many detainees in U.S. custody, most notably those in Iraq's Abu Ghraib prison, suffered from extensive abuse. While acknowledging some problems, the Bush administration stood firm and continued to insist that many of its more controversial interrogation techniques such as waterboarding (a technique in which water is poured over a person's face to simulate drowning) did not amount to torture.

Shortly after September 11, 2001, the Bush administration also implemented what later became known as the Terrorist Surveillance Program (TSP). This secret program allowed executive branch agencies to engage in electronic surveillance of suspected terrorists without warrants or any judicial supervision. Many critics argued that this program was an attempt to circumvent legislative and judicial oversight. They also claimed that it violated the Federal Intelligence Surveillance Act (FISA), the legislation designed to regulate the collection of foreign intelligence by the U.S. government. The program was eventually discontinued after its existence became public. Still, the administration defended its secret program, arguing that FISA didn't provide the needed speed and flexibility in the war on terror. The government sometimes needed to move quickly, officials argued, and the TSP allowed agencies to do just that.

Eventually, many of the Bush administration's controversial programs were challenged in federal court, and the U.S. Supreme Court handed down several decisions on their constitutionality. In *Hamdi v. Rumsfeld* (2004), the court held that the AUMF authorized the president to detain terror suspects as enemy combatants (even American citizens) but that suspects had the right to due process and the ability to challenge this "enemy combatant" designation before a neutral tribunal. In *Rasul v. Bush* (2004), the court ruled that Guantanamo detainees had the right to challenge their detention in U.S. federal court despite the fact that they were not technically being held on U.S. soil. In a related case, *Hamdan v. Rumsfeld* (2006), the court also struck down the system of military tribunals used to try many of the Guantanamo detainees, a system that had been unilaterally established by the Bush administration shortly after 9/11. Congress responded to the *Hamdan* decision by passing the Military Commissions Act of 2006, again authorizing Guantanamo detainees to be tried via military commission.

Even after leaving office, President Bush and Vice President Richard Cheney were adamant that their antiterrorism policies were the right course of action for the United States. Far from being apologetic of their actions, they steadfastly proclaimed that they would take same actions if they had to do it all over again. In his first days in office, President Barack Obama quickly repudiated a number of the Bush administration antiterrorism policies, issuing executive orders designed to close the detention facility at Guantanamo Bay and rejecting many of the harsh interrogation methods used by the Bush administration.

George W. Bush and the Federal Courts

During his eight years in office, George W. Bush had the opportunity to appoint more than 300 judges to all levels of the federal bench. President Bush also appointed two justices to the U.S. Supreme Court. In 2005, District of Columbia Circuit Court Judge John Roberts was nominated to replace Chief Justice William Rehnquist, who had died after a battle with thyroid cancer. That same summer, Justice Sandra Day O'Conner also resigned, allowing Bush to appoint Judge Samuel Alito to her position on the court. Despite these successes, Bush faced significant opposition from Democrats in the U.S. Senate on a number of his other appellate court nominees. Democrats charged that his nominees were "radically conservative" and out of the "judicial mainstream" of thought. Several were filibustered, which caused a handful of nominees to withdraw from consideration altogether. Eventually, a bipartisan group of senators called the "Gang of 14" reached an agreement that allowed most of Bush's judicial nominees to receive votes on the Senate floor and be confirmed.

The Roberts Court has issued a number of rulings that have pleased political conservatives. Two of the more notable ones touch on right to bear arms. In *District of Columbia v. Heller* (2008), the court struck down a Washington, D.C., ordinance banning firearms in the home and requiring weapons to be disassembled or otherwise disabled with mechanisms such as trigger locks. The court ruled that the Second Amendment protects the right of an individual—unconnected to any service in the militia—to possess a firearm in one's own house for the purpose of self-defense. Two years later, the court took the significant step of incorporating the Second Amendment, applying it to the states in *MacDonald v. Chicago* (2010). While the court left some issues unresolved, the fact that it recognized that the Second Amendment contained an individual right to own firearms was an important victory for advocates of gun rights.

Darren A. Wheeler
Ball State University

See Also: 2001 to 2012 Primary Documents; Homeland Security; Terrorism; Torture; USA PATRIOT Act of 2001.

Further Readings
Bush, George W. *Decision Points*. New York: Crown Publishing, 2010.
Maranto, Robert, et al. *Judging Bush* (*Studies in the Modern Presidency*). Palo Alto, CA: Stanford University Press, 2009.
Woodward, Robert. *Bush at War*. New York: Simon & Schuster, 2002.

Byrnes, Thomas

A famous New York City detective, police chief, and author, Thomas Byrnes was born in Ireland and immigrated to the United States as an infant. He grew up in New York's Fifth Ward along the Hudson River. He briefly served in the Civil War with Ellsworth's Zouaves, returned to New York, and joined the police force in 1863. Byrnes quickly rose through the ranks: He was appointed roundsman in 1868, sergeant in 1869, captain in 1870, inspector and chief of detectives in 1880, and superintendent of police from 1892 to 1895. Known for his charisma and strong personality, Byrnes exemplified the evolution of New York's detective force from an untrained group of watchmen to a disciplined military-like organization. Byrnes instituted a variety of high-profile reforms.

In 1880, Byrnes opened detective offices at 17 Wall St. and in the New York Stock Exchange Building in order to monitor and arrest thieves and pickpockets in the city's business district who preyed on bank messenger boys, depositors, and others cashing checks. Byrnes then established the "dead line"—any known thief or pickpocket found south of Fulton or Liberty streets was "dead" and the police could arrest him on sight. Aggressive enforcement of the dead line transformed street life in lower Manhattan. Crime dropped, and Byrnes became a hero among New York businessmen. His success convinced President-elect Grover Cleveland to place him in charge of presidential security during the 1885 inauguration ceremonies in Washington, D.C.

Byrnes also created a system of municipal espionage during the 1880s. His detectives infiltrated and monitored leisure resorts in the tenderloin nightlife district along Broadway and Sixth Avenue. He expanded and enlarged the "rogues' gallery," a photographic collection of criminal suspects posted on public display at the central police headquarters in Manhattan. He required pickpockets and other "professional criminals" traveling through New York to "register" with him and avoid any criminal activity while in the city. Before major parades, Byrnes's detectives waited in railroad depots and ferry stations in Jersey City, Hoboken, and New York and detained any suspected criminal. Defenders of Byrnes claimed that he was responsible for transforming New York's

Two detectives study portraits in the police "rogues' gallery" in July 1909. Thomas Byrnes improved and expanded this photographic collection of criminal suspects displayed at the New York City police headquarters in Manhattan.

detective force into an unparalleled crime-fighting organization, surpassing even London's Scotland Yard. Concerns about civil liberties mattered little to Byrnes. He was associated with harsh methods of criminal interrogation, often referred to as "the third degree" (some erroneously claimed Byrnes invented the tactic). Although Byrnes admitted to physically assaulting suspects at times, he insisted that the use of corporal punishment, sleep deprivation, and the denial of food and water were short-sighted and usually ineffective. "The 'third degree,'" he told reporter Frank Marshall White, "should be a psychic rather than a physical process."

After Allan Pinkerton, Byrnes was the most influential crime writer in the 19th-century United States. In 1886, he published *Professional Criminals in America*, an illustrated compendium of the leading underworld figures at the time. In 1891, he coauthored *Darkness and Daylight: or, Lights and Shadows of New York Life* with Helen Campbell and Thomas W. Knox. Byrnes even became the subject of story papers and melodramas, best exemplified by Julian Hawthorne's five novels allegedly "from the diary of Inspector Byrnes."

Byrnes was appointed New York City police superintendent in 1892, but immediately came under attack from the Rev. Charles Parkhurst and various reform groups. Byrnes responded by transferring precinct captains, instigating formal charges of corruption against certain inspectors and captains, and raiding brothels and gambling dens. These actions never placated Byrnes's critics. Byrnes testified before the Lexow Committee investigating municipal malfeasance in 1894 and not only admitted that the police department suffered from corruption but also that he personally profited from his position. He described how he turned $12,000 of savings into $300,000 with advice from Jay Gould and Cornelius Vanderbilt. Shortly thereafter, Theodore Roosevelt was appointed president of the New York City Board of Police and Byrnes resigned on May 27, 1895. Byrnes became an officer in the United States Casualty Co. after he left the force. He dabbled in real estate in New York and New Jersey, while occasionally providing law enforcement advice to police officials and New York City mayors. He died of stomach cancer in his home at 318 West 77th Street in New York on May 7, 1910.

Timothy J. Gilfoyle
Loyola University Chicago

See Also: Detection and Detectives; Interrogation Practices; New York; Professionalization of Police; Reform, Police and Enforcement; Roosevelt, Theodore (Administration of).

Further Readings
Byrnes, Thomas. *Professional Criminals of America.* New York: D. W. Dillingham, 1895.
Gilfoyle, Timothy J. *A Pickpocket's Tale: The Underworld of Nineteenth-Century New York.* New York: W. W. Norton, 2006.
White, Frank Marshall. "Inspector Byrnes and the Third Degree." *Harper's Weekly* (June 18, 1910).

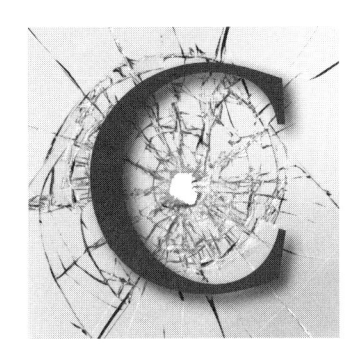

California

California is the third-largest U.S. state by area and the largest by population. The population of California in 2010 was 37,253,956, a 10 percent increase from 2000. California has an ethnically diverse population that is 57.6 percent white, 13 percent Asian, and 6.2 percent African American, with smaller numbers of other ethnic groups and people reporting multiple ethnicities; 37.6 percent of the population identified themselves as Hispanic or Latino (a person of any race can be of Hispanic or Latino origin), 26.8 percent were foreign born, and 42.2 percent spoke a language other than English at home. The median household income in 2009 was $58,925 (above the U.S. average), and 14.2 percent lived below the poverty line (comparable to the U.S. average).

Early History

Numerous Native American tribes lived in the area now known as California before the arrival of the Europeans. Many resisted the arrival of European settlers beginning in the 16th century, and the first colonizers, the Spanish, used military force to establish and sustain their missions in California. Several armed revolts against the missions were documented in the 18th century, as were the assassinations of several priests by Native Americans, before the mission system collapsed in the 19th century. However, the Native Americans suffered far more than the Europeans, with their numbers declining about 50 percent between the arrival of the Europeans and annexation of California by the United States at the conclusion of the Mexican–American War in 1848.

The California Gold Rush, which began after gold was discovered at Sutter's Mill in north central California in 1848, caused a huge increase in California's population, particularly in San Francisco, which was the official port of entry by sea for the state. Most of the gold mining claims were on public land, and as California was essentially without government other than that provided by military commanders, miners adapted a variety of codes governing issues such as the rights to a particular claim.

In 1850, California became a state, and one of its earliest pieces of legislation was the somewhat ironically named Act for the Government and Protection of Indians, which, among other things, devalued the legal testimony of Native Americans against whites, prohibited them from buying alcohol, and established the legal basis for kidnapping and enslaving Native Americans. Another early law required foreign miners to pay an onerous tax ($20 per month, when a good claim might produce $16 per day), an act specifically implemented to discourage or prevent Chinese, Mexicans, and other migrants from placing claims, a practice already in place before statehood. In 1854, the California State Supreme Court ruled that Chinese people, as well as African Americans and Native Americans, did not have the right to testify in court against whites. Chinese immigrants were also resented by white laborers, who saw them as economic competition; racist attacks on Chinese occurred regularly. The so-called Anti-Coolie Act (officially An Act to Protect Free White Labor Against Competition with Chinese Coolie Labor, and to Discourage the Immigration of the Chinese into the State of California) passed by the California legislature in 1862 imposed a tax of $2.50 per day on Chinese who worked in the mines or in any business. Tensions increased with the completion of the transcontinental railroad in 1869 because the thousands of Chinese who had been working on it joined the labor pool. In 1882, the United States passed the Chinese Exclusion Act (it was not repealed until 1943, by the Magnuson Act), which excluded Chinese immigrants from U.S. citizenship, made it difficult for immigrants to leave the United States and re-enter, and excluded Chinese laborers and miners from immigrating to the United States.

Police and Policing

The first statewide law enforcement agency in California was the California State Rangers, established in May 1853 to capture or kill Joaquin Murrieta, a Mexican bandit and his gang, known as the Five Joaquins. Murrieta was killed in July 1853, and the Rangers disbanded shortly thereafter. The California State Police (CSP) was founded in 1887 to protect state agencies, the governor, and the capitol building. The state police also patrolled the aqueduct systems, performed tax seizures, and provided investigative services. The California Highway Patrol (CHP)

The California Highway Patrol is sometimes called upon to assist local police in disasters and emergencies. These California Highway Patrol mobile field force officers performed annual training in crowd dispersal methods using smoke canisters at the Marine Corps Air Ground Combat Center in Twentynine Palms, California, on November 9, 2011.

was created in 1929 to enforce traffic laws on county and state highways with the goal of promoting safe and efficient use of the highway traffic system. The CHP also provides disaster and lifesaving assistance and assists in emergencies that are beyond the capacity of local authorities. By World War II, the CHP consisted of more than 700 uniformed officers. In 1947, the state established the Department of the California Highway Patrol, headed by a commissioner. The CHP was merged with the California State Police in 1995 and today has many responsibilities beyond those stated in the original mandate, including inspecting buses and trucks, educating the public about safety issues, and protecting the governor, state property, state employees, and visiting dignitaries.

As the population of California has increased (from 15.7 million in 1960 to 37 million in 2009), so have the number of crimes generally increased. Looked at in terms of the rate of different crimes per 100,000 population, it can be seen that the amount of crime relative to population has fluctuated over this period, changes attributed to various causes, including the crack epidemic that hit much of the United States in the 1980s, changes in policing patterns, passage of the three strikes laws that kept many criminals incarcerated and by definition not committing crimes in the civilian world, and (more controversially) changes in abortion laws that meant that fewer unwanted children were born in the socioeconomic classes mostly likely to commit violent crimes. In 1960, California had 3.9 murders per 100,000; in 1970, 6.9 per 100,000; in 1980, 14.5 per 100,000; in 1990, 11.9 per 100,000; in 2000, 6.1 per 100,000; and in 2009, 5.3 per 100,000. The rates of total violent crime (of which murders make up a small proportion) follows a slightly different pattern: in 1960 there were 239 violent crimes per 100,000 population; 474.8 per 100,000 in 1970; 893.6 per 100,000 in 1980; 1045.2 per 100,000 in 1990; 621.6 per 100,000 in 2000; and 436.6 per 100,000 in 2009. Of course, in any year the number of crimes reported varies widely by location: In 2009, Los Angeles County had 6.7 homicides per 100,000 while Ventura County (also in southern California) had a homicide rate almost 50 percent lower at 3.4 per 100,000.

Political Protest and Free Speech

In 1919, the California legislature passed the Criminal Syndicalism Act, which prohibited individuals from acting or organizing in ways intended to overthrow the government (many other states had similar laws at the time). In 1922 Anita Whitney was convicted under this act for her role in establishing the Communist Labor Party. She claimed that the act violated her right to due process and equal protection and appealed to the U.S. Supreme Court, which in 1927 ruled that the law was constitutional, declaring that the state had the right to control and punish those whose speech was intended to incite crime, disturb the peace, or threaten established government. However, this judgment was overruled in a later Supreme Court decision, *Brandenburg v. Ohio* (1969), in which the court ruled that speech could not be prohibited or punished unless it was judged likely to incite immediate lawless action.

The University of California, Berkeley (UCB), was a center of political protest in the 1960s, and the free speech movement was founded on the UCB campus in 1964. Some of the organizers had participated in civil rights actions in the south and questioned practices on their own campus, including the fact that faculty were required to take a loyalty oath and that political advocacy and fund-raising by students was severely restricted. In December 1964, a sit-in (a tactic borrowed from the civil rights movement) protesting the arrest of Jack Weinberg (a former student who had been sitting at a table soliciting donations for the Council of Racial Equality) took place in Sproul Hall and was the site of a famous speech by Mario Savio that advocated that students stop the "machine" of society. Hundreds of students were arrested, although they were released a few hours later, and UCB rules were revised to allow more political activity and discussion on campus.

In the following years, the UCB campus was the site of many protests against the Vietnam War, including a teach-in held in May 1965 attended by about 30,000 people. UCB students also participated in antiwar demonstrations off campus, including a May 5 march to the Berkeley Draft Board bearing a black coffin and numerous protests that included young men publicly burning their draft cards. Deliberately destroying or mutilating a draft card was made a criminal act in

1965 and, in the 1968 decision *United States v. O'Brien*, the U.S. Supreme Court ruled that the prohibition was not a violation of free speech.

More recently, students and some faculty at several branches of the University of California gathered in 2009 to protest a 32 percent increase in undergraduate tuition (pushing costs to more than $10,000 annually) as well as cuts in staff. Most of the demonstrations were peaceful, although some students were arrested for conducting sit-ins (at UCB, the University of California, Davis, and the University of California, Santa Cruz, among others), and a protest outside the home of the UCB chancellor resulted in property damage and eight arrests. Although the demonstrations drew publicity about the price hikes, they were not successful in rolling them back due to the California budget crisis.

Three Strikes and Drug Laws

California passed one of the nation's first "three strikes" laws in 1994 (Proposition 184), which specified life imprisonment for offenders convicted of three felonies. This law was amended in 2000 (Proposition 36) so that certain nonviolent drug offenders could receive probation and mandated treatment rather than incarceration. Another amendment (Proposition 66) to the three strikes law failed in 2004; it would have required the "third strike" to be a serious violent crime (not all felonies meet this definition). There is no general agreement on the usefulness of three strikes laws in reducing crime and whether other measures could achieve better results at lower cost. California also has tough laws regarding parole violations: A 2007 study found that parole violations were the reason for nearly two-thirds of prison admissions.

The three strikes law and severe enforcement of parole regulations contributed to overcrowding in California's prisons. About 25 percent of California's prisoners are serving extended sentences for second or third offenses, which are punished more severely under the three strikes law than first offenses. On May 23, 2011, the U.S. Supreme Court ruled in a 5–4 decision (*Brown v. Plata*) that the prison conditions were so bad they constituted cruel and unusual punishment, a violation of the Eighth Amendment to the U.S. Constitution. The majority decision cited the overcrowding and lack of medical and mental healthcare as causing needless suffering and death and ordered state officials to reduce the prison population to 110,000 (still 137.5 percent of capacity) from the 2011 level of more than 140,000. The state was given two years to accomplish this reduction, which Governor Jerry Brown stated he intended to do by moving nonviolent inmates and those convicted of relatively minor crimes into county facilities, with the state subsidizing the counties for the costs of incarcerating these inmates.

California opened its first adult drug court in 1991 and juvenile offender drug court in 1995. These courts have several goals, including providing treatment rather than incarceration for drug and alcohol offenses, integrating drug treatment with other rehabilitation services, reducing the number of children in the welfare system, and reducing the social costs of drug and alcohol abuse. Typically, possession offenders who complete the court-ordered treatment program are discharged without a criminal record.

California has allowed the use of medical marijuana since 2003. Patients or their caregivers are required to obtain a recommendation from their physician and are then issued a Medical Marijuana Identification Card, which allows them to purchase marijuana legally. As of 2011, 53,378 cards have been issued: 46,972 to patients and 5,697 to caregivers. Nonmedical use of marijuana has been somewhat decriminalized in California: Gift or possession of 28.5 grams or less is treated as an infraction carrying a fine of $100, while possession of larger amounts is a misdemeanor carrying a sentence of six months incarceration and a fine of $500.

Sarah Boslaugh
Kennesaw State University

See Also: 1851 to 1900 Primary Documents; *Brandenburg v. Ohio*; Chinese Americans; Chinese Exclusion Act of 1882; *Griffin v. California*; Hispanic Americans; *Hurtado v. California*; Native Americans; Racism; Three Strikes Law; *Whitney v. California*.

Further Readings

California Department of Public Health. "Medical Marijuana Program." http://www.cdph.ca.gov/programs/mmp/Pages/Medical%20Marijuana%20Program.aspx (Accessed June 2011).

California Native American Heritage Commission. "Short Overview of California Indian History." http://www.nahc.ca.gov/califindian.html (Accessed June 2011).

Dolan, Jack and Carol J. Williams. "No Easy Fix for California's Prison Crisis." *Los Angeles Times* (May 25, 2011). http://articles.latimes.com/2011/may/25/local/la-me-prisons-20110525 (Accessed June 2011).

Library of Congress. "The Chinese in California, 1859–1925." http://memory.loc.gov/ammem/award99/cubhtml/cichome.html (Accessed June 2011).

Liptak, Adam. "Justices, 5–4, Tell California to Cut Prisoner Population." *New York Times* (May 23, 2011). http://www.nytimes.com/2011/05/24/us/24scotus.html (Accessed June 2011).

University of California Berkeley Library. "The Pacifica Radio/UC Berkeley Social Activity Sound Recording Project: Anti-Vietnam War Protests in the San Francisco Bay Area and Beyond." http://www.lib.berkeley.edu/MRC/pacificaviet.html (Accessed June 2011).

Camden, New Jersey

Camden is a city in southern New Jersey that was incorporated in 1828. The city serves as the county seat of Camden County. Camden is situated near Philadelphia, Pennsylvania, and the Delaware River and has a population of roughly 77,344. Camden County was initially settled by the Dutch West India Company in 1626 at a time when the Dutch and Swedish competed for control of the fur trade in the region. The settlement of a Quaker colony at Philadelphia in 1682 encouraged trade between Camden (located in what was then West Jersey) and Pennsylvania through the introduction of ferries that helped to facilitate transportation, making Camden an important hub in the Philadelphia region for more than 100 years. The Port of Camden developed on the eastern shore of the Delaware River in New Jersey opposite the Port of Philadelphia.

The development of the Industrial Revolution in America through the 19th century brought railroads such as the Camden and Amboy Railroad and industries such as shipping, shipbuilding, food canning, and the manufacture of phonographs. Campbell Soup Company (1869), the New York Shipbuilding Corporation (1869), and RCA Victor (1901) were based in Camden during the height of the industrial era in the United States. Camden became a thriving industrial city in the early decades of the 20th century, with an expanding population, connected by transportation links to both Philadelphia and New York City.

Since World War II, Camden has been a city marred by the ravages of deindustrialization, high unemployment, poverty, crime, and urban decay despite more recent attempts at revitalization. Modern Camden is at the center of the social history of crime and punishment in the United States. Crime or some form of mismanagement has been documented at nearly every level in the city, including the police department, school system, and government. Three mayors have been jailed for corruption (the most recent in 2000) while the school system and the police department have both been made subject to state takeover amid the rise of violent crime. This has led some to label Camden as either a "failed" or "dysfunctional" city. Camden has been routinely listed as one of the most violent cities in the United States since the late 20th century. The social history of crime and punishment in Camden may be explained through a discussion of the changes in economics, industry, society, and politics from postwar deindustrialization to the present.

Economy and Industry

The economy and industry of Camden have been shaped by the geographic positioning of the city. Camden is located between two key waterways: the Delaware and Cooper rivers. This prime area facilitated the growth of the ferry system in and around Camden at places such as Coopers Point on Market Street, Federal Street, and Ferry Street from the late 17th century through the early 19th century. Some of the earliest buildings erected in Camden emerged first around the ferry industry, including taverns, hotels, and companies such as the Coopers Point Hotel built by Samuel Cooper in 1770 near Delaware Avenue. The ferries helped to connect Camden to emergent cities (such as Philadelphia and New York) and major towns in South Jersey. Industrial development through the

19th century brought improvements in transportation, urbanization, new immigrants, and manufacturing industries to Camden.

The railroads were a vital feature of industrial growth and development in 19th-century Camden. One of the first railroads in the United States, the Camden and Amboy Railroad, was built by inventor Robert L. Stevens (1787–1856) in New Jersey during the 1830s. This was the first railroad in New Jersey and the first railroad in the United States to connect major cities; it was built more than three decades before the Pacific Railroad connected Mississippi to California. The Camden and Amboy Railroad was followed by the Camden and Atlantic Railroad in the 1850s, bringing new business and passengers to the Camden ferries.

The rise of business and industry came with the railroads. In 1860, there were 80 manufacturers in Camden; by 1870, that number had risen to 125. Joseph Wharton's Camden Metal Works (American Nickel Works) began production in 1862 in Camden and served as a major supplier of nickel to the U.S. Mint for the manufacture of coins. In 1869, Joseph Campbell and Archibald Anderson formed a partnership to develop a canning factory that later came to be known as the Campbell Soup Corporation. Some other successful Camden businesses at the time included Henry Bottomley's Camden Woolen Mill, the Coopers Point Iron Works, and the New York Shipbuilding Corporation. New York Shipbuilding at its height in Camden employed 40,000 workers. In 1901, the Victor Talking Machine Company (RCA Victor) emerged in Camden and eventually became the world's largest manufacturer of phonographs and phonograph records for much of the early 20th century, employing 10,000 in Camden.

Though the Campbell Soup Corporation continues to make Camden its world headquarters, post–World War II Camden has suffered economically. The decline of industry and white flight from the city have contributed to its economic downfall. Currently, two of every five residents in Camden live below the national poverty line. Camden spends an estimated $17,000 per student per year in the Camden school district, yet only two-thirds of these students actually graduate high school. By 2006, Camden was listed as one of the poorest cities in the United States, with a large majority of residents living under the poverty line. The median household income in Camden was estimated at $18,000 in 2000, and in 2009, the unemployment rate was recorded at roughly 17 percent. The lack of economic opportunity as compounded by a crippling poverty has contributed to the changing sociopolitical landscape and the rise of crime in the city.

Society and Politics

Camden has a multiethnic and multiracial social history. The Lenni Lenape were the Native American inhabitants of the region. They engaged in hunting and gathering activities until their numbers began to dwindle because of European encroachment, disease, and the depletion of natural resources. The first European settlers were the Dutch, English, and Irish through the 1600s and 1700s. The ferry sites, including Daniel's Ferry,

A carpenter finishing a wooden radio cabinet in an RCA Victor factory in Camden, New Jersey, in 1937. In the early 20th century, RCA Victor employed 10,000 workers in 23 Camden factories.

Samuel Cooper's Ferry, and Roberts Ferry, served a vigorous Delaware River slave-trading business through the 1700s. German, Polish, and Italian immigrants came to the area through the 19th century. The rise of cities and urbanization contributed to a dramatic period of growth in Camden's history between 1870 and 1920, with the population increasing from 20,000 to 116,000. Immigrants from Italy and eastern Europe began to dominate the city in the 1920s, coupled with the Great Migration of African Americans to northern cities. Once teeming with a mixture of mostly British, Irish, and German migrants, modern Camden is primarily a city of African Americans (45 percent), Hispanics (43 percent), and foreign-born immigrants from places such as the West Indies and the Dominican Republic. In terms of politics, though it was once significantly Republican, Camden is a place that has become recognized as a stronghold of the Democratic Party.

The same industries that brought immigrants to Camden during the 19th century have now drained middle-class communities out of Camden, with key businesses having withdrawn from the city, in decline, or simply relocated elsewhere during the 20th century. RCA Victor, once maintaining 23 of its 25 factories inside Camden, was no longer headquartered in Camden after 1929. The New York Shipbuilding Corporation no longer made Camden home after 1967.

Camden has been operating under a mayor-council form of government since the 1960s, and in 1994, the council members were no longer elected at large. Instead, the city was divided into four districts, with one council member elected from each district. Mayor Milton Milan was jailed for corruption in 2000.

Crime and Punishment
Crime and punishment in Camden took a violent turn in the postindustrial era after World War II with the decline of industry and the rise of poverty. In fact, the first single episode of mass murder in U.S. history occurred in Camden. Howard Unruh, an unemployed World War II veteran, killed 13 of his neighbors in 12 minutes during a random killing spree that took place on September 6, 1949. Unruh was subsequently found not subject to criminal prosecution by reason of insanity and was sent to the New Jersey Hospital for the Insane (now Trenton Psychiatric Hospital), where he died in 2009 at age 88. Both the Trenton Psychiatric Hospital and the Riverfront State Prison have been instrumental institutions of punishment for Camden's criminals. The Riverfront State Prison was opened on Camden's north side in 1985 and closed in 2009 to make way for new commercial development along the waterfront. In 2002, Camden was ranked the third most dangerous city in the United States, and in two consecutive years, 2004 and 2005, Camden had the dubious distinction of being the most dangerous city in the United States, a milestone it reached again in 2009. The designation of "most dangerous city" is based on the statistics for violent crimes such as murder, rape, robbery, and assault.

Camden has experienced a high incidence of crime or impropriety in society, government, the police department, and education system. The rise of crime in Camden is directly linked to deindustrialization and the rise of poverty. Nearly a third or more of the city's residents live below the poverty line. Social scientists have long made the link between high rates of poverty and crime. Working and middle-class families began to abandon the city for places such as Cherry Hill once railroads, electric trolleys, and highways began to serve as avenues into the suburbs and out of the city. This was coupled with the mass decline of industry as compounded by racial tensions in the late 1960s, culminating in the Camden Riots in 1971. Several days of violence occurred in 1969 in response to rumors that an African American girl had been beaten by a white cop; in 1971, the actual beating death of a Puerto Rican motorist led to days of violent civil unrest through August. The two white police officers charged with the beating death of the motorist (Rafael Rodriguez Gonzales) were subsequently acquitted of manslaughter by a jury.

In the 1990s, less than 10,000 of the 50,000 manufacturing jobs brought by businesses such as RCA and New York Shipbuilding remained in Camden, and in the 2000s, Camden began to acquire a notorious reputation as the crime capital of America. The Port of Camden (South Jersey Port Corporation) has been under scrutiny for alleged improprieties and the school system and police departments of Camden remain under a state takeover. By 2003, according to

Revitalization plans in Camden, New Jersey, which averaged one of the highest crime rates in the United States in the late 2000s, include waterfront projects, new upscale housing and commercial developments, and Urban Enterprise Zones. This sign marked the site of an American Recovery and Reinvestment Act Project near a partially abandoned row of houses in inner-city Camden in March 2011.

the Federal Bureau of Investigation (FBI) report "Offenders Known to Law Enforcement," Camden had surpassed the national average in nearly every arena of violent crime several times over, including murder (6.69 times the national average), rape (1.9 times the national average), robbery (4.8 times the national average), and aggravated assault. In 2008, Camden had the highest crime rate in the United States with 2,333 violent crimes per 100,000 people (the national average was 455 per 100,000 at this time). The 2011 layoff of nearly 50 percent of Camden's police force has led to a rise in arson, burglary, rape, and aggravated assault.

Revitalization
The post–World War II industrial decline of Camden has given way to a vast revitalization plan despite the rising crime statistics. Major employers in the city include the Campbell Soup Corporation, the City of Camden, Rutgers University, the state of New Jersey, and Cooper University Hospital. The Port of Camden, with terminals at Beckett Street and Broadway and access to the Atlantic Ocean, continues to handle both international and national bulk cargo. The Campbell Soup Corporation's Campbell's Field is home to the minor league baseball team known as the Camden River Sharks and is situated on the waterfront along the Delaware River. This area also includes the Adventure Aquarium, the Susquehanna Bank Center, and the floating museum USS *New Jersey*. Some sections of Camden have also been designated as Urban Enterprise Zones to encourage redevelopment. There are also redevelopment plans in the works to produce upscale housing and more commercial businesses.

The city of Camden has undergone profound changes in its history. This is evident in the social, economic, and industrial past, including the rise of crime and punishment. Camden was once the industrial capital of New Jersey in many respects with ferries, railroads, electric trolleys, and thriving corporations. There is no doubt that Camden has harshly weathered the fate of deindustrialization, not unlike other great cities in the American experience.

Hettie V. Williams
Monmouth University

See Also: Crime Rates; New Jersey; Newark, New Jersey; Riots; Urbanization.

Further Readings
Anderson, Elijah. *Code of the Street: Decay, Violence, and the Moral Life of the City*. New York: W. W. Norton, 2000.
Baisden, Cheryl L. *Camden*. New York: Arcadia Publishing, 2006.
Gillete, Howard, Jr. *Camden After the Fall: Decline and Renewal in a Post Industrial City*. Philadelphia: University of Pennsylvania Press, 2006.
Sidarick, Daniel. *Condensed Capitalism: Campbell Soup and the Pursuit of Cheap Production in the Twentieth Century*. Ithaca, NY: ILR Press, 2009.
Wilson, William Julius. *When Work Disappears: The World of the New Urban Poor*. New York: Vintage, 1997.

Caminetti v. United States

During the 1890s and the first two decades of the 20th century, the U.S. Congress began to criminalize interstate commerce deemed harmful to society in general. Among the prohibitions were impure food and drugs, stolen automobiles, prostitution, and child labor. Lawmakers relied on two provisions of Article I of the U.S. Constitution to legitimize these statutes: the commerce clause and the necessary and proper clause. Farley Drew Caminetti was convicted of violating one of these laws, a verdict the U.S. Supreme Court subsequently upheld. National authority to do so remains controversial today, nearly 100 years later. Legal challengers asserted in federal court that such national policies violated the Tenth Amendment by invading "the powers … reserved to the states." At that time, these advocates had history on their side. With rare exception since 1789, states had protected the health, welfare, safety, and morality of persons residing within their boundaries from the criminal behavior of others.

The White Slave Traffic Act, also known as the Mann Act, was a significant example of an early-20th-century congressional policy that spawned constitutional conflict between Article I and the Tenth Amendment. Introduced by Republican Congressman James Robert Mann of Illinois, the proposal was enacted in 1910 and was signed into law by President William Howard Taft. The statute specifically invoked the commerce clause by providing that "any person who shall knowingly transport or cause to be transported, or aid or assist in obtaining transportation for, or in transporting, in interstate or foreign commerce, or in any territory or in the District of Columbia, any woman or girl" could be prosecuted for felonious conduct.

The U.S. Supreme Court first adjudicated the Mann Act in 1913. In *Hoke v. United States*, counsel for the petitioner asserted that the law was invalid on its face, as written, and argued that the federal government was attempting to interfere with the Tenth Amendment police power of the state of Texas to regulate the morals of its citizens. The interstate commercial element of the Mann Act was evident, however, in such references as "for the purpose of prostitution" and "with the intent and purpose to induce, entice or compel such woman or girl to become a prostitute." A unanimous court upheld the act, deciding that the statute was concerned with a "domain which the States cannot reach and over which Congress alone has power."

The Caminetti Case
The law was more ambiguous about the appropriate scope of application of the Mann Act. The statutory language pertaining to "debauchery or for any other immoral purpose" and engaging in "any other immoral practice," if divorced from

prostitution, raised serious questions about the potential for selective enforcement. Farley Drew Caminetti and Maury I. Diggs were convicted in 1913 in Sacramento, California, by jury verdict in separate trials for violation of the Mann (White Slave Traffic) Act. Their wives had informed law enforcement agents that their husbands were traveling with Lola Norris and Marsha Warrington—with whom the wayward husbands were having extramarital affairs—to Reno, Nevada. Upon arrival, the men rented an apartment, and arrests followed. On appeal to the U.S. Supreme Court in *Caminetti v. United States*, the convictions were affirmed in 1917.

A three-fifths majority sustained application of the Mann Act to the conduct of Caminetti and Diggs. In doing so, Justice William Day and the majority construed the intent of Congress to include interstate travel for the purpose of consensual extramarital sexual activity. Justice Day concluded that not to apply the law in this case "would shock the common understanding of what constitutes an immoral purpose."

Justice Joseph McKenna's dissenting opinion called attention to the tenuous relationship between the commerce clause and the facts of these cases. From his perspective, the intent of Congress in passing the Mann Act was to attack "commercialized vice as a business which used interstate commerce as a facility to procure or distribute its victims. These defendants were not so engaged." Not until 1986 did Congress amend the law by replacing "debauchery" and "any other immoral purpose" with "any sexual activity for which any person can be charged with a criminal offense."

Steven H. Hatting
University of St. Thomas

See Also: Fornication Laws; Mann Act; Prostitution, Sociology of.

Further Readings
Caminetti v. United States, 242 U.S. 470 (1917).
Grittner, Frederick K. *White Slavery: Myth, Ideology and American Law.* New York: Garland, 1990.
Langum, David. *Crossing Over the Line: Legislating Morality and the Mann Act.* Chicago: University of Chicago Press, 1994.

Capital Punishment

The United States is virtually unique among modern industrial democracies in maintaining the use of capital punishment. Both historically and in the contemporary world, the death penalty has had strong supporters as well as serious critics. Reflecting the contested status of the sanction, its use has varied depending on a number of factors, including crime rates, public sentiment, legal strictures, and geographical differences.

The annual number of executions in the United States has been on the decline since it reached a peak of 98 in 1999. In 2010, there were 46 executions in the nation, virtually all of them in the south. Only seven states executed more than one person. Texas alone was responsible for 37 percent of these deaths. It appears from the statistics that although some surveys indicate the persistence of support for capital punishment, in recent years, its use has become less frequent and more localized. Likewise, the number of offenders sentenced to death has also declined from 315 in 1999 to 114 in 2010. More than 85 percent of those death sentences were handed down in the south and the west. If juries are reflective of community sentiments toward capital punishment, the death penalty's popularity has decreased even in such traditional areas of support as Virginia, Georgia, and Missouri, which had no death sentences in 2010. In addition to a decline in both executions and death sentences, a number of anti–capital punishment governors were elected in recent years in California, Connecticut, Maryland, New York, Massachusetts, and Illinois. A number of opinion polls indicated a decline in support for the death penalty, especially when respondents were offered a life sentence without parole as an alternative.

Several reasons may be offered to explain why, according to a variety of measures, support seems to be declining. A number of high-profile cases have indicated that innocent persons are sentenced to death, and some have suggested that such wrongful convictions may actually lead to the execution of some who are innocent. The existence of alternatives such as life without parole makes the argument that death is necessary to protect public safety more tenuous. Likewise, many citizens are concerned about the cost of capital punishment when state budgetary problems lead to cutting other vital services such as education and law enforcement. A significant number are also concerned about the apparent arbitrariness of a system that disproportionately affects minorities, the poor, and the mentally ill.

Historical Background

Although capital punishment has been a fact of life in America from the earliest colonial period, its purposes, the rationales for its use, and the methods of execution have undergone many changes. To the earliest settlers who brought the English legal codes with them, capital punishment for a large number of crimes was simply a reality intended to serve a variety of purposes. It was meant to be a deterrent whereby potential offenders would be discouraged from criminal activity. It was intended as retribution, holding the lawbreaker responsible and requiring him to pay the price for his crimes. And it was designed to offer the opportunity for a sinner/criminal to repent and to end his life in a state of grace, which could spare him eternal damnation. Up until the late 18th century when prisons were developed, the death penalty served as the major punishment available for serious crimes. Few questioned its utility or its necessity, and both the theory and practice of capital punishment suggested that most people regarded criminals not as "others" different from law-abiding citizens, but as neighbors who had succumbed to the evil forces that could tempt anyone.

For free white persons sentenced to death, hanging was the usual form of execution. The event followed a standard ritual and generally brought a community together to witness the public drama. After the prisoner was brought to the scaffold, the sheriff read the death warrant and sometimes added some editorial comments of his own. One or more ministers would follow with sermons, setting out the moral lessons to be learned from the fate of the condemned man. Next, the offender would speak, offering his own interpretation of the failings that had brought him to such a miserable end. The crowd would sing hymns, and finally, with a hood draped over his head, the prisoner would be hanged. The whole ceremony could take hours and was typically conducted with the solemnity of a religious service. During the 17th and 18th centuries, parents were encouraged to bring their children to observe the hanging, as it was believed to be an especially effective way to teach about morality. However, even in the colonial period, some observers complained that the hanging ritual would often have a contrary effect if it instilled sympathy for the condemned man, who could seem to be a victim himself.

The crowds who observed executions represented all elements of the community; in fact, the event could serve a number of secular purposes. It might satisfy a curiosity about violence, even provide a sort of vicarious excitement in otherwise normal lives. It could show how the community made a statement of its disapproval of certain behaviors, thus reinforcing its solidarity. And it demonstrated the power of the state to punish those who defied the authority of the law. For people who were unable to attend an execution, the highlights would be available in published form—the sermon, the last words of the condemned man, and a description of the death itself could be profitable to publishers and could serve as exciting as well as efficacious reading to the public.

Although hanging was the most common method of execution, several other options existed during the colonial era. While witches had been burned at the stake in Europe, those convicted of witchcraft in America were—like most common criminals—hanged. The more dramatic punishments were reserved for persons found guilty of either petit treason (wives who murdered their husbands or slaves who killed their owner would be burned) or treason. In the latter case, the offender might be disemboweled and dismembered. His corpse could be left to decompose in public view. Slaves or Native Americans could be hanged in chains, as an added deterrent to members of their community. These examples served as a sort of "super capital punishment," intended to demonstrate that the crime was so horrible that "mere" death was insufficient as a response.

By the time of the American Revolution in the late 18th century, voices began to be raised questioning both the propriety and the utility of capital punishment. Enlightenment thinkers had emphasized the need for governments to establish rational systems based on a social contract that assumed human rights. One such influential thinker, Cesare Beccaria, wrote *On Crimes and Punishments* in 1764. Beccaria's work, which was widely read by the American founding fathers, argued that capital punishment was a violation of human rights. No one, he maintained, could give the state the power to take his life. He further claimed that the death penalty was ineffective as a deterrent. Life in prison accompanied by hard labor would, Beccaria argued, frighten a potential offender more than the prospect of a simple hanging. And, he noted, rather than discouraging violence, public hangings hardened citizens to brutality.

Although Beccaria's treatise did not lead to the abolition of capital punishment in the United States, along with other Enlightenment writings, it influenced policy makers to reduce its use to a few serious crimes: For example, Pennsylvania limited the use of capital punishment when it distinguished degrees of murder in 1794. The development of prisons in the 19th century provided an alternative sanction that seemed more consistent with the enlightened and humane society Americans hoped to create. In addition, many thoughtful people came to believe that crime was not simply a matter of free will but that instead, a malign environment could be responsible.

As a movement promoting the abolition of capital punishment developed, its proponents argued that crime was analogous to illness. The solution was not to kill the patient, but to remove him from the sources of contamination. Others tried to reconcile opposition to the death penalty with the Bible by citing the New Testament teachings favoring mercy rather than the Old Testament's endorsement of retribution. Although the idea of doing away with capital punishment altogether had some adherents, before the Civil War, only a few northern and midwestern states followed the 1847 example of Michigan and abolished it. In the south, there was little or no opposition.

Many authors note that the retention of capital punishment in the south is inexorably connected to the institution of slavery. While the southern states abolished the death penalty for most crimes other than murder committed by whites, black slaves were hanged at rates quite disproportionate to their population. They might be executed for rape, slave revolt, attempted murder, burglary, or arson, as well as for murder. Hangings were public and were intended to deter others from similar behaviors. State governments were required to reimburse owners for the cost of an executed slave. For that reason, many slaves were executed outside the system by lynching, while in other cases, states sold slaves outside the country to defray the cost of reimbursement.

The Nineteenth and Twentieth Centuries

While the debates over the use of capital punishment waxed and waned, the setting of executions in the north moved from the public square to the prison yard. The rise of the urban middle class in the 19th century was accompanied by attitudes that valued gentility and decorum. The violence of a public execution came to be regarded as barbaric, something well-bred people would not wish to see. Nor did members of the new bourgeois class approve of the behavior of vulgar crowds, who might drink and carouse during a hanging. Mobs might miss the moral lessons of a hanging and be brutalized instead. Such sentiments led authorities to move executions inside the prison walls, where only invited observers witnessed the death of the offender. The result was that the community no longer came together to participate in a ritual and make a moral statement. The responsibility for carrying out the punishment symbolically shifted from the public to the government. Some would argue, in retrospect, that the opponents of capital punishment made an unfortunate deal whereby hangings continued unabated, and the potential for abolition was reduced when they moved out of public view.

The effort to move executions from a public space into the confines of the prison was only the first change that altered the relationship between the community and the application of the death penalty. Some have suggested that as Victorians and modern Americans became less comfortable with death, it was only consistent that capital punishment became less visible and more sanitized. Technology, especially the development of the electric chair and the gas chamber, meant that executions would be carried out by "experts" in a closed room in a centralized location. Some states sought alternative means of death because of frequent reports that bungled hangings caused serious pain to the condemned person. At the end of the 19th century, a faith in science as the solution

Confederate Captain Henry Wirz was hanged for war crimes in the Civil War in November 1865, in the yard of Old Capitol Prison, the future site of the U.S. Supreme Court in Washington, D.C.

to many human problems and a belief in the wonders of electricity contributed to the notion that electrocution could provide a clean and "painless" way to put criminals to death. New York was the first state to execute a convict in the electric chair when William Kemmler was put to death in 1890. Prior to his execution, state and federal courts, including the Supreme Court, had ruled that death by electrocution would not violate any of Kemmler's rights. However, the procedure was badly bungled. The generator malfunctioned, and the electrician in charge of its operation ordered repeated surges of current. Kemmler's hair caught on fire, and witnesses reported the smell of burning flesh. Nonetheless, New York continued with the use of the electric chair, and 14 other states adopted the method before World War I. Most people inside and outside the criminal justice system viewed the electric chair as a progressive development. Perhaps some of this approval occurred because electrocutions were carried on behind closed doors, with no visual reports of errors in its application. With few exceptions, states located their electric chairs and therefore all their executions in a single prison, often far from the community where the crime had occurred.

Nevada adopted the gas chamber in the mid-1930s, and 11 states followed suit. The use of toxic gas promised a swift and painless death that would simply "put the convict to sleep." However, concerns about the safety of spectators as well as the expense of building and maintaining a gas chamber made the method somewhat impractical. In addition, after World War II and the Nazi use of lethal gas during the Holocaust, its appeal waned in the United States. With the use of the electric chair and the gas chamber, executions were not only concealed from the public but were more exclusively male. In virtually every case, everyone who participated in the killing—the warden, the technicians, the witnesses—was a man and an agent of the state. The relationship between the community ritual and the visibility of the punishment became more attenuated, making the argument for deterrence more difficult. Almost none of the witnesses were the sort of people for whom the deterrence message was intended.

If the argument that capital punishment was necessary to deter potential criminals was cast into doubt, scholarly work in the early 20th century also raised questions about the extent of individual responsibility for criminal behavior. Criminologists, psychologists, and other students of human behavior advanced theories suggesting that deviant behavior could possibly be correlated with inherited characteristics or, alternatively, with environmental factors. Both types of theory argued that individual offenders could not be totally responsible for their actions. If that were true, the death penalty as an instrument of retribution could not be justified. Such academic arguments seemed to influence the public's perception of criminal accountability. Juries were returning fewer death sentences, and in some cases where death was a mandatory punishment with a guilty verdict, juries were engaging in nullification and returning verdicts of "not guilty." As a result, states enacted statutes allowing juries more discretion in sentencing. Legislatures in 15 states abolished the death penalty before 1917. However, after World War I, seven states reenacted the sanction.

The issue was clearly a matter of political debate, but trends shifted frequently during the early 20th century. Publicity about a number of high-profile trials such as the Sacco and Vanzetti case where there were doubts about the defendants' guilt kept the issue in the public eye. By the mid-20th century, death sentences in both the north and the south had significantly decreased. However, in the south, African Americans continued to be sentenced and executed in disproportionate numbers.

The Role of the Supreme Court

Although the task of interpreting the Constitution falls to the Supreme Court, it did not address the issue of applying the Bill of Rights to the states until the mid-20th century. Before that time, the court tended to defer to the individual states' application of their criminal law despite the constitutional prohibition against cruel and unusual punishment in the Eighth Amendment. However, beginning with a series of decisions in the 1960s, the court tended to set national standards that protected the rights of the accused in the criminal process.

The concept that the death penalty might be inherently unconstitutional first came to the Supreme Court as a result of cases raised by the National Association for the Advancement of Colored People (NAACP). The NAACP had represented a number of African American men on trial for capital offenses. It gathered statistics showing the disparities in sentencing based on race. From the 1890s to the 1970s, more than 54 percent of those executed were "non-white." Among 4,736 illegal executions (lynchings), 73 percent of those killed were black. These percentages were grossly disproportionate in a society where African Americans made up 10 percent to 12 percent of the general population. Many observers argued that capital punishment was used as an instrument to maintain white supremacy. The NAACP claimed in the post–World War II period that the biased application of the death penalty violated "evolving standards of decency."

The court in a 1958 case, *Trop v. Dulles* (1958), had ruled that the definition of cruel and unusual punishment must "draw its meaning from the evolving standards of decency that mark the progress of a maturing society." In other words, the justices indicated that the test of whether a punishment violated the Constitution would be based on the changing (and presumably more humane and refined) attitudes of the contemporary society. Thus, when challenges to the death penalty were raised before the court, they almost always tended to reflect the argument that capital punishment no longer conformed to the views of the American people.

In 1963, the NAACP in *Rudolph v. Alabama* raised a claim that racial bias in capital sentencing violated the evolving American standards. The case concerned a black man sentenced to death for the rape of a white woman, a situation all too common in the south. Although the court declined to hear the case, three justices in a rare procedure wrote a dissent from that decision. Their opinion questioned whether executing a man for rape violated evolving standards.

Furman v. Georgia. *Rudolph* laid the groundwork for a landmark case nine years later. In *Furman v. Georgia* (1972), the court for the first time ruled on the constitutionality of the death penalty. It found that capital punishment *as applied* violated the ban on cruel and unusual punishment in a 5–4 decision. *Furman* involved three cases consolidated into one argument. Furman was a black man who had shot a white homeowner, apparently by accident, during a burglary. The other two cases involved rapes of white women by black offenders. All three defendants had been condemned to death by juries that enjoyed wide discretion in choosing sentences.

Each member of the Supreme Court wrote a separate opinion and, although five justices found the death penalty as administered unconstitutional, their reasoning varied widely. Justice William Brennan concluded that American juries voted for so few death sentences that its rejection showed that it violated evolving standards. Likewise, it was disproportionate to many crimes and its use could be arbitrary and biased. For Brennan, the court could simply formalize the consensus that the larger society had already reached. Justice William O. Douglas believed that a punishment that fell most heavily on unpopular minorities was in conflict with enlightened public opinion. Justice Thurgood Marshall found capital punishment both excessive and abhorrent. He wrote that if citizens were fully informed, they would find the death penalty unjust and unacceptable. Justices Potter Stewart and Byron White focused on the arbitrariness with which capital punishment was inflicted. The four dissenters made various arguments based on Federalism, which focused on the need to allow the states to determine their own criminal penalties based on popular sentiment within their jurisdictions.

Gregg v. Georgia. Reactions to *Furman* varied widely. Some saw it as a death sentence for capital punishment itself. Others saw it as a step toward standardizing criminal procedures across the states. Opponents claimed it was an outrage. After *Furman*, most scholars agree, capital punishment became more politicized. Support became a way for politicians to demonstrate their zeal for "law and order." The majority of states immediately began to write new laws intended to meet the constitutional standards for avoiding arbitrariness and uncontrolled discretion. Some states, including North Carolina, tried to avoid these concerns by creating a mandatory death penalty for certain offenses. The court rejected this approach in *Woodson v. North Carolina* (1976), holding that a mandatory sentence would not take individual circumstances into account. Instead, it upheld a revised capital statute from Georgia in *Gregg v. Georgia* (1976). The court ruled that the death penalty per se did not violate contemporary standards of decency and that the new law fixed some of the flaws identified in *Furman*. Essentially, the provision identifying specific aggravating factors that would make a crime death eligible, the bifurcated procedure separating the guilt phase from the sentencing phase of a capital trial, and the provision for automatic review of capital sentences satisfied the majority of the court that death penalty laws could be written to be compatible with the Constitution. The decision in *Gregg* revealed the court majority's deference to the principles of Federalism as they held that each state legislature can best evaluate the moral consensus in its state.

Since *Gregg,* the Supreme Court has worked from the assumption that the death penalty is constitutional. The complex structure of capital law that has emerged since the death penalty was reinstated in 1976 is essentially an attempt to reconcile the sometimes divergent requirements that it be both consistent with the Constitution and in conformity with local public standards.

Although "evolving standards of decency" provide a guideline for deciding whether a punishment conflicts with the Eighth Amendment, the question of how to measure those standards is a complicated one. The court often looks to laws passed by state legislatures to see if a majority of states prohibit or permit a certain category of punishment. However, in looking to evaluate the policies of states, the justices often disagree about how to count them. Some advocate counting all the states—those with the death penalty and those without—to find a consensus. Other justices argue for counting only pro–death penalty states to determine whether a certain application meets contemporary standards. Besides tabulating state laws, the Supreme Court also looks to jury verdicts, opinion polls, and scholarly research. Some members of the court also consider the policies of other nations and the standards of international law. Others say laws from outside the United States are irrelevant for interpreting our Constitution.

Proportionality. In a number of cases, the court considered the issue of proportionality—how to ensure that taking the life of the convicted person was not excessive in relation to the crime. Prior to *Furman*, rapists had often been punished with death, particularly when the offender was African American and the victim was white. Shortly after reinstating capital punishment, the court considered whether it was a constitutional penalty for the rape of an adult woman. In *Coker v. Georgia* (1977), the court ruled that the death penalty was a disproportionate sanction and that it therefore violated evolving standards of decency. *Coker* did not address whether capital punishment could be permissible for the rape of a child. The court considered that question in *Kennedy v. Louisiana* 2008. It ruled that although child rape is a heinous offense, if no murder was involved, execution violated the ban on cruel and unusual punishment. As only six states provided a death sentence for child rape, there was not a national consensus in favor of that sanction. And as no one had been executed for child rape since 1964, the court found that it violated contemporary standards of decency.

Other cases involving proportionality have considered whether someone who participated in a murder but did not kill or intend to kill anyone should be eligible for the death penalty. Here, the justices reversed themselves between the decision in *Enmund v. Florida* (1982) and *Tison v. Arizona* (1987). In the prior case, they held that capital punishment for an accomplice who did not kill nor intend to kill was disproportionate and therefore unconstitutional. In *Tison*, they ruled that a defendant who was a major participant in a murder but did not actually kill could be sentenced to death. The latter case seems to reflect the court's increasing willingness in the years since *Gregg* to allow more discretion to the local criminal justice community in determining death eligibility.

Cruel and Unusual Punishment. The court has also considered how the execution of some categories of offenders could violate the ban on cruel and unusual punishment. *Atkins v. Virginia* (2002) concerned the question of whether a person suffering from mental retardation could be put to death. The court ruled that such an execution did not conform to contemporary standards of decency and was therefore impermissible. However, the justices left it up to the states to decide how mental retardation would be determined. Thus, definitions and procedures vary widely among the states. Three years later, basing some of their reasoning on *Atkins*, the justices, in *Roper v. Simmons* (2005), found it was unconstitutional to execute someone who was a juvenile (under 18 years of age) at the time of the crime. In *Roper*, they cited not only state legislation and jury verdicts but also international law to support their ruling.

In *Ford v. Wainwright* (1986), the Supreme Court held it was unconstitutional to execute a person who was insane at the time of death, although it has not decided whether a convict may be medicated so he will be competent to be put to death. It also has not determined whether it is constitutional to sentence someone to death who was severely mentally ill (but not legally insane) at the time of the crime.

Many people might be surprised to learn that another area where the court has not ruled definitively concerns the execution of the innocent. In *Herrera v. Collins* (1993), the justices addressed that question. In that case, they held that a defendant claiming innocence must also show that his or her constitutional rights had been violated by improper procedures. He or she would not be allowed an appeal simply by offering evidence that he or she was factually innocent. Several justices wrote that executing an innocent person would be "perilously close to simple murder," but the majority did not reach that conclusion.

McCleskey v. Kemp. Perhaps the most important post-*Gregg* case was *McCleskey v. Kemp* (1987), which had the potential to challenge the whole capital punishment regime based on claims of racial bias. Warren McCleskey, who was African American, was charged with shooting a white police officer in the commission of a robbery. He based his appeal on a massive statistical report, the Baldus Study, which examined sentencing in Georgia and found that the killer of a white person was more than four times as likely to be sentenced to death as the killer of a black person. Earlier studies had focused on the race of the defendant. The Baldus Study showed that the race of the victim was an even stronger predictor of sentencing than the race of the defendant. It appeared to play an impermissible role in determining who would be sentenced to death. McCleskey argued that the bias in the system violated his constitutional rights guaranteed in the Fourteenth Amendment provision that no state may deny a citizen the "equal protection of the laws."

The Supreme Court in a 5–4 decision rejected McCleskey's claims, insisting that McCleskey would need to show bias in his own case, not only in the system. (This approach contradicted the rationale in *Furman*, which found the death penalty unconstitutional based on systematic arbitrariness.) The court also noted that although the Baldus Study found a "discrepancy that appears to correlate with race," the disparity did not result in an "unacceptable risk of racial prejudice." They suggested that if McCleskey's allegations of racial bias were followed to their logical conclusion, the whole criminal justice system would be at risk. Although three justices found the statistical evidence of prejudice "intolerable," the court as a whole did not. One might view the contrast between the willingness of the court to overturn the death penalty in *Furman* in 1972 with its cautiousness in *McCleskey* as evidence of a change in the national mood from one focusing on the rights of the accused to one that emphasized "law and order" in the late 1980s. However, a study of the relationship of race and capital punishment by the General Accounting Office in 1990 supported the findings of the Baldus Study.

Lethal Injection. After the reinstatement of the death penalty, many states sought a method of execution that would be less controversial than the electric chair. Most ultimately adopted lethal injection, which appeared to be clean and apparently painless. However, a challenge to the three-drug cocktail used in lethal injection and the method of its administration developed in *Baze v. Rees* (2008). Despite claims that the procedure carried a risk of significant pain, especially when done by untrained correctional personnel, the court found that the threat of pain was not "objectively intolerable." This decision is consistent with earlier rulings that the method of execution should be left to the states.

Current Status of Capital Punishment
Although it is possible to argue that the death penalty is still popular in the United States, surveys show that when offered the alternative of life without parole for convicted murderers, a majority of citizens favor that option. More than 30 years after its reinstatement, many remain

The gas chamber at San Quentin State Prison in California, shown here, was the site of 194 executions by gas, including those of four women, from 1938 to 1967. After a 1994 ruling barred the state from using the gas chamber, as it was found to be cruel and unusual punishment, lethal injections were instead administered inside the chamber until the completion of a lethal injection room in 2010.

concerned about the fairness with which capital punishment is administered. Additionally, as the cost of an execution exceeds the cost of a life sentence, state officials are weighing its value more critically. Finally, the possibility of executing an innocent person and numerous well-publicized exonerations have undermined public support.

Mary Welek Atwell
Radford University

See Also: *Coker v. Georgia*; Cruel and Unusual Punishment; Death Row; Electric Chair, History of; Executions; *Furman v. Georgia*; *Gregg v. Georgia*; Lynchings; *McCleskey v. Kemp*.

Further Readings
Banner, Stuart. *The Death Penalty: An American History*. Cambridge, MA: Harvard University Press, 2002.
Bedau, Hugo Adam, ed. *The Death Penalty in America: Current Controversies*. New York: Oxford University Press, 1997.
Bohm, Robert M. *Deathquest II: An Introduction to the Theory and Practice of Capital Punishment in the United States*. Cincinnati, OH: Anderson, 2003.
Del Carmen, Rolando V., et al. *The Death Penalty: Constitutional Issues, Commentaries, and Case Briefs*. New York: Lexis-Nexis, 2005.
Dow, David R. and Mark Dow. *Machinery of Death: The Reality of America's Death Penalty Regime*. New York: Routledge, 2002.
Garland, Robert. *Peculiar Institution: America's Death Penalty in an Age of Abolition*. Cambridge, MA: Belknap Press of Harvard University, 2010.
Kaufman-Osborn, Timothy V. *From Noose to Needle: Capital Punishment and the Late Liberal State*. Ann Arbor: University of Michigan Press, 2002.
Paternoster, Raymond, Robert Brame, and Sarah Bacon. *The Death Penalty: America's Experience With Capital Punishment*. New York: Oxford University Press, 2008.
Sarat, Austin. *When the State Kills: Capital Punishment and the American Condition*. Princeton, NJ: Princeton University Press, 2001.
Zimring, Franklin. *The Contradictions of American Capital Punishment*. New York: Oxford University Press, 2003.

Capone, Al

Alphonse Capone (1899–1947) was born in Brooklyn, New York, and was a notorious gangster who never made it to his 50th birthday. Although he was an elementary school dropout, Capone learned how to survive on the streets in a gang known as the Five Pointers. He became known for his toughness and his willingness to follow orders. He had an uncanny ability to sense danger, and his survival skills were sharpened on the backstreets of Brooklyn. His criminal career served as a model for organized crime members.

Capone's street name alias was "Scarface," a legendary calling card for his infamous criminal career. However, no one dared call him "Scarface" in his presence. The large scar running down the side of his face, along with his big eyes and penetrating glare, gave Capone a formidable appearance.

Climbing the Criminal Ladder
Capone's early mentor was Frankie Yale, who put the aspiring gangster to work in a Coney Island dance club. Capone earned his prominent facial scar during a bar fight over a crude remark he made to Frank Gallucio's sister. Gallucio struck Capone in the face with a knife. Capone apologized for the comment on orders of Frankie Yale, and learned a lesson: His controlled use of charm and violence became his new persona during his rise in the organized crime hierarchy.

Capone followed orders without hesitation, including orders to kill. He became a suspect in the murders of "Wild Bill" Lovett's White Hand Gang. Facing retaliation, Capone could stay and pay the consequences or flee New York and find sanctuary in Chicago. He wisely chose the latter. His murderous rise to the top and mob reign in the Chicago syndicate made him a gangster legend.

Capone's Chicago Outfit
Capone's Chicago mentor was Johnny Torrio, who in turn was assigned to "Big Jim" Colosimo, the kingpin of prostitution. Colosimo resisted the lucrative opportunities for bootlegging alcohol during Prohibition, leading his fellow mobsters to reason that he stood in the way of progress and profit. Colosimo was killed in his office over his resistance to cash in on the bootlegging alcohol

A mug shot of Al Capone in 1931. In November of that year, he was convicted of income tax evasion and sentenced to 11 years in prison; he served seven and a half years, partly in Alcatraz.

enterprise. In the power vacuum that followed, Johnny Torrio and Al Capone seized the Chicago rackets: Capone unleashed a campaign of terror and violence while Torrio tried but failed to play the role of peacemaker. In the ongoing gangland war, a rival Irish gangster, Dion O'Banion, was killed in a flower shop.

O'Banion's successor, Hymie Weiss, plotted to kill Torrio and Capone in retaliation for the flower shop murder. The ambush took place in downtown Chicago; however, Capone escaped without injury. Later that day, Torrio was shot five times in his home. Johnny Torrio survived the shooting, though he eventually stepped aside and retired as a millionaire, leaving Capone to be the sole boss of the Chicago outfit. Capone decided that Weiss needed to be eliminated for his own personal safety and survival. Weiss, while walking to his car, was confronted by two killers from the North Side Gang, and then was murdered gangland style with a machine gun and shotgun.

Capone prevailed in Chicago; his syndicate eventually reigned supreme. His operations, power, and influence infiltrated businesses and unions. The outfit emerged not as a corporate hierarchy, but more like a senior partnership comprising four men who eventually formed a variety of criminal partnerships to operate explicit criminal enterprises. The partnership of four ruthless organized crime figures included Al Capone, his brother Ralph Capone, Frank Nitti, and Jake Guzik, the accounting specialist. Illicit payoffs were divided equally with prescribed deductions for general expenses that included operational building space, clerks, and bodyguards. In addition, expenditures included political bribes and protection that allowed the criminal enterprises to flourish.

The St. Valentine's Day Massacre represents the classic Capone hit in the name of preserving his lucrative business interests. In 1929, George "Bugsy" Moran, the leader of a rival gang, and seven other gangsters were shot to death in Chicago's Clark Street Garage. Capone ordered the killings, and the hit included the assassinations of "Machine Gun" Jack McGurn and two other known killers: Albert Anselmi and John Scalise. The hit men drove a black limousine and entered the garage dressed in police uniforms. The unsuspecting gangsters inside offered no resistance to the "officers." They lined up against the wall and died in waves of bullets. Seven men were left dead; no criminal trial took place. Capone had an airtight alibi in Florida socializing with friends; he later personally murdered Anselmi and Scalise to cover his link to the St. Valentine's Day Massacre.

Capone's Arrest

The final assault on Capone did not advance from other gangsters, but from the federal government. President Herbert Hoover advocated the repeal of Prohibition as a means of controlling Capone. The Treasury Department assigned Special Agent Elliot Ness to track down and arrest Capone. Ness formed his "Untouchables" unit to uncover and shadow Capone's assets. The arrest team executed search warrants, conducted midnight raids, and collected evidence in support of Capone's arrest. Ironically, Al "Scarface" Capone was not tried and convicted for his involvement in many murders but for income tax evasion on $165,000 dollars of unexplained income.

Al Capone, the bully with a propensity for violence, was, in the end, not able to protect himself. He wandered in a state of senility throughout his Palm Island, Florida, mansion in gangster retirement. Capone, who suffered from syphilis and became unable to recognize his old gangster companions, refused treatment while serving prison time in Alcatraz. Al "Scarface" Capone lived in seclusion, and was totally incapacitated until his death at age 48 after a case of pneumonia and a resulting stroke in 1947.

Thomas E. Baker
University of Scranton

See Also: Alcatraz Island Prison; Bootlegging; Chicago, Illinois; Ness, Eliot; Organized Crime, History of; Prohibition.

Further Readings
Abadinsky, Howard. *Organized Crime*, 9th ed. Belmont, CA: Thomson/Wadsworth, 2010.
Bonanno, Joseph. *A Man of Honor: The Autobiography of Joseph Bonanno*. New York: St. Martin's Press, 2003.
Eig, Jonathan. *Get Capone: The Secret Plot That Captured America's Most Wanted Gangster*. New York: Simon & Schuster, 2010.
Franzese, Michael and Dary Matera. *Quitting the Mob*. New York: HarperCollins, 1992.
Lyman, Michael D. and Gary W. Potter. *Organized Crime*, 5th ed. Upper Saddle River, NJ: Pearson Prentice Hall, 2011.
O'Brien, Joseph F. and Andris Kurins. *Boss of Bosses*. New York: Simon & Schuster, 1991.
Schoenberg, Robert J. *Mr. Capone: The Real and Complete Story of Al Capone*. New York: Harper Paperbacks, 1993.

Carter, Jimmy (Administration of)

James Earl "Jimmy" Carter was the 39th president of the United States, serving from 1977 to 1981. Carter, a former peanut farmer, naval officer, and governor of Georgia, won the Democratic nomination in 1976 and defeated incumbent President Gerald Ford in the general election. He ran for reelection in 1980 but was defeated by Ronald Reagan.

Carter assumed office in the years following the Watergate affair with the goals of reestablishing trust and transparency to the office of the presidency. Economic stagflation and a focus on energy policy were key domestic issues. The Department of Energy was created during Carter's term in office. In foreign affairs, the Camp David Peace Accords, the Soviet invasion of Afghanistan, a foreign policy emphasis on human rights, and the Iran hostage crisis were key events.

Carter is also well known for his international humanitarian work after his presidency, having received the Nobel Peace Prize in 2002. Indeed, these themes of human rights, peace, and democracy can be seen in both the domestic and foreign policies that Carter pursued during his presidency. In the domestic arena Carter could fairly be labeled as liberal in the area of law and criminal justice, especially when compared to his immediate Republican predecessors. On the first day of his presidency, he signed a controversial general amnesty for those who had avoided the Vietnam draft. He was also an outspoken opponent of the death penalty both during and after his term as president.

Despite the fact that Carter is the only full-term modern president not to have the opportunity to appoint a justice to the U.S. Supreme Court, his impact on the federal judiciary was a distinct one. It was under Carter that the Omnibus Judgeship Act of 1978 was passed. This act created 152 new federal judgeships, including 35 at the appellate level. This act becomes more significant when Carter's appointment record is more closely examined. Carter greatly increased the number of women and minorities appointed to the federal bench. In fact, Carter appointed five times more women to the bench than all his predecessors combined. While subsequent Democratic presidents have built upon these numbers, it was the Carter administration that was really the first to nominate significant numbers of women and minorities to serve on the federal bench. It was also Jimmy Carter who appointed future Supreme Court Justices Stephen Breyer and Ruth Bader Ginsburg to the appellate federal bench.

Restoring Executive Trust

Carter was elected to the presidency in an era in which Americans were reevaluating the scope and desirability of presidential power in the wake of Watergate and President Richard Nixon's resignation from office. The Church Committee investigations of the mid-1970s revealed an extensive history of executive branch lawlessness in the area of government surveillance by the Central Intelligence Agency (CIA), the Federal Bureau of Investigation (FBI), and other government agencies. Over the course of several decades, executive branch agencies secretly implemented a host of programs designed ostensibly to counter domestic and international threats to U.S. security.

COINTELPRO was a counterintelligence program originally intended to target racist groups, Black Nationalist groups, and Communists. It included illegal eavesdropping, mailing anonymous threats to targets, disinformation, harassment, the fabrication of evidence, and the creation and dissemination of false documents. Operation CHAOS gathered information on political protesters, which resulted in more than 13,000 computerized files on more than 300,000 people.

Operation MERRIMAC targeted civil rights and peace organizations. In project SHAMROCK, Western Union and other wire service providers gave intelligence personnel at the National Security Administration (NSA) access to private messages. Project MINARET was an NSA database that contained computer files on more than 75,000 American citizens, including members of Congress. By 1968, almost every intelligence agency in the executive branch was spying in one form or another on nonviolent protesters. Abuses of constitutional rights and liberties were rampant in all of the above programs, and it was these widespread abuses that eventually prompted Congress and the courts to respond with increased oversight measures.

Carter ran as a Washington outsider and sought to bring about a renewed sense of trust and transparency to the office of the presidency. One example of this was the Federal Intelligence Surveillance Act (FISA) of 1978. FISA was an attempt to provide legislative and judicial restraints on presidentially ordered warrantless electronic surveillance while still providing presidents with the flexibility that they needed to gather foreign intelligence. FISA created the Federal Intelligence Surveillance Court (FISC) and the Federal Intelligence Surveillance Court of Review. Executive branch agencies wanting to conduct electronic surveillance to obtain foreign intelligence needed to obtain warrants from the FISC (absent exigent circumstances). These warrants have generally been quite easy to obtain, with the FISC denying only a handful from thousands of applications. After the terrorist attacks of September 11, 2001, President George W. Bush generated immense controversy when he initiated a secret warrantless electronic surveillance program that critics argued violated FISA.

Unfortunately, Carter found it difficult to shake the perception held by many Washington politicians and the national media that he was a nice guy but not one who was tough enough to be a forceful, effective president. Carter remained active in public affairs after his presidency. He founded the Carter Center, a nonprofit agency dedicated to advancing human rights around the globe. Carter worked as a U.S. emissary in North Korea, Haiti, Africa, and the Middle East, earning a Nobel Peace Prize in 2002 for his efforts. The extent of his work after his presidency has led some commentators to describe him as a more successful ex-president than he was president. Nevertheless, Carter's lifelong record on international humanitarian issues is one that few presidents can claim to match.

Darren Wheeler
Ball State University

See Also: 1961 to 1980 Primary Documents; Clemency; Ethics in Government Act of 1978; Ford, Gerald (Administration of); Internment; Watergate.

Further Readings

Fink, Gary and Hugh Davis Graham, eds. *The Carter Presidency: Policy Choices in a Post–New Deal Era.* Lawrence: University Press of Kansas, 2001.

Kaufman, Burton I. and Scott Kaufman. *The Presidency of James Earl Carter, Jr.* Lawrence: University Press of Kansas, 2006.

Zelizer, Julian. *Jimmy Carter: The American Presidents Series: The 39th President, 1977–1981.* New York: Times Books, 2010.

Chain Gangs and Prison Labor

Chain gangs were found in all regions of the United States in the last third of the 19th century, and legal provision for convict roadwork existed in all states except Rhode Island as late as 1923. Convicts were used in all types of road construction in western states such as Arizona, Montana, and Nebraska in the 1910s, but chain gangs were synonymous with the southern region where economic, racial, and climatic factors spurred their expansion in the early 20th century. For example, Georgia abolished its convict lease in 1908 and nearly 5,000 felony and misdemeanor convicts, 91 percent of whom were black, became available for roadwork. By 1910, every southern state legislature had authorized use of convicts for public works to replace the inefficient statute labor system that required male citizens to undertake roadwork every year.

Racism

Support for convict road labor came from civic groups, penal reformers, organized labor, and the Good Roads Movement. In the south, road labor in the fresh air and sunshine was often promoted as a healthy alternative to the increasingly discredited convict lease system and to idleness in the dank stone cellblocks of northern prisons. It was a more cost-effective alternative to housing able-bodied inmates in prisons with fewer work opportunities. It was also deemed particularly appropriate for black convicts, whose numbers continued to outstrip those of white prisoners, in a period when free African Americans were usually employed in unskilled positions at low wages (including road construction, sewer digging, and quarrying). African Americans arrested on charges of vagrancy and disorderly conduct as well as more serious property and personal violence offenses constituted a ready supply of labor to build roads for white planters, politicians, and industrialists. Chain gang labor was very much linked to the patronage politics of the southern Democratic Party in the approval of construction projects and the awarding of guard and other official jobs to party loyalists. It was also a key component of the systems of racial oppression and labor subordination that shored up white supremacy and racial segregation.

Chain gang labor became an integral part of southern states' plans for economic development, expanding farm-to-market routes, tourism, and urban growth in the 1920s and 1930s when millions of dollars of federal monies were apportioned to states for road and highway construction (the states had to provide matching funds). In January 1921, 628 prisoners were located in 24 road camps in Florida, and North Carolina had over 2,400 prisoners working on county chain gangs by October 1926. Lines of dirty, sweaty, exhausted, bare-chested men toiling on roads and in ditches and clad in black and white convict suits were common sights. The men were chained day and night at the ankles and together. They could wear up to 20 pounds of chains at a time. Shotgun guards on foot, horseback, or in trucks monitored their progress and watched out for escapees. Physical strength was vital for survival and to undertake the back-breaking work for 12–15 hours a day. African American chain gangs moved in time to the tempo of work songs, while white gangs might rely on counts or shouts. Chain gang labor had to be synchronized to avoid death or injury from fellow inmates randomly wielding pickaxes, shovels, and bush axes.

Conditions on the chain gang and in the road camps could be as brutal and harrowing as those under the convict lease system. In the early days, convicts were often housed in mobile steel-barred pie wagons on wheels with tiers of iron bunks, a zinc pan underneath for the toilet, and an open bucket for washing. Northern journalist John L. Spivak likened them to cages "in which a circus pens its most ferocious beasts." Out on the road, inmates relieved themselves in bushes at the side of the road, but only with a guard's permission. Prisoners who could not or would not complete their daily tasks were subject to corporal punishment, and the strap was a ubiquitous feature of chain gang life. The unsanitary camp conditions, physical punishments, and hard labor took its toll on inmates' health and mortality.

Criticism

There was growing criticism of chain gang labor and conditions from the 1910s. Opposition to chain gang labor, lynching, and racial oppression were key parts of influential left-liberal political movements in the south in the Depression years. However, Robert E. Burns's 1932 expose of Georgia's brutal chain gang system, *I Am a Fugitive From a Georgia Chain Gang!*, its adaptation as a Hollywood movie in 1933, and Burns's much-publicized extradition fight with the state of Georgia did much to increase opposition to southern penal practices in the 1930s and 1940s. Burns's experiences also illustrated that chain gangs of white convicts were not uncommon and were becoming more prevalent in the majority of southern states where numbers of white prisoners were increasing.

Most states constructed permanent road prisons in the 1930s and 1940s with marked improvements in material conditions, particularly sanitation, although they were still very basic. Inmates were transported to and from road construction or maintenance sites by truck. Southern states began to abandon chained labor squads in the period during and after World War II. Leg irons were removed from all but the most incorrigible inmates, striped suits and chains gradually disappeared, corporal punishment was replaced with the sweatbox, and the working day was gradually shortened. Yet, southern prison road labor was still hard and unrelenting as illustrated in Donn Pearce's iconic novel, *Cool Hand Luke* (1967), set in early 1940s Florida. States like Florida continued to utilize road labor prison gangs until the late 1960s, and "honor squads" of low-risk prisoners continued into the last third of the 20th century.

In the 1990s, several states in the south and west revived the classic chain gang of the 1930s. Chain gang revival was part of a series of measures designed to "get tough" on prisoners that enjoyed significant popular support in the context of frustrations over so-called molly-coddled prisoners

These young African American men were serving on a chain gang in the American south between 1900 and 1906. By 1910, every southern state legislature had authorized the use of convicts for public works, including Georgia, where 5,000 convicts were made available for road labor, 91 percent of whom were black.

that were taken up by politicians across the spectrum, public resentment at spiraling prison costs, and public weariness with prisoners' rights and rehabilitation programs. It also coincided with dramatic rises in the numbers of nonwhite state and federal prisoners. Inmates were set to work clearing roads and highways of litter and weeds. These tasks were similar to those of the "honor" squads, except chain gang inmates were literally chained at the ankles. Another common feature was the use of conspicuous uniforms, including old-fashioned black and white stripes and orange and pink jumpsuits. Critics charged that the primary purpose was not punishment but to deliberately humiliate inmates and create a demeaning public spectacle that could not effect rehabilitation.

Vivien Miller
University of Nottingham

See Also: African Americans; Convict Lease System; Corporal Punishment; Cruel and Unusual Punishment.

Further Readings
Burns, Robert E. *I Am a Fugitive From a Georgia Chain Gang!* Athens: University of Georgia Press, 1997.
Lichtenstein, Alex. *Twice the Work of Free Labor: The Political Economy of Convict Labor in the New South.* New York: Verso, 1996.
Myers, Martha A. *Race, Labor & Punishment in the New South.* Columbus: Ohio State University Press, 1998.
Pearce, Donn. *Cool Hand Luke.* London: Prion Books, 1999.
Spivak, John L. *On the Chain Gang,* 2nd ed. New York: International Pamphlets, 1934.
Steiner, Jesse F. and Roy M. Brown. *The North Carolina Chain Gang: A Study of County Convict Road Work.* Chapel Hill: University of North Carolina Press, 1927.

Chandler v. Florida

In *Chandler v. Florida* (1980), the U.S. Supreme Court ruled in a unanimous decision that the presence of a television camera in the courtroom or simply broadcasting or televising portions of a trial does not in and of itself constitute prejudice to the defendant or interfere with the defendant's right to a fair trial.

During the early 1980s, Florida was implementing an experimental pilot program to allow cameras in its courtrooms. In 1981, two Miami police officers were convicted of stealing $3,000 from a Miami Beach restaurant and challenged the new rules in Florida permitting cameras in the courtroom. Specifically, the defendants argued that the television coverage of their trial in and of itself had prevented them from receiving a fair trial. In *Chandler*, the court held that an absolute ban on cameras in the courtroom could not be justified based on the rationale that their use may pose a danger to the fair trial rights of a defendant, especially considering a judge's ability to control the media. Specifically, the court held that because it had no supervisory authority over state courts, its decision was limited to whether a constitutional violation had occurred. While the court approved the use of cameras in the criminal courtroom, the court reserved the right to hold that their use may, on a case-by-case basis, violate a defendant's right to a fair trial. Moreover, the court did not hold that a state was required to allow cameras in the courtroom.

Chandler v. Florida was not the first time the Supreme Court contemplated the constitutionality of cameras in the criminal courtroom. The prohibitions limiting the use of recording devices and cameras were instituted in the 1930s, in response to the outrageous press coverage of the trial of Bruno Hauptmann, who was charged with kidnapping the baby of Charles and Anne Lindbergh. As a result, the American Bar Association (ABA) adopted rules, known as Canon 35, prohibiting the use of cameras and other electronic equipment in courtrooms. These rules were adopted in most states. In 1952, the ABA rules were amended to include television. By the mid-1960s, the Supreme Court considered the constitutionality of the ban on cameras in the courtroom. Texas was one of a handful of states that sometimes permitted recording and photography in the courtroom. In *Estes v. Texas*, Billie Sol Estes was convicted of fraud and sentenced to 15 years imprisonment. Estes appealed on the grounds that he was deprived of a fair trial because his trial had been televised and broadcast. In *Estes*, at least a dozen cameras were present. The court agreed with Estes. During the mid-1970s, recording devices and cameras were barred from courtrooms in all but two states: Colorado and Texas. However, as technology improved, the experimental use of cameras in the courtroom also continued. Moreover, *Estes* was not explicitly overruled by *Chandler*.

In *Chandler*, the use of cameras in the courtroom was strictly regulated by an order from the Florida Supreme Court. Specifically, only one camera was present, and its location was fixed throughout the trial. Jurors were not permitted to be filmed, and recording of attorney and bench conferences was forbidden. Furthermore, the trial judge had the discretion to ban the coverage of certain witnesses, such as the victims of sexual assault. In all cases, a defendant retains the right to establish that the presence of cameras (or other media) violates, or compromises, his or her right to a fair trial. If the defendant establishes that the media compromises his or her constitutional right to a fair trial, an appellate court should reverse the conviction pursuant to *Estes*.

In 1991, the Courtroom Television Network, known as Tru-TV, premiered. It was the first commercial effort to televise selected trials nationally and to provide commentary by experts on what happens in the courtrooms of America. Millions of viewers have had access to the network, which has covered well over 1,000 trials. The advent of the Courtroom Television Network, along with several highly publicized trials such as the William Kennedy Smith rape trial and the O. J. Simpson murder trial, has led to questions and concerns about cameras in the courtroom and the transformation of trials into televised drama. By 2001, South Dakota became the 50th state to allow cameras in the courtroom to some degree. However, many states have limitations. For example, in Minnesota, if anyone in the case objects, the judge may keep cameras out.

Liz Marie Marciniak
Neil Guzy
University of Pittsburgh at Greensburg

See Also: Due Process; *Estes v. Texas*; News Media, Crime in; Television, Crime in.

Further Readings
Chandler v. Florida, 449 U.S. 560 (1980).
Dow, Marjorie and David Dow. *Cameras in the Courtroom: Television and the Pursuit of Justice*. Lanham, MD: Rowman & Littlefield, 2002.
Estes v. Texas, 381 U.S. 532 (1965).
Nasheri, Hedieh. *Crime and Justice in the Age of Court TV*. New York: LFB Scholarly Publishing, 2002.

Chapman, Mark David

Mark David Chapman was born to David and Diane Chapman on May 10, 1955, in Fort Worth, Texas. Chapman is well known as the man who shot and killed musician and former member of the Beatles John Lennon on December 8, 1980. After pleading guilty to the murder of Lennon, Chapman was sentenced to 20 years to life in prison and remains incarcerated at Attica Correctional Facility near Buffalo, New York. Although Chapman became eligible for parole in 2000, parole boards have denied his release six times. Guilty of a crime that shocked the nation, Chapman is considered by many to deserve lifetime imprisonment.

Mark David Chapman settled in Decatur, Georgia, with his parents and younger sister when he was 7. Both of his parents were present throughout his childhood, but Chapman has claimed that his father was often emotionally distant. Chapman became involved with drugs during his early teenage years, but by the age of 16 he was off drugs and became a born again Christian, working for several years as a camp counselor for his local YMCA. After graduating from high school in 1973, Chapman made an unsuccessful attempt at obtaining a college degree before returning to his hometown to work as a security guard. Suffering from depression, Chapman eventually moved to Honolulu, where he was briefly hospitalized in a mental facility following an unsuccessful suicide attempt in 1977.

After being discharged, Chapman began doing maintenance work for the same facility in which he had been hospitalized. While planning a vacation, Chapman met Gloria Abe, a Japanese-

American travel agent, and the two married on June 2, 1979.

While Chapman's motive for assassinating Lennon is not clear, several theories have been put forth. Some have asserted that Chapman was offended and enraged by Lennon's statement that the Beatles "were more popular than Jesus." However, there is little evidence to support this theory. Additionally, Chapman's obsession with J. D. Salinger's *The Catcher in the Rye* has been considered a potential contributor. This theory has been given more attention than the former because Chapman had a copy of the book on his person at the time of the murder. Finally, some indicate that Chapman was upset after reading Anthony Fawcett's *John Lennon: One Day at a Time*, which showed the style and wealth in which Lennon lived. Chapman's wife claimed that he perceived Lennon to be a hypocrite due to his wealth and lifestyle.

Though the exact motive for Chapman's crime is disputed, the circumstances of his crime are not. Chapman made one trip to Manhattan in October 1980 prior to returning to the city on December 6 of the same year. It was during this second trip that Chapman assassinated Lennon. He staked out the Dakota apartment building where Lennon lived with his wife, Yoko Ono, for two days before returning to the building on the evening of December 8. Lennon and Ono returned to their apartment around 10:50 P.M., at which time Chapman shot Lennon in the back four times. Chapman did not attempt to flee the scene and was restrained by security guards until police arrived. Lennon died in the ambulance on the way to Roosevelt Hospital.

Chapman was charged with second-degree murder in Lennon's death and, after being examined by a psychiatrist, was declared delusional but competent to stand trial. Initially, his attorney entered a plea of insanity. However, after several months of preparation for his trial, Chapman changed his plea to guilty in June 1981, and on August 24, 1981, he received a sentence of 20 years to life in a New York State Correctional Facility. Chapman remains in a special housing unit at Attica Correctional Facility and his next parole hearing was scheduled for 2012.

Amanda K. Cox
Pennsylvania State University, Altoona

See Also: Attica; Guns and Violent Crime; Insanity Defense; New York City; Violent Crimes.

Further Readings
Bresler, F. *Who Killed John Lennon?* New York: St. Martin's Press, 1989.
Jones, J. *Let Me Take You Down: Inside the Mind of Mark David Chapman, the Man Who Killed John Lennon.* New York: Random House, 1992.
Rosen, R. *Nowhere Man: The Final Days of John Lennon.* Oakland, CA: Quick American Archives, 2002.

Chicago, Illinois

Chicago's reputation for vice and corruption was born as it became the entrepôt of the northwest and grew with the city's rise as a commercial and industrial power. Famed for their innovations in agricultural processing, manufacturing, and retail sales, Chicago entrepreneurs took to less legitimate industries as well. The patterns of criminal activity that developed, and the social conflicts and attempts at study, reform, and control they fostered, all shaped and were shaped by the city's dynamic growth.

Chicago is located in the portage between the two major water systems of the Old Northwest—the upper Mississippi basin and the Great Lakes. It incorporated as a village in 1833 with 150 settlers. Though the city had but 25,000 residents by 1848, the conditions for its emergence as a commercial nexus were in place: the telegraph, the Illinois and Michigan Canal, oceangoing steamers, and railroad tracks. The city's unbridled growth reached 500,000 residents by 1880 and more than doubled during the next decade. Only after it reached 1.7 million in 1900 did growth slow to 25 percent for the next three decades before the population stabilized above 3.4 million from 1930 to 1970.

Early Law Enforcement
A murky relationship between politics and law enforcement developed early in Chicago's history. Mayor Levi Boone's attempt to enforce liquor regulations in 1855 led to the Lager Beer Riot, which spurred the replacement of the old system of law

A squad of Chicago mounted police lined up in a show of force around 1907. From 1875 to 1920, Chicago police killed three times as many people as local gangsters, committing one out of every 18 homicides, or 307 total. The city's overall murder rate was the highest outside of the south by 1920, at 9.7 per 100,000 persons.

enforcement—a salaried marshal coordinating the nighttime watch and nine daytime police—by the new Chicago Police Department. The new force, which grew from 80 officers in 1855 to more than 3,000 by the turn of the century, quickly became one of the most important institutions in establishing a new urban social order.

With officers wearing uniforms and a centralized chain of command, the police were able to perform a number of important tasks: Officers directed traffic and stopped runaway horses, and reunited lost children with their parents; police stations provided beds for the indigent. On the beat, officers mainly arrested drunks, vagrants, and other disorderly people who hung around the city's thousands of saloons. Such arrests could be demanding: Until 1880, when the call box and patrol wagon were invented, an officer might find himself with a belligerent arrestee and nothing more than a club to get him the up to half a mile to the station.

The police managed crime and vice rather than fighting it. Pickpockets and con men found ready prey among the many strangers in the city on business, and many travelers in turn sought out illicit recreation. Among Chicago's many houses of ill repute, Carrie Watson's parlor house and the Everleigh Club were the industry leaders. By 1911, the city had more than 5,000 prostitutes serving 5 million customers each year; their average weekly earnings of $25 were three times the mean female wage. Vice proliferated because it was often symbiotic with politics. In the 1870s, the city's biggest gambler, Mike McDonald, also ran the Democratic Party. Vice was segregated into its own districts, bringing to prostitution and gambling the same advantages that geographical concentration brought the stockyards. The most notorious district was "the Levee," where Michael "Hinky Dink" Kenna and "Bathhouse John" Coughlin ruled the First Ward from the 1890s to the 1920s by drawing graft and protection money from saloons, brothels, and gambling halls. "Big Jim" Colosimo rose from precinct captain to mob boss, running his many illicit operations out of the First Ward for nearly 20 years.

The embedding of policing within local politics was made possible by the exceptionally decentralized structure of both institutions. Wards overlapped police districts, and aldermen and ward committeemen reinforced their power by using the police to generate contributions. Gambling dens that refused to pay their tribute might find themselves suddenly subject to strict enforcement of the law.

Ward political machines centered on the city's thousands of saloons; 15 percent of alderman in 1874 were involved in the liquor business. "Hinky Dink" Kenna ran the Workingmen's Exchange Saloon. Saloons were the hub of social activity for Chicago's young workingmen, providing free meals, networking, paycheck cashing services, and recreation. An acceptance of illegal activity quickly became part of the department's institutional subculture for many reasons. Many policemen shared values with the men who hung out in saloons. National ties linked others of the 54 percent of police who were foreign born from 1890 to 1925. Tolerance pleased the political patrons of the officers—the men who sponsored them for their jobs and any promotions—by furthering the goals of the ward organization. It also could provide a supplement to the policeman's modest pay.

Early Crime and Punishment

Saloons were at the heart of a violent society in which drunken brawls were the leading cause of homicide before 1890. Violence permeated economic affairs, with labor and capital squaring off in the Great Railroad Strike of 1877, the Haymarket bombing in 1886, and the Pullman Strike of 1894. Although Chicago's businesses often went over the heads of the police department to Chicago's own Pinkerton Detective Agency, or even to state militia or federal troops, the Haymarket bombing solidified the police against labor radicalism. Resulting in the deaths of seven officers and injuries to 60 others, Haymarket created a bunker mentality in police culture and justified the creation of a Red Squad to collect intelligence on radicals. It remained in evidence when police killed 10 picketers at Republic Steel on May Day in 1937, and during the riot at the 1968 Democratic National Convention.

The influence of police culture was present in the high rate at which the police killed civilians in the line of duty. Overall, Chicago's homicide rate increased from 2.25 per 100,000 persons in 1875 to 9.7 in 1920—the highest rate outside of the south. The inclusion of new types of homicide (vehicular, abortion, and infanticide) accounted for only part of the rise. As murders multiplied, they also became more controlled, deliberate, and private, with domestic homicides and robbery-murders becoming the leading modes after 1890. Police officers were among the most lethal residents, committing one out of every 18 homicides—307 total over the period from 1875 to 1920. Police killed three times as many people as local gangsters, 2.5 times as many as were killed as a result of labor conflict, and killings by police outpaced killings of police threefold. A disproportionate number of their victims (21 percent) were from the city's 3 percent African American population.

Convictions were almost nonexistent (1 percent) in police killings and were rare for other homicides (24 percent of all homicides resulted in convictions). From 1875 to 1920, only 27 percent of individuals arrested by the police for a crime were convicted. Muckrakers attributed such failings to institutional corruption, but acquittals were often an expression of popular justice. This was especially true for homicides. As police improved at apprehending suspects—from 44 percent of cases in the 1870s and 1880s to 70 percent by the 1910s—the conviction rate decreased by 63 percent. More than 40 percent of suspects were released without indictment, and jurors convicted those who were tried only 36 percent of the time. However, against defendants considered particularly cold-blooded—wife-killers, robbery-homicides, those who killed police officers, and African American defendants—juries convicted at twice that rate.

In the 20th century, the proprietors of illicit commerce required flexibility to thrive. Reformers never took gambling lightly, and beginning with William T. Stead's exposé of the city during the 1893 World's Fair, *If Christ Came to Chicago* (1894), they attacked prostitution as well. Chicago's awful reputation came almost directly from their attacks. By the mid-1910s, Progressive pressure resulted in the breakup of the Levee (the city's red-light district), but this merely transformed vice. Automobiles and telephones, employed by a human network of saloonkeepers and pimps, made a more dispersed structure possible. Gamblers innovated as well, especially Mont Tennes, who used the telegraph to standardize off-track betting and used violence to consolidate his control of it.

Prohibition Era
The coming of Prohibition and the murder of Colosimo in 1920 by his lieutenant Johnny Torrio led to underworld consolidation and the quick rise of Torrio's subordinate, Al Capone. Bootlegging actually began as a diversified industry, run primarily by enterprising, young, usually immigrant men who had some experience in organized crime and were hungry for success. Liquor wholesalers soon turned to cartels to limit their investment risk: They divided territory, raised prices, reduced quality, and—especially—bought political protection (including payoffs to a rumored 50 percent of Chicago policemen). Bootlegging turned violent in Chicago in part because the decentralized structure of politics meant that there was no authority that could restrict grabs for more territory.

When William Dever became mayor in 1923, he destabilized the status quo by trying to enforce Prohibition. It was Capone, though, whose efforts to dominate the industry led to the "beer wars" from 1924 to 1930, punctuated by the St. Valentine's Day Massacre in 1929. This led the influential citizens group the Chicago Crime Commission to cement his historical reputation by naming him their Public Enemy No. 1.

In the early 20th century, Chicagoans built new institutions to address crime. The world's first juvenile court was established in 1899. Rather than finding children guilty and incarcerating them with adults, the court had the option of finding them delinquent, dependent, or neglected; judges could choose treatment from a variety of alternatives, including probation or placement in a reformatory. While the municipal court, which was founded five years later, did not transform the entire criminal court system, it did bring sociological jurisprudence to the lesser crimes, the governance of morals offenses (such as prostitution), and the behavior of boys who were too old for the juvenile court but not yet fully adults.

Just as influential in the history of criminology were the studies of delinquency done in the Sociology Department at the University of Chicago. Deploying an ecological understanding of social phenomena, the scholars of the Chicago school used the city as a laboratory for empirically studying various manifestations of crime and delinquency.

Race Relations
For Chicago's growing African American communities, the crackdown on segregated vice in the 1910s had unintended consequences. Chicago's strategic position in the rail network made it a major destination for African American migration, first from Kentucky and Tennessee and later from Louisiana, Mississippi, and Alabama. These migrants increased Chicago's African American population from 40,000 in 1910 to 278,000 in 1940, with the South Side Black Belt becoming increasingly crowded and racially concentrated. It also became the new vice district. Excluded from many other businesses, African American entrepreneurs invested in gambling and entertainment, especially in the policy wheel. Chicago's most powerful African American politicians of the 1920s, Oscar DePriest and Dan Jackson, were closely linked to both gambling interests and Republican Mayor William Hale Thompson.

The growing African American population was confronted with a massive rise in racially motivated crime. Between 1917 and 1921, there were 58 bombings in the name of restricting black residential mobility, which left two people dead, many injured, and much property destroyed. In the midst of this violence were five days of rioting in July and early August 1919, during which whites invaded black neighborhoods to injure, maim, and murder blacks. Before the violence ended, 38 persons were dead, 537 were injured, and more than 1,000 were left homeless. Nonetheless, the 17 indictments stemming from the riot all targeted African American men. After World War II, as Chicago's African American population grew to 813,000 by 1960, disputes over African American mobility once again led to racially inspired bombing or arson at a rate of one incident every 20 days.

Ironically, it was under the last of the nation's great political machines that the link between crime and politics was broken. Graft persisted during the reign of the Cermak-Kelly-Nash Democratic machine of the 1930s and 1940s. The mob took over slot machines, the racing wire, and many of the policy operations. According to the *Chicago Tribune*, there remained 1,000 gambling establishments in Cook County in 1959. When a group of Chicago policemen were discovered to be part of a burglary ring in the Summerdale district, Mayor Richard J. Daley used the scandal to clean house. Orlando W. Wilson, the nation's leading expert in police administration, was named commissioner and was given the political support to divorce wards from police districts, modernize communications, and put beat officers in squad cars.

Although Wilson created an environment that was intolerant of brutal methods and outright racism, long-standing tensions over police–community relations intensified before his retirement in 1967. Claims of discrimination were one source of friction: Although African American police officers roughly paralleled the percentage of African American residents in Chicago in the 1950s, they did not keep up with the city's rapid demographic change. During the late 1960s, African Americans and Puerto Ricans rioted in response to police treatment, leading Mayor Daley in one case to utter his famous "shoot to kill" order. The nadir came when Black Panther leaders Fred Hampton and Mark Clark were murdered in a midnight raid by police officers in 1969. The police were understood by those on the left to be a force of conservative counter reaction, symbolized by the Red Squad's spying on left-wing activists and the police riot at the 1968 Democratic National Convention.

Modern Chicago

From the 1960s to the present, suburbanization, deindustrialization, and rising income inequality have remade metropolitan Chicago. This structural transformation was accompanied by rising crime in the 1960s and 1970s. Homicide peaked

Chicago Police Department superintendent Jody Weis displayed these guns seized by Chicago police at a press conference on January 13, 2010. That year, the city experienced its lowest number of homicides since 1965, but six police officers were killed, the most in 25 years. Of all groups, African American men in the city are among the most likely to be victims of homicide.

in 1975, in 1981, and, again in 1992, each time at around 30 per 100,000 persons. After the latter, it began a long decline to half of its peak. Over this period, victimization rates for whites have remained remarkably stable and low; those for African Americans—especially men—grew to unprecedented heights in the early 1990s; and those for Latinos remained in the middle. Although Illinois maintains an incarceration rate well below the national average, there are more Chicagoans incarcerated today than at any other time in its history. The Cook County Department of Corrections alone holds more than 10,000 prisoners on a daily basis.

Policing has been a particularly important political issue over this period. By 1960, the department had more than 10,000 officers. In 1975, a federal judge concluded that the city had discriminated in the hiring of women, African Americans, and Latinos. Although the percentage of minority and female officers has increased in recent years, it has never reached parity with their percentages of the population. Over the past decade, claims of police brutality and discrimination were given credence amid revelations of the ongoing use of torture by a group of officers under Commander Jon Burge during the 1970s and 1980s. The Burge case has helped turn attention to the death penalty, as a number of his victims were sentenced to death based on confessions obtained through torture. While 171 Chicagoans were executed between 1840 and 1962, the practice has rarely been used since 1977 and may have ended since Governor George Ryan issued a moratorium in 2003.

Peter Constantine Pihos
University of Pennsylvania

See Also: 1851 to 1900 Primary Documents; 1941 to 1960 Primary Documents; Bootlegging; Capone, Al; Chicago Seven/Democratic National Convention of 1968; Everleigh Sisters; Gacy, John Wayne; Illinois; Leopold and Loeb; Nitti, Frank; Organized Crime, History of; Torrio, John; Wilson, O. W.

Further Readings

Adler, Jeffrey. *First in Violence, Deepest in Dirt: Homicide in Chicago, 1875–1920*. Cambridge, MA: Harvard University Press, 2006.

Asbury, Herbert. *Gem of the Prairie: An Informal History of the Chicago Underworld*. New York: Alfred A. Knopf, 1940.

Lindberg, Richard C. *To Serve and Collect: Chicago Politics and Police Corruption From the Lager Beer Riot to the Summerdale Scandal, 1855–1960*. Carbondale: Southern Illinois University Press, 1998.

Chicago Seven/ Democratic National Convention of 1968

In 1968, many groups protested the Vietnam War and fought for civil rights. It was the high-water mark of the Vietnam War for the United States with the Tet Offensive. It was also a year of great sorrow, because it saw the assassinations of two civil rights icons: Robert F. Kennedy and Martin Luther King, Jr. King, the spiritual and temporal leader of the civil rights movement for African Americans, was assassinated on April 4, 1968. Kennedy, the favored candidate for the Democratic nomination for president and the great hope for the youth of the nation to start the withdrawal from Vietnam and continue the civil rights movement, was assassinated on June 5, 1968. It was also the year of the 1968 Democratic National Convention and the year when one of the most infamous occurrences of police misconduct was televised to the entire nation. Riots broke out in over 100 U.S. cities.

Against this backdrop, the 1968 Democratic National Convention was scheduled to be held in Chicago from August 26 to August 29. The mayor of Chicago, Richard Daley, wanted to make the convention a national event to highlight the city. However, various social justice groups, focused around the Yippies, had made plans for holding a festival in Chicago to coincide with the Democratic National Convention to protest the Vietnam War. Other groups, including the Students for a Democratic Society (SDS) and the Black Panthers, were also involved. Mayor Daley, in response to the plans of the protesters, assured the media that they would not take over the streets of Chicago.

Prior to the start of the convention, Jerry Rubin, one of the Yippie leaders, announced that their nomination for president was an actual pig named Pigasus (the Yippies referred to the police as pigs). When the pig was placed on parade, Rubin and several others were arrested, resulting in Pigasus becoming a national media event.

With the start of the convention, approximately 10,000 demonstrators appeared. Mayor Daley had arranged for the Illinois National Guard to be present, and over 23,000 police and National Guardsmen met them. On August 28, at the rally in Grant Park, a boy lowered the American flag. The police attacked, broke through the crowd, and started to beat the boy. The protesters responded by pelting the police with rocks, food, and urine. A pitched battle broke out between protesters and the police, with one of the SDS leaders, Tom Hayden, exhorting the protesters to take the fight to the city if there was to be bloodshed. The police used tear gas, and many bystanders were injured. Newsmen Dan Rather and Mike Wallace were assaulted by the police. The protesters were taunting the police with the now-famous phrase "Hell no, we won't go," which changed to "Kill, kill, kill" as the violence became worse. The violence spread throughout the city, and for 17 minutes, the assault of the police against the protesters in front of the Hilton Hotel was broadcast on national television. At one point during the convention, Connecticut Senator Abraham Ribicoff stated that if George McGovern were nominated, the Gestapo tactics used in Chicago would not occur. Mayor Daley was reported to have cursed him in response.

The nation was shocked. Public opinion polls showed that the majority of Americans supported the actions of Mayor Daley, but too many people were incensed at the police conduct to forget the incident. An investigation was launched and the Walker Report was issued, which found much fault with the police. In the Walker Report, the phrase *police riot* was used to describe the behavior of the Chicago Police Department. One positive result was an increased national focus on the proper training for police officers.

Because of the riot, the U.S. Justice Department prosecuted a number of the leaders, who became famous as the Chicago Eight and then the Chicago Seven, after one defendant was dismissed for charges of conspiracy and incitement to riot. The defendants included such 1960s notables as Abbie Hoffman, Tom Hayden, Jerry Rubin, and Bobby Seale. The trial was a focus of media attention and became a circus due to the antics of the defendants and the defense mounted by their attorneys, who included famous civil rights attorney William Kunstler. All of the defendants were found guilty of incitement to riot but acquitted on the charges of conspiracy. Even the defendants' attorneys were sent to jail. All of the convictions were reversed on appeal, and the Justice Department declined to retry the case.

From a historical context, the 1968 Democratic National Convention and the Chicago Seven are monuments to the principle that there are limits to police conduct. Further, these events are considered one the major influences that began the modern professionalization of police departments in America through the use of education and training.

Wm. C. Plouffe, Jr.
Independent Scholar

See Also: Kennedy, Robert F.; King, Martin Luther, Jr.; Kunstler, William; Police, History of; Political Crimes, History of; Professionalization of Police; Riots.

Further Readings
Epstein, Jason. *The Great Conspiracy Trial*. New York: Random House, 1970.
Farber, David. *Chicago 1968*. Chicago: University of Chicago Press, 1988.
Kusch, Frank. *Battleground Chicago: The Police and the 1968 Democratic National Convention*. Chicago: University of Chicago Press, 2008.
Schultz, John. *No One Was Killed: The Democratic National Convention, August 1968*. Chicago: University of Chicago Press, 2009.

Child Abuse, Contemporary

The two major categories of child abuse are physical and sexual. Child abuse may initiate the next cycle and generation of adult abusers. Emotionally damaged survivors may engage in future child abuse, criminality, and violence. According to Childhelp, children are suffering from a hidden epidemic of child abuse and neglect. Over 3 million reports of child abuse are made every year in the United States; however, those reports may include multiple children. In 2007, approximately 5.8 million children were involved in an estimated 3.2 million child abuse reports and allegations. Almost five children die every day as a result of child abuse. More than three out of four are under the age of 4. There are many other forms of child abuse, including neglect, psychological maltreatment, and medical neglect.

Child Physical Abuse
The most frequent cause of death in children is physical abuse. Psychologists and social workers describe the physical abuse pattern as "battered-child syndrome." The telling signs of this syndrome are children exhibiting a pattern of bone fractures, subdermal hematoma, and soft tissue swelling. Sudden, near-death experiences should initiate further investigation and raise suspicion from medical and law enforcement professionals. Combinations of these symptoms represent positive indicators for child abuse and physical violence. In addition, the observation and documentation of prior recovered or healing injuries may indicate a future life-threatening attack.

Child abuse represents many cruel behaviors, from lesser assaults to sadistic torture. Investigators of possible child abuse incidents may discover that the injuries cannot be explained by guardians and remain inconsistent with factual evidence. Past injuries and bruises at varying degrees of coloration remain a strong indicator of child abuse. Generally, the first weapon of choice is the common belt attack, disguised as child discipline. The most subtle attack involves Munchausen syndrome, in which the mother presents an infant with a mysterious illness to doctors. However, she causes the emergency intervention to meet her own ego needs for attention. Another less obvious sign of physical abuse is shaken baby syndrome (SBS). This intentional and violent shaking of the child causes severe brain damage due to intracranial trauma. The violence and abuse may be precipitated by the child's continuous cries or screaming.

Burn Injuries
Deliberate burn injuries occur with children under the age of 10, with the majority of victims under 2 years of age. Children are burned for different reasons, which are generally related to twisted forms of deviant discipline. Burns may result from a caretaker's poor impulse control and anger over toilet training. There is an erroneous notion that the child will associate the punishment with toilet training compliance. In some cases, little hands may be forced into a pot of hot water as a punishment for playing near a stove.

Immersion burn patterns have a distinctive line pattern. They occur when a child is intentionally placed in a tub or sink full of hot water. Burn marks that are consistent with child abuse leave a pattern that cannot be hidden. The burn injury has a noticeable line of demarcation of uninjured tissue and injured tissue. In cases of deliberate immersion, the depth of the burn is consistent. Burn borders have defined "waterlines," with slight tapering of the depth at the edges. There may also be evidence of finger impressions/bruises on arms and shoulders resulting from the child trying to twist and turn from the hot water. These bruises indicate that the child was held in place by the caretaker. Generally, burns are located on the buttocks, between the legs, or on ankles, wrists, palms, or soles of the feet.

There may be a delay in medical treatment and inconsistent explanations from the caregivers. Close medical evaluation may find evidence of past child abuse. In addition, there may be a burn pattern that is inconsistent with the explanation of an accidental injury and evidence. The interview with the victim may reveal the identity, intent, and motivation of the offender(s). The possibility and incidence of death or serious injury is high in these burn cases.

Child Sexual Abuse
The average person views the child predator as wearing dark glasses and wearing a black trench coat. They summon mental images of the offender lurking in the shadows of an alley waiting for a child to appear. Child sadistic offenders exist; however, they do not appear any different than the average person on the street. More often, the offender knows the child, is an acquaintance, friend of the family, professional person of trust, or even

In the United States, physical abuse is the most frequent cause of death in children and almost five children die per day as a result of such abuse. In 2007 alone, about 5.8 million American children were involved in an estimated 3.2 million reports or allegations of child abuse. Three million reports of child abuse per year or more has become the average in the United States.

a family member. The child molester may engage in behaviors like touching or fondling to sadistic torture and rape. The terms *pedophile* and *child molester* may be applied interchangeably; however, the terms are different in their meaning and application. Pedophilia is a diagnostic mental disorder; the child molesters may not have this disorder.

According to the *Diagnostic and Statistical Manual of Mental Disorders III-R*, the child molester may be a pedophiliac, or the molester may be a situational offender. Pedophilia is a psychological attraction to children, a psychosexual disorder. Offenders have an intense attraction to children that is recurrent, including sexually arousing fantasies; their sexual targets rivet on prepubescent children. Pedophilia is a sexual desire or erotic craving of an adult who focuses on children. They are generally attracted to child victims between 8 and 10 years old and are not attracted to adults. In some cases, the children may even be as young as 2 years old. Child molesters may simply view children as opportunistic substitutes for their sexual gratification. Investigators have new investigative strategies for child sex offender cases. Investigators determine the modus operandi (MO), signature behavior, trademark, and behavioral activities linked to related cases. Crime analysis plus inductive and deductive reasoning techniques offer additional investigative opportunities. Analytical charting techniques offer new methods of analyzing behavioral evidence that link offenders to certain cases. Geographic information system (GIS) crime mapping identifies the geographical patterns of the offender's and victims spatial relationships. Social network analysis provides the means for identifying the offender's victims and relationships.

Conclusion

Police agencies are beginning to respond by assigning specialists to investigate crimes against children. Child abuse investigative strategies require interviewing the victim, caregivers, and coordinating the physical evidence with medical personnel. Accurate reporting serves as the backbone of any investigation, especially child abuse and predator investigations. Excellent reporting describes the acts that occurred between the offender and child. This means recounting the damage caused by the offender in the form of specific emotional symptoms and physical injuries.

Thomas E. Baker
University of Scranton

See Also: 2001 to 2012 Primary Documents; Child Abuse, History of; Child Abuse, Sociology of; Children, Abandoned.

Further Readings
American Psychiatric Association. *Diagnostic and Statistical Manual of Mental Disorders DSM-IV-TR*, 4th ed. Arlington, VA: American Psychiatric Publishing, 2000.
Baker, T. *Introductory Criminal Analysis*. Upper Saddle River, NJ: Pearson Prentice Hall, 2005.

Child Abuse, History of

Instances of child abuse have been documented as early as 322 B.C.E., during the era in which many believed that one's actions should promote quality of life for the greater good. Since then, child abuse and maltreatment have been part of virtually every culture and society. Protections against child abuse were instituted in the 1700s but were not effective until the mid- to late 1800s. Child abuse continues to be a social concern, despite the ongoing effort to reduce child abuse in the United States.

Colonization of the United States
In the 1500s and early 1600s, child abuse was widespread throughout the United Kingdom and Europe. The streets and rivers of England were often saturated with children who were not wanted by their parents. Furthermore, parents were able to discipline their children with any means they saw fit, often resulting in beatings, whippings, and burning. When the Puritans broke away from England and sailed to North America, these traditions and habits followed.

The majority of the first English colonists in North America were dependent children. Many of these children were homeless before coming to the colonies and remained so because of lack of funds and family. The English Privy Council issued an order to gather indentured and orphaned children and dispose of them in Virginia. Upon their arrival, indentured children were forced into shelters or remained homeless. Many infants did not survive past age 1 and approximately 50 percent of these children did not survive past age 20.

Life was especially complicated for orphaned children who found settlement in Virginia or Maryland. For example, Virginia desired to increase the number of wool and hemp products to create more revenue. The courts opted to appoint orphans and indentured children to workhouses, resulting in fewer children on the streets and cheap labor for manufacturers. This practice resulted in the desired outcome of increasing production; however, the bosses would whip and beat the children if they did not produce enough material or if they were slacking on the job.

Those families fortunate enough to find areas suitable for living made their children participate in the construction of housing and other labor necessary for family survival. The children working on the construction of homes or other projects were made to carry large pieces of lumber, despite their lack of muscle and proper help. It was not uncommon to find reports of child death as a result of labor accidents. In fact, when an accident occurred, fathers would give lashings to the child for making mistakes.

The familial structure of the new colonies was not unlike the familial structure of precolonial England. Fathers, or the eldest son, were the heads of the family and were the sole owners of property. Furthermore, the eldest son was typically the heir to the family fortune and women were often ineligable for property acquisition if a male in the family was alive. Because a man's house was considered his castle, he was free to do as he pleased, so long as he did not take a life.

Children in Colonial America
Children in colonial America faced the same challenges as those who first settled in the New World. Children were considered valuable assets because they could be used for work around the house. Nevertheless, children were often physically abused, neglected, and in some cases, sexually abused. Orphanages and almshouses were the

main forms of relief from this type of behavior, yet the conditions in these places were less than desirable. Children who avoided their homes or the almshouses often lived on the side of a road in cardboard boxes. It was often the case that at least one-quarter of the inhabitants in jails were children. This pattern of child abuse and neglect was seen throughout the colonial period and into the Civil War.

Civil War in the United States

Child abuse in the United States was widespread at the time of the Civil War. Male children were made to work on farms from sunrise to sunset, and female children learned the ways of the housewife for their future husbands. The children of slaves were subjected to much harsher rule than those of nonslave parents. African females and their female children were prostitutes, housemaids, and cooks. They were regularly beaten by slave owners and were sometimes loaned to other slave owners for prostitution. The prostitution of a slave began anywhere from age 10 to 14. Male slave children were made to work on the farm with the adult male slaves. Like the adults, they were beaten, cattle prodded, and sold at the will of the slave owner.

After the Civil War, the children of former slaves had little in the way of social support. The almshouse in Richmond, Virginia, was a place where African females who were pregnant could take refuge, but it was not uncommon for the nurses there to beat the children. Families who did not want their children would leave them at the almshouse, hoping that the nurses would give them a better life; however, the nurses often disposed of children by drowning, heavy medication, or starvation.

Industrial Revolution, Child Labor, and Abuse

The Industrial Revolution influenced the United States by creating more factory jobs. Children of the Industrial Revolution were faced with new tasks, which required them to develop new skill sets to make them more marketable in the workforce. This new requirement meant that children had to attend school to learn to read and write. Children were expected to behave in a certain manner while in school. Deviation in behavior often resulted in lashings or whippings by schoolteachers. When school recessed for the day, the children would either go to work or go back home for chores,

These "breaker boys" worked sorting impurities from coal by hand in the Woodward Coal Mines in Kingston, Pennsylvania, around 1900. Breaker boys were usually 8 to 12 years old.

depending on age and gender of the child. Unlike their counterparts, who typically were meant to stay at home and tend the house, male children were meant to go to work to provide for their family. Long hours and low pay were the norm of society, and even lower pay and longer hours were the norm for children. The bosses of mills would often strike children who were not producing enough goods or who were not working hard enough. When the children were finished with work for the day, they would also tend to chores at home, such as cooking, cleaning, or farm work. The combination of school, long work hours, and regular beatings by authoritative figures led to the child savers movement in the United States.

Preventing Child Abuse

Laws protecting children from harsh labor did not appear until the late 1800s in the United States. These laws reduced the number of hours a child could work per day and the total number of hours per week. These laws were derived directly from England's Factory Act, passed in 1831, which allowed children from the ages of 9 to 12 to work for 12 hours a day and for a maximum of 48 hours per week. Furthermore, statutes mandating that children attend school on a regular basis promoted children's well-being by valuing education for the young.

During the late 1800s, child abuse started to become more of a social problem, rather than a family problem. In 1874, the case of Mary Ellen in the United States was the beginning of the social reform movement to stop child abuse. After a neighbor witnessed the beating of Mary Ellen by her foster mother, the Society for the Prevention of Cruelty to Animals brought the case before the court. They argued that a child should have at least as many rights as an animal. The result of this case led to the creation of the Society for the Prevention of Cruelty to Children. It also led to a number of laws preventing and punishing child abuse in the United States. Many of the laws that have been passed categorize child abuse, sexual abuse, and neglect under the term *child maltreatment*. Additionally, the courts began considering the well-being of children by enacting *parens patriea*. This doctrine permitted courts to act in loco parentis, meaning that the court could act as if it was the parent of a child if there was a need to do so. Typically, a court would do so if there was evidence of severe abused or if a child was orphaned. This doctrine gave some assurance that children of the state were going to be protected from abuse and neglect.

Abuse in Modern Society

Modern child abuse is not unlike the forms of child abuse in previous decades. Regular reports of beatings, burnings, and accidental and purposeful deaths riddle the nightly news and newspapers. In the early to mid-2000s, the focus on child abuse shifted from parents to educators; namely, the clergy and schoolteachers. Catholic priests were scrutinized when reports of rape and sexual abuse surfaced in the media. Many priests were accused of raping young men who served as altar boys. Several public school teachers across the United States also became the targets of lawsuits when it was discovered that some children had been brutally raped by teachers. Though many of these accusations have since been invalidated, especially those against educators, society has recognized different forms of child abuse and the need to protect against them.

Despite having passed laws to prevent child abuse, there are still forms of child abuse commonly practiced through religion or as a habit of society. Male circumcision is thought of as child abuse by some. In this procedure, the physician removes the sheath of foreskin from the penis. This is done as a religious ceremony for the Jewish faith, and for non-Jewish families it is done out of tradition. Research concerning the effectiveness and cleanliness of circumcisions has shown mixed results. Some researchers have concluded that circumcisions of both males and females can lead to later complications in life, such as human immunodeficiency virus and acquired immune deficiency syndrome (HIV/AIDS) and infections, while others have found little evidence to support the health risks involved with the procedure. Circumcision is a widely accepted ritual in many countries, however, the risks involved with the procedure may be cause for concern.

Historians have documented the prevalence of child abuse as early as the Greek philosophers. Early attempts at punishing child abuse failed because of lack of enforcement of child abuse laws. The reform movements of the 19th century resulted in more cases being presented to the courts, better identification of child abuse, and legislation for harsher punishment of child abuse. In spite of reform, some modern societies continue to practice child abuse as either a religious ceremony or out of habit.

Thomas Zawisza
University of Arkansas at Little Rock

See Also: 1777 to 1800 Primary Documents; 2001 to 2012 Primary Documents; Child Abuse, Contemporary; Child Abuse, Sociology of; Infanticide.

Further Readings
Abbot, Edith. "A Study of the Early History of Child Labor in America." *American Journal of Sociology*, v.14/1 (1908).
Costin, Lela, Howard Jacob Karger, and David Stoesz. *The Politics of Child Abuse in America*. New York: Oxford University Press, 1997.
Radbill, Samuel X. *The Battered Child*. Chicago: University of Chicago Press, 1968.

Child Abuse, Sociology of

Child abuse, as a recognized sociological phenomenon, is relatively new. It wasn't until 1946 that American medicine recognized the intentional mistreatment of children as a real entity. This changed, in large part, due to John Caffey's seminal article in the *American Journal of Radiology* that documented a series of long-bone injuries and subdural hematomas in infants and toddlers consistent with our current understanding of child abuse. However, it was not until C. Henry Kempe et al.'s paper defining the battered child syndrome that our current view on child abuse took hold. Laws mandating the reporting of child abuse have since been put in place in all 50 states.

Until the Renaissance (and perhaps later), children were not seen as being different than their adult counterparts. They were often viewed as "small adults" and were treated as such in labor, personal responsibilities, and in methods of discipline. Only as the popular view of childhood evolved into one of childhood as a process of development did the views on discipline change. It was requisite that children be seen as separate from adults to have two separate disciplinary standards. What is now viewed as potentially abusive was not in times past. Differing cultures continue to have widely different views on what is or is not abusive.

In 1974, in line with the nation's evolving awareness of child abuse, Congress passed the Child Abuse Prevention and Treatment Act. Its definition includes the physical or mental injury, sexual abuse, or negligent treatment of a minor by those responsible for the child's welfare. The National Incidence Study (NIS), a comprehensive review of current incidence of child abuse in the United States, was mandated by this act. Currently in its fourth iteration, the NIS has two definitions for child maltreatment: the harm and endangerment standards. The harm standard defines abuse only if the child has already experienced some degree of harm. The endangerment standard, in contrast, also sees children as maltreated if they have been put at risk of harm. The maltreatment of children encompasses all areas of abuse: physical, sexual, emotional, and neglect.

While physical and sexual abuse are relatively easy to document and quantify, defining neglect is more difficult. Neglect universally includes the failure of a caregiver to provide food, clothing, shelter, medical care, or supervision. In addition to physical and emotional neglect, an increasing number of states (24 as of 2009) also have provisions for educational neglect. Yet fewer (seven) states have specific provisions defining medical neglect. Depending on local and regional reporting laws and dependency and criminal statutes, the definition of neglect becomes even broader.

National Incidence Study Results

Unfortunately, estimating the prevalence of any form of child abuse is exceedingly difficult. The majority of abuse cases go unreported or undiscovered, thus artificially deflating any reported incidence. The National Incidence Study, however, gives the best and most comprehensive data on child abuse available. Between 1986 and 1993, cases of abuse increased by more than 50 percent. However, it is unknown if this reflects a true increase in abuse cases or is more suggestive of an increase in awareness and reporting. In 2006, in contrast, there was a 19 percent decrease in reported cases of maltreatment. Despite potential underreporting biases, the numbers remain alarmingly high. Using the harm standard definition, nearly 1.25 million children were abused in the United States. Almost three million children were maltreated during this time using the endangerment standard, however. Of all reported cases, physical abuse was most common, followed by sexual abuse. In terms of neglect, educational neglect was most common (47 percent), a third were physically neglected, and a quarter were emotionally neglected.

In the case of sexual abuse, victims tend to be more heterogeneous as a group, and as a result, development of prevention programs has been more complex. A large focus has been on educating children at risk of being potential targets. In 2006, girls had a significantly higher rate of harm standard abuse than boys. An estimated 8.5 per 1,000 girls experienced harm standard abuse compared to 6.5 per 1,000 boys. In other words, girls' risk of abuse was 1.3 times that of boys. However, girls' overall higher risk of harm standard abuse is due primarily to their significantly higher risk of sexual abuse (five times greater than for boys).

White and black children had significantly different rates of maltreatment according to the harm standard during 2006. Approximately 12.6 per 1,000 white children experienced harm standard maltreatment, whereas this number was nearly double, or 24 per 1,000 for black children. The rate for black children was also significantly higher than that for Hispanic children (14.2 per 1,000), with black children 1.7 times more likely to experience harm standard maltreatment than Hispanic children. Other race categories (including American Indian or Alaska Native, Native Hawai'ian or other Pacific Islander, or mixed race) were represented too rarely to develop estimates for these groups.

The rate of harm standard abuse was also significantly higher for black children than for children in the other two racial/ethnic groups. An estimated 10.4 per 1,000 black children suffered harm standard abuse during 2006 compared to 6 per 1,000 white children and 6.7 per 1,000 Hispanic children. The abuse rate of black children is 1.7 times that of white children and 1.6 times that of Hispanic children. An estimated 14.7 per 1,000 black children experienced harm standard neglect during 2006 compared to 7.5 per 1,000 white children, a statistically marginal difference. Thus, black children had nearly two times the risk of harm standard neglect compared to white children.

Corporal punishment remains a controversial topic, partly due to the difficulty distinguishing between discipline and abuse. Despite this, more than 90 percent of American parents report having used physical discipline at least once, according to J. E. Lansford, and between 40 to 70 percent report using corporal punishment within a more limited time frame. Multiple studies have indicated a link to a higher incidence of externalizing disorders, aggression, and delinquency among those who experience corporal punishment. However, in cultures where corporal punishment is more accepted, this is not entirely the case.

Laws have been developed in every state in the United States defining mandated reporters. These individuals include personnel working in educational, legal, law enforcement, criminal justice, social services, medical, mental health, foster care, or child care fields. Provisions in these laws allow for mere "reasonable suspicion" that abuse or other maltreatment has occurred and provides immunity for acting in good faith. School professionals represent the largest group of mandated reporters (17 percent), followed by law enforcement (16.3 percent). Social services, medical staff, and mental health practitioners follow (10.2, 8.4, and 4.3 percent, respectively). Physicians, nurses, daycare personnel, and neighbors are frequently the ones to suspect and report neglect occurring to infants, toddlers, and preschool-aged children. Relatives, police officials, and close friends are frequently the ones to suspect neglect toward teens and young adults.

Effects of Abuse

Youth who experience maltreatment are at significant risk for both short-term as well as long-term deleterious consequences. According to the National Survey of Child and Adolescent Well-Being (NSCAW), more than 25 percent of children in foster care 12 months or more had a lasting health problem. More than 75 percent of foster children between 1 and 2 years of age were found to be at medium to high risk for problems with brain development, as opposed to fewer than 50 percent of children in a control sample. Given that the human brain experiences its greatest growth

An advocate works with a child abuse victim in 2009. As many as 80 percent of young adults with a history of abuse may suffer depression, anxiety, eating disorders, and suicide attempts.

in the first year of life, and continues to rapidly develop during early childhood, this is significant. In addition, fear, disruptions of attachment, and violations of trust can also have lasting consequences, including poor self-esteem, troubled relationships, and psychological symptoms including depression and anxiety.

These difficulties can carry on into adulthood. In one long-term study, as many as 80 percent of young adults with a history of abuse demonstrated symptoms, including depression, anxiety, eating disorders, and suicide attempts. Children who experience maltreatment are also more likely to develop antisocial traits. Parental neglect is also associated with borderline personality disorders and violent behavior. A number of studies have also suggested increased risk of the following outcomes: delinquency, risk-taking behaviors, teen pregnancy, poor academic performance, substance use, and psychiatric comorbidity. Child maltreatment also results in a cost to society. Financially, these costs are significant. A 2001 report by Prevent Child Abuse America estimates $24 billion per year, including costs associated with juvenile and adult criminal activity, mental illness, substance abuse, and domestic violence.

A number of programs have been developed over the past 40 years addressing prevention of child abuse and neglect with different strategies. These programs have focused on increasing parent and caregivers' knowledge and skills, changing societal norms, and increasing support for parents. Theories supporting these programs have varied from psychodynamic, learning, ecological, to environmental. According to D. Daro, psychodynamic theory suggests that if parents better understood themselves, they would be less likely to engage in abusive behavior, whereas gaining more knowledge about how to best care for children helping decreasing rates of abuse is supported by learning theory. Provision of greater material or social supports being of benefit is supported by environmental theory, whereas ecological theory suggests that a network of services to compensate for a variety of deficiencies would be helpful.

Jeremy Matuszak
Maya Strange
University of Nevada, Reno

See Also: Child Abuse, Contemporary; Child Abuse, History of; Children, Abandoned.

Further Readings
Daro, D. *Confronting Child Abuse.* New York: Free Press, 1988.
Kempe, C. Henry, et al. "The Battered-Child Syndrome." *Journal of the American Medical Association* (July 7, 1962).
Lansford, J. E. and K. A. Dodge. "Cultural Norms for Adult Corporal Punishment of Children and Societal Rates of Endorsement and Use of Violence." *Parenting: Science and Practice*, v.8 (2008).
Lewis, M. *Child and Adolescent Psychiatry: A Comprehensive Textbook*, 3rd ed. Philadelphia: Lippincott Williams and Wilkins, 2002.
Myers, J. E. B., et al. *The APSAC Handbook on Child Maltreatment*, 2nd ed. Thousand Oaks, CA: Sage, 2002.

Child Murderers, History of

Evidence of children who murder dates back to the 1700s with the case of William York, who in 1748 mutilated and stabbed to death 5-year-old Susan Mahew in Suffolk, England. A few other historic cases are of note. In 1874, Jesse Pomeroy killed a 4-year-old boy and a 10-year-old girl in Boston at the age of 14. During a home burglary in June 1945, 16-year-old William Heirens attacked an unsuspecting homeowner in Chicago and slit her throat.

American serial killer, Edmund Kemper, began his murderous career in 1963, at age 15, when he shot both of his grandparents in California. Another high-profile child murderer is 11-year-old Mary Bell, who strangled a 3-year-old and 4-year-old boy in Scotswood, England, during the summer of 1968. In March 1978, 15-year-old Willie Bosket shot and killed Noel and Moises Perez in New York, during attempted robberies, which led to the state's law changing so that juveniles as young as 13 could be tried as adults. In an inexplicable chain of events, 17-year-old Brenda Spencer, shot into a San Diego elementary school in 1979, killing two men, simply because she did not like Mondays. Additionally, in February 1993, there was the incident of two 10-year-olds, Robert Thompson and Jon Venables, who lured 2-year-old James Bulger away from a shopping center in northwest England where they sexually abused him and subsequently beat him to death with bricks, stones, and a metal bar.

In 1988, 15-year-old Rod Matthews of Massachusetts lured his 14-year-old neighbor into the nearby woods, where he beat him to death with a baseball bat for the thrill of learning what it was like to kill someone. Matthews later bragged to two friends of his actions and brought them to view the bludgeoned body. Matthews's impulsive homicide serves as an example of thrill killing, whereby a relatively normal juvenile randomly kills a stranger to experience some form of exhilaration. The 1986 cult-related torture killing of James Thimm in Nebraska was committed by 15-year-old Dennis Ryan and his father, Michael Ryan. As members of a deeply religious survivalist cult, Ryan and his father demoted fellow cult follower, Thimm, to rank of slave and subsequently tortured him to death. In the same year, 16-year-old Sean Sellers killed both of his parents in Oklahoma during a satanic ritual that he conducted while they slept. Thus, the prevalence of involvement in the occult is associated with past instances of juvenile-perpetrated homicides. While the motives of some juvenile murderers often appear nefarious, some youth-involved homicides are committed in the defense of others. For instance, in 1988, a 3-year-old boy living in Detroit retrieved his father's pistol from a nearby table to shoot and kill his father, who was brutally assaulting his mother.

Youth-involved homicide remains a contemporary problem, especially since homicide arrests for juveniles in the United States rose every year from 1984 to 1993. Current trends suggest that young people in the United States are killing more now than in the mid-1980s. However, homicides by juveniles are still quite rare in comparison to those committed by adults, especially when the youngest of juvenile homicide offenders are considered. Nevertheless, such brutal and violent murders committed by children bewilder a concerned public. In fact, the 2003 case of Lionel Tate, who killed his 6-year-old neighbor while reenacting professional wrestling moves he had seen on television, garnered immediate media attention. The 12-year-old Tate was facing life in prison without the possibility of parole until an appeal reversed the decision because his competency to stand trial as an adult had not been evaluated prior to trial. As a result, Tate was given one year of house arrest and 10 years of probation. This landmark case led many social and behavioral scientists, such as Thomas Grisso, Robert Schwarz, Laurence Steinberg, Franklin Zimring, and Elizabeth Cauffman to further develop research on how developmental maturity affects a juvenile homicide offender's ability to competently stand trial as an adult.

Risk Factors

While the term *youth* is often used to broadly include both juveniles and adolescents, there are distinctions between the two. The minority status of *juvenile* is defined by legislative statute and the federal government. This legal label is applied to children who have committed a crime while under the age of 18. On other hand, *adolescence* refers to a stage in human development when a child reaches puberty, which usually occurs by age 12 but can extend to age 19 or 20. The use of the term *children* typically refers to prepubescent youth.

Since the mid-1950s, research has revealed numerous factors associated with youth homicide. Lauretta Bender's research in 1959, which involved 33 children who committed homicide prior to age 16, found that roughly half of the subjects had been referred for psychiatric evaluation, where several were diagnosed with schizophrenia, epilepsy, chronic brain syndromes without epilepsy, and depression. Bender acknowledged several risk factors for child homicide offenders, which included a history of brain damage, schizophrenia, compulsive fire setting, mental retardation, unfavorable home environments, and personal life experience with a violent death.

Elsewhere, researchers identified different risk factors, such as intense self-destructive impulses, intense hostile reactions, immaturity, infantile rage, psychopathic tendencies, language and education deficits, inability to find alternatives to difficult life situations, availability of weapons, history of harming small animals, presence of an overly dominant mother, childhood maltreatment, living in poverty, and a history of making homicidal threats and fighting other children. These risk factors encapsulate the biological, psychological, and sociological underpinnings of child murderers.

Specifically, psychological deficits among juvenile murderers are explained by mental illnesses, psychoses, mood disorders, defective intelligence, and severe childhood trauma. These include factors like impaired ego development, unresolved dependency needs, displaced anger, the ability to dehumanize the victim, and narcissistic deficiencies. Biological dysfunctions include neurological impairments or brain injuries. Sociological factors refer to turbulent or disturbing home situations, family violence, spousal abuse, and parental abuse. Peer influences may also play a role in youth-involved homicide, since adolescence is a period of development where a youth undergoes great pressure to obtain peer acceptance and individual autonomy. In fact, peer rejection and ridicule were linked to the Columbine High School shootings, which took place in 1999.

Classifications
In 1989, Dewey Cornell and colleagues developed a typology for classifying juvenile homicide offenders into three categories based on the circumstances of the offense: (1) psychotic, (2) conflict, and (3) crime. In the case of the psychotic youth, he or she exhibits severe mental illness such as hallucinations or delusions, and psychiatric disorders play a large role in the person's homicidal tendencies because these conditions cause the youth to lose touch with reality. However, juvenile homicide offenders are rarely classified as psychotic. One example of a juvenile psychotic killer is the 1986 case of Patrick DeGelleke who, at the age of 15, murdered both of his adoptive parents by setting fire to their bedroom. Psychologists concluded that DeGelleke's knowledge of his parents' intent to institutionalize him threw him into a psychotic rage that resulted in his homicidal actions.

The conflict-related classification is reserved for youthful murderers who engaged in an argument or dispute that later resulted in the victim's death. For example, in 1998, 15-year-old Jonathan Miller attacked and beat 13-year-old Josh Belluardo as the two exited a school bus in Georgia. The assault was a result of an argument between the two boys that occurred while on the bus. The blows Belluardo sustained caused a hole in an artery at the base of his brain, which put him in a coma and later led to his death. Miller was sentenced to life in prison. Conflict-related offenders score higher on family dysfunction measures and seldom have a significant prior delinquency record.

Those offenders with circumstances categorized as crime-related are youth who kill while committing some other felony such as rape or robbery. A widely publicized Vermont case of rape eventuating into homicide took place in 1982 when 15-year-old James Savage and 16-year-old Louis Hamlin dragged two 12-year-old girls into the woods where they undressed them, tied them up, raped them, shot them with a BB gun, and stabbed them. One of the girls died. Crime-related offenders usually have school adjustment problems, substance abuse problems, and involvement in previous criminal activity. They tend to act with accomplices and to be under the influence of drugs during the murder.

Due to the seriousness of their offense, youthful murderers face the increased potential of being transferred to criminal court where they face adult sanctions. Traditionally, judicial waiver was the predominant method of transfer in the 1960s, and it entailed a review by a juvenile court judge of the youth's prior record, character, maturity, seriousness of the offense, his or her amenability to rehabilitation, the suitability of available programs at facilities, and the interest of public safety. However, between 1992 and 1995, automatic forms of juvenile waiver, such as prosecutorial direct file or statutory exclusion, became more commonly used; these waivers do not require any formal review of the youth's sophistication and ability to stand trial competently as an adult. Instead, the focus of automatic or mandatory waiver practices is to punish the grave crime of murder with severe sentencing in the hope of achieving deterrence and retributive goals. Competency to stand trial refers to the defendant's ability to assist counsel; the ability to reason and understand the legal proceedings against him or her; and the ability to adeptly make legal decisions. Research in the behavioral and social sciences has found that juveniles may not possess the developmental maturity necessary to be considered competent to stand trial as adults. Mandatory or automatic forms of waiver lack adequate guidelines to properly evaluate a youth's level of developmental maturity to be deemed fit for trial and thus place the juvenile defendant in peril of receiving long-term confinement without consideration of treatment and rehabilitation. Although the U.S. Supreme Court decided in the 2005 *Roper v. Simmons* case that defendants under the age of 18 are not eligible for the death penalty, youthful murderers may still receive a sentence of life without parole.

Treatment
Research between the late 1970s and the early 1990s revealed many effective treatments for child murderers. In 1992, Wade Myers identified four major areas of treatment for homicidal youth: psychotherapy, psychiatric hospitalization, institutional placement, and the use of psychopharmacological drugs. These four interventions can be effectively utilized to treat young killers, but must be tailored to account for the individual needs of the youth while attending to unique family situations, mental and learning disorders, and substance abuse and/or dependence. Psychotherapy has proven successful for youth with undifferentiated conduct disorder who also have prior emotional relationships with their victims and are suicidal. Psychotherapy is most effective for more mature youth who are capable of forming emotional relationships with others and can perform introspective self-examination.

Psychiatric hospitalization is usually used for preadolescent child murderers who appear psychotic and require psychopharmacological management. Hospitalization can allow mental health professionals to provide an appropriate setting to evaluate the youth and stabilize his or her homicidal impulses. Institutional placement is frequently used for adolescent murderers in order to provide a prosocial environment that aids their cognitive and emotional growth, which will permit them to better control their aggression. Psychotropic drugs, which require careful monitoring, can be used in addition to the above treatments in an effort to reduce aggression, stabilize mood, and alleviate the symptoms of mental disorders.

Brian G. Sellers
University of South Florida

See Also: Infanticide; Juvenile Justice, History of; Juvenile Offenders in Adult Courts; Murder, Contemporary; Murder, History of; School Shootings.

Further Readings
Bender, Lauretta. "Children and Adolescents Who Have Killed." *American Journal of Psychiatry*, v.116 (1959).
Davis, Carol Anna. *Children Who Kill: Profiles of Preteen and Teenage Killers*. London: Allison & Busby, 2008.
Grisso, T. et al., eds. *Youth on Trial: A Developmental Perspective on Juvenile Justice*. Chicago: University of Chicago Press, 2000.
Heckel, Robert V. and David M. Shumaker. *Children Who Murder: A Psychological Perspective*. Westport, CT: Praeger, 2001.
Heide, Kathleen M. *Why Kids Kill Parents: Child Abuse and Adolescent Homicide*. Thousand Oaks, CA: Sage, 1992.
Heide, K. M. *Young Killers: The Challenge of Juvenile Homicide*. Thousand Oaks, CA: Sage, 1999.
Knapp, A. and W. Baldwin. *The Newgate Calendar: Comprising Interesting Memoirs of Notorious Characters, Vol. 2*. London: J. Robins, 1825.
Moffatt, Gregory K. *Blind-Sided: Homicide Where It Is Least Expected*. Westport, CT: Praeger, 2000.
Ramsland, Katherine. (n.d.). "Court TV's School Killers." http://www.trutv.com/library/crime/serial_killers/weird/kids1/index_1.html (Accessed April 2012).
Sellers, Brian G. and Bruce A. Arrigo. "Adolescent Transfer, Developmental Maturity, and Adjudicative Competence: An Ethical and Justice Policy Inquiry." *Journal of Criminal Law & Criminology*, v.99/2 (2009).
Smith, D. and K. Sueda. "The Killing of Children by Children as a Symptom of National Crisis." *Criminology & Criminal Justice*, v.8/1 (2008).

Children, Abandoned

Child abandonment means giving up all claim and interest over an infant with intent of never reclaiming the baby. Mothers surrender offspring for various reasons: mental illness, for example, or poverty, particularly in societies with inadequate social welfare arrangements or in which adoption procedures are difficult or orphanages are rare or overcrowded.

An abandoned child, a foundling, is not to be confused with a runaway or an orphan. The prevalence of child abandonment in literature does not necessarily mean that the culture practices abandonment. Societies that long abandoned or never practiced it still have the literature and tradition. Even societies with no history of abandonment have myths of abandoned children living in luxury after being taken by supernatural beings.

Historical Context

Oedipus was abandoned after an oracular proclamation that the child would cause harm. Some mothers in Greek myth chose to hide the result of a god's rape. A jealous stepmother cast out Snow White. Commonly, the foundling is taken in by a lower-class person, often a shepherd, a rural start for an abandoned urban child. Extreme examples involve the rearing of the child by animals: Romulus and Remus by wolves, Tarzan by apes. Oedipus grows up to marry his mother. Snow White survives with the help of dwarves. A common twist, introduced by Euripides, is the happy reunion of the now-grown child because of his or her possession of a token.

In the 1980s, historians and anthropologists agreed that premodern societies practiced infanticide to control population, most commonly through exposure. Modern instances are rare but not unknown. In 1988, John Boswell's *The Kindness of Strangers* found that abandoned children included not only the deformed or those born outside "legitimate" relationships but "normal" babies as well. Boswell estimated 20 to 40 percent of Roman babies were abandoned—but most were rescued. Some became slaves, most were foster children. The kindness of strangers, as in the fairy tales, determined the fate of the child.

Even in seriously infanticidal societies, most children are not killed but abandoned, given at least a chance to survive. Religious authorities in countries dominated by Abrahamic religions (Judaism, Christianity, Islam) condemned infanticide as murder but had no proscription of abandonment.

Abandonment waned between 1000 and 1200 and then rose in the 13th century as population increased and economic hard times prevailed. Some Italian cities introduced foundling homes to reduce the likelihood of an unwed mother killing her infant to avoid social stigma or by parents too poor to care for another child. Foundling homes replaced the kindness of strangers as they spread through Portugal, Spain, and France. In the Enlightenment, foundling homes proliferated anew in Catholic Europe and Russia in response to a rise in exposures, up to 150,000 a year in Europe in the early 19th century, as illegitimacy and poverty rose. The mortality of foundlings in the first year in the homes was 50 percent.

In early-19th-century Protestant Europe and the United States, abandonment was rare. In Catholic Europe, abandonment was discreet until the mid-19th century, when asylums made abandonment a public rather than a private matter. When abandonment was public, the number of abandonments dropped sharply, as did the incidence of foundling mortality. Increased availability of contraception also decreased abandonments.

Industrialization generated unregulated work for children as young as 4 in mines and factories and as chimney sweeps. Often, the children were farmed out by workhouse managers. Charles Dickens became a child worker at age 12 when his father was in debtor's prison and regarded the experience as one of abandonment by his family, as reflected in the largely autobiographical *David Copperfield*. Reform in the early 19th century focused on the mines and factories but also on asylums; 19th-century England had asylums in virtually all major cities for the care of babies abandoned by unmarried or indigent mothers. Charles Dickens's *Oliver Twist* is the story of such a facility. In 19th-century Canada, indigent and abandoned British children were worked as agricultural apprentices in order to get the children off the dole and out of the unhealthy city air. Italian children worked in Paris, New York City, and elsewhere as figurine sellers and street musicians.

In 1853 minister Charles Loring Brace was determined to do something about the problem of "street Arabs." He founded the Children's Aid Society, which relocated more than 100,000 street children (maybe 150,000 to 200,000) to rural America between 1854 and 1929. Brace thought

The director of the Sprague Settlement House, which began providing vocational training and health services to needy families and children in 1910 in Providence, Rhode Island, cares for a recently abandoned infant while watching over a class of local girls learning to sew in November 1912. In the early 20th century, institutions for foundlings began to be replaced by more foster care and adoption.

the children would be welcome as an additional source of farm labor and that farmers would take the children into their homes. These efforts were the forerunner of foster care.

Modern Era

In antebellum U.S. cities, abandoned children were sent to the poorhouse. New York City on the eve of the Civil War had a foundling problem caused by rapid development, population increase, immigration, and mass poverty. Once aware that foundlings were a symptom of urban moral decay, religious reformers and public officials established four institutions for foundlings and infants. The asylums proved inadequate, and early in the 20th century, three of the four were closed. In New York, adoption replaced abandonment, and foster care replaced institutionalization. In Kansas in the early 1920s, the United Methodist Church opened the Kansas Methodist Home for Children in Newton to provide a farm environment for homeless and abandoned children. In 1960, it shifted to providing services to adolescents with social adjustment or emotional problems. In 1996, Kansas became the first state to completely privatize adoption, foster care, and family preservation, with Youthville holding a regional contract that included care of more than 1,000 children.

Modern law regards child abandonment as a serious crime because of its potential for direct harm to the child and because of the burden it places on society. Georgia classifies simple abandonment as a misdemeanor, with abandonment and subsequent leaving of the state a felony. In the 20th century, the definition of child abandonment moved beyond the actual physical giving up of the child. Abandoned children included street children, war victims, child prostitutes, refugees, and runaways seeking to flee unhappy home environments. For some, particularly during the 1980s and 1990s surge of "retrieved memories" of child abuse, living in a dysfunctional family constituted a cruel form of child abandonment. In 1996, the United States had 1 million street children. They are more likely to be arrested, to contract human immunodeficiency virus (HIV), and to abuse drugs.

Reduction Approaches
To reduce instances of child abandonment, many jurisdictions have introduced "safe haven" laws that identify hospitals, police and fire stations, and other facilities where an infant can be left, usually with no recrimination and often with no need to identify the mother. In 1999, Texas became the first state to enact a safe haven law. Some states allow the handing of a newborn to a doctor or police officer, some decriminalize the act, some allow for parental anonymity while others want identity to establish a medical history, and some set time or age limits. By 2006, 47 states had these laws.

In 2008, Nebraska was one of the last states to pass a safe haven law. The law was so loosely written that it included 17-year-old abandoned children; child welfare experts argued that it didn't deal with the causes, particularly of the abandonments of older children. Infants could be the result of an embarrassing teen pregnancy, but when a parent just left a child or teenager in the hospital for authorities, that was another matter. It smacked of the Depression era when parents bought children bus tickets and put signs on them asking that they be directed to Boys Town, the original safe haven. Federal funding of safe havens came in 2002 as a state option, not as a mandate.

Foster care is a more significant approach than safe haven. Before its safe haven law, Texas had 33 newborns abandoned a year, same with Illinois, with other state numbers closer to five to 10. A third died. Today, nearly half a million American children are in foster care. Foster care dates back more than 150 years. In the 1850s, New York City was home to thousands of street children who roamed in search of food, shelter, and money and were a source of disease and crime. They were street vendors of matches, newspapers, and rags, and their defense against street violence was to form gangs. Police arrested vagrant children as young as 5 and locked them up with adult criminals.

Foster care receives 40,000 infants a year. Not all children in foster care are physically abandoned; most are abused physically, sexually, or emotionally, then taken by the state from their parents. Foster care costs $25.7 billion a year, and child abuse and neglect cost an additional $100 billion. For this cost, former foster care children constitute a fourth of prisoners and 30 percent of homeless people. Four years after leaving foster care, half are unemployed, in part because foster care reduces the probability of finishing high school, virtually rules out completion of college, and increases sixfold the chance of teen motherhood.

The problems of child abandonment are worldwide and solutions are scarce. Urbanization and industrialization merely exacerbate the situation.

John H. Barnhill
Independent Scholar

See Also: Child Abuse, Contemporary; Child Abuse, History of; Children's Rights; Juvenile Justice, History of; Juvenile Offenders in Adult Courts.

Further Readings
Ball, Karen. "The Abandoned Children of Nebraska." *Time*. http://www.time.com/time/nation/article/0,8599,1859405,00.html (Accessed October 2011).
Child Welfare Information Gateway. "Infant Safe Haven Laws: Summary of State Laws, 2010." http://www.childwelfare.gov/systemwide/laws_policies/statutes/safehaven.cfm (Accessed October 2011).
Miller, Julie. *Abandoned: Foundlings in Nineteenth-Century New York City*. New York: New York University Press, 2008.
Panter-Brick, Catherine, ed. *Abandoned Children*. Durham, NC: University of Durham, 2000.
Youthville. "History." http://www.youthville.org/History/Default.aspx (Accessed October 2011).

Children's Rights

While many may believe that the concern for children's rights is a relatively recent phenomenon, it must be placed in its historical context. As early as 1919, the League of Nations established the Committee for the Protection of Children, and in 1923, the organization formally codified the rights of children in a series of proclamations referred to as the Declaration of the Rights of the Child, collectively endorsing a child's right—regardless of race or nationality—to survival, nutrition, shelter, healthcare, humanitarian relief, and protection from exploitation, as well as the right to grow up in an environment that fosters his/her material and spiritual development.

Early Social Reforms

However, concern for children's rights in the United States took root much earlier—at the same time that the first European colonies were being established and children were dying at astoundingly high rates. Settlers in Massachusetts attempted to define the legal relationships between children and parents. The "stubborn child laws" of the mid-1600s permitted parents to discipline children physically, including to the point of death, and defined the limited basis on which public officials could intervene. "Poor laws" inherited from England authorized parents who were unable to sustain their children to send their children out to work. Children were routinely seen as cheap and legal labor. And yet, by the late 18th and early 19th centuries, there were already numerous organizations denouncing child labor and agitating for the rights of children. The New England Association of Farmers, Mechanics and Other Workingmen condemned child labor in 1832, and by 1836, Massachusetts passed the first state child labor law requiring children under 15 who worked in factories to attend school for three months each year.

In the 1870s, social reformers tackled the problems of child labor and child delinquency and crime. These movements were in large part driven by the efforts of middle-class women whose faith in the continuation of the social order was tied to the apt rearing of children and the inculcation of proper social values. Many children who lived in cities spent their time in the streets. Labor unions, including the Knights of Labor and the Workingmen's Assembly in New York, rallied to the cause. The New York legislature passed compulsory school attendance legislation in 1874. In 1886, that state passed the Factory Act of 1886 prohibiting factory work by children under 13 years of age.

Twentieth-Century Advances

The most significant advance in the history of children's rights, however, was the entry of the federal government as a powerful and influential stakeholder. In 1906, a senator from Indiana introduced a federal child labor bill, but Theodore Roosevelt did not support the bill, and support among social reformers was also mixed. After a few years of continued efforts, President William Howard Taft signed into law a bill that created the U.S. Children's Bureau, as part of the Department of Commerce and Labor, to investigate and report on all matters related to the welfare of children. In 1938, President Franklin Roosevelt signed the Fair Labor Standards Act, limiting many forms of child labor.

In the early 20th century, experts were mobilized on behalf of children's rights. In 1909, William A. Healy, a doctor, was appointed director of the Juvenile Psychopathic Institute and announced that the institute would begin to research the causes of juvenile delinquency. Young people who ran afoul of the law were considered victims of their circumstances and perceived to be delinquents whose offenses were the result of neglect and poverty. They were guilty of undesirable behaviors, but they were not viewed as criminals. Focus was on the root causes of offending behavior, indicting parents for ineffectively socializing their children, thereby locating the legislation as part of the rise of the "child-saving movement" of the late 19th and early 20th centuries. The prosperity of the 20th century, declining mortality rates, and the rise of the teenager as a distinct social group defined a turning point in the relationship between children and American society. In particular, the 1920s saw young people—"flaming youth"—capture attention like they never had before.

Recognizing the rights of children—particularly legal rights—has been problematic given the dependent nature of children. As Michael

In the latter half of the 19th century, vagrant nondelinquent children could be sent to the New York Juvenile Asylum. These boys learned shoemaking at the facility sometime before 1905.

Grossberg put it, children are "double dependent: on their parents and on the state," thus not only creating a tenuous basis on which children might assert rights but also setting up a tension between parents and government about how best to recognize and protect the rights and welfare of children.

In 1944, the decision of the Supreme Court in *Prince v. Massachusetts* underscored the tensions between parents and state even as it articulated a legal basis to ensure the welfare of children. The court confirmed that government possessed broad authority to regulate the treatment of children, at the same time declaring that parental authority was not absolute. *Prince* established that the state's interest in protecting children through child labor laws superseded the constitutional right of parents to raise their children as they choose. Parental authority could be restricted when it was in the best interests of the child for the state to do so. On November 20, 1959—a date that was accepted as Universal Children's Day in 1954—the United Nations General Assembly adopted an expanded version of the 1923 League of Nations declaration, adding provisions regarding a child's right to an identity, family, and education, and the right to be free from discrimination. In *In re Gault* (1967), the U.S. Supreme Court established once and for all that perhaps there was justice for all. The court confirmed that juveniles accused of crimes possess many of the same fundamental due process rights as adults. These rights include the right against self-incrimination, the right to be arraigned on charges, the right to confront witnesses, and the right to be represented by counsel.

Conclusion
The struggle throughout the 20th century to comprehend, articulate, and define the rights of children has been a philosophical, moral, and legal struggle that has sought to separate the rights of children from other rights claimants. Some argue that children have the same rights as adults; others disagree and assert that children have no rights or at best only some of the rights enjoyed by adults. As worries about globalization, poverty, war, child soldiers, national security concerns prevailing over civil rights, and other historically specific debates shape our conception of human rights, it remains to be seen how these issues will impact and shape our conceptions of children's rights and our willingness to define them in law and social practice in the century ahead.

Donn Short
Robson Hall Law School

See Also: 1777 to 1800 Primary Documents; 1901 to 1920 Primary Documents; Child Abuse, History of; Children, Abandoned; Civil Rights Laws; Juvenile Justice, History of.

Further Readings
Alston, Philip. "The Best Interests Principle: Towards a Reconciliation of Culture and Human Rights." *International Journal of Law, Policy, and the Family*, v.8/1 (1994).
Eekelaar, John. "The Emergence of Children's Rights." *Oxford Journal of Legal Studies*, v.6/2 (1986).
Grossberg, Michael. *Governing the Hearth: Law and the Family in Nineteenth-Century America*. Chapel Hill: University of North Carolina Press, 1985.

Guggenheim, Martin. "A Brief History of Children's Rights in the United States." In *What's Wrong With Children's Rights?* Cambridge, MA: Harvard University Press, 2005.

Hamilton, Carolyn and Tabitha Abu El-Haj. "Armed Conflict: The Protection of Children Under International Law." *International Journal of Children's Rights*, v.5 (1997).

Hawes, Joseph. *The Children's Rights Movement: A History of Advocacy and Protection.* Boston: Twayne Publishers, 1991.

Hawes, Joseph and N. Ray Hiner, eds. *Growing Up in America: Children in Historical Perspective.* Chicago: University of Chicago Press, 1985.

Platt, Anthony. "The Rise of the Child Saving Movement: A Study in Social Policy and Correctional Reform." *Annals of the American Academy of Political and Social Science*, v.381/1 (1969).

Chillicothe Correctional Institution

The Chillicothe Correctional Institution is located in the city of Chillicothe, Missouri. It is the administrative seat of Livingston County and sits approximately 80 miles northeast of Kansas City. State highways 36 and 65 intersect at Chillicothe, making it a hub of political, economic, and commercial activity for the region.

The first visitors to the area established Chillicothe as a settlement in 1837, naming it after its sister city in Ohio. The city was incorporated in 1851. As Chillicothe grew, so did its prominence, attracting the attention of the state's political leaders. In 1887, the state legislature selected Chillicothe as the site of the State Industrial Home for Girls. It appropriated $50,000 to its construction and operation. The home was located two miles south of the town square, on what was later to become Third Street. Designed around the cottage plan (a design that allows residents to live in a smaller and more relaxed setting), the first dormitory was given the name of Marmaduke Cottage in honor of Governor John S. Marmaduke. By the early 1900s, three more dormitories had been completed, with the home being renamed the State Training School for Girls. Capacity grew to 225 residents. In addition to the existing dormitories, the school also consisted of a chapel, boiler house, and administration building.

In 1981, the home closed permanently, and the campus was updated and expanded to function as a women's prison. Known as the Chillicothe Correctional Center, this 525-bed prison housed minimum to maximum security inmates. After more than 20 years of operation, the old prison structure fell into disrepair, convincing state officials to construct a larger and more modern women's facility. After considering various proposals, state officials decided to vacate the old prison and construct a larger, more modern facility north of Chillicothe.

Before construction began, a tragic event marred the otherwise favorable reputation of the old facility and shocked the surrounding community. On September 10, 2006, two officers were involved in a domestic dispute that resulted in their deaths. Just before 3:30 P.M., outside the prison's library, a male officer approached his female roommate and fired two shots, striking her in the back. He then turned the gun on himself, firing one shot into his chest. Both officers were pronounced dead at the local hospital. At the time, officers were not required to pass through metal detectors and were only occasionally required to submit to security screening processes. The prison went into lockdown. Because this incident involved no inmates, and because all inmates cooperated as instructed, the lockdown soon ended. This shooting prompted a re-evaluation of the security measures at Missouri's prisons pertaining to correctional employees. The old facility continued to operate until the construction of the new facility was completed.

A groundbreaking ceremony for the new facility was held on October 24, 2006. Construction was completed in 2008 at a cost of $120 million. The new facility consists of four 256-bed general housing units utilizing 4-person rooms. It also contains a 240-bed unit (with 2-person rooms), a 76-bed administrative segregation unit, a 96-bed mental health unit, and a 200-bed reception and diagnostic unit. The new prison complex is made up of six single-story buildings, eight two-story buildings, and a 126,000-square-foot Central Services Building. The Central Services Building houses the prison's classrooms as well as its laundry, kitchen, culinary arts, and dining and religious areas. The new Chillicothe Correctional Center sits on 55 acres and was, at the time of its construction, the largest design-and-build project ever undertaken by the state of Missouri. The new prison employs approximately 315 security staff. Even though the new facility has an operating capacity of 1,636 inmates—nearly 300 percent more than the old facility—the use of architectural features and technological advancements has helped reduce the need for additional security personnel.

Transfers to the new facility began on the night of December 4, 2008. Approximately 150 specially equipped and highly trained correctional officers participated. Buses were dispatched two at a time. Transfers started at 10:30 P.M. and continued until the last offender arrived at 5:15 A.M. the next morning. The last two transports were of inmates housed in the old segregation unit. Extra security procedures were taken with these high-risk inmates, who were transferred by van. All transfers went smoothly and without incident. Shortly after the arrival of the 525 inmates from the old facility, another 550 from the Women's Correctional Center in Vandalia, Missouri, arrived. At the time, the Vandalia facility was operating in excess of 500 inmates over its designed capacity. The Missouri female prisoner population was 1,071 in 1996, ballooning to 2,522 in 2006—an increase of 150 percent (during the same 10-year period, the male population increased by 50 percent). Such an increase necessitated Missouri's building of a large prison and centralized processing center for female offenders.

Since the opening of the new facility, discussion has taken place about what to do with the old prison complex. Suggestions have ranged from its complete demolition to turning it into a home for mentally handicapped women, creating a transitional facility to assist female inmates during their return to society, or perhaps even creating an inpatient substance abuse treatment center for women. One proposal even calls for the entire site to be turned into commercial and residential housing units. A 15-acre plot on the north side of the old compound is now being developed into a medium-income housing subdivision.

Curtis R. Blakely
Truman State University

See Also: Corrections; Missouri; Racism; Women in Prison.

Further Readings
Glaze, Lauren E. *Correctional Populations in the United States 2009*. Washington, DC: Bureau of Justice Statistics, 2010.
Missouri Department of Correction. http://doc.mo.gov/division/dai/facilities_inst.php (Accessed May 2011).
Siegal, Larry and Clemens Bartollas. *Corrections Today*. Belmont, CA: Cengage, 2011.

Chinese Americans

Chinese Americans are a racial, ethnic, and cultural group making up part of the landscape of U.S. citizenry. While distinguished by their perceived cultural and geographical tie to China, Chinese Americans are also identified as part of a broader Asian American community. Historically, Chinese Americans' difference from and sameness to other Asian American ethnic communities (like Japanese Americans) has fluctuated depending on the political climate. U.S. law and policy, as well as social attitudes, have shaped Chinese Americans into a distinct and marginalized racial and cultural category historically criminalized as inassimilable aliens and foreign threats to the integrity of the United States.

Early Immigration
The category *Chinese American* was in part created and defined through the policing of early U.S. immigration and citizenship laws. With westward expansion, the need for undervalued labor in places like California met with free labor ideologies, which argued against slavery on grounds that advocated ideals of capitalism based in notions of free (white and male) labor. This antislavery sentiment often worked in tandem with anti-black racism on the west coast. The result of these sentiments impacted developing industries like railroads, mining, and agriculture by forcing employers to find ways of employing so-called cheap labor without depending on slavery or undercutting the labor of free (white and male) workers.

Nineteenth-century economic development in the west looked to indigenous and Mexican laborers, as well as Chinese immigrants to fill the need for cheap labor. While Japanese labor migration recruitment patterns sought peasants from rural areas to work in agriculture on the west coast and sugarcane plantations in Hawai'i, recruitment of "coolie" Chinese labor was often funneled into railroad and mining. Because the Chinese government had been weakened with the Opium War against Britain (1839–42) and the Taiping Rebellion (1850–64), it was not able to negotiate strong emigration treaties with the United States (in contrast to the Japanese government, for instance).

Federal immigration laws passed during the late 19th century restricted entry and naturalization along racial lines, helping to distinguish and criminalize Chinese Americans as outside the boundaries of the U.S. national body. For immigration officials, Chinese racial and cultural difference was read as a marker of inassimilibility, criminality, and sexual deviance, reasons used to justify exclusion, detention, and deportation. Such rationale informed the passage of the Chinese Exclusion Act of 1882, widely considered the first federal immigration law. With this law, all Chinese laborers were prohibited from entering the United States. Exceptions were made only for the merchant and wealthy classes and students. Thus, proving class status to gain entry after 1882 often meant fitting into immigration officials' preconceived ideas about what "respectable" Chinese would

Chinese American men pause to read announcements posted on a wall (right) on what was known as "the street of the gamblers" in San Francisco's Chinatown sometime between 1896 and 1906. Associations of a Chinese criminality were magnified by the myth of Chinatowns being distinct geographies plagued by vice and dominated by gangs.

look like. For example, the assumption carried by many immigration officials that wealthier Chinese women would have small, bound feet helped shape policing efforts at the border, where a physiology of respectability/criminality developed, which linked physical features with perceived class status and sexual morality.

As Chinese female sexuality was constructed as suspect, Chinese women were assumed to be prostitutes even when they presented legal documentation of their status as wives. Legal documentation was often not enough proof of respectability, and policing of Chinese immigrants, particularly women, was accompanied by physical and medical exams as well as interviews. Immigration scholars consider the early treatment of the Chinese on issues such as entry, permanent residence, and citizenship as establishing the blueprint for immigration law and practices.

This policing of immigration based on assumptions of a Chinese threat to the health and morality of the U.S. nation impacted the formation of Chinatowns as seemingly distinct, self-controlled, and self-governed areas separated from the rest of the city. The association of Chinese difference with exotic cultural proclivities, disease, and underground vice activities like gambling, opium, and prostitution was both a result of and shaped by media sensationalism, policing practices, and social science research.

The myth of Chinatowns as self-governed and distinct geographies housing vice, disease, and run by gangs (rather than police) further entrenched the associations of Chinese difference with criminality. For example, when such racial assumptions helped justify overpolicing of Chinatowns and Chinese (and often also Japanese) American communities, the adverse effects (drop in business, psychological and social impacts on the community) of overpolicing on "respectable" Chinese merchants was blamed on "tong violence" rather than on police harassment. Such associations of Chinatowns as self-governed, gang-run neighborhoods continued into late 20th-century representations of Chinese Triads (organized criminal networks) working within Chinatowns in the United States.

In the late 19th and early 20th centuries, the policing of Chinatowns helped entrench Chinese difference as linked to criminality, as well as to solidify what were otherwise very porous geographic, social, and political boundaries between so-called blighted city neighborhoods like Chinatowns and respectable ones. Such constructions of Chinese difference continue to inform Chinese American racial formation.

Citizenship Rights
In the the late 19th and early 20th centuries, the context of a shifting political and economic landscape resulting from westward expansion, industrialization, and urbanization helped posit Chinese Americans in politics and media as symbolizing the potential threat of a changing national body and citizenry. These anxieties manifest in media sensationalism and overpolicing of reports of Chinese men with white women, which helped the passage of the Mann Act (or White Slavery Act) in 1910 and is evident in examples such as D. W. Griffith's film, *Broken Blossoms* (1919). Popular representations of the Chinese threat to the health and future of the nation (symbolized through white women) differed from representations invoking African Americans. As in *Broken Blossoms*, Chinese masculinity was often constructed as an implied moral and cultural threat to whiteness as opposed to the more sexually overt depictions of African American masculinity as a physical threat, as Griffith's infamous film *Birth of a Nation* illustrates. Such depictions helped solidify constructions of the Chinese as foreign threats to the (white) American body, which were later used to justify eugenics and social purity movements and further immigration restrictions well into the 20th century.

The extension of citizenship rights to African Americans with the Fourteenth Amendment (1868) called into question the rights of U.S.-born Asian Americans. A key Supreme Court case testing both the application of the Fourteenth Amendment and the Chinese Exclusion Act, *Wong Kim Ark v. United States* (1898) involved a U.S.-born Chinese American who was denied re-entry under the Chinese Exclusion Act after visiting China in 1895, despite his U.S. citizenship. While the constitutionality of the Chinese Exclusion Act was not in question, the Supreme Court overturned the initial lower court ruling to prohibit Wong Kim Ark's re-entry. The decision included Asian Americans born in the United States as citizens with rights recognizable under the Fourteenth Amendment, though it did not extend naturalization rights to Chinese and other Asian Americans. Citizenship through naturalization continued to be withheld from Chinese until the 1943 Magnuson Act, when the politics of World War II helped shape Chinese Americans as allies against the figure of the Japanese enemy.

Following the U.S. government's official recognition of China as a wartime ally, the Magnuson Act repealed the Chinese Exclusion Act, though it did not lift the national origins quotas established in 1924, which barred all immigration from the region termed the Asiatic Barred Zone. This quota system was not lifted until the 1965 Immigration Act. The Magnuson Act thus did little to ease immigration restrictions, though it extended the right of naturalization to Chinese Americans. Part of the politics of the war, the 1943 act came as part of a broader cultural movement to deploy ethnicity to construct the Japanese as "bad" enemy aliens contrasted with a decriminalized image of the Chinese as "good" or model immigrant minorities. Notably, magazines such as *Life* published articles that provided physical measurements to distinguish "Japs from Chinese." Even with the end of World War II and the shifting geopolitics of the Cold War, notions of Chinese Americans as model minorities continued to saturate both the cultural and political landscape. As a cold war strategy, the U.S. government promoted the idea of Chinese Americans as model minorities so long as Chinese Americans were also aligned with the nationalist (rather than the communist) government. However, the image of the Chinese model minority worked simultaneously and alongside constructions of Chinese criminality as is evident in the popularity and longevity of the fictional character Dr. Fu Manchu, an evil Chinese mastermind featured in literature, film, and television throughout the first half of the 20th century.

The "Model" Minority

Such constructions of the Chinese as potential model minorities also helped the government shift civil rights claims into matters of cultural, rather than structural, deficiency. In 1966 amid nationwide civil rights protests, the popular magazine *U.S. News and World Report* published a story on the "success ... of one minority group in the United States," which contrasted Chinese Americans as models minorities against African Americans as failures. These constructions tied culture to the so-called criminal element of African American failure and the model element of relative Chinese success, which were also assumed to be visible on the body. Often noted by scholars of race and ethnic studies as an example of the ways the privileges of whiteness remain hidden, the construction of the Asian American model minority situated against the African American "monitored minority" is cited as one cultural and political argument used to argue against the need for civil rights reforms.

Despite these constructions of Chinese and, by extension, Asian Americans as so-called model minorities, the linking of Asian and Chinese difference to notions of a "foreign threat" continued to operate in shaping public understanding of Chinese Americans. Most notably, the economic restructuring of the 1970s and 1980s, which saw a dramatic shift in import/export relations with Japan, impacted how Chinese Americans were viewed by the broader U.S. public. In 1982, Vincent Chin, a Chinese American, was murdered by two white men who had recently lost their jobs in auto manufacturing in Detroit. Perceiving Chin to represent what the white men (Ronald Ebans and Michael Nitz) saw as the Japanese auto industry responsible for their job losses, the men beat Chin to death. The murder of Chin demonstrates the widely perceived construction of Chinese and Asian racial and cultural difference as perpetual outsiders in imagining U.S. national belonging, and the homogenizing function of racism. Despite the fact that Chin was not Japanese, but was raised in Detroit and worked in the Detroit auto industry, it was Chin's perceived racial difference that the men read as an indicator of his outsider status, which to the white men made Chin culpable for national (and their personal) economic hardships.

Further, the case of Vincent Chin demonstrates the ways race works to homogenize ethnic difference, where racial stereotypes of the Japanese as economic enemies impacted the daily lives of Chinese and other Asian Americans. The fact that the men responsible for killing Chin were sentenced only to probation and a $3,000 fine (they served no prison time) indicates that race plays an important role in configuring notions of criminality.

The criminalization of Chinese difference through the axis of national belonging also resonates in the 1999 case of Wen Ho Lee, a U.S. citizen who worked as a scientist at the Los Alamos National Laboratory before being accused of espionage. Lee was placed in solitary confinement for the theft of classified documents and charged with 59 different counts. Investigators were ultimately not able to find any evidence that Lee was acting as a spy or selling classified information. The charges against Lee were dropped, with the exception of one charge for mishandling sensitive documents, to which Lee pled guilty. After the ordeal, Lee filed his own lawsuit and won a $1.6 million settlement from both the federal government (for misconduct) and various news media organizations who leaked his name before he was charged with any crime. The targeting of Lee as a potential spy by both federal authorities and the news media helps continue to circulate constructions of Chinese Americans as suspect citizens and national outsiders. As with cases of Japanese Americans and internment during World War II, the Lee case demonstrates the racializing of Asian American difference as perpetual foreigners and suspect citizens even as these constructions work alongside stereotypes of Asian Americans as model minorities.

Throughout the late 20th century, Chinese difference was linked to criminality and suspect behavior, and these constructions continued to be informed by the political, economic, and social context. For example, the circulation of discourses around the Chinese triads gaining ground once again in Chinatowns during the 1980s and 1990s can be linked to the political context of the end of the cold war, where the Soviet threat loomed less large in contrast to the hypervisibility of Chinese difference as symbolizing both the economic and political threat of communism in a newly imagined global political landscape. Thus, the historical and contemporary linking of Chinese difference with criminal and foreign elements in public discourse is a continual process that reflects social, economic, political, and cultural national anxieties.

Julietta Hua
San Francisco State University

See Also: 1851 to 1900 Primary Documents; African Americans; Chinese Exclusion Act of 1882; Japanese Americans; Mann Act.

Further Readings
Chan, Sucheng and Madeline Hsu, eds. *Chinese Americans and the Politics of Race and Culture.* Philadelphia: Temple University Press, 2008.
Liu, Mary Ting Yi. *The Chinatown Trunk Mystery.* Princeton, NJ: Princeton University Press, 2005.
Shah, Nayan. *Contagious Divides: Epidemics and Race in San Francisco's Chinatown.* Berkeley: University of California Press, 2001.
Yung, Judy. *Unbound Feet: A Social History of Chinese Women in San Francisco.* Berkeley: University of California Press, 1995.

Chinese Exclusion Act of 1882

The Chinese Exclusion Act of 1882 was the signature piece of a body of legislation affecting the immigration of Asians to America. Signed into law by President Chester Arthur, the act established a 10-year moratorium on immigration from China of skilled and unskilled laborers and Chinese in the mining industry. It also provided that Chinese who were already in the country could not leave and re-enter without certification. The act raised a bar to citizenship by relieving state and federal courts of the power to grant citizenship to Chinese resident aliens. Unauthorized importation of Chinese was punishable by a $500 per person fine and no more than a year's imprisonment. The act also placed regulations on ships that might carry Chinese passengers or crew, barring them from setting foot on shore. The restrictions succeeded in limiting Chinese immigration and that of Asians in general, but it also produced human smuggling and the phenomenon of "paper sons," Chinese subject to bar or deportation who shed names and pasts to pass as the children of Chinese American citizens. Angel Island in San Francisco Bay served as the main processing center for Chinese entering or re-entering the country. The act was representative of the broader racism and suspicion affecting Asian Americans that periodically shifted ethnic focus but openly operated from the mid-19th century through World War II and resonated well afterward. Restrictions relaxed against the Chinese during the war, when China became an ally of the United States and American hostility refocused on Japan and Japanese Americans.

Chinese immigration to America swelled in the 19th century, fed by the steady disintegration of the Qing (Manchu) dynasty. As China crumbled under military and economic pressure from Western powers, internal dissent increased. After rebellions and the Opium Wars, the Chinese faced hunger and oppression from an increasingly desperate and fragile government and Western forces. This coincided with the 1848 California gold rush and frontier development that included railroad construction and the growth of countless American cities, towns, and industries. Chinese laborers sought success in the *Gam Saan* or "Gold Mountain" of California, often leaving wives and children behind. The immigrants were not welcomed in a nation already wracked by racism and an unresolved conflict over slavery. In the period of retrenchment after the Civil War and Reconstruction, white settlers, as well as immigrants considered marginally white during the period, turned concerns about labor, wages, race, and miscegenation into opposition to Chinese immigration. White workers and politicians argued that productive Chinese workers lowered wages for whites and reduced them to coolie labor. Eugenic arguments also emerged, warning that the Chinese were a diseased, inferior race that would rapidly reproduce and threaten the hegemony of whites through miscegenation.

Chinese and other Asians resisted the act in the courts, but Supreme Court decisions eventually smothered most challenges. In *Chae Chan Ping v. United States* (1889), *Nishimura Ekiu v. United States* (1892), and *Fong Yue Ting v. United States* (1893), the court affirmed the right of the United States to establish the immigration scheme. In *Lem Moon Sing v. United States* (1895), the court upheld an 1894 appropriation act that made the negative decisions of customs or immigrations officers final. In *United States v. Ju Toy* (1905), the Supreme Court ruled that the judgments of immigration officers and the secretary of commerce were final, even though a district court found that Ju Toy was a citizen. However, in *United States v. Wong Kim Ark* (1898), the court did rule that the act did not apply to a Chinese American born in the United States to resident alien parents. Under the Fourteenth Amendment, he was a citizen.

The Chinese Exclusion Act may be better understood in the context of related legislation. In 1875, the Page Act largely barred the immigration of Asian women. Ostensibly saving white men from Chinese prostitutes and protecting against forced labor, but also constructed to reduce miscegenation, it blocked almost all immigration by Asian women. The United States renegotiated the Burlingame Treaty on Chinese diplomatic relations in 1880, suspending Chinese immigration. The Geary Act extended the original Chinese Exclusion Act in 1892, and another extension in 1902 added a registration requirement for Chinese residents. Further legislative action in 1924 virtually arrested all Asian immigration. It was not until 1943 that the immigration impediments for Chinese were removed in the Magnuson Act.

This 1882 newspaper cartoon pointed out the unfairness of the Chinese Exclusion Act, depicting a Chinese man at the "Golden Gate of Liberty" above the caption "the only one barred out."

Eric Ashley Hairston
Elon University

See Also: Arthur, Chester (Administration of); Chinese Americans; Immigration Crimes; Racism.

Further Readings

Gyory, Andrew. *Closing the Gate: Race, Politics, and the Chinese Exclusion Act*. Chapel Hill: University of North Carolina Press, 1998.

Lau, Estelle. *Paper Families: Identity, Immigration Administration, and Chinese Exclusion*. Durham, NC: Duke University Press, 2007.

Wu, Frank H. *Yellow: Race in America Beyond Black and White*. New York: Basic, 2003.

Chisholm v. Georgia

Chisholm v. Georgia (1793) was one of the first important cases decided by the U.S. Supreme Court. In *Chisholm v. Georgia*, the court held that federal courts can hear suits when a citizen of one state sues another state. By a 4–1 decision, the court ruled that states did not have sovereign immunity and were subject to lawsuits from citizens of other states. The term *sovereign immunity* is a common law legal concept that states are immune from civil suit or criminal prosecution. Because of the potential litigation disaster, the decision was very unpopular and led to the adoption and ratification of the Eleventh Amendment in 1795, which overruled *Chisholm v. Georgia*. This was the first time that a Supreme Court decision was overruled by a constitutional amendment. The overturning of the *Chisholm* decision gave states sovereign immunity from being sued in federal court by citizens of other states without the consent of the state being sued. The case also illustrates the relative importance of the Supreme Court of the United States during the early years of the country.

Case Study

The case of *Chisholm v. Georgia* began in 1777 when Robert Farquhar of South Carolina sold supplies to the Executive Council of the state of Georgia for use by the army in the Revolutionary War. Georgia never paid its debt, and upon Farquhar's death, his executor, Alexander Chisholm, filed suit to collect payment from the state of Georgia in federal court. Georgia refused to even acknowledge the lawsuit for fear of giving legitimacy to the plaintiff, claiming that as a sovereign state, Georgia was not subject to the authority of federal courts. The governor of Georgia claimed that his state had not consented to the suit and was therefore immune from being sued on the grounds of sovereign immunity.

The case was heard in Georgia by Supreme Court Associate Justice James Iredell, who was riding circuit at the time. Iredell, like most of the justices, spent more time circuit riding than sitting as a member of the high court. Iredell found that the Georgia court lacked jurisdiction to hear the case because under Article III of the Constitution, only the U.S. Supreme Court can hear a lawsuit when a state is a party.

Upon appeal to the U.S. Supreme Court, only Chisholm's lawyer, Edmund Randolph, appeared. Randolph had attended the Constitutional Convention and introduced the Virginia Plan regarding the representation scheme to Congress. The court was asked to decide: Was the state of Georgia subject to the jurisdiction of the federal courts? The answer was inevitable since only one party of the dispute, Chisholm, appeared before the court. Having no choice, the Supreme Court entered a default judgment for Chisholm, ordering the state of Georgia to pay its war debt.

The Supreme Court decision was 4–1. Writing for the majority opinion was Justice James Wilson. Wilson, who had also attended the Constitutional Convention in Philadelphia and drafted the very jurisdiction language in question, ruled that the intent of the framers was to bind the states to the legislative, executive, and judicial powers of the national government. Any sovereign power was held by the people, not by the state government. Each—Chief Justice John Hay and Justices William Cushing, John Blair, and Wilson—wrote a separate opinion for the majority.

Justice Iredell angrily dissented. A southerner who believed in states' rights, Iredell reasoned that Article III did not alter the immunity of suit that states enjoyed. Just as the British king retained sovereign immunity at the time of the settlement of America, so did the states at the creation of the Union. Justice Iredell argued that the in the Judiciary Act of 1789, Congress authorized federal courts to issue writs "necessary for the exercise of their respective jurisdictions, and agreeable to the principles and usages of law." This, for Iredell, was the common law of the states, and Article III did not alter the immunity of states without their consent of being sued.

Eleventh Amendment

The reaction in the states was swift and negative. Fearing that the court's decision left the states vulnerable to lawsuits of monetary claims and debt collectors, a petition circulated among the states condemning the decision. A call to amend the Constitution and to pass state legislation to counter the court's decision came quickly. Congress responded by drafting and ratifying the Eleventh Amendment. By 1798, 12 states had ratified the amendment, with Pennsylvania and New Jersey rejecting ratification and two southern states, Tennessee and South Carolina, taking no action.

The Eleventh Amendment added to the Constitution in 1798 states that "the judicial power of the United States shall not be construed to extend to any suit in law or equity, commenced or prosecuted against one of the United States by Citizen of another State, or by Citizens or Subjects of any Foreign State." In short, the Eleventh Amendment guarantees sovereign immunity to the states from being sued in federal court without their consent. It has been reaffirmed, early on in *Hans v. Louisiana* (1890) and even recently in *Alden v. Maine* (1999).

The text of the Eleventh Amendment does not mention suits brought against a state by its *own* citizens. In *Hans v. Louisiana*, the Supreme Court ruled that the amendment reflects a broader principle of sovereign immunity. The court argued that sovereign immunity derives not from the Eleventh Amendment but from the broader structure of the entire Constitution.

The full breadth of sovereign immunity was explored in *Alden v. Maine*. By a 5–4 vote, the court ruled much like it did in *Hans v. Louisiana*. Writing for the majority, Justice Anthony Kennedy extended immunity to states sued by citizens of their state for federal violations. In *Alden,* the court chose not to use the language of the Eleventh Amendment but rather the common law immunity implicitly adopted by the framers of the Constitution. Writing for a four-justice dissent in *Alden,* Justice David Souter argued that states surrendered their sovereign immunity when they ratified the Constitution. The dissenting justices read the amendment's text as reflecting a narrow form of sovereign immunity that limited only the diversity jurisdiction of the federal courts. They concluded that the states are not insulated from suits by individuals by either the Eleventh Amendment in particular or the Constitution in general.

Today, the Supreme Court can only hear these cross-lawsuit cases if the state waives its immunity, which they do on a case-by-case basis, or consents to a lawsuit. The federal government has waived some of its sovereign immunity in the Federal Tort Claim Act, which allows a suit if the act of a federal employee is actionable under tort law. The Tucker Act waives immunity involving contract claims when one party is the federal government.

Priscilla H. M. Zotti
U.S. Naval Academy

See Also: Judiciary Act of 1789; Jurisdiction; Supreme Court, U.S.

Further Readings

Clark, B. R. "The Eleventh Amendment and the Nature of the Union." *Harvard Law Review,* v.124 (2010).

Jacobs, C. E. *The Eleventh Amendment and Sovereign Immunity.* Westport, CT: Greenwood Press, 1972.

Orth, J. V. *The Judicial Power of the United States: The Eleventh Amendment in American History.* New York: Oxford University Press, 1987.

Christie, Agatha

The English "Queen of Crime" and renowned author of detective novels, Agatha Christie created some of literature's most iconic characters and shaped how many people today imagine not only the genre of crime fiction, but also the nature of crime and the work of detectives. Born Agatha Mary Clarissa Miller on September 15, 1890, to an English mother and an American father, she left home in 1906 for a finishing school in Paris, her first formal education after a childhood tutor. At age 18, Christie turned to writing her first book while recovering from an illness and soon afterward began placing stories and poetry in magazines. At a dance at age 22, Agatha met her future husband, Archibald (Archie) Christie, a member of the Royal Flying Corps. They married on Christmas Eve, 1914, and Agatha moved to London when Archie went to war shortly thereafter. While working in a hospital dispensary, she learned about poisons, which became a central feature in many of her books. During this time, Christie also wrote her first detective novel, although she did not publish it until after the war.

In 1928, having had one child, Agatha divorced Archie after discovering his infidelity. In 1930, Christie met archaeologist Max Mallowan, marrying him the same year. Remaining together until her death in 1976, Christie traveled as part of her husband's archaeological team to clean and photograph their findings. Christie published her first detective novel, *The Mysterious Affair at Styles*, in 1921, introducing one of her most famous characters, Mr. Hercule Poirot, an eccentric and egotistic Belgian refugee living in England. As a former policeman, Poirot employs his skills of deduction and the art of interrogation to solve murders in some of Christie's most famous works, including *The Murder of Rodger Ackroyd* (1926), *Murder on the Orient Express* (1933), *The ABC Murders* (1936), and *Death on the Nile* (1937). Christie's second famed detective, Miss Jane Marple, appeared for the first time in a full-length novel, *Murder at the Vicarage* (1930). An English spinster and, unlike Poirot, an amateur investigator, Miss Marple draws on a studied understanding of human nature in combination with keen powers of observation and a modicum of nosiness. Christie later reported that she modeled Miss Marple on her grandmother.

In total, Christie wrote 66 detective novels featuring Marple and Poirot, along with scores of other novels, plays, and short stories. Her books typify the detective novel genre. In particular, she wrote her stories as puzzles, inviting the reader to act as detective from the pieces she laid out, though her novels characteristically culminate with surprising plot twists. Christie was a member and later president of the Detection Club, formed in 1930 by a group of British writers who pledged to give readers a fair opportunity to guess the perpetrator. Still, having helped create "rules" of fair play for the genre (such as giving the reader the same infor-

With 24,000 performances, many of them at London's St. Martin's Theatre, shown above, Agatha Christie's play The Mousetrap *is the world's longest-running show of any kind.*

mation as the detective), Christie was famous for breaking them; her stories frustrate readers when the detective reveals a crucial detail at the very end or when the narrator suddenly admits their guilt.

Credited as the best-selling writer of all time, with her work adapted many times to film and translated into more than 100 languages, Christie is the foremost figure in the development and increasing popularity of crime fiction as a literary genre. Preceded by Arthur Conan Doyle and joined by Dorothy Sayers and others, Christie's work encouraged readers to see the brilliant detective as the primary figure in investigation. That trope has recently undergone changes as technological developments (such as DNA testing and ballistics analysis) have emphasized the impartial collection of scientific evidence. Christie's overwhelming popularity extended to the United States, and has persisted, even as American audiences provided a ready readership for the "hard-boiled" sub-genre of crime fiction, including the unsentimental or more violent stories of Dashiell Hammett, Raymond Chandler, and later, Mickey Spillane. With her characters' keen insight into the motivations of criminals, Christie's work has also been associated with the fascination in and rise of psychological profiling, a tool used successfully in many real-life, high-profile investigations to identify and efficiently interview possible suspects. Some police have criticized the literary devices of crime fiction popularized by Christie and others for presenting a distorted picture of forensic work and raising false expectations among the public for how easily crimes can be solved.

Patrick Schmidt
IndiAna Gowland
Macalester College

See Also: Detection and Detectives; Dime Novels, Pulps, Thrillers; Literature and Theater, Crime in.

Further Readings
Christie, Agatha. *Agatha Christie: An Autobiography*. London: William Collins and Sons, 1977.
Morgan, Jane. *Agatha Christie: A Biography*. New York: Alfred A. Knopf, 1985.
Saunders, Dennis and Len Lovallo. *The Agatha Christie Companion: The Complete Guide to Agatha Christie's Life and Work*. New York: Delacorte Press, 1984.

Cincinnati, Ohio

Cincinnati, Ohio, is an Ohio River city, 255 miles downriver from Pittsburgh, Pennsylvania, and 83 miles upriver from Louisville, Kentucky, with a 2010 population of approximately 333,000. It has throughout its history been a city in transition, a trend that is as true today as it was in the 1780s. Over the centuries, numerous contributory factors caused by racial divides, population migration, substandard public education, poor governance, and serious economic and industrial decline have all contributed to Cincinnati's crime and punishment legacy.

Cincinnati's creation was a direct result of the opening of the Northwest Territory to settlement following the American Revolution. A riverfront location made it a convenient entry point for that first wave of settlers intent on forging new lives in what was then the western wilderness. The city was carved from an enormous 1788 land grant awarded by Congress to John Cleves Symmes (1742–1814). Other land speculators soon followed, hoping to find quick profits. In 1789, this emerging hamlet, which then consisted of only a few crude cabins, took the name Losantville, meaning "the place opposite the Licking River." In 1790, General Arthur St. Clair, governor of the territory, replaced the name Losantville with Cincinnati, in honor of the Roman hero-soldier, Lucius Quinctius Cincinnatus, and in recognition of the Society of Cincinnati, a Revolutionary War veterans' organization. In addition, St. Clair made Cincinnati the county seat of Hamilton County, which honored Alexander Hamilton, the nation's first secretary of the treasury. Cincinnati was also home to Fort Washington, an early base for defending the area from Ohio Indian tribes resistant to this settler expansion.

Police Force
Cincinnati was formally charted as a town in 1802, formed a rudimentary police force in the same year, and, in 1819, was incorporated as a city. Initially, the city's police force followed the night watch tradition but shift pay began in 1817, which was, after 1834, supported by direct commercial taxation. The early police reflected the English model, and in 1850, the post of police chief was established. During the 1850s, a more regular uniformed organization emerged. However, recruits largely came from the wards and precincts, which formed a structure easily influenced by local politics and politicians. Police positions were political plums subject to patronage perks associated with the "boss" system of urban government that characterized the late 19th and early 20th centuries. For example, in 1880, 219 of the 295 police were dismissed following a change in the political alignment. A more nonpartisan police structure did not see the light of day until after 1886.

A civil service exam for city police was introduced in 1902, and beginning in the Progressive Era, Cincinnati's police followed the national pattern of professional development and bureaucratization, which, it was argued, contributed

This African American boy lived near Cincinnati, Ohio, around 1942. The city's black population grew to almost 48,000 in the 1940s as a result of the Great Migration.

to declining crime rates. This process was also believed to counter petty levels of corruption such as bribes and street backhanders that occurred in urban policing, particularly evident during the Prohibition era. However, the more subtle levels of corruption involving perceived inequalities in the application of the law have continued to produce issues throughout the late 20th and early 21st centuries.

Racial Tensions
The city's economic base was strengthened after the War of 1812 with the arrival of riverboat steamers that allowed trade and traffic to travel both up- and downstream. The opening of the Miami–Erie Canal in 1827 provided further vital commercial infrastructure. Cincinnati in the 1820s was a frontier town with a rough edge. Lawlessness was common and was made worse by an abundant supply of distilled corn whiskey. In these early days, martial law was frequently employed to instill order. A significant early example of social unrest was the Cincinnati riots of 1829, which had clear racial overtones, a foretaste of divides that continue to mark the city's history. Fugitive slaves and free black residents in the city had grown from approximately 400 to more than 2,250 in the 1820s. As such, they competed with whites for the available jobs; this competition led to violent attacks and motivated the local authorities to require blacks to post bonds or leave at the risk of being expelled. Such circumstances set the stage for thousands of African Americans to leave the city for Canada, where they eventually established a base at Wilberforce in Ontario. This racial tension manifested itself again in anti-black rioting in September 1841 when the 2,200 city blacks were attacked by unemployed whites—an event that required militia intervention.

By 1830, the first waves of German and Irish immigrants brought the city's population to more than 46,000. A number of commercial enterprises, aided by the city's trade connections with the south, fostered further development, particularly in the meat-packing industry, which helped give Cincinnati the appellation "Porkopolis" and gave rise to one of America's great companies, Procter & Gamble. Because the city was surrounded by hills, Cincinnati's initial residential expansion was contained in the flat river basin. By the mid-19th century, downtown neighborhoods such as the Over-the-Rhine quarter became home to many German settlers. Since the 1960s, this district has witnessed repeated urban renewal schemes, and major investment drives continue in an effort to preserve its considerable 19th-century architectural legacy. Unfortunately, Over-the-Rhine has not yet become a genteel urban oasis for it remains ranked, according to some recent accounts, as the most dangerous neighborhood in all of America.

By 1850, Cincinnati's population exceeded 100,000, and its commercial success had gained it a reputation as the "Queen City of the West." Estimates from this era suggest that 27 percent of the population was German, followed by 12 percent Irish. The German influence was particularly felt in the city's cultural development and in its then-vibrant brewing industry. The German presence also stimulated mob violence in 1855 when anti-German crowds marched against the German community only to be stopped by the local militia. The city's German cultural orientation continued until World War I, when anti-German sentiments led to significant suppression of all things deemed German.

The coming of the Civil War stifled Cincinnati's trade relationships with the south and made it home to an active "Copperhead" movement sympathetic to the Confederacy. Its location, on the border of Kentucky, a slave state, also made the city a convenient depot for the Underground Railroad transporting runaway slaves to freedom in Canada. The city was home to several prominent abolitionists, including Harriet Beecher Stowe, James Birney, and Lyman Beecher, but its divided loyalties did not make for civic harmony. The additional threat of Confederate raids led to martial law being imposed in 1862.

Descent Into Corruption
After the Civil War, Cincinnati continued to grow. The city's population reached more than 200,000 in 1870. Newly constructed bridge and rail links with the south contributed to this expansion. Intense overcrowding made Cincinnati the second most densely populated city in the country, which increased late 19th century migrations to the neighboring hillside sections of the city. In addition, the city spread northward into the low-lying Mill Creek valley, which became a home to the city's industrial manufacturing base. However, during these years, Cincinnati's ambition to become a major national metropolis ended. New commerce and industry moved to other cities farther north. The decline in riverboat trade contributed to this state, as well as expanded railway links to the west through Chicago.

During the late 19th and early 20th centuries, the city became identified with municipal corruption and mismanagement. This was the era of bossism, led by George B. Cox, a Cincinnati tavern keeper, appointed in 1884 by Ohio Governor Joseph B. Foraker to lead the Board of Public Affairs. Cox dominated the city through his control of more than 2,000 jobs and numerous contracts. His influence and reach created a blatant climate of graft and corruption that was ended in 1924 when municipal reformers finally rid the city of old-style bosses, replacing them with a charter system of city manager–led government supposedly free of cronyism.

In this atmosphere of urban malaise, Cincinnati's judicial system was also suspect, and this led to a major riot by a mob outraged by what they saw as a corrupt verdict in a March 1884 murder case. Angry citizens armed themselves and marched on the courthouse, burning it to the ground, and attacked police. Barricades were erected, and three days of violence followed, leaving 56 people dead. The situation was finally ended with the arrival from Columbus of the National Guard. Besides riots, high levels of violence and soaring crime rates characterized life in Cincinnati during the late 19th century. With 93 murders in 1883, the city's level of violence was indeed staggering.

Urban Renewal
Cincinnati was part of the Great Migration, when nearly 2 million African Americans ventured north between 1910 and 1940 in search of better social and economic conditions. Cincinnati's African American population rose from 19,000 at the beginning of this period to nearly 48,000 in the 1940s. In residential terms, most of these new arrivals were concentrated in Bucktown on the eastern edge of downtown and in Little Africa on the western riverfront. This set a pattern of residential segregation that remained for most of the 20th century.

In the central business district, several commercial and public buildings were constructed during the 1920s and 1930s, yet the city's urban housing worsened, creating a major West End ghetto. Urban renewal and interstate road construction beginning in the 1950s began the steady dispersal of the black population to other city neighborhoods that offered cheap or government housing. Following World War II, city planners remained focused on downtown redevelopment, which eventually led to significant central business district and riverfront projects in the 1970s and 1980s. The Year 2000 Plan promised further downtown revitalization. However, in the midst of these revitalization schemes, geared to creating a vibrant downtown business district, the last half of the 20th century witnessed a two-thirds decline in the city's white population, which dropped from 425,000 to 175,500. Correspondingly during these years, the city's black population increased by 82 percent to 142,000. There

Cincinnati's population declined 10 percent from 1960 to 1970 and has continued to fall. This row of Italianate houses built in the 1890s in the West End of Cincinnati stood vacant in 1982, and the area was later redeveloped with mixed success. The pattern of segregation in housing that began during the influx of African Americans in the early 20th century has also persisted.

is the clear possibility that Cincinnati in the 21st century stands to become a black majority city. Of those whites who do remain, many represent a continued Appalachian presence that began during the World War II employment boom. More recently, there has been the arrival of a small Hispanic contingent.

Cincinnati's demographic experience presented clear evidence of the nation's post–World War II suburbanization phenomenon reinforced by increasing white flight to outlying neighborhoods beyond the city limits. From 1960 to 1970, a further 10 percent of the city population was lost through flight, and subsequent decades have continued this trend. African American rioting in 1967, 1968, and 2001 contributed to a further white exodus, which was worsened by a sense of rising, often racially linked, crime and violence in the downtown areas. Although there was a downward trend in overall crime statistics during the 1990s, since the 2001 riots, violent crime has increased and has been concentrated in certain neighborhoods, contributing to Cincinnati's reputation as the 19th most dangerous city in America.

Cincinnati police have been on the front line in trying to stem the criminal tide; however, they are perceived as being institutionally racist and prone to excessive use of force in dealing with a concentrated minority population. The resulting perceived absence of law and order threatens the city's corporate balance and tax base. Dealing with these urban challenges is made more difficult by a heavily indebted city government. Although an array of social programs and initiatives are periodically put forth, such attempts to reverse or alleviate circumstances that are viewed as contributory to crime have fallen short, suggesting that other issues might be at play. As in the nation as a whole, Cincinnati's crime successes are limited.

Theodore W. Eversole
Independent Scholar

See Also: Ohio; Racism; Riots; Urbanization.

Further Readings
Aaron, Daniel. *Cincinnati, Queen City of the West, 1819–1838*. Columbus: Ohio University Press, 1992.
Bronson, Peter. *Behind the Lines: The Untold Stories of the Cincinnati Riots*. Milford, OH: Chilidog Press, 2006.
Marcus, Alan I. *Plague of Strangers: Social Groups and the Origins of City Services in Cincinnati 1819–1870*. Columbus: Ohio University Press, 1991.
Miller, Zane L. *Visions of Place: The City, Neighborhoods, Suburbs and Cincinnati's Clifton, 1850–2000*. Columbus: Ohio University Press, 2001.
Ohio Historical Society. "Cincinnati Civil Disorders (2001)." *Ohio History Central* (July 1, 2005).
Taylor, Henry Louis, Jr., ed. *Race and the City: Work, Community, and Protest in Cincinnati, 1820–1970*. Urbana: University of Illinois Press, 1993.

Citizen Participation on Juries

In the United States, citizen participation on petit, or trial, juries is a cornerstone of the judicial system. Members of a jury deliberate and attempt to agree upon a verdict. If summoned, unless exempted or excused, all American citizens have a legal duty to serve on juries. However, the extent and manner of citizen participation on juries has varied and continues to evolve because of a myriad of both social and legal developments.

While the Sixth Amendment affirms the right to a jury and explicitly states that the jury be an impartial body drawn from a district where an alleged crime took place, the right to a jury trial was extended to all civil cases involving a dispute of $20 or more via the Seventh Amendment. In *Duncan v. Louisiana* (1968), the Supreme Court held that the Fourteenth Amendment afforded the right to a jury trial in criminal cases to any defendant tried in state court who, if tried in federal court, would require a jury. Later decisions established that any individual facing at least a six-month incarceration has a right to a jury trial. However, a state's constitution governs the right to jury trial in civil cases. Thus, states are able to determine the degree to which defendants being sued civilly must be provided a jury. As a result, in some states, citizen participation on juries involving civil disputes may be more limited.

Jury Qualification
Historically and even into the 20th century, citizen participation on juries was limited because early jury selection relied on the "key man" system. Techniques utilized under this system were heavily influenced and controlled by individual jury commissioners. As a result, jurors included only those citizens who the jury commissioner believed were of the appropriate intellect and character. Additionally, prior to the ratification of the Fourteenth Amendment, as well as the Supreme Court's decision in *Strauder v. West Virginia* (1880), only white men who owned a certain amount of property were eligible for jury service. With the passage of the United States Jury Selection and Service Act of 1968, voting lists replaced the "key man" system and were used to randomly generate jury lists in federal cases. However, this method also limited citizen participation by neglecting certain segments of the citizenry who were not registered to vote. Recently, efforts have been focused on selecting initial jury panels that reflect a more representative sample of the relevant citizenry population. Therefore, instead of relying on voting lists alone, tax rolls, records of welfare recipients, and rosters of licensed drivers are also used in attempts to gain a representative sample of the relevant population. Today, the vast majority of states utilize protocols similar to the federal act to generate jury lists.

Additionally, at one time, categorical exemptions were employed to keep certain citizens off juries. For example, citizens working in certain professions such as medicine or law were automatically excluded. Moreover, the exclusion of parents with primary child care obligations greatly limited the participation of female citizens on juries. The majority of these exemptions are no longer in place in most states. However, citizens under 18 or citizens convicted of felonies are not permitted to serve on juries.

During the jury selection process in both state and federal court, biased citizens who might decide cases subjectively must be excluded from serving on a jury. The ideal is a jury comprising citizens who are capable of being objective in regard to the parties and issues of a particular case. If a citizen demonstrates a bias, both sides have a right to prevent that citizen from serving on the jury. The general process of voir dire is utilized to identify and exclude partial citizens. Specifically, lawyers and/or the judge, by asking questions, work to identify and disqualify those citizens who have a bias and exclude these individuals for cause. Both sides may eliminate citizens from sitting on a jury via peremptory challenges. Although limited in number, peremptory challenges may be used in either civil or criminal matters and allow either side to exclude a citizen for any reason except race or gender. In *Batson v. Kentucky*, the Supreme Court created a new process for evaluating the use of peremptory challenges against racial minorities.

Additionally, although a completely random jury is not constitutionally mandated, a jury must be drawn from a fair cross-section of the community. According to *Duren v. Missouri*, to establish a prima facie violation of the Sixth Amendment fair cross-section requirement, a defendant must satisfy a three-pronged test. Specifically, the defendant must show (1) a group is distinctive in the community, (2) the group is underrepresented on the jury in comparison to its numbers in the community, and (3) that the underrepresentation is the result of the group's systematic exclusion during jury selection. Thus, this requirement, in

These women took part in the first all-woman jury in California. On November 2, 1911, in Los Angeles, they acquitted the editor of the Watts News *of printing indecent language. The inclusion of women was part of a trend toward making juries more and more representative of the general public in the 20th century.*

theory, further increases citizen participation on juries. Depending on the state, the size of a jury in both civil and criminal trials may vary between six and 12 members. Additionally, the vast majority of states require unanimous verdicts in criminal cases. However, a majority of states allow for less than unanimity in civil cases.

Jury Instructions

At the federal level and in most states, judges instruct the jury on the law at the end of the trial. Additionally, a judge may determine the length of time a jury is required to deliberate. Citizens participating on a jury are primarily finders of fact that apply the law as explained by the judge through his or her charge to the jury. Moreover, by participating on juries, citizens have the final word and do not have to explicitly state the reasons for their verdict. Jury nullification occurs when citizens on a jury acquit an individual who they believe based on the facts is guilty, because the jury believes the law or the application of the law is wrong. Jury nullification is relatively rare. In most states, citizens participating on a jury have a limited role, if any, in the punishment process. However, juries do participate in the punishment phase of capital cases. Additionally, in most states, the jury's decision concerning the imposition of the death penalty is conclusive. In civil cases, the citizens comprising a jury decide liability and award damages.

However, judges may have the right to reduce excessive damage awards or increase damages, though the latter is rarely utilized. Additionally, some states have placed limits on the amount of certain types of damages, such as punitive damages. Unlike a conviction, which may be overturned on appeal, a jury acquittal in a criminal matter is final.

In sum, jury service is an opportunity for citizens to learn about the law and participate in government. However, it should be noted that the percentage of both civil and criminal jury trials has steadily declined in recent years.

Neil Guzy
University of Pittsburgh at Greensburg

See Also: 1941 to 1960 Primary Documents; Appeals; *Duren v. Missouri*; Juries; Trials.

Further Readings

Abramson, J. *We, the Jury: The Jury System and the Ideal of Democracy*. New York: Basic Books, 1994.
Adler, Stephen J. *The Jury: Trial and Error in the American Courtroom*. New York: Times Books, 1994.
Batson v. Kentucky, 476 U.S. 79 (1986).
Daniels, Stephen and Joanne Martin. *Civil Juries and the Politics of Reform*. Evanston, IL: Northwestern University Press, 1995.
Duncan v. Louisiana, 391 U.S. 145 (1968).
Duren v. Missouri, 439 U.S. 362 (1979).
Guinther, Jon. *The Jury in America*. New York: Facts on File, 1988.
Hans, Valerie P. and Neil Vidmar. *American Juries: The Verdict*. New York: Prometheus Books, 2007.
Powers v. Ohio, 499 U.S. 400, 411 (1991).

Civil Disobedience

Civil disobedience occurs when a person refuses to obey a law or policy he or she believes to be unjust. Theoretically, there are three basic types of civil disobedience; in practice, the three types overlap somewhat. Integrity-based civil disobedience involves citizens engaging in protest against a law or policy they feel is immoral. Justice-based civil disobedience involves the disobeying of laws to obtain a denied right. Policy-based civil disobedience involves breaking the law in order to change a policy a citizen believes to be wrong. Civil disobedience has long been recognized as a fundamental right of American citizens. For instance, the Bill of Rights (1789) holds that citizens have the right to engage in civil disobedience if their conscience and the actions of government dictate it. Civil disobedience can take many forms, including pamphleteering and letter writing, demonstrations and marches, and worker strikes, as well as the occupation of public buildings. However, the exact nature of protest can vary considerably given the nature of the law or policy being demonstrated against. For example, campaigners for the legalization of cannabis have attended public demonstrations in possession of the drug, and furthermore, they have also been known to organize illegal medical cannabis dispensaries to promote cannabis usage to combat illnesses and diseases they argue it is effective in treating.

Practitioners of civil disobedience risk retaliatory acts, including perhaps most importantly the threat of physical violence and imprisonment. There is some disagreement between civil disobedience campaigners as to how a protester should respond to violence (from police or otherwise), as well as how protesters should submit to police arrest if it occurs. Some practitioners of civil disobedience argue that a campaigner must never engage in violence. Others argue it is sometimes necessary to protect oneself from aggressive and violent members of the public as well as from state-authorized violence committed by the police or armed forces.

Some practitioners of civil disobedience argue that a protester must not cooperate with police investigations or legal procedures, though others argue that it is necessary to cooperate so that the protesters can make their arguments heard. Some seek to make a political point by winning an acquittal or avoiding a fine, often using legal proceedings as an opportunity to inform observers of their reasons for breaking the law. There is also some debate among practitioners of civil disobedience as to whether a protester should plead guilty if he or she is charged—pleading guilty can be seen to imply wrongdoing, and a protester may well feel he or she is not doing anything wrong when engaging in civil disobedience, particularly when it is against a law or policy he or she feels is highly immoral.

Nonviolent Versus Violent Civil Disobedience

An important debate among civil disobedience campaigners revolves around the issue of nonviolent protest. Advocates of nonviolent civil disobedience reject completely the use of physical violence to achieve political goals. Voluntary human rights organizations that seek to promote civil liberties worldwide, such as Amnesty International, solely advocate nonviolent action. The use of nonviolent protest is held by some practitioners of civil disobedience to be a key measure by which the moral authority, social acceptability, and intellectual persuasiveness of their arguments can be demonstrated to other members of society, as well as, perhaps just as importantly, how their activities can be most clearly distinguished from the actions of terrorists. Practitioners of nonviolent civil disobedience use a diverse range of proactive protest methods in their campaigns, including sit-ins, blockades, and hunger strikes. Prominent campaigners who advocated nonviolent civil disobedience include Mohandas Gandhi, who led protests against British rule in India, as well as Martin Luther King, Jr., who followed Gandhi's lead in using nonviolent methods as he sought to win civil rights for African Americans. An important contemporary nonviolent movement was the Velvet Revolution, which led to the peaceful overthrow of the Communist government in Czechoslovakia in 1989. Similar success was obtained by the Singing Revolution, which occurred across Estonia, Latvia, and Lithuania in the early 1990s. During this time, protesters stood in front of Russian tanks and armed forces and sang national songs to help achieve independence. Such successes have been cited by the Dalai Lama as he has advocated nonviolence to gain freedom from Chinese rule for Tibet.

Not all civil disobedience campaigners have advocated nonviolent action. Leon Trotsky, Subhash Chandra Bose, George Orwell, and Malcolm X, among others, have all been ardent critics of nonviolent protest. They have variously argued that the poor and socially excluded have more to lose than the middle classes or rich elites when engaging in nonviolent action; that revolutionary change to society necessarily involves some element of physical violence; and that the right to self-defense is a fundamental human right. For example, during the 1960s' civil rights movement, Black Panther George Jackson argued that the nonviolent protests would not by themselves lead to social change. Similarly, Malcolm X clashed with American civil rights leaders over the issue of nonviolence, arguing that violence should not be ruled out when no other option remained. In a debate at the Oxford Union in 1965 titled "Extremism in the Defense of Liberty Is No Vice; Moderation in the Pursuit of Justice Is No Virtue," Malcolm X argued passionately that it was a crime for anyone being brutalized—as many African Americans were at the time—to continue to accept that brutality without doing something to defend themselves. Indeed, some civil disobedience commentators have argued that populist histories of social protest movements tend to ignore the involvement of more militant group members in both the Indian independence and American civil rights movements. Furthermore, it is arguable that violent protest and civil disobedience by citizens is justifiable when nation-states break international law and engage in war crimes such as torture and genocide.

The question of the conditions under which violent protest and civil disobedience are justifiable is a debate that is likely to continue for the foreseeable future. Justifications for violent protest and civil disobedience must be balanced against the recognition that the refusal of Gandhi and Martin Luther King, Jr., to engage in violence themselves, in spite of being physically assaulted and imprisoned, led to significant wider public sympathy and international support for their respective causes.

The Impact of Thoreau's *Civil Disobedience*

The history of civil disobedience in America reinforces the power of such forms of protest to engender social change. One of the earliest and most historically important examples of civil disobedience in America is the Boston Tea Party. In 1773, the British parliament passed the Tea Act, which levied a tax on tea in the then British colony of America. Protesters believed this violated their right to be taxed only by their own elected representatives and began a series of protests to stop the tea being imported into the country via key colonial ports, of which Boston was one. In no small part because the British governor in Boston, Thomas Hutchinson, refused to allow the tea to be returned to Britain, the protesters chose to destroy the tea by dumping it in the water. This act played a key role in galvanizing wider support for independence from British colonial rule. It was also drawn upon by Henry David Thoreau as inspiration for his famous 1849 essay *Civil Disobedience*. Thoreau had refused to pay poll taxes to his local tax collector, Sam Staples, as he was morally outraged with what he saw to be a corrupt American government that endorsed slavery and engaged in war against Mexico. He was sent to jail but was freed when a relative, without his knowledge, paid his debt. In *Civil Disobedience*, Thoreau sought to justify the viewpoint that citizens must not allow governments to act with impunity and rule as they please, and indeed, that citizens have a civic and moral duty to engage in organized protest and civil disobedience to fight social injustice. His arguments influenced many political activists, including Gandhi and Martin Luther King, Jr.

The Industrial Workers of the World (IWW) in the early 20th century followed Thoreau's lead and under a First Amendment free speech campaign sought to organize workers and publicly speak about labor issues, frequently in the face of violent repression by local government and business authorities. IWW members were frequently beaten and imprisoned for causing public disorder. Some IWW members were even kidnapped and covered in tar and feathers by local vigilantes paid by the business community to disrupt their activities. Yet wherever the IWW campaigned, it won the right to speak in public.

Thoreau's ideas also played a role in the women's suffrage movement in America during the late 19th and early 20th centuries. Lucy Stone and key members of the National American Woman Suffrage Association (NAWSA), alongside the National Woman's Party (NWP), engaged in protest and civil disobedience as they

A man wearing a placard reading "bread or revolution" on his hat at an Industrial Workers of the World rally in Union Square in New York City on April 11, 1914.

sought to secure equality and the right to vote for women. Many suffragettes endured physical violence and imprisonment for pursuing their political goals. Women finally gained the right to vote in 1920 through the enactment of the Nineteenth Amendment to the U.S. Constitution. However, the women's movement in America has continued to be active on a range of issues such as abortion, domestic violence, trafficking, and enforced prostitution, as well as the use of rape as a weapon of war.

Modern Civil Disobedience

The civil rights movement of the mid-20th century is another important moment in time for the history of civil disobedience in America. Martin Luther King, Jr., among others, engaged in numerous nonviolent protests such as the Montgomery Bus Boycott in Alabama, the Greensboro sit-in in North Carolina, and the Montgomery and Washington marches and public demonstrations. The civil rights movement is widely credited with achieving voting, employment, and home-ownership rights for African Americans.

Other important movements during this time included the anti–Vietnam War protests. Also bound up with the antiwar protests during the latter part of the 20th century was the antinuclear movement, which was against the use of nuclear energy and weapons. In 1982, more than 1 million people demonstrated in New York City's Central Park and called for an end to the arms race against the Soviet Union.

Aside from public marches and speeches, acts of civil disobedience in recent years have included maintaining peace camps near military bases and nuclear energy sites, as well as blockading and otherwise disrupting the transportation of nuclear materials. More broadly, the environmental movement in America has engaged in civil disobedience to protect animals and human beings from ecological harm, as well as to campaign against global warming. Although the movement is largely made up of nonviolent activists, some militant elements do exist.

The history of civil disobedience doesn't simply tell the story of how beliefs and values in the United States have changed and developed over the past 200 years—it also contains within it an important reminder of the power of nonviolent protest to engage in public debate and to help achieve real social change. Nevertheless, it must be acknowledged that it also reinforces that for some individuals, violence remains a legitimate form of protest.

John Martyn Chamberlain
Loughborough University

See Also: 1600 to 1776 Primary Documents; 1777 to 1800 Primary Documents; 1801 to 1850 Primary Documents; 1851 to 1900 Primary Documents; 1941 to 1960 Primary Documents; 1961 to 1980 Primary Documents; African Americans; Alien and Sedition Acts of 1798; American Civil Liberties Union; American Revolution and Criminal Justice; Anarchists; Civil Rights Laws; King, Martin Luther, Jr.; Malcolm X; National Organization for Women; Paine, Thomas; Political Dissidents; Riots; Strikes; Tax Crimes; Tea Act of 1773; Thoreau, Henry David.

Further Readings

Singer, P. *Democracy and Disobedience*. Oxford: Clarendon Press, 1973.
Sunstein, C. *Why Societies Need Dissent*. Cambridge, MA: Harvard University Press, 2003.
Thoreau, Henry David. "Civil Disobedience." In *Civil Disobedience in Focus*, Hugo A. Bedau, ed. London: Routledge, 1991.
Zunes, S. *Nonviolent Social Movements: A Geographical Perspective*. London: Blackwell, 1999.

Civil Rights Act of 1866

As of January 1, 1863, President Abraham Lincoln's Emancipation Proclamation freed the slaves in the Confederacy. Republicans were concerned, however, that winning the war would not permanently end slavery; thus, the Thirteenth Amendment was enacted, abolishing slavery and giving Congress power to enforce abolition. Section 2 of the Thirteenth Amendment was designed to eliminate the structural obstacles and practical impediments that existed under slavery—the so-called badges of slavery. After the war, southern culture did not easily embrace racial equality. African Americans were terrorized by the Ku

Klux Klan and other white supremacist organizations. Continued fear, hate, and racism led to the Black Codes, in which previous Confederate states enacted vagrancy and apprenticeship laws. Apprenticeship laws led to the institutionalization of African American orphans and abandoned children. Vagrancy laws resulted in the incarceration of unemployed African Americans. Overall, the Black Codes made African Americans unemployable, except to work for their previous owners or other white males.

In the post–Civil War South, the idea that African Americans were little more than chattel and savages was commonplace. Many whites believed that African Americans were becoming "uppity" because they stayed in the same hotels as whites and sat next to whites in church and at the theater. In addition to the continuation of racial inequality and discrimination through the Black Codes, there was a white backlash emboldened by vigilantism and violence.

Enactment and Prosecutions

In an atmosphere of white supremacy in the war-ravaged south, Congress overturned *Dred Scott v. Sandford* (1857) by enacting the Civil Rights Act (CRA) of 1866 over President Andrew Johnson's veto. Seeking to permanently enshrine the freedoms within the Thirteenth Amendment, the 1866 CRA granted newly freed slaves federal rights and removed obstacles to obtaining those rights. Known today as Title 18 U.S.C. Section 242, Section 2 of the 1866 CRA made it a federal crime for local or state government officials to violate the federally guaranteed rights (usually constitutional rights) of individuals.

The Reconstruction backlash from states' rights advocates kept the 1866 CRA relatively inactive until the middle of the 20th century. Even today, defendants are only prosecuted under Title 18 U.S.C. Section 242—per U.S. Justice Department policy—if federal prosecutors can show that state or local government officials acted under "color of law" and "willfully" with "specific intent" violated the victim's federally protected rights. Moreover, a Title 18 U.S.C. Section 242 prosecution occurs only when a "gross injustice has occurred." The "gross injustice" usually involves a state and/or local criminal justice official who avoided justice for committing a crime.

The 1866 CRA was designed to protect the federally guaranteed rights of African Americans and their white sympathizers from lawless local government actors. Such an application of the law existed in the case of *Screws v. United States* (1945), in which Sheriff Claude Screws arrested and beat to death an African American male. No state prosecution occurred, so the federal government stepped in to prosecute Screws. The "color of law" element was satisfied even though Screws acted outside the scope of his employment. Screws acted under "color of law" since "misuse of power possessed by virtue of state law and made possible because the wrongdoer is clothed with the authority of state law, is action taken under 'color of law'" (*United States v. Classic*, 1941). The federal right violated was the Fifth Amendment right to due process prior to the state taking a life. To meet the statutory requirements of Section 242, the crime must be intentional, willful, and specifically aimed at the victim.

Even though the 1866 CRA was designed to preserve equality and end discrimination, its impact was blunted by the U.S. Supreme Court's *Civil Rights Cases* (1883), which shifted civil rights enforcement power from the federal government to the states. As a result, Jim Crow laws allowed the continuation of race-baiting, lynching, extreme violence, and discrimination against African Americans until the civil rights movement of the 1960s.

Michael S. Vaughn
Sam Houston State University

See Also: African Americans; Civil Rights Act of 1875; Civil Rights Laws; *Dred Scott v. Sandford*; Johnson, Andrew (Administration of); Police Abuse; Racism; Supreme Court, U.S.

Further Readings

Cohen, J. "The *Screws* Case: Federal Protection of Negro Rights." *Columbia Law Review*, v.46 (1946).

Gressman, E. "The Unhappy History of Civil Rights Legislation." *Michigan Law Review*, v.50 (1952).

Kohl, R. L. "The Civil Rights Act of 1866, Its Hour Come Round at Last: *Jones v. Alfred*." *Virginia Law Review*, v.55 (1969).

Miller, D. A. H. "White Cartels, the Civil Rights Act of 1866, and the History of *Jones v. Alfred H. Mayer Co.*" *Fordham Law Review*, v.77 (2008).

Civil Rights Act of 1875

The Civil Rights Act of 1875 prohibited racial discrimination in public accommodations, including inns, modes of transportation, and theaters. The law was found unconstitutional by the Supreme Court in the 1883 *Civil Rights Cases*.

Following the emancipation of slaves and the passage of the Thirteenth, Fourteenth, and Fifteenth Amendments to the Constitution, Congress enacted several pieces of legislation designed to ensure that African Americans would enjoy the full rights of citizenship. The Civil Rights Act of 1875 provided that "all persons" would be entitled to use the "accommodations, advantages, facilities, and privileges" of public places, including inns, theaters and other places of entertainment, and forms of transportation. Policies restricting access to those venues must be "applicable alike to citizens of every race and color, regardless of any previous condition of servitude." The penalty for denying access to public facilities was a fine ranging from $500 to $1,000. Clearly, Congress was responding to the behavior of private businesses that separated the races as well as to state legislation that segregated people on the basis of race. They considered such discrimination both a violation of the Fourteenth Amendment's guarantee of equal protection of the law and the Thirteenth Amendment's ban on slavery and involuntary servitude.

Supreme Court Challenge

In the 1883 *Civil Rights Cases*, the Supreme Court found the Civil Rights Act of 1875 unconstitutional by a majority of 8–1. Justice Joseph Bradley wrote the opinion of the court, which held that discriminating in access to public accommodations is the act of private individuals and does not fall under the Fourteenth Amendment. The court's holding significantly narrowed the application of the Fourteenth Amendment's guarantee of "equal protection of the laws" by asserting that the amendment only prohibited unequal treatment by the states, but that it could not be read to prohibit discrimination by individual proprietors of inns, theaters, or modes of transportation. He wrote that Congress could only make laws in response to discriminatory actions by state legislators or by other state actors. It could not create codes of "municipal laws" that regulated the behavior of some private citizens and upheld the rights to social activities of others. Bradley made a "slippery slope" argument, stating that if Congress could pass civil rights laws, there was nothing to prohibit it from enacting codes of law for every possible situation. He distinguished the civil rights law from laws enforcing the right to vote or to serve on juries free from racial discrimination, as the latter examples would require that the state itself was directly involved in the forbidden discrimination.

Bradley also stated that the law could not be sustained under the Thirteenth Amendment's prohibition of slavery. Supporters of civil rights argued that discrimination in public places was one of the "badges of slavery," a form of bias that was held over from the laws that restricted the free movement of slaves. The Supreme Court also rejected this argument, stating that there was no similarity between servitude and the denial of the "accommodations or privileges" of staying at an inn, riding in a public conveyance, or attending a theater. The justices also maintained that it was time for former slaves to "take the rank of a mere citizen" and to stop "being the special favorite of the laws." They seemed to assume that no civil rights laws were necessary, but that African Americans would "be protected in the ordinary modes by which other men's rights are protected."

Justice John Marshall Harlan was the only dissenter in the *Civil Rights Cases*, as he was in *Plessy v. Ferguson* (1896). Harlan based his disagreement with the majority on several principles. He argued for judicial restraint, that the court should defer to the judgment of Congress in deciding which laws were "necessary and proper" to carry out the Constitution. Likewise, he argued that discrimination was indeed a "badge and incident of slavery," and that it was one of the "mischiefs to be remedied and grievances to be redressed" by the Thirteenth Amendment. In addition, he argued that the civil rights laws were permissible under the Fourteenth Amendment, which forbade the states from denying equal protection of the law. Inns and railroads, even if privately owned, were put to public use and were often licensed and regulated by the states. Therefore, the states were complicit in the policies of segregation practiced by those nominally private entities.

It was not until the Civil Rights Act of 1964 that the 1883 Supreme Court decision was rectified. In the 1964 act, Congress, mindful of the earlier decision, prohibited discrimination in public accommodations under its authority to regulate interstate commerce, not under the Thirteenth and Fourteenth Amendments.

Mary Welek Atwell
Radford University

See Also: African Americans; Civil Rights Act of 1866; Civil Rights Laws; *Plessy v. Ferguson*; Segregation Laws.

Further Readings
Lively, Donald E. *The Constitution and Race*. New York: Praeger, 1992.
Nieman, Donald G. *Promises to Keep: African Americans and the Constitutional Order*. New York: Oxford University Press, 1991.
Weiner, Mark S. *Black Trials: Citizenship From the Beginnings of Slavery to the End of Caste*. New York: Vintage Books, 2004.

Civil Rights Laws

The concept of civil rights refers to legal measures designed to protect citizens from arbitrary or discriminatory treatment by either a government or a private entity. Since the mid-19th century, the federal government has extended civil rights protections through executive orders, congressional legislation, constitutional amendments, and Supreme Court rulings. Together, such measures have established a legal framework for such protections. For most of U.S. history, they primarily aimed at protecting African Americans from discrimination but by the 1990s, the federal government had expanded the scope of civil rights protections to include, women, older workers, homosexuals, and the disabled.

Civil Rights Acts of 1866 and 1875

During the Reconstruction period following the Civil War, Congress acted to protect African Americans from oppressive actions by southern states. Those states had enacted measures known as the Black Codes—discriminatory laws that applied only to African Americans. The Civil Rights Act of 1866, passed over President Andrew Johnson's veto, established citizenship for all African Americans and banned states from enforcing discriminatory legislation. Fearful that the courts would strike down the law as unconstitutional or that a future Congress might repeal it, Congress passed the landmark Fourteenth Amendment (ratified in 1868) incorporating the terms of the Civil Rights Act of 1866 into the Constitution, thereby making it extremely difficult to eliminate. The Fourteenth Amendment established U.S. citizenship for all persons born or naturalized in the United States and banned states from unreasonably discriminating between classes of citizens or abridging the rights of any citizen without due process of law.

The last major civil rights legislation passed by Congress during the Reconstruction period was the Civil Rights Act of 1875. This measure banned racial discrimination in public accommodations such as inns, restaurants, theaters, and public transportation. Unlike previous civil rights policies, it regulated the behavior of private individuals and businesses.

From the end of the Reconstruction period in the late 1870s to the mid-20th century, no major civil rights legislation or policy was enacted by the federal government as the issue mostly lost favor with the public and Congress. Moreover, the judicial philosophy of the Supreme Court tended to limit the scope and effectiveness of the federal government to protect the civil rights of African Americans from discriminatory policies of states and private interests through narrow interpretation of both the Fourteenth Amendment and the commerce clause. In the *Civil Rights Cases* (1883), the court struck down the Civil Rights Act of 1875, arguing that Congress lacked authority under the Fourteenth Amendment to regulate discriminatory acts by private individuals and groups. Later, in the 1896 ruling in *Plessy v. Ferguson,* the court ruled that state laws requiring racially segregated transportation systems did not violate the Fourteenth Amendment if the quality of accommodations was equal, establishing the "separate but equal" doctrine. Such narrow rulings continued until the 1954 decision in

Brown v. Board of Education revised *Plessy* to strike down state laws requiring racially segregated public schools.

Presidential Action on Civil Rights

The federal government began to once again act to counter racial discrimination when in 1941, President Franklin Roosevelt established the Fair Employment Practices Committee, which forbade war industry contractors to discriminate in hiring and pay on the basis of race, religion, or national origin. In this first presidential directive on race since the Reconstruction period, Roosevelt was spurred to act by African American labor leader A. Philip Randolph's threat to organize a march on Washington. As its enforcement powers were limited, the committee's effectiveness proved a disappointment to many civil rights leaders.

Shortly after World War II, President Harry Truman pushed for a new national civil rights law, but that effort failed largely because of strong southern opposition in Congress and in his Democratic Party. Unable to get a bill through the committee system of Congress, Truman turned to his executive powers to promote civil rights. On July 26, 1948, he signed Executive Order 9981, which ordered all U.S. military installations, at home and abroad, to remove any policy that separated the races. This meant that all facilities, including barracks, mess halls, and bathrooms, would be racially integrated. Although Truman failed in getting a civil rights bill passed in Congress, he did contribute to bringing about more equality in the U.S. Armed Forces.

As Truman promoted civil rights policies through executive actions, the Supreme Court was evolving away from its narrow interpretation of the Constitution. In 1954, it delivered its landmark decision in *Brown v. Board of Education*, a case challenging state laws requiring racial segregation in public schools. Led by Chief Justice Earl Warren, the court rendered a unanimous decision, ruling the "separate but equal" standard to be unconstitutional. Consequently, the court ordered all levels of government—federal, state, and local—and particularly local school boards, to remove legal barriers to racial integration. Despite the unanimity of the court, many states, mostly in the south, resisted the order. For more than a decade, racial segregation continued in most southern public schools. Racial minorities would not get the relief they were looking for until the enactment of the Civil Rights Act of 1964.

President Dwight D. Eisenhower was cautious about advancing civil rights, believing such reform must come gradually as hearts and minds changed. However, he issued an executive order to desegregate public facilities in Washington, D.C., and he signed the Civil Rights Act of 1957, the first such legislation passed by Congress since the Reconstruction period. The latter measure mainly aimed to eliminate barriers to African American voting rights (only 20 percent of African American citizens were registered to vote). However, the act turned out to be largely ineffective and was ridiculed by civil rights activists. In order to overcome a southern filibuster in the Senate, its enforcement power had been watered down. Three years after enactment, African American voter registration had not increased.

Civil Rights Act of 1964

Like his Republican predecessor, Democrat John F. Kennedy was cautious when it came to civil rights issues. Although philosophically supportive, he was a political realist, generally fearful of alienating the southern wing of his party. His actions in support of civil rights were usually in reaction to events rather than proactive. In 1961, for example, he directed the Interstate Commerce Commission to enforce the Supreme Court's ruling in *Boynton v. Virginia*. That decision struck down as unconstitutional state and local statutes that mandated segregated bus and train stations on interstate routes. He took this action only after civil rights activists forced the issue with the so-called Freedom Rides, an exercise in civil disobedience against state segregation laws and a tactic the president opposed. The racist violence provoked by the Freedom Rides convinced Kennedy to act. The next year, violence again forced Kennedy's hand when he sent troops and federal marshals to the University of Mississippi to enforce a court order to allow an African American student, James Meredith, to enroll. Shortly before his tragic death, Kennedy called for Congress to pass a new and stronger civil rights law.

The request was fulfilled when President Lyndon B. Johnson, with Martin Luther King, Jr., standing by his side, signed into law the Civil

President Lyndon B. Johnson signing the 1964 Civil Rights Act on July 2, 1964, with Martin Luther King, Jr., standing behind him. In the following years, President Johnson also signed both the Voting Rights Act of 1965 and the Civil Rights Act of 1968 (the Fair Housing Act). The 1964 act reestablished many of the terms of the defunct Civil Rights Act of 1875.

Rights Act of 1964. The statute empowered the national government to safeguard civil rights in both the public and private sectors. It prohibited workplace discrimination, as well as discrimination in public accommodations based on race, color, religion, sex, or national origin, reestablishing many of the terms of the defunct Civil Rights Act of 1875. Any business—including theaters, motels, restaurants, or sports stadiums—that substantially affected interstate commerce was considered a place of "public accommodation" and was thereby subject to federal regulation. For example, the federal government charged a motel owner in downtown Atlanta, Georgia, for violating the 1964 civil rights law. The motel owner provided lodging for whites, but not for African Americans. The dispute ended up at the U.S. Supreme Court. The court was asked to address the issue of whether the motel business practices interfered with interstate commerce. The court ruled that the motel practices substantially disrupted the flow of interstate commerce because more than 70 percent of the motel's guests came from out of state. The *Heart of Atlanta* decision, coupled with other Supreme Court rulings, expanded the federal government's regulatory powers over civil rights issues. The Civil Rights Act of 1964 also helped speed compliance with the *Brown* decision. According to its provisions, public schools that were slow to desegregate no longer received financial support from the federal government until they complied with national policy. To enforce the provisions of the new law, Congress created the Equal Employment Opportunities Commission (EEOC).

A year after the enactment of the Civil Rights Act of 1964, President Johnson signed another major piece of legislation into law, the Voting Rights Act of 1965. For decades, many states, most notably in the south, had circumvented the

Fifteenth Amendment by enacting clever barriers to African American voter registration such as literacy test requirements and poll taxes, which effectively disenfranchised the vast majority of African American citizens. The voting rights law banned these devices and other legislative measures that states had used to suppress minority voting. Moreover, the law placed particular state and local governments with long histories of discriminatory practices under the supervision of the federal government. Any state or local governments covered by the law would have to get approval from the federal government before executing a new law that, for example, changed polling locations, modified voting qualifications, or redrew electoral districts. The Voting Rights Act has been amended and renewed many times since 1965. In 2006, the federal government renewed the act for another 25 years, despite strong opposition from several southern states and local communities.

The following year President Johnson signed into law the Civil Rights Act of 1968, commonly known as the Fair Housing Act. It prohibited discrimination in the sale, rental, or financing of housing based on race, national origin, and religion and later covered gender and disability.

Other Disenfranchised Groups
By the late 1960s, civil rights activists were addressing discrimination issues involving other aggrieved social groups such as women, older workers, homosexuals, and the disabled. As with the African American civil rights movement, the favored tools for changing policies were lawsuits based on the Fourteenth Amendment's equal protection clause and new federal legislation.

The first major federal civil rights initiative aimed at enhancing women's rights was the Nineteenth Amendment, which was ratified in 1920. It prohibited states from denying any citizen the right vote based on one's sex. Later, the Civil Rights Act of 1964 prohibited gender discrimination in the workplace, while Title IX of that law required equal opportunity of participation by both males and females in all educational programs and activities that receive federal financial assistance. The implementation of Title IX has been controversial. In order to ensure compliance, many colleges have eliminated certain sports programs for men such as wrestling in order to fund new programs for women. In 1973, the Supreme Court ruled in the landmark *Roe v. Wade* case that governments may not prohibit or restrict women's access to abortions during the early months of pregnancy.

In 1967, Congress addressed the issue of age discrimination in the workplace. The Age Discrimination in Employment Act (ADEA) prohibited job discrimination based on age against employees 40 years of age or older working for employers with 40 or more workers.

The Americans with Disabilities Act of 1990 (ADA) protected disabled citizens from being treated unfairly in the workplace or in public accommodations. The 1990 law mandated state and local governments, as well as private businesses with 15 or more employees in 1994, to make "reasonable accommodations" for any worker with a physical or mental disability that significantly limits a major life activity.

Although some states have enacted statutes to extend civil rights protection to homosexual citizens, there have been no federal civil rights laws that specifically address discrimination against homosexuals. National policy changes in this area have generally come from the federal courts and usually concern privacy and substantive due process considerations. Some have argued that homosexuals, unlike like African Americans or women, are defined by a freely chosen behavior and lifestyle for which there is no Fourteenth Amendment protection. Traditionally, Congress had banned homosexuals from service in the U.S. military, fearing their presence might create problems in discipline and cohesion. In 1993, after failing to persuade Congress to change the policy, President Bill Clinton issued a policy directive, later dubbed "Don't Ask, Don't Tell" (DADT), under which the military would not question its members concerning their sexual orientation or preference, but the individuals were prohibited from revealing publicly that they were homosexual. This compromise policy lasted until Congress repealed the DADT in December 2010 and removed the ban on homosexuals serving in the military.

Other issues targeted as civil rights violations by homosexual activists have been antisodomy laws and marriage laws of states. In 1993, the

Supreme Court struck down state laws banning sodomy in *Lawrence v. Texas*. Consensual sexual contact between adults, the court ruled, is protected from government interference through the substantive due process doctrine of the Fourteenth Amendment. Activists have also argued that state laws that do not allow same-sex marriage are discriminatory. Fearing some states would legalize gay marriages that would have to be recognized by all other states under the full faith and credit clause of the Constitution, President Bill Clinton signed the Defense of Marriage Act in 1996. It defined marriage for federal purposes between one man and one woman, and it stated that states did not have to recognize same-sex marriages that are recognized by other states.

The penalties for violations of previously discussed acts have included corrective measures such as court injunctions, equitable relief, ordered restitution of back pay, job reinstatement, or hiring of employees.

John Kelly Damico
Kyle Barbieri
Georgia Perimeter College

See Also: 1961 to 1980 Primary Documents; *Brown v. Board of Education*; Civil Rights Act of 1866; Civil Rights Act of 1875; *Katzenbach v. McClung*; *Lawrence v. Texas*; *Plessy v. Ferguson*; Segregation Laws.

Further Readings
Brooks, Roy L., Gilbert Paul Carrasco, and Michael Selmi. *Civil Rights Litigation: Cases and Perspectives*. Law Casebook Series. Durham, NC: Carolina Academic Press, 2005.
Lovey, Robert D., ed. *The Civil Rights Act of 1964: The Passage of the Law That Ended Racial Segregation*. SUNY Series in Afro-American Studies. Albany: State University of New York Press, 1997.
Mezey, Susan Gluck. *Disabling Interpretations: The Americans With Disabilities Act in Federal Court*. Pittsburgh, PA: University of Pittsburgh Press, 2005.
Mezey, Susan Gluck. *Queers in Court: Gay Rights Law and Public Policy*. Lanham, MD: Rowman & Littlefield, 2007.
Tsesis, Alexander. *We Shall Overcome: A History of Civil Rights and the Law*. New Haven, CT: Yale University Press, 2009.

Clayton Anti-Trust Act of 1914

The Clayton Anti-Trust Act of 1914 created the Federal Trade Commission and contained major amendments to firm up the antitrust statutes of the Sherman Anti-Trust Act of 1890. After much discussion and compromise, the act was supported by labor and agriculture interests and signed by President Woodrow Wilson on October 15, 1914. The Sherman Act was the first major regulatory legislation to govern business and it became apparent by 1914 that the law had some vague language that needed to be corrected to tighten up industry regulations. Wilson's predecessors Theodore Roosevelt (1901–09) and William Howard Taft (1909–13) worked hard during their administrations to break up the monopolies that developed in numerous industries prior to 1901. Monopolies became targets of the Attorney General's Office in both administrations, resulting in the breakup of the Standard Oil Trust, American Telephone and Telegraph, and the American Tobacco Company.

The Clayton Anti-Trust Act originated from legislation proposed by Henry Clayton (D-AL) the chair of the House Commerce Committee. The House and Senate both offered versions of the bill in 1914 and formed a compromise version in conference committee. The conference opted to restore the prohibition on price fixing and added a test to see how the differential would impact trade. Congress also opted to use a modified version of the House and Senate's regulation on holding companies. The major conciliation was the decision to use administrative regulation powers for the commission versus a criminal approach that would remove enforcement of criminal acts from the Attorney General's Office. A success for the unions came with the Clayton Act's prohibition of the Sherman Act's conspiracy of interstate trade statute being used against them when they voted to strike, impacting multiple states.

Congress passed the Clayton Act 35–24 in the Senate and 245–52 in the House. In its final version the law created a regulatory agency, the Federal Trade Commission, to help implement the law and regulate industry. Industry could no longer set prices to eliminate competition, the same managers could not be on the boards of competing companies or interlocking directorates, and companies could no longer hold stock in a corporation that was in direct competition with that company. The role of the Federal Trade Commission was to promote free and fair competition in industry. A concern related to monopolies was the economy being controlled by the business decisions of a few people.

Trust-busting, another term for breaking up monopolies, declined during the 1920s because the economy was booming. However, once the Great Depression started, President Franklin Roosevelt called for the commission to pursue any illegal activities being carried out by industry. In 1936, the Robinson Patman Act amended Section 2 of the Clayton Act, which discusses price and other forms of discrimination among customers and prohibits the practice (this was not clarified in the Clayton Act). Additional changes to the legislation passed Congress in 1950 under the Celler-Kefauver Act, which amended Section 7 of the Clayton Act to prohibit not only horizontal mergers (firms producing similar goods) but any form of merger that might impact competition like conglomerate mergers. In 1976, further amendments to the law were included in the Hart-Scott-Rodino Anti-Trust Improvements Act of 1976, which impacted Sections 15 and 18 of the law and also required premerger filings with the FTC.

The Clayton Anti-Trust Act of 1914 strengthened the Sherman Anti-Trust Act of 1890, which did not prove to be a strong-enough set of regulations to protect consumers and industry from the abuses of monopolies. This legislation fixed the loopholes in the original law and put tighter regulations in force. In correcting the problems, Congress created the Federal Trade Commission (FTC) to oversee and regulate industry. The FTC looks for violations and reviews complaints about price fixing, mergers, and acquisitions, and issues administrative penalties for violations. The 1914 legislation has been amended only three times: 1936, 1950, and 1976, to adjust language and to add a prohibition of conglomerate mergers and to require premerger filings with the FTC. The main role of this legislation is to prevent illegal activity by corporations that can damage competition.

Theresa S. Hefner-Babb
Lamar University

See Also: Antitrust Law; Sherman Anti-Trust Act of 1890; Wilson, Woodrow (Administration of).

Further Readings
An Act to Supplement Existing Laws Against Unlawful Restraints and Monopolies, and for Other Purposes. 63 STAT 730.
Sanders, M. Elizabeth. *Roots of Reform: Farmers, Workers, and the American State, 1877–1917.* Chicago: University of Chicago Press, 1999.
Winerman, Marc. "The Origins of the FTC: Concentration, Cooperation, Control and Competition." *Antitrust Law Journal*, v.71/1 (2003).

Clemency

Clemency in the United States encompasses many related procedures, including amnesty, commutation, pardon, remission, and reprieve. All involve forgiving someone for a crime or cancelling the penalty associated with his or her crime. When an individual has paid his/her debt to society or is considered deserving, executives at the federal or state level can choose to assist his/her cause through any of these mechanisms. In the United States, there have been multiple examples of executive clemency throughout history—some more memorable than others—depending on the different types of executive clemency available, explanations for why an executive may choose to exercise clemency, and additional factors that shape when clemency may be exercised.

Amnesty
Amnesty involves overlooking a person's actions in order to serve some greater cause. Many cities, for example, have weapons amnesty programs in which citizens can hand in weapons without having to worry about facing any legal questions from authorities regarding how they were obtained or why they were in their possession. Likewise, a citizen who observes a violent crime while committing a property crime may have his/her own transgression overlooked through amnesty in exchange for his/her willingness to cooperate regarding what he/she observed. The key facet to amnesty is

that one individual's actions are forgiven in order to fulfill some larger mission—whether it is having someone to testify regarding a murder or to help eliminate violent weapons on the streets.

Commutation, Remission, and Reprieves

Commutation has become a popular subject in the United States in recent years because of the actions of two prominent governors. When commuting a sentence, an executive is substituting one penalty for a crime with another. The key is that the individual remains guilty; only his or her punishment changes. The governors of Illinois and New Mexico both commuted sentences for all death row inmates to life without parole over concerns with potential executions of innocent individuals.

Remission is similar to commutation and involves a complete or partial cancellation of a punishment while the offender is still legally guilty. In its most basic form, remission involves a sentence being reduced. For example, if you are supposed to serve a two-year term but prison overcrowding leads to your being released after serving eight months, you have had your sentence remitted.

Reprieves are temporary postponements of a punishment and are most frequently granted when someone is facing execution in the immediate future and needs additional time to appeal. Again, a reprieve does nothing to remove guilt from an offender.

Pardons

Of the five procedures encompassed by clemency, pardons are the most prominent historically. Pardon powers are given to both federal and state officials. The president of the United States gains his ability to pardon from Article II, Section 2 of the Constitution, which gives the ability to grant reprieves in pardons for any offense except in cases of impeachment. An individual seeking a pardon will address the request to the president, who will receive a nonbinding recommendation from the Office of the Pardon Attorney (housed in the Department of Justice). Likelihood for success depends on the administration, but overall has decreased since the conclusion of World War II. Franklin Roosevelt offered more pardons than any other president with 3,687. Woodrow Wilson offered the second most at 2,480.

The Department of Justice recommends that an individual must wait five years after conviction before receiving a pardon. This, however, is only a recommendation. In normal circumstances, an individual needs to have served his/her entire sentence and shown an ability to lead a productive life. Technically, an individual could receive a pardon before even being charged, let alone convicted, for a crime. The actual request is technically unnecessary. The president could opt to pardon an individual who does not even wish to be pardoned if he sees fit. An individual must affirmatively accept a pardon for it to be recognized by the criminal justice system but that acceptance also carries with it an admission of guilt.

By accepting a pardon, an individual has many rights restored that may have been lost. While it helps eliminate the stigma and public perceptions to an extent, it is important to note that pardons do not expunge one's criminal record. As a result, the person must still disclose his/her conviction on forms and must count on state governments to remove any actions related to voting or holding public office. Simply receiving a pardon does not wipe clean a person's past or assist him/her in bettering his/her future. Since the pardon power of the president is only applicable to matters of federal law, state executives play an important role in regard to clemency through pardons. Most states grant their governors the power to issue pardons while some give this ability to an agency or board appointed by the governor.

From its initial creation, clemency through pardons was highly controversial. At the federal level, the founders—particularly Alexander Hamilton—remembered the many royal abuses of similar powers throughout Europe and feared that the same would occur in the United States if presidents were given the ability to follow suit. Today, watchdog groups focus on whether pardons are being issued consistently with fairly strict, publicly available guidelines so the process is as transparent as possible. After all, the entire idea is to instill mercy into the system where possible and to assist individuals in regaining their lives after paying their debt to society. Pardons at the state level are similarly controversial. In the early years, they were often used in the case of people sentenced to death for lesser crimes (such as robbery) to reduce capital punishment, but even these decisions were not always received well by the public. Writing long before the American experience, Cesare Beccaria found that pardons gave too much power to executive authority, through which they could opt to act in a humane manner. By doing so, however, they failed to set examples for the general public.

Considerations

Several factors can impact whether an individual receives clemency. Legal and technical explanations for clemency are often quite telling. In this category are individuals who were granted some form of clemency because of their innocence, mitigating factors, or disproportionate punishments. Irregularities at trial, insufficient evidence, mistaken identity, new evidence, confessions, no premeditation, the heat of the moment, insanity, intoxication, and nonequal punishment for participants can all serve as causes for legal/technical clemency to be granted. In most cases, these explanations do not invite much controversy, given the black-and-white nature of the decision.

Humanitarian compassion and mercy form another basis for granting clemency. While there is considerably more controversy surrounding these decisions, the appeal to morality and sympathy may help mitigate the negative feedback an executive receives in response to his/her action. Prisoners near death, those whose health threatens other inmates, and those who begin to suffer from mental illness after years in prison may qualify under this category. Many executives choose to grant clemency under this category around the Christmas season when they can clearly explain that they are acting out of compassion in a season of giving to help control any negative public responses.

Judgments of reform and rehabilitation are often the basis for clemency. The clemency claims in this category face the most public scrutiny since it is merely a subjective judgment on whether someone has been rehabilitated that determines whether to grant clemency. Just because an offender has found religion, works for charity, or vows to never commit a crime again is not a basis to assess accurately whether he/she has been truly reformed. For an executive to take a chance in granting clemency puts the executive's own political career on the line, as an opponent will be quick to point out any grants of clemency that lead to future criminal activity.

A series of factors can impact whether an executive is likely to grant clemency. The background, experiences, attitudes, and concerns of the executive are a major factor. Presidents may favor helping people from their state, for example. Or a governor who lost a childhood home to an arsonist may be less willing to grant clemency to individuals who have committed similar crimes. Perhaps most importantly, executives who enter office with tough-on-crime policy beliefs are typically the least likely to grant clemency. Largely, commentators have argued that by granting clemency in cases, tough-on-crime executives are not remaining consistent in the eyes of their followers and risk backlash. In this way, ideology and party identification can impact the frequency with which an individual executive grants clemency.

A separate set of factors are more overtly political in nature. These include things like public opinion, social status of the petitioner, or the outbreak of war. Public opinion, as in most cases, can help or hurt an individual's petition for clemency. Some high-profile petitions can become captivating to the American public and lead to organized efforts to persuade an executive one way or the other. If an executive grants a series of pardons and receives public backlash, he/she may choose to cut back on future pardons. While most Americans would like to believe that who you are would play little role in whether clemency was granted, evidence has shown that more prominent, socially connected petitioners are likely to be viewed favorably by executives.

Administrative considerations also factor into pardons. For example, the number of pardons granted will depend on the number of petitioners. Likewise, the individuals making initial recommendations to the executive can impact numbers. Some individuals, after all, are simply more likely to favor clemency than others. Through this category, we are reminded that clemency is a process with some protocols at the federal and state levels. As a result, there are many places where the system can ultimately influence its own outcomes.

Famous Examples of Clemency

One of the most famous pardons was granted by Gerald Ford to Richard Nixon in 1974. Despite Nixon's never being charged, let alone convicted,

Ford opted to pardon Nixon for misconduct that led to the Watergate scandal. Americans strongly disapproved of this action (especially since Nixon had selected Ford to be his vice president after Spiro Agnew resigned) and punished Ford at the polls as a result. Ford insisted that the pardon was necessary to fully allow the nation to move forward in the wake of the scandal.

Many other presidents have undertaken controversial pardons. Andrew Johnson opted to pardon thousands of former Confederate officials and military personnel following the Civil War. While not surprising given that Johnson was from Tennessee, this decision was unpopular in the north, where many Union families were still seeking revenge on the south for costing them so many lives. Likewise, Johnson was already viewed as being too favorable to the south, which only made this appear as another attack to the citizens of the north. Jimmy Carter granted amnesty to draft dodgers from the Vietnam era. This is important to mention because Carter chose to give amnesty rather than pardons, allowing the young men to return home without fear of facing any legal action. George H. W. Bush pardoned six individuals from the Reagan administration who were accused or convicted in relation to Iran-Contra. Again, the public was not sold on the decision—largely because Bush had served under Reagan with many of these men. Bill Clinton caught flack for commuting the sentences of 16 members of FALN (a Puerto Rican paramilitary organization) and another 140 individuals in his final hours as president. George W. Bush also raised eyebrows when he chose to commute the prison term of "Scooter" Libby, who was convicted in relation to the leak of Valerie Plame's identity while she was with the Central Intelligence Agency. With hundreds of acts of federal executive clemency having occurred in U.S. history, these represent only a small number. They do, however,

President Gerald Ford speaks to the House Judiciary Subcommittee during a hearing on pardoning former president Richard Nixon on October 17, 1974, in Washington, D.C. The controversial pardon for Nixon is one of the best-known examples of clemency. The president of the United States is given the ability to pardon in Article II, Section 2 of the Constitution.

help to present how controversial the decision can be for an executive.

At the state level, two of the most famous examples involve state governors commuting sentences in similar ways for very different reasons. First, in 1986, on his way out of office, Toney Anaya chose to commute the death sentences of all eight death row inmates in New Mexico. He had campaigned against the death penalty and was staunchly opposed to capital punishment—particularly in his own state. In 2003, two days before ending his term as governor, George Ryan of Illinois followed Anaya's path and commuted the sentences of all 167 individuals on death row in Illinois. He believed that the system was beyond repair and that the death penalty could never be administered fairly. Going even further, he pardoned four inmates because of their tainted murder convictions. Ryan made his decision after seeing an inmate exonerated—two days prior to his execution—by new evidence collected by students at Northwestern University. As these two examples make clear, state governors can have significant impact on policies within their states through the use of executive clemency.

Clemency was written into U.S. law to ensure that mercy was extended to individuals throughout the year at all levels of government rather than to one turkey by the president every November. While executive clemency is, and always will be, a controversial element in American democracy, when used properly, it offers an opportunity for the American criminal justice system to right past wrongs and reward individuals who have truly been rehabilitated. When abused, however, it opens up the potential for significant backlash for all parties involved.

William J. Miller
Southeast Missouri State University

See Also: Capital Punishment; Carter, Jimmy (Administration of); Courts; Discretionary Decision Making; Ford, Gerald (Administration of); Nixon, Richard (Administration of).

Further Readings
Burnett, Cathleen. *Justice Denied: Clemency Appeals in Death Penalty Cases*. Lebanon, NH: Northeastern University Press, 2002.

Crouch, Jeffrey P. *The Presidential Pardon Power*. Lawrence: University Press of Kansas, 2009.
Humbert, W. H. *The Pardoning Power*. Washington, DC: American Council on Public Affairs, 1941.
Moore, Kathleen Dean. *Pardons: Justice, Mercy, and Public Interest*. New York: Oxford University Press, 1997.

Cleveland, Grover (Administration of)

Grover Cleveland was the first Democrat to be elected president after the Civil War and the only one to serve two nonconsecutive terms (1885–89 and 1893–97). Deference and respect for the law played an important part in Cleveland's swift political ascent as mayor of Buffalo, New York, New York State governor, and president of the United States. Cleveland trained as a lawyer and served as a sheriff and district attorney of Erie County, earning a reputation as an honest and hardworking citizen who fought Big Business interests and political corruption. Yet, during his two administrations, his reputation as a defender of the common man suffered as a result of adverse economic conditions. Particularly during his second term, he had to face a severe economic depression and his harsh financial measures, together with his support for the gold standard, ultimately proved so unpopular that the president lost even the support of his own party. The working classes were particularly alarmed by Cleveland's repression of the Pullman Strike in Chicago in 1894 with the intervention of federal troops and the punishment of its charismatic young leader, Eugene Debs, with a six-month prison sentence. Most of them interpreted these incidents as a signal that the president was now enforcing the law to protect the interests of the rich.

Born in Caldwell, New Jersey, on March 18, 1837, Cleveland had to help support his family from a young age after his father died in 1853. However, thanks to an influential uncle, he got a job in one of the most respected law firms in Buffalo and was admitted to the bar in 1859, starting his own practice three years later. As a lawyer, he defended some members of the Fenian Brotherhood who had taken part in the raids of the late 1860s against British targets in Canada to put pressure on Britain to withdraw from Ireland. He also associated his name with the freedom of the press when he successfully defended the editor of a Buffalo newspaper against a libel suit. During his term as sheriff of Erie County, he personally carried out two hangings and gained the reputation of being a staunch fighter against political corruption. He consolidated such reputation during his terms in office as mayor of Buffalo and as governor of New York. These two positions were instrumental in launching Cleveland's successful run for the presidency in 1884.

Yet, particularly during his second, nonconsecutive term as a president, Cleveland gave the impression of having abandoned his crusade against corruption and of using the law to favor business interests. Even moderate progressives and reformers saw the decision to use federal troops to stop the Pullman Strike as the legal result of the laissez-faire capitalism that prevailed during the Gilded Age. This economic attitude prevented the passing of effective protective legislation for workers, who tried to make up for their inability to obtain better wages and improve working conditions by forming unions. The conflicts between labor and capital became harsher as a severe economic depression materialized in the late 1880s through the 1890s. The Pullman Strike represented the dramatic and irreconcilable clash between the interests of capital and labor, which legislation had failed to moderate.

The Pullman Place Car Company owned a town near Chicago where it housed its workers, providing them with accommodations and services. This paternalistic policy toward its workers allowed the company to exercise a high degree of social control over them and effectively reduced their capacity to negotiate their wages. When economic recession struck in 1893, the Pullman Company adopted the strategy to slash workers' wages up to 40 percent while leaving rents and prices in their model town unchanged. Led by the charismatic Eugene V. Debs, the workers voted in favor of the strike. Yet, George Pullman refused to negotiate with union leaders and, thanks to the second Cleveland administration, he was able to get legal approval of his conduct.

The intervention of U.S. Attorney General Richard Olney, who obtained a court ruling to prevent the strikers from obstructing the railways and withholding the mail, effectively banned the strike. Citing this ruling, President Cleveland ordered troops to Chicago with the stated task of protecting the mail but with the implicit duty of curbing the strike, which ended within a month after the troops had been sent. Taking this action, Cleveland overruled the progressive Governor of Illinois John Altgeld, who had planned to use state troops to control the strikers.

Luca Prono
Independent Scholar

See Also: Great Depression; Harrison, Benjamin (Administration of); Strikes.

Further Reading
Graff, Henry F. *Grover Cleveland*. New York: Times Books, Henry Holt, 2002.
Jeffers, H. Paul. *An Honest President: The Life and Presidencies of Grover Cleveland*. New York: William Morrow, 2000.
Nevins, Allan. *Grover Cleveland: A Study in Courage*. New York: Dodd, Mead and Co., 1934.

Cleveland, Ohio

Cleveland is a city in northern Ohio with a northern border on Lake Erie. Formerly a manufacturing center and transportation center, the city's fortunes sank along with the decline of heavy industry and the departure of much of the city's population after World War II. Cleveland was dubbed "the mistake on the lake" after several incidents, including the heavily polluted Cuyahoga River catching fire in 1969 and the city defaulting on federal loans in 1978–80, but the city has made a comeback since then and is today often cited as an example of a Rust Belt city that has successfully transitioned to a diversified economy. In 2006, Cleveland had a population of 444,313, a 6.9 percent decline from 2000 and a more than 50 percent decline from its population of 914,808 in 1950. The Cleveland-Elyria-Mentor metropolitan statistical area had a population of 2,077,240, making it the largest metropolitan area in Ohio. In the city of Cleveland, 51 percent of city residents were black, 41.5 percent were white, 1.3 percent were Asian, and the remainder were American Indian, Alaska Native, or multiracial; 7.3 percent were of Hispanic or Latino origins and 4.5 percent were foreign born. Only 69 percent of persons age 25 or older were high school graduates, and 11.4 percent were college graduates. Median household income was $26,535 and 27 percent of the population lived in poverty, as did 41.9 percent of children.

Cleveland Police Department

Prior to 1866, police services were provided in Cleveland by constables and volunteer night watchmen under the authority of a city marshal. In 1866, the Cleveland Police Department (CPD) was formed using the metropolitan system already in use in several large U.S. cities, in which a board of police commissioners was empowered to appoint a superintendent of police and patrol officers. The CPD assumed its modern form in 1903 when control of the department was granted to the city government.

Cleveland grew rapidly in the early 20th century (the population increased from 381,000 in 1901 to 831,000 in 1921) and so did the police department, from 388 in 1901 to 1,384 in 1921. The first women police officers in the CPD were appointed in 1923 but they were part of the Women's Bureau and were restricted to a few duties, including guarding women prisoners and witnesses and assisting in home investigations, and were not given the right to bear firearms until 1971.

The Mayfield Road Mob (named after a street in Little Italy) was the leading Cleveland crime syndicate beginning in the 1920s. They ran bootlegging and gambling operations and in the 1930s expanded into laundries, casinos, and nightclubs in cooperation with the Jewish-Cleveland Syndicate. In the 1920s and 1930s, the CPD adopted many new technologies and procedures and gained a reputation as one of the most progressive departments

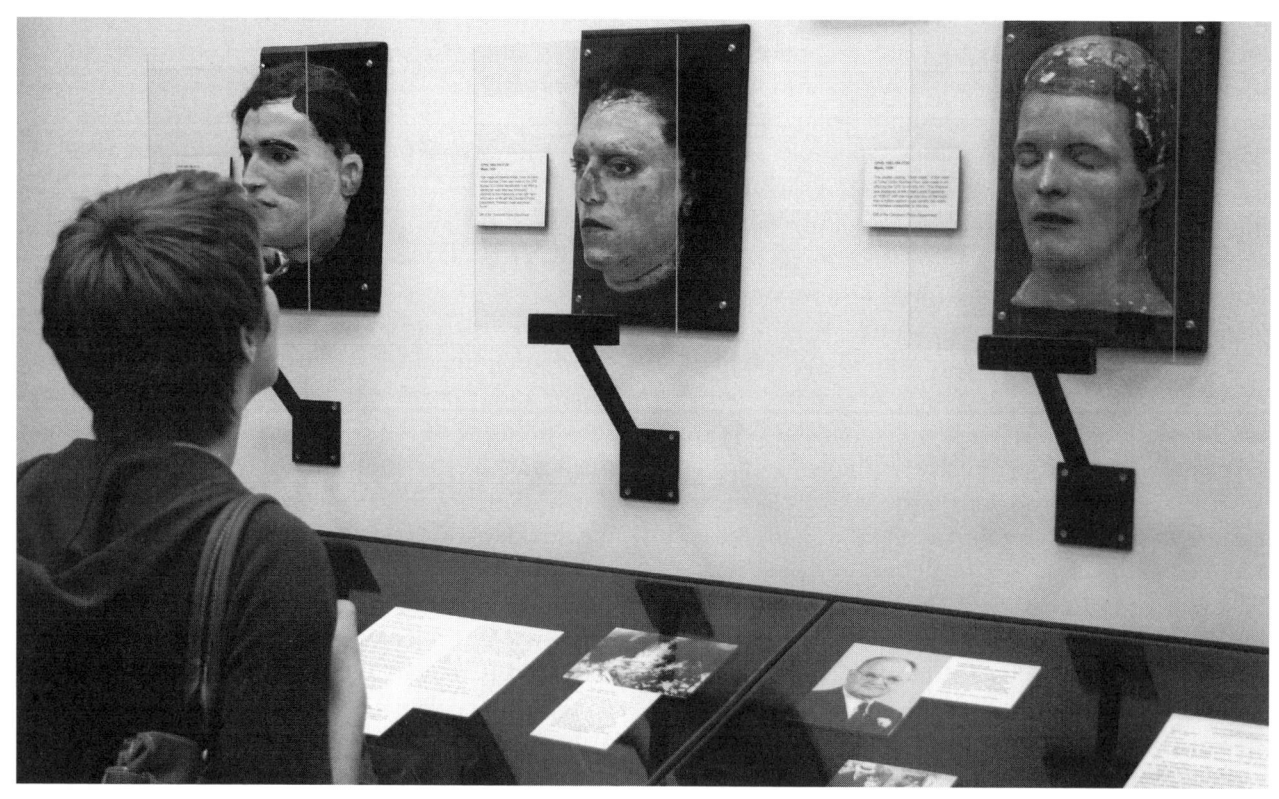

A visitor looks at a display of death masks of victims of the 1930s "Torso Murderer" at the Cleveland Police Museum in Cleveland, Ohio, in October 2007. The Cleveland Torso Murderer killed and dismembered at least 12 victims from 1935 to 1938, but his identity remains unknown, as do the identities of some of the victims.

in the United States. Eliot Ness was appointed safety director in 1935 and reorganized the CPD into a system of five police districts and 32 zones. Ness had one famous failure on his record, however: In the 1930s, the city was terrorized by an unknown killer (officially responsible for 12 deaths, although some believe there were more) dubbed the "Torso Murderer" because he beheaded and often further mutilated the bodies of his victims. The crimes were never solved but one suspect, Frank Dolezal, died while in police custody and another, a physician named Francis E. Sweeney who was a very strong suspect, voluntarily admitted himself to a mental institution.

In the 1950s, the CPD pioneered the use of automatic cameras in banks and stores to gather evidence of robberies, and in 1957, the St. Clair Savings and Loan holdup became the first bank robbery in history captured on film by hidden camera (it was activated by the sound of the bank alarm). Photographs of the holdup were printed in the local newspapers, and two of the robbers turned themselves in to the police within a few days. Most of the cash stolen was also recovered.

Race Relations

In the 1960s, racial tensions heightened in Cleveland, as they did in many other cities in the United States, and the relationship between Cleveland's growing black community and the police department deteriorated. The Hough Riots began on July 18, 1966, over a dispute within a café but quickly escalated into a large crowd, which the police were unable to control. The violence escalated to rock throwing, looting, vandalism, and fire setting, and on July 20, Cleveland Mayor Ralph Locher called in the National Guard to restore order. Four people were killed in the riot, 30 people were injured, and about 300 people were arrested. On July 23–28, 1968, an armed black militant group engaged in an action against the CPD known as the Glenville Shoot-out. This initial disturbance spread over a six-square-mile area of looting and arson, and in an attempt to calm matters Mayor Carl Stokes (the first African American to be elected mayor of a major U.S. city) announced that only black policemen and community leaders would be allowed into the area. This prevented further deaths, although looting and arson continued; ultimately, seven people were killed (all in the first day), 15 were wounded, and 63 businesses were damaged, with financial losses estimated at $2.6 million.

In 1977, the Cleveland Police Department was found guilty of discrimination in recruitment, hiring, and promotion, and after this time placed more emphasis on hiring minority officers. The CPD also instituted community policing programs in the 1980s and 1990s. In 1994, Patrick Oliver became the first black chief of police in Cleveland, and in 2001, Mary Bounds became the first female chief of police.

Crime

Crime in Cleveland has fluctuated over years with a general decline, as seen in much of the United States, over the past several decades. In 1980, there were 47 homicides and 1,187.8 robberies per 100,000 population, while in 1990 these rates had fallen to 26.1 and 972.5 per 100,000; in 2000, they fell to 15.3 and 644.4 per 100,000. However, Cleveland remains a relatively dangerous American city: According to the CQ Press rankings based on Federal Bureau of Investigation (FBI) statistics, in 2010, Cleveland had the 7th highest crime rate in the country with a score of 260.6 (where 0 would indicate an average crime rate and a positive number a higher than average rate). According to FBI statistics, in 2008, 6,193 violent crimes were reported in Cleveland, including 102 murders or nonnegligent manslaughters, 423 forcible rapes, 3,804 robberies, and 1,864 aggravated assaults. There were 25,071 property crimes reported in that year, including 9,102 burglaries, 10,686 larceny-thefts, 5,283 motor vehicle thefts, and 532 cases of arson.

Sarah Boslaugh
Kennesaw State University

See Also: African Americans; Ness, Eliot; Organized Crime, History of; Racism; Serial and Mass Killers.

Further Readings

Case Western Reserve University. "The Encyclopedia of Cleveland History." http://ech.cwru.edu (Accessed June 2011).

"City Crime Rankings 2010–2011." CQ Press. http://os.cqpress.com/citycrime/2010/citycrime2010-2011.htm (Accessed June 2011).

Porello, Rich. *The Rise and Fall of the Cleveland Mafia: Corn Sugar and Blood*. Fort Lee, NJ: Barricade Books, 2004.

U.S. Department of Justice, Federal Bureau of Investigation. "2008 Crime in the United States." http://www2.fbi.gov/ucr/cius2008 (Accessed June 2008).

Clinton, William (Administration of)

Criminal justice policy was central to Bill Clinton's (1946–) presidential administration (1993–2001). Coming into office after more than two decades in which the Republican Party had dominated political debates over crime by emphasizing policing and punishment, the Democratic Clinton administration was determined to demonstrate that it could provide tough and effective criminal justice. While the Clinton administration supported traditionally liberal positions such as gun control, it also ratified punitive programs more often associated with conservatives. At the same time, the Clinton administration had to deal with the emerging challenges of terrorism, both domestic and foreign. As a result, the Clinton administration continued a long-term trend of expanding the federal government's role in crime control.

Crime Prevention Efforts

In the early 1990s, Bill Clinton sought to position himself as being tougher on crime than the Republicans. As a candidate for president in 1992, Clinton—then the governor of Arkansas—flew back to his home state in the midst of the campaign to authorize the execution of a convicted murderer, signaling his political support for the death penalty. Candidate Clinton also proposed that the federal government should pay to hire 100,000 new police officers.

The Clinton administration initially enacted long-standing liberal goals. In 1993, Bill Clinton signed into law the Brady Handgun Violence Prevention Act, which passed after years of efforts by a coalition of gun control advocates and police leaders. When the law went into effect in 1994, it banned the sale of firearms to people who met certain conditions, including having prior convictions for felony offenses and prior institutionalization for mental illness. The law implemented a mandatory five-day waiting period before a purchaser could buy a gun, during which time a background check could be conducted. This waiting period was replaced with an instant background check in 1998.

Although Clinton's Attorney General Janet Reno came into office in favor of expanding crime prevention efforts, the administration as a whole quickly shifted toward a more punitive position. This occurred in the context of high crime rates. According to Federal Bureau of Investigation (FBI) statistics, in 1993, the absolute number of homicides in the United States reached an all-time peak. In addition, a series of widely publicized crimes in 1993 such as the kidnapping and murder of 12-year-old Polly Klaas by a previously convicted offender drew national attention. In this atmosphere, mandatory sentencing schemes such as three strikes rules—proposals that a third felony conviction should entail a mandatory extended or life term in prison, thereby preventing people like Klaas's killer from harming innocents—gained increasing public support. Voters in the state of Washington approved the first three strikes law in a November 1993 election, and President Clinton subsequently endorsed the concept in his State of the Union message in January 1994.

The Clinton administration most directly affected criminal justice policy through the Violent Crime Control and Law Enforcement Act of 1994. This omnibus crime law included funding for Clinton's proposal to add 100,000 new police officers through the Community-Oriented Policing Services (COPS) program. It also incorporated the Violence Against Women Act, which provided $1.6 billion for measures to reduce domestic violence. In addition, the 1994 crime law included funding for crime prevention programs and a controversial ban on some automatic weapons (which expired in 2004). In congressional debate, however, the law abandoned other elements favored by liberals such as racial justice provisions that would have allowed defendants to challenge sentences on the grounds that members of minority groups were disproportionately represented. The law also supported more conservative approaches to crime control such as linking funds for states to build additional prisons to provisions that states adopt tougher sentencing guidelines. It also required states to establish registries of convicted sex offenders. Finally, the law expanded the number of federal offenses subject to the death penalty.

The 1994 election of a Congress with a Republican majority limited the effect of the crime law. Subsequent budget decisions prevented most of the funds designated for crime prevention and prison building from being spent. In addition, the Republican Congress sought to convert COPS into block grants for states to spend as they wished on criminal justice programs; Clinton's threat to veto this change ultimately led Congress to create a separate block grant program in addition to the more directed COPS funds. By 1999, Justice Department reports showed that COPS had technically paid for 100,000 police officers, but that only about half were actually new positions; the others were replacements hired with the federal funds.

Terrorism and Federal Authority

Challenges posed by different forms of terrorism also shaped the Clinton administration's law enforcement policies. The Bureau of Alcohol, Tobacco, and Firearms and the FBI initially faced congressional and public criticism after 1993 raids on the Branch Davidian cult's compound near Waco, Texas, left 85 people dead. Federal agencies subsequently sought to avoid dramatic confrontations and primarily treated terrorist incidents as law enforcement matters. The 1993 bombing of an underground parking garage in the World Trade Center in New York City was handled through the arrest, trial, and conviction of the attack's main planner, Ramzi Yousef. Similarly, after the Alfred P. Murrah Federal Building in Oklahoma City was destroyed in 1995, that attack's main perpetrator, Timothy McVeigh, was arrested and tried on federal charges; he was convicted in 1997. Finally, federal authorities arrested Theodore Kaczynski in the Unabomber case in 1996 after he sent a series of bombs through the mail over several decades. Kaczynski pleaded guilty to federal charges in 1998.

The Clinton administration continued a trend toward expanded federal authority in criminal justice, which had traditionally been a matter for state and local governments. The 1994 crime bill and other legislation increased the number of offenses under federal jurisdiction. In addition, the federal prison system continued to grow. The number of federal prisoners nearly doubled under the Clinton administration, with most new inmates convicted on drug offenses. In addition, the federal government opened its first super-maximum-security (or "supermax") prison at Florence, Colorado, in 1994. Federal spending on criminal justice increased by more than one-third between 1992 and 2000.

A throng of emergency vehicles outside the World Trade Center when the underground parking garage was bombed on February 26, 1993, in a plot led by Ramzi Yousef.

David B. Wolcott
Independent Scholar

See Also: 1981 to 2000 Primary Documents; Gun Control; History of Crime and Punishment in America: 1970–Present; McVeigh, Timothy; Terrorism; Three Strikes Law; Violence Against Women Act of 1994.

Further Readings

Garland, David. *Cultures of Control: Crime and Social Order in Contemporary Society.* Chicago: University of Chicago Press, 2001.

Gest, Ted. *Crime & Politics: Big Government's Erratic Campaign for Law and Order.* New York: Oxford University Press, 2001.

Mauer, Marc. *Race to Incarcerate*, 2nd ed. New York: New Press, 2006.

Wright, Stuart A. *Patriots, Politics, and the Oklahoma City Bombing.* New York: Cambridge University Press, 2007.

Clinton Correctional Facility

Clinton Prison, as it was known until 1970, is the largest and third oldest of New York State's 70 correctional facilities. Often called Dannemora for the town in which it is located, or Little Siberia for the punishing northern climate of the region, Clinton Prison is a maximum-security facility that houses New York State's most violent and dangerous criminals.

Into the Mines

Built in 1845, Clinton quickly developed a reputation as a professional, no-nonsense institution known for its unique programs. However, prior to its national reputation, Clinton Prison was conceived in the midst of economic protest. With the recent perfection of the Auburn system of prison management, which boasted a prison industrial system capable of offsetting its operating costs by achieving factory efficiency, came an uproar of protests from local artisans and craftsmen, who frequently owned their own businesses and who saw the industrial production at nearby prisons as unfair competition. In an effort to appease these small business owners without destroying the profitable prison industrial scheme, lawmakers proposed a compromise by restricting the number of prisoners allowed to be employed in a prison workshop. However, the act, which was passed in 1835, failed to appease their concerns, and a subsequent amendment passed in 1842 that tightened the restrictions. It also proposed an idea developed by a local resident: that prisoners be sent to Clinton County, New York, and be employed in iron mines. In 1844, the legislature passed an act to establish a prison for the purpose of employing convicts in the mining and manufacturing of iron. A total of $17,500 was spent to purchase a mine in Clinton County along with 200 acres of land.

Ransom Cook, who had been commissioned to find the land and to design the institution, was appointed Clinton's first warden and agent and began preparations for building the prison yard. On June 3, 1845, Clinton's first 50 prisoners arrived, having been personally selected by Ransom Cook for their health and physical strength. Three weeks later, 44 convicts arrived from Auburn Prison. With nearly 100 prisoners to aid in the construction of the institution, progress was made quickly, and within 18 months a section of the first cellblock was made ready for occupancy. A kitchen, blacksmith shop, steam saw mill, and iron foundry were also completed during that time, and the nearby Lyon Mountain mine was opened.

Three years later, in January 1848, Cook was replaced by George Throop, who had been appointed by the new legislature to unify the administration of the Clinton, Auburn, and Sing Sing prisons. Unfortunately, the new administration, coupled with the remote location of the prison and the depletion of the iron mine, quickly led to the downfall of the mining project, and the state was forced to pay significant fees to send prison workers to adjacent mines. In 1876, prison inspectors declared the iron mining project at Clinton Prison to be a disastrous financial failure, resulting in closure of the mines in 1877. Production subsequently changed to making brooms, shoes, and other items to be used by other prisons in the state.

Rehabilitation and Reform

During the 50 years following the mining project, Clinton developed into one of the largest correctional facilities in the country; its capacity was doubled in 1881 with the addition of 656 prison cells. Moreover, with cases of tuberculosis at a steady increase during the following years, Clinton physicians were surprised by the full recoveries of several of the affected inmates. Reportedly because the healthfulness of the prison location, Clinton quickly saw an influx of ailing prisoners from other institutions, and a special tuberculosis hospital was constructed on prison grounds in 1918. In addition to treating tuberculosis, Clinton Prison also specialized in working with incorrigible prisoners and steadily received the worst criminals other prisons had to offer, including those with multiple felonies and those legally declared insane.

In July 1929, riots at Clinton and Auburn prisons led to calls for reform, and increasing emphasis was placed on rehabilitative programs. Consequently, Warden Thomas Murphy, who was appointed several years prior, required all inmates to attend school. He also ordered that Clinton Prison be rebuilt, with modern housing replacing the antiquated cellblocks. With the increased modernization of national prisons and the further development of rehabilitation services, several creative programming concepts were also developed. In 1977, the Merle Cooper program was introduced to help prisoners adjust to incarceration. In addition, the Assessment and Program Preparation Unit was developed to help address inmates' real or imagined fears of other prisoners and to help their transition into the general population. The location of the prison, which was built into a hillside, also provided for sporting activities unusual for prisons, including skiing, ski jumping, and bobsledding. Additionally, Clinton is known for another unusual tradition whereby small areas of the hillside, called "courts," were used by inmates to gather and socialize, play chess, and grow flowers and vegetables. Clinton housed approximately 300 such courts, which could accommodate up to six men. The courts have been identified as having played a key role in the management and social development of Clinton's inmate population.

Continuing Effectiveness

Clinton Prison has also been known to be the leader in modern rehabilitation and currently provides academic education, vocational training, and drug and alcohol treatment. In 1970, the facility's name was officially changed from Clinton Prison to Clinton Correctional Facility, and in 1989, Clinton became the 19th correctional facility to be accredited by the American Correctional Association.

Currently, Clinton houses up to 2,900 prisoners and provides housing for prisoners on death row. It remains a maximum-security prison and contends with its share of prison gangs, including the Bloods, Crips, Five Percenters, Trinitarios, and MS-13. It still houses New York State's most notorious criminals and has housed several famous inmates, including Charles "Lucky" Luciano, a key player in the establishment of Italian organized crime in America; Jesse Friedman, convicted of sexual abuse and sodomy of a minor and the subject of *Capturing the Friedmans*, a documentary of his crimes produced in 2003; Carl Panzram, a notorious serial killer; and Tupac Shakur, who served nearly a year for sexual abuse but was later released on appeal.

Kathrin Ritter
Todd Moore
University of Tennessee, Knoxville

See Also: Auburn State Prison; Federal Prisons; New York; Sing Sing Correctional Facility.

Further Readings

New York Correction History Society. "Facility Profile: Clinton." *DOCS/TODAY* (January 1999).

Village of Dannemora, New York. "Clinton Correctional Facility." http://www.villageof dannemora.com/clinton_correctional.html (Accessed September 2011).

Code of Silence

The code of silence, as it is known among police officers, is the unwritten rule that a police officer does not report, complain about, or testify against a fellow police officer. It is also commonly referred to as the "thin blue line." Any police officer who reports, complains about, or testifies against a fellow police officer is said to have crossed that line.

This Chicago police sergeant was heckled by spectators when he testified in defense of his fellow officers at a Senate Civil Liberties Committee hearing in Washington, D.C., on July 1, 1937, after the killing of 10 steel strikers in what became known as the Memorial Day Massacre. The code of silence may make it difficult for police officers in similar situations to testify against their fellow officers.

Those police officers who cross that line are usually tagged with various different names, all of them derogatory in the criminal justice lexicon. Some of these names are rat, squealer (with rather contradictory connotation to the 1960s and 1970s nickname for cops as "pigs"), whistle blower, and Serpico. Frank Serpico, as many people in the criminal justice field are aware, is the name of a famous New York City Police Department detective who reported widespread corruption involving New York City police officers and was subsequently not backed up on a drug raid, resulting in Serpico's being shot. Serpico had crossed the line and alienated himself from his fellow police officers because he had reported the corruption. Serpico and his actions have been immortalized in a book and a movie starring Al Pacino, yet it is still usually an insult when a police officer calls another police officer a Serpico.

It is interesting to note that organized crime or the Mafia have an almost identical code for the conduct of their members. This code of silence is called *omerta*. Members of organized crime or the Mafia are expected to keep quiet about their associates and activities when they are questioned, arrested, charged, tried, or convicted for their activities. The usual punishment for a crime family member who broke *omerta* was death, with the body being dumped in a location where it was certain to be found with a canary or a pigeon stuffed in the mouth. This was a warning to other members of the crime family who were considering breaking *omerta*.

Police officers, like organized crime and the Mafia, will punish fellow police officers who cross the thin blue line. Although being killed is not one of the usual retaliations brought against a police officer for crossing the line, the results can be just as devastating, as demonstrated by the experience of Frank Serpico. Retaliation against a police officer who crosses the line usually involves lack of backup on dangerous calls, assignment to undesirable jobs within the department, denial of promotion even if the applicant receives the highest score on the promotional examination, and discipline for minor infractions that other police officers would not be disciplined for.

Justifications

Police officers present a number of excuses in attempts to justify the code of silence. One of them is the idea of professional courtesy. For example, if a police officer stops a fellow police officer for driving drunk, he might not arrest him but, rather, will drive him home. Another excuse for keeping silent about the misconduct or criminal activity of fellow criminal justice officials is fear. For example, if a police officer brings a complaint against a fellow police officer for criminal activity, then the reporting police officer will justifiably be afraid that he might not receive backup on a dangerous call from the reported police officer or the reported police officer's friends.

This fear was highlighted by Frank Serpico in his testimony before the Knapp Commission on police corruption, where he stated that 10 percent of the cops are good, 10 percent of the cops are bad, and 80 percent of the cops wish they were good. Potentially honest criminal justice officials are also afraid, with justification, that they will not be promoted if they blow the whistle on their fellow criminal justice officials. A third excuse used by police officers to justify the code of silence is the pressure of the job and the proposition that because the public hates cops, police officers need to receive special consideration or breaks when they engage in misconduct, as the misconduct is supposedly not a result of any criminal intent by the police officer. A fourth excuse employed by police officers for the code of silence is that police officers, on some occasions, have to break the law to catch the criminals. Some decisions of the U.S. Supreme Court provide a little support for this position through the use of good faith and recognizing that police officers can engage in some deception when enforcing the law. For example, in *Frazier v. Cupp* (1969), the U.S. Supreme Court allowed a conviction to stand where the police lied to the suspect about his cousin implicating him in the crime. In *Oregon v. Mathiason* (1977), the Supreme Court ruled that it was not improper for the police to lie about finding the suspect's fingerprints at the scene of the crime. Further, in *Illinois v. Perkins* (1990), the Supreme Court held that it was permissible for an undercover police officer to pose as an inmate and that it did not invalidate the suspect's confession.

However, none of these excuses adequately counters the basic principle of civilized law that no person is above the law, no person is below the law, and all persons must be equally subject to the law. As the code of silence is not formally enshrined in the American criminal justice system, it can be argued that it is not a valid principle of criminal justice procedure. Unfortunately, the widespread recognition and employment of the code of silence illustrates that law cannot always ensure justice, and justice is all too frequently subject to the ethical quality of the persons holding office in that system.

Wm. C. Plouffe, Jr.
Independent Scholar

See Also: Equality, Concept of; Knapp Commission; Mollen Commission; Police Abuse; Professionalization of Police.

Further Readings
Albanese, Jay S. *Professional Ethics in Criminal Justice*. Upper Saddle River, NJ: Pearson Prentice Hall, 2008.
Dreisbach, Christopher. *Ethics in Criminal Justice*. New York: McGraw-Hill, 2009.
Klockars, Carl B. and Stephen D. Mastrofski, ed. *Thinking About Police*, 2nd ed. New York: McGraw-Hill, 1991.

Codification of Laws

Codification is the general process of collecting, arranging, and revising the laws of a nation or other specified jurisdiction into a systematically ordered legal code. A codification of laws attempts to be comprehensive, covering the entirety of a field of law. A codification also endeavors to consist of a logically consistent whole of rules and legal structures. In this sense, a system of codified law is able to make a break from the past, whereas an uncodified system typically retains aspects of historical legal traditions. Advocates of codification assert that codified law is more certain, harmonious, and knowable.

Ancient Codes

In ancient times, legal systems focused primarily upon the issues that societally seemed to be the most pressing. Accordingly, ancient laws concentrated on matters such as protecting private property, suppressing violent crimes, maintaining civil peace, and enforcing accepted moral standards like those concerned with family relations and religious observances. Individual laws were created as the need for them was perceived, but as they accumulated, it became difficult to be aware of all that might be applicable. Law codes were established, often by local rulers, to be more accessible and understandable to the populace. The scope of laws gradually expanded, such that it is difficult to find any areas of human conduct that are not, in some way at least, regulated by legal codes.

The Code of Hammurabi was carved in Akkadian cuneiform upon a black stone stele so that all who read it would know what was expected of them. It publicly proclaimed an entire body of laws that were arranged in organized groupings. Like many ancient codes, it began with an invocation to divine authority. Hammurabi was a king of Babylon who ruled from about 1728 B.C.E. to 1686 B.C.E. He ruled an empire stretching from Nineveh on the Tigris River to the Persian Gulf. Anyone within his kingdom could read it and know what the laws of the land were, including particular punishments for respective violations, several of which carried the death sentence. However, special laws applied only to select members of Babylonian society who had particular obligations such as nuns or physicians. Although the Code of Hammurabi is the best known, it was not the earliest Mesopotamian code of laws. Earlier Mesopotamian law codes that could have served as precedents for that of Hammurabi have been found, such as the Sumerian Code of Ur-Nammu from about 2050 B.C.E., one from Isin codified by Lipit-Ishtar around 1800 B.C.E., and another in Akkadian from Eshnunna.

Mosaic law of the ancient Hebrews, as presented in the Old Testament, has been shown

This detail from the top of the black stone stele that is inscribed with the Code of Hammurabi in cuneiform script shows Hammurabi (standing) with the sun god Shamash.

to have been influenced by Mesopotamian law codes; indeed, both list specific punishments for respective offenses with proportionality used as a guiding moral principle of punishment. The Mosaic Code, although said to be collected and codified by Moses, is claimed to have been written by God. Breaches of the Mosaic Code, accordingly, offend God, and all crimes are regarded as sins. The Mosaic Code is said to have been promulgated around 1250 B.C.E. The Mishnah, a collection of existing traditions and oral law, was a later (redacted ca. 220 C.E.) codification of Jewish Halakha law. These sorts of codes were attempts to reduce laws to a consistent and uniform whole.

Codes of law were created elsewhere across the ancient world; these, for example, include the Code of Nesilim written in Hittite around 1650 to 1500 B.C.E., the Law Code of Vishnu (*Vaisnava-dharmasastra*) composed around the 7th century B.C.E. in Kashmir, India, and the Gortyn Code from 5th-century B.C.E. Crete. The first comprehensive criminal code in China was the Tang Code created around 624 C.E. During the

19th century, the Ottoman Empire created a civil law code based on Islamic Sharia law.

Roman-Byzantine Law

The first known set of Roman laws was first written down around 450 B.C.E. This was known as the Law of the Twelve Tablets (*Leges Duodecim Tabularum*), which was posted in the Roman Forum so all Romans could read them. They served as the foundation for the constitution of the Roman Republic. The main significance of the Law of the Twelve Tablets was that it fixed in written form a large corpus of customary law.

Emperor Theodosius II (401–50 C.E.) ordered the codification of Roman-Byzantine law. This was known as the Ode of Theodosius (*Codex Theodosianus*) and was completed about 438 C.E. It was based on a review of primary sources of laws from the reign of Constantine to that of Theodosius II. However, the best-known codification was that known as the Code of Justinian. Emperor Justinian I (483–565 C.E.) ordered the compilation of the *Corpus Juris Civilis* (Body of Civil Law), which was completed about 534 C.E. It secured the status of Orthodox Christianity uniting church and state; it forbade specific pagan practices, including sacrifices. The Justinian Code became the basis for later legal systems of many countries. Other Byzantine law codes included the *Ecloga*, issued in the 8th century (circa 740 C.E.) by Leo III, and the *Basilika*, commissioned by Basil I and completed by his son Leo VI in the late 9th century.

Common Law

The notion of common law originated in the 11th and 12th centuries with the kings of England granting the authority to settle disputes. Gradually, the concept of legal precedent took hold in English thought and the doctrine of stare decisis, that previous decisions should be used to direct the adjudication of new controversies, served as the operating principle for common law courts. Thus, English common law was created by the customary practices of judges and not by legislated decisions. English colonists brought their common law traditions with them, and therefore, common law serves as the basis of the legal systems in the United States, the United Kingdom, and most of the countries that are members of the Commonwealth of Nations. Nevertheless, codifications have become common in many common law systems. Criminal codes, for instance, have been adopted in Australia.

Napoleonic Code

After becoming emperor of the French, Napoleon Bonaparte (1769–1821) in 1804 enacted a comprehensive codification and reformation of French civil laws, which in 1807 became known as the Code Napoleon. The Napoleonic Code clarified and standardized the body of law that applied to all French domains and territories. Prior to the Napoleonic Code, there were more than 400 legal codes extant throughout France, with common law more dominant in the north and Roman-based systems in the south. Further, the revolutionary regimes enacted thousands of pieces of legislation. Created after the French Revolution, the Napoleonic Code permitted freedom of religion, forbade hereditary feudal privileges, and ensured that governmental jobs be given to the most qualified. It also reaffirmed patriarchal authority, designating the husband as the ruler over the household.

The Napoleonic Code served as a secularized and uniform system of French law. It heavily influenced the codification of laws in other countries, notably those across western Europe, the Americas, and the Caribbean. For example, the Napoleonic Code was virtually copied and became the civil code of Haiti in 1825; of Oaxaca, Mexico, in 1827; and of the Dominican Republic in 1845. It also profoundly impacted the standards of legal practice in the state of Louisiana, as well as the Louisiana Code adopted in 1824. This was the first state code established in the United States.

In addition to the Napoleonic Code, several other codes were established for European nations during the late 17th and 18th centuries. The spread of codification was aided by the forces of the Enlightenment, which asserted the notion that human conduct could be regulated by means of adhering to structured rational systems. In 1756, for example, the Maximilian Code (*Codex Maximilianeus bavaricus civilis*) was established in the Duchy of Bavaria. In 1794, Frederick the Great (1712–86) promulgated the General National Law for the Prussian States (*Allegemeines Landrecht fur die Preussischen Staaten*), which compiled civil, constitutional, and penal law. However, these early codes generally covered a limited geographic region and contributed little to more widespread reform efforts. The Napoleonic Code, on the other hand, had a global impact.

Following the dissemination of the Napoleonic Code, other law codes were, in fact, adopted throughout much of Europe. After the breakup of the Holy Roman Empire of the German Nation as a result of the Napoleonic Wars, a similar codification effort in 1811 created the Austrian General Civil Code (*Allegemeines burgerliches Gesetzbuch*). In the early 19th century, following the establishment of these prominent law codes, there was a codification movement that spread across Europe and beyond, including the Americas. Advocates for codification at the time argued that laws codified by legislators would better reflect the will of the people than would case-by-case decisions by judges. Codification efforts continued in Europe as well, such as with the passage of the Spanish Civil Code (*Codigo Civil*) of 1889, the German Civil Code (*Burgerliches Gesetzbuch*) of 1900, the Swiss Civil Code (*Zivilgestzbuch*) in 1907, and so forth up to the Dutch Civil Code (*Burgerlijke Wetbock*) finally completed in 1992, and the work continuing within the European Union.

Codes of law were established elsewhere as well, many heavily influenced by the Napoleonic and German codes in particular. For example, in 1898, during the Meiji Restoration, Japan adopted a civil code (*Minpo*), influenced by that of the French. The Republic of China adopted a civil code after the Xinhai Revolution of 1911, one that was heavily influenced by that of the Germans. The Code of Canon Law (*Codex Iuris Canonici*) is the codification of the canonical legislation of the Roman Catholic Church; the first edition, known as the Pio-Benedictine, was released in 1917, and the Reformed edition in 1983.

American Legal System

The American colonists justified their rebellion against the British Crown by the assertion that the government of King George III (1738–1820) grossly violated their fundamental liberties, such as those guaranteed by the Magna Carta, which King John (1167–1216) had been forced by his barons to sign on June 15, 1215. The American colonists carried with them the principles of British common law. This was modified over time by the enactment of statutory changes. Criminal law, for example, consists of legislatively prescribed lists of crimes, which are clearly defined. Although the American Revolution severed the political unity between England and the United States, it did not break the continuity of legal tradition.

U.S. law consists of many levels of codified and uncodified varieties of law. In addition to the federal level, law codes can be adopted by state and municipal governments. When a state codifies its laws, the statutes contained in the code supersede previous laws. In 1848, New York passed the Field Code, devised largely by David Dudley Field, to serve as a systematic Code of Civil Procedure. Its adoption stimulated legal reforms and code enactment in other U.S. states. In fact, during the middle of the 19th century, there was an influential codification movement in the United States. For example, the Georgia Code was adopted in 1860. Individual municipalities can adopt locally enforceable codes. These include not only building codes, electrical codes, and fire codes but other areas over which local municipalities have jurisdiction.

The United States Code (U.S.C.) is a codification, by subject matter, of the general and permanent federal laws of the United States. The first edition of the U.S.C. was passed by Congress in 1926. The U.S.C. is prepared and published by the Office of the Law Revision Council of the U.S. House of Representatives. The office engages in positive law codification, a process intended to remove contradictions, ambiguities, and other imperfections from the law. Public laws are incorporated into the U.S.C. every six years. The U.S.C. is divided into 50 different titles based on the respective topics covered. Most federal criminal statutes, for example, are contained in Title 18. Procedural rules in the United States have been codified as well; these include the Federal Rules of Civil Procedure, the Federal Rules of Criminal Procedures, and the Federal Rules of Evidence. While the U.S.C. is a codification of laws created by Congress, regulations emanating from the executive branch are published in the *Federal Register* and codified in the Code of Federal Regulations (C.F.R.).

The American Law Institute is one of the leading organizations involved in the codification of U.S. laws. The National Conference of Commissioners on Uniform State Laws in collaboration with the American Law Institute developed and monitors the Uniform Commercial Code (U.C.C.). The U.C.C. is a comprehensive code that covers most areas of U.S. commercial law. Other model statutory projects of the American Law Institute have included the Model Code of Evidence, the Model Code of Pre-Arraignment Procedure, the Model Land Development Code, and the Model Penal Code.

As the law is dynamic, not static, codification of laws must evolve over time. The legislative process tends to amend statutes; however, updates often conflict with earlier versions, and as conditions change, the language of codes may become archaic. The process of recodification addresses the need to rewrite and reformat the law.

Conclusion

Codification of laws serves many useful purposes. A major benefit of codification is that laws can be collated and organized. A code of laws discloses the penalties that a society will inflict upon specific transgressions. More generally, a law code clearly announces the standards of public morality expected to be held by members of that social grouping. A code of laws also attempts to identify punishments commensurate with the severity of the respective offense.

Victor B. Stolberg
Essex County College

See Also: American Law Institute; American Revolution and Criminal Justice; Common Law Origins of Criminal Law; Constitution of the United States of America.

Further Readings
Friedman, Lawrence M. *A History of American Law.* New York: Simon & Schuster, 2005.
Legrand, Pierre. "Strange Power of Words: Codification Situated." *Tulane European and Civil Law,* v.9 (1994).
Schwartz, Bernard, ed. *The Code Napoleon and the Common-Law World: The Sesquicentennial Lectures Delivered at the Law Center of New York University December 13–15, 1954.* Union, NJ: Lawbook Exchange, 1998.
Steele, Francis R. "The Lipit-Ishtar Law Code." *American Journal of Archaeology,* v.51 (1947).

Zimmermann, Reinhard. "Codification: History and Present Significance of an Idea." *European Review of Private Law,* v.3 (1995).

Cohens v. Virginia

Cohens v. Virginia (1821) was a case that solidified the Supreme Court's power of judicial review. Washington, D.C., had a lottery that had been created by Congress. Virginia state law did not recognize the law that authorized the lottery. When Phillip and Mendes Cohen, who were brothers, were arrested, tried, and convicted in Virginia for selling lottery tickets, they appealed to the U.S. Supreme Court, arguing that national law was supreme and therefore their conviction was illegitimate. The Supreme Court heard the case, and the Virginia state attorneys, including one future U.S. Supreme Court justice, argued that states were sovereign and therefore state court decisions could not be reviewed by the national court. Specifically, they argued that the Eleventh Amendment to the Constitution prevented the Supreme Court from hearing appeals by citizens brought against their home state. Despite the claims of the state, the justices unanimously decided against Virginia.

At issue was the 25th section of the 1789 Judiciary Act, which allowed the Supreme Court to hear cases in which a state was challenging federal authority. The court's opinion, penned by Chief Justice John Marshall, declared that national law is supreme over state law, and when state law contradicts the Constitution, that law is void. Moreover, states are members of a nation and in some instances are sovereign, but in others they are not. Marshall reinforced the idea that it was necessary for the federal judiciary to ensure that state legislation and judicial decisions were within the bounds set by the national constitution. Additionally, according to Marshall, although the Supreme Court was provided the power of judicial review in the Constitution, the original intent of the framers, as evidenced in the *Federalist Papers*, was that the Supreme Court would have the power to decide the constitutionality of government actions.

Judicial review, first recognized in *Marbury v. Madison* (1803) and supported in *Martin v. Hunter's Lessee* (1816), remained controversial for years. In particular, some states did not want to become subservient to the national government, and therefore questioned the right and power of the Supreme Court to overturn laws and judicial decisions of the states. *Cohens* is but one case stemming from Virginia in which the state claimed equality or supremacy over federal law. In addition to its impact regarding the Supreme Court's judicial review power over the states, the case is noteworthy because it continued to recognize the states' right to have a major role in defining criminal law. Although the Supreme Court did reserve the right to review the Virginia decision, Marshall's opinion clearly notes that although Congress allowed the District of Columbia to have a lottery, Virginia had banned such practice. Because the Cohens were selling District of Columbia lottery tickets in Virginia in violation of state law, Virginia had jurisdiction to prosecute the interlopers.

Although John Marshall's opinion in *Marbury v. Madison* is more famous, his opinion in *Cohens* is one of his most highly regarded. However, several political opponents thought that Marshall ignored his own constitutional jurisprudence from prior decisions, most notably *McCulloch v. Maryland*. Additionally, some critics argue that Marshall purposefully misread the applicable Virginia statute, so that he and his Court could make a decision that was broader than the facts would suggest. *Cohens* served as the capstone to the Marshall effort to provide the Supreme Court with judicial review over the branches of the national government including the actions and judicial decisions of state governments. This allowed, and continued to allow, the Supreme Court the power of oversight of state laws, including criminal laws and defendant rights. The Supreme Court continues to hear and decide cases that profoundly impact defining characteristics of criminal law at the state and local levels.

Tobias T. Gibson
Westminster College

See Also: *Marbury v. Madison*; Marshall, John; *Martin v. Hunter's Lessee*.

Further Readings
Epstein, Lee and Thomas G. Walker. *Constitutional Law for a Changing America: Institutional Powers and Constraints*. Washington, DC: CQ Press, 2007.
Graber, Mark A. "The Passive-Aggressive Virtues: *Cohens v. Virginia* and the Problematic Establishment of Judicial Power." *Constitutional Commentary*, v.12/67 (1995).
May, Christopher N. and Allan Ides. *Constitutional Law: National Power and Federalism*. New York: Aspen Law and Business, 1998.
Roche, John P., ed. *John Marshall: Major Opinions and Other Writings*. New York: Bobbs-Merrill, 1967.
Schwartz, Bernard. *A History of the Supreme Court*. New York: Oxford University Press, 1993.

Coker v. Georgia

This landmark Supreme Court decision found the irrevocable imposition of the death penalty for the rape of an adult woman to be a violation of the Eighth Amendment, given that rape is a non-homicidal crime. The decision stems from the events of September 2, 1974, when convicted felon Ehrlich Anthony Coker escaped from Ware Correctional Institution outside Waycross, Georgia, where he was serving several sentences for aggravated assault, rape, kidnapping, and murder. Later that evening, at roughly 11 P.M., Coker entered the residence of Allen and Elnita Carver through an unlocked kitchen door. Armed with a board, Coker managed to tie up Mr. Carver in the nearby bathroom, after which he located a knife in the kitchen and threatened Mrs. Carver with the blade; he then raped her. Next, Coker stole money from Mr. Carver, gathered the keys to the Carvers' family car, and kidnapped Mrs. Carver as he fled. Able to break free, Mr. Carver contacted the police, and Coker was subsequently arrested. Mrs. Carver was not killed during the perpetration of these crimes.

Coker was charged with escape, armed robbery, motor vehicle theft, kidnapping, and rape. After hearing Coker's general plea of insanity, the jury found him guilty and a sentence of death by electrocution was decided. At this time, rape of an adult woman was still a capital offense under Georgia statute as long as one or more of the following aggravating factors were found to be present: (1) the rapist had a prior record of conviction for a capital felony, (2) the rape was committed during the commission of another capital felony, or aggravated battery, or (3) the rape was outrageously or wantonly vile, horrible, or inhumane in that it involved the torture, depravity of mind, or aggravated battery to the victim. In *Coker*, the jury found the first two of these aggravators to be present during Mrs. Carver's rape. Coker had prior convictions for three capital felonies and he committed capital armed robbery in concurrence with the rape. Upon appeal, Coker's conviction and sentence was affirmed by the Georgia Supreme Court. However, the Supreme Court of the United States granted a writ of certiorari to assess whether the application of the death penalty for the rape of an adult woman violated the Eighth Amendment to the U.S. Constitution.

The Eighth Amendment holds that excessive bail shall not be required, nor excessive fines imposed, nor cruel and unusual punishments inflicted. Thus, the cruel and unusual clause serves to prevent the abuse of judicial and legislative discretion in regard to sentencing punishments that may be either overly disproportionate or excessive in relation to the harm caused by the crime committed. The court applied a two-step test, where the first step sought to ascertain whether the goals of the punishment were met or if the punishment served to inflict needless pain and suffering; and the second step inquired as to whether the penalty was grossly disproportionate to the severity of the crime.

From the court's analysis, the majority opinion concluded that after *Furman v. Georgia,* only North Carolina, Louisiana, and Georgia kept rape as a capital offense. However, *Woodson v. North Carolina* and *Roberts v. Louisiana* invalidated the mandatory sentence of death for rape in those two states. Also, in no time in the past 50 years had the majority of states imposed the death penalty for the crime of rape. As a result of the proportionality test applied to *Coker*, the court found the application of the death penalty to be excessive and disproportionate for the crime of raping an adult woman. Finding rape to be the most reprehensible and heinous crime second to murder, the Supreme Court still ruled that it was unconstitutional to impose the death penalty for the crime of rape of an adult woman, where the rape victim was not also murdered. The court decided that while rape was deserving of serious punishment, it did not compare with murder. In the court's opinion, life of the rape victim is not beyond repair, whereas life is over for the murder victim.

Brian G. Sellers
University of South Florida

See Also: Capital Punishment; Cruel and Unusual Punishment; *Furman v. Georgia*; Rape, History of; Rape, Sociology of.

Further Readings
Bohm, Robert. *Deathquest III: An Introduction to the Theory & Practice of Capital Punishment in the United States*. Newark, NJ: Anderson Publishing, 2007.
Coker v. Georgia, 433 U.S. 584, 1977.
Ga Code Ann. § 26-2001, 1972.
U.S. Const. Amend. VIII.

Colonial Charters and Grants

The American colonies were brought into legal existence by means of colonial charters and grants bestowed by the British Crown. These documents granted proprietors and settlement companies the exclusive and broad authority to govern territories and punish crimes in accordance with prescribed royal allowances. They laid the foundations for colonial and state constitutions and greatly influenced the evolution of individual rights, criminal law, and representative democracy in America.

Early Charters
The first English charter granted in consideration of present-day America was "The Letters Patents of King Henry the Seventh Granted Unto Iohn Cabot and His Three Sonnes, Lewis, Sebastian and

Sancius for the Discouerie of New and Unknowen Lands." The charter, issued on March 5, 1496, granted John Cabot the right to sail under the English flag as a vassal of the Crown. Cabot was entitled to occupy and govern any discovered lands on behalf of the Crown—retaining exclusive rights, after a 20 percent contribution to the Crown, of all commercial profits. This general charter was preceded less than a decade earlier by the "Privileges and Prerogatives Granted by Their Catholic Majesties to Christopher Columbus" in 1492, by which Columbus was declared governor of any territory he discovered in North America and vested with authority to decide criminal cases and to punish offenders. Various contemporary charters and land grants were issued in consideration of present-day Canada, particularly the Newfoundland fisheries, with analogous investitures of governing rights.

If history is a guide to interpreting the intentions of these earliest royal charters and grants, the recipients were expected to govern discovered territories in a manner consistent with their maritime command of the fleet delivering them to their destination. As the captain of a ship at sea was vested with authority to govern his vessel in accordance with strict rules of discipline, so were colony builders granted sufficient authority to govern their subjects and territories. These early documents reveal prototypical features common to nearly all future colonial charters and grants. Their primary purpose was to encourage often perilous but potentially lucrative expeditions to distant lands by providing assistance to explorers and ensuring personal rewards for successful commercial discoveries. While the Crown retained full sovereignty and ultimate authority over the expedition and colony, charter and grant recipients were conferred broad discretion to implement laws and mete out punishments within governed territories.

Settling North America

The earliest American colonial charters were granted to trading companies—the latter-day version of explorers such as Columbus and Cabot. These companies were political corporations, and their charters were letters vesting governing authority over colonial settlements. The charters served as corporate constitutions vesting officers with discretion to determine colonial administration and legislation. This discretion was limited only by the mandate that colonial law submit to the laws of England.

James I's initial attempt to settle North America's eastern seaboard in 1606 relied upon a charter granted to the Virginia Company, which consisted of a pair of English joint stock companies known as the London and Plymouth Companies. The Virginia charter permitted the companies to establish settlements in North America and to govern colonial administration through corporate councils. Notably, the Virginia charter confirmed the enduring guarantee that subjects of the Crown born or living in the colonies possessed all of the rights, liberties, and immunities afforded to those remaining in England.

The Plymouth Company's settlement was abandoned after a single year, but the London Company enjoyed greater success in present-day Virginia and expanded its charter upon the former's

A 1762 painting of John Cabot, recipient of the first English charter for America. Charter holders had broad discretion to implement laws and inflict punishments in new territories.

dissolution. This second Virginia charter reiterated the power of the council residing in London to pass laws and expressly made available English courts of law for legal matters arising in the colonies. The London Company's officers in Virginia were granted explicit governing authority to conduct criminal procedures in order to punish and correct misbehavior. The charter anticipated the exercise of martial law in cases of rebellion and endorsed the administering of religious oaths in order to prevent the immigration of Catholics.

Upon the London Company's bankruptcy in 1624, the Virginia Company's charter was revoked, and Virginia became a royal colony. As such, the colony continued to enjoy a popularly elected assembly, but the prevailing governor and council were royally appointed and administered justice in accordance with royal prerogative. The Old Dominion would remain a royal colony until American independence.

In 1620, the abandoned Plymouth Company was resurrected as the Plymouth Council for New England with corresponding land grants and governing authorities commensurate with those provided by the Virginia charter. A far more successful venture, the council issued its own land grant for a plantation in Massachusetts Bay to the New England Company in 1628. However, conflicting territorial claims among competing companies caused the New England Company to seek a charter in place of its land grant. Charles I granted the charter in 1629 and thereby established the legal authority of the New England Company to govern Massachusetts Bay. In accordance with the Cambridge Agreement later that year, the Massachusetts Bay Colony became the first English charter colony to boast a board of governors that was not situated in England, permitting extensive local autonomy in the administration of criminal law.

The Charter of Massachusetts Bay mirrored the earlier Virginia charters, vesting power in the legislative General Court and elected officers to enact laws, punish offenders, and take all necessary actions to ensure peace and security. By 1634, the General Court was comprised of two deputies elected by each town, and the corporate structure of the trading company had largely been transformed into a system of representative democracy. In 1641, Massachusetts Bay adopted the first colonial legal code, the Massachusetts Bodie of Liberties, which declared the civil and religious foundations of rights, privileges, crimes, and punishments.

The Decline of the Charter System

Charles II issued the final corporate charters in America to the established colonies of Connecticut and Rhode Island in 1662 and 1663, respectively. Both of these documents sustained the traditions of earlier charters by granting extensive authority for self-government, including the administration of criminal law and penal sanctions. The charter of Rhode Island instituted unprecedented rights of religious liberty.

Aside from corporate charters, colonial America was also governed by proprietary charters that vested governing authority in lords proprietors. Proprietary charters resembled royal colonies except that a proprietor was substituted for the king. Proprietors arranged the form of government, appointed governing officers, and enacted legislation subject to the advice and consent of voting members of the colony. While colonists were generally afforded greater civil and religious liberty within these colonies, the authority to dispense criminal justice was largely consolidated in the proprietor. Pennsylvania, Delaware, New Jersey, and Maryland were founded as proprietary colonies.

However, by the late 17th century, colonial charters were regarded by the Crown as obstacles to royal governance of the colonies. In 1684, as a result of perceived colonial insubordination with regard to the Navigation Acts, Charles II voided the charter of Massachusetts Bay and began the process of converting the New England colonies into royal colonies under the Dominion of New England. Massachusetts Bay, the Plymouth Colony, and the provinces of New Hampshire and Maine were soon administratively unified with Connecticut, New York, and New Jersey.

The Dominion was dissolved with James II's overthrow in the Glorious Revolution of 1689. Connecticut and Rhode Island reinstated their corporate charters. King William III issued a charter unifying Massachusetts Bay and Plymouth as the Province of Massachusetts Bay. Though administered by a royally appointed governor, Massachusetts Bay continued to functionally operate under the forms of its vacated charter.

Nevertheless, royal provinces had replaced most charters by the time of the American Revolution. Provincial colonies governed by proxy agents of the Crown were authorized to assemble and dissolve provincial legislatures, veto acts thereof, and enact all necessary criminal laws consistent with the laws of England. New Hampshire, New York, North Carolina, South Carolina, Georgia, and Virginia were provincial colonies. Only Maryland, Delaware, and Pennsylvania retained proprietary charters, while Connecticut and Rhode Island retained corporation charters, and Massachusetts persisted as a hybrid royal colony under charter administration.

Upon independence, colonial charters were converted or consulted as the basis for state constitutions. The balance of individual rights and criminal sanctions that evolved under charter governance were codified in state and federal government.

Justin Paulette
Independent Scholar

See Also: 1600 to 1776 Primary Documents; *Book of the General Lawes & Libertyes;* Colonial Courts; Constitution of the United States of America; History of Crime and Punishment in America: Colonial.

Further Readings
Avalon Project. "Colonial Charters, Grants and Related Documents." http://avalon.law.yale.edu/subject_menus/statech.asp (Accessed April 2011).
Thorpe, Francis Newton. *The Federal and State Constitutions, Colonial Charters, and Other Organic Laws of the State, Territories, and Colonies Now or Heretofore Forming the United States of America, Volume 7.* Washington, DC: Government Printing Office, 1909.

Colonial Courts

In colonial British America, local county courts functioned as the primary unit of adjudication. The English colonists who came to America failed to transport the English system of common law, prerogative, and ecclesiastical courts to the colonies intact, and no exact counterparts to the English assize, prerogative, and chancery courts existed in 17th-century North America. Instead, local county courts (outwardly similar to English Quarter Sessions) performed a number of tasks that had previously been assigned to different branches of the English court system, and at the colony level, a higher judicial body, usually composed of the colony's leading male residents, functioned as a trial court for certain cases (usually involving felonious acts or property exceeding a certain minimum valuation) and as a supreme appellate court with the power to overturn lower rulings. As time passed, in the later 17th and 18th centuries, this simple system became more elaborate and more contentious as special-purpose courts (often staffed by English appointees), including Vice-Admiralty Courts, Courts of Oyer and Terminer, and Chancery Courts, were established in some colonies.

Throughout the colonial period, individual county courts served as the primary vehicle for distributing justice to the king's subjects in America. In each county, a number of justices—usually 12—held office, and monthly court sessions took place when a quorum of the sitting justices was present. The method of selection for justices varied from colony to colony, depending in part on whether the colony was a proprietary, corporate, or royal one. In New England, where the tradition of annual elections was strong, judges usually served for short periods of time. Farther south, members of county courts usually received their appointment from the colony's governor, although in royal colonies, the appointment had to be confirmed by the sitting monarch. The county court system (in which justices were originally called commissioners) was not implemented in Virginia until 1634 but was present throughout the southern colonies from that date until the end of the colonial period.

Regional Variations

Regional differences existed in the quality of individual appointed to the local bench. In the New England colonies, for instance, early justices tended to be members of the local Puritan congregations who sometimes possessed a formal university education and legal training. In the first generations, these included men who had attended university in England but, as the 17th century progressed, increasingly included locally educated New Englanders as well. These were men of property, local standing, and religiously orthodox beliefs; accordingly, the justice they dispensed as well as the local laws they interpreted often bore witness to orthodox Puritan theology.

In the southern colonies, the character of local justice differed significantly. The nature of Chesapeake settlement and the high mortality rates throughout the region meant that there was a smaller pool of potential justices and rapid turnover in the composition of the courts, especially during the first half of the 17th century. Some justices were men of good social background and education in England; many, however, were self-made men who had sometimes come as indentured servants or menial laborers but who rose in wealth and status over time. Contemporaries sometimes complained that these men were illiterate, unorthodox, unscrupulous, rude, and self-serving. Over time, as great families emerged at the helm of Chesapeake society, the composition of the courts changed; these younger justices had often received English educations, and the later 17th century witnessed an anglicization of the American colonial courts as lawyers better trained in English legal theory and method came to proliferate. Still, even in the late colonial period, the character of American frontier justice remained rough, with recent Scotch-Irish and German immigrants finding their way onto the bench along with migrants from the north and east who had moved south and west in search of improved fortunes.

Court Procedures
During the 17th century, a typical county court docket might include the recording of property deeds, the probate of local estates, and the empanelling of juries to hear legal suits. Courts simultaneously heard civil and criminal cases. Justices might negotiate boundary disputes and settle conflicting inheritance claims at the same time as they disciplined unruly servants and slaves, determined who would care for illegitimate children, punished gossips whose tales damaged personal reputations, punished cases of petty theft and criminal trespass, and ferreted out accused arsonists, rapists, and murderers from the local population. Plaintiff, defendant, and witnesses at one suit often served together later in the same session as jurors at another. Throughout colonial America, "court day" became an important occasion, one when the entire community—ranging from the wealthiest local grandees to the most humble servants—assembled to transact both legal business and personal affairs, a day filled with gravity as the court handed down its legal rulings and often afterwards with jollity as participants fellowshipped in local taverns and celebrated the outcome of their suits.

Much evidence suggests that the court rulings, fair or unfair, upheld prevailing local concepts of law and order. In New England, these most frequently reinforced local Puritan orthodoxy. Old Testament Mosaic law influenced both the way legislators wrote laws and the way jurors and judges interpreted them. In the southern colonies, court decisions and the punishments assigned guilty parties tended to uphold the hegemony of the planter elite by supporting their claims to real and chattel property and extending their dominion over servants and slaves.

Throughout colonial America, the court system also upheld the gendered norms of 17th- and 18th-century America. "Unruly" women—those who violated the religious norms of the northern colonies or more genteel ideals about elite women in the south—found themselves subject to a number of punishments intended to chasten them into proper behavior, including punishments for allegedly lewd and unchaste actions, for bearing children out of wedlock, for spreading malicious gossip, for promoting witchcraft, and for encouraging men to criminal activity. While women might testify in colonial legal disputes, they could not as a rule bring court suits on their own and could own property only under specific circumstances, usually as unmarried spinsters or, later in life, as widows.

Punishments
As in England, punishments for crimes—ranging from small fines and short stays in "gaol" to public flogging or execution—acted as deterrents intended to curb criminal activity and to promote law and order. Like their English counterparts, albeit on a lesser scale, American justices also used the majesty of their position and the mercy

allowed them in dispensing justice to commute sentences or to impose more lenient punishments than legally prescribed when strict adherence to the letter of the law ran contrary to prevailing local norms. Because many colonial legal statutes had been created with particular local issues in mind, courts also exercised considerable leeway in the application of these laws, and even when English laws appeared in simplified form in American legal codes, the realities of colonial life often led to rulings that could seem at odds with prevailing legal interpretations in England. One example is the case of Anne Orthwood, an English indentured servant who became pregnant while working on a plantation on Virginia's Eastern Shore; in interpreting legal liability in a case in which a pregnant Orthwood had been sold to an unsuspecting planter, the court reversed the prevailing English tradition of applying the principle of caveat emptor ("let the buyer beware") to sales in favor of caveat venditor ("let the seller beware"), a concept that better functioned to bolster the local social order and to support an unstable economy in a tumultuous and rapidly evolving society.

In the northern colonies, where population density was higher, where town meetings and religious congregations rivaled the county courts for local power, and where residents often lived in closer proximity to the true seat of provincial authority in the colony's capital city, the authority of the local courts was not as great as in the southern colonies, where the local county courts dominated local governance throughout the 17th and early 18th centuries. New England justices tended to serve shorter terms (often rotating off the bench annually), which limited their ability to dominate local society when compared with southern justices, who often held what amounted to life appointments. But even in the southern colonies, where a few powerful local families often tended to dominate the bench across several generations, the possibility of appeal to a higher authority existed when litigants questioned the validity of a local ruling.

Appeals

In each of the colonies, certain legal rulings could be appealed beyond the county officials who meted out local justice. In the southern colonies, the Governor's Council usually functioned as a supreme court to hear matters referred to it for appeal. The Governor's Council, a group of 12 of the colony's preeminent men, usually appointed for life or good behavior, advised the governor on policy matters and served as the upper chamber of the colony's bicameral legislature. Sitting in another capacity, these men also interpreted the laws they had helped create. Given their positions at the helm of the colonial ruling elite, these men issued rulings that often upheld the status quo, although they did occasionally reverse local rulings in particularly controversial decisions.

A similar system existed in the New England colonies. For instance, the Massachusetts Bay Charter of 1629 established a General Court, which would meet four times annually to conduct company business and issue local laws and ordinances. Elected annually, the General Court over time came to function as a legislature (bicameral after 1644), an administrative body, and a supreme court. As compared with the southern colonies, the Massachusetts Court of Assistants (in which the Governor's Council served as judges) differed chiefly in terms of the quality of men chosen for the office (with a preference for educated men of solid Puritan outlook), its frequently changing composition, and a tendency to interpret laws in a manner consistent with local Puritan theology. Following the Glorious Revolution, with the grant of a new charter to Massachusetts in 1691, the Puritan stronghold on the colony declined (and the court was also formally separated from the council), but the religious outlook of many of its members shaped the Court of Assistants into the Revolutionary era.

In the Dutch New Netherland colony (which after 1655 included struggling New Sweden), a different juridical system prevailed. Based on Roman-Dutch law, this system differed significantly from English common law, with one important feature being that it allowed women a greater economic and legal role in society. Many Dutch women worked independently, trading and operating businesses on their own, bringing both civil and criminal cases in their own right, and occasionally serving as legal arbitrators in cases involving other women. Because New Netherland was organized as a trading colony, resident officials were always responsible to higher

The Capitol building in Williamsburg, Virginia, shown after modern reconstruction. The first floor of the west building was used by the colonial government as a General Court in the early 1700s. During the 17th century, a typical county court might handle recording property deeds, probate of local estates, and empanelling of juries to hear legal suits.

authorities residing in the homeland. Within New Netherland itself, however, the court of New Netherland—which included the director general and council—had supreme authority. Over time, local courts (similar to the county courts in English colonies) were established, such as the municipal court created in New Amsterdam (New York City) in 1653. The New Amsterdam court, for example, consisted of the *schout* (a combination of prosecutor and sheriff), two *burgomasters* (co-mayors), and five *schepens* (aldermen), who (apart from the *schout*) fulfilled both legislative and judicial functions.

The English capture of the colony in 1664 brought gradual change, with Dutch law initially left in effect. The duke's laws, issued by future King James II in 1665, provided the first step in the transformation to English common law, which came to fruition after the second and final English capture of the colony in 1674. Although Dutch cultural influence remained significant throughout the Middle Colonies for the rest of the colonial period, attempts to anglicize the colony's legal operations were successful, largely bringing New York in line with other British colonies by the end of the 17th century.

Special Purpose Courts

As British America's colonial population increased and local affairs grew more complex, government officials created a number of special purpose courts throughout the colonies. The enforcement of the Navigation Acts after the middle of the 17th century created many problems. In 1675, Charles II had appointed the Lords of Trade, a subcommittee of the Privy Council, to enforce the Navigation Acts, and they sent Edward Randolph (who later became the first Surveyor General of Customs for all of North America) across the Atlantic as their special agent to ensure colonial compliance. Colonial assemblies interpreted Randolph's mandate as an invasion of their own administrative and judicial powers and objected to Randolph's presence.

During its brief existence in the 1680s, the Dominion of New England streamlined justice in the northern colonies, taking the power to empanel juries from local justices and giving it to sheriffs appointed by the Dominion's governor, Sir Edmund Andros, and establishing a special Admiralty Court with no jury to handle trade offenses.

In 1696, the English government made two important changes impacting colonial legal and judicial matters. William III created the Board of Trade as an intermediate body under the supervision of the Privy Council to oversee colonial administration, and in a controversial move, Parliament mandated the governors of Massachusetts, New York, Pennsylvania, Maryland, and Virginia to establish Vice-Admiralty Courts similar to the one established under the Dominion of New England to hear cases involving trade laws. New York established a Court of Chancery to hear equity matters in 1701, but most other colonies waited until after the American Revolution to establish such bodies. Still, throughout the 18th century, colonial elites continued to regard attempts to divest them of their judicial authority with alarm.

Under Governor Alexander Spotswood in the 1710s, Virginia's Governor's Council bitterly resisted Spotswood's effort to create a special Court of Oyer and Terminer that they believed violated their rights as the colony's highest court. Later, during the imperial crisis of the 1760s, it was likewise the threat to colonial "rights" represented by the order to establish Vice-Admiralty Courts that provoked alarm throughout British America following the Townshend Acts of 1767.

While there were important 17th-century variations in the Middle Colonies, where the first governments were proprietary ones and where the colonists were more socially and culturally diverse than elsewhere, throughout colonial British America, the courts imposed order in a rapidly changing, often unstable environment and profoundly shaped the character of everyday life. As society grew more complex in the later colonial period, so, too, did the court system. Efforts to anglicize the law brought greater uniformity in the 18th century, but by then, local traditions were so entrenched that eventually the role of the local court system itself would become part of the disputed terrain of the larger revolutionary conflict.

Thomas Daniel Knight
University of Texas—Pan American

See Also: 1600 to 1776 Primary Documents; Colonial Charters and Grants; Common Law Origins of Criminal Law; Court of Common Pleas; Court of Oyer and Terminer; Court of Quarter Sessions.

Further Readings
Billings, Warren. *A Little Parliament: The Virginia General Assembly in the Seventeenth Century.* Richmond: Library of Virginia, 2004.
Breen, Timothy. *The Character of the Good Ruler: A Study of Puritan Political Ideas in New England, 1630–1730.* New York: Norton, 1974.
Dalton, Cornelius, et al. *Leading the Way: A History of the Massachusetts General Court, 1629–1980.* Boston: Office of the Massachusetts Secretary of State, 1984.
Dayton, Cornelia. *Women Before the Bar: Gender, Law, and Society in Connecticut, 1639–1789.* Chapel Hill: University of North Carolina Press, 1995.
Greenberg, Douglas. *Crime and Law Enforcement in the Colony of New York, 1691–1776.* Ithaca, NY: Cornell University Press, 1976.
Salmon, Marylynn. *Women and the Law of Property in Early America.* Chapel Hill: University of North Carolina Press, 1989.

Colorado

The development of Colorado's early legal system was intimately tied to the land and its natural resources and to the settlers who moved into the state to pursue these resources. In the late 1850s, gold was discovered along the front range of and within the Rocky Mountains, leading to the creation of the provisional Jefferson Territory to govern the growing population. In December 1859, following a lynch mob's hanging of John Stoeffel for the murder of his brother-in-law over a bag of gold, the newly chartered city of Denver appointed its first marshal, William E. Sisty. That year, the Jefferson Rangers were created to protect gold shipments and otherwise maintain law and order throughout the Jefferson Territory. A series of local miners' and people's courts were established within this territory as early efforts at institutionalized justice.

In 1861, Congress officially established the Colorado Territory, with William Gilpin as the first territorial governor. The Jefferson Rangers became the Colorado Rangers (also called the Colorado Mounted Rangers); this unit still exists as an all-volunteer auxiliary unit authorized by statute to assist law enforcement and emergency and rescue services throughout the state. Today, there are 64 county police departments throughout the state of Colorado, as well as the Colorado State Patrol.

Early Conflicts

As new settlers poured into Colorado, conflicts between these settlers and Native Americans increased, and the U.S. Army was used to maintain order. On November 29, 1864, 650 Colorado troops attacked a friendly settlement of Cheyenne and Arapahoe Indians along the banks of Sand Creek. These troops were led by John M. Chivington, known as the "Fighting Parson." Approximately 150 Indians, mostly women, children, and the elderly, were killed; a subsequent congressional investigation found that they had been murdered in cold blood by the troops commanded by Chivington. The site of this atrocity, known as the Sand Creek Massacre, was dedicated as a national historic monument in 2007.

Colorado is also the site of one of the most deadly confrontations between striking workers and the state militia. Since the beginning of the 20th century, workers in mines and mills in Colorado began organizing and striking for better wages and working conditions. In 1913, the United Mine Workers organized a lengthy strike against Colorado coal companies. On April 20, 1914, the Colorado National Guard went to clear out a tent city occupied by striking miners and their families. The conflict escalated, and state militia killed a number of men, women, and children, some of them burned to death in their tents. The site of this Ludlow Massacre is now owned by the United Mine Workers and has been designated a national historic landmark.

A striking miner holding a white flag of truce approaches the body of a victim of the April 29, 1914, Ludlow Massacre as smoke rises from fires in the background.

Criminal Justice System

In 1868, the first prison was established by the Territorial Legislature in Canon City. The Colorado Territorial Penitentiary admitted its first prisoner in 1871, and the prison facility has been active since that time.

In 1876, Colorado became the 38th state to join the Union. In 1935, a separate Women's Prison was built in Canon City; this building now houses the Museum of Colorado Prisons. In 1903, one of the first juvenile courts in the United States opened in Denver; Ben B. Lindsey served as this court's first judge. This court was based on a similar model created in Chicago and focused on rehabilitation, rather than punishment of juvenile offenders. Judge Lindsey was an early advocate for juvenile justice; his legacy survives today, as the Colorado Department of Corrections operates a Youthful Offender System, diverting juvenile offenders from prison into rehabilitation programs. While the Colorado legislature eliminated the practice of sentencing juveniles convicted of murder to life without parole in 2005, this law was not retroactive. As a result, Colorado still has dozens of juvenile offenders convicted of murder who are serving life sentences without parole.

Until 1933, hanging was the method used for executions in Colorado. Colorado then became one of the first states to adopt the gas chamber, which replaced hangings until 1967. Lethal injection is the current method of execution; Gary Lee Davis (1997) was the last person executed in Colorado. There are currently three prisoners on death row in Colorado, which is located in the Colorado State Penitentiary in Canon City.

During World War II, Japanese Americans from California were interned at the Amache relocation camp near the town of Granada on the eastern plains of Colorado. This camp was established pursuant to Executive Order 9066, signed by President Franklin Roosevelt on February 18, 1942, two months after the bombing of Pearl Harbor. This order required that all west coast Japanese Americans were to be immediately relocated to inland camps to prevent their participation in espionage activities against the United States. Amache was open from August 1942 through January 1946 and housed 7,597 Japanese Americans.

The 1970s and early 1980s saw large population growth in the state, thanks to an increase in the mining and oil shale industries. During the 1980s and 1990s, a technology boom similarly resulted in an influx of new residents. Along with these new residents, the prison population in Colorado soared; in the past 15 years, the number of state inmates and parolees has tripled. As of June 30, 2011, the Colorado Department of Corrections had 22,610 adult inmates, with an additional 10,696 offenders on parole. In recent years, the Colorado Department of Corrections has focused on reducing recidivism rates through the adoption of evidence-based practices such as more effective offender diagnostic tools, motivational interviewing, and reentry programs that assist offenders in escaping the revolving door of prison.

Susan J. Tyburski
Women's College of the University of Denver

See Also: 1941 to 1960 Primary Documents; 1981 to 2000 Primary Documents; Executions; Japanese Americans; Juvenile Corrections, History of; Native Americans; Penitentiaries; Strikes.

Further Readings
Colorado Department of Corrections. "General Statistics." http://www.doc.state.co.us/general-statistics##Offender%20Population (Accessed September 2011).
Martelle, Scott. *Blood Passion: The Ludlow Massacre and Class War in the American West*. New Brunswick, NJ: Rutgers University Press, 2007.
Sherard, Gerald E. "A Short History of the Colorado State Penitentiary." Colorado State Archives. http://www.colorado.gov/dpa/doit/archives/pen/history.htm (Accessed September 2011).

Common Law Origins of Criminal Law

There are four major legal traditions in the modern world: the common law, the civil law, the socialist law, and the religious law legal traditions. Although many other different legal traditions have existed throughout history, these four traditions are representative of the major legal traditions that have developed over the course of history.

It must be realized that each of these four legal traditions consists of certain fundamental principles unique to that tradition, but they are not necessarily mutually exclusive. Some aspects of each tradition might be found in the other traditions. Indeed, many legal systems in the world may incorporate some aspects of each these traditions. Further, classification of a legal system as falling within one of the legal traditions is a function of determining which tradition not only predominates in that legal system but how that legal system developed over time.

Religious Law Legal Tradition
The religious law legal tradition is not limited to one religion. A number of major religions are recognized in the world today, including Buddhism, Hinduism, Judaism, Christianity, and

Islam. Throughout history, many other religions have been practiced. Each of the major religions that have been practiced throughout history have developed some form of laws and methods to enforce those laws. These two aspects of law are referred to as substantive law and procedural law. Substantive law is law that provides rights or mandates a duty. Thus, substantive criminal law usually defines what acts are criminal. In contrast, procedural law is law that specifies the methods used to enforce the law and adjudicate violations of it. In criminal law, the procedural law would state what steps are required to enforce the criminal law and what steps are required to adjudicate a violation of the substantive criminal law.

In the religious law legal tradition, the source of the substantive criminal law is usually the divine law. Usually, this divine law is codified in holy texts. For example, in Christianity, this would include the Ten Commandants; in Islam, it would be the Koran. Procedurally, as a general matter, under a religious law legal tradition, the courts would be subject to the religious leaders. The courts would not be independent government agencies, and changes to the religious law would come through religious leaders, who would interpret the meaning of that law.

Socialist Law Legal Tradition

For the purposes of this article, the socialist law legal tradition that is addressed refers to the Communist view of socialism. The socialist law legal tradition is a relatively new phenomenon, having its basic roots in Marxism and the Russian Revolution of 1917. Karl Marx was a political philosopher who lived during the 19th century and developed a theory of politics and economics that focused on the economic resources of a society and the division of these resources between the social classes. Marx's primary works were *Das Kapital* and the *Communist Manifesto*. Marx was an advocate of the basic principle that a society's resources should be shared by all of the populace and not concentrated in the hands of a few wealthy individuals. Marx was a vehement opponent of capitalism.

Under the socialist law legal tradition, the law is subordinate to the policies and principles of socialsm. Even though a person may be factually innocent of a crime, if a guilty verdict would help advance the socialsm ideals of the nation and an acquittal would damage the state, then a guilty verdict would likely be the result of any trial. The substantive law in such a tradition would likely include all of the criminal laws of common law and civil law nations, including murder, rape, and robbery, but it would also include laws that focus on advancing socialist principles. While the procedural law of a socialist law legal tradition would include some of the same aspects of a common or civil law tradition, such as a court trial, its functions would not be for the searching of truth and protection of the innocent but for the advancement of socialist ideals. Thus, the courts are not independent government agencies.

One must be careful to distinguish between the various uses of the term *socialism*. When the term *socialist* is used, it is usually used in the context of the welfare of the people, that is, for each person's welfare. In actual practice, there are three distinct uses of the term. For example, the Nazis, who were acknowledged fascists, actually used the terms *national* and *socialism* in the title of their political party, and in actual practice, it only meant that the individual person had no value and that the power of the state was paramount. The Communists, who are used as the primary example of a socialist government, used *socialism*, like the Nazis, as meaning that the individual had no value but, unlike the Nazis, believed that the overall good of all of the individuals was more important. Unfortunately, the Communists of the former Soviet Union, especially under Stalin, perverted much of Marx's philosophy, and the practical effect of the system was little different than Nazism. The third meaning of *socialism* is that demonstrated by the Scandinavian nations of Europe. In these nations, *socialism* refers to a government that provides extensive social services for the individual people, which include education, healthcare, and other social services. It is democratic in nature and is not totalitarian like fascism or communism.

Civil Law Legal Tradition

When the term *civil law* is commonly used in the United States of America, many people today accept it as meaning the law that is not criminal, that is, there is the criminal law and the civil law. In both cases, the law is generally found in codes or statutes. However, when the term is used with regard to a legal tradition, it refers to the historical development of the law through the use of actual codes or statutes rather than from the common law or customs, which is explained in the succeeding section of this article.

The civil law legal tradition has its roots in ancient Rome. Legend has it that Rome was founded in the 8th century B.C.E. by two brothers, Romulus and Remus. However, archaeological evidence indicates it existed for thousands of years before that time. The Roman Republic was founded in 510 B.C.E. with the Roman Empire coming into being in 27 B.C.E. With the founding of the Roman Republic, there began a historical period of great cultural development. Around 450 B.C.E., the Twelve Tables of laws were enacted. From that time, Rome developed more complex legal codes and courts to adjudicate violations of the law. Finally, in 527 C.E. under the Roman emperor Justinian, the Corpus Juris Civilis was created, which was a codified set of laws. With the Corpus Juris Civilis, all prior law was abolished, but this does not mean that previously recognized principles of law were ignored. In fact, many of these previously recognized principles of law were incorporated into the Corpus Juris Civilis. Many nations subsequently followed the civil law legal tradition, following the Roman law or enacting their own codes of laws. In France, during the reign of Napoleon Bonaparte, in 1804, the Napoleonic Code was enacted, which provided a comprehensive set of laws for the French criminal justice system. In modern times, many nations still adhere to the civil law legal tradition.

Thus, under the civil law legal tradition, the law was defined in a specific written code. The primary difference between the civil law legal tradition and the common law legal tradition is that the law under the common law legal tradition developed through customs of that particular society, as opposed to specific written statutes. However, this does not mean that nations that follow the common law legal tradition do not have codes or statutes. What is different between the two systems is how each system makes decisions and adjudicates criminal charges.

Common Law Legal Tradition
The common law legal tradition developed from the influence of several separate preexisting legal systems. These were customs, feudalism, and equity. Customs were those practices that were adopted by social groups, which eventually came to have the force of law. As the same customs were repeatedly enforced over time, they came to be accepted by that society as law. According to Sir William Blackstone, the famous English legal philosopher, such customs have existed since ancient times. The employment of these customs led to the use of precedents as controlling law in common law systems. Under feudalism, a monarch was owed fealty by subordinate lords, who in turn were owed fealty by their serfs. Disputes that arose between serfs were resolved by the local lord. Usually, these disputes were resolved by referring to the local customs in that fiefdom. Under equity, a separate system of courts developed. These

England was the primary source of the common law legal tradition. Today, important English criminal cases are tried at London's Central Criminal Court, or "Old Bailey," shown above.

courts were called courts of chancery (or equity) as opposed to courts of law. They flowed from the office of the chancellor of England. Courts of chancery could provide justice where courts of law would not. The chancellor could order parties to act or desist from acting to accomplish fairness, as opposed to granting relief according to law, especially where the law was unjust.

Thus, there was no code of equity that guided the chancellor in his decision but rather his sense of fairness and justice with reference to custom. Approximately a century after the Norman conquest of England in 1066, Henry II reformed the legal system such that the customs of the land would be fairly and consistently applied by the courts. These three legal systems, combined with Henry II's reforms, led to what is now known as the communal legal tradition.

England was the primary source of the common law legal tradition, which has been adopted by the Commonwealth of Nations—which includes Australia, Canada, and New Zealand—and the United States. The common law legal tradition was imported by the English colonists who eventually revolted and formed the United States of America.

In England and, thus, the common law legal tradition, there was no written legal criminal code. Most of the written laws concerned civil matters separate from the criminal law, although in its early years, there was no distinction between civil and criminal law in the common law legal tradition. However, over the centuries, the common law came to recognize a number of crimes: high treason, petty treason, sedition, murder, manslaughter, mayhem, arson, larceny, robbery, burglary, rape, assault, battery, riot, escape, breach of the peace, and blasphemy. Of course, there were many other crimes under the common law, but what is important to realize is that the crimes recognized under the common law are remarkably similar to the subsequent codifications of the criminal law in the United States of America and to the criminal codes found in civil law legal tradition nations.

Under the common law legal tradition, the same distinction between felonies and misdemeanors was present that is present in modern American criminal codes. However, in ancient England, during the development of the common law legal tradition, the punishments were much harsher. For almost all felonies, the punishment could be death.

Common Law Versus Civil Law

Even though the United States of America is a common law legal tradition nation, every jurisdiction in the United States has, for the most part, abolished all of the common law crimes that were brought over from England. Today, every jurisdiction has codified the criminal law and has abolished the common law crimes previously recognized. This does not mean that the United States is no longer a nation that follows the common law legal tradition.

The only exception in the United States to the common law legal tradition is the state of Louisiana. Because Louisiana was founded and developed by the French, it initially adopted the Napoleonic Code. Even after the Louisiana Purchase, when the United States bought the area from the French, Louisiana, at the state level, retained its adherence to the civil law legal tradition and still does so today.

The primary facet of the common law legal tradition is the employment of custom or, as it is called in modern times, precedent to adjudicate violations of the criminal law. In a common law legal tradition court, such as those found in the United States, where criminal codes have been adopted, although a criminal statute is the basis for the criminal charges against a suspect, the law is applied by reference to legal precedents. Legal precedents are previous court decisions that have interpreted and applied that statute. The reason for the use of legal precedents is that any criminal statute cannot possibly foresee and address all possible ways the crime in question could be committed. Accordingly, courts are allowed to use precedents to aid in the adjudication of violations of the criminal law. In contrast, courts in a civil law legal tradition nation would, at least in theory, only refer to the statute when adjudicating violations of the criminal law. The use of previous judicial decisions as legally binding precedents is called the principle of stare decisis.

It is interesting to note that, in the United States, with the abolishment and supplantation of the common law by codes and statutes, it would appear that the United States has essentially adopted the civil law tradition in all but name.

This process of codification of the common law in the United States began in the early part of the 19th century. However, the fundamental difference between the current system of American law and a strictly civil code nation is that precedents are still considered controlling over the interpretation and application of codes and statutes. Thus, the essential aspect of the common law, stare decisis, is controlling and the United States is still a fundamentally common law nation.

Criminal Law Through History

Even though the criminal law as recognized and as employed in the United States originated with the common law legal tradition as developed in England, England was not the source of all criminal law. Since ancient times, nations have recognized and codified criminal acts. Indeed, under the Code of Hammurabi, which was written approximately 4,000 years ago, numerous crimes and punishments for them were established. This is also true for each of the other modern legal traditions of religious law, socialist law, and civil law. Each has had its own criminal laws, although some traditions will recognize crimes that other traditions might not.

Wm. C. Plouffe, Jr.
Independent Scholar

See Also: Blackstone, William; Bodie of Liberties; *Book of the General Lawes & Libertyes*; Codification of Laws; Courts; Felonies.

Further Readings
Blackstone, Sir William. *Commentaries on the Laws of England*. Oxford: Clarendon Press, 1770.
Cardozo, Benjamin. *The Nature of the Judicial Process*. New Haven, CT: Yale University Press, 1921.
Hale, Matthew. *The History of the Common Law of England*. Chicago: University of Chicago Press, 2002.
Holmes, Oliver Wendell, Jr. *The Common Law*. Mineola, NY: Dover Publications, 1991.
Pound, Roscoe. *The Spirit of the Common Law*. Charleston, SC: Nabu Press, 2010.
Reichel, Philip L. *Comparative Criminal Justice Systems*, 5th ed. Upper Saddle River, NJ: Pearson Prentice Hall, 2008.

Community Policing and Relations

The United States is a constitutional republic founded on the premise that the government is entrusted with power that comes from the people to be used for the benefit of society; therefore, the government needs to be accountable to the people for how it uses power. An important role of the government is to provide for the safety and security of the public through the enforcement of law. The police are the agency of government that carries out this function. The police need the support and assistance of the public in order to effectively enforce the law and ensure the safety of the people. To do this, they need to work as partners with the community and collaboratively identify and solve problems within the community. However, the police have not always had positive relations with the community, and relations with the minority community in particular have been strained.

Racism and racial profiling, brutality, and corruption have been reccurring themes with American police throughout their history. The late 20th century has seen the police reach out to the community to improve community relations through community-oriented policing and similar ventures.

Early Police Relations

Modern paid policing in the United States began in the early 19th century. Social changes caused by the Industrial Revolution and urbanization brought increased crime and disorder to American cities. The system of constables and unpaid watchmen was ill-suited to deal with these issues, and following similar developments in England, U.S. cities began to develop formal police departments. Unlike England, however, American police departments developed in a decentralized fashion with each municipality creating its own police force. This has been called the political era of policing because these early police were closely allied with the politicians who appointed them and controlled their fate.

This epitomized the spoils system; patronage was the order of the day. This system served to foster racism, brutality, and corruption among police officers, particularly as these served the political power holders in society.

While there were many problems with policing in this period, police officers were close to the public. The primary method of patrol was by foot, with some locations utilizing horses or bicycles. This, by its very nature, enabled the police to work closely with citizens. When citizens needed police assistance, they usually knew where to find the officer in the neighborhood. Police performed many social service functions, and a large part of their role was public service. Police stations operated as homeless shelters and soup kitchens, providing aid to those who needed it. Police officers also worked with disobedient children and assisted the public in a myriad of other ways.

While the police were directly involved with citizens, it did not mean that they were active partners in the community. To the contrary, police were still beholden to the politicians who appointed them and kept them in their positions. To this end, police officers followed the dictates of those in power, even if they opposed the interests of the community. Often, this included intimidating citizens during elections to achieve desired results. The corruption of the police went hand in hand with political corruption, and there was no distinction between the two.

Nineteenth- and Twentieth-Century Policing

In the late 19th and early 20th centuries, concerns over corruption and abuses by the police led to frequent calls for reform. Several commissions investigated the police, and there were numerous demands to eliminate corruption and brutality in policing. Chief among them were proposals to separate politics from policing as it was felt that this was a primary cause of corruption. Some argued that the police needed to be removed from the public as much as possible since contact with them also could lead to corruption. This period of police history has been termed the reform, or professional, era.

The mission of the police in this era was narrowed to crime fighting, and many of the social service functions that the police formerly performed were removed to distance the police from the public. Police officers were told to maintain a professional attitude and detachment from the public. Further widening the gap between the police and the community were technological advancements that changed police service delivery methods. Patrol officers were placed into automobiles equipped with two-way radios and removed from foot patrols. Citizen use of telephones enabled them to call the police directly so they could be dispatched to calls for service. This spurred the development of random police patrol to deter crime, the police as crime fighters, and citizens as passive recipients of police services.

The changes of the reform/professional era did not lead to improvements in relations between the police and the community. The police were still perceived to be brutal and racist, and in minority communities, relations were outright hostile at times. Ironically, the changes that were meant to improve and professionalize the police only served to widen the gap between them and the community. Police were alienated from the community and were viewed with suspicion by many citizens. These feelings erupted in the decade of the 1960s as riots occurred throughout the United States. Events—including an unpopular war in Vietnam, a growing civil rights movement, and unrest on college campuses—fueled a distrust of government that spawned numerous civil disturbances that pushed police into the national spotlight. Police actions during these disturbances only exacerbated these feelings. In addition, there was a growing fear of crime in many communities and a belief that the police could do nothing to alleviate rising crime and violence. The decade saw several national commissions that studied the urban unrest and the criminal justice system, leading to recommendations that again spurred an agenda of reform.

Some police administrators recognized these issues and attempted to reach out the community. These efforts, termed police community relations programs, were endeavors to address community concerns and build relations with the community. As well-intentioned as these programs were, they often failed for a variety of reasons: lack of staffing, insufficient funding, and attempts at legitimizing past police practices. They were run as separate units in the police departments and were operated by staff rather than line officers, which meant that the officers in these units did not work the streets. While they attempted to foster good relations with the community, their efforts were frequently undone by police officers in the field who did not know, or even care, what the community relations officers were doing or saying. This caused even more damage as people felt that the police said one thing but did another.

Team policing, another attempt to build relations with the community, was tried in the 1960s and 1970s. This consisted of decentralization of the police and an increase in participation by the community. In its ideal form, the patrol force was reorganized into one or more semiautonomous teams that were assigned permanently to particular neighborhoods. The team was then responsible for handling all calls for service and crime in that area. The team was to work closely with neighborhood residents with the goal of building close relationships. With a few exceptions, team policing did not work, and most efforts failed, mainly because they did not differ from traditional reactive policing, they did not receive sufficient administrative support, and officers did not clearly understand their roles. Team policing did not last into the 1980s.

By the 1980s it was clear that reactive patrol was not working. Police were isolated and alienated from the community, and this was magnified by the automobile. The narrowing of the police mission to crime fighting and a focus away from service further pulled the police from the community. In many minority communities, the police were looked upon as an alien occupying force. Rising crime and violence increased fear of crime and citizen dissatisfaction with the police. Concerns over police use of force and violence continued, putting additional strains on community relations. These factors, combined with new research into police operations, led police departments to seek different methods of delivering police services.

Modern Community Policing Efforts
Research conducted in several aspects of police operations in the 1970s and 1980s challenged traditional assumptions regarding policing. Random police patrol, rapid response to calls for service, foot patrol and fear of crime, and the investigative function were areas examined with unexpected results that led to questions regarding policing. These findings suggested that the police needed to pay more attention to conditions that cause crime and disorder, and that random patrol might not be effective in addressing problems. Foot patrol studies showed that while it might not initially reduce crime, it did reduce citizen fear of crime, and improved relations between police and citizens. These all came together in the concept known as "broken windows." This theory states that the police must work proactively to address problems and the conditions that cause them, that they need to work in partnership with communities, and that fear of crime must be a police concern. Most importantly, the theory also recommended that attention be paid to disorder and quality of life issues since they contribute to fear of crime and citizen perceptions of the community and police.

By the 1980s, there was considerable movement toward community policing as a method to improve police service and relations with the community. The idea and meaning of community policing have evolved over the past 30 years as police departments have experimented with different ways to achieve its means and as academics and the federal government have studied its processes and effects with the goal of identifying best practices. Community policing has grown for many reasons. Police departments embraced the idea as a way to reduce crime and disorder and to foster better relations with the community. The public accepted it and welcomed having a say regarding policing in their communities.

A major factor in the growth of community policing has been the federal government program COPS (Office of Community Oriented Policing Services), which started in 1994. Since its inception, COPS has distributed in excess of $1 billion to promote community-oriented policing around the country. This money has been used to hire new officers, to start and maintain community policing programs, and to purchase new technology that assists in promoting community policing. In addition, COPS has funded numerous studies of community policing.

Community policing, simply defined, means a decentralized form of proactive policing working in partnership with the community to identify and solve problems, and having permanent police officers assigned to permanent places. Three ideas underlying community policing are citizen input, an enhanced and broadened police function, and

Bicycle police on patrol in the city of White Plains, New York, in November 2002. Moves toward increased foot and bicycle patrols, which allow for more face-to-face interaction with the public, and away from automobile patrols, which tend to isolate officers from their communities, have been emphasized in recent community policing efforts.

personal service. The emphasis is on working with citizens to improve the quality of life by reducing fear of crime and finding the causes of problems in the community and fixing them.

Elements of Community-Oriented Policing

There are four dimensions to community policing, each with several elements. The philosophical dimension implies that community policing is a philosophy rather than a program. It begins with citizen input, meaning that citizens have a say in their policing. Next is a broad police function, which suggests that policing is expanded to include dealing with issues that impact quality of life. Another component is personal service, policing that is tailored to the needs of the community.

The strategic dimension includes the elements that translate the philosophy into action. A reorientation in operations emphasizes face-to-face interaction with citizens over random patrol and finding ways to free officer time to achieve this. A geographic focus places officers into permanent areas rather than assignment by time of day. This also implies accountability for that area. A prevention emphasis places importance on proactive approaches that prevent crime and disorder rather than reacting after the fact.

The tactical dimension translates the philosophical and strategic dimensions into practice. The element of positive interaction stresses the need for officers to interact with citizens in positive, meaningful ways. This is related to the element of partnerships, which involves organizing the community and its organizations to jointly deal with quality of life issues. Problem solving is the final element. Problem solving is the process of getting to the root causes of problems and either eliminating them or reducing their harm.

The organizational dimension consists of changing and streamlining the organization to enable officers to carry out their mission. The structure and management of the organization need to change so that authority and responsibility are pushed down to line officers to allow them to act as "mini-chiefs" in their areas. Also, real-time information must be provided to these officers so that they may succeed in their mission.

Ongoing Challenges

While community policing has been practiced for approximately 30 years, it still faces challenges. One primary obstacle is that there is no clear definition of community policing. Police departments practice different forms of community policing, some of which may not be clearly defined as community policing, or may adopt only certain elements of it. True community policing is not just programs or projects; it is a philosophy. Some of this is attributed to police departments that claim to be practicing community policing, but actually are doing something different, such as aggressive policing tactics under the cover of community policing. Other departments may have adopted the language of community policing but have not changed organizational structures or value systems to be in line with true community policing. Because community policing is so difficult to define, it is difficult to accurately study, making its effectiveness difficult to measure.

Another challenge is funding: Community policing is labor intensive and expensive. Local governments are struggling with budget constraints in the 2000s, and the federal government has reduced funding as money is used for other programs. The downturn in the economy in the 21st century has hit state and local governments particularly hard. Tax revenues are down, and many communities have either laid off police officers or not replaced those who retire. Community policing is typically cut back as officers are needed for regular patrol duty. For example, Cleveland, Ohio, cut 250 police officers in the mid-2000s because of reductions in federal funding; Trenton, New Jersey, laid off 105 police officers as a result of budgetary problems. This is occurring in communities across the United States.

Finally, the focus on terrorism since September 11, 2011, has turned attention away from community policing as funds and other resources are dedicated to the war on terror. The federal government has not only shifted funding from community policing to homeland security, it has also asked local police do to more in this area, such as immigration enforcement, intelligence gathering, and guarding of likely terrorist targets. While some feel that community policing and antiterrorism policing can work together, others argue that they are incompatible and that only one style of policing can survive. Regardless of the direction that community policing takes, it is imperative that the police work closely with the public. Police need the support of the public to do their jobs effectively and are dependent on them for funding. Police are accountable to citizens for their use of power, and only by cultivating positive relationships can they work together to create an improved quality of life in their communities.

Marcel F. Beausoleil
Fitchburg State University

See Also: Automobile and the Police; Crime Prevention; History of Crime and Punishment in America: 1970–Present; Police, Contemporary; Police, History of.

Further Readings

Diamond, Drew and Deirdre Mead Weiss. *Community Policing: Looking to Tomorrow.* Washington, DC: Police Executive Research Forum and Community Oriented Policing Services Office, U.S. Department of Justice, 2009.

Fridell, Lorie and Mary Ann Wycoff. *Community Policing: The Past, Present, and Future.* Washington, DC: Police Executive Research Forum, Annie E. Casey Foundation, 2004.

Roberg, Roy, Kenneth Novack, and Gary Cordner. *Police and Society*, 4th ed. New York: Oxford University Press, 2009.

Wilson, James Q. and George L. Kelling. "Broken Windows: The Police and Neighborhood Safety." *Atlantic Monthly* (March 1982).

Community Service

Community service orders are sanctions that typically require youth or adult offenders to work for governmental or nonprofit agencies for a specified number of hours. Such orders are used frequently in both adult and juvenile justice systems in the United States, United Kingdom, Europe, Australia, and New Zealand.

Community service programs may vary in the types of work required from offenders, as well as in the degree of service obligations, usually measured in hours or less frequently in remuneration. Common forms of community service work include physical labor as well as semiskilled work, and less frequently involve skilled work. The duration of service obligations is typically determined by offense within any given municipality and may range from a few hours to hundreds of hours.

History

Community service orders were first used in Alameda County, California, in 1966 as an alternative for female traffic violators who faced jail time as a consequence of unpaid fines. In the late 1960s and early 1970s, interest in alternative sanctions continued to grow, and community service programs flourished. By the late 1970s, community service orders were being used in many juvenile and adult criminal courts in the United States.

Research suggests that public support for community service programs in the United States has remained strong since their initial use. However, the reasons for this support have shifted over time in relation to changing criminal justice philosophies. In the 1970s and early 1980s, for example, community service programs were supported as cost-effective and potentially rehabilitative alternatives to incarceration. Such programs received significant governmental support, and organizations such as the Law Enforcement Assistance Administration provided millions of dollars in assistance to jurisdictions in order to establish programs in support of these goals.

By the mid-1980s, however, support for community service as an alternative to incarceration had begun to wane. Initial research on community service had found little if any reductions in recidivism when compared to other sanctions such as short-term incarceration or community supervision. Other research suggested a "net-widening" effect of offenders sentenced to community service. Nevertheless, throughout the 1980s, the use of community service remained popular, less as a means of rehabilitation or an alternative to incarceration than as one of a growing number of punitive sanctions popular within the growing "tough on crime" turn in criminal and juvenile justice practices. The purpose of community service itself was thus largely reframed as one of retribution or deterrence. Along with other sanctions such as boot camps, house arrest, and intensive supervision, community service became increasingly viewed as a popular form of intermediate punishment between community supervision and incarceration.

More recently, community service has gained support from some advocates of restorative and community justice approaches. Beginning in the late 1970s, several notable works emerged from Albert Eglash and others that argued for a restorative use of community service focused on repairing harms caused to victims and successfully reintegrating offenders into their communities though the use of service work. Research on restorative applications of community service has focused on its use as a symbolic or even literal type of restitution to the community and on its ability to foster interactions between community members and offenders. Within restorative justice, however, the use of community service is not unanimously supported. Some proponents of restorative justice have argued that community service, whatever its merits, fails to directly address the harms caused to victims. Others have pointed out the problem of old wine in new wineskins, arguing in effect that community service programs that use work crews or other punitive practices have simply been relabeled as restorative for the reason that they have some tangible benefit to the community.

Community Service Outcomes

The majority of research on the use of community service programs has focused on whether such programs decrease recidivism. Overwhelmingly, such research indicates either a small reduction or no net increase in reoffending. Other research on community service has focused on individual indicators—for example, rates of completion—as

These young offenders were assigned to clear snow from a set of stairs as part of a community service program in January 2010. Studies of community service program results have overwhelmingly found either a small reduction or no net increase in reoffending. Other research has made a connection between reduced recidivism and rates of offender satisfaction with their service assignments.

well as community indicators—for example, the contributions of offenders to nonprofit or public agencies measured in hours or in the monetary value of service work. One of the best-known studies on community service is Douglas McDonald's research on the Vera Institute service program in New York City, published in 1986. McDonald's research found that this program at the very least did not increase recidivism, that it was able to effectively divert many offenders from incarceration, and that it was able to provide significant cost savings to the city in the form of more than 60,000 hours of unpaid labor. A more recent study of community service as used by Vermont Reparative Probationers found high rates of program completion for offenders (91 percent) and high rates of agency satisfaction for organizations involved in this program (94 percent).

Survey, assessment, and participant observation research on participant involvement in community service programs has been cautiously positive. One study of 19 adult community service programs in the United States found that both offenders and victims believed the requirements of such programs were fair, and offenders who completed the programs by and large viewed their experience as useful. A study on the use of youth restorative community service in Deschutes County, Oregon, found that this program was able to address and serve immediate community needs, such as the building of low-income housing, and also found significant community support in the form of both time and funding from community volunteers and organizations. A study on the use of youth restorative community service in Clark County, Washington, focused on the transition from work crews to service projects where youth worked side by side with community members and found that such work increased rates of completion for youth offenders, solicited substantial community volunteerism in service projects, and allowed community organizations to propose projects that met local community needs.

International research on the use of community service has also found high levels of offender satisfaction with service work in countries such as New Zealand and Scotland. Research from Scotland on the use of community service has also found an important connection between reduced recidivism and rates of offender satisfaction with service assignments, suggesting that how offenders perceive the quality and purpose of their community service work may contribute to lower rates of reoffending.

William R. Wood
University of Auckland

See Also: Corrections; Courts; History of Crime and Punishment in America: 1970–Present; Juvenile Corrections, History of; Law Enforcement Assistance Administration; Probation; Rehabilitation; Sentencing.

Further Readings
Bazemore, G. and D. R. Karp. "A Civic Justice Corps: Community Service as a Means of Reintegration." *Justice Policy Journal*, v.1 (2004).
Tonry, M. and M. Lynch. "Intermediate Sanctions." *Crime and Justice: A Review of Research*, v.20 (1996).

Compton, California

Compton is a city in Los Angeles County, California, located south and east of downtown Los Angeles. The 2006 population was 95,701, a 2.3 percent increase since 2000. The area of the city is approximately 10 square miles. The largest racial group in Compton is African American (40.3 percent), but the largest ethnic group is Hispanic or Latino (56.8 percent; people of Hispanic or Latino origin can be of any race). The city also has a growing Pacific Islander community (1.1 percent). In 2000, 31.4 percent of the population was foreign born. The median household income in Compton is $31,819, well below the California average of $47,493, and 28 percent of the population lives below the poverty line (versus 14.2 percent for California as a whole). A higher percentage of firms in Compton are owned by African Americans (27.8 percent) and Hispanics (37.4 percent) than in California as a whole (3.9 percent and 14.7 percent, respectively).

The area that is now Compton was originally claimed for Spain but was ceded to the United States after the Mexican–American War in 1848 and was incorporated in 1889. The first settlers were primarily white, but African Americans began migrating to the area in larger numbers in the 1940s, settling mainly in the western side of the city, while the eastern side remained largely white. The first African American was elected to the City Council in 1961 and in 1969 Douglas Dollarhide became the first African American mayor. In 1973, he was succeeded by Dora A. Davis, the first African American female mayor of metropolitan city.

In 1952, Compton received an All American City honor from the Civic League, and in 1960, the median income was twice that of Watts (a primarily African American area in the city of Los Angeles, located about 11 miles north of Compton), while unemployment was also much lower. In these years, the city offered a stable working-class and middle-class environment to its residents. In 1963, Compton elected its first black mayor. However, after the Watts riots in 1965, many business owners and middle-class residents, both African American and white, left the area, and unemployment and crime both rose. Compton became a center of gang activity: The Crips were founded in 1969 Watts (now known as South Central Los Angeles, and the Bloods in 1970 on Piru Street in Compton. The emblematic color of the Bloods, red, is the school color of the Centennial High School in Compton.

In the 1980s and 1990s, Compton became a symbol of urban decay and gang violence. A survey by the RAND Corporation in 1982 declared Compton a disaster area, and a 1992 survey found that half of all black men ages 21–24 in Compton were affiliated with gangs. Compton's negative image was crystallized by the 1988 album *Straight Outta Compton* by the rap group N.W.A., which ushered in the era of "gangsta rap" and achieved double platinum status despite minimal airplay due to profanity and violent lyrics (including the controversial track "F*** tha Police").

In 1991, the murder rate in Compton was three times that of the city of Los Angeles. Over 50 people were killed in the riots following the acquittal of four white Los Angeles Police Department officers for the beating of Rodney King (which was captured on videotape and played repeatedly on television during the trial), but partly in response to this extreme violence, the Crips and Bloods agreed to a truce. Crime declined in much of the Los Angeles area in the 1990s and Compton was no exception. Although gang membership remained high—with an estimated 65 gangs and 10,000 members in Compton in 1998—the number of murders committed in Compton declined to 48 in 1998 (versus 87 in 1991) and to 28 in 2008. The drop in crime was attributed to several causes, including the waning of the crack epidemic, California's three strikes law (Proposition 184), which took effect in 1994, and California's ban on semiautomatic weapons that took effect in 1989.

In 2000, the Los Angeles County sheriff's department took over policing of Compton due to a scandal involving Compton Mayor Omar Bradley, later convicted on felony corruption charges. The city is patrolled by 79 deputies and a gang unit with 38 members, and significant efforts are devoted to community policing, which has improved the relationship between the city residents and the force. However, the overall crime level in Compton remains high relative to other U.S. cities. According to the CQ Press rankings (based on Federal Bureau of Investigation [FBI] statistics from 2009), in 2010, Compton had the eighth highest crime rate in the country with a score of 260.13 (where 0 would indicate an average crime rate and a positive number a higher than average rate) and the second-highest crime rate among cities with populations of 75,000 to 99,999. According to FBI statistics, in 2008, 1,738 violent crimes were reported in Compton, including 28 cases of murder or non-negligent manslaughter, 48 forcible rapes, 595 robberies, and 1,067 aggravated assaults; 3,333 property crimes were reported in that year, including 896 burglaries, 1,409 larceny-thefts, 1,028 motor vehicle thefts, and 95 cases of arson.

Sarah Boslaugh
Kennesaw State University

See Also: African Americans; Gangs, Contemporary; Gangs, History of; Gangs, Sociology of; Racism; Riots.

Further Readings
Bennett, Jessica. "Straight Into Compton: How the Country's Murder Capital Got Its Groove Back." *Newsweek* (March 24, 2009).
CQ Press. "City Crime Rankings 2010–2011." http://os.cqpress.com/citycrime/2010/citycrime2010-2011.htm (Accessed June 2011).
Public Broadcasting Service. "Crips and Bloods: Made in America." http://www.pbs.org/independentlens/cripsandbloods (Accessed June 2010).
U.S. Department of Justice, Federal Bureau of Investigation. "2008 Crime in the United States." http://www2.fbi.gov/ucr/cius2008 (Accessed June 2008).

Computer Crime

Virtually unknown 20 years ago, computer crime has rapidly become part of daily life. Computer crime, also known as cybercrime, includes a range of criminal activity associated with computers or networks. Cybercrimes include the theft of property or identity, stalking and bullying, child pornography, and the distribution of illegal goods and services. Computer crime also includes denial of service attacks, securities fraud, and a variety of emerging issues regarding copyright and intellectual property. Due to the disruptive potential of crimes directed at businesses or governments, computer crime also raises concerns about terrorism or cyber warfare.

Although technological breakthroughs have always created new opportunities for criminal behavior, the pace of change has accelerated because of rapid advancements in processing power, access to technology, and the expansion of networks used to access computer-based technology. This technology allows criminals to operate more efficiently and effectively, often with minimal surveillance. Because these crimes are not detected or investigated through traditional law enforcement tools, they present a significant challenge for the justice system.

According to Federal Bureau of Investigation (FBI) estimates, U.S. businesses spend around $67 billion each year dealing with computer theft and malicious programs such as viruses and spyware. The Internet Crime Complaint Center (IC3), a partnership between the FBI, Bureau of Justice Assistance, and National White-Collar Crime Center, also estimates a total loss of $559 million in 2009 related to a variety of frauds, including scams asking for advance fees associated with a large return from a fake lottery or estate, nondelivery of merchandise or payment, and other crime related to consumer goods and services. The number increased substantially in 2009, more than doubling the 2008 estimate of $265 million.

Computers as Targets of Cybercrime

The targets of computer crimes include both individuals and organizations. Crimes against individuals target the person's property, or in the case of stalking and bullying, the person is the target. The computer itself was the target of many of the first cybercrimes. Cybercriminals, often motivated by curiosity and challenge more than by personal gain, exploited opportunities to access other computers. The infringement on the privacy of others, which may include damage to files, software, or other property, is known as hacking. The first hackers were younger computer users who engaged in hacking as a hobby that provided an opportunity to develop and demonstrate their computer skills. The initial hackers were not interested in harming

An instructor at the U.S. Department of Defense Cyber Investigations Training Academy in Linthicum, Maryland, teaching methods of forensic analysis of cybercrime in September 2010. Changes in the National Information Infrastructure Protection Act as a result of the USA PATRIOT Act have made it easier to investigate and prosecute certain cybercrimes.

others. In fact, they were often helpful in efforts to identify and reduce security risks.

Cybercriminals soon moved beyond simply accessing other computers to a more active effort to control these computers or the networks to which they are attached. Computer viruses and worms, transferred through the exchange of infected files or embedded in Trojan horses or other seemingly benign files, have the potential to quickly spread from one system to another. Once infected, files and information on the computer are altered or destroyed as the virus actively seeks other computers to infect. A virus can hide and replicate itself, wait harmlessly until activated, delete or transfer files and information, post messages on the user's screen, and interfere with the use of printers or other peripherals. In a cycle of development often demonstrating escalating skill levels, individuals, businesses, and governments have spent billions on the development of antivirus and antispyware software, often staying just a step ahead of cybercriminals.

Vandalism and defacement are also examples of crimes directed at computers. Cybervandalism ranges from sending destructive viruses and worms to hacker attacks designed to disrupt or destroy entire computer networks. Vandals may delete information needed by legitimate users or install programs that deny users from accessing this information. Hackers may also vandalize a Website or personal computer in order to display political, religious, or other malicious messages.

Hacking has reached a global level, often targeting businesses or governments. For example, a hacker group known as Anonymous successfully organized denial-of-service attacks that disrupted service at Visa and MasterCard after these corporations stopped allowing donations to WikiLeaks. Like WikiLeaks, Anonymous and similar groups use the Internet to highlight what they see as illegal or unethical corporate or government behavior. Although these organizations target computers, their actions also demonstrate the use of computers as a tool for protest and/or financial gain.

Computers as Tools for Cybercriminals

Rather than targeting the computer or network, other computer crimes use technology as a tool for the completion of a crime. These crimes include fraudulent use of credit and debit cards, unauthorized access to bank accounts, and theft from accrual, conversion, or transfer accounts. Because of the prevalence of technology, cybercriminals can steal millions of dollars by using technology to skim a few cents, or less, from billions of routine transactions performed every day.

While embezzlement and fraud are not new crimes, technology has changed the rules. Similarly, stalking and bullying are examples of existing crimes that have evolved to take advantage of technological tools. Cyberstalking refers to the use of the Internet, e-mail, or other electronic communication methods to stalk another person. Some stalkers pursue minors through online chat rooms, while others harass their victims through social networking or other online or electronic communication. Cyberstalking can range from simple harassment, threatening or intimidating a victim, or repeated attempts to communicate with the victim. Since computers and the Internet provide a safe haven for the cyberstalker, while also providing a place to exhibit uninhibited conduct, this crime can be difficult to identify and address.

Stalking and exploitation have grown to the extent that these crimes reach beyond inexperienced computer users to impact individuals who assume they are well protected and fully aware of threats encountered with the use of technology. Although stalking and exploitation have always been challenging issues for the justice system, the use of technology in order to complete these crimes creates an enormous challenge. Similarly, bullying has always been a challenge for parents, schools, and the justice system. Cyberbullying inflicts and compounds the harm of traditional bullying but does so through the medium of electronic text.

Cyberspying, another growing concern associated with both crime and privacy, involves accessing computer files or using the Internet to gather private and confidential information. While hackers may access confidential information through illicit means, many willingly share a large amount of information on Facebook and other sites with social networking features. For example, crime may occur when an individual posts vacation pictures celebrating a trip. This announcement also notifies friends and others that the potential victim's house may be empty. On a larger scale, techniques used by cybercriminals may include data mining, which involves the analysis of cumulative data about an individual's financial history, habits, preferences, and other unique traits.

Technology has also provided new opportunities for cybercrime associated with child pornography, money laundering, gambling, and the distribution of illegal substances. In addition to new laws and policies, law enforcement has responded to this category of computer crime by taking advantage of the privacy that is so attractive to cybercriminals. For example, child predators have been targeted by investigations in which law enforcement officers pose as children in an attempt to lure predators to a certain location for an arrest. Gaming Websites have also been infiltrated, and charges brought, as a result of similar sting operations.

Opportunities for Cybercrime
Other computer crimes are the result of the massive opportunity created due to the widespread use of computers and technology. These crimes are committed by groups or individuals actively involved in cybercrime as well as citizens who break the law, willingly or otherwise, because it has become so easy to do so. Computer theft and the black market for technology are simple examples of this type of criminal activity. Similarly, technology has advanced to the point where amateurs can easily engage in counterfeiting. As with other types of cybercrime, the justice system has responded to these challenges by relying on technological advances that make it more difficult to profit from breaking the law.

Crimes in this category also target industries, individuals, and businesses in order to engage in criminal activity ranging from music trading, software piracy, and other infringement of copyright and intellectual property rights. These crimes occur, in part, as the result of confusion about ownership. For example while an individual knows it is wrong to steal a computer, the ownership of software, music, and movies is not immediately apparent. It can also be difficult to define a victim when the crime is limited to downloading music from Websites using programs that facilitate file sharing.

The policy response to this type of cybercrime includes education, increased threats, and reliance on technological advances that monitor the sharing of digital media. This monitoring can lead to a DMCA (Digital Millenium Copyright Act) warning, an informational first step provided by the Internet provider, potentially followed by legal action. While the DMCA increases penalties for online copyright infringement and criminalizes efforts to defeat copyright protections, the initial policy response to this type of cybercrime includes the opportunity to learn about copyright laws. The cybercriminal, who may be a computer-savvy child with a great music collection, has the opportunity to conform to these laws before facing further legal action. The DMCA also addresses repeat behavior by authorizing both civil and criminal penalties, including imprisonment and fines up to $1 million.

Identity theft is another example of a crime that relies on the ubiquitous use of computers and technology. Identity thieves use a variety of electronic tools, often relying on the individual's limited understanding of computers, to collect social security numbers, credit card information, and other unique information to gain access to a person's financial data. Phishing, one of the best-known tools used by cybercriminals, uses e-mail or Websites to steal personal and financial information. Computer criminals have become increasingly sophisticated in their efforts to make it difficult to distinguish legitimate e-mail and Website content from illegitimate ones, so Internet users have been forced to become similarly creative, educated, and suspicious in order to protect themselves from cybercriminals.

While the majority of Internet users have learned to identify and avoid these risks, much as people have learned to minimize risk in the nonvirtual world, phishing and related scams only need to succeed for a small number of people when the scam is operating on a global level. Research supported by the financial services industry reports that more than 11 million adults were victims of identity theft and fraud in 2009. The total cost of these crimes was more than $54 billion. The number of victims actually decreased considerably in 2010, down to just over eight million people, but the cost of identity fraud increased to $631 per incident, up 63 percent from the previous year. The decreased number of incidents may be attributable to increased security by the general public and financial institutions, although the increasing cost of such crimes can be financially devastating for victims.

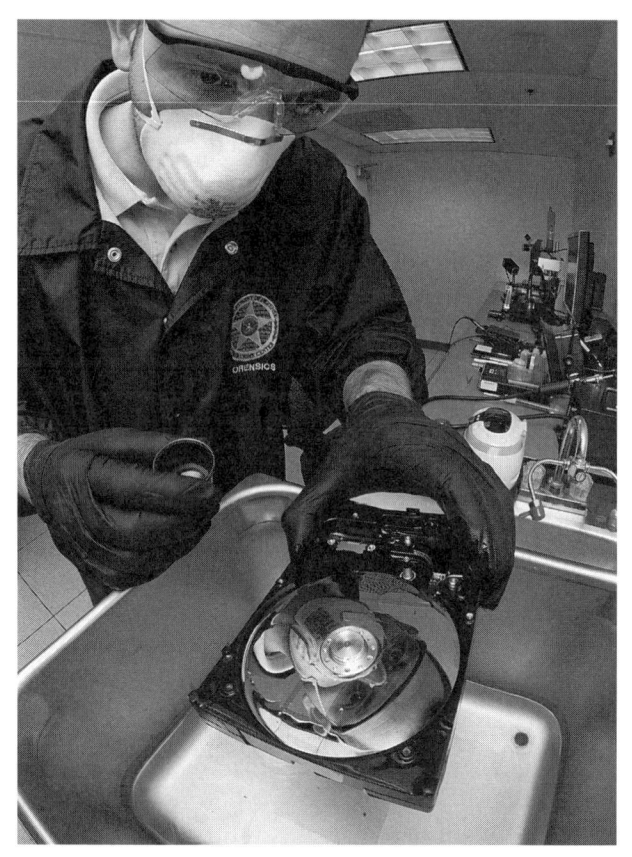

A forensic technician cleaning a hard drive in a 91 percent alcohol/9 percent water solution. Such cleaning may allow for the recovery of crucial evidence in an investigation.

Responding to Computer Crime

While law enforcement agencies are typically bound by geography, computer criminals can treat the whole world as their target. While leading to a vast number of potential victims, the global nature of cybercrime leads to unique challenges for the justice system.

Like computer crime, the enforcement of cybercrime is evolving. Based on the uniqueness of this criminal activity, Congress has treated computer-related crime as a distinct federal offense since 1984. Identity theft became a federal crime in 1998, with most states passing similar laws against identity theft since then. The attacks of 9/11 also impacted the definition of, and response to, computer crime. The USA PATRIOT Act amended parts of the National Information Infrastructure Protection Act in order to make it easier to investigate and prosecute crimes against crucial computer systems.

Federal and state law enforcement agencies have also increased their efforts to collaborate in a variety of ways, including the coordination of activities completed by law enforcement agencies involved in investigating cybercrime. Local police departments have also responded to new challenges by creating specialized units focusing on specific types of cybercrime, with undercover officers actively involved with the investigation of gambling, child pornography, and the distribution and sale of illegal goods and services.

Though contemporary techniques have increased the effectiveness and efficiency of justice agencies charged with responding to cybercrime, critics are concerned that these efforts have compromised the privacy and liberty of U.S. citizens who have not engaged in criminal activity. While the level of intrusion and surveillance citizens will tolerate may depend on the perception of risk, computer crime has rapidly become a massive problem and people may not fully comprehend the risks to both security and liberty. Cybercriminals have also demonstrated the ability to respond very quickly to new opportunities for criminal gain, in spite of increased efforts to stop their behaviors.

As with other questions about crime, there are issues regarding the balance of security and liberty. Although the justice system has a long history of protecting rights in the face of threats, cybercrime has accelerated these efforts to uncomfortable levels, and there will be continued policy changes in response to the challenges of computer crime.

Kenneth W. Mentor
University of North Carolina

See Also: Confidence Games and Frauds; Identity Theft; Pornography; Terrorism.

Further Readings

Balkin, Jack M., James Grimmelmann, Eddan Katz, Nimrod Kozlovski, Shlomit Wagman, and Tal Zarsky. *CYBERCRIME: Digital Cops in a Networked World*. New York: New York University Press, 2007.

Bloss, W. P. *Under a Watchful Eye: Privacy Rights and Criminal Justice*. Westport, CT: Praeger, 2009.

Britz, Marjie T. *Computer Forensics and Cyber Crime: An Introduction*, 2nd ed. Upper Saddle River, NJ: Prentice Hall, 2009.

Clarke, Richard and Robert Knake. *Cyber War: The Next Threat to National Security and What to Do About It*. New York: HarperCollins, 2010.

Federal Bureau of Investigation. *The IC3 2009 Annual Report on Internet Crime*. Washington, DC: Federal Bureau of Investigation, 2010.

Kerr, Ian, Valerie Steeves, and Carole Lucock, eds. *Lessons From the Identity Trail: Anonymity, Privacy, and Identity in a Networked Society*. New York: Oxford University Press, 2009.

Knetzger, Michael and Jeremy Muraski. *Investigating High-Tech Crime*. Upper Saddle River, NJ: Prentice Hall, 2008.

McQuade, Samuel C. *Understanding and Managing Cybercrime*. Upper Saddle River, NJ: Prentice Hall, 2006.

Solove, Daniel J. and Paul M. Schwartz. *Privacy, Information, and Technology*. New York: Aspen Publishers, 2008.

Taylor, Robert, et al. *Digital Crime and Digital Terrorism*, 2nd ed. Upper Saddle River, NJ: Prentice Hall, 2011.

Comstock Law

In 1873, Congress passed An Act for the Suppression of Trade in, and Circulation of, Obscene Literature and Articles of Immoral Use, better known as the Comstock Law or Federal Anti-Obscenity Act. The act expanded upon 1842 legislation designed to impede the importation of "obscene" materials, 1865 legislation to curb the thriving wartime "obscenity" business, and 1872 legislation that included "obscene" postcards. Upon the initiative of Anthony Comstock (1844–1915), Congress expanded the legislative purview by broadening the definition of obscenity to include information concerning abortion and birth control.

Comstock moved to New York City after the Civil War. Dismayed by an urban life fettered with prostitution, "obscene" novels and pamphlets, and pornography, Comstock became a leader in the New York Society for the Suppression of Vice, founded in 1872 and sponsored by the Young Men's Christian Association. Blending traditional Christian moral language with new concepts of state regulation of issues previously considered private, Comstock convinced numerous philanthropists that not only vice but also abortion and birth control undermined public morality. Comstock included the latter two because he believed the younger generation's reading of "lascivious" material reflected increasing promiscuity that could be concealed with contraceptives and abortion. He latched onto the postal office because he feared the privacy entailed there allowed people to transmit morally offensive materials.

Congress obliged Comstock and passed the act with little discussion and no roll-call vote. No federal restrictions on abortion or birth control existed prior to 1873, and many legislators were unaware that the act included these two matters, believing instead that it merely strengthened regulation of pornographic and other indecent materials. President Ulysses Grant signed the law on March 4, 1873. The act eliminated "nefarious and diabolical traffic" in "vile and immoral goods" from the postal service. It banned the selling or distribution of materials that could be used for abortion or birth control; forbade importation, mailing, and interstate transportation of obscene books, articles, and literature, including those dealing with contraceptives and abortion; and empowered the U.S. Postal Service to censor any such materials. The law carried a fine of between $100 and $5,000 for each offense, or jail and hard labor for at least one year and not more than 10.

This law passed within the historical context of antiobscenity and social purity crusades. Reformers looked to the federal government to regulate issues they believed were undermining the moral fabric of American society—a society experiencing rapid change as a result of industrialization, urbanization, and immigration. The law fit well within the growing concerns of elite white Anglo-Saxon Protestants who feared their inundation by increased fertility among the lower classes, especially among immigrants considered racially and morally inferior. In addition to this moral aspect, Congress passed the act to substantiate its right to regulate the interstate flow of "lewd" and vulgar materials through the postal system.

Enforcement

Enforcing the Comstock Law proved difficult. Congress appointed Comstock as a special agent of the U.S. Postal Service from 1873 until 1915, but the lack of funding for additional agents made implementation onerous. His main tactic was entrapment: He wrote to doctors pretending to be a young pregnant woman, seduced, abandoned, and in need of abortion information. When doctors accepted cash from the letter and mailed back abortive preparations, Comstock arrested them. Yet juries were often reluctant to find defendants guilty. Even Grant pardoned nearly 50 percent of those indicted for contraceptive violations; President Rutherford B. Hayes similarly pardoned some defendants.

Attempts to repeal the law, however, were unsuccessful. In 1876, the National Liberal League protested the law as unconstitutional because it imposed specific moral and medical mandates. Nearly a half century later, Mary Ware Dennett and the Voluntary Parenthood League worked to introduce the Cummins-Vaile Bill in 1923 to repeal Comstock as an infringement on free speech and press. Margaret Sanger and the National Committee on Federal Legislation attempted to amend the law to exempt medical professionals. Her campaign from 1929 to 1935 became moot with federal court decisions. While *Bours v. United States* (1915) laid a foundation, the case of *United States v. One Package* (1935) exempted doctors from the contraceptive aspects of the law, thereby allowing hospitals and freestanding birth-control clinics to multiply, and *Bolger v. Youngs Drug Products Corp.* (1983) declared that preventing Americans from receiving truthful contraceptive information was harmful. In 1971, Congress eliminated the reference to birth control from the law; in 1994, it increased the fine for the abortion provision from $5,000 to $250,000 for a first-time offense; and in 1996, it extended the abortion stipulation to the Internet.

Although the law remains, the government takes little action to enforce it. Even during the law's height at the turn of the 20th century, millions of women ignored it, evidenced by the continued decline in the fertility rate of white and black women, especially among the urban middle and upper classes.

While usually associated with abortion and birth control, the law also censored other aspects of society. Agents raided low-rent pornography shops and cheap mail-order pornography services; censored art, with Paul Emile Chabas's "September Morn" in 1912 as one example; and banned books mailed to libraries and bookstores. The law targeted classics such as Aristophanes's *Lysistrata*, Rabelais's *Gargantua and Pantagruel*, Chaucer's *Canterbury Tales*, Boccaccio's *Decameron*, DeFoe's *Moll Flanders*, the *Arabian Nights*, Rousseau's *Confessions*, and Voltaire's *Candide*. Modern authors such as D. H. Lawrence, John Dos Passos, William Faulkner, F. Scott Fitzgerald, Oscar Wilde, Ernest Hemingway, John Steinbeck, and Eugene O'Neill also faced censorship; most famously, James Joyce's *Ulysses* came before Judge John Woolsey, whose decision in 1933 that the book was not obscene initiated a change in legislative and judicial interpretations of free speech with regard to obscenity. Still, courts were slower to overturn these aspects of the law than the contraceptive aspects. In *Miller v. California* (1973), the Supreme Court declared that works were obscene if they lacked serious artistic merit, violated contemporary moral standards, or portrayed sex in a blatantly odious manner.

Simone M. Caron
Wake Forest University

See Also: Abortion; *Griswold v. Connecticut*; *Roe v. Wade*; *United States v. One Book Called "Ulysses."*

Further Readings
Beisel, Nicola. *Imperiled Innocents: Anthony Comstock and Family Reproduction in Victorian America*. Princeton, NJ: Princeton University Press, 1997.
Reagan, Leslie J. *When Abortion Was a Crime: Women, Medicine and Law in the United States, 1867–1973*. Berkeley: University of California Press, 1997.
Tone, Andrea. *Devices and Desires: A History of Contraceptives in America*. New York: Hill & Wang, 2002.

Confession

The pursuit of a confession from a criminal accused is a pivotal development in the early stages of law enforcement's "often competitive

Harry F. Powers, known as the "Bluebeard of Quiet Dell," confessing to murder in Clarksburg, West Virginia, in August 1931. He later recanted but was hanged in 1932 for multiple murders.

enterprise of ferreting out crime." Framed from a legal perspective, a confession is a statement made by an alleged suspect who is the focus of a criminal investigation, which is adverse to the penal interests of the accused. *Black's Law Dictionary* defines a confession as "a criminal suspect's oral or written acknowledgment of guilt, often including details about the crime," which usually concerns "the truth of the main fact charged or some essential part of it." Once obtained, the state prosecution may seek to utilize the out-of-court statement against the accused at trial. Therefore, it is critically important that the confession be made voluntarily or willingly, free from any coercion, and as a by-product of the confessor's free will and choice.

Anglo-American legal jurisprudence has carefully developed standards to ensure confessions are competent to be received as evidence at trial and to safeguard against any of the inherent evils that arise from the rigors of custodial interrogation. The main concerns underlying the confession of an accused arise from the dynamic pressures surrounding the making of such an admission. Jurisprudential experience with the criminal procedure, as well as psychological and sociological insight into human factors, have exposed the grave likelihood that an accused may render a confession as a result of intense interrogation, the incommunicado ambiance of police questioning, the pressures of coercion, and/or the attendant perplexity and confusion of confrontation rather than as a lucid and introspective choice by the confessor. Despite advancements in the quality and training of law enforcement officers with regard to interrogation techniques, many legal scholars and jurists have recognized that police interrogation still takes place in secluded settings that are unfamiliar to the suspect, who is separated from any familiar faces and stripped of any meaningful support.

With these concerns as the foundation of confessional jurisprudence, the overriding principle since common law has been trustworthiness. Trustworthiness was the traditional doctrine used by courts in England and the United States to exclude confessions. The trustworthiness doctrine emphasized the notions of freeness and voluntariness as the cornerstones that make a confession credible. American criminal procedure was in need of some constitutional bases encompassing the law of confessions, which extended beyond the common law to ensure greater protections.

Due Process Clause

The due process clause of the Fourteenth Amendment to the U.S. Constitution provides in pertinent part, "[N]or shall any State deprive any person of life, liberty, or property, without due process of law …" In the context of confessions, this language has a profound implication, the meaning of which has been shaped and interpreted by various decisions from the U.S. Supreme Court. The protection of by the due process clause of the Constitution has been made applicable to and is binding upon the several states.

In the earliest seminal decision, *Brown v. State of Mississippi* (1936), a farmer named Raymond Stewart was discovered beaten to death on the grounds of his home in Kemper County, Mississippi, on March, 30, 1934. Outraged by the brutal killing, town locals turned vigilantes sought to bring someone to justice. A mob assembled and pursued three African American males—Ed

Brown, a tenant on the deceased farmer's land, Yank Ellington, and Henry Shields—whom they suspected committed the heinous crime. The mob, accompanied by a deputy sheriff, confronted Ellington. He vehemently denied the accusations and maintained his innocence. The group of vigilantes, backed by the color of law, repeatedly hung Ellington from a rope tied to a tree and let him down only for sporadic rests. Demanding that he confess, the mob then tied him to a tree and violently whipped him. He continued to protest his innocence. Although he was released, the deputy, accompanied by a member of the unruly mob, returned two days later to arrest Ellington. En route to take Ellington to jail, the deputy detoured and proceeded to whip him yet again, and threatened the beating would continue until he confessed. Finally, Ellington agreed to comply with the deputy's desires and confess to any statement as directed by the deputy. All three men were arrested for the murder.

At the trial, the defendants testified about the brutal tactics that surrounded the making of their coerced confessions. The prosecution did not refute the defendants' account of the interrogation tactics. By the same token, the defense neither moved to suppress the confessions nor sought a mistrial. As such, the defendants were convicted and sentenced to death. An appeal was taken to the Mississippi Supreme Court, which upheld the trial court's conviction based on a failure to timely object to the confessions. The defendants' attempt to have the state's high court review its decision proved futile. Finally, an appeal before the U.S. Supreme Court was granted.

In *Brown*, the U.S. Supreme Court established that brutal police tactics in any form employed to coerce a confession from a suspect directly contravene and violate the explicit demand of the due process of law under the Constitution. Consequently, any coercive police conduct that would reasonably elicit from a suspect a statement that is not the product of free will and choice violates due process and renders any resulting confession a nullity. The due process of law dictates that an involuntary confession acquired through coercive means is inadmissible in a criminal trial. The *Brown* decision would shape the legal landscape of confessional law for years to come.

In the decades that followed the *Brown* decision, the due process limitation was interpreted to have several objectives, which constituted a complex system of values: (1) the trustworthiness concern of a confession that is procured through unfair means or gross violations, which is presumptively unreliable; (2) the due process concern of deterring future police misconduct; (3) the voluntariness of the confession under the totality of the circumstances—an analysis which, among other things, included the relevant characteristics of the suspect and his or her susceptibility to the pressures of police tactics.

Fifth Amendment to the U.S. Constitution

The self-incrimination clause, also referred to as the privilege against self-incrimination, of the Fifth Amendment to the Constitution of the United States of America provides that no one "shall be compelled in any criminal case to be a witness against himself." Taken at face value, this constitutional protection seems to only encompass being made a witness against oneself in a court of law, not in a police interrogation room or elsewhere. However, in *Bram v. United States* (1897), the U.S. Supreme Court overturned a conviction on Fifth Amendment grounds and found that there was no meaningful distinction between compulsion inside as opposed to outside a courtroom. Although the precedent of *Bram* existed, and was argued by the defense attorneys in *Brown*, courts were reluctant to apply the Fifth Amendment as a constitutional power source of exclusion. Aside from the plain meaning of the text, another reason for not invoking the self-incrimination clause was the historical and original intent of the Fifth Amendment as a proscription on the power of the federal government rather than a grant of power.

Following decades of meager precedential value—during which it was not yet accepted that the protections of the federal Constitution were binding upon state courts—the self-incrimination clause was revived in the momentous decision of *Miranda v. Arizona* (1966). In *Miranda*, the Supreme Court was confronted with deciding the constitutionality of law enforcement officers interrogating criminal defendants while in custody, or otherwise having their freedom curtailed, without being notified of their right to counsel. Along with *Miranda*, the Supreme Court decided three other consolidated cases: *Westover v. United States*, *Vignera v. New York*, and *California v. Stewart*.

In the case of Ernesto Arturo Miranda, officers arrested him based on circumstantial evidence loosely connecting him to the kidnapping and rape of an 18-year-old victim. Police officers interrogated Ernesto Miranda for two hours, at which point he orally confessed to the crime and signed a sworn written statement, which included a provision that his confession was free and voluntary and not the product of coercion, threat, or physical harm. The officers never informed Miranda—neither prior to nor during the interrogation—of his right to the assistance of counsel, his right to remain silent, or that any statements he made would be used against him. At trial, the prosecution attempted to introduce Miranda's written confession as evidence against him. Miranda's court-appointed lawyer, Alvin Moore, argued that the confession should be excluded on the grounds that it was not free and voluntary since he was not properly informed of his rights. The trial court overruled the objection, and Miranda was convicted and sentenced to a term of imprisonment. Following the conviction, Miranda appealed to the Arizona Supreme Court, which affirmed the conviction since the trial court found he did not specifically seek the assistance of an attorney. The U.S. Supreme Court granted him an appeal.

The *Miranda* court, in a 5–4 decision with Chief Justice Earl Warren penning the opinion for the majority, established a series of warnings or prophylactic safeguards to ensure the right of an accused against compelled self-incrimination under the Fifth Amendment. The reason the warnings are often referred to as prophylactic is because they are not explicitly mandated by the

At the moment when questioning by law enforcement becomes "custodial interrogation," defined as "questioning initiated after a person has been taken into custody or otherwise deprived of his freedom of action in any significant way," Miranda warnings become necessary. Not only must a suspect be warned of his or her rights prior to interrogation but the rights entailed in those warnings must be expressly waived by the suspect before any interrogation takes place.

text of the Fifth Amendment but instead are judicially created mediums to ensure the protections of the Fifth Amendment are afforded. In unpacking the reasoning for the majority, Chief Justice Warren carefully examined various police manuals and texts, which proved valuable insight into the police practices of the day. The police techniques depicted psychological ploys and manipulative tricks calculated to tire the will of a suspect during interrogation. Some examples include the proverbial good cop–bad cop routine, the unassuming false friend, and blatant misrepresentations or lies regarding other evidence against the accused. Under such circumstances, the court reasoned that it was necessary to have protective devices or warnings that mitigate the inherently coercive atmosphere of custodial interrogation.

The *Miranda* precedent demanded that a suspect, prior to any custodial interrogation, be warned that (1) he/she has the right to remain silent, (2) anything said by him/her may be used against him/her in a criminal prosecution, (3) he/she has the right to consult with an attorney and (4) counsel will be appointed if he/she cannot afford to retain one himself/herself. Not only must a suspect be warned of his/her rights prior to interrogation, but the court also held the rights entailed in those warnings must be expressly waived by the suspect before any interrogation takes place.

Two significant concepts to the *Miranda* decision are custodial interrogation and waiver. Pinpointing the moment that interrogation by law enforcement becomes custodial is central to triggering the necessity for *Miranda* warnings. Custodial interrogation means "questioning initiated after a person has been taken into custody or otherwise deprived of his freedom of action in any significant way." The court has clearly distinguished situations where a suspect is the focus of police investigation from custody by explaining that in the former, *Miranda* warnings are not required if the investigative efforts of police officers occur before the suspect has been taken into custody. Courts utilize an objective standard to determine custody in which the relevant inquiry is whether a reasonable person in the suspect's position would feel believe he/she was in police custody of the quality associated with formal arrest—not whether the suspect subjectively felt he/she was in custody or free to leave.

Criticisms

Miranda has garnered both support and disfavor. On the one hand, *Miranda* serves a useful and instructive purpose by reinforcing the rights of the citizenry in the daily practice of police officers. By the same token, *Miranda* helps ensure that the uneducated segments of our society are essentially warned of what is at stake during interrogation. Furthermore, *Miranda* provides uniformity, predictability, and constancy in the court system and in the case law. These warnings have been embraced by all facets of popular media and culture, so much so that most people have a working understanding of their rights. On the other hand, prosecutors, politicians, law enforcement groups, scholars, and the public at large felt the *Miranda* decision unnecessarily hindered police investigations and provided suspects with a loophole to escape liability. Critics predicted that the ruling would "handcuff the police," and that police efforts would be thwarted because suspects would refuse to talk or go free based on what critics perceived to be a technicality.

Initially, the decision took center stage in the political arena. During the 1968 presidential campaign, Richard Nixon commented the *Miranda* decision "had the effect of seriously ham stringing [sic] the peace forces in our society and strengthening the criminal forces." The Senate Judiciary Committee held hearings into the benefits and drawbacks of the *Miranda* requirements and ultimately concluded that crime would not be effectively decreased if criminals who have voluntarily confessed are released on mere technicalities. Various efforts in the legal and legislative forums were made to overturn *Miranda*.

Challenges to *Miranda*

The greatest challenge the *Miranda* ruling faced was the threat of repeal by Congress. In response to rising crime rates and an influx of urban riots, Congress passed the Crime Control and Safe Streets Act of 1968. Congress made an explicit attempt to repeal *Miranda* as applied in federal prosecutions. The law provided that confessions that were given voluntarily could be used in federal court regardless of whether the suspect was warned of his rights as required under *Miranda*. Perceiving *Miranda* to be nothing more than a procedural matter, the federal government argued that Congress maintains the enumerated power to create, modify, or set aside any judicial rules of evidence and procedure. In *Dickerson v. United States* (2000), approximately 34 years after the pronouncement of *Miranda*, the viability of the warnings as a constitutionally compelled rule was called into serious doubt. In deciding whether Congress possessed the constitutional authority to repeal *Miranda*, the Supreme Court reasoned that *Miranda* was constitutionally compelled and that the legislature had no authority to supersede the judiciary's interpretation and application of the Constitution.

Today, *Miranda* remains vitally prominent and relevant in the context of law enforcement interrogation and confessional jurisprudence. As recently as 2010, the Supreme Court addressed whether *Miranda* warnings are insufficient, and as such a constitutional violation, when the warnings omit the suspect's right to the presence of counsel during interrogation and instead narrowly advise the suspect of the right to presence of counsel prior to questioning. Justice Ruth Ginsburg, writing for the majority, explained that *Miranda* only requires law enforcement officers to clearly inform suspects of their right to consult with counsel and to have counsel present during interrogation. Thus, the Tampa Police Department's *Miranda* warnings at issue in the case were sufficient to reasonably convey to a suspect the right to have an attorney present.

Right to Counsel Under the Sixth Amendment

In *Brewer v. Williams* (1977), the Supreme Court held that confessions and admissions elicited from a suspect after the right to counsel has attached must be suppressed if the incriminating statements were elicited without the presence of counsel or without a proper waiver by the suspect of his right to counsel. The Sixth Amendment standard serves as a basis for exclusion of confessions that is independent of the voluntariness and *Miranda* standards.

The Sixth Amendment right to counsel standard for suppression of incriminating statements requires the following judicial inquiry: (1) whether the right to counsel has attached at the time of the statement, (2) whether the suspect has made an effective waiver of the right if it has attached, and (3) whether the conduct of the police or their agents violates the right to counsel if no waiver has been made.

Armando Gustavo Hernandez
Independent Scholar

See Also: *Brown v. Mississippi*; Constitution of the United States of America; Defendant's Rights; Due Process; Interrogation Practices; Lynchings; *Miranda v. Arizona*; Police Abuse.

Further Readings

Berkemer v. McCarty, 468 U.S. 420, 104 S. Ct. 3138, 82 L.Ed.2d 317 (1984).
Bram v. United States, 168 U.S. 532, 18 S. Ct. 183, 42 L. Ed. 568 (1897).
Brewer v. Williams, 430 U.S. 387, 97 S. Ct. 1232, 51 L.Ed.2d 424 (1977).
Brown v. State of Mississippi, 297 U.S. 278, 56 S. Ct. 461, 80 L. Ed. 682 (1936).
Colorado v. Connelly, 479 U.S. 157, 107 S. Ct. 515, 93 L.Ed.2d 473 (1986).
Dickerson v. United States, 530 U.S. 428, 120 S. Ct. 2326, 147 L.Ed.2d 405 (2000).
Garcia, Alfredo. "Is Miranda Dead, Was It Overruled, or Is It Irrelevant?" *St. Thomas Law Review*, v.10/461 (1998).
Garner, Bryan A., ed. *Black's Law Dictionary*, 9th ed. Eagan, MN: West, 2009.
Johnson v. United States, 333 U.S. 10, 68 S. Ct. 367, 92 L.Ed. 436 (1948).
Miranda v. Arizona, 384 U.S. 436, 86 S. Ct. 1602, 16 L. Ed.2d 694 (1966).

Confidence Games and Frauds

Confidence tricks, *con games*, and *confidence games* are terms for fraudulent activities where the intention of the swindler is to gain items of value through means of deception, confidence, or trust. Confidence gaming requires at least two players; the confidence game, therefore, is in fact a game. The operator of the con is known as the "swindler" or con artist, and the victim is called the "mark." The confidence trick is a game of chance where the risk of losing is minimized through a set of rules and rehearsal by the swindler. The more times the con artist plays the game, the more likely he or she will be successful.

Confidence games differ from other types of fraudulent crimes such as white-collar crimes, check frauds, and pyramid schemes. All of these have some aspect of similarity with one another and are often considered to be in the same type of crime category; however, confidence gaming requires the deceiver to be a talented wordsmith and actor. Furthermore, the con artist accepts his or her role and actively engages in the world of con artistry, whereas the white collar criminal generally does not confide in others.

Selecting a mark is usually accomplished by two swindlers. The first swindler gains the confidence of the mark so that he or she will be comfortable in engaging in a scheme. The second swindler is the target of the scheme. In the end, the mark puts his or her money at risk in the hope of a large gain. This can be illustrated with the following scenario: The first befriends the mark and invites him or her to a poker game. He informs the mark that the individuals playing are not very good and that a large sum of money can be made. The swindler's partner is one of the poker players who acts as an unskilled player and intentionally loses money throughout the poker game. After some type of signal between the two swindlers, one swindler urges the mark to make a large bet, only to lose it to the swindler's partner.

Confidence games are categorized as either short-scale or large-scale games. Short-scale games usually involve a quick scheme, taking from a few minutes to a week to complete. These types of schemes usually involve one or two swindlers and a mark. Large-scale schemes include elaborate plans that may take weeks or months to develop. These schemes are aimed at maximizing the amount that the swindler can extract from his or her marks. The most common forms of short-scale scams are the pigeon drop, three-card monte, and large-scale schemes include the bait-and-switch and apartment swindle.

Vice and Confidence

The earliest forms of confidence games in the United States were those of vice. In the early 1800s, gambling halls became popular among young males in New York City. These halls offered two of the most popular confidence games: three-card monte and the shell game. It was not uncommon to also have prostitution rings associated with gambling halls. Though these places were illegal in America, they were able to continue by bribing the authorities. Like the Prohibition period that was to come in the next century, law enforcement officials would also partake in the gambling halls, further promoting its survival.

Three-card monte is a confidence game in which the object is for the mark to pick the correct playing card from a choice of three cards. The dealer shows the mark which card he or she is to pick, rearranges the cards face down, and the mark is to choose the correct card. During the process of the game, the dealer uses sleight of hand to trick the player into choosing the wrong card. The game itself is run by two or more swindlers. The first swindler is the game operator, and the second is an audience member. To lure the potential marks in, the fake audience member plays a few rounds of the game and is allowed to win. Once the mark enters the game, the team will then attempt to extract as much money from the mark as possible, using persuasive tactics.

Though confidence games have been observed throughout history, the first confidence trick formally recorded, and described as such, was in 1849. William Thompson, a New York conman, was arrested for tricking a man out of his watch. Thompson approached a man on the sidewalk, struck up a conversation, and asked him if he would trust him with his watch until tomorrow. Once the item was in his possession, Thompson walked off laughing. Irate, the man informed the authorities of the theft and later arrested Thompson. Once on trial, the New York Herald wrote a story about Thompson and how he tricked men by gaining their confidence. Thus, the confidence man was born.

Before the modern era of confidence games, three-card monte was one of the most popular confidence tricks; however, as confidence games became more popular, so did the streets. Business for the conman declined as a result of increased competition, resulting in the emergence of the dollar store swindles of the 1870s. Here, the conman would buy a store and stock vanity items for

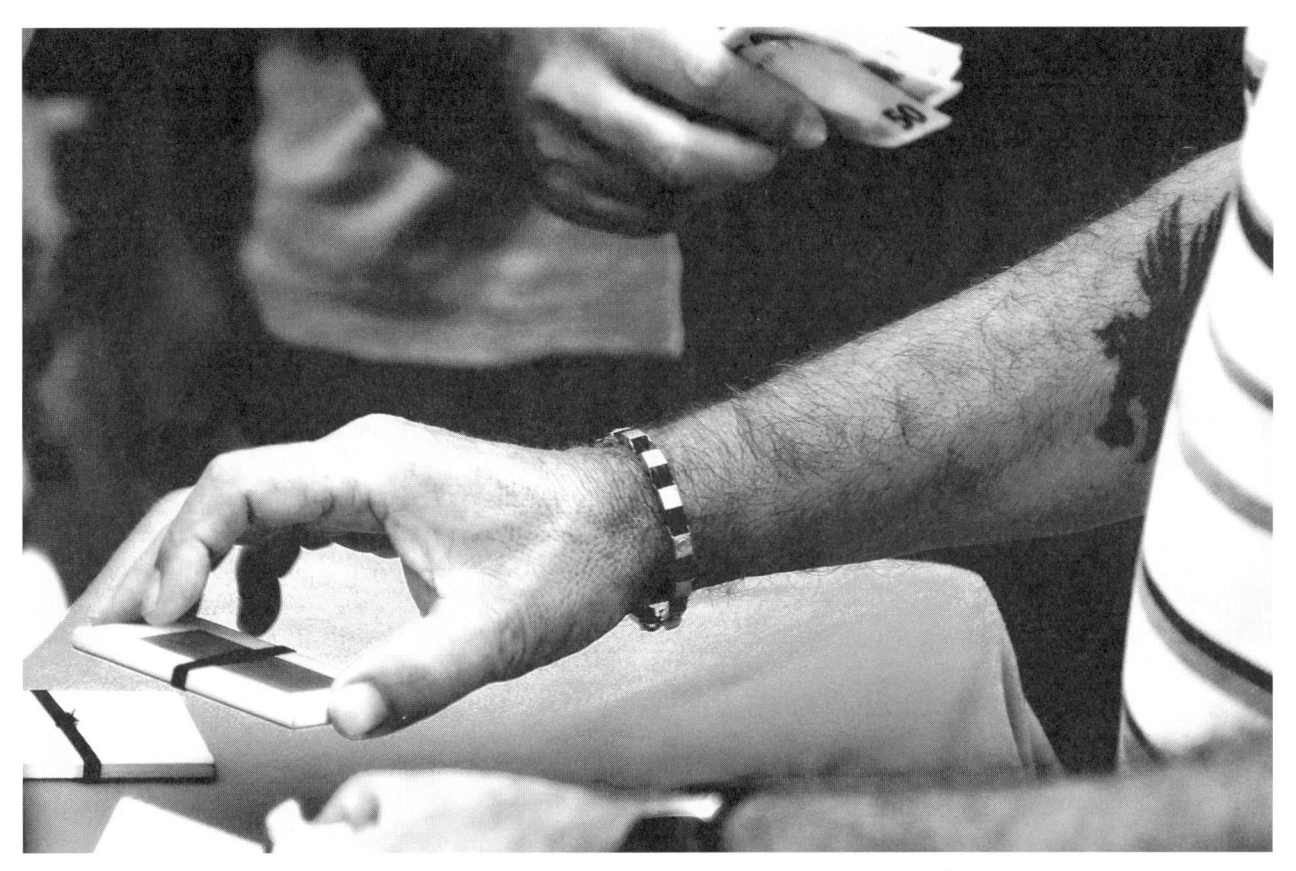

A three-card monte dealer at work at a street market in 2009. Swindlers and con artists are often first involved in other types of crime and may be recruited in jail or by an acquaintance, typically at around age 30 or older. The use of violence is rare, but it is occasionally used to prevent a mark or another swindler from going to the police, rather than as a means of gaining money.

a mere dollar. Once a mark was lured into the store, the conman would shift the mark's focus from the merchandise to the three-card monte.

The bait-and-switch is used to trick the mark into paying for a more expensive service or item when the mark has agreed to an initial lower price. The swindler lures the mark in by persuading him or her to buy an item or service because of a special deal. The swindler then tells the mark that the item or service is no longer available at the special price and that the mark now has to pay for the item or service at regular price. Marks are more difficult to trick with this type of confidence game versus other types of confidence games because it requires the swindlers to be able to pitch an item to the mark and for the mark to agree to buy the item.

In the apartment scandal con, the swindler and accomplices trick several marks into renting an apartment that the swindler does not have the right to rent out. The first part of the confidence trick is having the swindler rent an apartment. The swindler visits apartments for rent and, with persuasive discussions and false information, rents one. The swindler takes out an ad in a newspaper or Website showing the apartment for rent. This confidence game is difficult to accomplish because the swindler must be aggressive when showing the apartment to the mark and must sell the features of the apartment. If successful, the swindler may convince several marks to rent the apartment and put up a large sum of cash for the first month's rent.

Perhaps one of the most famous Internet cons was the Nigerian 419. Originating in Nigeria, but practiced in various countries around the world, the 419 scam is a scheme to relieve multiple marks of their money. In this scam, the con artist produces mass e-mails telling about a large sum of money that is held in an African bank account or deposit box. The swindler then asks the mark for help in transferring the money into a legitimate bank account. In return, the mark is promised a share of the money. When successful, the swindler receives the bank account information from the mark, eventually relieving the mark of his or her money. This confidence trick acquired its name from the Nigerian Criminal Code 419, which prohibits impersonation of an official for financial gain.

Cooling-Off the Mark
Swindlers set up confidence games with the intention of never having to interact with the mark after the confidence trick is finished. Often times, the mark will be hustled and no report to the authorities will be made because he or she broke the law in undertaking the confidence game or because of embarrassment. There are times, however, when the mark threatens to call the police or to take other types of action. When this occurs, it is important for the swindler to be able to cool off the mark so as not to draw unwanted attention.

The Code of the Confidence Game
The code of the confidence game is one held by each of its practitioners. Generally, a swindler avoids working in another swindler's area. Moreover, swindlers rarely report other swindlers to authorities or use another swindler as a mark. When this occurs, the person is referred to as a "niner," someone who is willing to swindle another confidence artist or someone who reports a confidence artist to authorities. An example of the usage of this term is, "He would nine ya in a heartbeat."

Confidence men and women often look out for one another in times of need. When a confidence man or women is outed by a mark or is caught by the authorities, others come to the criminal's aid. This is typically done by collecting money and giving it to the person's closest friend for bail or attorney's fees. Once the swindler is out on bail, it is almost impossible for him or her to pay back the money because it is given anonymously. It is expected that he or she will do the same for another when the time comes.

The practice of confidence gaming would not survive without partnerships. Swindlers often are members of a con artist "circle," with several members filling different roles. For example, one person may have a specialty in cooling off the mark, while another is able to lure in the mark with ease; these people may be referred to as the "roper" or the "outside man." Desired traits are the ability to fill several roles and the ability to improvise based on the situation. A partnership between con artists does not come without risk. Partners usually come to an agreement as to how much money each is going earn from the schemes. Most often, an even split of money is agreed upon; however, some give a larger portion of the earning to his or her partner to avoid conflict. The basis of a good partnership is founded in the ability to trust the partner and in making him or her feel useful and well paid.

The use of violence within the realm of confidence gaming is shunned by many members. There are times when confidence men and women use violence to prevent a mark from going to the police or when another member of the circle is about go to the authorities with information. When violence does occur, it is out of necessity and not as the means of gaining money. The use of violence is thought of as undignified and something a simple thief would commit. Swindlers agree that the con game is just a game; if you lose, be a good sport about it.

The Life of a Con Artist
The life of a con artist is hectic and often mobile. Con artists usually begin their career around age 30. It would be rare to find a person who is a professional at confidence games before age 25. Professional confidence men and women argue that a person younger than 30 does not have enough life experience to participate in confidence games. Many of these people are recruited in jail or by an acquaintance who is a swindler. Often, the con artist begins as a gambler or is involved with other types of crime similar to confidence gaming, and then becomes a professional con artist.

When the person is fully involved in schemes, it is typical to not be stationary for a long period of time. It is likely that the con artist will move to new cities and use other confidence men and women to help build a reputation within the network of confidence men and women. If con artists marry at any point during their career, they will travel to other nearby cities, instead of swindling in their neighborhood.

Con artists rarely completely retire. Many are still active well into their 60s and have a steady income other than using confidence tricks. Others, however, have made a large enough profit to live comfortably into their old age. Older con artists are more likely to buy a home, get a steady job, and be married with children. These con artists realize that living a conventional life is important for the continuation of the confidence game as a practice. Having a steady income and a family makes a person more legitimate within society and in the eyes of the law.

Thomas Zawisza
University of Arkansas at Little Rock

See Also: Fraud; Gambling; White-Collar Crime, History of; White-Collar Crime, Sociology of.

Further Readings
Blumberg, Abraham S. "The Practice of Law as Confidence Game." *Law & Society Review*, v.1/2 (1967).
Gasser, Robert Louis. "The Confidence Game." *Federal Probation*, v.27/22 (1963).
Halttunen, Karen. *Confidence Men and Painted Women: A Study of Middle-Class Culture in America, 1830–1870*. New Haven, CT: Yale University Press, 1982.

Connecticut

Connecticut, the fifth state in the United States, was established in 1788. Connecticut covers 5,018 square miles and has a population of approximately 3.5 million residents. There are eight counties with 164 towns and 21 cities in the state. Connecticut's major cities are the capital city of Hartford, New Haven, Bridgeport, Stamford, and Waterbury. Located in the northeastern part of the country, Connecticut borders Massachusetts to the north, Long Island Sound to the south, Rhode Island to the east, and New York to the west. Boasting one of the countries lowest unemployment rates, Connecticut is ranked as one of the top states for personal income. It is known for educational opportunities at the elementary and secondary levels as well as for excellent colleges and universities. Yale University, an Ivy League institution established in 1701, is located in New Haven, Connecticut. Other private universities such as Wesleyan in Middletown are nationally recognized.

As with other states, crime rates in Connecticut are declining. The total number of crimes reported in Connecticut was 96,514 in 2008, while in 2009 there were a total of 92,689 crimes reported to the Federal Bureau of Investigation (FBI). In 2009, there were 10,508 violent crimes and 82,181 property crimes. Connecticut had 107 murders, 651 forcible rapes, 3,990 robberies, and 5,760 aggravated assaults in 2009. The city of Hartford had the greatest number of murders.

Police
Established in 1903 by legislation signed by Governor Abiram Chamberlain, the Connecticut State Police Department is one of the oldest state police departments in the United States. In 2003, the Connecticut State Police celebrated its 100th anniversary. The department began when five law enforcement officers were hired to fight the growing problems of illegal liquor manufacturing and gambling in the state. An old mansion near the state capital of Hartford served as the first police department. Officer pay was minimal, with most officers paid $3 a day for their service. The emphasis on crime prevention and safety in Connecticut rose with the increasing population in the state. Twenty years after the first state law enforcement officers were hired, police numbers had grown to 80 officers. Today, Connecticut State Police officers are divided among 12 troops across the state.

In 1941, the Auxiliary State Trooper Program was established in order to guard the shorelines from enemies prior to World War II. More than 1,200 volunteers were recruited, and at the end of the war, these troops were reassigned to barracks throughout the state. In 1988, the Auxiliary State Trooper program ceased recruitment; 56 volunteer troopers are in service today. Their duties consist of crash scene and traffic stop assistance, traffic control, disaster relief, and special detail support for state officers. Auxiliary troopers are required to maintain the same training standards as state law enforcement officers.

Overall, according to the FBI, there were a total of 10,556 individuals employed by police departments in Connecticut in 2009. Of those employees, 8,622 were law enforcement officers.

These officers were employed in 104 agencies. In addition to state and local police officers, Connecticut also employs 35 capitol police officers. The state capitol opened in 1878; however, the State Capitol Police Department was not established until 1974. State capitol police officers are stationed in the Hartford, and they work closely with Hartford police as well as Connecticut State Police officers.

The largest cities in Connecticut employ the greatest numbers of both civilians and officers. The cities of Hartford, New Haven, Bridgeport, Waterbury, and Stamford have the largest police forces in the state. In 2009, Hartford had 448 officers, followed by New Haven with 423 officers, Bridgeport with 409, Waterbury with 291, and Stamford with 284 officers.

Hartford has the oldest police department in Connecticut. Similar to other colonies, the original police forces in Connecticut consisted of constables and citizen patrols. Men were assigned as night watchmen who watched for fires and suspicious persons. The Hartford Police Department dates back to 1636, when Samuel Wakeman was appointed to the position of constable. In the summer of 1860, the first official police force was established. In most cities, an organized police force developed in the 1800s. This organization was in response to the growth of the population, increases in immigration, and the emergence of economic class divisions.

The entrance to an underground cell at Connecticut's infamous Old Newgate Prison, where Loyalists were held during the Revolution. It was the first state prison in the United States.

Punishment

There are approximately 21,000 offenders under the custody of the Connecticut Department of Corrections, with approximately 18,000 inmates housed in correctional facilities. Overall, the Connecticut Department of Corrections is responsible for 18 correctional facilities for juveniles and adults. The average daily cost of housing an offender in Connecticut is $90, compared to approximately $33 to supervise an offender within the community. Contrary to the trend in the United States, the prison population in Connecticut has been declining since 2008. Connecticut's Office of Policy Management (OPM) projects that this moderate decline will continue, with the prison population in Connecticut experiencing a 2 percent reduction in 2012. Further, in February 2010, the State Criminal Justice and Planning Division completed a study on recidivism within the Connecticut Department of Corrections. Approximately 16,000 sentenced offenders were followed for a three-year period after they were released from a prison facility in 2005. The study found that almost 37 percent of the offenders were reincarcerated within three years after release from prison. Additionally, the chance of recidivism of an offender was reduced if the offender spent time under supervision within the community toward the end of the sentence.

Along with state correctional facilities, Connecticut is home to one federal correctional facility located in the town of Danbury. The Danbury Federal Correctional Institute currently houses an all-female population of approximately 1,000 low-security inmates. This facility, nicknamed "Club Fed," has housed such notable inmates as Leona Helmsley, G. Gordon Liddy, Michael Milken, and Sun Myung Moon.

Connecticut is one of 35 states in the United States that have the death penalty, and along with New Hampshire is one of only two New England states with this punishment. However, while Connecticut has the death penalty sanction, it is rarely used. In 2005, Connecticut carried out its first execution since 1960 when Michael Ross was put to death for killing four women. Ross spent 18 years on death row before his execution, when he became the first inmate in Connecticut executed by lethal injection. Lethal injection is the state's official method of execution, and there are currently 10 inmates awaiting execution at Northern Correctional Institution in the town of Somers.

Connecticut is also home to Newgate Prison in East Granby. Built in an abandoned copper mine, Newgate Prison is considered Connecticut's first prison institution and America's first state prison. Newgate Prison housed inmates between 1773 and 1827 and was declared a national historic landmark in 1972. Political prisoners, Tories and Loyalists, were held at Newgate during the Revolutionary War, and Confederate soldiers were held there during the Civil War. While primarily a male institution, female inmates were housed at Newgate for three years starting in 1824 until the facility was closed in 1827.

Newgate Prison is now a tourist attraction run by the Connecticut Commission on Culture and Tourism. While the majority of the prison is in ruins today, visitors can still view the guardhouse and enter the copper mine where inmates were held in solitary confinement. While Newgate was deemed one of the most secure prisons in the colonies, several escapes and escape attempts are said to have taken place there. Newgate housed more than 800 inmates throughout the course of its history. It was well known for horrific living conditions that included vermin, bunks of wet straw, floors covered in slime, and inedible food. Harsh punishment at Newgate consisted of flogging, a reduction in food, hanging by the heels, extra sets of hand and leg irons, and solitary confinement.

Melissa E. Fenwick
Western Connecticut State University

See Also: 1851 to 1900 Primary Documents; Capital Punishment; Crime Rates; Penitentiaries; Prisoner's Rights.

Further Readings
Gaskins, R. "Changes in Criminal Law in Eighteenth-Century Connecticut." *American Journal of Legal History*, v.25/4 (1981).
State of Connecticut Office of Policy Management, Criminal Justice Policy and Planning Commission. "2011 Annual Correctional Population Forecast Report." http://www.ct.gov/opm/lib/opm/cjppd/cjresearch/populationforecast/2011_forecast_report_final.pdf (Accessed February 2011).
U.S. Department of Justice "Crime in the United States 2008." http://www.fbi.gov/about-us/cjis/ucr/crime-in-the-u.s/2008 (Accessed February 2011).
U.S. Department of Justice. "Crime in the United States 2009." http://www.fbi.gov/about-us/cjis/ucr/crime-in-the-u.s/2009 (Accessed February 2011).

Constitution of the United States of America

The U.S. Constitution, at the time it was adopted on September 17, 1787, did not address crime and punishment issues in great detail. Article I (Legislative), Section 9 stipulates that the "privilege of the writ of habeas corpus shall not be suspended, unless when in cases of rebellion or invasion the public safety may require it" and that "no bill of attainder or ex post facto law shall be passed." Habeas corpus requires that cause be shown for detaining an individual; a bill of attainder declares an individual guilty of a crime and subjects him/her to punishment without a trial; and ex post facto laws declare some action illegal after the fact. Further, Article III (Judicial), Section 2 specifies that the "trial of all crimes ... shall be by jury; and such trial shall be held in the state where said crimes shall have been committed." Aside from these brief passages, the unamended Constitution is silent on crime and punishment issues.

That the authors of the Constitution felt it necessary to include these restrictions on government power to protect individuals' rights is evidence of the historical context in which the Constitution was written. Although many of the legal rights that were adopted in the Constitution were already law in England, there is an important distinction to be made between the rights of subjects and the rights of citizens. In a monarchy, subjects receive their rights from the Crown. Therefore, the rights of subjects can be abused by the Crown, which was happening in the colonies. In a republic, citizens have natural rights that are guaranteed, and the government's function is to protect these rights. The document that guarantees and protects these rights is the Constitution of the United States of America. While the authors of the Constitution believed the previously mentioned protections were sufficient, others disagreed.

That the Constitution did not address crime and punishment issues more specifically was one point of contention between the Federalists and the Anti-Federalists—with the Federalists arguing that state constitutions would protect citizen rights and the Anti-Federalists arguing that citizens needed legal protection from the federal government as well. In order to gain support from the Anti-Federalists, a compromise was reached. The compromise called for amending the Constitution, after it was ratified, to include what has come to be known as the Bill of Rights. On September 13, 1788, the Constitution was ratified by 11 of the 13 states, and the Bill of Rights came into effect on December 15, 1791.

Bill of Rights
The Bill of Rights consists of 10 amendments to the Constitution. Of these, the Fourth, Fifth, Sixth, and Eighth Amendments specifically address crime and punishment issues. The Fourth Amendment guards "against unreasonable searches and seizures" and stipulates that "no Warrants shall [be] issue[d], but upon probable cause … and particularly describing the place to be searched, and the persons or things to be seized." The Fourth Amendment specifically addresses past abuses of general search warrants or a writ of assistance. In addition to being general in nature, a writ of assistance did not expire. As such, law enforcement officials could search anywhere and for any reason without limitations on what was seized and used against the accused in criminal prosecution. By guarding against unreasonable searches and seizures, guaranteeing a threshold of probable cause before a warrant can be issued, and stipulating the place and person or things to be seized, the Fourth Amendment limits the government's ability to prosecute individuals without sufficient cause and secures individual rights against unwarranted criminal charges.

The Fifth Amendment guarantees the rights of citizens in criminal cases. Specifically, the right to a grand jury indictment "for a capital, or otherwise infamous crime . . . nor shall any person be subject for the same offense to be twice put in jeopardy of life or limb, nor shall be compelled in any criminal case to be a witness against himself, nor be deprived of life, liberty, or property, without due process of law." Grand juries and due process were not new concepts as both can be traced to the Magna Carta. Although not new, the inclusion of both in the Fifth Amendment is important. Because grand juries are composed of a jury of peers, not government officials, indictments (a formal charge of a crime) cannot be pursued by the government alone. Protection against double jeopardy restricts the government from charging an individual with the same crime after an acquittal. Without double jeopardy, the government would be able to prosecute an individual for the same crime until it achieved a guilty verdict. Finally, protections against self-incrimination guard the accused from providing evidence that can be used against him/her in criminal proceedings.

The Sixth Amendment ensures the right to a fair trial. These rights include the "right to a speedy and public trial, by an impartial jury … [that the accused] be informed of the nature and cause of the accusation; to be confronted with witnesses against him; to have compulsory process for obtaining witnesses in his favor, and to have the assistance of counsel for his defense." An individual's right to a speedy and public trial by an impartial jury limits the government's ability to hold the accused for prolonged periods of time while it builds its case and guarantees that trial proceedings will be open and fair. In order to ensure fairness in the proceedings, the accused has a right to review the indictment levied against him/her, to cross-examine witnesses testifying against him/her, to present witnesses defending his/her innocence, and to have legal representation in his/her defense.

The Eighth Amendment stipulates that "Excessive bail shall not be required, nor excessive fines imposed, nor cruel and unusual punishment inflicted." The Eighth Amendment is almost

An original copy of the U.S. Constitution, which delineates the rights and processes of crime and punishment in the American legal system, can be seen at the National Archives, shown here.

indistinguishable from a provision in the English Bill of Rights of 1689, which states that "excessive bail ought not be required, nor excessive fines imposed, nor cruel and unusual punishments inflicted." Excessive bail is prohibited under the assumption of the accused being innocent until proven guilty of a crime, while excessive fines can be linked to the prohibition against cruel and unusual punishments. In short, the punishment must fit the crime committed.

While most of the crime and punishment rights outlined above are absolute, others are not. For example, bail can be denied under certain circumstances. In addition, the accused can waive some of these rights—trial by jury, assistance of legal counsel, and self-incrimination, to name a few. Further, because the Supreme Court interprets the Constitution, crime and punishment rights have changed and evolved throughout the history of the United States of America.

Supreme Court Interpretations

Examples of how Supreme Court interpretations have affected the rights discussed are plentiful. For instance, where the Fourth Amendment protection against unreasonable search and seizure is concerned, *California v. Greenwood* (1988) gave law enforcement agencies more leeway in collecting evidence. The question presented to the court in *Greenwood* was whether law enforcement could search a suspect's trash without a warrant and use evidence secured in the warrantless search to obtain a warrant. The court ruled that the warrantless search of Greenwood's trash was legal on the grounds that it was on the street and open to inspection by "animals, children, scavengers, snoops, and other members of the public."

Where the Fifth Amendment is concerned, specifically the self-incrimination clause, *Griffin v. California* (1965) provides a good example of the court finding for the defendant. Griffin was on trial for murder and, under advice of counsel, refused to testify. In closing arguments, the prosecutor implied to the jury that Griffin's refusal to testify was evidence of guilt. Griffin was convicted and was sentenced to death, but the Supreme Court found in Griffin's favor, saying what the jury "may infer when the [trial] court solemnizes the silence of the accused into evidence against him is [dangerous]."

The Sixth Amendment right to have the assistance of counsel has evolved through Supreme Court rulings as well. *Powell v. Alabama* (1932) and *Gideon v. Wainwright* (1963) illustrate this evolution well. Powell was one of nine African American males accused of raping a white woman. The day of the trial, Powell's attorney refused to represent him. When an attorney willing to represent Powell was secured, he was given 30 minutes to meet with Powell before the trial. Powell was convicted and was sentenced to death. Among other due process issues addressed, the court ruled that defendants facing the death penalty be guaranteed counsel regardless of ability to pay. Gideon was arrested for attempting to break and enter a poolroom with the intent to commit a misdemeanor, which was a felony in Florida. Gideon, illiterate and indigent, was denied request for counsel and made to represent himself in the criminal proceedings. He was convicted and was sent to prison. In the *Gideon* case, the court extended the guarantee of counsel regardless of ability to pay to include all defendants facing felony charges.

Where the Eighth Amendment is concerned, specifically the cruel and unusual punishment clause, two cases illustrate how Supreme Court interpretations can change within a short period of time—*Furman v. Georgia* (1972) and *Gregg v. Georgia* (1976). In the *Furman* case, the court ruled that the death penalty constituted cruel and unusual punishment and was therefore unconstitutional. Justice Thurgood Marshall stated that the death penalty was "excessive, unnecessary, and offensive to contemporary values." Four short years later in the *Gregg* case, the court reversed itself and found that "punishment of death does not invariably violate the Constitution."

As these cases illustrate, the Supreme Court, through judicial review, interprets the Constitution, which can alter crime and punishment procedures and rights. In some instances, the court restricts the government's ability to pursue justice (*Griffin, Powell, Gideon,* and *Furman*), while in other instances, the court expands the government's ability to pursue justice (*Greenwood* and *Gregg*). Regardless, the Constitution remains the governing document on crime and punishment issues.

Conclusion
While many of the historical origins of the American legal system can be traced to English common law and the Magna Carta, the Constitution of the United States of America delineates the rights and processes of crime and punishment in the American legal system. It is the function of the U.S. Supreme Court to interpret the Constitution and the Bill of Rights to determine that each citizen is afforded the full protection of the law.

Lee W. Payne
Stephen F. Austin State University

See Also: Anti-Federalist Papers; Bill of Rights; Defendant's Rights; Due Process; *Furman v. Georgia; Gideon v. Wainwright; Gregg v. Georgia; Griffin v. California;* Habeas Corpus, Writ of; *Mapp v. Ohio; Miranda v. Arizona;* Rule of Law; Supreme Court, U.S.

Further Readings
Chemerinsky, Erwin. *Constitutional Law: Principles and Policies.* New York: Aspen Publishers, 2006.
Ides, Allan and Christopher N. May. *Examples & Explanations: Constitutional Law Individual Rights,* 5th ed. New York: Aspen Publishers, 2009.
Stone, Geoffrey R., Louis M. Seidman, Cass R. Sunstein, Pamela S. Karlan, and Mark V. Tushnet. *Constitutional Law,* 6th ed. New York: Aspen Publishers, 2009.

Convention on the Rights of the Child

The United Nations (UN) Convention on the Rights of the Child recognizes and protects the civil, cultural, economic, political, and social rights of children. The most current convention advances the autonomous rights of children, beyond the welfare-oriented paternalism of earlier conventions. Children are defined as persons under the age of 18, unless an earlier age of majority is recognized by the signatory country's laws.

An earlier precedent was the Declaration of the Rights of the Child of 1924, a nonbinding resolution from the League of Nations. In 1959, the UN General Assembly unanimously adopted new text of the Declaration of the Rights of the Child, but it was still not legally binding. In 1978, Poland submitted the draft text of a new convention on the rights of children, coinciding with the International Year of the Child in 1979. The UN Commission on Human Rights organized a working group on the convention that included unprecedented involvement by nongovernmental organizations (NGOs).

The convention was adopted and opened for signature, ratification, and accession by the UN General Assembly Resolution 44/25 of November 20, 1989. The convention entered into force on September 2, 1990. It has been ratified by every UN member state except Somalia and the United States. The convention's 54 articles consist of guiding principles, categories of rights, and implementation details.

Provisions

Nondiscrimination is the first of four guiding principles and requires each child to be treated equally without reference to his/her race, gender, language, religion, political belief, origin, property, disability, or birth status, or the status, activities, opinions, or beliefs of the child's family or legal guardians. The second is that the best interest of the child must be the primary concern in making decisions that affect the child. Third is that governments must ensure children have the right to life, survival, and development. Fourth is respect for the views of the child. Children's input should be sought, and their opinions should affect the decision-making process.

The first of four categories is protection rights. Criminal justice–related issues are covered in this category. Article 37 covers detention and punishment and ensures children are not "subjected to torture or other cruel, inhuman or degrading treatment or punishment"; prohibits capital punishment or life imprisonment; states that "arrest, detention or imprisonment ... shall be used only as a measure of last resource and for the shortest appropriate period of time"; notes children should be housed separately from adults; declares children have access to their family through visits and correspondence; and guarantees prompt access to legal assistance and the judicial system.

Article 40 focuses on the juvenile justice system. Part I states that the system should respect children's rights, account for their younger age, and promote reintegration into society. The second part calls for presumption of innocence, prompt notification of charges; access to legal assistance, hearing before an independent legal authority, protection against self-incrimination, the right to call and question witnesses, the right to interpreters, and the right to privacy. Part III promotes the establishment of a juvenile justice system specifically designed for children, including a minimum age for criminal responsibility and the use of alternative methods, rather than relying on judicial proceedings. The last part recommends alternatives to institutional care be made available, such as counseling, probation, foster care, and training programs.

References are made to protective rights for adoption, child labor, drug abuse, kidnapping, and rehabilitation of child victims. Protection rights related to sexual exploitation and the abduction, sale, and trafficking of children are both augmented by the Optional Protocol on the Sale of Children, Child Prostitution and Child Pornography. The use of children as armed combatants is prohibited for those under the age of 15. The Optional Protocol on the Involvement of Children in Armed Conflict raises the age of involvement to 18. The United States has signed and ratified both optional protocols.

The United Nations Children's Fund (UNICEF) defines participation rights as "ensur[ing] children are entitled to the freedom to express opinions and to have a say in matters affecting their social, economic, religious, cultural and political life. Participation rights include the right to express opinions and be heard, the right to information, and freedom of association. Engaging these rights as they mature helps children bring about the realization of all their rights and prepares them for an active role in society."

Survival and development rights, as recognized by UNICEF, "are the resources, skills and contributions necessary for the survival and full development of the child." They include rights to adequate food, shelter, clean water, formal education, primary healthcare, leisure and recreation, cultural activities, and information about their rights. These rights require not only the existence of the means to fulfill the rights but also access to them. Specific articles address the needs of child refugees, children with disabilities, and children of minority or indigenous groups.

Implementation

To implement convention obligations after ratification, countries review their laws related to children. The review process examines the educational system, health and social services, and legal structure to ensure minimum standards set by the convention are met. The review also evaluates funding to ensure that adequate resources are available for educational, health, legal, and social services. The review process has led to the creation of new laws in some countries and expansion and strengthening in others. Article 41 ensures that existing laws that already guarantee higher standards than the convention are not abandoned in favor of the convention's minimum standards.

Monitoring of treaty obligations takes the form of periodical reports to the UN Committee on the

Rights of the Child. The committee consists of 18 children's rights experts who act in a personal capacity despite being nominated and elected by country representatives. Countries submit their reports within two years of ratification and every five years after. The committee has created report guidelines.

A number of weaknesses of the convention have been acknowledged. There are no provisions for petitions by individuals or interstate petitions. Critics point to the lack of specific, strong rights for girls. The committee suffers from its limited ability to independently research, rather relying on nongovernmental organizations to confirm the veracity of country reports, and the body has fallen behind schedule, as has the submission of many country reports. Lastly, the broad nature of the convention's economic and social rights has led to complaints by countries trying to meet the rights of children and by child proponents, who claim that countries often do not do enough to meet those specific rights of children.

Chad M. Kahl
Illinois State University

See Also: Children's Rights; Juvenile Corrections, History of; Juvenile Justice, History of.

Further Readings
Buck, Trevor. *International Child Law*, 2nd ed. London and New York: Routledge, 2011.
Fottrell, Deirdre, ed. *Revisiting Children's Rights: 10 Years of the UN Convention on the Rights of the Child*. Boston: Kluwer Law International, 2000.
LeBlanc, L. J. *The Convention on the Rights of the Child: United Nations Lawmaking on Human Rights*. Lincoln: University of Nebraska Press, 1995.
United Nations Children's Fund (UNICEF). "Convention on the Rights of the Child." http://www.unicef.org/crc (Accessed February 2011).

Convict Lease System

Under the system of convict leasing, persons convicted of criminal offenses were contracted out to private businessmen, planters, and corporations to serve their prison sentences laboring in coal and phosphate mines, turpentine farms, lumber and naval stores operations, brickyards, sawmills, and sugar and cotton plantations. In return for an annual fee for each prisoner that was paid to local and/or state governments, these private entrepreneurs were to work, clothe, house, and discipline men, women, and children. Several northern states, including New York, leased some of their prisoners in the decades after the American Revolution, but convict leasing was associated more with the southern states in the decades after the Civil War, where, for example, they were contracted to construct railroads in the late 1860s and 1870s. In the last third of the 19th century, convict leasing acted as a bridge between a displaced agricultural slave economy in the region and a free labor society with nascent industrial and manufacturing concerns. It was also firmly wedded to the political agendas of conservative southern white Democratic governments.

The former Confederate states experienced rising levels of property and interpersonal violence offenses in the immediate aftermath of the war and during the Reconstruction period. In the context of extremely weak state governments with deep financial problems, war-damaged and dilapidated penitentiaries that were expensive to rebuild and maintain, severe labor shortages, and four million former slaves no longer under the control of white planters, southern state governments viewed the convict lease as an all-encompassing solution. The system of leasing convicts to private employers offered cash-strapped governments a means of profiting from the labor of prisoners, dispensing with expensive penitentiaries, and controlling the free black labor supply.

Some historians, such as David Oshinsky and Douglas Blackmon, view convict leasing as merely another form of racial slavery. It rested on corrupt networks of sheriffs, judges, and labor agents who used criminal justice systems to provide entrepreneurs with a reliable source of labor. By the 1880s, African Americans comprised over 90 percent of state prison populations in Alabama, Georgia, and Florida.

Private employers acquired their convict laborers through a public bidding procedure, usually every two to four years. Many convicts were subleased to other contractors at a profit to the

These wagons, which were lined with bunks, were home to a group of African American laboring convicts in Pitt County, North Carolina, in the fall of 1910. The wagons could be moved from one location to another depending on the work project. The armed guards and bloodhounds shown would hunt down any escapees.

original purchaser. Profit was the main driver of convict leasing. It was a system of punishment that was always characterized by brutality, violence, race subordination, and labor exploitation. Employers had few incentives to provide anything more than basic shelter, food, and clothing for their charges. There were considerable variations in convict leasing practices. Generally, inmates were housed in itinerant and unsanitary camps in remote rural areas near phosphate, lumber, or railroad construction operations or in more permanent but equally unsanitary structures near mines and plantations. Labor squads worked from dawn until dusk, subsisted on meager rations, were often clothed in rags, and slept in vermin-infested cots. Corporal punishment or the lash was a central feature of the lease in all southern states. Death rates and numbers of escapes were both high.

From its inception, convict leasing was subject to criticism; for example, from governors and legislators over lessees' failures to pay fees or comply with rules and regulations. Over the decades, legislative investigations and newspaper exposés led to calls for reform that were supported by church ministers, physicians, boards of health, and progressive reformers. More fundamental moral and political criticisms over private corporations reaping financial rewards from public lawbreakers and sustained calls for abolition of convict leasing appeared during the 1890s alongside the rise of the Populist Party. The American Federation of Labor also waged a highly successful campaign against unfair prison labor practices and unfair competition with free labor. Prisoners demonstrated their opposition through work slowdowns, strikes, and open rebellion, as in the Tennessee coalfields in the late 19th century.

Southern governments responded by tightening rules and regulations and increasing state oversight of leasing and subleasing. Incentives to induce good prisoner behavior included free Sundays, paid extra work, pardons, and "gaintime" schedules where sentences could be reduced by a specified number of days per month. Yet, support for leasing declined in the early 20th century as alternative forms of prison labor, including prison farming and chain gang labor, gathered support in southern states. Whereas nine southern states leased their prisoners to private contractors in 1898, only Florida and Alabama continued to do so by 1913. There is debate over the extent to which humanitarianism played a role in the decline of convict leasing as it became less profitable compared to publicly funded convict road labor in the 1910s and 1920s, as Matthew Mancini and Alex Lichtenstein have noted. However, the much-publicized murders of white convicts at the hands of brutal prison guards in these states in 1923 and 1924 provided the final important catalyst for abolition of convict leasing in the south. Nevertheless, other forms of peonage endured longer in the region.

Vivien Miller
University of Nottingham

See Also: African Americans; Alabama; Chain Gangs and Prison Labor; Corporal Punishment; Georgia.

Further Readings
Blackmon, Douglas A. *Slavery by Another Name: The Re-Enslavement of Black Americans From the Civil War to World War II*. New York: Doubleday, 2008.
Curtain, Mary Ellen. *Black Prisoners and Their World: Alabama, 1865–1900*. Richmond: University of Virginia Press, 2000.
Lichtenstein, Alex. *Twice the Work of Free Labor: The Political Economy of Convict Labor in the New South*. New York: Verso, 1996.
Mancini, Matthew J. *One Dies, Get Another: Convict Leasing in the American South, 1866–1928*. Columbia: University of South Carolina Press, 1996.
McLennan, Rebecca M. *The Crisis of Imprisonment: Protest, Politics, and the Making of the American Penal State, 1776–1941*. Cambridge: Cambridge University Press, 2008.
Oshinsky, David M. *"Worse Than Slavery": Parchman Farm and the Ordeal of Jim Crow Justice*. New York: The Free Press, 1996.
Shapiro, Karin A. *A New South Rebellion: The Battle Against Convict Labor in the Tennessee Coalfields, 1871–1896*. Chapel Hill: University of North Carolina Press, 1998.

Coolidge, Calvin (Administration of)

Calvin Coolidge, Jr., (1872–1933) was the 30th president of the United States (1923–29). He held various local, state, and federal political posts prior to becoming president. John Calvin Coolidge was born in Plymouth Notch, Vermont. He was the elder of two children of John Calvin Coolidge, Sr., and Victoria Josephine Moor. He graduated from Black River Academy in 1890, attended Amherst College, and graduated cum laude in 1895.

Coolidge moved to Northampton, Massachusetts, because of its location near a courthouse. He decided not to attend a formal law school but rather apprenticed with a local law firm, Hammond and Field. He was admitted to the Massachusetts Bar in 1897. In 1898, he opened his own law office with practice interest in transactional law. He was elected as a Republican city councilman in Northampton in 1898. In 1905, he was formally introduced to Grace Anna Goodhue, and they were married on October 4, 1905, in Burlington, Vermont. The couple had two sons: John, born in 1906, and Calvin, Jr., born in 1908.

In 1910, Coolidge was elected mayor of Northampton. As mayor, he increased salaries for teachers, slightly decreased taxes, and managed to retire some of the city's debt during his first term. He was elected and served in the Massachusetts State Senate from 1912 to 1915. He was the lieutenant governor of Massachusetts from 1916 to 1918. He was nominated for governor of Massachusetts in 1918, and his campaign emphasized law and order, fiscal conservatism, opposition to Prohibition, and support for American involvement in World War I, among other positions.

In 1919, Coolidge was elected governor of Massachusetts. One of his greatest challenges as governor was to deal with the crime and criminal justice aspect of the Boston Police Strike of 1919. Displeased with their working conditions, the Boston police officers walked off the job September 9, 1919, leaving the city unprotected. Consequently, crimes of violence, arson, and lawlessness followed, with business store windows smashed and stores' contents vandalized and looted. Other trade unions, including firemen, streetcar men, and telephone and telegraph operators, all had grievances and threatened to join the police strike. As violence continued through the nights of September 10–11, gamblers openly played dice in the streets and snatched women's handbags. In South Boston, gunfire killed two people and wounded others, with a death total overall reaching nine.

At the request of Boston Mayor Andrew Peters, Coolidge deployed almost 5,000 troops to control the chaos and criminality that besieged the city. Coolidge's actions during the strike and after in reconstructing the police department earned him a reputation as a man of decisive action and thrust him into the national spotlight as a presidential figure.

Presidency

In 1920, the Republican Party nominated Senator Warren G. Harding of Ohio as its presidential nominee and Calvin Coolidge as its vice presidential nominee. Coolidge's party won the election in 1920, and he became vice president in 1921. President Harding died on August 2, 1923, while on a speaking tour. On August 3, 1923, Coolidge's father, John Coolidge, a notary public, administered the oath of office to his son in the presence of Mrs. Coolidge and several others, making him president.

As president, Coolidge's first message to Congress in December 1923 was a call for isolation in foreign policy and tax cuts, economic growth, and limited subsidies to farmers. His administration dealt with resistance to Prohibition, which lasted from 1920 to 1933. That era was associated with corruption and violence from criminal gangsters, bootleggers, and rumrunners, as well as an overall chaotic situation in the American criminal justice system. As president, Coolidge gained a reputation as a small government, low taxes, conservative politician, and also as a person who said very little. He was credited as the president who restored public confidence, dignity, and prestige to the White House after the scandals of his predecessor's administration. In a number of his annual addresses, Coolidge called attention to the civil rights of African Americans and challenged Congress to exercise powers of prevention and punishment against the lynching of African Americans based on racial hatred. He left the presidency and returned to Northampton in 1929. On January 5, 1933, he died of a heart attack at age 60.

Felix O. Chima
Prairie View A&M University

See Also: Boston, Massachusetts; Harding, Warren G. (Administration of); Prohibition.

Further Readings
Felzenberg, Alvin S. "Calvin Coolidge and Race: His Record in Dealing With Racial Tensions of the 1920s." *New England Journal of History,* v.55/1 (1988).
Gilbert, Robert E. "Calvin Coolidge's Tragic Presidency: The Political Effects of Bereavement and Depression." *Journal of American Studies,* v.39/1 (2005).

Corporal Punishment

The use of corporal punishment occupies a controversial place in the history of the United States. Government-sanctioned corporal punishment has been used for millennia. Often, these punishments tended toward brutal and theatrical public spectacles. By the time the American colonies had separated from England, a vast transformation in punishment was under way. Gone were the grotesque spectacles of ritualized barbarity that often typified pre-Enlightenment European criminal justice. In their place, the relative banality of imprisonment rose to dominance. Even so, one holdover from the previous era, flogging, remained common in many spheres.

Flogging in U.S. History

Flogging was retained as a way to impart discipline to many vulnerable constituencies. Reports from the 19th century describe routine flogging of slaves, prisoners, members of the military, women, and children. The parental right to physically discipline children was circumscribed only by vague admonitions to avoid excessive force. This practice carried over to school officials. Even now, many states still permit the use of physical punishment to chastise students. Slaves were often subject to the cruelest forms of physical discipline. Women, owing to their inferior legal status, also faced physical punishment from their husbands, fathers, and the state. While slaves, women, and children were often subjected to corporal punishment in an arbitrary manner, members of the military were systematically flogged until the mid-1800s. In 1775, the Continental Congress authorized whipping aboard American naval vessels by permitting officers to strike enlisted men with up to 12 lashes. Shortly thereafter, a naval court-martial was allowed to assign whipping as a punishment. During this same period, the U.S. Navy vastly expanded the number of crimes punishable by flogging.

As a punishment for convicted criminals and as a means to discipline prison inmates, corporal punishment proved to be equally enduring. Setting aside its use inside prisons, the American movement against the use of corporal punishment as a sanction in lieu of prison gained momentum in the years between 1820 and 1850. Fueled by a potent combination of Enlightenment philosophy and Utilitarian social theory, religious leaders, educators, and the medical establishment spoke out against excessive and barbaric physical punishment. A growing public distaste for the practice prompted restriction and outright abolition of corporal punishment against soldiers, students, and juvenile offenders. In response to growing public opposition, Congress eventually restricted the use of whipping in the U.S. Navy, abolishing it formally in 1853. The U.S. Marine Corps would not ban all forms of direct physical punishment for another century. Likewise, many state and local school systems modified regulations to move away from corporal punishment. Adolescents were no

A crowd watches as a man is whipped while restrained at a whipping post in Delaware in the early 20th century. Delaware continued to allow whipping as a punishment for certain crimes as late as 1963 and did not ban it entirely until 1972. However, no offender has actually been subject to corporal punishment in almost 60 years.

longer subject to whippings and other punishments such as shackling but were instead diverted to the growing institution of juvenile court.

Whipping Continues in Some States

Despite this trend away from corporal punishment, whipping laws remained in some state systems as late as 1972. Although the practice was in effect discontinued by the early 1950s, Delaware approved whipping as a punishment for certain crimes as late as 1963. Until the practice was finally banned in 1972, the Delaware Supreme Court recognized growing opposition to corporal punishment but left to the legislature the question as to whether it violated the state constitutional prohibition on cruel and unusual punishment. Even with the state's relative recalcitrance to embrace prevalent punishment norms regarding corporal punishment, no offender has been subject to corporal punishment in almost 60 years. Even in the face of abandonment in most other realms, corporal punishment died a hard death in American prisons. As seen above in the matter of Delaware's criminal justice history, the U.S. Constitution recognizes the right of each state to legislate its own punishments. This right can only be abrogated if it is proven that a particular punishment is cruel and unusual under the terms of the Eighth Amendment. Therefore, one might expect judges and legislatures to permit a broad range of punishments, provided they were demonstrably neither cruel nor unusual. As applied to a given state's right to discipline prison inmates, this doctrine permitted corporal punishment inside many American prisons until the 1960s.

Resistance to Corporal Punishment

In *Talley v. Stephens* (1965), Arkansas state prison inmates challenged the use of corporal punishment citing due process (Fourteenth Amendment) claims. Their base allegation was that being beaten by correctional staff amounted to punishment without being afforded due process. In response, a federal judge ordered not that corporal punishment be banned altogether, but that its use be restricted until adequate safeguards were established for its application. Just three years later, another Arkansas case, *Jackson v. Bishop* (1968), sealed the fate for corporal punishment in American prisons. *Jackson v. Bishop* concerns an injunction brought against the superintendent of the Arkansas State Penitentiary, O. F. Bishop, to cease using the strap (a long, flat leather whip) to discipline prisoners. The court of appeals held, among other things, that any use of the strap (even when due process of the Fourteenth Amendment was demonstrated) violated the Eighth Amendment of the Constitution that prohibits cruel and unusual punishment, simply because it was cruel.

A brief examination of three court cases demonstrates how American courts have chosen to navigate the qualitative aspects of being punished as a prison inmate. In the case of *Ingraham v. Wright* (1977), the U.S. Supreme Court noted that while prison brutality is part of the total punishment to which an individual is subjected for his crime, the protection afforded by the Eighth Amendment is, nevertheless, limited after incarceration. As such, only unnecessary and wanton infliction of pain constitutes cruel and unusual punishment in the context of incarceration. Some scholars have argued that this holding yields a kind of legal paradox in that the court's position seems to affirm the infliction of harsh conditions, especially violence, upon inmates as an intrinsic part of prison, whereas specifically administered violent or harsh punishments would likely be deemed unconstitutional. Along this same line of reason, some have argued the court's failure to perceive the variety of possible punishments is well demonstrated in its assumption that all corporal punishments are the same, and that they are all synonymous with torture. Even in the light of these landmark court cases, the possible revival of corporal punishment is periodically explored by U.S. lawmakers. While none of these efforts has advanced the cause beyond discussion, its continual reemergence speaks to its place in the history of American criminal justice.

Matthew Pate
State University of New York, Albany

See Also: 1600 to 1776 Primary Documents; 1851 to 1900 Primary Documents; Cruel and Unusual Punishment; *Gates v. Collier*; History of Crime and Punishment in America: 1783–1850; Prisoner's Rights.

Further Readings

Colvin, Marc. *Penitentiaries, Reformatories, and Chain Gangs: Social Theory and the History of*

Punishment in Nineteenth-Century America. New York: Palgrave Macmillan, 2000.

Garland, David. *Punishment and Modern Society: A Study in Social Theory*. Chicago: University of Chicago Press, 1993.

Ingraham v. Wright, 430 U.S. 651 (1977).

Jackson v. Bishop, 404 F. 2d 571 (1968).

Newman, Graeme. *Just and Painful: A Case for Corporal Punishment of Criminals*. Monsey, NY: Criminal Justice Press, 1995.

Scott, George. *The History of Corporal Punishment—A Survey of Flagellation in Its Historical Anthropological and Sociological Aspects*. London: Boughton Press, 2010.

Talley v. Stephens, 247 F. Supp. 683, Dist. Court, ED Arkansas (1965).

Corrections

Corrections is typically considered the third major component of the criminal justice system (with law enforcement and courts being the first and second, respectively). Corrections are those sentencing options for someone who has been convicted of a crime and can include financial penalties and reimbursement (fines and restitution), community/public service hours, community-based sanctions (probation, parole, or house arrest), intermediate sanctions (work-release and restitution centers, boot camp programs), institutional corrections (jails and prisons), and capital punishment (the death penalty). Corrections consists of both the pretrial and posttrial management of offenders charged with and convicted of criminal offenses. According to data from the Bureau of Justice Statistics, there were 7.2 million adult offenders under correctional supervision in the United States (those persons on probation, on parole, or incarcerated in jails or prisons) at year end 2009. According to the American Correctional Association, the purpose of corrections is to enhance social order and public safety.

Early Correctional History

Corrections and punishment can trace their origins to ancient Greece. Punishments at that time were carried out in public and included execution, denunciation of the offender, banishment and exile of the offender, public shaming, the confiscation of the offender's property, and corporal punishments, including stoning offenders and throwing them over cliffs. Old Testament punishments included corporal punishment as well, including beating and blinding the offender, and capital punishment that included beheading the offender, burning the offender at the stake, crushing the offender to death with heavy weights, drowning the offender, and crucifixion.

Confiscation of the offender's property was practiced at this time as well. In early Rome, both corporal and capital punishments were practiced, which included decapitating or hanging the offender, clubbing (beating) the offender, burning the offender at the stake, and throwing offenders over cliffs. In some instances, offenders were required to pay compensation to the victim for any loss caused by the offender.

Punishments during these eras were considered theatrical performances as they were carried out in public in a carnival-type atmosphere (the rationale was that if the public observed the punishment and sanctioning of an offender, they would be deterred from then engaging in criminal behavior); these public punishments were often considered social events of sorts where the public would gather to observe the macabre punishments as a form of entertainment.

Punishment at that time had various levels of severity. The least was flogging, which involved the offender being whipped using either leather whips or the cat-o-nine-tails. Branding, in which the offender was branded with a symbol or letter noting the type of offense he had been convicted of, was considered an appropriate correctional measure. For example, if an offender was convicted of stealing, he would be branded with a "T" in his right palm. The rationale was that if an individual was ever required to testify or appear before the court, either as a defendant or a witness, and was required to swear or be affirmed in court, he would raise his right hand. The brand would then be visible by the court and would indicate that the offender had been previously convicted of an offense. Mutilation involves afflicting the offender with corporal punishment, sometimes consistent with the offense committed. For example, a thief may have a hand cut off; a liar may have his tongue removed. Instant death (the fourth in terms of level of severity) included hanging, beheading, or strangulation. Finally, lingering death was the most severe punishment; the offender was put to death slowly and often was tortured beforehand. This may have included burning the offender alive or breaking the offender on the wheel (a procedure that broke all of the offender's major bones).

Torture played a key role in corrections and punishment during the Middle Ages and included stretching offenders until their joints separated (on a device known as the rack) or crushing the offender by placing heavy stones on his chest. Exile and transportation were used, sending offenders out of the country. For example, England sent its offenders to the American colonies or Van Diemen's Land off the Australian coast. During the 1500s, penal bondage emerged as a form of punishment that involved all forms of incarceration. From 1550 through 1700, houses of corrections were formed to incarcerate vagrants (at the time, it was a crime to be vagrant). Those who could not document that they had a viable means of support were placed into a bridewell (workhouse). Prisons emerged once there was a philosophical shift from punishment of the body to punishment of the soul.

Goals of Corrections

There are five commonly held goals of corrections in terms of punishment. Deterrence is preventing crime through the threat of punishment. There are two types of deterrence: general and specific. General deterrence is where the court punishes the offender to dissuade the remainder of society from committing criminal offenses. Specific deterrence is where the offender is punished in such a way so as to dissuade him/her from committing a subsequent offense. Retribution is the premise that punishment should be the act of taking revenge on the criminal and adheres to the doctrine of *lex talionis* ("an eye for an eye"), in which the offender receives his just deserts for his offense. Rehabilitation is the goal of reforming the offender through fundamental changes and addressing any mental health, substance abuse, or behavioral challenges he/she may have that may be causing or influencing his/her criminal behavior. The goal is to "correct" behavior of offenders through treatment, education, and training, yet provide some level of punishment. For example, a condition of probation may be to require an offender to complete substance abuse treatment or anger management courses. Restoration focuses on the victim and seeks to make the victim and all affected by the offender's crime (e.g., society, community) whole again, either through financial reparations or restorative justice. Incapacitation seeks to reduce the likelihood that an offender is able to offend again, through physical barriers and restraints, or through court or other government-imposed restrictions.

Corrections in the United States is typically divided into nine distinct eras. The Penitentiary era (1790–1825) focused on rehabilitation and deterrence of offenders. This era was characterized by offenders serving their time in prisons designed on the congregate system (Auburn system), in which offenders worked and ate together in silence, or the separate system (Pennsylvania system), in which offenders lived and worked in their cell and in silence. The Mass Prison era (1825–76) focused on incapacitation and deterrence, including inmate labor. From 1876 through 1890, the Reformatory era focused on rehabilitation of the offender. During this era, parole gained in popularity, as did indeterminate sentencing, in which offenders were sentenced to an unspecified sentence range (e.g., 5–10 years). Depending on the offender's behavior in custody, he/she would serve the minimum sentence or the maximum (rewarding productive and compliant behavior with the minimum sentence). The Industrial era (1890–1935) focused on incapacitation and included contract labor, state use labor, and the convict lease system. The Punitive era (1935–45) focused on retribution through strict punishment and the offender being in custody. From 1945 through 1967, the Treatment era focused on rehabilitation and included the medical model of treating offenders (i.e., rehabilitation). The Community-Based era (1967–80) emphasized reintegration of offenders into the community through halfway houses, work-release centers, and community service. The Warehousing era (1980–95) focused on incapacitation of offenders with parole being abolished and sentencing guidelines prescribing specific and mandatory sentences. Finally, from 1985 through the present, the Just Deserts era has focused on retribution. This era is marked by determinate sentences (fixed sentences), truth in sentencing laws, and three strikes legislation.

Community-Based Corrections
Community-based corrections are those sanctions that afford the convicted offender an opportunity to remain in the community with the possibility of receiving therapeutic support programs. Those offenders sentenced to a community-based sanctions can be formally supervised by community corrections professionals (such as a probation officer, parole officer, or other case manager) and are subject to terms and conditions ordered by the court, parole commission, or other governing body. The most popular community-based corrections sanctions are probation and parole. Of the 7.2 million persons under correctional supervision at year-end 2009, 70 percent (just over 5 million offenders) were on either probation (4.2 million) or parole (819,000).

Probation. Probation is considered the most widely used sentencing option, and it is a criminal sanction in which the offender remains in the community subject to terms and conditions imposed by the court; probation is an alternative to incarceration. Probation can be supervised (in which the offender is monitored by a probation officer or other community corrections professional) or unsupervised (where the offender is not monitored). While the terms and conditions vary from jurisdiction to jurisdiction and offender to offender (e.g., based on the offense or the offender's challenges), there are standard conditions of probation (required of all offenders, regardless of their offense, special needs, or previous convictions) that require the offender to (1) be gainfully employed or enrolled in a program of study, (2) commit no criminal offense and notify the court and/or probation officer if charged with a new offense, (3) pay a fine, cost of court, restitution, or other fees, (4) report as directed to the court, probation official, or other community corrections professional, (5) notify officials of any change in address and/or employment, (6) not possess any illegal weapons, (7) maintain family obligations (e.g., child support), and (8) remain within the court's jurisdiction unless given permission to leave by the court and/or probation officer. Punitive conditions of probation are those that increase the punishment of the offender based on the severity of the offense.

Therefore, the offender may be sentenced to complete community service hours as a condition of probation, or the offender may be required to observe a curfew, or be placed on intensive probation (a more restrictive form of probation). Treatment conditions of probation (such as requiring the offender to participate in substance abuse treatment or mental health counseling) attempt to reverse the offender's self-destructive behavior.

Probation as a community-based sanction can trace its origins to Boston, Massachusetts, in the 19th century. In 1841, John Augustus, a Boston shoemaker and a member of the temperance movement against alcohol, would often visit the Boston courts to observe the daily hearings, operations, and business of the courts. There, he observed that many offenders were often held over for court or remained in custody because they could not afford to pay the fine or other monetary assessment ordered by the court. Augustus then decided to approach the judges and ask if the courts would consider releasing the offender if Augustus promised to "monitor" them while they were released and ensure that they did not get in further trouble. It is estimated that by the time of his death in 1859, Augustus supervised 2,000 offenders over the years. Boston led the nation in establishing probation as a statutory sanction: The first state law prescribing probation and a full-time paid probation officer was passed in Massachusetts in 1878. By 1925, probation was available for juveniles in every state and for every adult by 1956.

Parole. Parole is the conditional release of an offender from an active jail or prison sentence. Parole can trace its origins to the 18th century, when English judges transferred the custody of inmates to contractors who were paid to transport the prisoners to the American colonies and in turn sell the services of the offenders to the highest bidder. These offenders would have to work for the high bidder until the end of their sentence. However, once the Revolutionary War started in 1775, the British offenders were fighting for the colonists against England, and thus the practice ended. From 1775 through 1856, offenders were transported to penal colonies such as Norfolk Island in Australia. Navy captain Alexander Maconochie was appointed the superintendent of the penal colony, and he implemented a marks system in which an offender could be released from custody early if he earned good marks for improved behavior (much like the indeterminate sentencing policies of today). In 1854, Sir Walter Crofton, who directed the Irish prison system, implemented conditional release of the offender if he reported to local authorities weekly once he was released, committed no new criminal offense, earned an honest living, produced documentation of his ticket of leave, and did not change residence without notifying officials. Massachusetts authorized the first parole legislation in the United States in 1837. At the Elmira Reformatory in New York (which opened in 1876), the institution's superintendent, Zebulon Brockway, developed a classification system in which the offender was categorized based on earning good marks for productive behavior. Brockway determined his impression of the inmate during a one-on-one interview and, eventually, a parole hearing before Brockway and five other staff members. The 1920s through the 1930s were marked by organized crime, Prohibition, and media criticism of crime in the United States. As a result, President Herbert Hoover established the Wickersham Commission to examine these issues facing the criminal justice system. One of the recommendations of the Wickersham Commission was that there be uniformity in state parole practices through the creation of central policy-making boards in the states.

Rows of separate cells in cellblock nine of the Eastern State Penitentiary, in Philadelphia, Pennsylvania, which was built in 1829 and promulgated the separate "Pennsylvania" system.

Advantages and Disadvantages. There are a number of advantages and disadvantages for community-based corrections. Community-based corrections are more cost effective than incarceration. Nationwide, the average cost to house an offender in a jail or prison is $62 per day, far more than $2 to $3 per day for probation. Community-based corrections are also advantageous because there is a reduced criminalization of offenders as they are not subject to socialization with more hardened offenders behind bars. Another advantage of community-based corrections is that the offender can maintain family ties. Parents are able to remain in the home to raise their children (whereas incarcerating the parent may result in the children being placed with other family members or in foster care). Community-based corrections are advantageous because they allow an offender to work, thereby providing for the family; paying restitution, court costs, and fees; and contributing to the tax base. The offender also has a greater opportunity to receive therapeutic and professional services. In prison, there are few programs available to offenders, and those that are available have limited availability based on the large numbers of offenders in prison seeking to participate. Disadvantages of community-based corrections are that these sanctions can be considered a lack of punishment. There is a social liability in that offenders do remain in the community and often reoffend, sometimes committing violent acts. According to the Bureau of Justice Statistics, 52 percent of offenders recidivate, being rearrested for a parole violation or new offense within three years of being released from jail or prison.

Intermediate Sanctions
Intermediate sanctions are those punishments that are not as lenient as community-based corrections but not as restrictive as institutional corrections. The offender is not completely confined to a correctional facility around the clock and has some freedom in the community. Some of the most popular intermediate sanctions are halfway houses, work-release and restitution centers, and boot camps. Intermediate sanctions grew from the need to create alternative sentencing options that did not involve the incarceration of offenders and were more harsh and restrictive than traditional community-based corrections.

Halfway houses are residential programs, located in the community, in which the offender may serve a portion of his/her sentence as a condition of probation or as a condition of early release (e.g., parole, post-release supervision). The offender is ordered to reside in the house, where he is subject to supervision by house staff and any other conditions imposed by the court or sentencing authority, yet he is free to work and to go to school or training programs. Boot camps are paramilitary programs of intensive physical training and include an educational component in which offenders can complete a GED, earn a high school diploma, or pursue other vocational skills. These programs average 90 days, and their goal is to instill discipline, respect, and other skills to foster successful transition once the offender returns to the community.

Institutional Corrections
Institutional corrections are those punishments that involve the offender serving an active sentence in a correctional facility. There are primarily two types of institutional corrections: jails and prisons. Jails are typically local or county facilities that house those offenders who are awaiting trial or convicted offenders serving short-term sentences. Prisons are typically state or federal facilities that house convicted offenders serving long-term sentences. Institutional corrections are often considered an "American" invention as they were developed as a result of a push in the colonies to focus on punishment of the spirit versus punishment of the body during the 1700s. Prisons are total institutions in that offenders work, play, eat, recreate, and sleep together on a continual basis.

During the 1980s, several high-profile, violent offenses by parolees led citizens to demand that the criminal justice system, politicians, and society "get tough" about the recidivism of offenders on parole. That, coupled with President Bill Clinton's signing the 1994 Violent Crime Control and Law Enforcement Act, led to the abolishment of parole. One of the components of the Violent Crime Control and Law Act included $10 billion in funding to the states for corrections spending if those states created provisions or changed their sentencing laws to mandate that offenders serve their sentences in their entirety without provisions for good time, gain time, or parole. However, practitioners and policy makers came to the realization that offenders were being released from prison without any supervision, monitoring, or therapeutic support upon their release. Likewise, there were not any incentives for offenders to continue not to get in trouble (apart from the threat of a new conviction and the punishment sanctioned as a result of the same) as the offender was no longer subject to the authority of the parole commission or other sentencing authority. In 2007, President George W. Bush signed the Second Chance Act, which created federal funding for government agencies and organizations, including faith-based organizations, to provide re-entry programs for offenders in an effort to address the issues and challenges of releasing offenders from prison without any resources in place to assist in their transition back to society.

Re-entry programs promote the reintegration of offenders back into the community once they are released from jail or prison. Re-entry programs differ from parole because parole is a supervision status, which can be revoked if an offender fails to comply with the terms and conditions of his release, and re-entry programs are in place to assist the offender in his transition back to society. Re-entry programs not only prepare offenders for life after prison but reduce future criminality by addressing their challenges of obtaining gainful employment, teach life skills needed (e.g., money management, soft skills needed to deal with other individuals), and put community support resources in place for the offenders.

In the United States, the responsibility for the administration of corrections varies from jurisdiction to jurisdiction. At the federal level, the U.S. Probation Office is responsible for administering probation in each of the U.S. district courts. The Federal Bureau of Prisons is responsible for administering the various federal correctional facilities and penitentiaries. At the state level, most states have a department of corrections, which is responsible for administering the state prisons. Yet probation and parole can be administered through the state's executive branch of government, state judicial agencies, or local executive or judicial agencies. In some states, probation is administered by a combination of these agencies and organizations or may even be a private function, contracted by the states to a private organization.

Capital Punishment

Capital punishment is the ultimate sanction, in which the offender is sentenced to death for his/her offense. The first execution in the United States was Captain George Kendall in the Jamestown Colony in 1608 (he was executed for being a spy for Spain). According to the Bureau of Justice Statistics, at year-end 2009, there were 3,173 offenders on death row in 36 states and in the Federal Bureau of Prisons. Currently, the death penalty is a sanction in 36 of the 50 United States and the federal criminal justice system. Lethal injection is the most common form of execution (allowed in all 36 states). Seventeen of the states give the offender an alternative form of execution in addition to lethal injection, including electrocution (in nine states), lethal gas (in four states), hanging (in three states), and firing squad (in two states). Most of the offenders on death row (1,708) were convicted in southern states, followed by those convicted in western states (940). It is believed that the numbers are as high as they are in these regions because of traditional, conservative views of punishment, retribution, and justice.

Capital punishment as a sentencing option is still widely accepted in the United States, although support for it has declined over the past 30 years. Internationally, capital punishment is not widely accepted, with the United States being the only Western democracy and the only country in North America that executes offenders. Critics of the death penalty argue that it violates the Eighth Amendment of the Constitution, citing that it is cruel and unusual punishment; the U.S. Supreme Court upheld the practice in 1976 in the landmark case *Gregg v. Georgia*. Per the U.S. Supreme Court, the death penalty is constitutional if (1) the court is informed about an offender's criminal background and history, (2) there are standards to guide the trial court in the sentencing decision, (3) the state appellate court must review every death sentence, and (4) the court is made aware of mitigating factors.

The United States does have a history of executing juveniles. George Junius Stinney, Jr., was convicted of the murder of two young girls in April 1944 and was executed in June 1944 at the age of 14 (he was the youngest person executed in the 20th century), despite questions about his ability to commit the murder based on his size, physical attributes, and the alleged method by which the victims were executed. There was also a question about his mental competence. However, in 2005, the U.S. Supreme Court in *Roper v. Simmons* declared it unconstitutional to execute individuals for crimes committed under the age of 18.

In 2002, the Supreme Court also held in *Atkins v. Virginia* that it was unconstitutional to execute persons who are mentally challenged/mentally impaired. In the court's decision, Justice John Paul Stevens, writing for the majority, cited public views against executing this population and changes in several state statutes that were reflective of the view that this was cruel and unusual punishment.

Special Needs Offenders

Special needs offenders are those offenders who provide challenges to the agencies that provide services to them and to the community corrections professionals who work with them based on physical, mental, social, or health challenges. These offenders include substance-abusing offenders, elderly offenders, mentally ill and mentally challenged offenders, as well as offenders with communicable diseases.

Substance-abusing offenders are those offenders who suffer from dependency on one or more substances, including alcohol, as well as legal and illegal drugs. According to the U.S. Department of Justice, 83 percent of all jail and prison inmates abuse or are addicted to drugs and/or alcohol. In addition, 25 percent of all federal and 33 percent of state inmates were under the influence at the time of their arrest, and 50 percent had used drugs within one month prior to the time of their arrest.

Elderly offenders are those offenders age 50 and over. It is estimated that one-third of all offenders are age 50 and older. As a result, some states have developed geriatric prison facilities, which can provide the long-term care needs of elderly inmates and protect these inmates from younger, stronger, and more violent offenders.

Mentally ill offenders are those offenders who have experienced a recent history or symptoms of a mental health problem and its occurrence within the past 12 months. It is estimated that 50 percent of all jail and prison inmates have a mental health disorder (schizophrenia, major depression, bipolar disorder, or post-traumatic stress disorder [PTSD]), and there are eight times more mentally ill individuals in jails and prisons than in mental hospitals. The Los Angeles County Jail spends $10 million per year on psychiatric medication because constitutional standards require that offenders be treated for physical and mental health disorders. This likely mirrors the community-based corrections population, and community corrections professionals work with these offenders, often visiting them in their residence and workplace and during office visits. With government budget cuts prompted by the economic challenges facing most states, there has been an emphasis to deinstitutionalize mentally ill individuals, causing them to remain in the community and often engage in criminal behavior.

Offenders with communicable diseases are a challenge to both institutional and community-based corrections in that diseases attributed to airborne pathogens such as tuberculosis or hepatitis can be easily transmitted by inmates living in close confines. Because of sexual contact (which occurs regardless of policies prohibiting the acts), sexually transmitted diseases are often spread in prison. Likewise, inmates have these diseases upon being admitted to the correctional facilities and are seldom screened. Other communicable diseases such as human immunodeficiency virus and acquired immune deficiency syndrome (HIV/AIDS) pose a risk for corrections in that they can be transmitted to staff, inmates, and visitors through sexual contact with the inmate or through the inmate placing his/her blood in the drink or food of other parties.

Nicola Davis Bivens
Johnson C. Smith University

See Also: Capital Punishment; Community Service; Parole; Prisoner's Rights; Probation; Sentencing.

Further Readings
Champion, Dean J. *Probation, Parole, and Community Corrections*, 6th ed. Upper Saddle River, NJ: Pearson Prentice Hall, 2007.
Glaze, Lauren E. *Correctional Populations in the United States 2009*. Washington, DC: Bureau of Justice Statistics, 2010.
Schmalleger, Frank and John Ortiz Smykla. *Corrections in the 21st Century*, 5th ed. New York: McGraw-Hill Higher Education, 2009.
Siegal, Larry and Clemens Bartollas. *Corrections Today*. Belmont, CA: Cengage, 2011.
Snell, Tracy L. *Capital Punishment 2009—Statistical Tables*. Washington, DC: Bureau of Justice Statistics, 2010.

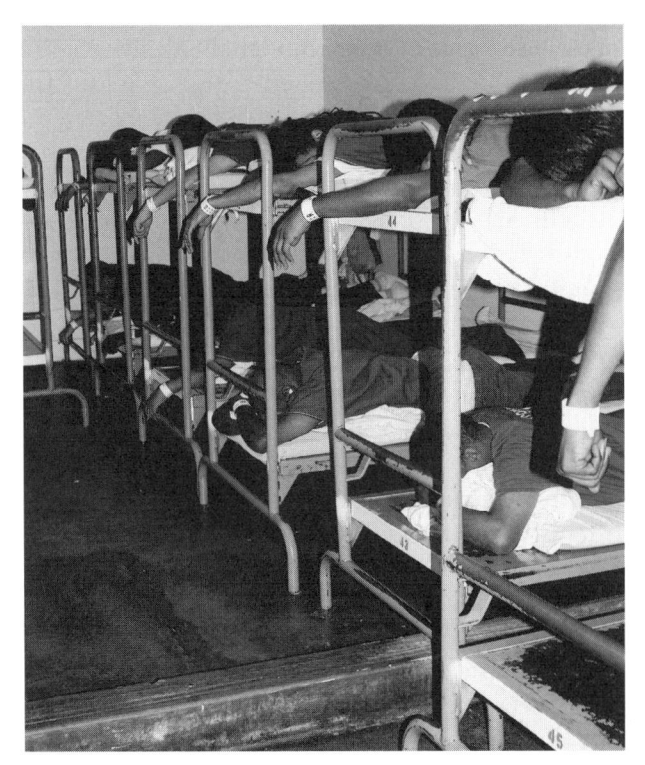

With 50 percent of all U.S. inmates suffering from a mental health disorder, the Los Angeles County Jail, shown above, is forced to spend $10 million a year on psychiatric medications.

Corruption, Contemporary

Corruption is the practice of using influence or money to cause officials to do what they would otherwise have not done or to accelerate what they would already have done. The first of these cases is considered more serious than the second, although this is still illegal. Corruption can affect every sector of society and can be found in both the public and private sectors. In the 21st century, the United States has scored as having a relatively low level of corruption and is a member of a second group of countries somewhat behind the leading economies of Sweden, Norway, Australia, and Canada, among others. Nevertheless, there are still plenty of causes for concern in the strong and opaque relationships between some corporate interests and certain politicians, in the new forms of corruption that are possible, and in the continued issue of public discourse being negatively affected by the continued use of falsification and oversimplification by some commentators.

The Federal Bureau of Investigation (FBI) claims that public corruption remains one of its principal targets because of its role in eroding trust in government institutions and the poisonous effect such lack of trust has on society. Meanwhile, corporate lobbyists continue to try to water down the provisions of the Foreign Corrupt Practices Act (1977) and other anticorruption measures. The Supreme Court itself, notably in the 2006 *Garcetti v. Ceballos* decision, has made government suppression of corruption difficult by permitting retaliation against whistle-blowers. The post–September 11 environment has been used to justify many practices that were previously considered outrageous.

Financial Industries

Owing to the high levels of cash available, the volume of transactions, the complexity of many new financial instruments, and the informational asymmetries existing, there remain powerful incentives for rogue individuals to cheat the public or even institutional customers. Bernie Madoff, for example, organized a Ponzi scheme in which customers were fraudulently repaid with money drawn from newer customers. Madoff was subsequently convicted and given a 150-year prison sentence, but the significance of his career lies in the complexity of contemporary financial services and their separation from the scrutiny of nonspecialists. Even specialist attorneys and prosecutors find it difficult to take into account all the different interactions involved; people less conversant with the issues find it extremely difficult to make proper judgments about what may or may not have happened. Combined with the drastic reduction in regulation of the finance industry and the enormous increases in income inequality created by repeated tax cuts for the very richest in American society, a number of finance industry executives came to feel a sense of impunity that contributed to the banking crisis of 2007–08 and its subsequent disastrous impact on countries around the world. Some efforts were subsequently made to reform the industry by, for example, breaking up those banks deemed to be "too big to fail," but these efforts are widely considered to be inadequate.

Cash-Based Industries

Cash-based industries offer a particular incentive for operators to commit minor or even major acts of corruption because cash can easily be transferred from one hand to another without appearing on any books. These industries, including casinos, establishments offering sexual services, or others in which patrons may be reluctant to leave their personal details, are also associated with the laundering of money by criminal gangs. Prostitution and drug money, for example, can be reworked through such industries, and cash payments can also be made to officials charged with regulating the businesses to turn a blind eye to infractions. Such activities are often associated with newly arriving migrants, who may find it difficult to obtain alternative sources of employment and who are vulnerable to exploitation and in urgent need of money quickly.

Military-Industrial Complex

In the years following the terrorist attacks on the United States in 2001, a vast increase in military action overseas and homeland security domestically have provided a wide range of opportunities for well-connected military goods and services providers that have raised new fears of a corrupt relationship between industry and government. These fears were intensified by the opacity with which many contracts were awarded and operations organized, because of the pretext of security, as well as the use of private-sector companies such as Blackwater (now renamed Xe) that have hired large numbers of former service personnel to provide guarding and security services in Iraq and other overseas trouble spots, while also bolstering their position in the United States. This company, which is not alone in the field, has been accused of numerous acts of unwarranted violent aggression overseas, and the thought of its heavily armed personnel being deployed on American streets to keep order in the wake of natural disasters has prompted concern.

Police Corruption

Recent work on corruption in the American police has argued for a broader definition of corruption, which, like the treatment of the military-industrial complex, includes some actions not previously considered to be corrupt. Malfeasance, for example, can include many illicit activities conducted with a view to completing official tasks. Falsifying statements or manufacturing evidence, for example, would be classified as corruption according to this thinking. Police departments might succumb to systemic corruption either through the desire to prosecute individuals believed to be guilty but for whom evidence is insufficient, or because of desire for personal gain. The temptations are more severe in the case of cash-based industries such as sale of illegal drugs. However, the problems of police corruption have declined over the years as measures enforcing accountability and transparency have become more effective.

Recent high-profile cases such as the execution of Troy Anthony Davis reveal the suspicion with which many people view statements made by at least some of the police in some circumstances. Davis was convicted of the August 1988 murder of a Savannah, Georgia, police officer and was sentenced to death. In the years after his conviction, many of the witnesses in the case recanted their statements and accused the police of coercing their testimony, casting doubt on his guilt. In 2011, Davis was denied his final appeal for a new trial and was executed by lethal injection in the midst of mass protests and pleas from such notable figures as former President Jimmy Carter and Archbishop Desmond Tutu, among others.

Popular Media

It has been argued that the normal issue of bias in the popular media has been stretched to the extent that it should now be referred to as "media corruption." The dividing line appears to be when falsehoods are deliberately passed off as truths and facts are deliberately traduced for the sake of ideological bias. The best-known examples of this involve the talk radio sector, which is strongly associated with the extreme political right, and the Fox News Network, which also has a pronounced right-wing agenda and, according to its critics, deliberately produces inaccurate reports that suit its ideology better. Man-made global climate change is one issue that has attracted the charge of media corruption in that it is alleged that corporate agencies with an interest in promoting fossil fuel use have persuaded media outlets to claim that a debate exists among scientists concerning the existence of global climate change, its cause, and what can be done to combat it, when such debate does not exist in a meaningful sense.

Corporate Social Responsibility

American business tends to prefer a contractual basis to underline its activities, and this approach extends to the provision of laws and regulations. Laws now expressly forbid American people or corporations, participating in any form of bribery or corrupt practices wherever they might happen in the world. Despite some high-profile exceptions, this approach has proved quite successful in most parts of the world, although the reservations related to military services mentioned above should be retained. At the same time, the continued spread of information and Internet technology have made it much more difficult for business entities to keep activities secret anywhere in the world. Although it remains difficult to attract widespread media coverage in the United States for stories critical of corporate behavior, it is possible to bring it to the attention of state authorities, who in due course will bring about investigations and prosecutions when these are warranted.

Companies, especially large companies, have reacted to a changing marketplace by creating and propagating campaigns of corporate social responsibility (CSR) to demonstrate their benign intentions toward the environment and society at large. Although not all of these programs are entirely sincere or indeed of any real use, it does indicate the current belief in business that, as the knowledge-based economy approaches, intangible assets will be increasingly valuable to businesses and, of these assets, the most obvious is the reputation of the company. It is believed and taught in many business schools, therefore, that any gain that might be obtained from an act of corruption is greatly outweighed by the negative consequences to the organization if the wrongdoing is discovered and made known.

Computer-Mediated Corruption

One of the most significant differences between contemporary forms of corruption and those of the past is the ubiquity of computer-mediated communication as part of everyday life. People intending to take part in some form of corrupt practice are now likely to deal with each other through some kind of electronic means rather than on a face-to-face basis. The transmission of money or other resources might also be conducted by computer rather than being physically transferred from one party to another. This change has made clear differences in the type and nature of evidence that may be obtained by legal authorities in pursuing a prosecution. From a human perspective, computer-mediated communication has greatly widened the range of possible contacts, but the communication is often on a very shallow level with limited amounts of trust and, hence, increases the likelihood of cheating other people.

John Walsh
Shinawatra University

See Also: 1961 to 1980 Primary Documents; Computer Crime; Corruption, History of; Corruption, Sociology of; Madoff, Bernard; Technology, Police.

Further Readings

Brown, Ed and Jonathan Cloke. "Critical Perspectives on Corruption: An Overview." *Critical Perspectives on International Business*, v.7/2 (2011).

Dion, Michel. "Corruption, Fraud and Cybercrime as Dehumanizing Phenomena." *International Journal of Social Economics*, v.38/5 (2011).

Henriques, Diana. *The Wizard of Lies: Bernie Madoff and the Death of Trust*. New York: Time Books, 2011.

Punch, Maurice. *Police Corruption: Exploring Police Deviance and Crime*. London: Routledge, 2009.

Transparency International. http://www.transparency.org (Accessed September 2011).

Corruption, History of

Corruption is generally defined as an act that is evil or wicked or that involves dishonesty or violation of a duty or trust. This is a very broad definition and can include almost any act and, as a general matter, can include criminal acts. It also includes any number of acts that, although dishonest or unethical, are not crimes. Indeed, *corruption* is a term that is not legally defined, as specific criminal acts are defined. Thus, the term can and does have a broad meaning and is frequently applied in many different contexts, although it is generally limited to acts involving government officials and agencies. In the context of crime, it can have various applications.

Corruption and Crimes

In the context of crime, corruption is usually not used for generic crimes such as murder, rape, kidnapping, arson, battery, assault, robbery, burglary, or simple theft, although such crimes would be encompassed in a broad definition of corruption. The term *corruption* can be and frequently is applied to certain crimes that involve the violation of a trust or a fiduciary relationship. These crimes usually involve embezzlement, bribery, extortion, malicious prosecution, abuse of process, insider trading, and malfeasance or abuse of office.

Embezzlement is usually defined as the crime of theft by a person who holds a position of fiduciary responsibility such as a banker or a trustee but can be applied against government officials. Bribery is usually defined as the payment of money to a person in a position of trust, such as a government official, to influence that person's behavior in his or her official capacity in a particular manner. The crime of extortion is frequently defined as when a government official demands money in exchange for performing a certain act or failing to execute a duty. Malicious prosecution is usually defined as the initiating of criminal charges against a person for an unethical or unlawful motive such as personal hatred, even though the criminal charges are technically correct. Abuse of process is similar to malicious prosecution but is more expansive in that it can involve the employment of other government processes to harm another person. Malfeasance or abuse of office occurs when a government official intentionally engages in some unethical or illegal activity for his or her own or another's personal gain or purposes, such as the harm of another person, even if the act is technically legal. Malfeasance is not a crime in some jurisdictions and may only constitute a civil offense.

Corporations and commerce present a different problem regarding corruption than government agencies and officials. Many acts that would be considered corrupt or illegal when committed by a government official are not corrupt when done by a corporate official. However, there are crimes that are uniquely associated with corporations and commerce. For example, the crime of insider trading occurs when people with secret information concerning certain corporations or securities use that information to gain an unfair advantage in the purchase or sale of securities—this is a crime. Another example is the crime of embezzlement, which is defined as the theft of money that is entrusted to a person or entity such as a bank. Those persons or entities who hold such a trust are called fiduciaries.

Corruption is also used when describing unethical activities such as conflicts of interest, to include nepotism and cronyism, which might not constitute an actual crime. Nepotism is the employment of a relative rather than hiring the most qualified person for a job. Cronyism is the hiring of people based on their personal or professional contacts rather than on their qualifications. Although nepotism and cronyism are not illegal in private corporations, some political entities have laws against nepotism. But cronyism is usually not illegal, even though it is generally recognized as not fair or equitable, and is even widely accepted in political systems that allow for "political spoils" to the winners of elections. Conflicts of interest usually involve situations in which a government official might have a personal or financial interest in the matters before that official. Many political entities have laws or regulations that prohibit conflicts of interest. In the modern world, one of the biggest problems is the awarding of lucrative government contracts. Because government contracts are so profitable, with payments amounting to billions of dollars, many corporations will do anything to win them. There are many examples of politicians and bureaucrats being caught in the web of government contracts.

Corruption can be and is frequently viewed as a government-based phenomenon (to especially include political corruption). Corruption by government officials tends to be viewed as more serious than corruption in the private sector, at least in certain democratic nations. Moreover, political corruption can include activities by a government that suppress or oppress the citizenry for the enrichment and benefit of government officers and powerful private entities. Political corruption also includes tampering with elections or improperly influencing the creation or selection of a political system or leader. Of course, the view of such activities must be interpreted through the nature and philosophy of the political system present in that country. What might be corrupt in one country (e.g., capitalism in a communist regime) might not be corrupt in a country holding different political values.

Political Corruption in Early America

Political corruption has been with America since its founding. A brief representative list of events and legislative enactments up to the start of the 21st century provides the flavor of political corruption in American history.

One of the first major corruption scandals in America involved President John Adams and the Federalist Party. The opposing Democratic-Republican Party, led by Thomas Jefferson, had been criticizing Adams and his administration. Also, Adams and the Federalists were concerned about the French Revolution causing problems in the newly formed United States of America. In response, Adams and the Federalists enacted the Alien and Sedition Acts of 1798, which, among other results, criminalized criticism of the president or the government. Subsequently, a number of Democratic-Republicans, including several publishers, were arrested and convicted. The political reasons for the Sedition Act were obvious when the expiration date of the statute—one day prior to the expiration of Adams's term—came to light. As a result, the Federalists were swept from office in the next election, and Jefferson, the new president, pardoned all of the people convicted under the Sedition Act.

New York City in the 1860s was the location of one of the most famous corruption scandals in America. The power brokers of New York City had created a massive political machine known generically as Tammany Hall. The name *Tammany Hall* came from a political society known as the Tammany Society that was founded in 1789 and opposed the Federalists. Over the years, it developed into a corrupt political organization that did not gain power until the 1850s. It specialized in political patronage and corrupt business dealings involving city money, such that the name *Tammany Hall* became synonymous with political corruption. Corruption by Tammany Hall included but was most certainly not limited to political favors, police payoffs, and election fixing. The power of the Tammany Hall political machinery reached its height in the 1860s. Despite efforts at reform, it continued to exist in one form or another until the 1960s, when it was finally extinguished.

After the Civil War, Ulysses S. Grant, the victorious commander of the Union army, was elected president in 1868. Grant's administration was considered one of the most corrupt in American history, becoming ridden with political scandals. Grant was primarily accused of being incompetent in the selection and appointment of subordinates and of abusing his authority by protecting family members and cronies.

The Credit Mobilier scandal in 1872 was another major national political corruption scandal. Credit Mobilier was a company started in the early 1860s to build a transcontinental railroad across the United States. The construction of the railroad was burdened with enormous unnecessary costs. To prevent any congressional investigations and to obtain favorable legislation, numerous congressmen were showered with bribes, gifts, and stock. After several years the railroad began to experience huge financial losses, and in 1872, the scandal broke in the newspapers. Congressional investigations resulted in the expulsions of two congressmen from the House of Representatives, who were viewed as scapegoats. No criminal charges were brought against any other person. President Ulysses S. Grant, whose administration was under severe criticism for corruption, was not implicated.

In 1875, the Whiskey Ring scandal broke in St. Louis, Missouri. It was discovered that a large number of government agents were involved in the siphoning of tax revenues from the sale of whiskey. Treasury Secretary Benjamin Bristow had conducted a secret investigation to prevent the suspects from being warned because so many government officials were involved. More than 350 people were arrested, resulting in more

This 1885 cartoon shows Uncle Sam in a swamp filled with symbols representing such scandals as the Whiskey Ring, while a man points to a statue of Abraham Lincoln freeing a slave.

than 200 indictments. President Grant was not informed of the investigation prior to the arrests. When the prosecutions started, Grant interfered in them to the extent of firing the special prosecutor who was handling the trials as well as Bristow himself. Only a few people were convicted.

In 1883, as a result of the extensive corruption in the Grant administration and the assassination of President James Garfield by a disappointed office seeker, Congress enacted the Civil Service Act of 1883. Up to that point, appointments to the government bureaucracy were a result of the "spoils system," in which a government job was obtained by favors from the primary officeholder. With the advent of the civil service, it became more difficult to fire government employees after an election with a new party taking office, and the seeds of a professional bureaucracy were planted.

Twentieth-Century Corruption

The Tillman Act of 1907 was the first attempt by the Congress to limit spending in campaign finance. Because of the widespread corruption in elections, especially from corporations and banks giving gifts to political campaigns, Congress attempted to limit the influence of these entities on elections to public office. This was shortly followed by the Publicity Act of 1910, which not only revised the Tillman Act but also required the disclosure of campaign contributions and spending.

With the passage of the Volstead Act of 1919, the manufacture and sale of alcohol became illegal in the United States. As a result of the Volstead Act, organized crime expanded its operations from gambling and prostitution to include bootlegging to address the demand for alcohol, which many people in America still wanted despite the law. This expansion into bootlegging also brought a new perspective to corruption in America, which is illustrated by events in Chicago in the 1920s and the early 1930s. It has been estimated that the Chicago mob, personified by Al Capone, operated more than 10,000 speakeasies in the city. The problem was so widespread, with the corrupt assistance and protection of the Chicago Police Department, that the federal government eventually moved in to enforce the law and stop the violence. In 1933, in recognition that some forms of vice cannot be controlled, the Volstead Act was repealed.

The Teapot Dome Scandal, which occurred from 1923 to 1929, was one of the most famous political corruption scandals in America. Earlier in the century, a number of areas in the United States had been set aside for the development of oil, one of which was called the Teapot Dome. In 1920, President Warren Harding appointed Albert Fall to be his secretary of the interior. Fall was friends with several oilmen. Fall convinced Harding to transfer control of the oil reserve areas to the Department of the Interior. After apparently accepting bribes, Fall leased some of the areas to his friends. The oil reserves were estimated to be worth $100 million, for which Fall received payments of almost $500,000. When the secret deals became public, there was a massive public outcry. Harding died in 1923 his successor, Calvin Coolidge, appointed a special prosecutor to investigate the matter. As a result, Fall was convicted and sent to prison, though his friends were acquitted.

During this time period, Congress continued its attempts to regulate corruption in elections. The Federal Corrupt Practices Act of 1925 repealed the Tillman Act of 1907 and the Publicity Act of 1910, adjusted the spending limits for federal candidates, and mandated disclosures of campaign contributions and expenditures. The Hatch Act of 1939 prohibited federal employees from working on campaigns of candidates for federal offices and prohibited the coercion of contributions from federal employees.

The early 1950s saw an income tax scandal during the administration of President Harry Truman. Allegations of corruption at the Internal Revenue Service (IRS) became public along with accusations that the Department of Justice was refusing to investigate the IRS. Truman appointed a special prosecutor to investigate the matter, but when the special prosecutor attempted to investigate the Department of Justice, the attorney general refused to cooperate. Truman fired the attorney general and appointed another one, who took over the investigation, despite accusations of a cover-up. As a result of the investigation, only one minor Department of Justice official was fired.

Chicago is a place where political corruption is considered by many people to be standard operating procedure. It is personified by the administration of Mayor Richard J. Daley, who served for

21 years from 1955 to 1971. Daley is considered to be the last old-style political boss. He was in charge of the Democratic Party in addition to being mayor and exercised an incredible amount of power.

Although he was frequently accused of being heavy-handed, undemocratic, and politically corrupt, which included accusations of fixing the election for President John F. Kennedy and being responsible for the police riot at the 1968 Democratic National Convention, he was honored as a man who protected Chicago and had a number of positive accomplishments. Although a number of his assistants were jailed for corruption, Daley was never convicted.

Corruption in the Modern Era

At the start of the 1970s, Congress enacted the Federal Election Campaign Act of 1971. This law established stricter standards for the monitoring and reporting of campaign finances. It also limited the contributions by individuals and political action committees. The act was amended in 1974 to address the abuses of the Nixon campaign after the Watergate scandal.

The 1970s ushered in a new era of corruption in America. The Watergate scandal exploded in 1972. President Richard Nixon was forced to resign under the threat of impeachment after it was discovered that the Republican Party was responsible for the burglary of the Democratic National Committee headquarters in the Watergate Hotel in Washington, D.C. Congressional hearings followed after the matter was widely publicized by two *Washington Post* reporters, Bob Woodward and Carl Bernstein. Nixon appointed a special prosecutor, Archibald Cox, who was eventually fired when he tried to compel Nixon to reveal certain tape recordings, after Nixon forced the resignations of various government officials who refused to fire him.

This firing later became known as the Saturday Night Massacre. In dramatic testimony before Congress, former Nixon lawyer John Dean provided testimony that sealed Nixon's fate. President Gerald Ford's subsequent pardon of Nixon is considered the primary reason Ford was not given a full term as president. Watergate is considered the watershed for political cynicism in modern America.

In 1975, following the Watergate scandal, there was a mood in the country for increasing oversight of government activities. In 1975, the Church Committee was formed in the U.S. Senate and was tasked to investigate allegations that the Central Intelligence Agency (CIA) had plotted assassinations of foreign leaders and was involved in subverting foreign governments, and that the CIA and the Federal Bureau of Investigation (FBI) were involved in spying on American citizens. The most infamous FBI operation was COINTELPRO, in which the FBI engaged in covert surveillance of American citizens for political reasons. The results shocked America and resulted in significant changes to increase accountability of covert activities and law enforcement. Much of the Church Committee report is still classified.

In the aftermath of the Watergate scandal, Congress enacted the Ethics in Government Act of 1978. This law prohibited officers and employees of the government from soliciting or accepting anything of value from any corporation or person that conducts business with the government. This law also established the Office of Independent Counsel to investigate violations of law by government officers. It provided for the appointment of a special prosecutor by a panel of three judges.

The 1970s saw the expansion of investigation into government corruption by the FBI. From 1978 to 1980, the FBI conducted a sting operation against various U.S. congressmen, which was called ABSCAM. FBI agents posed as Arab sheikhs and offered bribes to the various congressmen for help in gaining entry into the United States and for the purchasing of casinos. A number of congressmen were convicted. A subsequent congressional investigation into whether the FBI entrapped the congressmen was unsuccessful. ABSCAM is considered to be one of the most effective sting operations in the history of investigations of political corruption.

The Iran-Contra scandal lasted from 1986 to 1993 and was probably the biggest embarrassment of President Ronald Reagan's administration. Up until 1986, officials in the Reagan administration had been secretly and illegally shipping arms to Iran. This occurred during the Iranian Hostage Crisis, and the arms shipments were justified on the grounds that they were intended to secure the release of the hostages. Another purpose was the funding of the Contras, a group of rebels in Nicaragua who were being supported in their revolt against the government of Nicaragua. After the revelation of the shipments, the resulting political carnage was devastating. Fourteen Reagan administration officials were indicted, with 11 being convicted, including Defense Secretary Casper Weinberger. Reagan was never charged or convicted. Some of the convictions were overturned on appeal, and the remaining people who were convicted were pardoned by the next president, George H. W. Bush, who was Reagan's vice president. Interestingly, some of those who were pardoned later became officials in the administration of President George W. Bush.

Protesters calling for Richard Nixon's impeachment near the U.S. Capitol in 1973. After the national trauma of the Watergate scandal, Congress enacted the Ethics in Government Act of 1978.

Throughout the 1980s, there was a serious financial crisis with savings and loans in the United States. Charles Keating was the chairman of Lincoln Savings and Loan, which was under investigation by the federal government. In 1989, Lincoln Savings and Loan collapsed, costing the United States more than $3 billion. Keating had made numerous donations to various politicians. Five U.S. senators, who came to be known as the Keating Five—a group that included John McCain—attempted to intervene on behalf of Keating. Although none of the senators were charged or convicted of any crimes, they were reprimanded and/or criticized by the Senate for their actions.

In 1989, the Housing and Urban Development scandal was brought into the public light. The Department of Housing and Urban Development, which was formed in 1965, was, among other things, responsible for assisting the poor with housing projects. One of these programs was Title 8. It was revealed that a Reagan appointee, Judge Samuel Pierce, Jr., had overseen a massive campaign of fraud, embezzlement, influence peddling, and preferential treatment relative to Section 8 housing. Although Pierce was never charged with a crime, it is estimated that the fraud cost the United States between $2 billion and $8 billion.

With the 1990s came a new president—Bill Clinton. However, political corruption and scandal still appeared. From 1993 to 2001, the Whitewater scandal occupied much of the nation's time and attention. Bill and Hillary Clinton were accused of being involved in an extensive land fraud deal that occurred before their move from Arkansas to Washington, D.C. One of their associates had used money from Madison Savings and Loan to secretly finance the land deal. Some of the money was alleged to have been improperly used for the Clinton campaign. Madison Savings and Loan later collapsed, costing the United States $68 million. An independent prosecutor was appointed to investigate the matter, while several committees in Congress conducted investigations. Eventually, several Clinton associates were sent to jail; the Clintons were never charged or convicted, although the final report indicated that they were involved in the fraud.

In recognition of the corrupting influence of lobbying and the ineffectiveness of previous legislation, Congress enacted the Lobbying Disclosure Act of 1995. This act required the registration of and disclosure by lobbyists who were attempting to influence the government.

Corruption in the Context of Crime

In the context of crime, corruption in the nation's law enforcement agencies has been widespread. A primary example is the continuing effort in New York City to address corruption. In 1894, the Lexow Committee conducted an investigation into police corruption and found that election tampering, bribes for assignments and promotion, brutality, and bribery for gambling and prostitution were widespread in the New York City Police Department dating back to the 1850s. In 1913, the Curran Committee investigated murder by the police, the police extorting protection payments from citizens, bribes, payoffs concerning gambling and prostitution prosecutions, and the rather unique situation of assigning officers to investigate complaints against themselves. In 1932, the Seabury investigation addressed bribes to and extortion by the police department, lawyers, judges, and politicians to fix criminal prosecutions.

Perjury was found to be widespread in the police department. In 1954, the Helfand investigation was formed to investigate protection payments extorted by the police department and widespread perjury. In 1972, the Knapp Commission, made more famous by the events surrounding Frank Serpico, found extensive perjury and bribery by the police involving prostitution, drugs, and gambling. Payoffs inside the department were frequent for promotions and medical retirements. In 1994, the Mollen Commission found that the police engaged in systematic burglary, robbery, and drug trafficking. It also found that the police engaged in perjury and brutality and had a code of silence and cover-ups that prevented internal investigation into corruption. The Mollen Commission also found that it was impossible for police departments to investigate themselves.

Conclusion

There is no doubt that corruption in America has been and is widespread, continuing, and widely accepted, if only informally. Corruption is part of the political and governmental culture of America despite the many attempts to address it. And it appears to be widely accepted as a part of the law enforcement community. It is ironic that corruption is so ingrained in the very governmental agencies that are intended to stop crime. Indeed, history seems to show that it will never be effectively stopped.

Wm. C. Plouffe, Jr.
Independent Scholar

See Also: 1961 to 1980 Primary Documents; Code of Silence; Corruption, Contemporary; Corruption, Sociology of; Ethics in Government Act of 1978; Knapp Commission; Mollen Commission; Political Crimes, Contemporary; Volstead Act; Watergate.

Further Readings

Allen, Oliver E. *The Tiger: The Rise and Fall of Tammany Hall*. Boston: Addison-Wesley, 1993.

Binstein, Michael and Charles Bowden. *Trust Me: Charles Keating and the Missing Billions*. New York: Random House, 1993.

Burns, Eric. *The Spirits of America: The Social History of Alcohol*. Philadelphia: Temple University Press, 2003.

Chin, Gabriel, ed. *New York City Police Corruption Investigation Commissions 1894–1994*. Buffalo, NY: Hein, 1997.

Dash, Samuel. *Chief Counsel: Inside the Ervin Committee—The Untold Story of Watergate*. New York: Random House, 1976.

Grossman, Mark, ed. *Political Corruption in America*. Amenia, NY: Grey House, 2008.

McCarthy, Laton. *The Teapot Dome Scandal*. New York: Random House, 2008.

Royko, Michael. *Boss: Richard J. Daley of Chicago*. New York: Dutton, 1971.

Sirica, John J. *To Set the Record Straight: The Break-in, The Tapes, The Conspirators, The Pardon*. New York: Norton, 1979.

Corruption, Sociology of

Corruption involves using money, power, or influence to cause an official to act differently from how his or her duties would normally require. It can occur in the private or public sectors and can involve both accelerating what would have happened anyway and changing a decision that should have been made. Clearly, people who are able to wield such power, influence, and money are most able to cause corruption, and this is a crime that has much less involvement with the poor. Corruption in the private sector has become quite closely involved with white-collar crime both domestically and internationally. A conflict of interest occurs when an individual or institution is charged with providing an impartial decision but has a connection with one or more of the other actors involved, which tends to prevent impartiality. A lobbyist writing legislation represents a conflict of interest.

Political Corruption

It should be acknowledged that much of the rest of the world considers the American political system to be inherently corrupt—but that does not mean that they overlook the corruption in their own systems. This is because of the close cash nexus between politicians and lobbyists and the lack of binding ideology among the large parties that means candidates customarily run as individuals rather than as members of a party with a defined partly line and known principles that would guide behavior in situations that are still emergent.

Political corruption tends to center on the ability of lobbyists to persuade representatives to pass or reject legislation in a way that benefits them and that does not meet that the legal requirements. As lobbying has become more professional in the modern age, the relationship between politicians and lobbyists has become not just more intense and multivalent but also much longer-lasting in time. One of the principal reasons many political posts have term limits placed upon them is to try to inhibit this type of relationship, and it is problematic that many leading positions are open-ended in nature. As the relationship continues, people become more familiar with each other's desires, intentions, and goals, and this has the effect that, like a long-term personal relationship, it is no longer necessary for one party fully to express desires and wishes to the other party. When understanding is present without anything being said and certainly nothing documented, then it is much easier for the relationship to slide into a corrupt one without it being apparent at any particular stage that the line has been crossed.

This form of corruption is most commonly associated with corporate interests, which have used their influence throughout American industry to resist the regulation that protects consumers from dangerous products or the negative externalities of their actions, to restrict or deny freedom of association or collective bargaining for their workers, or in the endless demands for tax cuts for themselves and subsidies to protect them against more-competitive foreign firms. However, some labor unions have also exerted their influence in corrupt ways, notably the International Teamsters Union, which has attracted an unwanted reputation for both corruption and violence. These cases show the weakness of a relationship in the public sphere that is not properly transparent and subject to investigation and, preferably, limited in time. Since positions of influence in America have been most commonly held by rich, middle-aged, white men, most cases of corruption have focused on the actions of rich, middle-aged, white men. However, investigations of corruption around the world have demonstrated that there are people of all genders, ethnicities, religions, and any other demographic factor willing to become involved in corruption on either side of the relationship, and there are no demonstrable differences among people in this regard. Instead, it is all about the money and the power.

One of the most prominent examples of corruption of this sort is seen in the administration of President Warren Harding (1921–23), when a significant number of his long-term political allies, who became known as the Ohio Gang, were appointed to high office. "Gang" members profited from rents obtained from their actions, although it is not clear whether Harding himself was complicit in these actions or just negligent. An earlier example is the administration of Ulysses S. Grant (1869–77), under whose rule nepotism and rent-seeking by political appointees was apparently rife.

The relationship between political supporters and office appointments has continued to be problematic at all levels of government. Transparency and scrutiny by courts and media have been weapons used to combat this form of corruption, although it can hardly be said that the battle has been won. Former Illinois Governor Rod Blagojevich, for example, was found guilty of a variety of corrupt practices in 2011. Numerous officials were indicted and prosecuted during the Reagan (1981–88) and Nixon (1969–74) administrations, in particular, though no administration has been free of its own scandals. Often, corrupt practices were tied to other illegal or unethical activities, sometimes in the interest of ideological purposes (as in the Iran-Contra scandal during the Reagan administration) and sometimes just in the interest of personal gain (as the Blagojevich case seems to indicate).

Attempts to Limit Corruption

To deal with corruption at the corporate level, various laws have been introduced to add transparency to corporate practices and also to prevent bribery, notably through the 1977 Foreign Corrupt Practices Act. As business became more internationalized and non-Western states became prominent as both potential markets and suppliers of goods, American corporations found themselves drawn more or less willingly into corrupt practices, when, for example, gift-giving exchanges escalated or bribes were openly solicited by private- or public-sector officials. The principle enforced now is that any corrupt practice by an American corporation is punishable in a domestic court no matter where in the world it took place and who was involved in such an act. This principle is becoming popular around the world and, in combination with the empowering effects of the Internet and mobile communication devices, companies are becoming obliged to pay close attention to the nature of their supply chains to make sure they are not linked in any way not just with corruption but with trying to hide the use of sweatshop or child labor, polluting other countries, or exploiting their resources in an unsustainable way.

People who attempt to reveal wrongdoing and corruption by organizations are known as whistleblowers. Such people are often subject to considerable pressures to keep them quiet, either through intimidation or being involved in peer groups that privilege loyalty to the organization above normal standards of behavior. Consequently, several laws have been introduced to protect and regulate the interests of whistleblowers, including the 1912 Lloyd–La Follette Act and the Sarbanes-Oxley Act of 2002, in addition to clauses or provisions in various other pieces of legislation. Increased job insecurity in the wake of lower levels of unionization, together with corporate attempts to monopolize the thoughts of employees and keep them from being broadcast publicly, deter many people from speaking out as they might otherwise do. Incidents of workplace bullying, for example, reveal that many people will tolerate abuse shown to others if it seems to mean they themselves will not be persecuted.

Small-Scale Corruption

In the case of small-scale corruption, officials with discretionary ability have in some cases accepted bribes of different kinds to turn a blind eye to crimes or to manipulate the resources to which they have access. During Prohibition, for example, organized criminals running illegal alcohol production and distribution services often used bribery to induce police to leave them in peace to conduct their operations. The same is true of cash-based illegal or semilegal industries throughout history. This includes such activities as gambling, prostitution, and the use of drugs. Even when the activities are, strictly speaking, legal or the involvement of an individual as a customer has not been criminalized, business operators are reluctant to have police involvement since this leads to scandal, and potential customers are scared away. In these cases, the type of people involved are also those involved in the industries concerned, and there is a link between illegal, gang-related activities and marginalized members of society, such as members of recently arrived ethnic minorities who lack the network connections or influence to obtain decent work. Since most criminal gangs prey on their junior members, the actual money used to pay bribes is extorted from the sex workers or drugs runners at the ground level. Sex workers, in particular, are vulnerable to this kind of extortion, especially when they have been trafficked from overseas, have no official standing in America, and thus have no opportunity to appeal to the authorities or to anyone else.

In the case of nonpolice officials, the type of influence that can be brought to bear includes a combination of cash payments and other inducements. Nearly all academic institutions have organizational memories, usually anecdotal in nature, in which male teachers request or are offered sexual favors from female students (other configurations are possible but are less common) in return for better grades or other rewards. The same situation exists in many workplaces, and it is often the case that prosecutions are almost impossible to achieve because any case reduces to one person's word against another, and this is very difficult to adjudicate. However, suspicion that many people, especially men, abuse their position to obtain such favors from female staff was part of the motivation leading to the rise of the political correctness campaign.

This campaign was aimed in part at raising the consciousness of people concerning incidents of potential abuse and corruption and, by stigmatizing certain forms of language and behavior, to minimize the opportunity for potential offenders to do so. This has been largely successful in most American workplaces and classrooms that are properly monitored and in which workers and students have proper representation. Going into 2011, however, various high-profile cases involving leading American politicians and foreign officials have demonstrated the continuing willingness of many high-status men to abuse their power by enticing, soliciting, or even forcing women into providing sexual favors to them.

Conflicts of Interest

The dividing line between urging a certain decision to be made and a conflict of interest has become notoriously difficult to determine. The nature of gift-giving culture in Asian business and society, in particular, was influential in leading to the Foreign Corrupt Practices Act (1977), which aimed to outlaw any form of incentive provision in making commercial decisions anywhere in the world. Codes of ethics have been adopted in a variety of professions in which similar situations might be found: for example, market researchers, travel agencies, and medical doctors. As the amount of money increases, the thought given to noncriminalized incentives also increases. A medical doctor given the latitude to select between competing pharmaceutical products for a number of patients represents an important market opportunity. Hollywood producers and people in similar positions, notoriously, ask for sexual favors from young actors in return for a career boost. Historically, American society has turned to binding contracts, legislation, and the law to try to minimize these problems and, in partnership with investigative journalism, some important abuses of power have been discovered.

John Walsh
Shinawatra University

See Also: 1961 to 1980 Primary Documents; Corruption, Contemporary; Corruption, History of; Political Crimes, Sociology of; Sexual Harassment.

Further Readings
Kaikati, Jack G., et al. "The Price of International Business Morality: Twenty Years Under the Foreign Corrupt Practices Act." *Journal of Business Ethics*, v.26/3 (2000).
Trounstine, Jessica. *Political Monopolies in American Cities: The Rise and Fall of Bosses and Reformers*. Chicago: University of Chicago Press, 2008.
Washburn, Jennifer. *University, Inc.: The Corporate Corruption of Higher Education*. New York: Basic Books, 2006.

Counterfeiting

Though relatively rare now, counterfeiting once flourished on a staggering scale in the United States. Beginning in colonial times and continuing well into the 19th century, counterfeiters manufactured innumerable imitations of coins and paper money that entered into circulation via extensive criminal networks. They operated with relative impunity, thanks to an unusual combination of lax law enforcement, limited federal oversight of the money supply, and a general tolerance for "making money" that dated to colonial times. Only during the Civil War, when the nation began issuing the first federal paper currency, did counterfeiting attract a more sustained and ultimately successful campaign to suppress it. Beginning in the early 20th century onward, counterfeiting ceased to play a major role in the criminal economy, a state of affairs that remained the rule, with rare exception, until the present day.

Bills of Credit in the Colonies

The rise of counterfeiting in the United States dates to the 17th century, when criminal entrepreneurs began churning out imitations of the European coins then in circulation, substituting lead and other base metals for silver and gold. After individual colonial governments began issuing paper money or "bills of credit," counterfeiters began imitating them as well. By the 18th century, counterfeiting had evolved into a reasonably sophisticated, capital-intensive enterprise that relied on a network of manufacturers, wholesalers, and dealers in counterfeit coins and notes, as well as the people who passed them into circulation (known as "utterers," "passers," or "shovers").

Though colonial authorities made periodic attempts to suppress the trade or design bills that defied imitation, these campaigns met with limited success. The absence of a significant police presence and the lack of secure jails both contributed to the problem. So, too, did the limited cooperation between the individual colonial governments. It was not uncommon, for example, for a colonial government to ignore counterfeiters who imitated other colonies' bills of credit, and counterfeiting rings were quick to turn these jurisdictional lacunae to their advantage. On the rare occasions when they caught and convicted counterfeiters, colonial governments rarely imposed the kind of draconian punishments common in Europe. Their reluctance to do so may reflect a genuine ambivalence about the place of counterfeiters in colonial society. Throughout the 17th and 18th centuries, the colonists repeatedly complained of shortages of money. Counterfeiting, however illicit, may have met a very real need for a sufficient medium of exchange.

Counterfeiting played an important role in the American Revolution. When the colonies broke away from Britain, the Continental Congress turned to the printing press to finance the coming war. As Congress issued growing amounts of paper money, counterfeiters put their own imitations into circulation. Some of these counterfeiters may have operated with the encouragement, if not outright support, of the British. These imitations hampered the war effort and contributed to the dramatic depreciation of the Continental dollars by the final years of the war. Similar problems plagued paper money issued by the individual states.

Bank-Issued Tender

The postwar years brought significant change to the world of money and counterfeiting. The U.S. Constitution banned state-issued bills of credit and vested the federal government with control over the money supply as well as the power to punish counterfeiters of the coins and securities of the new nation. Yet the government rarely did so, largely because it did not issue paper money of its own. Nor did it mint significant numbers of coins. Instead, most money in circulation originated with private banks chartered by state legislatures, each of which issued paper money in a variety of denominations and designs.

In ceding control to the states, the federal government made prosecution of counterfeiting a local matter, even as counterfeiters continued to operate across state and eventually national lines. Beginning in the 1790s, counterfeiters set up numerous "manufactories" just north of the border between Vermont and Canada. This region, a relatively lawless and remote area, became home to a growing number of rural manufactories of counterfeit notes. The most famous of these were clustered along a dirt road known as Cogniac Street, a few miles beyond the border. The criminal enclaves based there employed numerous engravers, printers, and signers of notes who sold their wares through a complicated network of "boodle carriers" (people who carried the money south from Canada), wholesalers, retailers, and shovers.

Banks pooled their resources to combat the problem, and they worked with local authorities in the United States to prosecute counterfeiters. Still, their efforts rarely yielded anything more than the conviction of a handful of low-level retailers and shovers, few of whom received prison terms beyond three or five years at most. Moreover, few counterfeiters convicted served out their prison terms, thanks to pardons by state governors. This reluctance to punish is puzzling but may reflect a deeper ambivalence about banks and banking at this time. Fraudulent banks were not uncommon in this era, and there was no hard and fast distinction between a bank that issued worthless paper and a gang of counterfeiters who did the same. Even legitimate banks often refused to redeem their notes in times of financial panic or distress. In this larger atmosphere of fraud and

A member of the Secret Service division of the U.S. Treasury examines confiscated counterfeit currency in October 1938. Soon after its founding, the U.S. Secret Service conducted one of the most successful law enforcement campaigns ever when it arrested and convicted numerous high-level counterfeiters in the 1870s and 1880s.

instability, counterfeiters found courts and juries reluctant to convict them.

Nonetheless, by the early 1830s, the growing operations of gangs of counterfeiters in Canada sparked a coordinated crackdown by a consortium of banks and law enforcement officials on both sides of the border. After several successful (and well-publicized) raids, the region lost its monopoly over the counterfeit economy. In response, many counterfeiters began shifting some of their engraving and printing activities to remote regions in the midwest where limited law enforcement, a scarcity of money, and a general skepticism of banks and banking prevailed. Counterfeiters in these regions generally focused on banknotes, though they also manufactured bogus coins.

At the same time, counterfeiters established workshops in the nation's burgeoning cities. Many things drew them to places like New York and Philadelphia: the growing anonymity of urban centers, the absence of an effective police force, the presence of many legitimate engravers and printers who could be lured to work in the counterfeit economy, and a growing population of poor people who passed counterfeit notes to supplement their income.

By the 1850s, New York, and to a lesser extent Philadelphia, harbored extensive gangs of criminals who manufactured, vended, and passed counterfeit notes. Satellite gangs also emerged in cities like Chicago, Cleveland, and St. Louis at this time.

The counterfeit economy of urban areas was sophisticated. In general, new notes would be commissioned by criminal partnerships headed by a "capitalist" who advanced the funds necessary to hire an engraver and print the money. Wholesalers and retailers would then purchase the counterfeits at a significant discount on their face value and then sell them at a higher price to growing armies of "shovers" who put the notes into circulation in grocery stores, bars, and other local retail establishments. Men typically dominated the manufacture and sale of counterfeit notes, but a growing number of women, most of them from the ranks of the working poor, put many of the notes into circulation.

On the eve of the Civil War, counterfeiting assumed new guises. By this time, approximately 10,000 different banknotes floated in circulation, making it hard to remember the appearance of a genuine note, much less a counterfeit. Counterfeiters exploited this chaos, issuing new kinds of bogus currency that relied on artful erasures and substitutions. They took genuine notes of defunct banks and altered them to imitate more solid banks; they "raised" denominations on genuine notes; and increasingly, they issued notes of fictional banks with plausible-sounding names. These notes, while not counterfeits in the conventional sense of the word, were generally considered to be as dangerous, if not more so, than conventional imitations of banknotes and coins.

Greenback

The Civil War set the stage for the destruction of the counterfeit economy. Over the course of that conflict, the North issued a new, federal currency known as the greenback. Congress also sanctioned the creation of national banks that would issue a common, uniform currency meant to replace the currency issued by the state-chartered banks. These radical reforms of the monetary system had profound implications for the craft of counterfeiting: Anyone who preyed on these currencies posed a direct threat to the sovereignty of the nation-state. In fact, the legislation that created the greenback and the national banknotes spelled out much harsher penalties for counterfeiting, including lengthy prison terms and onerous fines.

Nonetheless, counterfeiters had plenty of incentives to imitate the new notes. Whatever the risks, the new national currencies could be counterfeited in much greater volumes. The allure of far greater profits led counterfeiters to create a number of dangerous imitations, but for the first few years of the war, the federal government effectively ceded the problem to corrupt and inept local law enforcement authorities, and counterfeiters ran into little resistance at first. Counterfeiters generally ignored the currency of the South, with the exception of a handful of legitimate printers who sold millions of dollars of bogus Confederate notes to federal soldiers headed to the battlefield.

In 1864, the warden of the Old Capitol Prison in Washington, Colonel William Wood, pushed for a more concerted federal campaign against the counterfeiters of the federal currency. A protégé of Secretary of War Edwin Stanton, Wood eventually obtained permission to recruit and direct a new, national police force dedicated to prosecuting counterfeiters. This organization, soon known as the U.S. Secret Service, moved aggressively to combat counterfeiting. Under Wood's tenure, it hired dozens of operatives to catalog and destroy the counterfeit economy that threatened the new federal currencies.

This took an unprecedented amount of detective work, and during the first few years of its existence, the Secret Service interviewed thousands of suspects and secured hundreds of convictions. A controversial figure, Wood was eventually replaced by a succession of far more competent and bureaucratic chiefs, each of whom widened the assault on the counterfeit economy. In one of the most successful campaigns in law enforcement history, the Secret Service arrested and convicted scores of high-level counterfeiters in the 1870s and 1880s and hounded many others into retirement, including famed counterfeiters like William Brockway.

By the early 20th century, counterfeiting ceased to pose a threat to the nation's currency. It experienced a minor revival from the 1910s onward, when criminal syndicates underwritten by the Italian Mafia started to manufacture counterfeits on a large scale. While they never posed as serious a threat as the gangs of the 19th century, they enjoyed considerable success, particularly during the Great Depression, when the market for counterfeit notes, presumably driven by economic need, thrived. Counterfeiting then went into a sustained decline from the 1940s through the 1980s.

While counterfeiting experienced a minor revival in the 1990s after the widespread adoption of digital scanners and personal computers, domestic counterfeiting remains something of a rarity. In the 21st century, most counterfeiters of American currency operate beyond the borders of the United States, seeking out lawless locales much the way their predecessors did in centuries past.

Stephen Mihm
University of Georgia

See Also: 1851 to 1900 Primary Documents; 1921 to 1940 Primary Documents; Confidence Games and Frauds; History of Crime and Punishment in America: Colonial; History of Crime and Punishment in America: 1850–1900; Secret Service.

Further Readings
Johnson, David. *Illegal Tender: Counterfeiting and the Secret Service in Nineteenth-Century America.* Washington, DC: Smithsonian Institution Press, 1995.
Mihm, Stephen. *A Nation of Counterfeiters: Capitalists, Con Men, and the Making of the United States.* Cambridge, MA: Harvard University Press, 2007.
Scott, Kenneth. *Counterfeiting in Colonial America.* New York: Oxford University Press, 1957.
Smith, Laurence Dwight. *Counterfeiting: Crime Against the People.* New York: W. W. Norton, 1944.

Court of Common Pleas

The Court of Common Pleas, the King's Bench, and the Court of Exchequer were the three superior courts of common law in England. Criminal matters were handled by the King's Bench, while the Exchequer dealt with tax collection and rent. All three were lodged in Westminster Hall from 1395 to 1882. Henry II established the Court of Common Pleas in 1178 to hear civil cases involving pleas, or suits, between citizens, and the Crown used this court when it took civil action against a citizen. This court was responsible for shaping English law. It employed numerous functionaries and acted as an early law school. The superior court structure held until the passage of the Judicature Act of 1873, when it was dissolved. In the United States, four states have courts called Courts of Common Pleas: Delaware, Ohio, Pennsylvania, and South Carolina.

Delaware
The Courts of Common Pleas are trial courts divided into criminal and civil jurisdictions. Courts with criminal jurisdiction have original, general jurisdiction over motor vehicle offenses and criminal misdemeanors, with the exception of most drug offenses. Original jurisdiction means that the court has the authority to be the first to try the case and rule on it directly; general jurisdiction means that it has the ability to hear a wide variety of cases.

Courts with criminal jurisdiction handle preliminary hearings for the Superior Court. These courts also have appellate jurisdiction over two lower courts, the Alderman's Court and the Justice of the Peace Court. Appellate jurisdiction means that it can hear cases from lower courts in order to affirm or reverse the actions of those courts.

Common pleas courts with civil jurisdiction hear civil actions not exceeding $50,000, cases in which a person has been accused of being a habitual offender under the motor vehicle code, and petitions for name changes. They also hear appeals from Justice of the Peace Courts and administrative appeals from the Division of Motor Vehicles.

Ohio
The Courts of Common Pleas are Ohio's trial courts. Each of the state's 88 counties houses one. There are four divisions: general, domestic relations, juvenile, and probate. The General Division hears criminal as well as civil cases when the suit is for more than $15,000. It has original, general, and appellate jurisdiction. The Domestic Relations Division has limited jurisdiction (meaning that it is restricted to the types of cases it may hear) over cases dealing with marriage and family matters. The Juvenile Division has limited jurisdiction over matters involving people under 18 years of age who

have been charged with delinquent acts (i.e., acts that would be crimes if they were committed by adults). It also hears cases concerning abused and incorrigible children, paternity, neglect, failure to pay child support, and contributing to the delinquency of a minor. The Probate Division has limited jurisdiction over issues such as adoption, marriage licensing, and the determination of mental competency.

Pennsylvania

As in Ohio, Pennsylvania's Courts of Common Pleas are the trial courts, hearing major criminal and civil cases. There are 60 judicial districts, most serving one county, although seven districts serve two counties. Similar to General Division courts in Ohio, Pennsylvania courts have original, general, and appellate jurisdiction. These courts also deal with a variety of other cases, including juvenile delinquency, child abuse and custody, divorce, and estates.

South Carolina

The South Carolina Court of Common Pleas is a civil court within the state's circuit court. The criminal court is known as the Court of General Sessions. South Carolina is divided into 16 judicial districts. The Court of Common Pleas has general jurisdiction over civil cases involving more than $7,500. Administrative support is provided by the clerk of the courts, which schedules trials, maintains records of military discharges, and collects and pays out money as ordered by the court.

James Geistman
Ohio Northern University

See Also: Appellate Courts; Common Law Origins of Criminal Law; Courts; Jurisdiction; Juvenile Delinquency, History of.

Further Readings

Baker, John H. *An Introduction to English Legal History*, 4th ed. Oxford: Butterworths, 2002.
Carter, Lief H. and Thomas F. Burke. *Reason in Law*, 7th ed. Upper Saddle River, NJ: Pearson, 2005.
South Carolina Judicial Department. "Circuit Court." http://www.judicial.state.sc.us/circuitCourt/index.cfm (Accessed August 2011).
State of Delaware. "Welcome to the Delaware Court of Common Pleas." http://courts.delaware.gov/commonpleas (Accessed August 2011).
Supreme Court of Ohio. "Judicial System Structure." http://www.supremecourt.ohio.gov/JudSystem (Accessed August 2011).
Unified Judicial System of Pennsylvania. "Common Pleas Court." http://www.pacourts.us/T/Common Pleas (Accessed August 2011).

Court of Oyer and Terminer

The Court of Oyer and Terminer (literally translated as "to hear and determine") originated from English law; these courts were used to prosecute criminal offenses of an extraordinary and/or serious nature. The judges of assize sat on these commissions (along with some others) and were charged with the duty to inquire about the situation and prosecute those found guilty. Trials of treason, felonies, and misdemeanors that were committed in the areas specified by the commission were tried in these courts. First, the inquiry section of the court processes was conducted by a grand jury. Once the grand jury indicted, the commissioners of the court then heard and decided upon the petit jury.

In Scotland, commissions of the Court of Oyer and Terminer can be established by the crown in cases of treason and misprision of treason per the Treason Act of 1708. This act created a shared law of high treason after the uniting of Scotland and England in 1707 created the kingdom of Great Britain. The commission must have three lords of justiciary to begin proceedings. Courts of Oyer and Terminer have been used historically in Scotland on many occasions, namely the Radical War of 1820.

Salem Witch Trials

The American Court of Oyer and Terminer was established in 1692 by Governor William Phipps during the Salem witch trials in Massachusetts. The commission appointed John Hathorne, Nathaniel Saltsonstall, Bartholomew Gedney, Peter Sergeant, Samuel Sewall, Wait Still

Winthrop, and Lieutenant Governor William Stoughton to examine the claims of witchcraft in the small town. During the subsequent trials, Cotton Mather wrote a formal letter to the court appealing for the desistance of the use of spectral evidence—claims of images that were visible only to the witchcraft victims who had supposedly been attacked by the specter. The use of this type of evidence was common in English law but never had a decisive role in proceedings. Nonetheless, Mather's request was dismissed, and the trials continued at an accelerated rate.

Later that year, Reverend Increase Mather, the president of Harvard College, condemned spectral evidence as being of use in court and urged caution prosecuting those accused of witchcraft in his "Cases of Conscience." Mather stated that "It were better that 10 suspected witches should escape, than that one innocent person should be condemned," a position that eventually led to the demise of the Court of Oyer and Terminer.

After the condemnation posed by Increase Mather, Governor Phipps recanted the use of spectral evidence in the witch trials and later released the accused and banned further arrests for witchcraft. The Court of Oyer and Terminer was terminated a mere five months after its inception, and the witch trials of Salem, Massachusetts, were declared unlawful by the general court.

In later years, Governor Phipps requested that Increase Mather record all knowledge about the Salem witch trials through obtained official records. The resulting publication *Wonders of the Invisible World* was based directly on the trials.

Melissa J. Mauck
Sam Houston State University

See Also: Colonial Courts; Court of Quarter Sessions; Courts; History of Crime and Punishment in America: Colonial; Massachusetts; Salem Witch Trials.

Further Readings
Bouvier, John. *A Law Dictionary: Adapted to the Constitution and Laws of the United States.* Philadelphia: T. & J. W. Johnson, 1839.
Boyer, Paul S. and Stephen Nissenbaum, eds. *Salem Village Witchcraft: A Documentary Record of Local Conflict in Colonial New England.* Evanston, IL: Northwestern University Press, 1972.

Court of Quarter Sessions

The Court of Quarter Sessions, sometimes known as general sessions, is a local court in the United States that has criminal jurisdiction and sometimes presides over local administrative matters, such as the development and repair of roads. The court gets its name from its English predecessor. The link between English and early American legal systems illustrates that American leaders felt comfortable using familiar English legal institutions to help establish judicial procedures in the colonies and, later, the United States. To understand the court's role in the United States, it is useful to look at its place in the English legal system.

The Court of Quarter Sessions in the United Kingdom sat four times a year, dating from the 14th century, usually at the county level. These courts existed until the 1970s in the United Kingdom. The court had criminal jurisdiction for crimes that needed to hold a jury trial to be dealt with, but it could not preside over crimes that were of a very serious nature, such as those constituting a sentence of life in prison or capital punishment. The Quarter Sessions also had some civil jurisdiction, such as designating the repair of roads and overseeing county institutions like jails and lunatic asylums. The Court of Quarter Sessions in the United States ran in a very similar fashion to that in the United Kingdom.

Several states in the United States, like Pennsylvania and New York, used the Court of Quarter Sessions to preside over local criminal matters. For instance, Pennsylvania held Quarter Sessions until 1968 when the state constitution enacted that the Court of Quarter Sessions be moved under the jurisdiction of the Court of Common Pleas in each county. New York underwent a similar reform of its court systems in the 1960s.

Looking at the use of the Court of Quarter Sessions in Pennsylvania provides an example of how these local criminal courts were used in the United States. In 1683, Philadelphia and the surrounding counties established the Court of Common Pleas to oversee civil matters and the Court of Quarter Sessions to preside over criminal cases. The Quarter Sessions would meet every three months in each county. Justices of the peace for these courts were generally appointed by the governor. The trials in the Court of Quarter Sessions empanelled a jury of 12 men who had to be unanimous in their decision to designate a guilty verdict as opposed to merely a majority rule. This court heard all criminal matters, including very minor transgressions, except those of a more heinous nature, such as the capital crimes of murder and treason. In the colonial era, these more serious crimes were heard by the Supreme Court in Pennsylvania in which the judges would hold commissions of Oyer and Terminer. After the American Revolution, a separate Court of Oyer and Terminer heard the capital crimes. Criminal jurisdiction was split, then, between the Court of Quarter Sessions and the Court of Oyer and Terminer.

Particularly in Philadelphia, the Court of Quarter Sessions was, at times, renamed or the criminal jurisdiction given to other courts, such as during 1838–43. During these years, the Quarter Sessions relinquished its criminal jurisdiction to the Court of General Sessions and its successor, the Court of Criminal Sessions. By 1843, the Court of Quarter Sessions regained its jurisdiction over local criminal matters until its consolidation with the Court of Common Pleas in 1968.

In addition to its criminal jurisdiction, throughout the 18th century and into the 19th century, the Court of Quarter Sessions in Pennsylvania also had growing county administrative duties. These were similar to the administrative responsibilities held by the English Court of Quarter Sessions. Some of these duties included the opening of new roads or bridges, examining county officials' record books and punishing them for any misuse, the establishment of election districts, and the official licensing for businesses such as taverns or peddlers. In essence, the Court of Quarter Sessions also acted as a form of county government, as was typical in most of the southern colonies.

Erica Rhodes Hayden
Vanderbilt University

See Also: Court of Common Pleas; Court of Oyer and Terminer; Courts.

Further Readings
Carp, Robert A., Ronald Stidham, and Kenneth L. Manning. *Judicial Process in America*, 7th ed. Washington, DC: CQ Press, 2007.

Marietta, Jack D. and G. S. Rowe. *Troubled Experiment: Crime and Justice in Pennsylvania, 1682–1800*. Philadelphia: University of Pennsylvania Press, 2006.

Courts

Courts are created to provide justice and protection of the law through the civil and criminal justice systems. The differences between civil and criminal courts will be highlighted, but the focus of this entry is about criminal courts. In the United States, criminal courts operate at the state and federal levels, known as the dual system of justice. The state and federal systems are divided into three tiers—trial, appellate, and supreme—each with its own functions and duties. Throughout the history of courts, their duties have been similar, but the processes of how the courts actualized the duties has changed.

Specifically, court processes shifted between due process and crime control models and courtroom workgroup members managed their roles in working together. Examples of how the court process has changed over time include specialized courts and sentencing structures. These topics display the historical importance and evolving nature of the federal and state courts in the United States.

Civil Versus Criminal Court Systems
The civil and criminal court systems engage in similar actions but have different purposes and types of cases. Civil courts deal with personal issues between individuals and/or businesses, where the individuals or businesses represent themselves or can hire an attorney. Civil law is all law outside of criminal law. Civil courts have various types of cases, including general (e.g., contracts, personal injury, and damaged property), family (e.g., divorce and child custody), juvenile (e.g., child abuse and neglect), small claims cases (e.g., suits for smaller monetary amounts), and probate (e.g., wills and trusts).

Criminal courts work with criminal law violations; criminal law deals with criminal behavior. The city, state, or federal government takes action

The photo shows the U.S. Supreme Court in 2009, including Sonia Sotomayor (top right), who was confirmed in August of that year. Every year, about 4,000 to 7,000 cases are petitioned to be reviewed by the U.S. Supreme Court, but the court's nine justices decide to hear only the approximately 100 cases that they find most important that year.

against the person accused of engaging in criminal behavior and is considered the representative of the individual victim(s) of the crime because crimes are viewed as actions against society and the common good, not just the individual. The governmental entity that is in charge of the crime is dependent upon what type of offense was committed, whether it was a city ordinance violation, state crime, or federal crime. Criminal courts operate to determine the guilt of defendants and sentence offenders. Criminal courts function separately at the state and federal levels of government and are divided among trial courts, appellate courts, and superior courts.

Organization of the Federal System
The U.S. Constitution in Article 3, Section 1 establishes the right of a supreme court and other inferior courts to operate in the United States to deal with law violations as necessary. The federal court system deals with federal crimes and constitutional issues through its three tiers of U.S. district courts, U.S. courts of appeals, and the U.S. Supreme Court, with the majority of the cases dealing with civil issues.

U.S. district courts are the trial-level courts for the federal government. There are 94 district courts in operation across the United States, with most states having multiple district courts as decided per their population. As trial courts, the U.S. district courts hear cases about criminal federal law violations, civil rights abuses, and crimes that involve interstate movement. Within the United States, however, the majority of crimes committed are in violation of state laws, not federal laws. Thus, the majority of the cases heard at this level of court are civil in nature, dealing with constitutional right concerns such as petitions for habeas corpus in which prisoners ask the federal courts to review the constitutionality of their imprisonment.

U.S. courts of appeals, or circuit courts, are divided into 13 judicial circuits throughout the United States. These courts are in charge of hearing federal appellate cases covering substantive and procedural constitutional issues that occurred during federal district court proceedings. The U.S. courts of appeals do not concern themselves with original jurisdiction, meaning they do not retry cases or determine guilt; instead, they review trial cases to ensure that rights were not infringed upon. A panel of justices reviews the written petitions of attorneys and oral arguments to determine if the original decision of the trial court should be upheld or overturned. If the decision is to uphold the trial court's decision, nothing extra happens with the case. However, if the decision is overturned, cases can be reopened and remanded to the original court or dismissed.

The U.S. Supreme Court is the highest appellate court and is known as the "court of last resort." In the U.S. Supreme Court, there are nine justices who preside over all of the cases and are appointed to life terms by the president of the United States and confirmed by the Senate. Cases are petitioned to be reviewed by the U.S. Supreme Court from the state and federal systems. The U.S. Supreme Court only hears cases from state systems when an important substantive constitutional issue is in question. The justices select which cases they want to review; typically, 4,000 to 7,000 cases are petitioned to be reviewed by the U.S. Supreme Court each year, but only about 100 cases are chosen by the justices. The justices select the cases they view as the most pertinent constitutional issues, with their decisions shaping the direction of law within the United States. These landmark decisions have been entered on such pivotal issues as segregation, abortion, birth control, and the meanings of legal concepts like cruel and unusual punishment and legal search and seizures. Once decisions have been entered by the court, they become precedent for all other courts at the state and federal level to follow when similar legal issues arise.

History of the Federal System

Prior to the creation of the federal court system, the executive and legislative branches operated without separation; the judiciary branch was a function of Congress under the articles of the Confederation. It was not until after the first Constitutional Convention and the adoption of the U.S. Constitution that a separate judiciary branch existed. Article 3 of the Constitution, however, only created the Supreme Court and left the development of other types of courts to future decisions and compromises of Congress. Under the Judiciary Act of 1879, the legislative power of the United States created the lower-level federal courts.

Even though separate, the Supreme Court justices were required to oversee the operation of the circuit courts in what became known as "circuit riding." The justices would travel to different circuits to hold court in each of the three districts twice a year. Per Congress, this would ensure that all justices would understand the complexities and concerns of the local system, which would allow them to be more effective in the Supreme Court. This proved to be a difficult task in colonial years when a lack of secure transportation in the growing nation made the trips lengthy and unsafe; justices would retire from the bench to stop riding the circuit. This practice by the Supreme Court justices was abolished with the Judicial Act of 1801 but then reconfirmed with the Circuit Court Act of 1802. The 1802 act, however, also stated that Supreme Court justices did not need to be present for circuit courts to hear cases and increased the number of districts to six; district judges were hired to preside over the courts.

Although the Supreme Court decided only 50 cases during its first decade of operation, this number rapidly increased with the developing roles and duties of the court. The varied functions of the justices and movement across the districts created a backlog of cases in the courts. As time progressed, it was decided that circuit riding was ineffective and that the system needed to be redesigned. Throughout the mid- and late 1800s, including the implementation of the Evarts Act of 1891, the Supreme Court, circuit courts of appeals, and federal district courts developed their individual roles and actions.

During the development of the three levels of courts, the Supreme Court was charged with determining the functions and purposes of courts. The early cases of the court were fraught with battles over the powers of the courts as well as arbitrating differences between states, businesses, and political powers. It was these early years, however, that built the foundation of the court's power and its influence as a policy maker. Some of the first decisions entered shaped the power of the courts, including the rights of original jurisdiction (the ability of the court to overview the actions of Congress) and judicial review (ability to ensure that state legislation is constitutional).

The Supreme Court also has been charged with ensuring that due process rights of citizens, especially those involved in the criminal justice system, are upheld, using the Fourth, Fifth, Sixth, and Eighth Amendments as a framework for decisions. For instance, the cases of *Terry v. Ohio* (1968) and *Arizona v. Gant* (2009) aided the construction of what are illegal search and seizures, whereas *Weeks v. United States* (1914) and *Mapp v. Ohio* (1961) resulted in the exclusionary rule that evidence from illegal actions cannot be used in courts. In connection to the Fifth Amendment, the case of *Miranda v. Arizona* (1966) established rules for how police can legally interrogate individuals without concern of self-incrimination, and the 2010 cases *Berghuis v. Thompkins* and *Maryland v. Shatzer* fine-tuned the implementation of the Miranda warnings. The right to council as identified in the Sixth Amendment was not extended to all defendants until *Gideon v. Wainwright* (1963) and *Argersinger v. Hamlin* (1972); these two decisions effectively created the public defender. With regard to the Eighth Amendment, individuals have a right to bail that is not excessive as defined by cases such as *Stack v. Boyle* (1951) and *Bell v. Wolfish* (1979), whereas the other clause of not bearing cruel and unusual punishment has been outlined by influential decisions such as *Francis v. Resweber* (1947), *Harmelin v. Michigan* (1991), and *Roper v. Simmons* (2005). All of these decisions helped to shape the functions of the criminal justice system and the operation of the state courts in protecting the constitutional rights of defendants.

Organization of the State System
The state court system is similar to the federal court system in having three tiers with distinct duties. State courts were created and operate as a distinct system from the federal court system because of the dual court system. In addition, state criminal courts operate individually and distinct from all other states. Although different states operate in various manners, a typical court process does exist. The three levels of state courts are trial courts, appellate courts, and state supreme courts.

The trial courts can be broken into two levels of courts that can be called minor courts or courts of general jurisdiction, and major courts or courts of limited jurisdiction. The minor trial courts usually are not operated at the state level and instead deal with municipal violations at the city level. Some examples of these courts are municipal courts, magistrate courts, and police courts. These courts work with less serious violations and, at times, civil matters. Less serious offenses are city or municipal violations that include traffic violations, trespassing, and disorderly conduct. When an individual is guilty of a municipal violation, the punishment is normally a fine.

Major courts are the typical trial court of the state and conduct court processes for defendants charged with state crimes, including misdemeanors and felonies. The trial courts are known by different names throughout the states such as superior courts, courts of common pleas, and circuit courts. Trial courts have a formal process to determine guilt of a defendant that begins with charging the individual, pretrial procedures, trial processes including the verdict, and ends with sentencing the individual. Individuals who are found guilty of a misdemeanor or felony criminal offense are subject to receiving penalties that range from fines to house arrest to probation to prison to death sentences.

The next court level is the intermediate appellate court or court of appeals. This court has the duty of hearing cases in which offenders bring grievances of constitutional issues that occurred during the trial process, such as judicial errors, prosecutorial misconduct, and defense attorney incompetence. The appellate court acts as a check to ensure defendant rights were protected during trials. Not all states have appellate courts, and instead constitutional issues are heard by the supreme courts.

The highest state court is the state supreme court or the court of final resort. These courts are the final stop in the state criminal court system to ensure that due process and constitutional rights are upheld for defendants in trial processes. If cases are not resolved at this level, cases can be transferred to the federal system.

History of the State System
The history of each state system is unique, as is the organization and operation of each of the court levels previously explained. Commonalities,

however, do exist in the creation of the state court system. Most states developed their court system at the time the state's constitution was ratified. The similarities between state systems result from connections to English common law as a foundation for building the court systems in the original colonies. State courts began with the idea of having one person controlling the decisive power of the court while creating the roles of juries and prosecutorial attorneys to aid with the procedural aspects known in state courts. The means to become judges and attorneys were not formalized, and often social power was enough to hold the position without consideration of education or employment experience. Those attorneys who gained experience went to general colleges in England or had apprenticeships with practicing attorneys in the United States. There was a lack of strict and formal guidelines of what it meant to pass the bar or be an attorney.

As state courts continued to mature between the Revolutionary War and the mid-1800s, legislative powers increasingly removed justices and stopped courts from engaging in free enterprise; decisions and practices were watched over to ensure that the courts were enforcing laws as desired by the legislature. The role of attorneys became more professionalized as law schools began to be built in successful law offices in the late 1700s and as established curricula in universities in the mid-1800s, but the practice of apprenticeships still ruled the means to become a lawyer. Thus, state courts had concerns with being impartial purveyors of justice as the courts were not yet professionalized and lacked true formal systems of justice.

It was not until the early 1900s when judges were able to hold more autonomous powers over the courts, but these powers were often shared with those in the courtroom workgroup. In response to growing cities and urban areas, the courts had to find means to make their workload manageable while ensuring the rights of those involved in the system. During this time the roles of judges and attorneys became more formalized and attuned to requirements of educational pursuits. More universities began to develop educational programs for attorneys, but achieving college education prior to a law degree is a more recent development. The mid- to late 1900s were marked with a growth in the professional and social prestige of attorneys; professionalization was a direct consequence of educational requirements as well as the ethical standards of the American Bar Association. Although many judges do have backgrounds in law, it is important to note that trial judges have different requirements across the states, but higher-level state courts have educational and experiential requirements. One major change during this time was the development of a public defender in the 1960s and 1970s; it was not until this time that all defendants were afforded the constitutional right to an attorney even if they were unable to afford one. Another modification of the late 1990s was the development of specialty courts, where specific concerns or cases were dealt with.

Specialized Courts

Specialized courts are trial courts that deal with particular issues of the defendant, crime, and/or case and have been in existence since the late 1980s, with a larger movement in the late 1990s and 2000s. They move away from the traditional stance of the court and criminal justice system as being focused on retribution, punishment, and adjudication. Specialized courts are created to aid defendants in rehabilitative and restorative efforts that rebuild the defendant's life and help him/her move away from criminal lifestyles. Some examples of specialized courts are drug courts, domestic violence courts, mental health courts, and veteran courts. Numerous states have been creating these types of specialized courts to allow individuals with these types of concerns to be funneled out of the traditional trial court system and into the specialized court to receive treatment, supervision, and case management to reduce concerns of recidivism while diverting the defendant away from the system.

Specialized courts can be viewed as problem-solving courts where the courtroom actors, including the judge, prosecutor, and defense attorney, develop bonds with the defendant and his/her life. Information is gathered to determine the best means to aid the defendant. Judges do more than enter decisions as they monitor the defendant's progress and focus upon life outcomes instead of verdicts and sentences. For instance, in mental health courts, judges make certain that the defendant is obtaining necessary treatment and require numerous court dates to congratulate success or to ensure increased compliance with requirements for defendants not engaged properly with treatment. The courtroom workgroup works with the community, each other, and the defendant to provide a wrap-around model of care.

Overall, research about specialized courts, especially drug courts, domestic violence courts, and mental health courts, has demonstrated success. Defendants who are engaged with the processes and procedures of these courts tend to have lower recidivism rates and increased successes in life, including employment. However, when individuals do not work with the court, penalties do exist. Sanctions often include jail days, fines, termination of involvement with the programs, and prosecution in traditional courts for the original offenses.

Courtroom Workgroup

In the courtroom workgroup are employed individuals of the court who work together to ensure an effective and efficient court process. These individuals include judges, prosecutors, defense attorneys, and various support staff and administrators who each have their own set of duties and obligations.

Judges are leaders of the courtroom. Judges may be elected or appointed and are to be impartial voices and decision makers during pretrial, trial, and sentencing stages of the court process. Their duties include presiding over court cases, deciding verdicts in nonjury cases, and assigning sentences to guilty defendants. Although judges are viewed as the most powerful courtroom workgroup members, they would be unable to complete their job without the aid of the other courtroom workgroup members.

The attorneys of the courtroom include prosecutors and defense attorneys. Prosecutors work for the city, state, or federal government. Their role during the court process is to make charging decisions, engage in plea negotiations, and present the case against the defendant. Defense attorneys can be private or public and work for the defendant. It is their responsibility to uphold the rights of the defendant, research evidence, engage in plea negotiations, and exploit weaknesses in the prosecutor's case.

Support staff members of the courtroom are those individuals who aid with the smooth functioning of the courtroom but are not tied directly to the pretrial, trial, and sentencing processes. They engage in the ancillary functions of the courtroom such as scheduling, recording, and providing information during court processes. Support staff includes bailiffs, court clerks, court administrators, court reporters, and expert witnesses.

Due Process Versus Crime Control Models

In the criminal justice system, there is a debate between how the system should work and how it can function. This debate includes the processing of defendants through the court process, especially within state trial courts, and is understood best as the due process model versus the crime control model.

The due process model of justice states that rights should be upheld at all times for all people. In the court system, this means that defendants should be afforded their due process rights guaranteed by the Sixth Amendment in the U.S. Constitution. All defendants are granted the right of a speedy and impartial trial by a jury of their peers and must be presented with and allowed to confront all witnesses with the protection of a defense attorney. Although some of these rights are difficult to define and put into practice, the overreaching meaning is that the defendant's rights are protected at all stages of the trial; when rights are not enacted properly, the system has broken down, and the grievance must be fixed by the appeals processes at the state and federal level. In addition, all defendants should be treated equally, all steps of the court process should be questioned to ensure rights were protected, and precedence of court procedures should be abided.

The crime control model suggests that the system operates in an efficient and productive manner; it gives a picture of assembly line justice in which defendants move in and out similarly to factory production of car parts. Courts become duty- and goal-oriented and less focused upon the individual. The formal court process becomes minor to the overall desire of pushing defendants through the system. Whereas the due process model operates more through the formal trial court processes and individualized justice, the

The east courtroom of the Howard M. Metzenbaum U.S. Courthouse in Cleveland, Ohio, in 2009. The Supreme Court, circuit courts of appeals, and federal district courts developed their individual roles and actions in the mid- and late 1800s. However, the courts were not yet professionalized and lacked true formal systems of justice.

crime control model appreciates plea negotiations and devalues the individualization of justice.

It is difficult to state which one of these models the court process more closely resembles, especially because of the diverse nature of justice in each state and in different courtrooms. Yet it is safe to conclude that the court system is a myriad combination of these two models. The due process model provides a checkpoint and goal for how justice should be served for each defendant, while the crime control model depicts a means for the system to work without huge backlogs and to operate with appropriate levels of resources. Defendants are able to have rights upheld in an efficient manner, and other procedures such as the presence of the defense attorney and appeals process ensure rights are not trampled upon. This hybrid model of justice also ensures that the attorneys as well as the judge and other courtroom workgroup members work together to create fair and equal justice.

Adversarial Process

Connected to the models of justice is the picture of a court as an adversarial process. Numerous aspects of the court process were created to demonstrate separation of powers among the judge, prosecutor, and defense attorney. Think of how most movies and television shows depict the courtroom atmosphere; they usually picture the attorneys against each other, fighting for their cause without concern for the others involved in the process, with the judge as the ultimate arbiter deciding which attorney is correct. This depiction of the adversarial process does have some truth to it, but overall it is not how most courts and courtroom workgroups operate on a daily basis.

The adversarial process is used to determine guilt of the defendant by having the prosecutor represent the state's (and victim's) cause to demonstrate guilt of the defendant while the defense attorney represents the defendant to show the weaknesses of the prosecutor's case. These two attorneys work to benefit their client while the judge ensures that legal procedures are met. However, as suggested in the discussion of the due process and crime control model, all must work together to have an efficient system of justice that does not break down because of the number of cases and defendants in the system. Therefore, although aspects of the adversarial process are intact, the court system and its workgroup members more often work together in an amicable process.

Sentencing Structures
With the beginning of trial courts at the state and federal level also came the ability of the system to regulate the types of punishments received by offenders for the crimes they have committed against society. The court processes were created to ensure that the rights of citizens were upheld though a just and fair process. Through the history of the court, various arguments and concerns have arisen about the ability of the court to uphold these most basic functions of the court. One example that demonstrates the operations of the courts through the due process and crime control models as well as its continued regulation of itself is sentencing structures.

Early in the court system's history, judges were afforded the right to have sole discretionary decision making over the sentence received by offenders. This type of sentencing is referred to as indeterminate sentencing, because there is a lack of legal mandates placed upon the types of sentences assigned to offenders except that the punishment cannot be cruel and unusual and should fit the crime. Beginning in the 1980s, public outcry led to legislators and other governmental officials asking for more legal guidance to be given to judges in their sentencing duties because of disparities and discrimination that were found in sentencing practices. By the mid-1990s, most states and the federal government shifted sentencing practices to determinate or fixed sentencing structures. These types of sentencing structures limited the discretion judges were afforded in sentencing decisions by legislation providing guidelines and proscriptions about appropriate sentences for various types of crimes.

Determinate sentencing structures were created to lower the disparities and discriminatory practices of judges that were found with unbridled discretion. However, another consequence of determinate sentencing is a movement away from individualized justice and the adversarial court processes while moving toward the efficiency expected in crime control models of justice. Determinate sentencing structures have not made the improvements with respect to disparities that were desired; sentencing outcomes still are not equal among differing populations in society. Determinate sentencing has allowed for efficiency of the system and created a larger need for the courtroom workgroup to be amicable and less adversarial. More recently, however, the U.S. Supreme Court has entered decisions suggesting that when determinate sentencing is highly proscriptive and structured (e.g., federal guidelines), it does a disservice to the defendant's right to justice and infringes upon his/her constitutional due process rights to an individualized court process. Although geared more toward the federal guidelines, other states have been examining their guidelines to ensure constitutional rights are upheld in their jurisdictions.

Conclusion
Courts must ensure that rights are protected and that the need for an efficient system does not disregard the need for fairness and justice in the process. The court system was created by the Constitution as well as decisions of the federal and state governments to protect due process rights of defendants that were infringed upon without formal court systems. Throughout history, the court process has moved along with public policy as well as dictated public policy through its regulation of laws. The court system, as shown in the example of sentencing structures, is a revolving process attempting to find the best balance between the due process model and the crime control model of justice to create an efficient, rights-oriented version of justice and equality in all of its duties and processes. In addition, the court system can be highly regimented and focused on punishment as determinate sentencing structures demonstrate, but also it can be a place for forgiveness, restoration, and rehabilitation as shown in specialized courts. Both of

these demonstrate the reason courts exist to aid society in finding a just means to deal with the concerns of its members.

Jennifer L. Huck
Indiana University of Pennsylvania

See Also: Appellate Courts; Court of Common Pleas; Judges and Magistrates; Legal Counsel; Sentencing; Sentencing: Indeterminate Versus Fixed; Supreme Court, U.S.

Further Readings
Berman, Greg and John Feinblatt. *Problem-Solving Courts: A Brief Primer.* New York: Center for Court Innovation, 2001.
Carp, Robert A., Ronald Stidham, and Kenneth L. Manning. *Judicial Process in America*, 6th ed. Washington, DC: CQ Press, 2004.
Spohn, Cassia and Craig Hemmens. *Courts: A Text/Reader.* Thousand Oaks, CA: Sage, 2009.

Courts of Indian Offenses

Courts of Indian Offenses were the first courts in Indian Country resembling the Anglo-American legal system. Indian nations had previously regulated criminal behavior using social and religious rites, mediation, and restitution; beginning in the 1880s, however, the courts established a forum for prosecuting criminal charges, including many traditional Indian customs and religious practices newly outlawed under the courts' criminal code. Courts of Indian Offenses arose not in express statutory authorization, but in the early administrative practices of the Bureau of Indian Affairs.

After decades of military oversight, the Bureau of Indian Affairs was placed under civilian control when the Interior Department was established in 1849. The bureau's transfer from the Department of War resulted in the creation of Indian agents to oversee Indian Country. Quarrelling chiefs increasingly turned to these agents to arbitrate disputes not resolved through traditional tribal means, laying the foundation for the court. Although not formally sanctioned, this practice was recommended by the first secretaries of the interior, who regarded Indian agents as local justices of the peace.

Indian agents also helped shape Courts of Indian Offenses by creating a class of Indian police to carry out their instructions. Through this newly won police force, agents were able to exercise control over American Indians while introducing Anglo-American jurisprudence to Indian Country. The rise of Indian agents corresponded with the decline of traditional tribal political and legal institutions, prompting administrators in Indian Country to recognize the need to establish a court system to regulate life on reservations. Deeming traditional tribal rites and customs an obstacle to the government's effort to assimilate Indians, the Interior Department formulated rules to govern tribal affairs while bolstering the proliferation of Anglo-American law.

By 1883, Courts of Indian Offenses became a standard component of the Bureau of Indian Affairs' administration of reservations. In addition to outlining the courts' organization and

A Native American chief of police in uniform surrounded by tribal members in traditional dress at the Pine Ridge Agency in South Dakota around 1891.

procedure, the department's rules stipulated only that potential jurists not be polygamists and provided brief civil and criminal codes, which outlawed many remaining traditional practices. The resulting Courts of Indian Offenses thus established a forum in which native peoples were prosecuted for engaging in tribal rites, dances, and other customs.

The need for courts also arose from the bureau's management of Indian Country. The allotment process dispersed families across reservations, making it difficult for communities to observe traditional conflict resolution practices. As a result, Native peoples increasingly turned to Courts of Indian Offenses to resolve disputes. Moreover, the sale of reservation land to non-Indians introduced new residents to Indian Country, further compelling American Indians to turn to the courts for redress.

As reservations became more complicated, so too did the Courts of Indian Offenses, plagued by jurisdiction dilemmas and growing financial troubles. Founded on the general authority of the Interior Department and lacking statutorily defined jurisdiction, the courts were frequently challenged. Nevertheless, in their 51-year history, no legal challenge proved successful, in large part due to the commissioner's strategic avoidance. The status of the courts remained correspondingly unstable, especially because Congress repeatedly failed to appropriate sufficient funds to guarantee their efficacy. Calls for law in Indian country, therefore, often meant a need for assimilation and acculturation. In light of the offenses prosecuted, the courts operated more as instruments of oppression than traditional courts in either the Indian or Anglo-American traditions. *United States v. Clapox*, 35 Fed. 575 (D.C. Ore. 1888), one of the only cases tried that deals directly with the legality of the courts, even describes the tribunals as educational and disciplinary instruments, specifically distinguishing the courts from those provided for in the Constitution.

Sometimes called "CFR courts" because they followed the regulations established by the Code of Federal Regulations, the courts were commonly staffed with Indian judges, who were often appointed by agents as a reward for assimilation. Well-known Indian leaders were also appointed to lend credibility to the courts. The ultimate judgment in most cases, however, lay primarily with the agent. Courts of Indian Offenses were established for nearly all Indian tribes, except the Five Civilized Tribes and a handful of others that had recognized governments and courts. Other reservations maintained courts only temporarily, in part because of limited congressional funding. Nevertheless, at the courts' peak around 1900, approximately two-thirds of all reservations had courts. As public concern for the poor conditions on Indian reservations mounted in the late 1920s, however, the administrative abuses in Indian Country were increasingly criticized. The resulting reform movement culminated in the passage of the Indian Reorganization Act, which formally abolished Courts of Indian Offenses in 1934.

Matthew H. Birkhold
Princeton University, Columbia Law School

See Also: Indian Civil Rights Act; Indian Removal Act; Native American Tribal Police; Native Americans.

Further Readings
Johansen, Bruce Elliott. *The Encyclopedia of Native American Legal Tradition*. Westport, CT: Greenwood Press, 1998.
O'Brien, Sharon. *American Indian Tribal Governments*. Norman: University of Oklahoma Press, 1989.
Richland, Justin B. and Sarah Deer. *Introduction to Tribal Legal Studies*. Lanham, MD: AltaMira Press, 2010.

Coverture, Doctrine of

Coverture is a legal term with origins in the British common law. It established the legal status of married women with respect to the exercise of personal rights to enter into contracts, conduct business, function as a member of a community, and incur criminal liability. Coverture also limited women's capacity to purchase and inherit property and was used to deprive women of a remedy for domestic violence. In the common law tradition, married couples became one person with the legal status of the wife merged into that of her husband, who took almost unlimited legal control over the wife's earnings, contractual rights and obligations, capacity to sue, and property. In addition, the husband became responsible for the wife's debts and assumed her liability for criminal and tortuous acts. Thus, married women ceased to have legal standing, and their status was covered by the husband. Coverture governed the legal status of women during the American colonial era through American jurists' reliance on the work of Sir William Blackstone. In the United States, policies restricting the civil, criminal, economic, and social status of women prevailed throughout the 19th century. As a result of reform efforts during the early decades of the 20th century, states began to dismantle coverture laws through legislation recognizing the personal liberties and property rights of women. Furthermore, by the mid-20th century, courts began considering some remaining gender discriminatory policies as violations of the Fourteenth Amendment's equal protection clause.

Women as Chattel

The American experience with coverture begins with the British common law and its establishment upon the American continent at the Jamestown colony in 1603. Under the common law of England, women held the position of chattel property. That condition followed women across the Atlantic. In the 18th century, American jurists relied heavily upon William Blackstone's organization of the common law, titled *Commentaries on the Laws of England* (1769). Blackstone defined coverture as the suspension of a woman's legal status during marriage to such an extent that she could not sign legal documents, obtain an education, or work for wages without her husband's consent. If allowed to work, her wages belonged to her husband. Since the legal status of a wife did not exist apart from her husband, coverture even prevented a husband from contracting with his wife because to do so would suppose she had separate existence from him, and no man can make a legally binding contract with himself. Furthermore, a married woman could not sue or be sued apart from joining her husband as a party. The style of court cases reflected that restriction (e.g., the early products liability case, *Thomas and Wife v. Winchester*, 6 N.Y. 397 (1852), in which the injured party was Mrs. Thomas. Her husband filed the lawsuit, which she joined).

However, the systems of law established in England and America did not completely deprive women of rights. The law identified numerous exceptions to the doctrine of coverture, although not all of these acknowledged the independent agency of women. For example, if a woman could demonstrate that her husband had induced her to commit a crime, she would be exempt from punishment. While all property brought into a marriage became the property of the husband upon marriage, a wife was legally entitled to a portion of that property upon the husband's death. Thus, a husband could not sell property without his wife's consent, and consent often required a wife's signature on a deed or contract accompanying a statement attesting that she signed of her own free will.

Property Rights for Women

Throughout the 19th century, the legal structure based on coverture began to slowly unwind as state governments gave women greater control over their earnings and property (e.g., the Illinois Married Women's Property Act of 1869). During the same period, however, courts enforced the doctrine of coverture with respect to personal rights. For example, when considering cases of divorce and domestic violence, state courts upheld the legal principle that a married woman has no legal status apart from her husband. In the 1862 North Carolina case *Joyner v. Joyner*, the court held that an allegation of physical violence might not be enough to grant a divorce if the wife provokes her husband. The court stated that "the law gives the husband power to use such a degree of force as is necessary to make the wife behave herself and know her place." In support of this arrangement, the court recited the common law doctrine of coverture, noting that a husband will be held liable for the criminal offenses of his wife, that a wife cannot make a will disposing of property, but that a husband may not sell land without the wife's consent. It concluded that "the law gives this power to the husband over the person of the wife, and has adopted proper safeguards to prevent an abuse of it." By the end of the 19th century, however, state courts began to treat physical violence in the home as criminal behavior.

An executive group of the National Woman's Party meeting around 1920, before their February 1921 convention in Washington, D.C. The convention called for the abolition of coverture laws, among other improvements in women's legal, social, and economic status. It was not until much more recently that the Supreme Court struck down some of the last remnants of those laws when it banned gender discriminatory policies in the assignment of work-related and survivor benefits and educational opportunities.

Removal of Coverture Laws

During the early decades of the 20th century, women's rights movements campaigned against coverture laws. Long after the Nineteenth Amendment granted women suffrage in 1920, coverture laws continued to determine the legal rights, duties, and responsibilities of men and women for broad areas of civil and economic life. Reformers sought the removal of such laws at the state level. In 1921, the abolition of coverture laws headlined the program of the National Woman's Party's Washington, D.C., convention. These efforts resulted in almost all states abolishing coverture by statute and recognizing women's property rights independent of their husbands. But vestiges of coverture remained. Courts routinely made decisions on child custody, alimony, and welfare policies based on gender distinctions.

In the 1972 case *Forbush v. Wallace* (405 U.S. 970), the Supreme Court of the United States held that states have the power to require women to use their husband's surname on all legal documents. However, in more recent decisions, the court has found state government policies that discriminate on the basis of gender unconstitutionally abridge the equal protection clause of the Fourteenth Amendment. The court has struck down gender discriminatory policies in the assignment of work-related and survivor benefits and educational opportunities. These are the last remnants of an age-old legal system of state sanctioned inequalities between men and women dating back to the American colonial era.

Hans J. Hacker
Arkansas State University

See Also: Blackstone, William; Colonial Courts; Domestic Violence, History of.

Further Readings

Blackstone, William. *Commentaries on the Laws of England*. Book 1, Chap. 15. "Of Husband and Wife." http://www.lonang.com/exlibris/blackstone/bla-115.htm (Accessed May 2011).

Harvard Business School. "Women, Enterprise, and Society: Marriage and Coverture." http://www.library.hbs.edu/hc/wes/collections/women_law/marriage_coverture (Accessed May 2011).

Joyner v. Joyner, 59 N.C. 322 (1862).

Crabtree v. State

Crabtree v. State is a criminal law case decided on February 8, 2002, by the Court of Appeals of Indiana. The majority opinion clarified the degree of reasonable suspicion of criminal activity that is necessary to justify an investigatory stop of a suspect by law enforcement officers.

In the early morning hours, two Indianapolis police officers responded to an anonymous complaint of African American males loudly playing a car stereo. Ervin Crabtree was observed hiding behind a parked car. The car was not in operation and there was no noise, though one of its doors was ajar. Several people took flight when an approaching officer's presence was made known, but none were in close proximity to Crabtree. When the officer shined a flashlight on Crabtree and ordered him to raise his hands, Crabtree threw aside a plastic bag before lying down on the ground. Upon Crabtree's refusal to comply with several verbal commands, the officer drew his handgun and placed him in handcuffs. The plastic bag that had been thrown aside was found to contain cocaine, and another bag of marijuana was found on the seat of the car behind which Crabtree had been hiding.

At trial, Crabtree was charged with drug related offenses and sought to suppress the cocaine and marijuana evidence. The motion was denied and Crabtree appealed. Crabtree raises two issues on appeal: first, whether a person has been subjected to an investigatory stop when spotted by a flashlight and ordered to raise his hand but refuses to comply and throws away an object; and second, whether reasonable suspicion exists to justify an investigatory stop when an officer is responding to a group of people loudly playing a car stereo, but encounters a single person hiding behind a car from which no music is heard. The Court of Appeals held that the altercation constituted an investigatory Terry stop but ruled that the stop was justified by the officer's reasonable suspicion of criminal activity. The Court of Appeals of Indiana affirmed the lower court's decision.

As a matter of law, the court confirmed that an appellate review of a denied motion to suppress evidence does not allow for a reweighing of evidence. Conflicting evidence is reviewed in a manner most favorable to the trial court's ruling and uncontested evidence is considered in a manner most favorable to the defendant. Review of a decision to admit evidence despite a motion to suppress is considered under an abuse-of-discretion standard, but the ultimate determination of reasonable suspicion to conduct an investigatory stop is reviewed de novo. The court held that Crabtree was subjected to a Terry stop, by which an officer briefly detains an individual for investigatory purposes based upon reasonable suspicion of criminal activity. In the case of *Terry v. Ohio*, reasonable suspicion was determined by objectively weighing whether an officer's actions were initially justified and reasonably related in scope to the justifying circumstances. A crucial factor was whether a reasonable person would feel free to end the detainment and leave the officer's presence.

The court subsequently found that the officer had reasonable suspicion to justify the Terry stop. The Fourth Amendment's reasonable suspicion requirement was deemed satisfied if the totality of the circumstances known to the officer would suffice to lead a reasonably caution person to believe that criminal activity had occurred and that the officer's conduct was appropriate. In a dissenting opinion, Judge J. Darden denied the existence of a reasonable suspicion that would justify the investigatory stop. Noting that reasonable suspicion must be based upon more than inchoate and unspecified suspicion, Darden objected that evidence of criminal activity was lacking. The officer admitted that Crabtree's crouching behind a car was consistent with legal activity and the order to raise his hands was intended to ensure the officer's own safety rather than a response to criminal suspicion. Darden thus held the stop to be invalid from its inception and refused to speculate as to whether subsequent events supplied the necessary reasonable suspicion for the investigatory stop. The majority holding has been substantially upheld on these merits by later courts.

Justin Paulette
Independent Scholar

See Also: Indiana; Police, History of; *Terry v. Ohio*.

Further Readings
Cook, Joseph, Paul Marcus, and Melanie Wilson. *Criminal Procedure*, 7th ed. Albany, NY: Lexis-Nexis, 2009.
Crabtree v. State, 762 N.E.2d 241–Ind: Court of Appeals (2002).
Terry v. Ohio, 392 U.S. 1 (1968).

Crime and Arrest Statistics Analysis

Criminologists and criminal justice system officials rely on crime statistics to obtain greater insight into currently existing crime levels and to determine whether rates of crime are increasing or decreasing over time. Criminologists utilize crime data to help test current theories of criminal behavior and to help them develop newer theories as they learn more about general crime trends. Law enforcement officials use crime statistics to help determine the extent to which existing crime control policies are effective or ineffective at deterring crime and to help make decisions about where to allocate their limited resources. The three most common methods for measuring crime are arrest statistics, self-reports of offending surveys, and victimization surveys. Each method has advantages and disadvantages, with no single measure of crime being a perfectly reliable measure of the extent of criminal behavior.

Since the pioneering works of Adophe Quetelet in the early 1800s, criminologists have utilized aggregate-level crime statistics as a means of gauging the moral health of nations. Quetelet was a Belgian astronomer who, along with lawyer André-Michel Guerry, first utilized judicial statistics to observe a consistency in crime rates in France and Belgium between 1826 and 1829. This systematic collection of national judicial statistics on prosecutions and convictions came to be known as "moral statistics" and were influential in the development of current methods of crime data collection.

Arrest Statistics

In the United States, the U.S. Census Bureau was the first national agency to collect crime data beginning in the 1850s. Data collection focused on counting the number of individuals committed to jails, houses of correction, and penitentiaries. While these basic census counts were informative, police in the United States at this time were not collecting reports of crime in any systematic or uniform fashion across jurisdictions, nor did the classifications of crimes conform to any one legal definition.

As a means of addressing the public's perception about the amount of crime, the International Association of Chiefs of Police (IACP) formed the Committee on Uniform Crime Records in 1927 to develop a system for collecting uniform police statistics. The result was a data collection method that would report both the number of offenses reported to police and the number of those offenses that resulted in an actual arrest. Police departments anticipated that these reports would dispel the notion that juvenile and adult crime in the United States was out of control and reinstill confidence in police efforts to control crime. Today, the Federal Bureau of Investigation's (FBI) Uniform Crime Report (UCR) collects information from approximately 16,788 law enforcement agencies, covering 97 percent of the U.S. population. Issues such as nonreporting by individual departments, as well as problems with the collection of data on the part of some agencies, often lead to the elimination of some, or even the entirety, of a state's crime data to become ineligible for recording in the UCR.

In 1958, the FBI constructed a composite offense index that sums eight individual offense categories into an overall crime index: murder, forcible rape, robbery, aggravated assault, burglary, larceny-theft, motor vehicle theft, and eventually arson, which was not added to the index until 1979. All of the remaining offenses are included in a list of 21 categories, which are known as Part II offenses. Currently, the FBI's Uniform Crime Reporting program lists the number of offenses known to police and the number of arrests police then make. The UCR also provides information about these offenses at the city, state, and county level as well as the age, sex, and race of persons arrested by police. Because Part II offenses are so numerous, the UCR does not collect data on the number of reports of these offenses to police and only reports the number of actual arrests.

Information from the UCR is often reported either as absolute numbers or as rates per 100,000 population to control for changes in the population composition. These crime rates then allow for comparisons of crime rates across cities and states of varying sizes. Finally, the UCR reports the number of crimes cleared by arrest. Crimes are considered by police to be "cleared" when there is either an arrest of a suspect or there are exceptions that are beyond the control of law enforcement, such as the death of a suspect, which makes a future arrest implausible. In other words, a clearance rate refers to the proportion of reported crimes that have been "solved." The arrest of one person often clears several crimes, such as a burglar who had broken into several homes. Conversely, the arrest of several people may clear only one crime, such as when the police arrest three people for an aggravated assault.

In 1988, a more contemporary approach to measuring crime using police arrest data known as the National Incident-Based Reporting System

A San Francisco police officer making notes at a June 2009 protest against healthcare cuts in California where 17 disability activists were arrested. The FBI's Uniform Crime Report (UCR) collects information from approximately 16,788 law enforcement agencies, covering 97 percent of the U.S. population, and including information on the age, sex, and race of persons arrested by police.

(NIBRS) was introduced. The purpose of NIBRS is to develop a more detailed crime-reporting program that would address some of the data-collection problems in the UCR. The more contemporary NIBRS system of data collection goes into much greater detail than the summary-based UCR system. NIBRS includes 46 offenses (labeled "Group A" offenses) within 22 offense categories, whereas UCR only has eight index offenses classified as Part I offenses. Another important distinction between the two systems is that while the UCR does not differentiate between completed and attempted crimes, the NIBRS does. While the NIBRS is still being implemented nationwide, the traditional UCR reporting format is still being used extensively. As of 2007, the FBI has certified 31 states to participate in NIBRS.

Self-Report Surveys of Offending

Although official arrest statistics like the UCR and NIBRS have historically provided insight into nationwide characteristics of particular types of offenses, the ability of these arrest statistics to accurately measure trends in the entire scope of criminal behavior came into question and spawned the development of self-report surveys. Early studies utilizing self-report data revealed that arrest data vastly underestimated the extent of delinquency in the United States, especially for minor crimes, which are less likely to become known to the police or result in an arrest. Even when police catch offenders, there are several factors that influence whether they actually make an arrest, such as the seriousness of the offense and the offender's prior record. These early self-report surveys revealed that the study of criminal arrest trends ignored a substantial amount of unmeasured crime—crime that official data simply did not even recognize. Criminologists often refer to this unidentified crime as the "dark figure" or "hidden figure" of crime.

In response to concerns among criminologists that arrest statistics were measuring trends in police and reporting behavior rather than actual changes in offending behavior, the development of self-report studies of delinquency gained popularity in the late 1940s and 1950s with the work of James F. Short and F. Ivan Nye. Short and Nye's use of self-report data challenged many conventional assumptions about the extent and nature of crime, especially when it came to the study of less serious offenses. Self-report surveys have given researchers a more complete picture of crime trends by revealing estimates of a greater proportion of the crime committed by individuals, both serious and minor, regardless of whether those behaviors are ever reported to police or result in an arrest. Self-report data also give researchers a more complete picture of subjects' attitudes toward topics such as educational aspirations, interpersonal relationships, occupational aims, government, and levels of friends' delinquency, along with individuals' reports of their own criminal behaviors.

Researchers obtain self-report data by asking groups of individuals (often high school students) about the extent of their offending behavior in the past. Sometimes the subjects are interviewed, but most often they fill out questionnaires about their behavior. Most self-report surveys focus on crimes committed during the previous year, to minimize problems with memory. In almost all cases, self-report surveys are anonymous or the researchers assure respondents that their answers will remain confidential. There are a substantial number of longitudinal self-report surveys of delinquency, such as the National Youth Survey Family Study (NYSFS), the National Survey on Drug Use and Health (NSDUH), and the Monitoring the Future (MTF) survey. The majority of these types of studies are panel studies where one group of youth, such as high school seniors, is repeatedly given a similar survey each year over several years. Surveys like the MTF survey have been distributed each year since the mid-1970s.

While more modern versions of the self-report survey have improved on early versions of self-report surveys, they also have the increased potential of suffering from testing effects. As youth fill out the surveys each year, there is the potential that many juveniles will eventually learn that the more delinquency they admit to, the longer it will take them to fill out their questionnaire. As a result, many juveniles who would otherwise admit to delinquent acts underestimate their delinquency simply to finish the survey more quickly.

There are other difficulties with self-report surveys beyond individuals simply not wanting to fill out the questionnaire. Another concern is with exactly how subjects experience specific events and the extent to which they feel those events are serious enough to report. For example, an 11-year-old may recall a recent scuffle in the schoolyard and indicate on the survey that he has gotten into a serious fight at school within the last 12 months. However, as that individual gets older, the types of behavior considered relevant or severe enough to mark down on a survey as a "serious fight" may be quite different. What an 11-year-old sees as a "serious fight" may be quite different to that same individual when he or she is 21 years old. Finally, since many self-report surveys are given to seniors during high school, the criminal behavior of many serious delinquents such as dropouts or those who have already entered the criminal justice system do not appear, as they are not present to take the survey.

Victimization Surveys
A final method used to study trends in criminal offending is victimization surveys. A typical victimization survey asks respondents to report on their experiences as victims of crime. Researchers began collecting data on victimizations in the 1960s and the federal government started compiling victimization data on an annual basis in the early 1970s through the administration of the National Crime Victimization Survey (NCVS), originally called the National Crime Survey (NCS). The NCVS is administered by the U.S. Census Bureau on behalf of the Bureau of Justice Statistics (under the U.S. Department of Justice).

Twice each year, the NCVS obtains data from a nationally representative sample of roughly 49,000 households comprising about 100,000 persons age 12 and older on the frequency, characteristics, and consequences of criminal victimization in the United States. The NCVS asks respondents to report crime experiences during the previous six months in an effort to improve the accuracy of recalling specifics of events. Many crimes that can be measured by arrest statistics or self-reports of offending are not measured in victimization surveys because there is no immediate, direct victim. For example, measures of crimes such as drug abuse or prostitution are not included in the NCVS as they could be considered "victimless" crimes. Similarly, some situations make it impossible to interview the victim, such as homicide victims or situations of retail theft where a company rather than an individual was the victim.

Victimization surveys have provided criminologists and law enforcement with valuable information that could not be gained from other data sources. Questions are asked regarding whether the victim and offender knew each other, where and what time of day the victimization occurred, whether the victim resisted the offender, whether or not the police were called, why the crime was or was not reported to police, and whether the offender was under the influence of drugs or alcohol or used a weapon. Although victimization surveys help to provide more insight into crimes that may never be reported to police, many victims of crime are resistant to report their victimizations to the NCVS for reasons such as embarrassment, fear of repercussion, and fear of getting the law involved.

Collecting data about the extent of crime is not a simple undertaking. Official police arrest data, self-report data, and victimization data should not be seen as incompatible, but instead the strengths of each method should be viewed as complementary to the weaknesses of the other. Together, all three methods yield a more complete picture of overall trends of criminal offending than a single method can provide. Knowledge about how researchers collect data and the strengths and weaknesses of that data can help researchers and law enforcement gauge the type of data that will provide the best estimate of the extent of crime or trends in crime for a particular crime or situation.

Ryan K. Williams
University of Illinois, Springfield

See Also: Crime in America, Causes; Crime in America, Distribution; Crime in America, Types; Crime Rates; Federal Bureau of Investigation; International Association of Chiefs of Police; Uniform Crime Reporting Program.

Further Readings
Federal Bureau of Investigation. "Uniform Crime Reports." http://www.fbi.gov/about-us/cjis/ucr/ucr (Accessed May 2011).
Menard, S. and D. S. Elliott. "Data Set Comparability and Short-Term Trends in Crime and

Delinquency." *Journal of Criminal Justice*, v.21/5 (1993).

Mosher, C., T. Miethe, and D. Phillips. *The Mismeasure of Crime*. Thousand Oaks, CA: Sage, 2002.

Short, J. F. and F. I. Nye. "Extent of Unrecorded Juvenile Delinquency. Tentative Conclusions." *Journal of Criminal Law, Criminology and Police Science*, v.49 (1958).

Crime in America, Causes

Crime is a major social problem in the United States affecting the quality of life and daily interactions of its citizens. The importance of crime is evidenced, in part, by the rise of academic criminal justice and criminology degree programs throughout American institutions of higher education since the 1970s. Whereas criminal justice is primarily concerned with addressing and responding to crime across the three major prongs of the criminal justice system (law enforcement, the courts, and corrections), the discipline of criminology is the study (*ology*) of crime (*crimin*) and related phenomena. Crime causation is a central concern for criminologists, who seek to identify the leading and contributing factors that explain or are associated with crime. Crime is a complex and multifaceted phenomenon, so it is not surprising that numerous causes and correlates have been identified and debated. In general, the causes of crime are considered in terms of factors internal and intrinsic to individuals or social forces external to a person, commonly referred to as the "nature versus nurture" debate.

While criminal abnormalities and personalities are addressed by psychology and, to a far less degree, biology, the scientific treatment of crime in America is primarily engaged by sociological criminologists. As a subfield of sociology, the practice of criminology is typically engaged with theory-methods symmetry according to the axioms of social science. Criminologists usually narrow research focus by dichotomizing crime into one of two general categories: criminality or crime rate. Whereas criminality refers to the amount and dispersion of crime attributable to the behavior of a group of people (as designated by age, gender, employment status, race/ethnicity, educational attainment, citizenship, criminal history, socioeconomic status, and a host of other indicators), crime rate denotes criminal offenses that are specific to a geographic locale such as a city, county, state, or justice system–designated jurisdiction, for example, a police precinct.

When trying to account for crime, regardless whether the focus is on a group of people or a place, criminologists seek to explain the fluctuation (i.e., variability) in crime levels and rates rather than to generate definitions or specifications of crime. The goal of accounting for the variability of crime entails a research process involving creating hypotheses that specify relationships composed of cause-and-effect elements. These relationships are then examined through data collection and quantitative, qualitative, or mixed methods analysis that inform whether the contended hypotheses are valid. Valid hypotheses, in turn, are combined to construct theories, which are basically formal explanations of crime.

The process of theory construction and theory testing is primarily engaged according to a variable analysis logic, wherein researchers strive to identify which factors (independent variables) correlate with a crime or an index of crimes (dependent variables) as indicated by statistically significant relationships. Because crime, like other forms of human behavior, is such a multifaceted reality, a single factor never fully explains all of the variability, thus necessitating identification of combinations of factors that collectively better specify why crime increases or decreases. Criminologists consider crime fluctuation spatially (across place) and temporally (over time). Assembling multiple factors into coherent explanations is referred to as modeling, often related in the formulaic expression of multivariate analysis. As noted in the overview of criminological theory below, which essentially is a chronological account of the study of crime causation in America, a wide range of factors, social forces, and dynamics are thought to account for criminal phenomena.

Sociological Explanations of Crime

The Italian Cesare Beccaria (1738–94) and the Englishman Jeremy Bentham (1748–1832) are remembered for framing what is known as the classical school of criminology, a perspective grounded in the central concepts of deterrence and free will. Much of applied criminology involves consideration of how the application of the elements of deterrence (certainty, severity, and celerity) condition decisions to offend and how crime prevention initiatives might be more effective.

The classical school has proved consequential for the evolution of criminological thought in two regards: (1) crime is no longer thought to be a function of religion, superstition, or myths that place the solution to crime and related problems beyond the control of man and (2) crime is to be considered, at least in part, the result of free will. Viewing crime as a result of free will means that it is something that can be explained as a result of rational choice–centered decision making. Criminal rational thought infers a determination of gains versus risks, suggesting that crime is related to elements impacting the decision to offend such as the amount and relative value of criminal proceeds and the likelihood of getting caught in the act.

American Criminology

In the evolution of American criminology, positivism began replacing the classical approach to crime during the 1920s, largely due to the rise of the Chicago school, an academic movement resulting from a series of groundbreaking studies conducted within and around the University of Chicago Sociology Department. From the 1920s through the 1940s, the Chicago school demonstrated that crime results from social ecology,

A police officer stands behind three young gang members who were arrested for suspicion of involvement in a fatal shooting in Brooklyn, New York, in 1959. In the 1950s and 1960s, the emergence of gangs and the resulting study of subcultures became a leading focus of crime causation theories as urban, lower-class males were profiled as likely gang members.

particularly the social disorganization that characterizes urban life. The social ecological approach to crime does not focus on the ways in which criminals and noncriminals differ in terms of intelligence, physical characteristics, and personality, instead examining and exploring economic disadvantage, community cohesion, and social stability. The Chicago School crime studies of H. Shaw and D. McKay (1924), D. Merton (1938), and E. Sutherland (1939) grounded U.S. criminology in sociology and established a dominant paradigm (model of inquiry) oriented toward environmental and interactional causes of crime.

Shaw and McKay used Ernest Burgess's "concentric zone" theory to direct their investigations of juvenile delinquency and to develop a forerunner to social disorganization theory. Social disorganization is defined as a community's failure to organize in order to prevent social problems from occurring because of poverty, residential mobility, and racial/ethnic heterogeneity. Social disorganization theory explains why some communities or neighborhoods are more vulnerable to crime than others, with research in this tradition focused on identification of informal network and collective efficacy issues. Focus on order maintenance and crime prevention are policy steps derived from disorganization theory, known more commonly now as environmental criminology.

The legacy of social disorganization theory is Lawrence Cohen and Marcus Felson's routine activities theory, which focuses on macrolevel social change conditioning opportunistic situations to motivate an individual to commit crime. According to routine activities theory, there is a conventional order of everyday events that creates predictable circumstances where crime is both more and less likely to occur. According to routine activities theory, three conditions must be present at the same time and place in order for crime to occur: (1) a motivated offender, (2) a suitable target (person or object), and (3) a lack of effective guardianship. Eliminating or significantly reducing the level of any one of these three elements theoretically invites crime and serves as a good example of how criminological theory has direct implications for crime prevention, such as target hardening strategies, which really are just suitability manipulation efforts.

The 1950s and 1960s

Ronald Akers and Robert Burgess, revising Sutherland's differential association theory with a new social learning theory during the mid-1960s, explained specifically how individuals learn by examining variations in social structure, culture, and locations of associations. Akers and Burgess observed the influence of these factors on key social learning variables such as differential association, imitation, definitions, and reinforcements. Social learning theory specifies that learning processes are contextually similar across social structure, interaction, and situation by producing both conforming and deviant behavior.

In the 1950s and 1960s, the emergence of gangs became a leading focus of crime causation theories as urban, lower-class males were profiled as likely gang members, and the sociological term *subculture* came to be used in reference to these unconventional groups. Albert Cohen's subculture of delinquency theory, Richard Cloward and Lloyd Ohlin's differential opportunity theory, and Walter Miller's focal concern theory are main contributions to what is a notably American line of criminology inquiry based in the notion of the cultural transmission of criminogenic values. The subcultural perspective acknowledges that middle-class values define social norms and proscribe quality of life standards that are reflected in the concept of the American dream. Subcultural theories suggest that everyone does not have equal opportunity to attain the American dream of upward mobility and thus people experience stress and frustration. Theoretical work in this Durkheimian anomie tradition predicts how individuals of lower socioeconomic class status face blocked opportunities and turn to unconventional alternatives (i.e., crime) to achieve needs and desires. People with similar attitudes congregate and form collective solutions to shared problematic situations—therein creating alternate values, beliefs, and rules that define and form a delinquent subculture.

Subcultural theories derive from and are thus similar to Merton's use of Emile Durkheim's anomie concept to theorize deviance in the 1930s. Durkheim defined "anomie" as deregulation and normlessness in society due to breakdown of rules and morals, with Merton redefining the term as a discrepancy between goals and means as a result of the way society is structured. Merton predicted that anomie leads to dissatisfaction, frustration, conflict, and ultimately, deviance. This approach to crime became known as strain theory, with constant and rapid social change prompting multiple revisions such as reverse strain theory, which purports that crime and delinquency can also be a result of too much positive assistance that can be defined as pressure to perform. Anomie and subcultural perspectives both emphasize that people are not naturally inclined to commit crime, but rather external forces compel individuals to deviate from social norms—a view that was challenged by the introduction of social control theories during 1960s.

In 1969, Travis Hirschi extended Thomas Hobbes's belief in the social contract and that people are expected to be deviant because they are rational and driven by efforts to realize gratification. Hirschi unveiled a theory anchored in the inner workings of the social bond. This social bonding explanation of crime hypothesizes that internalized norms, conscience, and desire for approval restrain individuals from delinquent behavior and encourage conformity. Because the social bond serves to control behavior, the perspective is known as social control theory, and it explains why some people are not prone to criminal behavior rather than focusing on why certain individuals are deviant.

Recent Developments
In 1990, Michael Gottfredson and Hirschi published a revision of social control theory in a book titled *A General Theory of Crime*, which proposed that levels of self-control internalized early in life determine who is apt to commit crime. This self-control theory purports that it is human nature to opt for pleasure over pain, but our self-control assists in evaluating short- and long-term consequences to prevent impulsive acts. Gottfredson and Hirschi's self-control perspective is distinct from most other criminological theories because their theoretical approach considers the type of parenting a person experienced rather than sociological factors to predict levels of self-control.

Another identified cause of crime is the natural result of class inequality that is inherent to capitalist societies. Known as critical criminology, the social thought of Karl Marx has shaped various class conflict–based theories examining the relations between the bourgeoisie (wealthy, elite) and proletariat (working) social classes. According to the Marxist perspective, various social problems, including crime, are caused by the constant, reifying competition between upper and lower classes with the minority ruling class using advantage and power to exploit and alienate the majority working class. Critical criminology emphasizes that criminal law is created and enforced to benefit the powerful and oppress the weak, leading to hostility within societies and, ultimately, participation in crime. In this view, much of the everyday crime is considered an expression of political inequality, with criminals seen as helpless victims of an uncaring society.

Theoretical Integration and General Theories
Theoretical criminology systematically analyzes explanations for crime and provides an extensive understanding for variation in offenders and crime occurrence. The previously discussed theories each better explain some crime types (violent or property) and specific offenses with no single theory offering a full account of either criminality or crime rate. Accordingly, contemporary criminological theory construction involves theoretical integration as reflected in general theories of crime. Theoretical integration refers to the regrouping and reconfiguration of single theories of crime into grander theories so as to offer fuller elaborations. As various theories are linked and interwoven, criminologists develop explanations that offer ever greater breadth and scope in terms of range and applicability. Moving forward, research on the causes of crime in America will be increasingly interdisciplinary. Biological and psychological traits such as personality, impulsivity, genetics, and body chemistry have received increased attention over the past decade both as independent and in conjunction with sociological orientations. Accordingly, the current state of crime causation analysis in the United States and internationally is situated in the concept of biosocial theory toward better understanding how genetic and social factors coalesce to foster crime.

J. Mitchell Miller
University of Texas, San Antonio
Kristina M. Lopez
Texas State University

See Also: Crime in America, Distribution; Crime in America, Types; Crime Rates; Criminology.

Further Readings

Copes, H. and V. Topalli. *Criminological Theory: Readings and Retrospectives.* New York: McGraw-Hill, 2010.

Miller, J. M., C. J. Schreck, and R. Tewksbury. *Criminological Theory: A Brief Introduction.* Boston: Pearson Education, 2008.

Scarpitti, F. R., A. L. Nielsen, and J. M. Miller, eds. *Crime and Criminals: Contemporary and Classic Readings in Criminology,* 2nd ed. New York: Oxford University Press, 2009.

Vold, G. B. and T. J. Bernard. *Theoretical Criminology,* 3rd ed. New York: Oxford University Press, 1986.

Crime in America, Distribution

Despite the images sometimes seen in the media, crime in the United States follows some relatively predictable patterns. For example, in any given year, there will be much more property crime than violent crime, and men will be arrested more than women. While crime is not a new phenomenon, the definition of what constitutes a crime, and the salience of certain crimes, changes with policy shifts and public opinions. Law enforcement and the public's concern over street crime means that official data collected by police and government agencies focus on property and violent crime. According to those data, all types of crime have been decreasing since the 1990s for all groups and across all regions, though not uniformly. Property crimes have been decreasing since about the 1970s, whereas violent crimes did not start rapidly decreasing until the 1990s. Those rates have varied by location, with higher crime rates consistently reported by the south and west over the northeast and midwest, and urban centers over rural areas. Crime rates also vary by social groups, with poor men of color overrepresented in official crime data. Although crime in the United States is a complex phenomenon, criminals still behave in some predictable ways.

How Crime Patterns Are Understood

Crime data used to identify crime patterns are collected by a variety of sources, each giving a slightly different picture of offending. Most crime data reported in the news are collected by the Federal Bureau of Investigation (FBI) through the Uniform Crime Reports (UCR) or the National Incident-Based Reporting System (NIBRS). The Bureau of Justice Statistics (BJS) also collects information on victimization experiences of those from a large national sample of households for the National Crime Victimization Survey (NCVS), and there are various self-report surveys, where those surveyed report the crimes they have committed. Unfortunately, reliable data are not available for all crimes, including professional, organized, and white-collar offending. Therefore, the public tends to fear and focus on street crime over white-collar offending, although such offenses have a much higher social cost. For the crimes that are most often studied, official, victim-based, and self-report data each are collected in a different way and therefore show some differences in crime rates.

The UCR collects information on crimes known to police. Because UCR data track offenses known to the police, law and enforcement policies and victim-reporting practices as well as offender behavior are reflected in these data. Violent crimes are more likely to be reported than minor crimes, so the UCR reflects the amount of serious violent crime more accurately than less serious violent and property crimes. The UCR also asks law enforcement to record only the most serious crime that occurred during an incident. If an offender breaks into a house, steals a TV, and shoots the homeowner, only the shooting will be reported in the statistics. This also means that the UCR reports serious violent crime more accurately than other types of crime.

NIBRS collects much more detailed information about crime incidents, allowing law enforcement and researchers to make connections between victims and offenders, among other relationships. It also collects information for all of the crimes that happen in an incident, not just the most serious. This gives a more detailed picture of crime, but because far fewer jurisdictions participate in the data collection, the numbers do not necessarily reflect crime happening all over the United States. Participation in the UCR and/or NIBRS is voluntary, and law enforcement practices and policies may mean uneven or inconsistent reporting. Using self-report data, such as the NCVS, more than half of violent crime (such as rape, assault, and robbery), and even more property crime (such as larceny, motor vehicle theft, and arson), never gets reported to the police.

The NCVS randomly surveys households across the United States, asking individuals age 12 and older about whether certain crimes have happened to them and/or their household. While these data capture a view of crime not filtered by law enforcement, it is also possible that there are data inaccuracies related to the victims' reporting and interpretation of events and issues with personal recollection. Victims tend to be more willing to report offenses that were serious and those perpetrated by strangers. Even though all of the numbers are not in sync, the patterns and trends reported in both official and victim-based data sources are often similar. Self-report data give an even different picture, as such studies ask respondents to report on their own delinquencies and offending. Such studies tend to focus on minor and more common forms of delinquency. In general, self-report data show that crime is underestimated by police data, and that the race, class, and gender differences found in official data are often exaggerated, especially class.

Patterns of Crime by Type

For crimes on which data are consistently collected, rates of property crimes (damaging or taking property of another person) are consistently much higher than rates of violent crimes. According to victimization survey data, less serious crimes are not reported as often, so the difference looks even bigger using data collected by police. Those same survey data show that property crime makes up about three quarters of all victimizations; official data show that property crimes constitute well over 80 percent of crimes known to the police. Of the property crimes, the one most often reported to the police is larceny-theft, followed by burglary. Homicide, though it receives a disproportionate amount of attention by the media, is the smallest category of all serious crimes.

The discrepancy between high minority arrest and imprisonment rates compared to self-report data that show smaller or no race differences points to bias in the U.S. criminal justice system.

Patterns of Crime Across Time

Overall, crime trends, as reported from the biggest data sources, have followed a distinctive pattern. From about 1830 to 1860, there was a gradual increase in the crime rate, especially for violent crime. Following the Civil War, the crime rate increased significantly for about 15 years. From 1880 until about the time of World War I, the number of crimes reported went down, other than spikes around the beginning and ending of the war. The crime rate steadily declined until about 1930, when the United States experienced a crime wave during the Great Depression. According to the UCR, crime rates gradually increased between the 1930s and 1960s, followed by a faster increase through the 1970s. The homicide rate, which had gone against the trend and decreased between the 1930s and 1960s, also had a sharp increase in rate through the 1970s.

Crime peaked in the 1990s and has been declining ever since. The UCR and NCVS have both shown decreases in property and violent crime since the mid-1990s. Self-report data appear to be more stable than the UCR; they also show that people may be offending at significantly higher rates than the FBI is able to capture in their data sources.

In addition to broad changes over time, there are also smaller fluctuations in crime within a given year. For example, most reported crime happens in the warm summer months of July and August. That is a time when teenagers (who commit higher rates of offending) are out of school, more people are spending time together, and homes are left vacant during summer vacations. The two exceptions seem to be murder and robberies, which also have high rates during December and January.

Patterns of Crime Across Place
Just as crime rates vary over time, they are unevenly distributed by place. Rates of offending vary between the United States and the rest of the world, they vary by regions within the United States (the south and west tend to have higher rates than the midwest and northeast), and they vary by demographic attributes within those regions (urban areas have higher rates than rural areas). It is very difficult to compare U.S. crime rates with other countries because there are differences in how each country defines crimes, and there are widely varying perspectives between nations on the value of life and property. Some efforts have been made to overcome these differences, including one major international survey of victimization. Although it is difficult to know exactly how the United States compares to other countries, it seems that the United States consistently has among the highest rates of homicides and incarcerations compared to other developed nations. Some criminologists theorize that the variance between regions within the United States occurs because cultural values vary by region, while others argue it is because of economic differences across regions. Large urban areas have the highest rates of violent crimes, by far, and rural areas have the lowest crime rates on average. Even so, a small number of rural areas have violent crime rates that meet or exceed those of large cities. Cities outside metropolitan areas typically fall between urban and rural rates.

Patterns of Crime Across Social Groups
Just as there are differences in crime across areas, there is variation in crime rates across groups of people within the United States. The most commonly studied differences are between gender, age, race-ethnicity, and class categorizations. Criminological research aims to identify the social factors that cause these differences among population subgroups.

Using both official and other data sources, for almost every crime, men offend at much higher rates than women. In victimization studies and official data, men account for around 80 percent of violent crimes and almost 70 percent of serious property crimes. In self-report data, males consistently report more offending, and more serious crimes, than females. Criminologists theorize the differences could be due to gender socialization and opportunities to offend. When women do offend, their offending tends to be less serious and is more likely to involve crimes tied to women's stereotypical roles in society, like sex work, consumer fraud, and shoplifting.

As with gender, age is another strong correlate of crime. Young people are arrested at a much higher rate than any other age group. Offenders begin in their childhood, rapidly increase offending in late adolescence, then slow down starting with early adulthood. Property crime commission tends to peak a couple of years earlier than violent offending, and property crime arrests drop off more rapidly than arrests for violence. As age increases beyond adolescence, the likelihood of being arrested decreases greatly; criminologists call this "aging out" of crime. Robert Agnew, a criminologist, says that this peak in offending during adolescence can be tied to the unique lives of youth in modern, industrial societies. Youth in these cultures are given many of the privileges of adulthood, yet also experience less supervision as their demands and social networks increase. Although there is variability across nations in the age at which crime peaks, it nearly always is during late adolescence.

Official crime data show that members of minority groups are overrepresented in property crime arrests, and especially in violent and drug crimes. Based on other data sources, criminologists affirm that young, lower-class men of color have disparately high rates of homicide and robbery.

People of color disproportionately experience economic inequality and disadvantaged living conditions, which have been connected to criminality. However, regarding the more common minor offenses, self-report surveys found that minority members generally report lesser or similar rates of minor offending than their majority counterparts. For example, white youth have the highest rates of substance use, whereas African American adolescents report among the lowest levels. The discrepancy between high minority arrest and imprisonment rates compared to self-report data that show smaller or no race differences suggests some amount of bias in the criminal justice system. The United States has a long history of racial stereotypes and media portrayal of young men of color as dangerous, drug addicted, and criminal. Thus, the same action performed by both a white and a black youth could be seen as a "stunt" for the former and a "crime" for the latter. Such stereotypes can influence decisions made by victims to invoke the law and personnel at every level of the criminal justice system, from law enforcement to judges and members of juries.

The association between class and crime almost seems like common sense, as one might believe those in lower classes have the most motivation to commit crimes. That perspective seems validated by the higher arrest rates of those from lower income areas. The use of self-report data, which originated in the 1950s, has complicated this perception among criminologists, although it has not changed public discourse. Whereas class differences are more apparent for serious crimes like homicide and robbery, social class differences are lesser for more common forms of offending. The connection between class and offending is also exaggerated by the disproportionate attention given to street crime over white-collar offending. Although difficult to estimate, societal harm due to corporate and elite crime is thought to be far more damaging in terms of lives lost and financial costs than street crimes.

Criminologists use a variety of data sources to define how crime is distributed systematically across places, historical periods, and social groups in the United States. This endeavor is complicated because definitions of crime differ over time and across places and because each data source measures a slightly different aspect of criminal behavior. However, all sources agree on several enduring patterns of crime. The most serious crimes, like homicide and robbery, occur infrequently, whereas less serious crimes like larceny and burglary occur more often. Crime is concentrated in urban centers, although not absent from rural areas, and more prevalent in the southern and western United States. Crime rates in the United States have declined precipitously since the mid-1990s. Even so, the United States has higher crime and punishment rates compared to other industrialized nations. The demographic profile of the typical offender is a young male; offending rates of females and older people are considerably less. Minorities and the lower class are overrepresented in arrest data. Differences between race, class, and gender appear smaller when using self-report data that is unfiltered by law enforcement practices and better at representing minor forms of offending.

Jennifer Schwartz
Meredith Conover Williams
Washington State University

See Also: Crime in America, Causes; Crime in America, Types; Crime Rates; Juvenile Delinquency, Sociology of; Uniform Crime Reporting Program; Women Criminals, Sociology of.

Further Readings
Agnew, Robert. "An Integrated Theory of the Adolescent Peak in Offending." *Youth and Society*, v.34 (2003).
Elliot, Delbert and Suzanne Ageton. "Reconciling Race and Class Differences in Self-Reported and Official Estimates of Delinquency." *American Sociological Review*, v.45 (1980).
Gove, Walter R., Michael Hughes, and Michael Geerken. "Are Uniform Crime Reports a Valid Indicator of Index Crimes? An Affirmative Answer With Minor Qualifications." *Criminology*, v.24 (1985).
Hindelang, Michael. "Variations in Sex-Race-Age Specific Incidences of Offending." *American Sociological Review*, v.46 (1981).
Steffensmeier, Darrell and Emilie Allan. "Gender and Crime: Toward a Gendered Theory of Female Offending." *American Review of Sociology*, v.22 (1996).

Crime in America, Types

Crimes are classified into various typologies that are used for different purposes, such as legislation and research, as well as specialized law enforcement and prosecutorial initiatives. Typologies of crime can suggest strategies for preventing and controlling crime and can contribute to understanding how and why crimes are committed and the effects of crime on individuals, families, and communities. Crime typologies guide studies of the causes of crime, people's membership in criminal organizations, the impact of programs and punishments on crime rates, and the distribution of crimes across periods of time and across places.

A crime is a definitive act or omission, defined by law for the protection of the public, and made punishable by the state in a judicial proceeding in its own name. Parsed into its basic elements, this definition illuminates the nature of crime and how it differs from other kinds of rule-breaking or deviant behavior. A crime can be an act of commission (e.g., robbery, burglary, or theft) or omission (e.g., child neglect, tax evasion, or failure to register as a sex offender). A crime must be provable in a criminal court in order to bring to justice an individual alleged to have committed the crime (i.e., the defendant). Thus, a crime (the alleged action or inaction) must be substantiated by legal evidence before an individual can be processed through the criminal justice system (arrested, indicted, tried, convicted, and sentenced).

A behavior constitutes a crime only if it is defined as such by the law or a criminal statute. In addition, for suspects to be charged with a crime, their behavior must have been defined as a crime at the time the behavior occurred. In other words, people cannot be charged with a crime if their behavior was not statutorily defined as illegal at the time the act was committed, even though the act is now defined as a criminal one. Charging people with a crime retrospectively is unconstitutional. Hence, ex post facto laws are prohibited.

The state is responsible for redressing the harm that results from criminal activity by prosecuting and helping to convict and punish people who are found guilty of a crime in a judicial proceeding. Only the state can charge people suspected of committing a crime, and only the court can convict and punish people found guilty of committing a crime. Individuals who seek personal vengeance against a criminal—outside the court or legal system—can themselves be charged with a crime (e.g., harassment or assault).

Felonies and Misdemeanors

The most basic typology of crime is built on the law and places offenses into categories of crime severity for sentencing purposes. The most serious crimes are felonies. Felonies consist of any crime that is punishable by a year or more of incarceration in a state prison. The more serious the felony, the higher the class (e.g., class 1 through class 4, in descending order of seriousness) and the longer the prison term as a potential punishment. People convicted of a felony are not automatically sentenced to prison, but they are eligible for imprisonment. In fact, most offenders convicted of a felony are sentenced to probation, a community-based sanction that monitors offenders under conditions of release stipulated by the court (e.g., curfews, participation in drug treatment, fines, or restitution). A conviction for a crime in the highest felony class, often called class X, results in a mandatory prison sentence. A conviction for a capital crime, also a felony, can carry the death penalty (the ultimate punishment).

The least serious crimes are misdemeanors, punishable by up to one year of incarceration in a county jail. Like felonies, misdemeanors are also classified into categories of severity (e.g., class A through class C, in descending order of seriousness); the more serious the misdemeanor, the more likely the perpetrator will be sentenced to a period of incarceration. Also, as is the case with felonies, most people convicted of a misdemeanor are sentenced to a community-based sanction (e.g., court supervision). In addition, they are also likely to receive a monetary sanction, usually in the form of a fine.

Violent, Sex, Property, Hate, and Drug Crimes

Other classifications of crimes place offenses into categories that largely reflect the target or focus of the crimes but are mostly unrelated to the severity of the crimes (i.e., both felonies and misdemeanors can be placed in the same category). Examples of such crime types are violent crimes, property crimes, drug crimes, and sex crimes. Violent crimes are also termed crimes against person and are generally considered more serious than crimes against property, because violent crimes involve harming or threatening to harm a victim. Violent crimes include homicide, which is taking the life of another person (purposefully, knowingly, recklessly, or negligently). Murders can be perpetrated with varying degrees of intent (deliberateness); the greater the degree of intent, the higher the level of offender culpability and the greater the likelihood of a severe punishment. For example, first-degree murder (by definition, with premeditation and purposefulness) by death or life in prison; whereas negligent homicide (without premeditation, purposefulness, or intentional malice) might be punishable by a term of incarceration, but never by the death penalty. Other violent crimes include aggravated criminal sexual assault (i.e., rape), which is compelling a person to engage in sex by physical force or threat of force; robbery, which is taking a person's property by force or threat of force; battery, which is inflicting bodily harm or injury on another person with a weapon or other means; and assault, which is threatening another person with bodily harm. The commission of robbery, battery, or assault with a weapon is referred to as an "aggravated" crime.

Sex offenses are another type of crime against person; they vary greatly in terms of their nature and severity. They can often be violent; for example, rape, which is also classified as a crime against person, is a sex offense. Sexual abuse is regarded as an extremely serious crime; it consists of fondling, kissing, or touching a minor in a sexual manner (contact with breasts, buttocks, or genitalia) or forcing a child to engage in oral or anal sex (sodomy) or masturbatory acts. Possessing, selling, or trading photographs of children for sexual gratification falls under the definition

A member of the U.S. Coast Guard opening a 60-pound bale of cocaine seized in a large antidrug operation in the Caribbean Sea in June 2008. Drug crimes are differentiated between drug-defined crimes such as possession, sales, and trafficking, and those that are associated with drug abuse and dependence, called drug-related crimes.

of child pornography. The exposure of genitalia in public (exhibitionism or indecent exposure) or watching others without their knowledge or consent (voyeurism) for explicitly sexual purposes are generally considered sex crimes of lesser severity and rarely result in prison terms.

Property crimes are the most common offenses reported in the United States. Similar to violent crimes, property offenses can also be placed into several subcategories. Theft (larceny) is taking another person's property without the person's knowledge or consent. Unlike robbery victims, theft victims typically have no contact with perpetrators. If they do, they are unaware of the contact; for example, a victim of pickpocketing might bump into the thief, but is unaware of the victimization during the encounter. Theft from stores (i.e., retail theft) is also called shoplifting. Car theft is its own category of crime, mostly for insurance purposes. Due to the appreciable value of automobiles, this crime is called grand theft auto; the term *grand* refers to the worth of a stolen object, usually in excess of $250 to $500 in value, depending on the state statute. Burglary involves theft from a home, store, car, or garage, following forced or unlawful entry. Only structures can be burglarized; only people can be robbed. Arson involves the deliberate burning of a structure (home, garage, store, or church) or vehicle by igniting an incendiary device or manipulating electrical wiring or utilizing other mechanical means for causing a fire. Arsonists can be motivated by revenge, profit (which occurs when property is insured for fire damage), or thrill seeking (such as pyromania, an impulse control disorder).

Hate crimes are driven by bias or prejudice, not by profit or anger against a specific individual. Perpetrators target victims on the basis of their actual or perceived race, sexual orientation, religious affiliation, or national origin. Hate crimes can be directed against a person (e.g., through acts of assault, battery, or murder), or against a property (e.g., through acts of vandalism, such as spray painting a swastika on a synagogue or torching a gay bar). In 1990, President George H. W. Bush signed into legislation the Hate Crime Statistics Act, mandating the reporting of hate crimes as a separate category of offenses in the Federal Bureau of Investigation's (FBI) Uniform Crime Report. The Violent Crime Control and Law Enforcement Act of 1994 created a specific category of hate crime: "crimes of violence motivated by gender."

Drug crimes involve the possession, sale, or distribution of illicit substances—in order, from the least to the most serious in terms of criminal penalties. Drug distribution done on a large scale and across long distances (across borders and oceans) is called drug trafficking. Most criminal statutes separate marijuana laws from controlled substances laws, which include, for example, cocaine (powder and crack), methamphetamine, opiates (e.g., heroin), and phencyclidine (PCP). Selling drugs near school or church property (drug-free zones) is considered more serious than selling drugs in other public places.

Another way to classify drug crimes is to differentiate between actual drug crimes, called drug-defined crimes, and those that are associated with drug abuse and dependence, called drug-related crimes. The former constitute drug offenses, such as possession and sales; whereas the latter constitute offenses committed to obtain money to purchase drugs, such as robbery, burglary, or theft. The relationship between drug crimes and violent acts can also be classified as pharmacological (e.g., the effects of the drug lower inhibitions or exacerbate paranoia, thereby increasing the risk of violence) or economic (e.g., armed robbery is committed to obtain money to purchase drugs). Systemic violence is caused by competition—usually between rival street gangs—to control drug markets.

Victimless Crimes

Although they are in a category of their own, drug crimes are usually included in a class of offenses known as victimless crimes, in which offenders willingly participate in a criminal transaction by exchanging money for illegal goods or services. For example, people arrested for drug possession seek out the substance that they have purchased, often at great expense and in high-risk places or situations. Prostitution (a sex crime) is also classified as a victimless crime; it involves the exchange of money for sexual services. The behavior itself, consensual sex between adults, is legal when no payment is made for the sexual acts performed. In a few counties in the state of

Nevada, prostitution is legal and operates out of state-regulated and licensed businesses known as brothels. Similarly, gambling is also a victimless crime. However, unlike prostitution, which is legal in only a few jurisdictions in the United States, gambling is legal in nearly every state in the country. Many states operate lotteries and numerous cities, towns, and Indian reservations operate gambling casinos.

The difference between victimless and nonvictimless crimes is related to two other broad categories of crime called *mala in se* and *mala prohibita*. The former are crimes recognized as inherently or naturally evil, such as hurting others (violent crimes) or stealing the property of others (property crimes). *Mala prohibita* crimes are objectionable on moral grounds; they are labeled as offenses only because they are defined as such by law. These offenses fall mostly into the victimless crime category (drugs, prostitution, and gambling).

Organized Crime
For research and prosecutorial purposes, crime can be classified on the basis of the perpetrators' characteristics or the methods of criminal activity. Organized criminal activity, or organized crime, is a collective enterprise in which groups of offenders engage in systematic, planned criminal pursuits within a well-defined organizational structure and hierarchy of leadership. Traditional organized crime, exemplified by the Italian American La Cosa Nostra, once consisted of organized crime families in several large cities in the United States, including the five families of New York City as well as families in Chicago, Philadelphia, Cleveland, Kansas City, New Orleans, and Miami.

At one time, these families wielded considerable political power and infiltrated the leadership ranks of major labor unions. La Cosa Nostra monopolized various illegal markets, engaging in labor racketeering and controlling legitimate businesses (construction, music, waste removal, clothing, and food) through intimidation, extortion, and violence. In addition to its criminal mainstays—gambling, loan sharking, and prostitution—La Cosa Nostra has been involved increasingly in sophisticated crimes such as stock manipulations, phone card theft, and health insurance fraud. Major street gangs are another example of an organized criminal group.

White-Collar Crimes
White-collar crimes are committed by professionals who hold legitimate positions of power, authority, and trust, allowing them to take advantage of people in fraudulent schemes that can cost victims millions or billions of dollars. White-collar crimes are differentiated in name from "street" or "predatory" crimes. Unlike street crimes, white-collar crimes are committed in an office by men wearing suits and ties—hence, the term *white-collar*. Corporate administrators, bank and real estate executives, commodities traders, and stock brokers are but a few examples of the positions held by white-collar criminals. White-collar criminals act for self-gain (for example, embezzlement) or for the benefit of a business (for example, corporate price-fixing). Victims of white-collar crime include employers, consumers, and financial institutions. Such crimes can also significantly damage the economy and the environment. Under the identification doctrine, entire corporations can now be treated as legal entities and charged with white-collar crimes.

The Ponzi scheme, one of the oldest white-collar crimes, involves a fraudulent investment operation that pays initial investors dividends that are not based on actual profits, but on the investments of subsequent victims. The offender attracts would-be investors by promising high financial returns that are not attainable through traditional investments. A recent example of a Ponzi scheme was the Madoff scandal, costing victims/investors more than $20 billion in losses.

Computer Crime and Terrorism
Two of the more recent types of crime are Internet crime, also called cybercrime, and terrorism. The World Wide Web created a number of new opportunities for criminal pursuits. Computers can be a vehicle or tool for other types of crimes, such as fraud. The Nigerian Letter Fraud scheme involves e-mails from Nigeria that offer recipients a share of the millions of dollars that the author—a self-proclaimed government official—is attempting to transfer out of Nigeria illegally. The official asks the "fortunate" e-mail recipient to wire money to expedite the transfer of these dollars; in the vast

majority of these cases, the money will never be traced or recovered. Other kinds of crimes facilitated by the Internet include identity theft, which involves using people's banking or credit card information to steal their assets, and infecting computer systems with viruses (computer programs that can copy themselves and damage a computer) in order to wreak havoc in government agencies or companies. A computer virus can be spread to personal computers simply out of maliciousness. Spyware can also be surreptitiously installed on personal computers to track the users' habits and interests for commercial gain.

Although legal definitions of terrorism are nebulous, such acts are generally characterized by violence, mayhem, and destruction against innocent victims. This is generally done for the purpose of instilling fear in order to advance political, religious, or ideological causes and to raise the profile of the groups that claim responsibility for the terrorist acts. The random, brutal, and public nature of the violence is calculated to have paralyzing effects on the citizenry. Targets are often selected for their symbolic value, such as in the 9/11 attacks on the World Trade Center and Pentagon.

Arthur J. Lurigio
Loyola University Chicago

See Also: Burglary, Contemporary; Child Abuse, Contemporary; Codification of Laws; Computer Crime; Crime in America, Distribution; Crime Rates; Criminalization and Decriminalization; Gambling; Larceny; Murder, Contemporary; Organized Crime, Contemporary; Prostitution, Contemporary; Race-Based Crimes; Uniform Crime Reporting Program.

Further Readings
Brenner, Susan W. *Cyber Crime: Criminal Threats From Cyberspace*. Westport, CT: Praeger, 2010.
Dabney, Dean A. *Crime Types: A Text/Reader*. Florence, KY: Wadsworth, 2003.
Hagan, Frank E. *Crime Types and Criminals*. Thousand Oaks, CA: Sage, 2010.
Lynch, James P. and Lynn A. Addington. *Understanding Crime Statistics: Revisiting the Divergence Between the NCVS and UCR*. Cambridge: Cambridge University Press, 2006.

Crime Prevention

Crime prevention is recognized as any action designed to reduce the actual level of crime, perceived levels of crime, or fear of crime. Its effects are a priori (i.e., proactive techniques) to future crime. Conversely, crime control is the maintenance or management of crime in society. Its effects are ex post facto (i.e., reactive techniques) to existing crime problems. While crime prevention can be broad, it focuses on efforts to alter the environment in order to reduce crime. These efforts involve actions of individual citizens, small groups of citizens, and entire communities.

Crime prevention encompasses both formal and informal strategies. Formal approaches are often planned, carried out by criminal justice officials, regulated by law or policy, and utilized to enforced explicit norms and values (i.e., criminal law). Informal approaches tend to be carried out by all members of society, unregulated, and used to enforce all norms of society. Crime prevention efforts can also be designed to encompass formal and informal strategies, and thus, prevention techniques are often seen on a continuum. At the formal end of the crime prevention spectrum are conventional maintenance efforts of the traditional criminal justice system. Moving along the continuum to less formal activities are such tactics as community-oriented policing initiatives, citizen patrol, and neighborhood watch groups. At the informal end of the spectrum are self-protection and risk-avoidance strategies of individual citizens.

Environmental and community crime prevention programs have emerged because of a myriad of factors. Citizen participation in crime reduction initiatives was encouraged and motivated by the political and social climate of the 1960s and 1970s. Furthermore, community prevention efforts were also encouraged by issues involving the formal criminal justice system. The justice system has often been criticized for being ineffective because of its reactive and punitive nature. Operating and maintaining the criminal justice system is also expensive and resource-intensive. Money and time are spent investigating existing crimes and prosecuting, trying, and housing criminal offenders rather than on strategies to reduce or eliminate crime. Finally, because of recent "get tough on crime" movements such as the war on drugs, determinate sentencing, three strikes laws, truth-in-sentencing laws, increased incarceration, and longer prison sentences, the formal justice system routinely operates at full capacity.

Many community crime prevention efforts are rooted in criminological theory. While traditional theories of crime focus on the offender and offender motivation (e.g., biological, psychological, and sociological factors), opportunity theories of crime emphasize the physical characteristics of the criminal event (e.g., spatio-temporal patterns of victims and offenders, and environmental influences). The most recognized opportunity theories of crime include Lawrence Cohen and Marcus Felson's routine activity theory, Derek Cornish and Ronald Clarke's rational choice theory, and Paul Brantingham and Patricia Brantingham's crime pattern theory. The three most utilized applications of these theories have been formulated through Oscar Newman's defensible space, C. Ray Jeffery's "crime prevention through environmental design" (CPTED), and Clarke's situational crime prevention.

Routine Activity Theory

Lawrence Cohen and Marcus Felson developed a criminological perspective based on the routine activities of people and changes in activity structures. They compared these changes to crime rates from 1947 to 1974. The authors posit that criminal behavior is routine and it is interdependent with other pro-social routines. Crime, therefore, is a result of the structures of "everyday life." Further, they contend that everyday life affects the extent to which three necessary elements must converge in time and space: (1) a motivated offender, (2) a suitable target, and (3) the absence of capable guardianship.

The motivated offender is taken as a given by Cohen and Felson, but the exposure between people (potential offenders and victims) is variable. Crime rates, thus, are a function of rates of exposure, target suitability, and a lack of able guardianship. For property offenses such as theft, the suitability of a target is determined by its value and portability. Guardianship refers to the capability of a person to guard his or her property by keeping it under surveillance or preventing access to it.

The authors specify several factors that emerged during this era that contributed to the alteration of routine activities in society. More women joined the labor force and enrolled in higher education, which fostered an increase in unattended households during the daytime. There was a greater production and consumption of goods, which created an increase in available targets. Moreover, the new items being produced (e.g., personal electronics) were also made smaller and lighter. This makes theft crimes easier. Further, there was a decrease in the number of people getting married. This meant more single people living alone; they also tend to be outside the home more often, which increases their likelihood of committing crime or being a victim of crime.

Cohen and Felson found support for their theory. They concluded that the increases in crime during that period (especially residential burglary and robbery) were associated with the routine activities of everyday life. Subsequent empirical tests of routine activity theory have suggested that aggregate crime rates and individual victimization can be attributed to the normal routines of people in society. These variables include the number of nights spent outside the home, the number of valuables carried outside the home, the number of portable household goods, and the lack of preventive maintenance (e.g., locks, security systems, and neighborhood watches).

Rational Choice Theory

While routine activity theory posits that variation in one's activity can alter crime, rational choice theory focuses on human agency; that is, the decision-making processes of humans, specifically criminals. It seeks to understand the dynamic components of involving oneself in committing crime, decisions directly related to the crime event, and the decision to desist from crime.

Cornish and Clarke state that rational choice theory concerns both crime and criminality, and it seeks to explain why motivations can change. It accounts for all types of crime, stresses the importance of situation and opportunity, and has direct policy implications. Rational choice theory has six basic tenets: (1) crimes are purposive and deliberate acts with an intention of benefiting the offender, (2) offenders do not always succeed in making the best decisions because

George Kelling and James Wilson's "broken windows" theory holds that increases in the number of minor crimes, such as littering or graffiti as seen in this pedestrian tunnel in Philadelphia in 2009, may lead some residents into antisocial behavior if they feel it will go unpunished and can lead to more serious forms of crime.

of risks and uncertainty, (3) offender decision making varies considerably with the nature of the offense, (4) involvement decisions are quite different from event decisions, (5) involvement decisions can be divided into three stages (initiation, habituation, and desistence), and (6) event decisions involve a sequence of choices made at each stage of criminal acts.

Crime Pattern Theory
Criminal behavior is typically not random in both motivation and geographical space. Recent research has demonstrated that relatively few "hot spots" produce the most crime and the most calls for police service. In a study by Lawrence Sherman, 50 percent of all calls for service in Minneapolis occurred in 3 percent of the places within the city. Moreover, all auto thefts were committed in 2.7 percent of places, all robberies were committed in 2.2 percent of places, and all rapes were committed in 1.2 percent of places within the city. Thus, the locations of many crimes are capable of being predicted. Crime pattern theory and offender search theory both add to routine activity theory by describing how and where offenders and victims come into contact with one another, creating the possibility of criminal opportunity.

The daily activities of offenders and law-abiding citizens are often structured around nodes and paths. Nodes refer to the specific places where individuals typically congregate (e.g., home, work, school, and places of entertainment). Paths refer to the roads and pathways that connect nodes to other nodes. Humans tend to be creatures of habit and often traverse the same route to and from their nodes. Moreover, humans typically do not stray too far from home. The probability of target selections becomes less and less as potential offenders get farther and farther from home.

Crime is most likely to occur at nodes or along paths because there they yield the greatest availability of offenders and targets. Offenders will often search for crime in search areas that are based off an offenders' typical type of target. Offenders will also commit crimes where their search areas overlap with their target areas. These places of convergence are based upon patterns of movement within the environment. Opportunity theories of crime contend that illegal behavior is largely a function of the structure of opportunity. Some offenders can actively create their own illegitimate opportunities, and thus, some crime may be best explained as a response to a situation in which the attraction of a particular crime may be too good to dismiss.

Broken Windows Theory

Situational and ecological factors that create or facilitate opportunities for crime have become vital elements of study for criminologists. George Kelling and James Wilson's "broken windows" theory details how neighborhood image impacts crime and crime prevention. Their central thesis is that unchecked social disorder is the primary cause of serious crime. Areas marked by unrepaired physical deterioration may lead to decreased participation in maintaining order among residents. This decrease in collective efficacy can lead to increases in delinquency, rowdiness, and vandalism.

This general disorder can lead to further neighborhood deterioration and further withdrawal among residents. Disorderly behavior, which goes unregulated and unchecked, signals to residents that the area is unsafe. The downward spiral begins not with serious offenders but with disreputable or disorderly persons (e.g., panhandlers, drunks, prostitutes, and addicts). Though the risk of criminal offending by these persons may be low, residents no longer feel safe walking down the street. Fearful residents will then avoid certain locations and withdraw from public life. By withdrawing from their roles of mutual support with their fellow neighbors, residents surrender the social control they had formerly helped maintain. With community safety now undermined, the area becomes vulnerable to increases in disorder and other serious crimes. In essence, serious crimes are able to flourish in areas where disorder and general incivility have gone unchecked.

Increases in the number of "broken windows" (e.g., graffiti, trash, or dilapidated housing) may lead some residents to conform to antisocial behavior if they feel it will go unpunished. It may also lead to outside offenders moving into the neighborhood who are attracted by the neighborhood's vulnerability to crime. Finally, "broken windows" can lead to more serious forms of crime if offenders are realizing that less serious crimes are going unnoticed.

Crime prevention initiatives focused on fixing the "broken windows" may involve residents or community groups but mainly concentrate on police tactics, such as zero-tolerance policing, quality-of-life policing, community-oriented policing, and problem-oriented policing. Zero-tolerance policing focuses on maintaining order through aggressive police action, whereas community- and problem-oriented policing relies mainly on citizen input, evidence-based policing, and fixing the root cause of the disorder. For Kelling and Wilson, order maintenance would not simply mean fighting serious crime but rather fighting the disorder and general incivility that undermined neighborhood social control in the first place. Some academics (e.g., Kelling) point to New York City's dramatic crime drop in the 1990s as evidence for zero-tolerance policing, but other academics claim that much of the crime drop would have happened anyway.

Environmental Crime Prevention

In the early 1970s, environmental crime prevention flourished with the published works of C. Ray Jeffery and Oscar Newman. In 1971, Jeffery coined the phrase *crime prevention through environmental design* (CPTED) and used it for the title of his book. He was followed by Newman in 1972 with his classic book, *Defensible Space*. Each helped to clarify how to design new buildings, structures, and neighborhoods more carefully so they did not foster crime. They also encouraged property owners to fix old places to reduce their crime problems.

Defensible space pertains to an environment that is under control of its residents, and Newman carefully considers a set of strategies for achieving such an environment. He suggests that community crime prevention is a function of four elements: territoriality, natural surveillance, image, and juxtaposition. Territoriality refers to the demarcation of space and its proper usage along with the development of residents' sense of ownership. Natural surveillance is the ability of residents to observe activity from inside or outside their homes. Image refers to the appearance, maintenance, and condition of the neighborhood (civility versus incivility). Juxtaposition refers to the positioning of structures within the broader environment.

To achieve defensible space, community developers and property owners must take these elements into consideration. Newman suggests that to properly achieve a "defended space," structures within communities must provide for the delineation of space for particular users (e.g., public versus private space). Private spaces (e.g., homes) are better for crime prevention because the area is better guarded. Provisions should also be made so that residents can naturally observe the area from inside and outside their homes. Finally, space should be created and maintained so that it is not isolating or stigmatizing (i.e., no "broken windows"), and residential buildings should be properly placed next to "safe" areas. Aspects of the physical environment that can influence these elements include access, site and street design, disorder, and boundary markers.

Situational Crime Prevention

In combining rational choice and human agency perspectives within environmental contexts, Ronald Clarke suggests that to reduce crime, society must reduce an individual's opportunity to commit crime. Although people differ in their motivations and dispositions to offend, Clarke argues actual criminal acts depend on situational factors. People may come from varying backgrounds, but all persons must still decide to break the law in any given situation; the nature of the situation can affect their decision making. To that end, he developed a new perspective of crime prevention, one that took situational variables into account.

Situational crime prevention focuses on the criminal event, whereas traditional theories center on the criminal offender and sources of individual motivation. This perspective promotes the importance that physical environments play in encouraging or inhibiting criminal activity and suggests that changes to the environment can reduce criminal opportunity. Clarke's focus on opportunity differs from other perspectives in that the reduction efforts being made are directed at repeated and highly specific forms of crime based upon analysis of crime patterns. The focus is also much more on reducing the opportunity than it is on fostering collective efficacy or informal social control.

Crimes are more likely to occur if they are easier to commit, have low risks of detection, provide attractive rewards, and are encouraged by the immediate environment. Altering the opportunity structure may be best utilized through situational crime prevention. Specifically, situational crime prevention is comprised of opportunity-reducing measures directed at specific forms of crime. It involves the management or manipulation of the environment in systematic ways to make crime more difficult and risky and/or less rewarding. The general concepts of this technique focus on the implementation of safety measures that help protect people and property by making criminals feel they will be unable to successfully commit crimes. If there are enough safeguards being implemented to reduce temptation or cause a high probability of failure or detection, then the rational choice for a criminal would be to avoid committing the act.

Situational crime prevention seeks to decrease specific crimes at specific places by focusing on five preventative techniques: (1) increasing the effort, (2) increasing the risks, (3) reducing the rewards, (4) reducing provocations, and (5) removing excuses. Increasing the effort made by potential criminals to commit crime can be done through measures of target hardening (e.g., locks and tamper-proof packaging) and controlling the access to facilities (e.g., electronic card access).

Increasing one's risk of detection can be achieved through the strengthening of informal (e.g., neighborhood watch groups) and formal (e.g., red-light cameras) surveillance. Reducing the rewards one might get as a result of a criminal act can be accomplished through measures of concealing or removing targets (e.g., a removable car radio) and by identifying or marking property. Reducing one's provocation for crime can be achieved by avoiding disputes, neutralizing peer pressure, and reducing stress. Finally, removing excuses for crime can be implemented by setting rules (e.g., rental agreements), posting instructions (e.g., "Private Property"), assisting compliance, and controlling drugs and alcohol.

Christopher M. Donner
University of South Florida

See Also: Community Policing and Relations; Crime Rates; Criminology; Deterrence, Theory of; Fear of Crime; Theories of Crime; Wilson, James Q.

Further Readings
Blumstein, Alfred and Joel Wallman. *The Crime Drop in America*. New York: Cambridge University Press, 2006.
Brantingham, Paul, and Patricia Brantingham. *Patterns in Crime*. New York: Macmillan, 1984.
Clarke, Ronald. *Situational Crime Prevention: Successful Case Studies*. New York: Harrow & Heston, 1992.
Conklin, John. *Why Crime Rates Fell*. Boston: Allyn & Bacon, 2003.
Cornish, Derek, and Ronald Clarke. *The Reasoning Criminal*. New York: Springer-Verlag, 1986.
Felson, Marcus. *Crime and Everyday Life*. Thousand Oaks, CA: Pine Forge Press, 1998.
Jeffery, C. Ray. *Crime Prevention Through Environmental Design*. Beverly Hills, CA: Sage, 1971.
Kelling, George and Catherine Coles. *Fixing Broken Windows*. New York: Simon & Schuster, 1996.
Newman, Oscar. *Defensible Space: Crime Prevention Through Environmental Design*. New York: Collier Books, 1973.
Skogan, Wesley. *Disorder and Decline: Crime and the Spiral Decay in American Neighborhoods*. New York: Oxford University Press, 1990.

Crime Rates

Crime rates refer to the collection and publication of data on criminal offending, usually measured in rates per 1,000 or per 100,000. The use of rates as opposed to raw numbers allows researchers to determine the prevalence of specific crimes within a defined population or jurisdiction. Such rates are particularly useful for measures of crime over time as well as for the comparison of specific crimes or crime types between two or more different populations.

Measuring Rates of Crime

Official Data. The first systematic attempts to record and measure rates of criminal offending were undertaken in the middle of the 19th century. In 1825, France began to collect national data on rates of criminal prosecutions and convictions, and Great Britain began to collect data in the 1850s on "crimes known to the police." The United States also had begun collecting judicial data on rates of crime by the latter part of the 19th century, but it wasn't until the 1920s that the government began to seek a way to systematically record, measure, and make available statistics on rates of criminal offending. For a variety of reasons, most notably because judicial records were seen as further removed from the act of crime itself than were police records, the recording of crime was standardized under the auspices of the Federal Bureau of Investigation (FBI). Beginning in 1931, the FBI began its annual publication of its Uniform Crime Report (UCR), which compiled statistics on criminal arrests from local, state, and federal law enforcement agencies.

Today, the UCR consists of data from over 17,000 police agencies that report on crimes known to the police, arrests, and crimes cleared by the police. Information reported in the UCR includes type of offense, region, and jurisdiction of offense, and in the case of arrests, the age, gender, and race of the offender. Historically, the UCR has also grouped crimes into more serious (Index I) crimes and less serious (Index II) crimes, as well as compiling indexes for "violent crime" and "property crime."

Since its inception, the UCR has served as the benchmark of official data on crime rates. However, official data (including the UCR) have several limitations. It has long been recognized that official measurements of crimes known to the police constitute only a small part of the overall crime that occurs. Criminologists refer to this unknown amount as the "dark figure" of crime. Other problems include varying policing strategies (i.e., beat cops versus vehicle patrols) that may lead to differences in the amount of crime known to police; differential policing or enforcement that may result in skewed data on certain demographic groups or communities; and the "inflation of seriousness" whereby policing agencies frequently charge offenders with the highest offense possible in the expectation that they will likely plea-bargain to a lower charge. One notable problem with the UCR in particular is the "hierarchy rule," where only the most serious crime in any single incident is reported, even when there may also be several less serious offenses. Other problems in the UCR include lack of data on relationships between offenders and victims, lack of detailed demographic information on victims, and lack of information regarding drug or alcohol use by offenders. Also, controversially, the UCR's definition of rape does not include male victims.

More recently, the FBI has implemented the National Incident-Based Reporting System (NIBRS) to address some of the problems in the UCR. NIBRS does not use the hierarchy rule. Rather, it collects information about crimes based on "incidents" rather than single offenses, allowing for a more comprehensive recording of both events and information on offenders and victims. It has an expanded recording of more serious (Type A) and less serious (Type B) offenses, including information on drug and alcohol use. It also differentiates between "attempted" and "completed" crimes, while the UCR does not. Finally, it includes males in its definition of rape. As of 2004, approximately 5,300 law enforcement agencies contributed to the NIBRS, representing 20 percent of the U.S. population.

Self-Report Data. In the 1940s, researchers began to measure rates of criminal offending in ways that did not involve reliance on policing agencies. In 1946, Austin Porterfield compared rates of "self disclosed" juvenile delinquency in college students against disclosed rates of adjudicated delinquents and found that these rates were more similar than official records suggested. Subsequent research by James Short and Ivan Nye in the 1950s confirmed that crime was more uniformly distributed among the population than evidenced in official data. They also developed a standardized instrument by which disclosed rates of criminal activity could be measured through the administration of an anonymous "self-report" survey. The use of such surveys has consistently demonstrated the underrecording of crime rates in official measures, and with varying reliability they have provided researchers with a second important measure of crime rates. Examples of well-known self-report surveys include the National Youth Survey, started in 1967 and used annually since 1976, as well as the Monitoring the Future project started in 1975.

Self-report surveys have several advantages over official data. Primarily, they are able to record and measure many crimes that go unreported to the police. Second, self-report surveys allow researchers to design survey instruments in ways that can test hypotheses on the etiology of crime and characteristics of offenders. Third, self-report surveys are often able to capture a larger amount of data than official records provide. However, they are not without their problems and limitations. Self-report surveys rely on the recollection of respondents, who may remember dates, places, or incidents incorrectly. Also, some researchers argue there is a trend that finds respondents overreporting their involvement in less serious crimes, and underreporting their involvement in more serious crimes, particularly sexual crimes and homicide. Finally, while hundreds of such surveys have been undertaken, differences in sampling and instrumentation make them difficult to use for comparative purposes.

Victim Data. Victim data utilizes surveys to inquire into the type and frequency of victimization of respondents. In 1972, the Bureau of Justice Statistics implemented its biannual National Crime Victimization Survey (NCVS). Today, the NCVS collects information from approximately 85,000 households and 150,000 persons per year. Households participate for three years, and individuals over the age of 12 are surveyed every six months. Questions in the survey include types of crimes experienced by victims; victim relationship to offenders; demographic data and characteristics of victims, offenders, and others in the household; attitudes toward crime and the police; and whether or not the crime was reported.

The NCVS is generally considered to be the most accurate and reliable single measure of crime in the United States. It records "personal crimes," including rape and sexual attack, robbery, aggravated and simple assault, and purse-snatching/pocket-picking; and "property crimes," including burglary, theft, motor vehicle theft, and vandalism. It does not record arson or homicide. Since 1972, the NCVS has consistently demonstrated a higher level of crime than is reflected in official data. For example, research conducted in the 1970s using the NCVS in eight U.S. cities found rates of assault to be 15 times higher than reported to police, and rates of robbery nine times higher. Another important finding of the NCVS has been that many people do not report crimes to the police because they do not believe it will make a difference or because they think the crime was not serious enough.

As with other self-report surveys, the NCVS relies on the recollection of respondents. This can lead to problems where respondents may conflate incidents of victimization, report crimes that may not have occurred (i.e., a lost wallet that is reported as stolen), not report particularly shameful types of victimization such as rape, or not report crimes that may implicate family members. Respondents are also asked to report crimes within the previous six months, and this can result in both under and overreporting due to misrecollection of when the victimization occurred.

Crime Trends

Establishing definitive rates of crime prior to the systematic collection of official and other data is difficult. Historians of crime, with few exceptions, suggest that crime rates in 18th- and early-19th-century America were for the most part significantly higher than those of the 20th century. Beginning in the mid-19th century, historians have found divergent crime trends between some major older metropolitan areas such as Boston and Buffalo, New York, which saw a general reduction in recorded violent crimes throughout the latter part of the 19th century, and rural areas (in particular, the southern states) or newly emerging urban centers, where crime rates frequently rose during this time.

Data from the first half of the 20th century in the United States evidences several trends. Most generally, crime began to decline overall at the end of the 19th century (and in some places earlier), and remained relatively low with a few

Unemployed people protesting in Camden, New Jersey, in 1935. The Great Depression saw an increase in crime but the relationship between crime and unemployment is ambiguous.

exceptions over the next 60 years. Historians have noted the short-term suppressant effect of major wars on crime rates, as well as the increase in crime rates (particularly property crime) in times of economic hardship—in particular, the Great Depression. However, there is considerable debate as to why crime apparently fell in the late 19th century and remained relatively low until the 1960s. Some historians suggest that the growing efficacy of modern police forces was significant in this decline, but others have noted that violent crime, in particular, began to decrease in several urban areas prior to the advent of modern police departments. Other explanations for the general reduction of crime in this period include the early growth of a middle class and subsequent suburbanization of northern cities; the growing assimilation of immigrant populations; the growth of civil organizations, including churches, unions, lodges, and clubs; and the growing stability of labor patterns and occupations (with the exception of the Great Depression).

Following World War II, crime rates rose in many European countries in the 1950s. Between 1945 and the early 1960s in the United States, however, rates remained relatively stable until the early 1960s, when both violent and property crime began a precipitous climb. In 1960, the violent crime index was 161 per 100,000. By its peak in 1991, this rate was 758 per 100,000. Property crime followed a similar trend, with 1,726 per 100,000 in 1960 and a peak of 5,350 in 1980, with only a gradual decline until the mid-1990s. Yet just as precipitously as crime rates climbed after 1960, they began to fall again in the mid-1990s. By 2009, violent crime rates had returned to 1973 levels, and property crime rates were at the same level as 1968.

UCR, self-report, and victimization data vary, but all confirm that the growth and subsequent decline in crime was real. Some argue that the increase in crime was due to the growing number of young people as a result of the Baby Boomer generation (1946–64). Sociologists have long recognized that young people (particularly young men) are responsible for a disproportionate amount of crime. The demographic bulge of maturing young people in the 1960s and 1970s, it is argued, led to an increase in crime rates during this time, as well as to a decrease in crime rates as the median age moved upward in the United States as Boomers started to age. Yet, while there is agreement that the growth and aging of Boomers has played a part in these changing trends, there is debate as to the degree of effect. Problematically, for example, birthrates at the beginning of the 20th century were even higher than during 1946–64 and life expectancy shorter, yet crime rates remained relatively lower, even in the Great Depression.

Some historians have argued that the Boomer generation was different, however, not only for its increased birthrates, but also for the changing culture values, including an emphasis on individualism and, in some cases, opposition to authority. The growth of social movements such as the civil rights movement and Black Panthers reflected, respectively, the fracture of the promises of the postwar boom in the 1960s as well as the growing despair of joblessness and growing poverty in the 1970s. In this respect, many criminologists have linked the growing crime rates of the 1970s and 1980s to growing poverty rates, particularly within minority communities, which also subsequently decreased during the 1990s along with rates of crime. However, the historical evidence on the relationship between crime and both unemployment and poverty is ambiguous. In some historical cases, crime has increased with poverty (particularly during the Great Depression), but in other cases it has not. A possible explanation put forth by some criminologists is that smaller recessions and periods of unemployment frequently lead to conditions where people are home more often and thus less likely to either commit or be victims of many types of crime, while more serious economic downturns such as depressions or prolonged poverty may serve as a tipping point at which otherwise law-abiding people begin to engage in criminal activity.

Other Theories

Aside from age and economics, several other theories exist as to the rise and fall of crime in the latter part of the 20th century. Most of these theories suggest that there is no single causal factor in the rise and subsequent fall of crime rates but rather a series of social, cultural, political, and demographic convergences and divergences that have in some cases been more instrumental and in other cases less so. For example, many criminologists point to the rise of the number of police officers as well as to changes in policing strategies in the 1990s as causal factors in the decline of crime.

The massive growth of incarceration, beginning in the 1980s, is also frequently cited as a factor in declining crime rates, although there is substantial debate as to the degree of this effect. Franklin Zimring, for example, has pointed out that Canada's crime rates also decreased at similar levels to the United States, even while its comparative rate of incarceration was significantly lower.

The economist Steven Levitt has argued that among other factors, the receding epidemic of crack cocaine and the legalization of abortion under *Roe v. Wade* in 1973 resulted in significantly lower crime rates beginning in the 1990s. In the case of abortion, Levitt argued that the decrease in unwanted births has resulted in a decrease of unwanted children at risk of future criminal activity. More recent research, however, has cast some doubt on this theory due to methodological errors in his work as well as to mistaken assumptions about the effects of abortion on crime rates.

Conclusion

While the three primary means of determining crime rates have increased in reliability and validity over the last 50 years, particularly when used together, they have arguably led to a wider divergence of explanations for general crime trends. Yet such divergent analysis of general crime rates often masks the fact that research on specific types of crime has yielded more definitive and concrete explanations. For example, decreases in burglary and larceny have been widely attributed to the relative decreasing value of electronics and other consumer goods over the last two decades. On the other hand, the growing arrests for marijuana possession over the last two decades are more likely explained by changes in drug laws and policing tactics than by any real increase in use, which self-report surveys show as decreasing beginning in 1985 and remaining relatively low throughout the early 21st century. Not all changes in rates of specific types of crime are so easily explained, but the development of multiple means of measuring rates has allowed researchers to know more about crime than at any time in the past.

William R. Wood
University of Auckland

See Also: Abortion; African Americans; Automobile and the Police; Black Panthers; Boston, Massachusetts; Civil Rights Laws; Crime and Arrest Statistics Analysis; Crime in America, Causes; Crime Prevention; Great Depression; *Roe v. Wade*; Violent Crimes.

Further Readings

Chambliss, William. "The Politics of Crime Statistics." In *The Blackwell Companion to Criminology*, Colin Sumner, ed. Oxford: Blackwell, 2004.
Levitt, Steven. "Understanding Why Crime Fell in the 1990s: Four Factors That Explain the Decline and Six That Do Not." *Journal of Economic Perspectives*, v.18/1 (2004).
Mosher, Clayton J., Terance D. Meithe, and Dretha M. Phillips. *The Mismeasure of Crime*. Thousand Oaks, CA: Sage, 2002.
Zimring, Franklin. *The Great American Crime Decline*. Oxford: Oxford University Press, 2007.

Crime Scene Investigation

The fundamental premise of a crime scene investigation is that perpetrators often leave clues during the commission of a crime. The smallest detail that may seem insignificant to the general public may provide vital information to crime scene investigators. Details from the crime scene will help investigators determine if the case in question resulted from criminal activity. If criminal activity is established, investigators carefully and thoroughly sift through the evidence in hope of apprehending a suspect.

Basic Procedure

The basic features of a crime scene investigation include the recognition, documentation, collection, packaging, and preservation of evidence left behind after the commission of a crime. After the commission of a crime, the first responder determines if the perpetrator is still in the vicinity of the crime scene, seeks to locate and assist any injured parties, and identifies any potential witnesses. Once those determinations have been made, the crime scene is secured in order to do an initial walk-through to assess the area. Investigators may physically secure the crime scene by placing ropes, tape, barricades, or law enforcement personnel around the perimeter to prevent the scene from being contaminated. Investigators and other personnel may also utilize protective gear if safety hazards have been identified at the scene. After the initial evaluation of the crime scene, investigators work to ensure that all physical evidence is discovered, investigated, and secured for scientific evaluation and comparison. Limiting the number of personnel entering the scene is essential for safeguarding the evidence and minimizing contamination. The proper collection, packaging, and preservation of evidence are essential so that physical evidence is not altered, misplaced, or lost.

Crime scene investigations are often long, tedious processes that involve precise documentation of the crime scene in order to directly or indirectly lead to potential suspects in order to solve cases. The documentation process may include photography, video, sketches, diagrams, and/or methodical notes. Recent developments in computer software even allow investigators to create a 360-degree panoramic image of the crime scene and how the crime may have unfolded. These various processes all combine to ensure that the details of the crime scene are permanently archived for further analysis. These processes aid investigators in examining the crime scene long after the area has been cleaned or officially disposed of.

Scientific Advances

In the past couple of decades, police have increasingly been relying on science in the collection, identification, and analysis of evidence retrieved from crime scene investigations. In addition to indirect clues, crime scenes may yield direct clues such as weapons, bullets, tire tracks, fingerprints, shoe prints, hairs, fibers, bite marks, blood splatter, or DNA from biological material. These clues can then be analyzed to identify or exclude suspects. The sophistication of these techniques drastically reduces the criminal's ability to elude justice. Prior to forensic evidence and advancements in science, many investigators relied on confessions, eyewitnesses, informants, and hunches.

The identification, measurement, and comparison of projectiles and firearms in the discipline of ballistics is one area of the scientific fight against crime. Advancements in science have increased the ability of investigators to match shell casings, bullets, and calibers to specific weapons and their corresponding owners. Forensic examiners can also examine the rate and range of fire, nature of bullet wounds, and the chemical residues that linger after discharge. These analyses have progressed tremendously with technological advances in lasers, complex computer software programs, and genetic engineering. The field of ballistics helps investigators determine if a case involving a firearm is a result of an accident, suicide, or murder.

Modern fingerprint analysis was first conducted in 1892 and was used as a sole means of identification in crime scene investigations by the early 1900s. The use of fingerprint analysis as a form of criminal identification has sparked considerable debate and controversy over the years. Critics argue that many of the central assertions of fingerprint examiners have not been thoroughly verified or tested in a number of important ways. The main controversial issue surrounding fingerprint analysis revolves around laboratory protocols. Some of the skepticism stems from the fact that fingerprint examiners lack objective standards for evaluating whether prints match. This is based on the fact that there is no uniform approach to deciding what counts as a sufficient basis for making an identification. Fingerprint examiners may also have inconclusive laboratory results stemming from the evaluation of partial, smudged, distorted, or incomplete prints. Nonetheless, fingerprint identification has a long role in the history of crime scene investigations.

Deoxyribonucleic acid (DNA) profiling is one aspect of forensic evidence that has significantly grown in importance for criminal investigations and court proceedings in recent history. DNA testing was formulated by British geneticist Alec Jeffreys in 1984 and was first used in a criminal case in the United Kingdom in the same year. DNA analysis has been especially important in cases involving rape and murder and has vastly transformed criminal investigations over the past few decades. Nonetheless, DNA testing is not without it criticisms. The reliability and accuracy of many of the processes involved in analyzing and interpreting DNA evidence have been hotly contested within recent years. Although many researchers contend that DNA testing is the most accurate of the forensic sciences, different interpretations of one DNA sample can be made by different experts. Calculating the probability of a match is one of the main criticisms of DNA profiling. Analysts must determine the frequency with which a genetic pattern is likely to occur in the general population and then base the probabilities accordingly. The accuracy of DNA evidence relies heavily on the individual analysts and laboratory equipment available for use. Many departments do not have the equipment, personnel, resources, or funding needed for DNA analysis. The mere presence of DNA at a crime scene does not by default prove guilt. Biological material left at a crime scene may have been left prior to the commission of a crime or even planted afterward. Nonetheless, biological material left behind at a crime scene is one of the biggest leads an investigator can obtain.

Application in the Courtroom

Many courts, when dealing with this type of evidence, apply the ruling of *Frye v. United States*, which contends that evidence derived from a novel scientific technique may be presented to a jury only if the court first determines the technique has gained general acceptance in the particular field to which it belongs. This ruling was implemented to make sure juries were safeguarded against misleading scientific testimony. A report by the National Research Council, *The Evaluation of Forensic DNA Evidence*, recommended that laboratories be accredited by professional boards such as the American Society of Crime Laboratory Directors. In addition, the report recommended proficiency tests be regularly administered and the results given to the courts. The report further recommended that research be conducted on how to present data on probabilities and genetics to juries in order to aid them in understanding the complexities of the information presented.

Wrongful convictions can occur because of inept criminal investigations, eyewitness errors, unethical conduct by police and prosecutors, inadequacy of counsel, or plea bargains. These injustices raise concerns and criticisms about the integrity and ethicality of our criminal justice system. Fortunately, the development of DNA technology has increased the number of people who have

This fingerprint examiner with the U.S. Army Criminal Investigation Division compares a latent fingerprint, left, and a recorded fingerprint, right, in a lab at Kandahar Air Base in Afghanistan in May 2010. Fingerprint analysis is considered controversial by some because of a lack of objective matching standards but continues to be an important tool in crime scene investigations.

been exonerated after being falsely convicted and imprisoned. The creation of the Innocence Project in 1992 has led to more than 200 exonerations of wrongly convicted prisoners by analyzing DNA evidence. DNA analysis is therefore viewed as a reliable mechanism for apprehending and securing convictions of criminals and is seen as one of the most important aspects of criminal investigations. Although DNA evidence has been very influential in the criminal justice system in convicting the guilty and exonerating the innocent, it is only one aspect of forensic science. Criminal investigators investigate all leads, possibilities, and evidence in hope of securing a strong case to be presented at trial.

Portrayals in the Media
Many researchers argue that the public has become captivated with crime scene investigations and the wide range of scientific techniques used by law enforcement as a result of the plethora of crime shows on television. This public fascination led to prosecutors and defense attorneys contending that jurors are becoming more reluctant to convict defendants without forensic evidence presented at trial. This reluctance to convict defendants without forensic evidence is what many call the "*CSI* effect." This term began in 2003 when the television program *Crime Scene Investigation* became popular. During this time, many attorneys have claimed that jury members based the decision to convict or acquit a suspect entirely on whether forensic evidence was found at the crime scene. Many have argued that forensic evidence may help the prosecutor's case because jury members often believe that forensic evidence is accurate and infallible. Following the same line of reasoning, many have argued that a lack of forensic evidence hinders criminal cases because jurors expect some type of forensic evidence to be present for a prosecutor to have a strong case. Although the existence of a *CSI* effect has been disputed by some critics, it nonetheless demonstrates the emergence of science as an investigative tool in aiding crime scene investigations.

Contrary to real life, television dramas often portray crime scene investigations as being a speedy and straightforward process. In actuality, criminal investigations may be hindered by individuals' failing to leave evidence behind or

Crime scene investigations may turn up such evidence as tire tracks, weapons, bullets, shoe prints, fingerprints, hairs, fibers, bite marks, blood splatter, or DNA.

cleaning up after the commission of the crime. In other cases, officials may be burdened by inadequate funding and/or resources that may negatively affect the process of analyzing various types of evidence after the investigation. Some experts have claimed that criminals may even watch crime shows such as *CSI* in order to escape detection. Analyzing evidence is also more time consuming than portrayed through the media. Investigators may take weeks, months, or years to compile enough evidence to go to trial in hope of securing a conviction. Cases lacking sufficient evidence may remain unsolved for decades and ultimately be forgotten. Crime shows may give a distorted view of how criminal investigations are carried out in the field. For instance, regardless of how criminal investigations are conducted on television, law enforcement personnel, investigators, and forensic scientists all have their own education, training, and methods. The majority of forensic laboratories do not perform multiple analyses because of cost, demand, and/or insufficient resources. Most investigators cannot devote all of their time and resources to a single case and are thus overloaded with cases.

The Department of Justice's Bureau of Justice Statistics found that in 2002 there were more than half a million backlogged cases in forensic labs. This is a surprising statistic considering that the tests were being processed at or above 90 percent of the expected completion rate. Another problem from the amount of backlogged cases includes having ample computers, software, and personnel to safely store and track the evidence after criminal investigations have been completed.

Conclusion

Forensic evidence is increasingly becoming a fundamental part of the criminal justice process. Research has shown that forensic evidence tends to be very influential at trial and is thus viewed as an important part of crime scene investigations. The National Institute of Justice recommended to the federal government that research be conducted to address basic principles, error rates, and standards of procedure to ensure a more efficient means of handling evidence collected during criminal investigations. Although every crime scene is unique, scientific crime scene investigations are the best methodology for ensuring proper investigative techniques for unraveling the clues to the method, motive, and suspect of a crime.

Jacqueline Chavez
Mississippi State University

See Also: Ballistics; Fingerprinting; Forensic Science; Police, Contemporary; Private Detectives.

Further Readings

Kruse, Corrina. "Producing Absolute Truths: CSI Science as Wishful Thinking." *American Anthropologist*, v.112/1 (2010).
Lawson, Tamara F. "Can Fingerprints Lie? Reweighing Fingerprint Evidence in Criminal Jury Trials." *American Journal of Criminal Law*, v.31 (2003).
Mirsky, Steve. "Crime Scene Investigation." *Scientific American*, v.292/5 (2005).

Sjerps, M. and A. D. Kloosterman. "Statistical Aspects of Interpreting DNA Profiling." *Statistica Neerlandica*, v.57/3 (2003).

Criminalization and Decriminalization

Criminalization is the legislative decision to make a noncriminal act into a criminal act. Decriminalization is just the opposite; it is the legislative decision to make a once criminal act into a noncriminal act. This decision may also be a judicial one. Judges have the power to criminalize and/or decriminalize behavior. In some instances, that decision may be more informal (as to not sentence persons for acts that the judges deem unworthy of punishment), and therefore they do not strictly enforce them. In other cases, the legislature can change the application of law. Law enforcement officers might more overtly change the treatment of offenders in their decision making; that is, using their discretion to enforce or not enforce the law. Thus, changes can be made in theory and/or in practice. There have been many examples of each of these decisions over the course of American legal history.

Prohibition

One of the best-known examples of criminalization and decriminalization regards the manufacturing, sale, and transportation of alcoholic beverages. Prohibition was the first and only time in the history of the United States that a constitutional amendment was repealed. In the 1920s, during the time known as Prohibition, and for a period of 14 years, alcohol production was forbidden. The move to criminalize this behavior developed from a group called the Women's Christian Temperance Union, which was made up of mostly women, fed up with their husbands spending their earnings on alcohol. The American Temperance Society was formed in 1826 and the Anti-Saloon League lobbied for Prohibition in the early 20th century. These organizations did not demand changes in drinking habits, but instead asked for changes in the laws passed by politicians in the legislature. Crimes were also associated with intoxication and

The mayor of Zion City, Illinois, personally pouring out bottles of beer in front of a camera at an event during which 80,000 pint bottles of beer were publicly destroyed during Prohibition.

the prevention of accidents in the workplace was a goal of criminalization. However, there was no amendment to establish national Prohibition (until 1918 with the Eighteenth Amendment). During Prohibition, offenders faced the destruction of their stills and products. Fines and jail time could also be imposed. At first, this happened on a state-by-state basis. By 1916, over half of the states had statutes that prohibited alcohol. The Eighteenth Amendment to the Constitution established Prohibition, but the law did not go into effect until the Volstead Act was passed in 1919, so there was time for people to buy cases of alcohol legally to store for future use.

As with most behavior, sanctioning often does not prevent it from happening. Instead, it just brings the behavior into hiding. This is exactly what happened during Prohibition. Gangsters opened speakeasies as places for people to drink (drinking alcohol itself was not illegal), and enforcement agents were not successful in dealing with the problem, because they were often underpaid and willing to accept bribes.

Those with power would hire rumrunners (men who could smuggle in rum from the Caribbean and whiskey from Canada) to bring alcohol into the United States. Gangsters and everyday people were violating the law. Almost as quickly as the law went into effect, there was opposition to it. Organizations formed to repeal the ruling, but the Great Depression and the stock market crash in 1929 were the largest impetus for change; making alcohol legal again would allow the government to tax citizens and would open up new jobs for them. By 1933, the Twenty-First Amendment to the Constitution was ratified (repealing the Eighteenth Amendment), once more making alcohol legal. Thus, the criminalization of alcohol in 1920 led to the decriminalization of alcohol in 1933.

Criminalization/Decriminalization Process

The process of criminalization is a means of creating social order. It defines and classifies acceptable behavior. In fact, there are more criminal laws today than in any other time in American history, and these laws are becoming increasingly intrusive into the private lives of citizens (e.g., control over smoking in public places, and even within one's car if a minor is in that car).

In some ways, crime control has become an industry, especially with the development of technology. For example, once cell phones were invented, people wanted to use them in their cars. However, once it was deemed a distraction to drive and hold a phone in one's hand, the act of doing so became a punishable offense. Companies had to develop hands-free devices so that people could talk on the phone but still keep their hands on the wheel. At first, this behavior was criminalized in ordinances, and then was extended to statutes.

Changing the designation from criminal to noncriminal (and back) can be both a social and an economic process. The creation of a law and the enforcement of that law must be acceptable to the majority. However, there are often changing social and moral views. If not viewed as harmful any longer, an act might be decriminalized. A fine or other penalty might still be associated with the behavior, however, such as requiring a permit before decriminalizing an act.

The decriminalization of certain crimes demonstrates how the ruling class has had much control of the definitions of crime. The plight of women and minorities has been difficult, especially in other countries. For years, abortion, witchcraft, adultery, and seduction were seen as crimes by women. Yet, behaviors that amounted to domestic violence and sexual harassment were not. Today, there are still some countries that stone women for being raped (because they are accused of committing adultery), and there are still classes of people who believe that the criminal justice system may treat some matters as crimes (even if the behavior was not considered criminal in the past).

Women's Rights

Another example of decriminalization, and one that is still a controversial subject today, is the right to abortion. Early secular law ruled abortion a crime only if the wife obtained one without her husband's knowledge. Abortions of the past were not outlawed in all cases. In the Middle Ages, penance was imposed in ecclesiastical courts, but there was no corporal punishment assigned. However, once medical evidence was produced, scientific knowledge supposedly demonstrated that life began at fertilization. Thus, the 18th century saw stricter abortion laws. Over time, some countries became more liberal in their legislation, generally allowing abortion; but overall, there was government control over abortion. It was not until the 1973 case *Roe v. Wade* that the U.S. Supreme Court struck down state laws banning abortion. This case determined that banning abortion violated the right to privacy. However, many countries do require certain criteria be met for an abortion to be considered legal (e.g., a 24-hour waiting period, parental notification, and the distribution of information on fetal development). Even in countries that ban abortion, it is usually allowed in cases of rape, incest, or risk of maternal death.

Legislation has been passed regarding the right of a woman to breast feed in public. Before an amendment was signed into law in 1999, government funds were used to prohibit women from breast-feeding in public because it violated indecent exposure laws. It took 10 more years, but by 2009, a majority of states had enacted statutes that permit the public exposure of the breast for breast feeding infants so that mothers are exempt from prosecution. In addition, employers are required to allow break time for their employees to breast feed their children in a private area.

Euthanasia and Prostitution

In general, it is a crime to commit a homicide, unless it is justified or excused. In the case of euthanasia (or assisted suicide at the request of the patient), some governments have legalized voluntary euthanasia. The use of pain medication to relieve suffering or withholding life-sustaining treatment with patient consent is considered legal. However, euthanasia remains a criminal homicide, if only in name.

Prostitution is another crime that has been criminalized and decriminalized, depending on the location and politics. Decriminalization means that laws regarding prostitution are removed. States collect tax in legal prostitution (instead of a pimp). Decriminalization of prostitution has occurred in Australia and New Zealand, and is thought to decrease brothel owners' hiring illegal, underage, or trafficked women. However, some research shows that it has promoted sex trafficking and child prostitution. Brothel prostitution was also instituted in the Netherlands. The United States is one of the few countries with laws against prostitution.

Until the 1960s, attitudes against prostitution were based on morals, risk of venereal disease, and the belief that prostitution led to additional crimes. Today, there have been strong arguments in favor of prostitution, such as the ability to regulate it (through medical testing of prostitutes, control and restrictions, and decreased risk of exploitation). Some argue that women would be more likely to report rape or assault if prostitution were decriminalized. However, any woman (prostitute or not) can report rape under current law. Legal status does not change the shame associated with such a career. The decision to criminalize or decriminalize the behavior often depends on community sentiment. Strong arguments have been made in support of legalizing prostitution, but more important might be the need for stable housing, social services, medical treatment, and job training for women, to provide them with alternatives.

Marriage Laws

Polygamy is another crime that has seen legislative changes that vary by location. In the United States, polygamy is illegal in all 50 states. However, under Islamic law, a man can have up to four wives. Polygamous marriages are recognized in almost 50 countries (mostly Muslim and African nations). Pakistan, Saudi Arabia, Yemen, Qatar, Egypt, Kuwait, Iraq, and Iran are just a few others that accept this practice. Interestingly, the United Kingdom and Australia do recognize polygamous unions performed in other countries (if those countries permit them).

The practice was formally abolished in 1890 in a document labeled the Manifesto, but many people still remain in illegal polygamous marriages, especially American Muslims. In Utah, for example, the Morrill Act, which was an Anti-Bigamy Act, was passed in 1862. The Edmunds Act was passed 20 years later. It punished polygamy as a misdemeanor with a fine of up to $300 and/or six months in jail. Mormons could not obtain statehood for Utah unless they officially ended the sanctioning of plural marriage. However, these laws only led to the unofficial practice of polygamy. Thus, Mormons continued to practice polygamy (in defiance of federal law). However, even after the establishment of the Morrill Act, and the 1882 Edmunds Act that strengthened the laws against bigamy and polygamy are not enforced by most governments. Changes in the criminalization of this behavior could impact the enforcement against it in the future.

Related to marital issues is the matter of same-sex marriage, which has legally been prohibited in many states. Yet, some states have decriminalized it. Until 2004, the marriage of same-sex couples was illegal. Some states do allow civil unions, and some offer domestic partnerships. However, 36 states have statutes that prohibit gay marriage, even if they have not taken action against "offenders." Gay marriage is legal in Massachusetts, Connecticut, Iowa, Vermont, Maine, and New Hampshire.

Marijuana

Decriminalization of marijuana use has been studied at length. Portugal was the first European country to officially abolish criminal penalties for possession of drugs, including marijuana and cocaine. The country replaced jail time with therapy. Although the Netherlands is known for marijuana "coffee shops," Holland has never actually legalized cannabis; the law simply isn't enforced against the shops. Since 1973, 13 U.S. state legislatures have decriminalized marijuana possession (or use of small amounts): Alaska, California, Colorado, Maine, Massachusetts, Minnesota, Mississippi, Nebraska, Nevada, New York, North Carolina, Ohio, and Oregon. This means no jail time, arrest, or criminal record is applicable in these locations.

Similar policies have been enacted internationally. In Australia, penalties have also been reduced. Evidence suggests that removal of criminal penalties for marijuana does not increase its use or affect the drug of choice for users. In fact, expenses for arrest and prosecution for marijuana possession offenses have been reduced without any impact on use. However, some research does find an increase in use among adolescents. Only time will tell if other states and countries will follow the decriminalization route or if the locations that have decriminalized marijuana will criminalize it in the future. For now, fear of apprehension, the cost of marijuana, and the difficulty of obtaining it do not seem to affect the decision to use it, and its use has been regulated for those with medical needs.

Conclusion

What or who is considered a victim is socially constructed and thus can change over time. Those who advocate the rights of the accused might say that certain behavior has been over-criminalized and should not be enforced. Sometimes, interpretations of the law are so broad that innocuous behavior can be construed as criminal. For those who advocate for the victim, there is an assumption that the criminal justice system must be more forceful in treating certain matters as crimes. Moreover, the view of whether an act is criminal is often based on politics, that is, the sentiment of the ruling class. Those theories vary depending on the evidence that is presented and on political change. If there is a modification to scientific or medical evidence, then certain behavior may be treated differently overnight. It will be interesting to see which behaviors become criminalized over time and which become decriminalized. Those decisions will have been socially constructed and based on political and economic factors.

Gina M. Robertiello
Felician College

See Also: 1941 to 1960 Primary Documents; Abortion; Prohibition; Prostitution, Sociology of; *Roe v. Wade*; Victimless Crimes; Volstead Act.

Further Readings
Amster, Randall. *Lost in Space: The Criminalization, Globalization, and Urban Ecology of Homelessness.* New York: LFB Scholarly, 2008.
Baker, Dennis J. "The Moral Limits of Criminalizing Remote Harms." *New Criminal Law Review*, v.11/3 (2007).
Kobler, John. *Ardent Spirits: The Rise and Fall of Prohibition.* New York: Da Capo Press, 1993.
Ringdal, Nils J. *Love for Sale: A World History of Prostitution.* New York: Grove Press, 2004.

Criminology

Emerging as a field of inquiry in Europe in the late 1700s, criminology is currently defined as a subdiscipline of sociology or as the science that studies crime, criminal activity, and social reaction to crime. Since its beginning, criminology has overlapped considerably with sociology and criminal justice.

However, criminology has developed as a discipline more specifically related to the causes of crime, whereas criminal justice is generally concerned with applied outcomes such as policing, correction, and reinsertion of criminals. In fact, criminology and criminal justice have developed a mutually beneficial relationship that has contributed to general sociology.

While in Europe criminology was seen more as a medical, psychiatric, and legal field, in the United States it was soon identified as a subdiscipline of sociology. By the 1960s, criminology was introduced as an independent doctoral degree at the University of California at Berkeley, and by the 1990s more than 1,000 universities were offering separate degrees in criminology.

Although criminology theories are classified in a variety of ways and criminologists have elaborated perspectives that can draw from more than one school of thought, there is a general consensus on the following classifications: the early main criminological theories (demonological, classical and neoclassical, ecological, and economic), biological theories, new biological or biosocial theories, psychological theories, sociological theories, and critical theories (labeling, conflict, feminist, and neo-Marxist).

Early Criminological Theories
Demonological Theory. The earliest theories on criminology are classified as demonological because they refer to possession, sin, and evil as explanation of crime. These theories rely on supernatural causalities of crime such as demoniac influences and/or witchcraft as inscribed in the theological approach classified, but not advocated, by the French sociologist Auguste Comte (1798–1857). This was at a time when social control was primarily assured by religion and kinship. The typical procedure for the ascertainment of criminal responsibility was the trial by ordeal, in which the accused was subjected to dangerous and painful experiences (i.e., walking on fire or holding a red-hot iron, dipping their hands in boiling water, or dipping in a stream with a millstone around their necks). The logic was that if the accused was innocent, God would intervene and save or heal him or her.

Classical and Neoclassical Theory. In the 18th century, the classical theory of criminology challenged the theological approaches to crime and deviance by stressing rational explanation revolving around the concept of free will of criminals. From the same approach stems the notion of individual responsibility for one's action and the commensurability of the punishment with the crime. Cesare Beccaria (1738–94), with his work *Of Crime and Punishment* published in 1764, and Jeremy Bentham (1748–1832) both had a profound impact on European and American criminology, criminal justice, and penology by advocating the abandonment of unjust suffering, torture, slavery, and the death penalty. Only adequate, swift, and proportionate punishment, they argued, would deter criminal behavior.

Neoclassical theory, as a continuation of classical theory, generated social reforms based on the concepts of human rights and rationalism, elaborated in the Enlightenment. Not only is criminal behavior caused by one's free will, but also criminals consider the costs and benefits of their actions while making decisions. Rational choice theories, for the first time, pointed to the context and circumstances of the crime, which may characterize the typology of crimes (i.e., domestic assault differs from robbery and burglary). Stress was also put on deterrence, not only through punishment, but also by an array of preventive measures that would reduce criminal activity and was defined as situational criminal control: securing buildings, controlling access to property, and adopting procedures of identification. Notions of crime deterrence were formulated as expressions that would become well known, such as "just deserts," also called *lex talionis*, or punishment proportionate to or resembling the offense is what wrongdoers deserve.

Ecological Theory. The ecological school of criminology was interested in the dynamics between human organisms and their physical environment. It was also called statistical, cartographic, and geographical because it was the first school of thought to apply statistical data and to rely on maps for its investigation of the causes of criminality.

André M. Guerry (1802–66) is regarded by many as the author of the first scientific work on criminology because his analysis was based on the French official crime statistics, which were notoriously difficult to access. Not very different from the contemporary Marxist theories, the findings of ecological theories pointed out the close relationship between crime and the upper stratum of society. However, Guerry's contribution was quite detailed in establishing a correlation between property crimes and urbanized areas, and violent crimes and rural areas. By systematically using statistics on crime, Lambert Adolphe Jacques Quetelet (1796–1874), who is remembered as the precursor of modern criminologists and was the author of the *Treatise on Man and the Development of his Faculties* (1835), successfully challenged the classical theories that insisted on the free will of criminals. He showed that crime is consistently the outcome of a group of sociological variables: gender, age, class, and economic factors. Guerry's and Quetelet's ecological theories advocated social investment into the improvement of physical and environmental contexts. Other ecological theories relied on moon cycles, climate, and astrology but remained inconclusive.

Economic Theory. Early economic theories in criminology, inspired by Karl Marx (1818–83), refuted the biological approach by arguing that crime is the product of inequalities stemming from capitalism. However, Marx's writings do not address crime in any depth. Economic criminological theories, treating crime as a social problem, have applied Marxist dialectical materialism and argue that the causality of crime must be sought in the exploitation of the proletariat by capitalist bourgeoisie.

The Dutch philosopher Willem Bonger (1876–1940) figures among the prominent names of early Marxist criminology. In his work *Criminality and Economic Conditions* (1910), he denounced criminal law as protecting the interests of landowners and hence contributing to perpetuating the inequalities created by capitalism. Pre-capitalist societies, being essentially altruist and based on consensus, were not afflicted by crime as much as capitalist societies. Social revolution, as a natural consequence of capitalism, was seen as the solution par excellence to many problems, including crime, afflicting society. Marxist criminology has been criticized for underestimating the gravity of crime and for naively arguing that the elimination of poverty and inequality would automatically reduce crime.

Biological Theories
Inspired by Auguste Comte's positivism, which was attracting worldwide consensus, biological and psychological theories dominated the late 19th and early 20th centuries. The scientific method, diagnosis of pathology, and treatment were the three elements favored by positivist approaches, whose principal streams in criminology were identifiable as biological and psychological theories. Albeit quite controversially, Cesare Lombroso (1835–1909) has been often indicated as the founder of modern criminology. In spite of his focus on criminal law reforms more than

on the analysis of crime, Lombroso is remembered for the principle of atavism as the cause of criminality. *The Criminal Man* (1876) is perhaps the most recognized contribution by Lombroso. Essentially evolutionist, Lombroso argued that criminals were atavistic human beings born criminals and identifiable by particular biological features and physical appearance such as big jaws, prominent superciliary arches, high cheekbones, and insensibility to pain. *The Female Offender* (1895) was among the first criminology studies on women. Women are depicted as inferior and likely to be even more atavistic than men. Perfectly in tune with his times, Lombroso contributed to the emergence of social Darwinism, that is, the application of the theory of evolution to society. The criminal was seen as the one who struggles to adjust to society and is therefore ill or defective. Thus, with Lombroso, criminology becomes a branch of medicine.

Enrico Ferri (1856–1929) and Raffaele Garofalo (1852–1934) furthered Lombroso's theory by locating four categories of criminals: insane, born, occasional, and passion-driven. Ferri also included both the individual and environmental variants. Both Ferri and Garofalo sympathized with fascism and supported the physical elimination of the unfit and their offspring. Little credit is given nowadays to Lombroso and the Italian school of criminology. Not only was their use of statistics not rigorous, but their stress on physical features for their typology of criminals completely disregarded the impact of environmental and societal factors such as malnutrition and poverty.

Contemporary to Lombroso, Charles Goring (1870–1919), Richard Dugdale (1841–1883), and Henry Goddard (1866–1957) also engaged in theories supporting the biological heredity of criminality. Goring's *The English Convict* (1913) compared about 3,000 convicts with students, soldiers, and hospital patients on the basis of personal physical features, personal histories, and mental abilities. Although he refuted Lombroso's classification of criminals, his theory of feeblemindedness as a cause of criminal behavior did not show convincing results. Dugdale and Goddard authored two case studies of families of criminals. By tracing the kinship of criminals, they meant to show that the offspring of the feebleminded were irremediably flawed and hence unfit for society. Their uncritical adhesion to positivism and Darwinism made their fortune but they remained flawed by the overestimation of dominance principles. Lombrosian theories have been considered the dark age of criminology.

New Biological or Biosocial Theories

Biological theories had a revival in the late 20th century and the new biological or biosocial theories still have their advocates. Different from the early biological theories, most biosocial theories take into account the social environment and recognize the limited impact of biological factors for certain types of crimes. Among these was the disturbing trend involving surgically removing or altering the brain tissue in an attempt to influence personality or behavior of criminals and deviants.

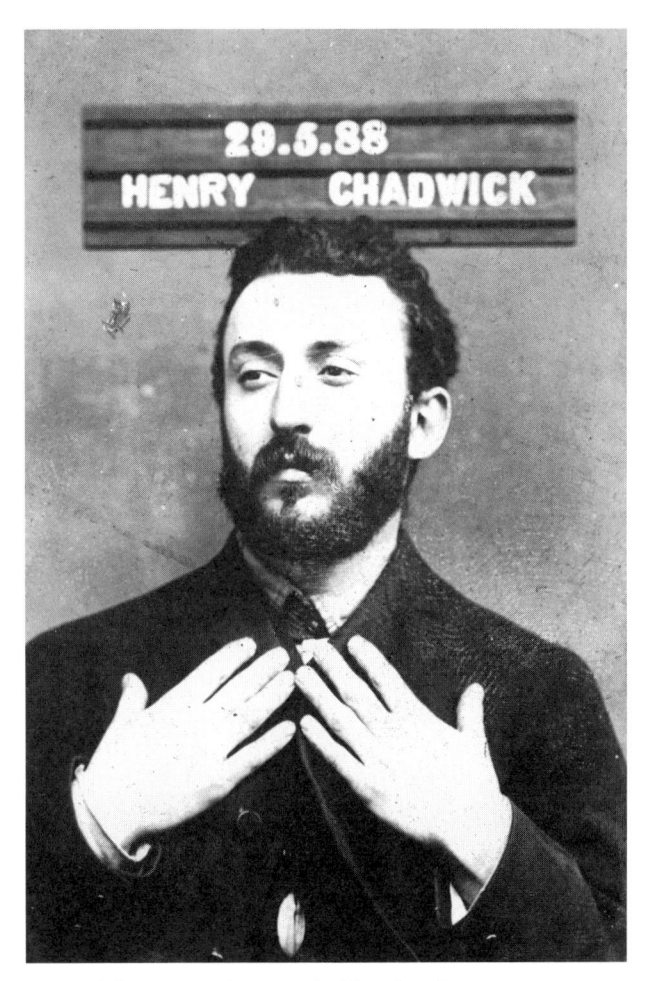

An English prisoner photographed for identification purposes in Manchester in 1888. The late-19th-century stress on physical features for the typology of criminals has since been discredited.

Perhaps the best-known case is that of actress Frances Farmer, who, was forced into psychiatric treatment in the 1940s, allegedly including a lobotomy, essentially because of her independent personality.

Twin studies also belong to the trend of new biological theories and contribute to the nature versus nurture debate. These studies investigate the life of criminals who have twins in order to detect biological similarities in their hereditary environment. Similarly, with adoption studies, attempts were made in order to show that the behavior of adoptees tends to match the personality of their biological parents. Other biological factors that have been taken into consideration are diet (i.e., sugar consumption), environmental pollution, hormonal imbalance, learning disabilities, and menstrual cycle. In spite of the fact that occasional neobiological studies have shown some interconnection between biological factors and criminality, biological explanations of deviance tend to be inconclusive, potentially dangerous, and less convincing than social and cultural factors.

Psychological Theories

While Charles Darwin was the principal reference for the biological school of thought, many psychological theories have been inspired by Sigmund Freud (1856–1936) and Burrhus Frederic Skinner (1904–90). However, most psychological theories were hybrid in the sense that they borrowed not only from a variety of authors but also from different schools of thoughts. The perfect example is that of Hans Eysenck (1916–97), who merged early classical theory and psychology by proposing two kinds of paradigmatic personalities: the extroverted and the introverted. Eysenck argued that the extroverted personality is most prone to crime and less responsive to guiding and conditioning. He advocated the use of modern psychology to encourage positive behavior and fight criminality.

Psychological theories continued through the late 1970s; perhaps the most recent representative of this trend has been the work of psychologist Samuel Yochelson (1906–76) and psychiatrist Stanton Samenow (1941–). Drawing from early criminological theories, Yochelson and Samenow claim that environmental and economic factors are irrelevant and revive the free will component of crime's causality. Although Yochelson and Samenow formulate a finite number of thinking patterns that seem to characterize the personality of criminals, they have not insisted on the causality but on the treatment of criminals through programs that would lead them to assume responsibility for their actions. In fact, contrary to economic theories, most psychological theories show a tendency of not challenging the dominant social order (consensus model) and of using psychological techniques to diagnose criminality as a pathology to be treated in view of social rehabilitation of criminals.

Sociological Mainstream Theories

Different from psychological theories, sociological theories do not favor the interpretation of crime as pathology because they tend to direct their attention and criticism to societal components that are likely to generate criminal behavior.

Robert King Merton (1910–2003), an American sociologist, argued that anomie, or personal feelings of "normlessness," is caused by society's pressure to achieve material aims without providing individuals with adequate means. His concept of anomie generated the strain theories, so called because of their focus on the situation of strain produced by the discrepancy between means and aims in the life of an individual. The difficulty or impossibility of reaching the goals that society impresses on individuals produces five possible modes of personality adaptation: conformist, innovator, ritualist, retreatist, and rebel. The conformist, quite unsurprisingly is the only mode that is not problematic because he or she accepts not only the aims indicated by society but also the limitations of the means. The innovator accepts the aims of society but does not accept their limitations and looks for alternative means, whose typical examples are the activities of organized crime, fraud, and forging identities. The ritualist personality accepts the means to such an extent that the achievement of the goals becomes irrelevant. The retreatist personality, typical of drug addicts and chronic alcoholics, refuses both the aims and the means and ends up with begging, stealing, or borrowing. Finally, the rebel personality rejects both means and aims but engages in the pursuit of new alternative goals and paths for achieving them: typically, the revolution.

Robert Agnew (1953–) has innovated considerably the strain theory by showing that the discrepancy between means and goals does not lead necessarily to criminality. Agnew's reformulation of the theory includes many more variables and goals that are not necessarily materialistic. By stressing the fact that individuals tend to be frustrated and upset when they do not reach their goals systematically, Agnew reasserts the link between strain and crime and also proposes policy recommendations.

Subcultural criminological theories were inspired by the application of Merton's definition of anomie to the study of specific deviant groups such as juvenile gangs and marginal classes. Albert Cohen's *Delinquent Boys* (1955) elaborates a theory on the reaction of the lower stratum of society, which is unable to share middle-class values and therefore becomes prone to deviant behavior in the quest for self-esteem. Travis Hirschi and Michael Gottfredson are the most prominent figures among control theorists. Their widely known book *A General Theory of Crime* (1990), starting from a large spectrum of criticism of all previous schools of criminological thought, claims to have discovered the essential feature of crime in the absence of self-control. The latter is usually acquired during childhood or in early life to such a degree that restraining from criminal activity becomes an almost permanent feature of the individual's personality.

Without departing from the notion of self-control, developmental and life course (DLC) theories, a theoretical model that investigates an individual's history in order to analyze the influence of early events of life on the future decision-making process, have encouraged a series of longitudinal studies looking at personal life as a sequence of events that impact one another. Development and life course theories were developed at the end of the 20th century on the basis of pioneering studies on children's development carried out at Berkeley in the 1960s. They try to isolate the factors that have an impact on the manifestation of deviance in the course of an individual's life and suggest that, on the basis of developmental sequences, it is possible to detect situational factors, such as temptation and friction, that are crucial for policing and deterrence.

Critical Theories

Critical theories include four major approaches: the labeling perspective, conflict theory, feminist, and radical (neo-Marxist) perspectives. A general consensus among these different perspectives seems to revolve around the idea that crime is a label often attached to the less privileged stratum of society in order to protect the interests of dominant groups. Crime is, therefore, not necessarily viewed in negative terms, because it is the rational response to the situation of unfairness and inequality in capitalistic societies.

Labeling Theories. The sociologist Howard S. Becker, born in Chicago in 1928, is usually indicated as the one who laid the foundation of the labeling theory. Also known as social reaction theory, the labeling theory departs from the majority of earlier theories by arguing that crime and deviance are not concerned with acts or behaviors but instead with the practice by dominant groups of society to label minority groups as deviant. Thus, deviance is instigated by the negative reaction of society that labels minority and marginal groups and leads them to commit crime. The modalities and contexts of labeling can be either formal (e.g., law courts, police stations, or state jurisdictions) or informal (e.g., family and social entourage). Labeling theories have isolated some patterns regarding the greater impact of formal labeling, of male-offending females, and race-related perception of the gravity of deviant behavior with consequent increase of the probability of deviant behavior. Criminality and deviance are not any longer approached as aspects of personality or as status but instead as the outcomes of the process of tagging, identifying, and segregating.

Conflict Theory. Inspired by Georg Simmel (1858–1918) and Ralph Dahrendorf (1929–2009), conflict theorists have expanded Marx's perspective on crime as the inevitable outcome of capitalism. Austin Turk, Richard Quinney, Thorsten Sellin, and Georg Vold are usually indicated as the major representatives of this trend, featuring the common distrust in the social contract between the state and citizens. Conflict theories

These suspected criminals were photographed together by the New York City Police Department in May 1933. Criminology in the United States became a subdiscipline of sociology but by the 1960s it had become an independent doctoral degree at the University of California, Berkeley, and by the 1990s, more than 1,000 universities offered separate degrees in criminology.

have developed in several directions, but the notion of conflict among individuals and social classes because of the variety and difference of interests pursued by each of them seems to be a common stance. Turk argued that some degree of conflict between social groups struggling for the monopoly of authority is beneficial because it allows the scrutiny of the ones who detain power. Sellin maintained that increased opportunities for conflict would stem from the increasing diversity in society. Vold suggested that conflict exists because of the struggle between different social groups to control the authority to govern society and further their own self-interest. Not always directly related with criminology, conflict criminology theories were soon the object of criticism for being too idealistic.

Feminist Theory. Feminist criminologists have attracted attention to the uncontested connection between masculinity and crime. Feminist criminology has included studies on women as criminal offenders, women as victims of crime and deviance, and women as professionals in the system of criminal justice. By focusing on the context of women's emancipation, Freda Adler (1934–) argued that the more women were provided with social and economic opportunities, the more they would become prone to deviance and crime. Feminist approaches had a great impact on the theory of power-control as articulated by John Hagan, whose view is that crime is the outcome of two factors: power expressed in function of class, and control expressed in function of family. Hagan's theory stresses the need to look at the structural foundation of crime. Crime itself implies a power relationship. To perpetrate a crime means to impose one's power on others, while to be punished for a crime means to be subjected to somebody else's power. Crime is, furthermore, not one-dimensional but has to be defined as a function of class, gender, and race. Hagan has attempted to explain the lesser role of women in criminality with the description of power dynamics at the interior of the family. Conventional patriarchal families, in which the role of the mother is confined to the home, would tend to provide more freedom to boys and greater control on girls who are closely supervised by their mothers and therefore are less prone to deviance. The egalitarian family characterized by an equal repartition of power between mother and father would allow similar access to experimentation and risk taking with indulgence in criminal behavior. Similarly, in single-parent, female-headed families, children would experience a lesser degree of control and therefore similar access to crime and deviance by boys and girls. However, Hagan's conclusion that women experiencing social mobility are more prone to deviance has been criticized for not explaining the overall lesser rate of their participation in criminal acts.

Radical (Neo-)Marxist Perspectives. Radical (Neo-)Marxist perspectives on crime tend to look at class struggle as the source of what is only labeled as crime and they argue for the need to attract the public's attention to what real crime is, namely, the violation of human rights, imperialism, over-evaluation of the rule of law, capitalism, racism, and sexism.

Livia Holden
Lahore University of Management Studies

See Also: Crime in America, Causes; Crime in America, Types; Crime Prevention; Crime Rates; Criminalization and Decriminalization; Critical Legal Studies Movement; Cruel and Unusual Punishment; Deterrence, Theory of; Fear of Crime; Theories of Crime.

Further Readings
Agnew, Robert. *Pressured Into Crime: An Overview of General Strain Theory*. Los Angeles: Roxbury Publishing, 2006.
Beccaria, Cesare. *Of Crime and Punishment*. 1764.
Becker, Howard S. *Outsiders: Studies in the Sociology of Deviance*. New York: Free Press, 1963.
Bonger, Willem. *Criminality and Economic Conditions*. Boston: Little, Brown, 1905.
Cohen, Albert. *Delinquent Boys: The Culture of the Gang*. New York: Free Press, 1955.
Goring, Charles. *The English Convict: A Statistical Study*. London: H.M.S., 1913.
Gottfredson, Michael. *Control Theories of Crime and Delinquency*. New Brunswick, NJ: Transaction, 2003.
Hirschi, Travis. *Causes of Delinquency*. Berkeley: University of California Press, 1969.
Lombroso, Cesare. *L'Uomo Delinquente*. Milano: Hoepli, 1876.
Merton, Robert King. *Social Theory and Social Structure*. New York: Free Press, 1949.
Quetelet, Adolphe. *Recherches Sur la Population, les Naissances, les Décès, les Prisons, les Dépôts de Mendicité, etc., Dans le Royaume des Pays-Bas*. 1827.
Quinney, Richard. *Bearing Witness to Crime and Social Justice*. Albany: State University of New York Press, 2000.
Yochelson, Samuel and Stanton Samenow. *The Criminal Personality*, Vol. 1. *A Profile for Change*. New York: Jason Aronson, 1977.

Critical Legal Studies Movement

The critical legal studies movement has developed as an academic, legal, and political project that seeks to challenge the terms of dominant legal discourse. Critical legal studies (CLS) scholars (sometimes referred to as "Crits") are interested in power and how law intersects with society. While much of legal scholarship is focused on explaining law, the critical legal studies movement is interested in critiquing law and changing society. CLS has roots in Marxism and aligns in many ways with other critical approaches such as feminist critical theory, postcolonial theory, queer theory, critical criminology, postmodern critique, and, to some degree, critical race theory.

Critics of CLS claim that CLS undermines confidence in our legal system and erodes public perceptions of the law's ability to promote equality and justice. However, proponents of CLS claim that the goal of a critical approach has the purpose of addressing what they perceive to be false assumptions about the neutrality of legal discourse and the autonomy of individuals.

Development

CLS developed with roots in legal realism and the antiwar movement of the 1960s. It is a part of the realist response to natural law and positive law jurisprudence. CLS posits that law is a discourse that cannot be detached from social, historical, and political context. Legal scholar Mark Kelman explains that CLS challenges law as a force of "legitimation" and the ways that law can make the contingent and unjust seem natural and just. From this perspective, law is ideological and epistemic; it does not just reflect norms, beliefs, and values but generates them. CLS has sought to demystify dominant Western ideologies about the certainty and legitimacy of legal decision making. The first conference on critical legal studies took place in 1977 at the University of Wisconsin, Madison. The ongoing annual conventions of CLS are characterized by interdisciplinary gatherings of scholars and activists with varied attachments to Marxism and Deconstruction.

One important CLS contention is that law is indeterminate. The "indeterminacy thesis" is a claim that legal rules do not really determine the outcome of legal disputes. It emerged as a critical response to the positivist notion that law is separate from politics and that legal reasoning is absolute. Indeterminacy thesis argues that legal resources are inherently incoherent, with legal structures based on binary oppositions and legal disputes often resolved in split decisions or procedural complications. The "indeterminacy debate" was in the spotlight in the 1980s and cast doubt on the neutrality of law and, more broadly, on modernity's claims to universality, rationality, and reason.

Many traditional legal theorists have been uneasy with the CLS attack on the legitimacy of legal authority. Mainstream legal authority has promoted a depiction of law as derived from historical figures (such as the founding fathers) and ordered progress. Another facet of mainstream legal thought is its embrace of liberalism's conception of universal equality and rights. Additionally, mainstream legal theory has mostly presumed law to be distinct from and in service of society. Countering these presumptions of traditional legal theory drives much of the CLS scholarship. According to Mark Kelman, much of the scholarship in CLS has the purpose of proving that legal doctrine is fraught with irresolvable contradictions of liberalism, including a positivistic commitment to rules in the face of fluctuating social standards, and commitment to individual values under the mask of objective truth. Many Crits, including Duncan Kennedy and Robert Gordon, have argued that legal education does little to challenge liberal ideology and may actually be complicit in maintaining entrenched legal justifications of hierarchy. These CLS scholars charge that the sterile discussion of appellate cases in law school ensures a disconnect from the real-life consequences of legalistic thought.

Related Theories

Critical race theory covers a spectrum of contestation and coalition with the CLS movement. Kimberle Crenshaw, in her work on critical race theory (CRT), describes opposition to liberalism and rule-of-law ideology as a point of alliance. These schools of thought share an understanding of law as a source of white supremacy. However, there are divergent points between CLS and the CRT perspective, especially in terms of a critique of rights. For CLS, the notion of legal rights is indeterminate and composed of contradiction. Many CLS scholars argue that the existence of formal "rights" will not of itself produce social change; it may in fact legitimize inequality and serve the interests of the wealthy and elite. CLS tends toward transformative efforts for social justice, focusing on substantive equality rather than equal access. In contrast, for critical race theorists combating disenfranchisement of African Americans, the notion of exercising rights has been an important component of inclusion. Mobilization around rights was an effective aspect of black empowerment and the success of the civil rights movement. While CRT and CLS diverge on various aspects of the role of rights in social justice, they coalesce on a critique of liberalism.

Feminist legal theory also has both alliance and divergence with the CLS movement. The predominant distrust of rights in CLS has been criticized by many feminist scholars in the quest for equal rights. Much success in feminist strategies is indebted to liberal feminism, which relies on the construct of a universal "woman" and has been useful in exposing law's maleness and exclusivity. On the other hand, postmodern, antiessentialist feminist critiques align with CLS to disrupt liberalism's notion of experiential consistency and community. Like CLS activists, feminists are often divided on the question of whether law can be useful as a transformative strategy or is fundamentally inimical to transformative social change effort.

Recent extensions of CLS include prison studies and global studies scholarship. Transnational prison abolition work, rooted in CLS, is a growing response to the global struggle for political and economic justice. This critical approach to criminology shares anticapitalist, anti-imperialist, and antiracist ties with CLS. In this conception of justice, resistance is formulated around criminalization, colonization, and capitalism. Scholar-activist Angela Davis argues that prison expansion in recent decades is linked to ideologies of racism and global capitalism. She suggests that the "prison industrial complex" (PIC) refers to the relationships between prisons, government, corporations, media, and the pursuit of profit. CLS is critical of penal expansion as expensive, ineffective, and rooted in the false neutrality of the legal system. Critical prison abolitionists see prison economy as more than the sum of all jails, but as comprising a whole set of relationships involving systems of education, medicine, and law in the service of global capitalism.

Continuing Debate

CLS scholars have brought the "critique of rights" to contemporary human rights discourse. There have been many successes of rights-based approaches to justice, including abolition of legalized slavery, civil rights for African Americans, suffrage for women, and humane regulation of work conditions. However, CLS scholar David Kennedy challenges rights-based discourse as "a drop of liberation in an ocean of oppression" and calls for more substantive formulations of justice. Many CLS movement activists and scholars emphasize that the professionalization of human rights work and the ascendance of penal policies has meant exclusion of more progressive and communitarian approaches to justice. From a CLS perspective, giving priority to liberal ideas of equal rights and procedural fairness is insufficient to combat problems of institutional racism and sexism; they argue instead that economic and material equality are preconditions for justice.

Many critical scholars view the current legal system as a rhetorical structure that serves to legitimate hierarchy and inequality. They have worked to present challenges to both the formalism of positive law jurisprudence and the alleged neutrality and objectivity of natural law jurisprudence. The critical legal studies movement has many times succeeded in the objective of challenging bias and privilege in the law. The longstanding themes of the CLS movement, accompanied by new, radical insight, offer alternatives to the traditional approaches to justice.

Mary Jo Wiatrak-Uhlenkott
University of Minnesota

See Also: 2001 to 2012 Primary Documents; Equality, Concept of; Libertarianism; Race, Class, and Criminal Law; Theories of Crime.

Further Readings
Barnett, Hilaire. *Introduction to Feminist Jurisprudence*. London: Cavendish, 1998.
Davis, Angela. *Abolition Democracy: Beyond Empire, Prisons, and Torture*. New York: Seven Stories Press, 2005.
Gordon, Robert. "New Developments in Legal Theory." In *Politics of Law: A Progressive Critique*, D. Kairys, ed. New York: Pantheon, 1982.
Kelman, Mark. *A Guide to Critical Legal Studies*. Cambridge, MA: Harvard University Press, 1987.
Kennedy, David W. "The International Human Rights Movement: Part of the Problem?" *Harvard Human Rights Journal*, v.15/99 (2001).
Kennedy, D. and K. Klare. "A Bibliography of Critical Legal Studies." *Yale Law Journal*, v.94 (1984).

Cruel and Unusual Punishment

Those who are convicted of a crime are vulnerable to the punishments inflicted upon them and are not in a position to easily protect themselves from extremes of punishment. To protect these people, the Eighth Amendment prohibits the infliction of punishment that is cruel and unusual. The phrase *cruel and unusual* is particularly effective because it allows interpretation according to an evolving standard. Therefore, although it was included in the Constitution to protect against punishments in use in the 1700s that the framers found offensive, it is used today to challenge the death penalty.

History of Cruel and Unusual Punishment
The prohibition against cruel and unusual punishment can be traced back to the principle of *lex talionis* (retaliation), which holds that a person's punishment should equal the harm caused by his action. This principle is seen in the Magna Carta as well as other 13th and 14th century documents. The Constitution's prohibition against cruel and unusual punishment is very similar to that in the English Bill of Rights of 1689. Records of discussions around the time the Constitution was drafted indicate that the framers intended to include the principle of *lex talionis* and prevent the use of punishments that were disproportionate to the crimes committed.

Despite its long history and consistency with historic principles, the wording of "cruel and unusual" in the Constitution has caused considerable debate. The phrase is vague and subject to interpretation. When the Constitution was drafted in the late 1700s, punishments such as drawing and quartering, branding, and ear cropping were falling out of use but not yet outlawed. Although the framers of the Constitution intended to protect against these punishments, standards of decency had altered the idea of "cruel and unusual" by the time the words were adopted into the Constitution. Thus, the phrase must be interpreted to determine the punishments that are considered "cruel and unusual" at any particular time. This necessity for interpretation was recognized by the Supreme Court in *Trop v. Dulles*, 356 U.S. 86 (1958). Realizing that the concepts of "cruel" and "unusual" evolve with society, the Supreme Court interprets the phrase according to "evolving standards of decency." Although this allows courts flexibility in determining inappropriate punishments, it puts them in the position of having to make a subjective judgment of attitudes and morals. To add impartiality to this task, the Supreme Court has assessed the enactment and repeal of laws concerning the punishment in question, as well as the frequency with which the punishment is administered.

In addition to being vague about the punishments to be prohibited, the "and" in the phrase causes confusion in determining the standard of judgment to be used. One interpretation would be that punishments that are cruel and punishments that are unusual are to be prohibited. An alternate interpretation is that a punishment has to be both cruel and unusual to be prohibited. It was not until 1989, in *Stanford v. Kentucky*, 492 U.S. 361 (1989), that the Supreme Court clarified that a punishment must be both cruel and unusual to be prohibited. This position was reiterated two years later in *Harmelin v. Michigan*, 501 U.S. 957 (1991), when the Supreme Court acknowledged that a punishment may be cruel but not unusual and, therefore, not prohibited by the Eighth Amendment.

During the last part of the 20th century, the Supreme Court also attempted to provide standards for determining whether a particular punishment was cruel and unusual. The first effort was in *Furman v. Georgia*, 408 U.S. 238 (1972). In his concurring opinion, Justice William Brennan defined a cruel and unusual punishment as one that violates human dignity, is imposed arbitrarily, is not considered acceptable by contemporary society, and is not proportional to the crime. In *Solem v. Helm*, 463 U.S. 267 (1983), the Supreme Court held that a punishment is proportional to the crime if the gravity of punishment meets the gravity of the crime and the punishment is consistent with punishments for similar crimes in the same jurisdiction and the same crime in other jurisdictions. These comparisons of the punishment to other punishments are consistent with the Supreme Court's position that the punishment must be both cruel and unusual to be prohibited.

Application of Cruel and Unusual Punishment
Throughout its history, the Supreme Court has been asked to determine whether various punishments are cruel and unusual. In some cases, this involved weighing the punishment against the crime. For example, in *Weems v. United States*, 408 U.S. 238 (1910), a sentence of 15 years in a Philippine prison, where the inmates were shackled and

expected to perform hard labor, was judged to be disproportionate to the crime of forgery. In other cases, the Supreme Court considered the punishment itself. Revocation of citizenship and forfeiture of associated rights was found to be a cruel and unusual punishment in *Trop v. Dulles*, 356 U.S. 86 (1958). More recently, the Supreme Court failed to find California's three strikes law, which mandates or increases prison terms for repeat offenders, to be cruel and unusual punishment in *Ewing v. California*, 538 U.S. 11 (2003).

Recently, the majority of the debate about cruel and unusual punishment has focused on the death penalty. The death penalty is at a comparable stage of acceptability as many of the punishments at the time the Constitution was written. Although the death penalty has not been prohibited as cruel and unusual punishment, primarily because it does not meet the criteria of both cruel and unusual, society is beginning to see it as unacceptable. Consistent with this view, the Supreme Court has limited both sentencing associated with the death penalty and the application of the death penalty itself.

The Supreme Court began limiting the sentencing procedures when the death sentence was involved as early as the late 1970s. In *Woodson v. North Carolina*, 428 U.S. 280 (1976), the Supreme Court ruled against a mandatory death sentence as punishment for a crime because it did not allow consideration of the defendant's character or the circumstances of the crime. Through subsequent cases, the Supreme Court has clarified the circumstances and character that are to be considered mitigating circumstances that should be considered before sentencing a person to death. Regarding the defendant's character, the sentencing jury is to consider any emotional problems, violent family background, learning difficulties, and IQ. Defendants should also have the chance to raise any doubts about their guilt and their good behavior. Prior imprisonment of the defendant is not to be considered because it is not necessarily associated with guilt.

Special procedures have also been attached to the process of sentencing when the death penalty is involved. Defendants are to receive prior notice that the death penalty will be included in sentencing options so that they can appropriately prepare and present their defense and sentencing arguments. Although defendants are not allowed to present new evidence during the sentencing hearing, victim impact statements are also not allowed, since they could lead to the arbitrary imposition of a death sentence. Furthermore, instructions to the jury in death penalty cases cannot be vague and must clearly explain the alternate punishments, such as prison without the possibility of parole. Instructions must also provide the jury with information about weighing aggravating and mitigating circumstances to avoid arbitrary sentencing. Sentencing in death penalty cases must be individualized.

Limitations placed on the application of the death penalty indicate that the Supreme Court is responding to America's changing attitudes. The death penalty was found not to be a cruel and unusual punishment, and therefore constitutional, in *Furman v. Georgia*, 408 U.S. 238 (1972), which

The concept of "cruel and unusual" has evolved over time with society. This pillory was in use as late as 1889 in Delaware, a state that also allowed whipping until the mid-20th century.

was decided at a time when the death penalty was supported by a majority of Americans. Five years later, another Georgia case, *Coker v. Georgia*, 433 U.S. 584 (1977), considered the death penalty for rape cases. In this decision, the Supreme Court found the death penalty to be a cruel and unusual punishment for rape because Georgia was the only state to impose death for rape, and it did so in only 10 percent of the rape cases. Five years later, in *Enmund v. Florida* 458 U.S. 782 (1982), the Supreme Court used similar logic to rule against the imposition of the death penalty if the defendant participated in a crime but not the associated murder. Two death penalty challenges were reviewed by the Supreme Court in 2008 that brought them closer to a determination of cruel and unusual punishment. In *Kennedy v. Louisiana*, 128 S. Ct. 2641 (2008), the Supreme Court admitted that there was a national consensus against imposition of the death penalty for child rape and that as a punishment it did not meet the goals of retribution and deterrence. Although the court did not feel that the defendants in *Blaze v. Rees*, 553 U.S. 35 (2008), met the required burden of proof to show that death by lethal injection was cruel and unusual punishment, it felt that execution when an alternative and feasible method was available did constitute cruel and unusual punishment.

When assessing whether sentencing a juvenile to death was cruel and unusual punishment, the Supreme Court considered state practice as well as its potential deterrent effect. The Supreme Court prohibited execution of children under the age of 16 in *Thompson v. Oklahoma*, 487 U.S. 815 (1988), reasoning that their age and associated lack of education minimized their ability to evaluate the consequences of their conduct. But in determining the acceptability of the death penalty for those over the age of 16, the Supreme Court focused more on state practice. In *Stanford v. Kentucky*, 492 U.S. 361 (1989), a lack of historical evidence against the execution of juveniles and evidence of the practice by the majority of states led them to the conclusion that execution of juveniles was not prohibited. However, recognizing the change in public attitude, the court reversed itself less than 20 years later. Combining the logic used in the previous two cases, the Supreme Court found in *Roper v. Simmons*, 543 U.S. 551 (2005), that states had either prohibited the death penalty entirely or prohibited its application to juveniles, and that its effectiveness on juveniles was limited due to their underdeveloped sense of responsibility and character.

The Supreme Court used a similar combination of practice and deterrent effect in determining whether the death penalty was cruel and unusual punishment for the mentally impaired. In its first effort to address this issue, *Penry v. Lynaugh*, 492 U.S. 302 (1989), the court found that mental retardation did not warrant prohibition of the death penalty, but should be considered as a mitigating factor at sentencing. Thirteen years later, the Supreme Court recognized changing public attitudes and found execution of the mentally retarded to be cruel and unusual punishment in *Atkins v. Virginia*, 536 U.S. 304 (2002). In a format that it would follow three years later when it prohibited the death penalty for juveniles, the Supreme Court considered the increased number of states prohibiting the death penalty for the mentally retarded and the infrequence of its use where it was allowed, as well as the ineffective deterrent value as a result of the diminished mental capabilities. However, the Supreme Court also recognized the result of the *Penry* decision by commenting that the mentally retarded were not able to effectively argue mitigating circumstances and thus were more likely to be wrongfully executed.

Kathleen Barrett
Georgia State University

See Also: Capital Punishment; *Coker v. Georgia*; Corporal Punishment; Deterrence, Theory of; Electric Chair, History of; Executions; *Furman v. Georgia*; Three Strikes Law.

Further Readings
Brodenhamer, David J. and James W. Ely. *The Bill of Rights in Modern America*. Bloomington: Indiana University Press, 2008.
Cusac, Anne-Marie. *Cruel and Unusual: The Culture of Punishment in America*. New Haven, CT: Yale University Press, 2010.
Levy, Leonard William. *Origins of the Bill of Rights*. New Haven, CT: Yale University Press, 1999.
Smith, Rich. *The Eighth Amendment*. Edina, MN: ABDO Publishing, 2008.

Cruelty to Animals

Criminal justice generally focuses on how humans treat one another, but one aspect of criminal justice centers on how humans treat nonhuman animals. Initially, American law did not prevent cruelty to animals, but during the 19th century, states gradually, albeit limitedly, protected animals against abuse. Because of the efforts of the animal advocacy movement, governments since the 1980s have expanded criminal prohibitions against harming animals, but enforcement of cruelty laws varies considerably, and there is significant controversy over how far prohibitions on animal cruelty should extend.

For most of Western civilization, legal and political philosophy regarded animals as property; therefore, humans were free to wantonly abuse the animals they possessed. This view of animals as property was exported to colonial America, and as a result, colonial law and the law of the early American republic continued to allow humans to physically harm their animals. States did ban mistreating another person's animal, but those laws were not concerned with animal welfare; rather, harming another person's animal was tantamount to destroying his physical property. Even the few state statutes that banned abusing wild animals or animals in one's possession were not concerned with the suffering of the animals. Instead, the state legislatures were worried that mistreating animals would eventually lead to mistreating humans.

Shortly after the Civil War, activists, particularly Henry Bergh of New York, became concerned directly about animal welfare; consequently, they sought to expand anticruelty legislation. Bergh was inspired by English philosophers, such as Jeremy Bentham, who emphasized the immorality of animal suffering. After a trip to Europe, Bergh recognized how political organizations could help prevent cruelty to animals. In 1866, Bergh founded the American Society for Prevention of

The American Society for Prevention of Cruelty to Animals (ASPCA), whose activities included providing water for these New York City carriage horses in July 1911, convinced the New York legislature to pass animal cruelty laws that prohibited neglect of animals as well as wanton cruelty. The state allowed the ASPCA to enforce these laws and even to arrest the most severe violators.

Cruelty to Animals (ASPCA), which successfully lobbied the New York legislature to pass meaningful animal cruelty laws. Unlike previous laws that weakly addressed animal cruelty, New York's anticruelty statutes included all animals regardless of ownership, banned animal fighting for sport, prohibited neglect of animals in addition to wanton cruelty, and required that old animals be humanely euthanized. Although violations of the New York laws were only misdemeanors, the state did empower the ASPCA to enforce these laws, seize mistreated animals, and even arrest the most severe violators. Throughout the late 19th century and the first half of the 20th century, most states enacted statutes similar to New York's anticruelty laws and empowered local ASPCA organizations to enforce them. This activity protecting animal cruelty occurred primarily at the state level, but by the 1960s, the federal government also banned animal cruelty by passing the Animal Welfare Act and the Marine Mammal Protection Act.

Animal Advocacy

The most significant changes in animal cruelty law commenced because of the efforts of the animal advocacy movement that emerged during the 1970s. Unlike the animal welfare movement that had developed during the 19th century, which called for more humane treatment of animals used by humans, this new movement advocated the more radical view of completely eliminating human use of animals. Moreover, this contemporary movement used more aggressive tactics to reduce animal cruelty.

Inspired by Peter Singer's landmark book *Animal Liberation*, groups such as People for the Ethical Treatment of Animals (PETA) and the Animal Legal Defense Fund (ALDF) increased their efforts to combat the animal cruelty that occurred in the fields of agriculture, entertainment, and scientific research. Members of PETA engaged in undercover operations to expose the cruel treatment of animals used in these endeavors. Most significantly, in 1981, a member of PETA worked undercover in a scientific research laboratory and publicly exposed the extremely cruel conditions in which monkeys were kept. The state of Maryland charged the lead researcher, Dr. Edward Taub, with animal cruelty, and he was convicted on six counts. Although the convictions were ultimately overturned on appeal, largely on procedural grounds, Taub was the first person in the United States convicted of animal cruelty because of the conditions of a laboratory.

The animal advocacy movement has grown since the 1980s, and it has focused on expanding criminal sanctions and penalties against animal abusers. It lobbied state legislatures to increase animal cruelty violations from misdemeanors to felonies, and almost every state has now adopted felony animal cruelty statutes, although a few states still do not consider animal cruelty to be a felony. Animal advocacy groups have also sought the passage of state ballot initiatives to ban all animal fighting and require better treatment of farm animals.

Despite these changes, controversies over animal cruelty still exist. High-profile cases, such as National Football League (NFL) quarterback Michael Vick's conviction and prison sentence for dog fighting, have brought the issue of animal cruelty to the public's attention, but activists contend that budget cuts to local enforcement agencies and public indifference have resulted in spotty enforcement of existing cruelty laws, with tremendous variation across jurisdictions. Moreover, animal advocacy groups seek to expand the definition of animal cruelty to include any use of animals in agriculture, entertainment (especially circuses and rodeos), and scientific research. However, because those endeavors are so ingrained in the American economy and culture, these efforts to expand the definition of animal cruelty have been unsuccessful.

Steven Tauber
University of South Florida

See Also: Blood Sports; Child Abuse, History of; Fish and Game Laws; History of Crime and Punishment in America: 1783–1850; New York.

Further Readings

Favre, David and Vivien Tsang. "The Development of Anti-Cruelty Laws During the 1800s." *Detroit College of Law Review*, v.1 (1993).

Singer, Peter. *Animal Liberation: The Definitive Classic of the Animal Movement*. New York: Harper Perennial Modern Classics, 2009.

Waisman, Sonia S., Pamela D. Frasch, and Bruce A. Wagman. *Animal Law: Cases and Materials*, 3rd ed. Durham, NC: Carolina Academic Press, 2006.

Cummings, Homer

Homer Stille Cummings (1870–1956), a native of Chicago, was a noted lawyer and politician who served in elected and appointed office at the local, state, and national levels. Cummings graduated from Yale University Law School in 1893 and began practicing law in Stamford, Connecticut. In 1901, he was elected to his first of three terms as Stamford's mayor. Although his tenure in office was not without its accomplishments, he earned greater notoriety serving as a state's attorney for Fairfield County, an office to which he was named in 1914.

While serving in this position, Cummings was responsible for prosecuting Harold Israel, who was charged with murder. The victim, a popular local Catholic priest, was shot in the head at point-blank range while taking his daily evening walk on February 4, 1924. Based on witness accounts, the police focused their attention on Israel, who was already in custody for vagrancy and possession of a concealed .32 caliber pistol—a weapon matching the type used in the crime. Despite what appeared to be overwhelming physical evidence and eyewitness testimony gathered by police, as well as a confession from the accused, Cummings embarked on his own investigation. His review included interviewing witnesses a second time to determine the truthfulness of their stories, hiring ballistics experts to determine if Israel's pistol shot the fatal bullet, and requesting the examination of the accused by physicians to determine his capacity to commit the crime. The inquiry led Cummings to conclude that Israel was not responsible for the murder and to ask that the charges be dismissed. In 1947, 20th Century Fox produced the film *Boomerang*, directed by Elia Kazan and starring Dana Andrews and Jane Wyatt, depicting the events of the case.

Cummings later served as both vice chairman and chairman of the Democratic National Committee and was instrumental in winning support for Franklin Delano Roosevelt's bid for the Democratic nomination for president in 1932. For his efforts, Roosevelt originally selected Cummings to serve as governor-general of the Philippines. However, when Roosevelt's original choice for attorney general, Senator Thomas J. Walsh of Montana, suffered a fatal heart attack, Cummings was asked to head the U.S. Department of Justice. As attorney general, Cummings earned recognition for leading the charge, with Federal Bureau of Investigation Director J. Edgar Hoover, to reform elements of federal criminal law. Faced with a public shocked by a number of violent and notorious crimes, Cummings proposed nearly a dozen bills that won the approval of Congress. Signed by Roosevelt in the spring of 1934, the combined legislation leveraged various federal powers to prohibit illegal activity that involved interstate transportation or communication or was an assault on a federal institution or employee. Cummings offered a defense of his program in his 1937 book *We Can Prevent Crime*.

Cummings also helped lead the Roosevelt administration's unsuccessful defense of many of the novel laws passed as part of the New Deal reforms meant to ameliorate the effects of the Great Depression. Frustrated by the defeat of his programs by the U.S. Supreme Court, Roosevelt engaged Cummings in a project to develop a proposal to reshape and remake the membership of the bench to enable the president to nominate justices who might look more favorably on reforms passed by Congress at the behest of the administration.

Beginning in January 1935, Cummings and several of his assistants worked in secret to develop a plan to pack the court with several new justices. Cummings and his aides hatched a plan, originally proposed by the Wilson administration more than two decades earlier, that would allow the president to appoint an additional justice for each current member of the court who was 70 years of age and had served at least 10 years on the bench. Although this proposal was part of a larger restructuring of the federal judiciary, the administration's political motivations were clear in spite of explanations that the change was meant to relieve the workload for aging members of the bench. Despite large Democratic majorities in both the Senate and the House of Representatives, Roosevelt's plan met significant resistance. The administration eventually tabled the proposal when the Supreme Court ended its habit of invalidating the Depression era policies sponsored by Roosevelt.

Cummings continued in his position as attorney general until 1939, when Roosevelt began making changes to his cabinet. Before resigning his post, Cummings asked the Federal Bureau of Investigation to unearth information about Harold Israel. Investigators found him working as a miner in Pennsylvania with his wife and two children.

Charles F. Jacobs
St. Norbert College

See Also: Great Depression; Roosevelt, Franklin D. (Administration of); Supreme Court, U.S.

Further Readings
Cummings, Homer S. *We Can Prevent Crime: The American Program.* New York: Liberty MacFadden, 1937.
Kunstler, William M. *A Case for Courage.* New York: William Morrow, 1962.
Shesol, Jeff. *Supreme Power: Franklin Roosevelt vs. the Supreme Court.* New York: W. W. Norton, 2010.
Whitehead, Don. *The FBI Story.* New York: Random House, 1956.

Cunningham, Emma

Emma Cunningham (1818–87), a mother of five, was accused of the gruesome murder of her lover, Harvey Burdell, a financially secure New York dentist. Burdell was found strangled and stabbed to death on January 31, 1857, in his four-story boarding house at 31 Bond Street, where Cunningham served as his landlady. The grisly details of the crime and the lurid details of the couple's tumultuous relationship, which were publicly divulged during the subsequent legal battles that included two criminal proceedings and an estate battle, were splashed across New York newspapers and captured the attention of New York residents for nearly a year.

Emma Augusta Hempstead was born in Brooklyn to devout Methodists Christopher and Sara Hempstead. She was a young girl, probably between 17 and 19, when she and widower George Cunningham, who was 21 years her senior, were united, although when and if they were ever formally married remains unclear. Nevertheless, the two lived as man and wife and had five children. The first, Margaret Augusta, was born in 1839; she was followed by Helen, Georgiana, and boys William and George, Jr. Although they had lived in relative comfort among the elite for a time, George Cunningham's badly managed business ventures and extended illness meant that even the modest insurance policy he left her following his uneventful death in 1854 at the age of 57 would not support the family.

A widow at the age of 33, Cunningham relocated her children several times in the months that followed in a desperate attempt to find a suitable husband—and a source of much-needed financial support. Although she failed to gain a marriage proposal, she did find a companion in Burdell, who lavished her with attention and took her to Saratoga Springs, a popular retreat among New York's elite, during the summer of 1855.

Burdell, born in 1811, began his dental practice with his brother John, but the two became entangled in a bitter dispute. Burdell opened his own practice and became successful, if unscrupulous. Cunningham and Burdell, both of whom were manipulative and scheming, made for a volatile couple. When they returned from the trip to Saratoga Springs, Cunningham was pregnant and hopeful that the two would be married. Instead, she had an abortion and moved into the Bond Street boarding house, becoming Burdell's landlord, but it was an uneasy relationship and the two were at odds almost immediately.

Sensational Trial
New York prosecutors argued that Cunningham and John Eckel, a resident at the 31 Bond Street boarding house who was said to be having an affair with Cunningham, were responsible for stabbing Burdell 15 times. Cunningham faced prosecution twice. During the trial, evidence was presented that Cunningham had charged Burdell with rape and with breach of contract for failing to marry her. Testimony also suggested that officials had mishandled the collection of evidence and the investigation of the crime. The defense accused the prosecution of misconduct, painting Cunningham as a twice-widowed victim. Her attorney claimed that there was evidence that there were other potential suspects who had greater motive and opportunity

to murder Burdell, but that the prosecution had failed to do a proper investigation. Although the public was convinced of Cunningham's guilt, she was twice acquitted of Burdell's murder. Eckel was released without ever facing a trial.

During her trial, Cunningham had produced evidence of a marriage to Burdell and claimed to be pregnant with his baby in an effort to establish a credible claim to his estate. Cunningham continued to carry out her ruse, even after the trial. Cunningham and her personal physician unwittingly enlisted the services of another physician working with the district attorney to produce a newborn that she could claim was the product of her affair with Burdell.

A sting operation was put in place, and Cunningham laid claim to a newborn who presumably was born to an indigent woman. Cunningham and those who assisted her were arrested shortly after obtaining the newborn. Her fakery finally revealed, her claims to Burdell's estate were denied. Following the trial, she was disgraced. In 1859, she moved to San Francisco, where she met and married William E. Williams. She returned east after his death in 1883. Burdell's murder was never officially solved, and Cunningham died a poor woman at the age of 69 in 1887. Burdell and Cunningham are buried in Brooklyn's Green-Wood Cemetery.

The sensational trial is the subject of two fictionalized accounts: Raymond Paul's *The Bond Street Burlesque: A Historical Novel of Murder (1987)* and Ellen Horan's *31 Bond Street: A Novel* (2010).

Tracey-Lynn Clough
University of Texas at Arlington

See Also: New York; Women Criminals, History of; Women Criminals, Sociology of.

Further Readings
Duke, Thomas Samuel. *Celebrated Criminal Cases of America*. San Francisco, CA: James H. Barry Co., 1910.
Feldman, Benjamin. *Butchery on Bond Street: Sexual Politics and the Burdell-Cunningham Case in Antebellum New York*. New York: Green-Wood Cemetery Historic Fund in Association with the New York Wanderer, 2007.

Customs Service as Police

From its earliest days as a nation, the United States has employed mechanisms to monitor its borders to secure commerce and collect import duties on items being brought into the country, as well as to investigate those involved in attempts to avoid paying import tariffs and more complex smuggling operations. The history of the agencies responsible for these tasks can be explored in two stages: the establishment and operation of the U.S. Customs Service, which was at its inception primarily concerned with collecting revenue for the government and its operations, as well as conducting investigations of failures to do so; and the creation of the Department of Homeland Security, during which the U.S. Customs Service was dismantled and

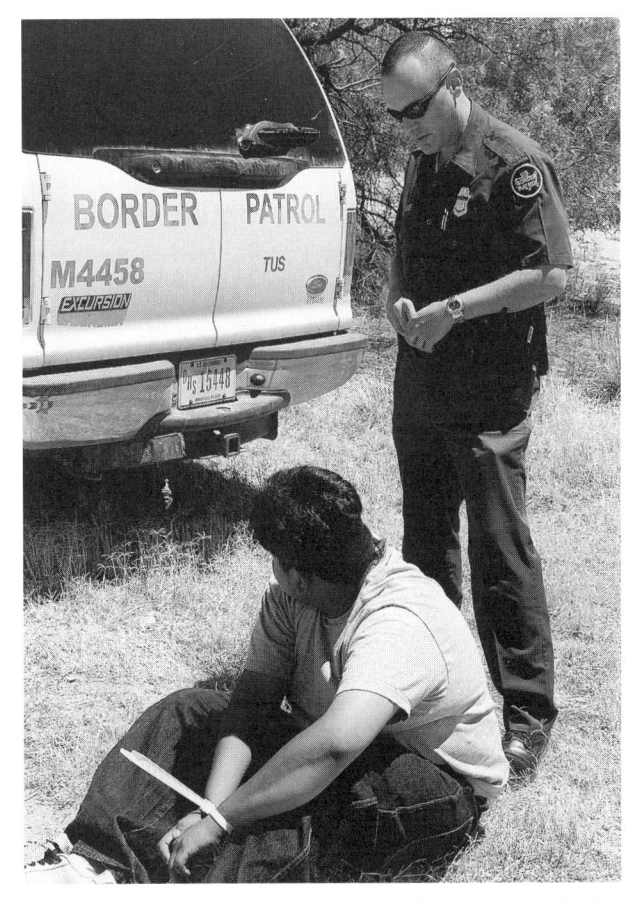

An agent with the U.S. Border Patrol, which is now part of U.S. Customs and Border Protection, arresting a Mexican national for transporting drugs into the United States.

reassembled into two separate agencies, U.S. Customs and Border Protection and U.S. Immigration and Customs Enforcement, both of which have primarily a national security focus. In both the previous and current incarnations, customs officials have been required to work with representatives from other law enforcement agencies on numerous complex criminal matters in order to satisfy overlapping goals.

The U.S. Customs Service was established upon the passage of the Tariff Act of 1789, which was the first major piece of legislation passed by the First Congress of the United States. This act established a schedule of tariffs, or duties, to be levied against goods imported into the country. Soon thereafter, Congress identified 59 official ports of entry that would fall under the jurisdiction of an entity to be known as the Collectors of Customs, which would be responsible for collecting duties on all items brought through these ports at the appropriate rate as designated by the import duty schedule.

The Collectors of Customs was a precursor to the U.S. Customs Service (as it was eventually renamed at the turn of the 19th century). The collector of customs and other high-ranking positions within the organization were prestigious and powerful political appointments. Lower-ranking positions within the organization, however, were often filled on the basis of politics and were granted by federal, state, and local politicians in exchange for patronage and loyalty. This state of affairs did not completely end in many regions of the country even after the agency came under civil service in the late 19th century.

The establishment of duties on imported goods was intended to have a certain protectionist effect for the developing American manufacturing base, but more importantly, at that time there did not exist a formal stable mechanism of funding the government. Import duties were perceived as a reliable stream of revenue for the fledgling nation to cover the costs of its debts and to support its developing infrastructure. Import duties were the major source of income for the U.S. government over the course of the next century, until the permanent introduction of the income tax in 1913.

The U.S. Customs Service's role in preserving national interests was clear: By monitoring trade activity across the country's border, it not only provided a source of revenue for the government but also helped facilitate commerce and protect the nation's economy. Meanwhile, the agency was responsible for preventing attempts to avoid paying import duties and for investigating individuals flouting the law with smuggling activities. In the mid-19th century, the agency was responsible for immigration law enforcement as well, but by the late 19th century, those responsibilities were moved to the agency that eventually evolved into the Immigration and Naturalization Service.

The U.S. Customs Service grew to be one of the largest, most visible law enforcement agencies in the country. It was responsible for physically monitoring several hundred different ports of entry (which included vehicular and pedestrian entry points, airports and seaports, railways, and postal facilities accepting mail from outside the United States) not only to collect import duties when appropriate, but to interdict and seize any individuals attempting to enter the country illegally or under false pretenses, as well as any items (whether plant, animal, or inorganic) that might threaten U.S. agricultural, environmental, public health, or economic interests.

Homeland Security Era

In the aftermath of the terrorist attacks on September 11, 2001, there was a dramatic organizational change within federal law enforcement. The Department of Homeland Security (DHS), which began operations in early 2003, was established with the primary mission of protecting the United States from domestic terrorism and improving the nation's readiness to respond to all serious emergencies, whether natural or man-made. All of the law enforcement agencies within the DHS would share the common goals of preventing and/or investigating activities that could undermine domestic safety and security. While some existing agencies were essentially unchanged when they were moved to DHS, others were dramatically reorganized.

The U.S. Customs Service was one of the agencies most dramatically affected by these changes. It was disbanded and reassembled into two separate and independent agencies, both of which are concerned with the same set of federal laws surrounding customs and immigration issues, albeit with very different specific tasks: U.S. Customs and Border Protection (CBP), with a border-based patrol, interdiction, and deterrence focus: and U.S.

Immigration and Customs Enforcement (ICE), which has solely investigative responsibilities. In performing their duties, CBP and ICE can be considered two sides of the same coin in that they share an interest in the same types of criminal law violations, but they are indeed two separate and autonomous agencies that are required to share information and work together on specific cases.

CBP retained its presence at all ports of entry but now focuses its efforts solely on detection and interdiction. It is no longer involved in investigations; rather, such activities were reassigned to the newly formed ICE. Although officially the agency's primary responsibility is to actively prevent terrorists and terrorist weapons from entering the United States through formal entry points, such apprehensions are relatively rare occurrences. Most of the daily activities of CBP officers involve other national security interests, such as detecting illicit narcotics or firearms smuggling (which, if discovered, are referred to the Drug Enforcement Administration and the Bureau of Alcohol, Tobacco, Firearms and Explosives, respectively); interdicting individuals attempting to enter illegally; preventing dubious plants, foods, or animals from passing into the country's interior; and collecting of import duties.

Within CBP is the Border Patrol, which was originally managed within the U.S. Department of Labor when it was established in 1924; its initial focus was preventing illegal entry into the country through the borders shared with Canada and Mexico. The agency's responsibilities included physically monitoring these land borders as well as approximately 2,000 miles of coastal borders surrounding the Florida peninsula and the island of Puerto Rico. Although the Border Patrol is a subunit of CBP, it operates with a fair amount of autonomy. Its responsibilities are identical to those of CBP, with one significant exception: Whereas CBP officers are stationed at formal, official ports of entry, Border Patrol agents comprise mobile units that travel along the U.S. border between ports of entry. Border Patrol agents, therefore, are particularly likely to encounter individuals attempting to enter the country in an effort to evade detection of some kind of illicit activity by officials at ports of entry. Although Border Patrol agents might hypothetically encounter individuals attempting to smuggle taxable goods as part of a scheme to avoid paying import duties, the vast majority of persons they encounter are either independently attempting to violate immigration laws, are part of a human trafficking scheme, or are involved in drug trafficking activities.

ICE was established by the dismantling and reassignment of duties that were once within the jurisdiction of the U.S. Customs Service and U.S. Immigration and Naturalization Service. It is primarily an investigative agency, staffed with nonuniformed agents with a specific interest in probing allegations of federal immigration and customs laws violations. Much of ICE's efforts revolve around apprehending individuals who have illegally entered the country or who entered legally but have remained past the terms of their visas. ICE also investigates individuals involved in cross-border human trafficking. However, the agency is also the entity responsible for investigating individual violations of customs laws as well as more complex smuggling schemes; particular cases are generally brought to their attention by CBP officers (after the seizure of items at a port of entry alerts them to smuggling activity) or other law enforcement agencies.

Miriam D. Sealock
Towson University

See Also: 1961 to 1980 Primary Documents; Border Patrol; Bureau of Alcohol, Tobacco, Firearms and Explosives; Bush, George W. (Administration of); Drug Enforcement Administration; Federal Policing; Homeland Security; Immigration Crimes; Smuggling; Tax Crimes; Terrorism; Washington, George (Administration of).

Further Readings

Department of Homeland Security. "Quadrennial Homeland Security Review Report." https://secure.nccrimecontrol.org/hsb/planning/Planning%20Documents/Quadrennial%20Homeland%20Security%20Report%202010.pdf (Accessed January 2011).

U.S. Customs and Border Protection. "U.S. Customs and Border Protection." http://www.cbp.gov/xp/cgov/home.xml (Accessed January 2011).

U.S. Immigration and Customs Enforcement. "U.S. Immigration and Customs Enforcement." http://www.ice.gov (Accessed January 2011).

Czolgosz, Leon

On September 6, 1901, at the Pan-American Exhibition in Buffalo, New York, Leon Czolgosz fired two shots at President William McKinley. McKinley died September 14, of gangrene poisoning, the third president in 36 years to be felled by an assassin. Czolgosz's trial began September 23, in the New York Supreme Court, in Buffalo, and ended the next day. During his incarceration, a physical examination revealed no signs of insanity and thus no insanity defense was undertaken. Czolgosz, however, never met with his defense team until the day of his trial. Czolgosz also did not take the witness stand. He was found guilty of murder and there was no appeal. He was electrocuted at Auburn Prison on October 29. His body was incinerated with acid and buried in an unmarked grave.

Not much is known of Czolgosz's life prior to the assassination. There is no extant birth certificate. It is commonly assumed that he was born in Detroit in 1873. His father, Paul, and his mother, Mary, née Nowak, arrived separately from Poznan, Prussia, in 1873. The family was Catholic. Mary died circa 1883 or 1885. Paul then married Katren Meltzfaltr, whom Leon disdained. Paul and Mary had nine children (seven sons and two daughters) and Paul and Katren had two sons. Leon was the first of Paul and Mary's children to be born in the United States.

Leon Czolgosz had little formal education. He briefly attended a Catholic school, attended public school on and off for about three years, and also attended night school for about three months in the late 1890s. He regularly attended church and was familiar with the Bible, although he abandoned any interest in religion in the late 1890s. He was fond of reading newspapers, the *Peruna Almanac*, which told him his lucky days, and Edward Bellamy's *Looking Backward*, though it is unknown if he read it in Polish or English.

Czolgosz worked on a family farm and in factories, starting at age 12 or 13. By the mid-1890s, he was earning about a dollar a day, working 12-hour shifts in a factory in Cleveland. He was laid off in 1896 but was later rehired under the name Fred Nieman. Czolgosz used a number of aliases—variations on Nieman—most likely because his name was difficult to pronounce, though it has also been suggested that Nieman was his mother's maiden name and that he used aliases because he was part of a conspiracy. Czolgosz quit working in 1898 because of ill health. In November 1898, he went to see a doctor, complaining of a chronic cough. He purchased an inhaling machine. The doctor suspected emphysema but found no evidence of it. At his trial, Czolgosz seemed to twitch, and throughout his life, he appeared dreamy and would suddenly fall asleep. After his trial, some doctors suspected Czolgosz had epilepsy, but this is unproven.

In his prison confession, Czolgosz said that he did not believe in the republican form of government and admitted to being an anarchist. McKinley was the fifth head of state or government since 1894 to be assassinated by an anarchist, though Czolgosz belonged to no anarchist club, party, or organization. In May 1901, Czolgosz admitted to an acquaintance that he had not read any anarchist literature. But because he asked so many questions regarding anarchism's tenets, the established anarchists in Chicago thought him a spy and warned anarchists, through the anarchist press, to stay away from "Nieman." Emma Goldman, who met Czolgosz in July 1901 under his alias Nieman, rejected Czolgosz's use of violence, but wrote of him with affection after his death. After the assassination, Goldman and a number of prominent anarchists were arrested on suspicion of aiding and abetting Czolgosz but were later released. The fear of anarchist violence persisted after Czolgosz's death. In 1903, Congress passed the Immigration Act, which excluded from the United States anarchists, epileptics, beggars, and importers of prostitutes.

Cary Federman
Montclair State University

See Also: Anarchists; Booth, John Wilkes; Guiteau, Charles; McKinley, William (Administration of).

Further Readings
Briggs, L. Vernon. *The Manner of Man That Kills*. 1921. Reprint, New York: Da Capo Press, 1983.
Channing, Walter. "The Mental Status of Czolgosz, the Assassin of President McKinley." *Journal of Insanity*, v.59/2 (1902).
Goldman, Emma. "October Twenty-Ninth, 1901." *Mother Earth*, v.6/8 (1911).

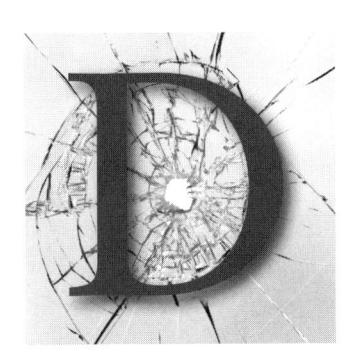

Dahmer, Jeffrey

Jeffrey Dahmer (1960–94) was one of the most notorious serial killers of the 20th century. The particularly gruesome nature of his crimes attracted widespread attention following their discovery and his arrest in Milwaukee, Wisconsin, in 1991. Born May 21, 1960, in Wisconsin, Dahmer spent much of his youth in Bath, Ohio. As a child, he grew aloof and unhappy, jealous of his brother and burdened by an overbearing father. He was known to bring home and store the remains of dead animals and reportedly committed acts of cruelty against animals. Alcoholism took root in high school. Dahmer's first murder occurred shortly after his high school graduation in 1978, when he picked up a hitchhiker, Steven Hicks, had sex with him, and then bludgeoned him with a barbell when Hicks wanted to leave. After just one semester at Ohio State University, Dahmer spent two years in the army, but he was honorably discharged due to his alcoholism.

In 1982, Dahmer moved into his grandmother's home in Milwaukee until she asked him to leave on account of his late hours and the bad smells coming from the basement—he had killed three times in this period. Just a day after moving into his own apartment in 1988, Dahmer was arrested and later served 10 months for sexually assaulting a 13-year-old boy. Upon his release, and in a new apartment, the violence began to accelerate. Many of Dahmer's murders followed a gruesome pattern. After drugging and strangling his 17 victims, Dahmer would then dismember their bodies, often having sex with the corpses. He stored some remains, such as skulls and testicles, as trophies; other remains he cooked and ate. He disposed of the bulk of the bodies by dissolving them in a large vat of acid.

Dahmer's crimes evaded detection despite the late-night noises and smells. Two neighbors did alert police one evening when a 14-year-old Laotian boy stumbled naked out of Dahmer's apartment, heavily drugged and bleeding. Dahmer persuaded officers to release him back to his care and then killed the boy moments after they departed. The police finally arrested Dahmer in July 1991 after a would-be victim overcame the effect of the drugs, fought off Dahmer, escaped, and directed police to the apartment.

Inside his bedroom, police discovered rotting remains, skulls, and photos of the dismembered bodies of some of his victims. Dahmer plead not guilty by reason of insanity and he gave a detailed confession of all his murders. A jury found him sane and he received 15 consecutive life sentences. After his conviction, business groups in Milwaukee gathered the funds to purchase Dahmer's possessions, which were promptly destroyed, and the apartment building was demolished. Dahmer and a fellow prisoner were killed by a third inmate while the trio cleaned the prison's gym.

The causes of Dahmer's crimes have been the subject of much discussion. Though some scholars have found his cannibalism and hoarding of body parts consistent with other murderers who feel no guilt and collect trophies from their victims, others have found it difficult to explain his actions in terms of a readily identifiable psychological condition. However unhappy or abnormal his childhood, most view his upbringing as an insufficient explanation. Many point to self-hatred, related to struggles with his homosexuality, as one factor. Psychologists question whether people like Dahmer have inherent psychopathic tendencies or develop them through life. The Dahmer case is frequently cited as an example of a jury rejecting an insanity plea because of the potential for the accused to re-enter society.

Dahmer has remained a cultural reference point over two decades. Much of Dahmer's notoriety, compared even to other serial killers, stems from the dismemberment, necrophilia, and cannibalism displayed in the murders. Aspects of Dahmer's activities parallel that of Ed Gein, the Wisconsin murderer who inspired the Alfred Hitchcock movie *Psycho*. Critical appraisals of the Dahmer episode suggest that this fixation on the horrific nature of his crimes obscures the racism present in Dahmer's motivations (many of the men he killed were African American or Asian American gay men). Sociologists and other critics also noted that the difficult relationship between the police and African Americans and gays in Milwaukee allowed Dahmer to avoid arrest, particularly in the near-miss when officers trusted Dahmer over the concerns of black neighbors.

Patrick Schmidt
Samuel Brier
Macalester College

See Also: Famous Trials; Insanity Defense; Serial and Mass Killers; Violent Crimes; Wisconsin.

Further Readings
Hickey, Eric. *Serial Murderers and Their Victims.* Belmont, CA: Wadsworth, 2010.
Masters, Brian. *The Shrine of Jeffrey Dahmer.* London: Hodder & Stoughton, 1993.

Darrow, Clarence

Attorney Clarence Darrow was born on April 18, 1857, in Kinsman, Ohio, to Amirus and Emily Darrow. Raised in an agnostic working-class home, Darrow attended Allegheny College and one year of law school at the University of Michigan. Although Darrow obtained a degree from neither Allegheny College nor the University of Michigan, he studied law and entered the Ohio bar in 1878. For the first nine years of his career, Darrow practiced in Ashtabula County, Ohio. In 1887, Darrow relocated to Chicago. His move to Chicago was motivated both by career ambitions as well as a desire to work with John Peter Altgeld, who would later become governor of Illinois in 1892. Specifically, Darrow had read and was inspired by Altgeld's text *Our Penal Machinery and Its Victims*, which attacked the criminal justice system as being biased in favor of the wealthy.

Chicago transformed Darrow, and he was greatly impacted by the suffering of the poor and the imprisoned. In the late 1880s, Darrow acted as a public speaker while embracing various social and political reform movements. By 1890, Darrow had been hired as the general attorney to the Chicago and North Western Railway. However, in 1894, Darrow defended the president of the American Railway Union, Eugene V. Debs, who had been charged with contempt of court in relation to the Pullman Strike. As a result, Darrow's employment with Chicago and North Western Railway ended. This trial marked the beginning of a period in Darrow's career in which he fiercely advocated the interests of labor and its leaders. For example, in 1907, Darrow defended William Haywood, another influential labor leader. Haywood had been charged with the murder of Frank Steunenberg, a former governor of Idaho. Darrow's meticulous cross-examination of the state's main witness was crucial to Haywood's acquittal.

Additionally, in 1910, Darrow defended trade unionists and brothers James and John McNamara, who were accused of bombing the *Los Angeles Times* office building and killing over a dozen employees of the newspaper. Organized labor vociferously proclaimed the innocence of the McNamara brothers. However, Darrow convinced the brothers to plead guilty in an attempt to avoid the death penalty. Many leaders in the

Clarence Darrow in 1913, around the time he was frequently defending labor leaders and trade unionists. Darrow's other interests included racial equality, the rights of criminals, capital punishment, and the protection of individual liberties.

labor movement were shocked by the confessions of the McNamara brothers, as well as by Darrow's defense. Moreover, Darrow found himself in the middle of a controversy when he was charged with jury tampering in relation to the McNamara trial. Although never convicted, both his work on the McNamara case and his subsequent legal battle served to transition Darrow away from defending labor leaders and toward high-profile criminal cases. Over the next several years, Darrow continued to build his criminal defense practice. During World War I, Darrow represented several individuals charged with antiwar activities and was a vocal critic of the Espionage Act of 1917.

In 1924, Darrow defended two wealthy teenagers, Nathan Leopold, Jr., and Richard Loeb, who faced the death penalty. Darrow stridently opposed the death penalty. However, the case was difficult because the defendants had confessed to brutally murdering 14-year-old Robert Franks. In spite of the brutal details of the crime and the defendants' confessions, Darrow masterfully mitigated the punishment to life in prison, while eloquently condemning the death penalty. More precisely, Darrow managed to save both from the death penalty by convincing them to plead guilty and by utilizing experts in psychology during the trial. These expert witnesses assisted Darrow in successfully arguing that social and psychological pressures were primarily responsible for the defendants' acts.

Just a year later, in *State of Tennessee v. John Thomas Scopes*, Darrow joined the defense team for a high school biology teacher, John T. Scopes. Scopes was on trial for violating a Tennessee law, the Butler Act, which made it illegal to teach evolution in a public school. Former Democratic presidential candidate William Jennings Bryan was a member of the prosecution's team. The trial captured the friction between religion and science. During the trial, Bryan even attempted to use the Leopold-Loeb case in an effort to buttress his argument that evolution was morally wrong. Darrow called William Jennings Bryan to the stand as a witness. Darrow was relentless in questioning the former presidential candidate about his literal interpretation of the Bible; the confrontation lasted for over an hour.

At the end of the trial, Scopes was eventually convicted and fined $100. Only five days after the trial, William Jennings Bryan died in his sleep. In another high-profile case, Darrow joined the defense team of black physician Dr. Ossian Sweet and his brother Henry. Both brothers were facing murder charges. Ossian Sweet had purchased a home in a primarily white neighborhood of Detroit. After an angry white mob gathered around Sweet's new home, an individual within the mob was shot and killed. Both Sweet brothers, as well as all other individuals in the Sweet home at the time of the shooting, were charged with murder. Darrow's skillful direct examination of Ossian Sweet, along with a riveting closing argument, helped both Sweet brothers escape conviction.

After Darrow's retirement from the practice of law, President Franklin D. Roosevelt appointed him chair of a commission to study and review the operation of the National Recovery Administration. Additionally, Darrow chaired the opening session of the American Inquiry Commission, which was established to study the disturbing events occurring in Germany during the mid-1930s. Darrow wrote several books, including *Crime, Its Cause and Treatment*, *The Prohibition Mania*, and *The Story of My Life*. Although not always victorious, Clarence Darrow took into account human nature, human emotion, and societal forces when advocating a cause or for an individual. Darrow's battles in the courtroom encompassed issues of racial equality, the rights of criminals, the appropriateness of capital punishment, and the protection of individual liberties. Darrow died in 1938, at the age of 81.

Neil Guzy
University of Pittsburgh at Greensburg

See Also: 1921 to 1940 Primary Documents; Capital Punishment; Espionage Act of 1917; Famous Trials; Legal Counsel; Leopold and Loeb; Scopes Monkey Trial; Trials.

Further Readings
Darrow, Clarence. *The Story of My Life*. New York: Da Capo Press, 1996.
Driemen, John E. *Clarence Darrow*. New York: Chelsea House, 1992.
Tierney, Kevin. *Darrow: A Biography*. New York: Crowell, 1979.
Vine, Phyllis. *One Man's Castle: Clarence Darrow in Defense of the American Dream*. New York: Amistad, 2004.
Weinberg, A. and L. Weinberg. *Clarence Darrow: A Sentimental Rebel*. New York: Atheneum, 1987.

Davis v. State

The fundamental issue in the case of *Davis v. State* has to do with the protection provided by the Second Amendment. The appellant (i.e., Davis; the person seeking to have the decision reversed) was traveling via wagon on the highway toward the town of Fayetteville, Arkansas, from his home in 1885. Before arriving at his destination, however, he borrowed a navy pistol, which he did not try to conceal as he made his way to the wagon and continued on his travels. During his trip, he kept the pistol on the seat to his side as well as under the seat. During this time, there was a statute that regulated the use of firearms. More specifically, it stipulated that weapons were to be concealed and only to be used for self-defense when embarking upon a journey, which was an exemption to the statute. However, Davis was indicted for wearing and carrying a weapon. In other words, his trip was not deemed a journey, which would have exonerated him from any wrongdoing. The defense argued that the appellant had the right to bear arms and defend himself. To strengthen their argument, they centered on two core issues: first, limiting the use and possession of a firearm was disputed as a violation of the appellant's Second Amendment right. Second, the law was argued as being adhered to incorrectly. In other words, the law was referring to the concealment of weapons with the exception of moments when a person feels the need to defend him- or herself. However, the appellant was charged with wearing and carrying a gun, not with failing to conceal a weapon or having embarked on a journey.

The standard for what constitutes a journey was not clarified, despite its apparent relevance. For instance, though the distance between the appellant's home and his destination is not known, Davis was reported to have obtained the pistol while he was within 12 miles of his destination. However, this issue was deemed insignificant and the jury was not instructed to consider the question pertaining to a possible exemption stemming from a clause that allowed for the possession of a weapon for self-defense. However, the jury was instructed that the appellant was guilty if the pistol was within his reach, which the defense argued contradicted the true nature of the law. Other decisions related to this case include *Carr v. State*, in which the exception to the statute was clearly stated: travelers are able to protect themselves while traveling on the highway. Also, to clarify the misunderstanding surrounding what constitutes a journey, *Wilson v. State* declared that it is impossible to outline a specific distance that will properly characterize a journey. Instead, it was decided that each case must be dealt with individually because the circumstances in each will ultimately make the difference during the decision-making process. The Second Amendment protects against the prohibition of the right to bear arms. More specifically, an individual has the right to possess a firearm and does not have to be serving in the militia at the time of possession. This right was included within the Bill of Rights out of fear that the federal government would one day attempt to disarm the citizens and thus leave them at the mercy of the standing army.

As a result of the above arguments, the Arkansas Supreme Court ruled that the appellant was not indicted for failing to conceal a weapon or embarking on a journey; rather, the issue was simply being in possession of a weapon. However, the court stated that the law preserved the right of people to protect themselves while traveling on highways. The court also recognized that no rule or law can be developed or implemented that will accurately depict the true nature of a journey. In their ruling, the court argued that a journey can take one day or several, for this reason, it is impossible to establish a standard that clearly defines a journey. However, since the appellant was traveling outside the scope of his neighbors, family, and friends, and was detained during the day, the court ruled that under these circumstances, this constituted a journey. Ultimately, due to a lack of evidence, the original judgment was reversed and a new trial was ordered.

Amy S. Eggers
University of South Florida

See Also: Arkansas; Bill of Rights; Gun Control; Guns and Violent Crime.

Further Readings
Carr v. State, 34 Ark. 448, 36 Am. Rep. 15 (1879).
Davis v. State, 45 Ark. 359 (1885).
Wilson v. State, 68 Ala. 41 (1881).

Dayton, Ohio

Dayton is located in Montgomery County, the fifth most populated county in Ohio. With a 2010 population of 141,527, Dayton is the sixth-largest city in the state. The population is approximately 53.4 percent white and 43.1 percent African American with minimal numbers of other ethnic groups. Dayton is home to Wright-Patterson Air Force Base and thus caters to significant industrial, aerospace, and technological research. Dayton also has a large service economy that includes insurance and legal sectors and a nationally ranked healthcare system.

Dayton is the birthplace of the Wright Brothers, who invented powered flight. The work of the Wrights started a long record of aviation accomplishments that have earned Dayton a reputation as the "birthplace of aviation." The first parachute jump, first solo instrument landing, night flying advances, world altitude records, and pioneering in aerial photography are all noted in Dayton's heritage as an aviation hub. Since the 1980s, Dayton's population has been in decline caused by a loss of manufacturing industries and the national economic downturn.

Nineteenth Century

With the admission of Ohio into the Union in 1803, Montgomery County was formed. Dayton was incorporated in 1805, with a government of seven trustees acting as council, a supervisor, and a marshal. Although Dayton was incorporated in 1805, the foundation of the local police service began with the appointment of the first constable, Cyrus Osborn, in 1797. At this time, Newcom Tavern, built by Colonel George Newcom, served as the town's courthouse and jail, with white prisoners lowered into a dry well and Indian prisoners bound and held in the corn crib. In 1803, Newcom was appointed Dayton's first sheriff.

Dayton is the home of the Montgomery County Jail. First built as a log cabin on the courthouse lot in 1803, in 1811 the jail was removed to allow a combination jail and sheriff's office. In 1834, a stone jail with four cells was erected; it served the city and county for 10 years, until a new jail was built in 1844 that allowed for 60–70 prisoners. In 1869, another jail was built and equipped with gallows that held public hangings; the last hanging in Dayton occurred in 1877. In 1965, the current county jail was built in Dayton; it was renovated in 1993 and in 2004 and has a 900-prisoner capacity.

In 1805, James Miller was appointed Dayton's first marshal. A marshal remained Dayton's only peace officer until 1818, when a deputy marshal was added. For the next 16 years, the marshal and deputy marshal were the entirety of Dayton law enforcement. In 1834, Joseph L. Allen became the first walking patrol beat officer. In 1840, Dayton was incorporated as a city. At this time, its population was more than 6,000 and the police force consisted of a marshal and deputy marshal assisted only by watchmen and citizens. By 1848, Dayton's population reached 10,000, and the city approved six watchmen, one for each city ward, to assist the marshal, deputy marshal, and two constables in law enforcement duties. After a rash of burglaries occurred in the mid-1850s, the city council authorized the mayor to appoint up to four watchmen for each of the six city wards.

The Dayton Police Department was officially established in 1873 when the Ohio General Assembly passed a law creating the Ohio Board of Police Commissioners. At this time, a new metropolitan police force was formed, consisting of a captain, acting superintendent, two sergeants, and 20 sworn officers to police Dayton's more than 25,000 residents. In these days, patrolmen were assigned 12-hour work shifts and worked seven days a week with minimal vacation time. Foot patrol was the only method of patrol, and officers were expected to purchase their own uniforms and equipment. In 1883, when Dayton's population reached 38,000 citizens, the police force mobilized its first horse-drawn patrol wagon.

Twentieth Century and Beyond

In 1886, Dayton purchased the Gamewell System, a police telegraph. Considered the greatest modern improvement in police service delivery, the $25,000 system consisted of 64 patrol boxes placed around the city. When a lever was pulled, a telegraph signal transmitted the call box number and location to the central exchange. In 1901, the Red Light Signal System enhanced the Gamewell System. Red lights were located on telegraph stations across the city, and when the lights were turned on by central exchange, patrolmen were required to contact headquarters for instructions. Although the Gamewell System was the primary method for dispatching officers for the next 50 years, by the 1970s, new portable radio dispatch systems rendered call box communications a technology of the past. Dayton was the first police force in the nation to have its entire fleet of squad cars equipped with two-way radio

The Dayton Police Department introduced its first police cars in 1918; this modern squad car was typical of those used in the city in 2011. Dayton had the 20th-highest crime rate in the United States in 2010, with 1,509 violent crimes being reported, including 34 murders, 92 forcible rapes, 782 robberies, and 601 aggravated assaults.

communication. Also, by 1977, the Dayton police force of nearly 500 had 50 African American and 28 women officers. In 1901, Dayton adopted the Bertillon system for criminal identification. This system relied on anthropometry, and specific body parts thought never to change were measured and cataloged for identification. In 1910, Dayton introduced motorcycles to its police units; in 1918, the police force purchased several automobiles for patrol; and in 1919, the Henry fingerprint system replaced the Bertillon system.

In 1933, John Dillinger was gaining infamy for bank robberies across Ohio and Indiana, and Federal Bureau of Investigation (FBI) director J. Edgar Hoover named him Public Enemy No. 1. On September 22, 1933, Dillinger was visiting his girlfriend, Mary Longnecker, at her residence in Dayton when two Dayton police detectives, Russell Pfauhl and Sgt. Charles Gross, finally arrested him.

According to the CQ Press rankings, based on FBI statistics from 2009, in 2010, Dayton had the 20th-highest crime rate in the country with a score of 191.14 (where 0 indicates an average crime rate and a positive number a higher than average rate). In 2010, 1,509 violent crimes were reported in Dayton, including 34 murders, 92 forcible rapes, 782 robberies, and 601 aggravated assaults. Finally, 8,891 property crimes, including 3,380 burglaries, 4,840 larcenies, 671 motor-vehicle thefts, and 203 cases of arson, were reported in 2010.

Patrick O'Brien
University of Colorado Boulder

See Also: Cincinnati, Ohio; Cleveland, Ohio; Crime Rates; Dillinger, John; Ohio; Police, Contemporary; Police, History of.

Further Readings
"City Crime Rankings 2010–2011. CQ Press. http://os.cqpress.com/citycrime/2010/citycrime2010-2011.htm (Accessed September 2011).
Dayton History. "Carillon Historical Park." http://www.daytonhistory.org (Accessed September 2011).
Dayton History Books Online. http://www.daytonhistorybooks.com/index.html (Accessed September 2011).

Grismer, Stephen. "Dayton Police History." http://dph-foundation.web.officelive.com/Documents/Part%203-%20History%20Section.pdf (Accessed August 2011).

Death Row

Death row, often a separate unit within a prison, houses individuals who have been sentenced to death for commission of a capital crime. As of 2011, 3,279 inmates were on death row in the United States. The number of death sentences has dropped dramatically since 1993, when 287 defendants were placed on death row, in comparison to 112 in 2009. Of the 7,773 prisoners awaiting execution between 1977 and 2009, 15 percent were executed, 5 percent died from causes other than execution, and 39 percent received other dispositions, such as having their convictions overturned or their sentences commuted.

Although a handful of states do not operate their death rows on a punitive-segregation model, most continue to follow a common practice from the 19th century, which required a condemned prisoner to spend the final months preceding execution in solitary confinement, primarily in the hope of forcing the prisoner into self-reflection that might help him repent before death. Today, the conditions of confinement on death row are often as austere as they were in the 1800s. Prisoners awaiting execution are generally isolated from other prisoners, often spending as much as 23 hours each day alone in their cells, except when medical or legal reasons otherwise dictate. The cells are small; in Florida, for example, a death row cell is 6 feet by 9 feet by 9.5 feet high. Food is usually prepared and delivered to death row inmates by prison trustees (inmates who are well behaved and deemed dependable to complete minor tasks within the prison). These conditions are comparable to solitary confinement, except that the latter is designed to be an acute form of punishment for a restricted time period for general-population prisoners.

Condemned prisoners are typically distinguished from other prisoners by color-coded clothing. They are generally excluded from recreational, educational, and employment programs, although a handful of death row units allow prisoners to participate in media interviews and/or highly limited recreation. Most are permitted to receive mail after screening by correctional officials. Visitations are also highly restricted, if they are permitted at all. Death row inmates are usually counted at least once per hour since many attempt suicide. They are escorted in handcuffs whenever they leave their cells, and the only time they are not restrained is in the exercise yard or the shower. Some institutions allow capital prisoners to have cigarettes; more recently, some prisons have also allowed access to snacks, radios, and closed-circuit televisions.

Execution Process

Once a state's governor signs a death warrant—a writ authorizing the execution of a judgment of death—the condemned is moved to a "death watch cell," a cell closer to the execution chamber where security is heightened; in many facilities, deputies provide 24-hour supervision. It is customary that prior to execution, an inmate may request a last meal; however, in an attempt to avoid profligacy, some states limit the meal's cost. Additionally, on the eve of execution, condemned inmates are usually permitted one legal and one social phone call.

States vary with regard to the preparation and processes used on the day of an execution. Most states allow the condemned person to select a fixed number of family, friends, and a spiritual adviser to act as witnesses at his/her execution. Most states also invite the victim's family to witness the execution, as well as representatives from the state and the media. All witnesses are mailed an information packet detailing the execution date, time, and processes so that they are informed about what will take place.

On the day of execution, witnesses are briefed in person about the condemned's offense, last meal, the witnesses in attendance, and execution procedures. Precautions are taken to ensure that the victim's and offender's witnesses remain separate during the entire process. Typically, multiple state actors (often correctional employees) serve as executioners. This redundancy helps ensure that no one knows who was actually responsible for the execution. Medical personnel are typically present to pronounce death, although in some states, medical professionals refuse to participate in any aspects of an execution. Once pronounced dead, the body is then transported for autopsy. Witnesses are escorted to a secure room for an opportunity to gather their thoughts. Most states allow witnesses to speak to media representatives if they so desire. They are then escorted from the facility.

The Death Row Phenomenon

Death rows were designed for short-term confinement of the condemned, often up to no more than three months, while a prisoner under a capital sentence exhausted last-minute appeals and requests for executive clemency. But after the adoption of the Fourteenth Amendment, providing due process rights to state prisoners, multiple appeals became commonplace, and the time spent awaiting execution grew from an average of six months to approximately two years between the 1950s and the mid-1970s. Since that time, the average stay on death row has lengthened exponentially. The extensive judicial review of death sentences after the 1976 case *Gregg v. Georgia* is partially responsible for the fact that death row inmates routinely spend between 10 and 20 years awaiting execution. The 52 inmates executed in the United States in 2009 spent an average of 14 years and one month on death row, about 30 months longer than those executed in 2008. Jack Alderman, executed September 16, 2008, spent nearly 34 years on death row, the longest time between sentencing and execution in U.S. history, although others with pending executions have been on death row even longer. Advances in technology have also contributed to long death row incarceration periods. DNA exonerations, for example, have heightened concerns about the potential execution of the innocent. As of August 2011, there have been 273 post-conviction DNA exonerations in U.S. history. The most common causes of wrongful convictions include eyewitness misidentification, invalidated or improper forensic science, false confessions/admissions, government misconduct, misinformation from informants, and poor lawyering. Yet, in *District Attorney's Office for Third Judicial Dist. v. Osborne* (2009), the U.S. Supreme Court held that prisoners have no right to obtain DNA evidence for testing that could prove they are innocent, even if paying for the testing themselves.

These guards are shown escorting a prisoner outside the numbered death row cells at California's San Quentin State Prison in 2010. In 2011, 3,279 people were on death row in the United States. Among all inmates awaiting execution, 29.1 percent were between the ages of 30 to 39, 51 percent were 25 to 44, 1.2 percent were under the age of 25, and 2.6 percent were older than 65. The average age at the time of arrest for the capital crime is 28 years.

Psychologists and lawyers have argued that extended periods of confinement and uncertainty of death—referred to as the "death row phenomenon"—can have profound and detrimental psychological effects, including marked decreases in cognitive functioning, dehumanization, mood disorders, delusions, and suicidal ideations and/or suicide attempts. Jens Soering, a German citizen charged in 1985 with murder in Virginia, fled to the United Kingdom and argued to the European Court of Human Rights that the protracted period on death row was as psychologically damaging as torture. The court ruled in his favor, citing the death row phenomenon. He was extradited in 1990 with the sole condition that he would not be sentenced to death. Canada and South Africa imposed the same condition on extraditions in 2001.

In a dissent to a denial of certiorari in the 2009 case *Thompson v. McNeil*, Justice John Paul Stevens argued that the average time spent on death row highlights the "fundamental inhumanity" and "unworkability" of the death penalty. Justice Stephen Breyer had expressed similar sentiments in his dissent from the denial of certiorari of two 1999 cases in which two inmates, who had spent 20 and 25 years on death row, argued that their prolonged stays on death row constituted cruel and unusual punishment. No majority decision of the U.S. Supreme Court, however, has ever agreed with these sentiments, although other countries have. In 1993, the British court of last resort for Caribbean Commonwealth countries ruled that it was "inhumane and degrading" in a manner constituting double punishment to execute a prisoner who had spent more than five years on death row. As a result, all such death row inmates have their sentences commuted to life in prison. For the same reasons, the president of Kenya commuted more than 4,000 death sentences in 2009.

The extensive judicial processes and special correctional procedures involved in capital cases make death sentences extremely costly. Most studies conclude that it costs two to four times more to try, convict, incarcerate, and execute a capital offender than it does to imprison an inmate for life without the possibility of parole. For example, Florida executed 44 people between 1976 and 2000 at a cost of $24 million per execution. This $1.056 billion cost amounts to approximately $51 million each year beyond the cost of incarcerating all first-degree murderers for life in the state.

Death Row Inmates
Racial and ethnic disparities in death sentences account, in large part, for the racial and ethnic composition of the death row inmate population. Of the 1,235 prisoners executed between 1976 and January 1, 2011, 696 (56 percent) were white, 427 (35 percent) were black, 91 (7 percent) were Hispanic, and 24 (2 percent) were "other." Blacks are significantly overrepresented in proportion to their prevalence in the U.S. population by an overall ratio of 3.5 to 1; in some states, however, the ratio is much higher, ranging from 5 to 1 in Connecticut to 29 to 1 in Utah. Blacks and Hispanics are significantly more likely to be condemned to death for the same crime than a white defendant. This is especially the case in interracial murders; only 15 whites have been executed for killing a black victim while 247 blacks have been executed for killing white victims. In spite of these disparities, the U.S. Supreme Court upheld the death penalty over due process and equal protection challenges in *McCleskey v. Kemp* (1987), reasoning that no constitutional violation takes place unless particularized discrimination can be proven in a specific case.

Direct telephone lines labeled "Attorney General," "Supreme Court," "Warden," and "Governor" and topped with red lights were installed for last-minute communications at the newly constructed Lethal Injection Facility at California's San Quentin State Prison in 2010. Partly because of lengthy judicial reviews of death sentences after 1976, condemned inmates may spend between 10 and 20 years awaiting execution. The 52 inmates executed in the United States in 2009 spent an average of 14 years and one month on death row.

Death row inmates are overwhelmingly male, revealing extreme gender differences in the way capital cases are handled. Even though women commit roughly 10 percent of all known homicides, only 12 women have been executed since 1976. In 2009, women comprised only 1.9 percent of the total death row population.

Of inmates under sentences of death, 42 percent graduated high school, 36 percent reached a 9th to 11th grade educational level, and 14 percent reached the 8th grade level or less; 9 percent received some college instruction. Almost 55 percent of death row inmates never married; 20.5 percent were either divorced or separated, 21.9 percent were married while on death row, and 2.8 percent were widowed. Only 8.6 percent of death row inmates had a prior homicide conviction at the time they were sentenced to death; 65.7 percent of them, however, had prior felony convictions.

Among all inmates awaiting execution, 29.1 percent were between the ages of 30 and 39, 51 percent were 25 to 44, 1.2 percent were under the age of 25, and 2.6 percent were older than 65. The average age at the time of arrest for the capital crime was 28 years. The 2005 U.S. Supreme Court decision in *Roper v. Simmons* restricted the death penalty to defendants who were at least 18 years of age at the time they committed their crimes. Prior to that case, however, 200 juvenile offenders had been sentenced to death in the post-*Furman* era; half of such sentences were handed down in Texas, Florida, and Alabama.

Of these, 17 were executed for crimes committed while 16 or 17 years of age, all of them were male, and three-quarters of them were minorities. At the other end of the spectrum, capital prisoners over age 65 present significant problems for the justice system. Seniors are housed in death row with other condemned prisoners, not in the geriatric units available for general population inmates. The constitutionality of executing seniors who suffer from dementia and other age-related impairments is questionable, especially in light of the Supreme Court's 1986 decision in *Ford v. Wainwright*, which held that the Eighth Amendment forbids capital punishment of offenders who became mentally incompetent, reasoning that execution of those who do not understand the reasons for doing so was cruel and unusual.

In the 2002 case *Atkins v. Virginia*, the U.S. Supreme Court held that executions of mentally retarded criminals were prohibited by the Eighth Amendment. In spite of *Atkins* and *Ford v. Wainwright*, clinical studies report that between one-quarter and two-thirds of death row inmates possess borderline intellectual functioning and upward of 85 percent suffer from an Axis I disorder as classified by the American Psychiatric Association in its *Diagnostic and Statistical Manual of Mental Disorders*.

Janet Ruiz
Henry F. Fradella
California State University, Long Beach

See Also: 1961 to 1980 Primary Documents; 1981 to 2000 Primary Documents; Capital Punishment; Clemency; Corrections; Cruel and Unusual Punishment; Electric Chair, History of; Executions; *Furman v. Georgia*; *Gregg v. Georgia*; Hanging; Sentencing.

Further Readings
Cunningham, Mark D. and Mark P. Vigen. "Death Row Inmate Characteristics, Adjustment, and Confinement: A Critical Review of the Literature." *Behavioral Sciences and the Law*, v.20/1–2 (2002).
Paternoster, Raymond, Robert Brame, and Sarah Bacon. *The Death Penalty: America's Experience With Capital Punishment*. New York: Oxford University Press, 2008.
Roberts, Marie Mulvey. *Writing for Their Lives: Death Row U.S.A.* Champaign: University of Illinois Press, 2007.
Walker, Ida. *The Death Penalty: Essential Viewpoints*. Edina, MN: ABDO Publishing, 2008.

Declaration of Independence

The Declaration of Independence is probably the most treasured and revered document in the history of the United States. With this document, the colonists declared their independence from

Great Britain and the American Revolution was justified, which resulted in the formal independence of the thirteen colonies from King George III and Great Britain and the eventual creation of the United States of America. In fact, the American Revolution had already started with the battles of Concord and Lexington before the Declaration of Independence was signed. Moreover, King George III had already issued a Proclamation of Rebellion against the thirteen colonies the year before, in 1775.

Ratification
The Continental Congress, the legislative body formed by the founding fathers, enacted the Declaration of Independence on July 4, 1776, in Philadelphia, Pennsylvania. It was signed by numerous leaders of the colonies. However, the enactment of the declaration was not a foregone conclusion. Some of the colonies were wary of signing a formal document proclaiming their independence. The Declaration of Independence was a dangerous document. For, as Benjamin Franklin is said to have stated: "If we do not hang together we most certainly will all hang separately." Any man who signed the Declaration of Independence was signing his death warrant if the revolution were lost.

Although a committee by the Continental Congress was appointed to write the Declaration of Independence, Thomas Jefferson is credited with writing the greatest part of it. After the draft was approved by the committee, it was sent to the full Congress for ratification. Twelve of the colonies voted for ratification, with New York abstaining because the New York delegation had not received permission to vote for it. New York ended up ratifying the Declaration of Independence a week later.

The majority of the Declaration of Independence lists the grievances of the thirteen colonies against King George III and Great Britain. Although many of these reasons, today, would not likely justify a revolution, they were sufficient in the minds of the founding fathers. The Declaration of Independence is renowned not for the list of grievances it presents but for several basic principles that form the basis of the political philosophy of the founding fathers and the nation they founded.

Principles
The first, and arguably the most important, principle set forth in the Declaration of Independence is that under the natural law and God, all men are entitled to have equal and separate station in life; when their current political circumstances deny them this right, they are entitled to sever those political bonds. This principle leads directly into the second principle of the Declaration of Independence, which is that all men are created equal and endowed with certain inalienable rights. This clause presents the fundamental importance of the individual and that men are entitled to certain rights that cannot be taken from them. The third principle is that each man has certain inalienable rights, which include the right to life, liberty, and the pursuit of happiness. The fourth principle is that the purpose of government is to secure those rights, not to oppress the people for the benefit of the few who occupy the upper echelons of society. The fifth principle is that when a government becomes destructive of these ends (i.e., protecting the life, liberty, and the pursuit of happiness of its citizens), then the people have the right to alter or abolish that government.

This right to change the government was founded on the Magna Carta, a political document written in the 13th century that allowed the nobles to rebel against the king if he oppressed them. Further, the idea of natural rights was expressed by English legal philosopher Sir William Blackstone, who, before the American Revolution, codified the English common law in his *Commentaries in the Laws of England*. Also, prior to and concurrent with the American Revolution was a philosophical period in Europe known as the Enlightenment. The Enlightenment included many famous social and political philosophers, such as John Locke, Baron Montesquieu, and Jean-Jacques Rousseau, who championed individual rights and liberty. Thus, the basic principles espoused in the Declaration of Independence were not new and had been previously recognized in English history and in the philosophy of the Enlightenment.

This right to revolt, which was specifically recognized in the Declaration of Independence, was implicitly recognized by the enactment of the individual right to keep and bear arms in the Bill of Rights. However, since that time, the U.S. Supreme Court has declined to formally recognize the right to revolt and has refused to consider the Declaration of Independence as a legally binding instrument, as is the Constitution and the Bill of Rights. This posture is understandable, as it appears incongruous for a court of a nation to rule that it is legal to revolt and abolish that nation's government. Thus, in one sense, it is difficult to say that the Declaration of Independence has had a lasting historical impact on the criminal justice system in America. However, that does not diminish the power or authority of the Declaration of Independence concerning its expression of American political philosophy.

The Declaration of Independence has greatly influenced many Americans in their passionate belief in the American political and legal system as the best in the world because the formation of the American nation was based on such revolutionary principles as individual liberty and freedom.

Wm. C. Plouffe, Jr.
Independent Scholar

See Also: Bill of Rights; Blackstone, William; Civil Disobedience; Constitution of the United States of America; Jefferson, Thomas (Administration of); Magna Carta.

Further Readings
Bailyn, Bernard. *The Ideological Origins of the American Revolution*. Cambridge, MA: Harvard University Press, 1992.
Countryman, Edward. *The American Revolution*. New York: Hill & Wang, 1985.
Maier, Pauline. *American Scripture: Making the Declaration of Independence*. New York: Knopf, 1997.
Plouffe, William C., Jr. "A Federal Court Holds the Second Amendment Is an Individual Right: Jeffersonian Utopia or Apocalypse Now?" *University of Memphis Law Review*, v.30 (1999).

Defendant's Rights

A defendant is the person charged with a crime by a prosecutor or grand jury. Until the time of charging, which marks the beginning of adversarial proceedings, he or she is known as a suspect. The rights of defendants are set forth in the Fifth and Six Amendments to the Constitution, although their origins exist in antiquity and English common law. The Fifth Amendment guarantees a defendant due process of law, freedom from self-incrimination, and protection against double jeopardy. The Sixth Amendment guarantees a fair, speedy, and public trial by an impartial jury; knowledge of the charges against him/her; representation by counsel; the right to be present at the trial and to confront witnesses; and procedures for obtaining witnesses.

American jurisprudence is adversarial. It is a "battle" between the prosecution and defense in which the judge acts as a relatively passive referee. It is governed by three major principles of procedural due process: the presumed innocence of the defendant, the burden of proof on the prosecution, and the level of proof beyond a reasonable doubt.

The Fifth Amendment
The concept of due process originates in the Magna Carta (1215), in which the king asserted that the government could not take away a person's property or freedom "except by the lawful judgment of his peers or by the law of the land." The phrase "due process of law" was substituted for the phrase "the law of the land" in the 1354 revision of the Magna Carta. Due process of law has to do with fundamental fairness in the way in which the government deals with the defendant. There are two types of due process: substantive and procedural. Substantive due process requires that the laws themselves be fair and constitutional. Procedural due process requires that the procedures by which the laws are applied be fair, as well. Legal authorities must satisfy a set of requirements when depriving someone of his/her freedom.

The concept of freedom from self-incrimination (also known as the right to remain silent) is deceptively simple: Government cannot force citizens to testify against their will. A fairly late addition to English law, freedom from self-incrimination came about as a result of Puritan John Lilburne's trial before England's Star Chamber. After refusing to take the oath ex officio, which meant that defendants had to swear to answer truthfully before they were questioned, Lilburne was pilloried and whipped. This led Parliament to declare Lilburne's punishment illegal, disband the Star Chamber, and recognize the right against self-incrimination. Although many other Puritan settlers had been persecuted by the British government, the Massachusetts Bodie of Liberties, which consisted of Puritans, allowed the use of torture to obtain confessions in capital cases. James Madison likely had both British and colonial history in mind when he included this clause in the Fifth Amendment. This right is the basis of the Miranda warnings, by which a suspect is informed that he or she has "the right to remain silent." It prohibits the state from forcing a defendant to confess his/her crime.

The government is prohibited from prosecuting a person twice for the same crime (also known as protection against double jeopardy). Although the concept can be traced to antiquity and is considered a core principle of common law, English law defined it narrowly to apply only to capital felonies. In the U.S. Constitution, it applies to all crimes. In the United States, this right was not made applicable to the states until 1969, in *Benton v. Maryland*. The doctrine demands that the state "get it right" when it prosecutes someone, because it will not get another chance.

The Sixth Amendment

The origins of the right to a speedy trial may be found in the Magna Carta and the Virginia Declaration of Rights of 1776. Although the Constitution does not specify exactly what is meant by a "speedy trial," the federal government and the states have set guidelines intended to move trials quickly through the system. If the prosecution cannot meet the requirements, a case may be dismissed. Some reasons for a speedy trial are to prevent defendants who cannot make bail from languishing in jail (which increases the cost to the state and to the families of the accused); to ensure that witnesses are available and that their memories are accurate; and to protect the public from criminals who are out on bail. Despite this right, many courts have large case backlogs, and cases often take a long time.

While not mentioned in English legal documents, the right to a public trial was considered a common law privilege. It first appears in the Pennsylvania Constitution of 1776 and is important for several reasons. First, it allows the community to see that justice is being carried out, which can have a deterrent effect on future criminals. Second, it guarantees that the defendant is not treated unfairly by prosecutors and judges. Unfair treatment was common during the Spanish Inquisition and Star Chamber proceedings. The right to a public trial is not an absolute right, since seating in the courtroom is limited to the courtroom's capacity, judges have discretion over who may be in the courtroom, and the judge may deny access to spectators who are disruptive or whose presence is intended to intimidate witnesses. The press cannot be denied access to the trial, but judges can impose limitations in order to keep order and protect the defendant's rights. Judges also decide whether cameras will be allowed in the courtroom. Juveniles do not have the right to a public trial, although some states do not close juvenile trials to the public.

The origins of the right to a fair trial by an impartial jury may be traced to Viking and Norman conquerors of England, although it did not become an integral part of English law until it was included in the Magna Carta. Prior to this, jury members were witnesses to a defendant's trial. The defendant might have to do battle or undergo a physical trial such as taking a rock out of a pot of boiling water. Guilt or innocence would then be determined by how quickly the person's skin healed. By the 17th century, trial by jury had become an integral part of English law, so much so that it was a key element in the constitutions of the original 13 states. It served as a check on government power. In *Duncan v. Louisiana* (1968), the Supreme Court argued that a jury greatly lessens the chance of unfairness on behalf of the judge or the prosecutor.

An impartial jury is one that has not had its judgment influenced unduly by publicity surrounding the case. A judge may limit the effect of such publicity by changing the venue, sequestering the jury, granting a continuance, imposing a "gag rule," or controlling the press. Changing the venue means moving the trial from one locale, such as a county, to another in an effort to find an impartial jury. Sequestering the jury means keeping the jury together for the duration of the trial under the watchful eye of the court in order to prevent

A lawyer stands to argue the case of a female defendant charged with murder at a trial in Annapolis, Maryland, in 1871. The Fifth Amendment guarantees a defendant due process of law, freedom from self-incrimination, and protection against double jeopardy, while the Sixth Amendment guarantees a fair, speedy, and public trial by an impartial jury; knowledge of the charges against him or her; representation by counsel; the right to be present at the trial and to confront witnesses; and procedures for obtaining witnesses.

members' being exposed to media reports about the trial. Granting a continuance means postponing the trial in order to allow publicity to subside. Imposing a "gag rule" means that the judge forbids the attorneys, police officers, witnesses, and jury who are affiliated with a trial from speaking publicly about the trial. Controlling the press means limiting the access of the press.

The right to be present at the trial and to confront accusers is based both on the consideration of due process and on the confrontation clause of the Sixth Amendment. In order to exercise the rights to confront and obtain witnesses, the defendant must be physically present at his/her trial. Their origins may be found in Roman law and in Blackstone's *Commentaries on the Laws of England*. Both sources stress the importance of examining witnesses face to face in order to arrive at the truth. Defendants who are able to hear and see a witness testify against them may likely prepare a better defense. Also, a witness who testifies in front of a defendant may be more likely to understand the importance of testifying truthfully.

In recent years, the court has decreed that in cases in which confrontation with the defendant may be difficult or impossible for the witness, the witness need not be in the courtroom with the defendant. In *Maryland v. Craig* (1990), a case in which Craig was being tried for the sexual abuse of a 6-year-old, the judge determined that the child would suffer too much distress to be able to testify effectively. The child was allowed to testify in another room in front of the prosecutor and defense attorney while the judge, jury, and defendant observed via closed-circuit television from the courtroom. The right to be present may be forfeited by defendants who disrupt or abscond from their trials.

The right to compulsory procedure to obtain witnesses is relatively new in American jurisprudence. It was not until after the Revolutionary War that some state constitutions permitted defendants to call witnesses in their defense and gave them power to bring those witnesses to the trial. When James Madison included this right in an early version of the Bill of Rights, it was accepted without discussion. This right gives subpoena power to the defense equal to that of the prosecution in order to compel witnesses to testify on their behalf.

The right to counsel, too, is relatively new. In English law, defendants had no right to an attorney except under certain circumstances, and then they had to hire their own. After 1688, only defendants charged with treason were granted the right by Parliament to have an attorney. In the American colonies, defendants were generally prohibited from hiring an attorney, although some colonies appointed attorneys in certain cases. One shortcoming of the Constitution, in the eyes of many Americans, was its failure to offer enough protections of individual rights, one of which was the right to counsel. Consequently, it was included in the Sixth Amendment.

The right to counsel is unique among Sixth Amendment rights in that it applies beyond the scope of the trial. The Supreme Court has identified critical stages in the criminal justice process during which a suspect or defendant is in need of an attorney to protect his/her rights. At the investigation stage, the suspect has a right to counsel during police interrogation. At the pretrial stage, the suspect has a right to counsel once the proceedings against the defendant have turned adversarial (i.e., during the arraignment, the preliminary hearing, identification processes, and when submitting a guilty plea).

Originally, the right to counsel meant that a defendant had a right to an attorney as long as he or she could afford one. Certain landmark cases led to a different interpretation of the right, in light of the difficulty that a layperson would have in defending himself or herself before the power of the state. The finding in *Powell v. Alabama* (1932), the first "Scottsboro Boys" case, was that a defendant in a capital case must be assigned counsel if he or she is unable to afford it. In *Gideon v. Wainwright* (1963), the Supreme Court found that indigent defendants in felony cases were to be assigned an attorney. In *Argersinger v. Hamlin* (1972), the court expanded this right to misdemeanor defendants. In *In re Gault* (1967), the court found that a juvenile who stands a chance of being incarcerated in a state institution has a right to counsel. Essentially, anytime a defendant is in danger of losing his or her freedom, he or she has the right to representation by an attorney at state expense. In addition, a person who has been convicted of a crime has a right to counsel for his/her first appeal.

A defendant may waive his/her right to counsel, as long as he or she can satisfy the court that he or she clearly understands what it means to give up the right to counsel and that he or she is doing so voluntarily. A defendant may act as his/her own counsel, or "pro se" (meaning "for himself"). Again, however, the court must be satisfied that the defendant is aware of his/her right to counsel, that he or she is making a valid waiver of that right, and that the defendant is competent to do so. Along with the right to counsel is the presumption of effective counsel. Defendants who are convicted are often unhappy and believe that their attorney did not represent them effectively. This belief is difficult to prove, however. In *Strickland v. Washington* (1984), the court ruled that a defendant must show that the representation provided by his/her counsel prevented him/her from receiving a fair trial. As this is quite difficult to show, most appeals on the grounds of ineffective counsel fail.

James Geistman
Ohio Northern University

See Also: Arraignment; Bill of Rights; Common Law Origins of Criminal Law; Constitution of the United States of America; Due Process; *Gideon v. Wainwright*; Prisoner's Rights; Scottsboro Boys Cases; Suspect's Rights; Trials.

Further Readings
Carp, Robert A. and Ronald Stidham. *Judicial Process in America*, 8th ed. Washington, DC: CQ Press, 2010.
del Carmen, R. V. *Criminal Procedure: Law and Practice*, 8th ed. Belmont, CA: Wadsworth, 2009.
Harr, J. Scott and Kären M. Hess. *Constitutional Law and the Criminal Justice System*, 4th ed. Belmont, CA: Wadsworth, 2008.

Delaware

One of the smallest U.S. states, Delaware is also one of the most densely populated states, with more than half of its 900,000 residents living in affluent New Castle County. Many of Delaware's legal records and laws from the colonial period have been lost to the historical record. For some of that period (1664–1704), Delaware (originally a Swedish colony, but then owned by the English) was part of Pennsylvania and operated under its laws; dissatisfied with that, Delaware seceded from Pennsylvania, but continued under English control during the Revolutionary War. Many of its early statutes in the 18th century were passed in order to clarify the legal environment, because Delaware courts had previously operated under Swedish, English, and Pennsylvanian laws.

Crime

As in some of the other former colonies, the post–Revolutionary War period saw more legislative activity, clarifying the state's relationship to English common law and individuating its legal codes. For instance, in the post-Pennsylvanian colonial period, a sodomy law had been enacted that affirmed that English common law—which called for the death penalty—would be upheld in Delaware. This was revised in 1826 as part of a wide-scale revision of Delaware criminal law, and the death penalty for sodomy was reduced to a maximum of three years in prison and a $1,000 fine.

The Revolutionary War also led to the partial outlawing of slavery in Delaware. The war had disrupted the economy, and wheat (which didn't depend on slave labor) replaced corn and tobacco (which did depend on slave labor) as the state's biggest cash crop. The new state leaders outlawed the importation of slaves in the state's new constitution, and in 1789, slave ships were barred from Delaware ports. The laws made it increasingly hard to sell slaves in order to discourage the slave trade, and by the turn of the 19th century, any Delaware slave sold out of state was automatically freed—essentially making those sales impossible. Despite this, attempts to abolish slavery entirely, beginning in 1792 and repeatedly attempted, failed until the Civil War.

Early law enforcement in Delaware consisted of constables responsible for keeping the peace during the day, and a night watch—often just one watchman per town, or in larger towns like Wilmington, one watchman per ward—with similar duties at night. Hours were long (typically 12 hours) and job duties might include other town chores: The night watch of Wilmington, for instance, was also responsible for lighting and trimming the wicks of the town's street lamps. During the 19th century, these constabulary forces were gradually replaced by city police, though they did not resemble a modern police department until late in the century. Until then, police constables were appointed and dismissed by local government—the mayor or town council, depending on the locality—which too often led to men being appointed to the police force by a new mayor as a political favor. Only when the state legislature passed the Metropolitan Police Act in 1891 were Delaware police departments professionalized, with a board of commissioners to oversee them, and a law requiring that officers be terminated only for just cause, with the right to a hearing to plead their case. Only two years after the act, the first female police officers, called matrons, were hired. Although their primary function was to guard female prisoners, they were sworn officers with the same powers as male officers. In the 20th century, the state's highway traffic police force was created (in 1919, reorganizing as the Delaware State Police in 1923), and local police departments added detectives. The Police School of Instruction was founded in 1916 as the state's first police academy, and a forerunner of the SWAT team was instituted in Wilmington in 1922, with a special division of officers trained in submachine guns and other specialized weapons.

During Prohibition, the state created the Department of Prohibition in order to enforce the new alcohol restrictions. After Prohibition's repeal, there was little formal alcohol regulation in the state for 20 years, during which time the few basic regulations that did exist (particularly those dealing with licensing and taxation) were overseen by "revenuers." They were frequently corrupt bureaucrats who attained their positions through political connections. The Delaware Alcoholic Beverage Control Commission was created in 1955 to move away from this and to respond to a new concern over youth drinking as parents around the country worried about the specter of juvenile delinquency.

Over the next few years, the licensing and regulation system was overhauled and formalized, and in the following decades, agents of the Division of Alcoholic Beverage Control were made police officers with statewide jurisdiction. In the 1990s, they were further tasked with the enforcement of tobacco laws, especially to enforce the 1998 mandatory federal Synar Amendment, which required states to test at least 10 percent of the tobacco retailers in their borders to ensure that they were not selling tobacco products to minors. In 2004, the division was reorganized and renamed the Division of Alcohol and Tobacco Enforcement. Its investigations include alcohol and tobacco offenses, organized crime, tax evasion, prostitution, gambling, and the manufacture and distribution of fake IDs.

Punishment

During the ramp-up of the war on drugs in the 1980s, Delaware adopted legislation imposing mandatory minimum sentences for a number of drug crimes, feeling that there was too little consistency across the sentences handed out by judges and that stricter punishments would be an effective deterrent. From 1981 to 2008, the average daily prison population in Delaware had risen from 1,562 to 7,100, at a cost to the taxpayers of about $30,000 per inmate. By 2008, 80 percent of the prison population was estimated to be in need of substance abuse treatment, but only half received it, and of varying quality and efficacy, contributing to a 60 percent recidivism rate.

In 2010, the state began rolling back those mandatory minimums in the case of first-time offenders; it also reclassified drug possession of small quantities as a misdemeanor, rather than a felony. Further, the new sentencing structure prevented prosecutors from charging a defendant with multiple crimes with mandatory minimum sentences, instead using a variety of base charges modified by aggravators, in order to avoid disproportionately long sentences. The new sentencing structure also more clearly delineated between the crimes of drug use and the crimes of drug dealing.

At the same time, while some states have begun to move away from drug criminalization, the new Delaware drug laws are actually stricter in specific areas. Increased penalties were added for distributing drugs near schools or parks or for drug dealers who resisted arrest with violence. Maximum sentences for the illegal sale of prescription drugs were increased. And a new crime was defined: allowing one's dwelling to be used as the site for drug deliveries.

National Drug Policy Director Gil Kerlikowske at the signing of the Delaware Prescription Monitoring Act on July 22, 2010. The act created a new state monitoring database for frequently abused drugs such as OxyContin, Adderall, and Percocet.

Delaware was the last state to end the use of flogging as a punishment. By the 20th century, flogging had become very rare, but remained on the books as a sentencing option for 25 crimes. Abolished in 1972, it had been used as recently as 1964.

Delaware's Department of Corrections is a unified corrections system, meaning that there is no separate regional, county, or municipal corrections or jail system, nor a separate probation system. The state takes responsibility for all corrections business and community-based sanctions. Most offenders serve their time in jail (sentences of less than one year), rather than prison (sentences of one or more years), and a large number of those held in jail are defendants awaiting trial who cannot make bail. Parole was abolished in 1990, except for those inmates whose sentences had been imposed prior to that year. The state's oldest correctional facility, the Sussex Correctional

Institution (SCI), was founded in 1931. In 1997, Delaware's first and thus far only correctional boot camp was added to the SCI site. The boot camp is home to 100 inmates designated "cadets," nonviolent offenders, and first-time drug offenders who are given a regimented, military-style routine of exercise, substance abuse treatment, education, and community service.

Delaware is a state that practices capital punishment. The death penalty was reenacted in 1974 after temporarily being suspended after the 1972 Supreme Court decision in *Furman v. Georgia* made extant death penalty statutes unconstitutional. Predating the 1976 Supreme Court cases that clarified the relationship between capital punishment and constitutionality, this 1974 law proved faulty when evaluated by the Delaware Supreme Court in light of those decisions, and in 1977, the legislature passed a new death penalty statute modeled on the law that the Supreme Court upheld in 1976's *Gregg v. Georgia*. Hanging was the method of execution until 1986, when the legislature passed a law allowing the convicted to choose between hanging or lethal injection. In 1991, when a jury returned a guilty verdict but failed to sentence the defendants to death in *Robertson v. Delaware*, the legislature amended the death penalty statute to eliminate jury sentencing, an amendment that was applied to capital trials already pending, since it was adjudicated that the change was procedural. The statute was amended again in 2002, when the Supreme Court ruled in *Ring v. Arizona* that a jury must find the factors that make the death penalty an eligible sentence. The new law, which remains in effect, requires that a jury unanimously find a statutory aggravating circumstance; it then makes a recommendation to the judge, who has ultimate sentencing power.

Bill Kte'pi
Independent Scholar

See Also: 1921 to 1940 Primary Documents; 1961 to 1980 Primary Documents; American Revolution and Criminal Justice; Capital Punishment; Corporal Punishment; Hangings; Supreme Court, U.S.

Further Readings
Blume, John H., et al. "The Death Penalty in Delaware: An Empirical Study." Cornell Law Faculty Publications. http://scholarship.law.cornell.edu/lsrp_papers/110 (Accessed September 2011).
Munroe, John A. *History of Delaware*. Lanham, MD: Lexington Books, 2006.

Democratic National Convention of 1968

See Chicago Seven/Democratic National Convention of 1968.

Dennis v. United States

During World War II, the Soviet Union and the United States were allies in the fight against Nazi Germany. The fact that the Soviet Union was a communist nation was not a major problem during the war. Communism was, however, gaining in popularity in the United States, so Congress enacted the Smith Act in 1940, which made it a crime to advocate, aid, advise the violent overthrow of the U.S. government, or belong to any association that advocated such a violent overthrow. After the end of World War II, with the Soviet isolation of Eastern Europe, the construction of the Berlin Wall, the trials of the Rosenbergs for espionage, and the Soviet Union's development of atomic weapons, a second Red Scare descended upon America. Shortly after World War II, President Harry S. Truman created the Federal Employees Loyalty Program to help address the perceived problem of communist spies in the government. This Red Scare was brought to its zenith by the activities of Senator Joe McCarthy and the House Un-American Activities Committee during the 1950s.

Eugene Dennis was a longtime member of the Communist Party in America. By the end of World War II, he had become the General Secretary of the Communist Party USA. As a member and general secretary, he engaged in numerous political activities on behalf of the Communist Party. In 1947, Dennis voluntarily appeared before the House Un-American Activities Committee. At that time, Congress had two bills under consideration to outlaw the Communist Party. When questioned by the committee, Dennis refused to answer any questions about his name, date of birth, or place of birth. As a result, the chairman of the House Un-American Activities Committee ordered that a subpoena be served on Dennis for April 9, 1947. On the appointed date, Dennis failed to appear. The committee reported the failure to appear to the House of Representatives and the House certified the report of nonappearance to the U.S. Attorney for the District of Columbia for prosecution.

Dennis and 11 other leaders of the Communist Party USA were indicted, arrested, and brought to trial on charges of violating the Smith Act. Prior to the start of the trial, Dennis asked the trial court to transfer the case to another district on the grounds that he could not receive a fair trial as government employees comprised the majority of the population of the District of Columbia and were subject to President Truman's Federal Employees Loyalty Program and possibly biased because of his status as a communist. The trial court denied the motion. During the trial, the government had difficulty proving that Dennis actually advocated the violent overthrow of the U.S. government, causing the government to rely on quotations from Marx and testimony from other witnesses that Dennis had privately advocated this. Dennis was then convicted at trial of willfully refusing to testify before the House Un-American Activities Committee, in violation of the Smith Act. Dennis appealed to the U.S. Supreme Court on the grounds that he was denied a fair and impartial jury.

On appeal, the Supreme Court affirmed his conviction. What is remarkable about the decision in the *Dennis* case is that both the two concurring justices and the two dissenting justices criticized the application of the clear and present danger test announced in the decision of the U.S. Supreme Court in *Schenck v. United States* in 1919 when considering the free speech clause of the First Amendment in criminal cases. Essentially, the dissenting justices and later decisions of the Supreme Court took cognizance of the lack of immediacy to the threat of violent overthrow of the government. It would not be until the case of *Brandenburg v. Ohio* in 1969 that the requirement of imminence of the threat would be formally recognized as a requirement for such speech not to be protected by the First Amendment. However, the *Dennis* decision is also historically important in the American criminal justice system in that it illustrates that constitutional civil rights are frequently, if not always, in danger in times of national political hysteria, as illustrated by the decision of *Schenck v. United States*.

Wm. C. Plouffe, Jr.
Independent Scholar

See Also: Civil Rights Laws; Political Crimes, History of; Political Dissidents; Political Policing; *Schenck v. United States*.

Further Readings
Fried, Albert. *McCarthyism, the Great American Red Scare: A Documentary History.* New York: Oxford University Press, 1990.
Haynes, John Earl. *Red Scare or Red Menace? American Communism and Anti-Communism in the Cold War Era.* Chicago: Ivan R. Dee, 2000.
Rabban, David. "The Emergence of Modern First Amendment Doctrine." *University of Chicago Law Review,* v.50 (1983).

Deportation

Legally understood as a civil procedure rather than criminal punishment, deportation—and the spatial-political banishment it entails—nonetheless has interacted with forms of law and social/territorial control since European colonization of the Americas. Proponents of deportation have seen it as a "second line" of defense against illegal immigration and the self-evident right of a sovereign polity to control its territory and population. Critics have seen it as an effort to create an amorphous mechanism of state control over labor markets and global populations: a means to repress political radicals; enforce a shifting, contested, moral order; and practice social-Darwinist racial eugenics.

Colonial Poor Laws
In the colonial period, governments set provisions on who might enter their lands and who might

be forced to leave. They feared that European nations were deporting their convicted criminals into the colonies, and colonial laws dictated that prospective migrants convicted of crime would not be allowed to land. Impoverished travelers fared little better. Colonial deportation evolved from English law and the concept of "jus solis"—membership based on birth. More specifically, the English poor laws justified expelling those people seen as likely to become a drain on parish coffers. Unwed pregnant women not born in the locality where they resided might be forced out so that citizens would not have to care for the mother or the child she bore. As with the control of criminals, these approaches were transferred to U.S. state and federal law. In 1794, Massachusetts required that arriving paupers be returned to their natal towns "or to any other State, or to any place beyond the sea, where he belongs."

Alien and Sedition Acts

Federal deportation laws first focused on political belief with the Alien and Sedition Acts (1798–1801). Under the acts, noncitizens thought to pose a threat to the nation could be deported at the president's discretion. Though highly contentious and not widely enforced, the acts prompted a number of noncitizens to leave the country. Thus, while U.S. law developed regulations on noncitizens' political beliefs, it strengthened the practice of noncitizens' "voluntary" departure when more forcible measures loomed.

Chinese Exclusion Act

In the late 19th century, white citizens, believing that national integrity was under threat, passed a series of restrictive immigration laws. Though the 1875 Page Act was geared toward the exclusion of unfree Chinese "coolie" laborers, it also forbade the arrival of criminals, prostitutes, and other "immoral classes." The 1882 Chinese Exclusion Act prohibited the immigration of the Chinese as a racial group, though it did differentiate by class: merchants and diplomats could still enter. The 1891 Immigration Act and the 1892 Geary Act compounded the legal bases for Chinese and many others' deportation. Subsequent acts expanded the range of excludable and deportable categories, including criminals, the insane, the epileptic, those deemed "likely to become a public charge," and, with the ascendance of scientific racism, those judged biologically or morally "unfit." Noncitizens convicted of crime after arrival were readily despised for wrongdoing, compounded by ethno-racial and national difference. Conviction of crimes of "moral turpitude"—a widely interpreted category—also became a deportable offense. The laws lengthened the time period during which the growing list of people might be expelled, and some offenses were made retroactively enforceable. The Palmer Raids, a series of antiradical sweeps in 1919–20, expelled a great many dissidents as "enemy aliens," but also prompted liberal response that mitigated, for the time being, the harshest measures of political deportation, and would eventually give rise to modest protections for potential deportees.

Nativism

The 1930s saw a massive upswell of nativist expulsion, combining formal deportation with informal "repatriation." An estimated 1 million Mexicans, many of whom were born in the United States and thus were citizens, were removed from the nation early in the Depression to protect jobs for white citizens. Sweeps in state institutions also intensified. Immigration declined as jobs became scarce, but with the 1940s and following the Alien Registration Act, European migrants experienced a period of relative tolerance. Immigrants who had shown "good moral character" or whose spouses or children were citizens might be granted stays of deportation. Undocumented Mexicans, maligned as "illegal aliens," benefited little from this shift. In World War II, Japanese internment was based on earlier alien enemy acts, though most internees were citizens.

During the cold war, the McCarran-Walter Act (1952) extended existing deportation provisions and revitalized the threat of expelling political dissidents. It also restricted administrators' discretion to prevent deportation, and amnesty was limited to those cases in which deportees would suffer "exceptional and extremely unusual hardship." Ordinary hardship was seen by lawmakers as appropriate to those deemed to threaten cold war security.

Political and Economic Refugees

The 1965 Immigration Act created new opportunities for legal arrival on the bases of family

These Mexican men were being prepared for deportation at a U.S. Customs and Border Protection holding facility. Those who are deported on criminal grounds face imprisonment if they attempt to return. The sentence is 10 years if they reenter the United States illegally and is increased to 20 years if they have been convicted of an aggravated felony. Related crimes, such as the use of false documents, harboring undocumented immigrants, or falsely claiming U.S. citizenship, are also punishable by incarceration.

reunification and skilled labor needs, and migrants from Latin America and Asia responded in considerable numbers.

Others found legal asylum as refugees from communist regimes. Deportation capacities expanded in the 1970s and 1980s, partly in response to these new migratory streams. In the 1980s, a great number of refugees from the United States' Latin American cold war allies came under harsh scrutiny and were threatened with deportation. In the late 1980s and 1990s, attention returned to Mexican nationals at the bottom of stratified labor markets. This came alongside a public rhetorical return to the deportation of "criminal aliens." It closely paralleled the war on drugs, and, later, the war on crime, becoming an analogue to the mass incarceration that nonwhite citizens would face. Provisions against criminal aliens were solidified in 1996 with the Antiterrorism and Effective Death Penalty Act and the Illegal Immigration Reform and Immigrant Responsibility Act. Like the laws passed at the turn of the 20th century, each led to a massive increase in deportation. There were hundreds of thousands of deportations each year in the early 21st century.

Terrorists

Since September 11, 2001, deportation related to military matters was explicitly politicized in the "extraordinary rendition" of accused terrorists to Guantanamo Bay and other secret sites. Deportation continues to reflect tensions over immigration, perceptions of security, economic health, the shifting racial bases of the population, and the meaning of the nation itself.

Ethan Blue
University of Western Australia

See Also: Alien and Sedition Acts of 1798; Border Patrol; Chinese Exclusion Act of 1882; Homeland Security; Immigration Crimes.

Further Readings

Balderrama, Francisco E. and Raymond Rodríguez. *Decade of Betrayal: Mexican Repatriation in the 1930s*. Albuquerque: University of New Mexico Press, 1995.

De Genova, Nicholas and Nathalie Peutz, eds. *The Deportation Regime: Sovereignty, Space, and the Freedom of Movement*. Durham, NC: Duke University Press, 2010.

Dunn, Timothy J. *The Militarization of the U.S.-Mexico Border, 1978–1992: Low-Intensity Conflict Doctrine Comes Home*. Austin, TX: CMAS Books, 1996.

Gutiérrez, David G. *Walls and Mirrors: Mexican Americans, Mexican Immigrants, and the Politics of Ethnicity*. Berkeley: University of California Press, 1995.

Hutchinson, E. P. *Legislative History of American Immigration Policy, 1798–1965*. Philadelphia: University of Pennsylvania Press, 1981.

Kanstroom, Daniel. *Deportation Nation: Outsiders in American History*. Cambridge, MA: Harvard University Press, 2007.

Ngai, Mae M. "The Strange Career of the Illegal Alien: Immigration Restriction and Deportation Policy in the United States, 1921–1965." *Law and History Review*, v.21/1 (2003).

DeSalvo, Albert

Albert DeSalvo, the self-professed Boston Strangler, was born on September 3, 1931, to Charlotte and Frank DeSalvo. Albert's father was an abusive alcoholic who once sold Albert and two of his sisters into slavery to a Maine farmer. The children remained captive for months before returning home. Frank DeSalvo taught Albert to steal at a young age and frequently brought prostitutes into their home. Albert witnessed his father having sex with prostitutes and had his first sexual encounter around the age of six with another child. Albert frequently ran away from home to escape his father's brutality, until finally enlisting in the army in 1948.

Albert met Irmgard Beck while stationed in Frankfurt, Germany, and they eventually married, moved back to the United States, and had two children, Judy and Michael. DeSalvo was honorably discharged in 1956 after allegations of sexual misconduct. In addition to his deviant sexual appetite, DeSalvo would occasionally burglarize homes. DeSalvo was arrested twice in 1958 for breaking and entering and received suspended sentences for both crimes. In the late 1950s, DeSalvo posed as a representative from a modeling agency as a way to gain entrance into the homes of young women. DeSalvo would then seduce the women or offer to take measurements of their body. Although he never assaulted any of these women, the police were called with complaints about a representative failing to follow up after DeSalvo's visit.

DeSalvo was arrested again in 1961 in Cambridge, Massachusetts, and charged with breaking and entering and lewd and lascivious behavior. DeSalvo was subsequently sentenced to 11 months in prison. On June 14, 1962, the killer who would eventually be known as the Boston Strangler took his first victim in a series of stranglings that baffled police and terrorized the city. Anna Slesers, 55, was found dead by her son in her Boston apartment after being sexually assaulted and strangled with a cord from her housecoat that was tied as a bow. There was no sign of forced entry and robbery was ruled out as a possible motive. The Strangler then continued on a series of murders whereby he would sexually assault and strangle women with their own clothing. There seemed to be no apparent motive and victims were both young and elderly. In 1964, DeSalvo was arrested for a string of sexual assaults in Massachusetts and Connecticut. These sexual assaults were known as the Green Man crimes as a result of DeSalvo wearing his green work clothes during the commission of the crimes.

While serving time at Bridgewater State Hospital for the Green Man crimes, DeSalvo and fellow inmate George Nassar had an unusual conversation that led Nassar to believe DeSalvo was the Boston Strangler. Soon after, Nassar contacted his attorney, Lee Bailey, with his suspicions. Although initially reluctant, Bailey interviewed DeSalvo shortly thereafter at the Bridgewater State Hospital. During the interview with Bailey, DeSalvo eventually confessed to 13 murders (11 known Strangler murders as well as two additional killings). With the exception of a few mistakes, DeSalvo provided detailed descriptions of the crimes, including information that had never been released to the general public. Although DeSalvo never provided a concrete motive for his criminal behavior, he at times would attribute his behavior to his wife, sexual impulses, and childhood.

Although DeSalvo confessed to the Strangler killings, the police lacked any concrete evidence tying DeSalvo to the crimes and he was never tried for these killings. DeSalvo was transferred from Bridgewater State Hospital to Walpole Prison in Massachusetts after being sentenced to life for rapes unrelated to the stranglings. On November 25, 1973, DeSalvo was found dead in his cell after being stabbed six times through the heart in a prison brawl after only serving six years. Eyewitnesses never came forward after DeSalvo's death, and inmates at the prison failed to provide any meaningful information leading to a suspect. Decades later, Strangler victim Mary Sullivan was exhumed in order to extract DNA for testing against DeSalvo's. In 2001, tests revealed that the DNA sample from Sullivan's body did not match that of DeSalvo's. Even though it did not completely exonerate DeSalvo, it shed doubt on whether he killed Sullivan or was even the true Boston Strangler. The controversy remains, and the Boston police have not officially closed the Strangler case.

Jacqueline Chavez
Mississippi State University

See Also: Boston, Massachusetts; Famous Trials; Massachusetts; Murders, Unsolved; Serial and Mass Killers; Sex Offenders; Violent Crimes.

Further Readings
Gerold, Frank. *The Boston Strangler.* New York: New American Library, 1966.
Knappman, Edward W. *Great American Trials.* Canton, MI: Visible Ink Press, 2003.

Detection and Detectives

Along with prevention of crime, detection of the criminal is an essential police function. Before modern patrol forces developed in England and the United States, all police who operated during the daytime were detectives. The only force expected to prevent crime by their presence was the night watchmen. Though officially public officers, constables were attached to courts and received fees paid by the victim. Usually, the detective officer had connections in the underworld that were especially useful in cases of burglary or robbery. After talking to his informants, he then confronted the suspect, offering not to arrest him if he returned the property, sometimes letting him retain a portion. The victim recovered some of the property or its value, and the detective kept some as an additional fee.

This was perfectly legal, but reformers were critical. In 1749, English magistrate Henry Fielding created the Bow Street Runners, a force of six men working under his supervision. These detectives were paid out of government funds, and Fielding meant them to supplant the "thief takers," who sometimes, like the notorious Jonathan Wild, worked both sides. The Bow Street Runners, disbanded in 1839, pioneered modern detection. Fielding started a crime reporting function and began publishing the *Covent Garden Journal*, which incorporated descriptions of wanted criminals, similar to the Federal Bureau of Investigation's (FBI) Most Wanted bulletins.

In both England and the United States, many feared detectives as either corrupt colluders with the underworld or secret police who spied on political activities. In England, by the early 19th century, reformers focused on the idea of prevention of crime by regular, professional, uniformed day and night patrols. The preventive ideal was realized in the 1829 Metropolitan Police Act, an innovative piece of legislation specifically designed for the civilian policing of the populace of London.

At first, Sir Robert Peel's legislation was not popular, but eventually the "Bobbies" won at least the acquiescence of Londoners. Nevertheless, fears of detectives lingered, and the new police did not create its first detective branch until 1842. This decision eventually led to the creation of the Criminal Investigations Department (CID) in 1878. Sir Robert Peel and his Metropolitan Police Act of 1829 set precedents for detectives all over the world.

Detectives in the United States

Similarly to Britain, the United States began its urban policing with constables and night watchmen. In 1845, the New York City Police Department (NYPD) became the first police department to offer 24-hour service. This force did without a specialized detective branch for many years, regular officers being "detailed" for special detective duty. Making deals with underworld characters became illegal, "compounding a felony," when preventive forces were established. Detectives continued to rely on the old method because of its practicality, which contributed to the persistent problem of corruption and considerable public suspicion. Some former constables became private detectives, who served victims wanting more efficient or unpublicized recovery of their property.

In New York, it was not until 1857 that the police department authorized and assigned 20 patrol officers as detectives. Other cities like Chicago (1861) soon established detective forces. NYPD detectives organized the rogues' gallery system, which included photographs of criminal offenders arranged by criminal specialty. The detectives studied these photographs to recognize them on the street. By the early 20th century, police detective units were utilizing the latest scientific methods, such as the Bertillon identification system, and fingerprinting and forensic techniques as they developed over the years. Thomas Byrnes, an enterprising NYPD detective captain, published *Professional Criminals in the United States* in 1886, a book that included pictures, descriptions, and methods of operations of criminals. His book encouraged criminal intelligence sharing among other jurisdictions. In the early 1900s, detectives were highly specialized, various urban departments forming vice squads, drug squads, anarchist and red squads, and Italian squads to deal with organized crime. Detectives of this era were not fussy about suspects' constitutional rights. "Third degree" interrogation methods, forms of mental and physical torture, were widely exposed by the Wickersham Commission in 1930, but persisted long after that.

Federal law enforcement did not have detectives until after the Civil War. In 1865, the U.S. Secret Service emerged to prevent and suppress counterfeiting. During 1894, the Secret Service was occasionally involved in guarding President Grover Cleveland. That duty did not become permanent until 1901, after the assassination of President William McKinley.

An early FBI agent reporting on his surveillance of a building using a field radio telephone around 1939. J. Edgar Hoover established the Scientific Crime Laboratory and the National FBI Academy to train field investigative agents in 1932.

The Bureau of Investigation, which eventually became the Federal Bureau of Investigation (FBI), was established in 1908 and paved the way for other investigative agencies. J. Edgar Hoover became the director of the bureau in 1924. He set the foundation for the FBI, which became one of the most prestigious investigative agencies in the United States. Director Hoover concentrated on crimes of high publicity that promised early solution. His focus was on bank robberies and kidnapping. He was primarily responsible for creating the "G-man" (government investigator) public image. Hoover portrayed the G-man as the nation's incorruptible crime fighter. In addition, Hoover established the National FBI Academy to train field investigative agents, as well as the Scientific Crime Laboratory, in 1932. The Uniform Crime Reports established by the FBI were important factors in coordinating crime statistics among police agencies in the United States. The crime laboratory located at Quantico, Virginia, has the most recent scientific technology available.

Director Hoover also focused on political policing, having been one of the organizers of the Red Raids of 1919–20. He never lost his hatred of communism, and during the cold war, the FBI organized operations against communists, leftists, and even liberal leaders like Martin Luther King, Jr. These campaigns were secret, relying on informers and agents provocateurs. Hoover saw himself as an expert on communism, and his *Masters of Deceit* had a profound influence on American thinking. Not only was he popular, but Hoover had embarrassing information about the different presidents he served, making him the longest-term federal official by the time of his death in 1972.

Private Detectives
Several factors created the need for private investigators. First, big-city corruption and graft were rampant, and police officers were directly involved. Police detectives could suppress, manipulate, and ignore criminal investigations and citizen complaints. Detectives, because of their underworld connections and the political nature of police forces, were particularly susceptible to corruption by saloonkeepers, brothel owners, and members of organized crime enterprises. Vice reformers especially received no official help, so they hired private individuals to uncover illicit activities. Second, criminals would cross jurisdictional lines to avoid detection and arrest. Third, there was little criminal information and cooperation among police jurisdictions. In 1846, two former St. Louis detectives established the first private detective agency. The need was clear for private detectives; however, Allan Pinkerton took the service to a higher standard of professionalism. Pinkerton's trademark emblem was an open eye and with a slogan underneath: "We never sleep." Thus, the trade jargon "private eye" became associated with private investigators. Born in Scotland, Allan Pinkerton was the son of a police sergeant, but he supported the working-

Mary A. Shanley, celebrated undercover New York City detective, meets New York Mayor Fiorello H. La Guardia in 1937. Shanley was known for catching pickpockets and thieves, pulling her regulation police revolver out of her handbag.

class political movements of the early 19th century. Eventually, he got into trouble for his politics and fled with his wife to America, surviving a shipwreck. He started a successful barrel making company. While he was owner of that business, his initiative led to the arrest of counterfeiters. This gave him an appetite for police work, his father's profession, and changed his life and American policing forever.

Pinkerton established his agency in 1852, at first working for railroads seeking to stop employee theft and later "troublemaking." He earned national and international respect for meticulous detective work. Some of Pinkerton's accomplishments include discovering and preventing an assassination attempt on President-elect Abraham Lincoln in Baltimore. During the Civil War, he infiltrated Confederate lines to obtain valuable military intelligence. Pinkerton's pursuit of Butch Cassidy (Robert Parker) and the Sundance Kid (Larry Longabaugh) forced them to flee the United States. They were eventually killed in a gun battle with Bolivian soldiers in 1909. The underside of Pinkerton's and other private detective agencies included spying on labor organizers and breaking strikes with hired thugs.

A Pinkerton detective's most famous spying operation was against the Mollie Maguires, a violence-prone organization of Pennsylvania coal miners. His testimony led to the hanging of some of the leaders in 1877. The infamous Pinkerton strike-breaking efforts during the Homestead steel strike of 1892 prompted considerable criticism. Congress even passed an "Anti-Pinkerton" law in response, but industrial spying and strikebreaking by private detective agencies such as Burns and Baldwin-Felts continued through the 1930s.

Forensic Science Contributions

Forensic science is an essential tool of detective work, which has increased in effectiveness as the field has developed. Massachusetts police investigating the murder of Lizzie Borden's parents in 1892 could distinguish cow from human blood on a hatchet, but they did not make use of the new technique of fingerprinting. Forensics developed steadily in the later 19th and early 20th centuries to reach the complexity of today.

In 1856, William Herschel, a British official in India, noted that the pattern of palm prints and fingerprints of an individual never changes, regardless of his or her age. Herschel eventually applied his knowledge to the identification of criminals. In 1900, Edward Henry developed the Henry fingerprint classification system. Henry published *Classification and Use of Finger Prints*, which eventually replaced Bertillon's anthropometric measurement system.

In 1879, Alphonse Bertillon developed a system of anthropometry, or exact physical measurements of the human body. He believed that the sum of these measurements would yield an individual formula that could identify a specific person or criminal. Though popular for several years, the Bertillon system was eventually discredited by contradictions in measurements taken by different individuals.

An Argentine police officer, Juan Vucetich, discovered fingerprints at a crime scene and was able to match them with prints in the department's files. He established the first fingerprint bureau in 1892.

Hans Gross published *Criminal Investigation* in 1893, a primary field publication for detectives that was translated into English in 1906. This book became the major source for criminal investigations, and remains highly respected.

In 1910, Edmond Locard established the first forensic laboratory. Locard's Exchange Principle suggests that when a criminal offender encounters a crime scene, a transfer of trace evidence takes place. Moreover, criminals contribute trace evidence and take trace evidence with them when they depart.

James Watson and Francis Crick inaugurated a new era of genetics and DNA research in 1950. Forensic scientists focused on DNA applications in 1985, and research into the structure of human genes by Alec Jeffreys and his colleagues added a new dimension. They discovered that portions of the DNA structure of certain genes could serve as a unique point of human identification, similar to fingerprints. This discovery led to solving cold cases from earlier decades. It also proved the innocence of many people convicted of crimes, including several on death row. DNA analysis is not perfect, but many people assume that it consistently reveals the truth.

Detection Methods Today

Procedures today vary according to the complexity of the crime and nature of the criminal. Criminal investigative analysts focus on major violent serial crimes. For example, the analyst provides psychological profiles in serial murder, rape, child molestation, and serial arson cases. Broader than the profiling process, it also involves the collection of psychological clues and physical evidence. Investigators develop offender traits, characteristics, and typologies that stem from crime scenes, victim statements, and autopsies. Analysts review crime scene reports and forensic evidence to make observations concerning criminals' reasoning. They can then target or eliminate suspects. The end purpose is to provide criminal information on

Crime analysis focuses on street crimes such as burglary, robbery, larceny, theft, and automobile theft. This form of analysis is primarily concerned with recognition of crime patterns. Crime analysts assist investigators in targeting the location of offenses, and in identifying emerging offense patterns. Their work involves crime mapping, targeting potential offenses, and preparing crime alerts and bulletins. Crime analysis is a systematic attempt to examine crime patterns and criminal behavior. The analyst identifies necessary and critical information related to crime patterns. He or she examines hot spots, crime clusters, and trends, and provides criminal information to field officers and detectives. This intelligence assists the investigative process, criminal apprehensions, and the successful case clearance rate of criminal cases.

Future Implications

Technology available to detectives will be increasingly sophisticated. The shift to detection in terrorist investigations encourages new technology and information sharing. Interagency cooperation, shared resources, and criminal intelligence require advanced computer technology applications. Centralized services and improved computer software offer maximum opportunities for timely criminal and terrorist detection and detective work. Computer crime-mapping technology provides detectives with the ability to correlate data and potential future crime hot spots. Geographic information systems (GIS) pinpoint crime incidents according to a specific location. GIS and tactical computer mapping permits detectives to establish geographical insights into crime patterns.

GIS crime-mapping technology continues to unlock potential criminal patterns. Crime-mapping software can visualize case-related data and descriptive crime patterns that can produce investigative leads. The GIS data may suggest questions in the interrogation process that might close cases. GIS and crime analysis mapping combine the interpretation of related incidents. Crime mapping spatial analysis might locate time factors and travel patterns for serial offenders. Crime mapping can bring disparate pieces of information together into a specific MO, criminal pattern, and case linkage to related offenses. The

U.S. Army Criminal Investigative Division special agents gathering potential DNA evidence at a crime scene for processing at the Army Criminal Investigation Laboratory.

offender motivation, modus operandi (MO), and psychological signature clues. The term *signature* represents a serial offender's calling card. The offender engages in psychological and compulsive behaviors that he or she must perform to obtain satisfaction. These behaviors occur because of personal needs that reflects the criminal's personality. Signature behaviors are generally excessively violent, sexually oriented, or both. These unique behaviors assist in case linkage.

Such information can further the interrogation process. This kind of analysis can create opportunities for related case linkage and prosecution. In addition, the psychological profile can assist prosecutors in the courtroom, should the offender take the witness stand.

criminal's MO may enable investigators to build a case in reverse order to explain the origins of the crime pattern and estimate future outcomes. Specialists can apply criminal geographic targeting (CGT) to locate suspects who work or reside in the crime cluster. Investigators apply a computerized spatial and statistical model that can connect the hot spots or events of a crime series. Then, it may be possible to trace the travel patterns to the offender's residence or workplace. Called a jeopardy surface, or geoprofile, this analysis provides an optimal criminal search process.

Conclusion

At first feared as spies, detectives have become an essential element of police work and their activities and responsibilities have expanded and become more complex over the years. Detection has become far more efficient than in the past, but unfortunately, sometimes the old problems of abuse of power and corruption resurface. Detectives, both official and private, continue to be significant, if sometimes ambiguous, figures in American popular culture.

Wilbur R. Miller
State University of New York, Stony Brook
Thomas E. Baker
University of Scranton

See Also: Ballistics; Bertillon System; Burglary, Contemporary; Byrnes, Thomas; Crime Scene Investigation; Federal Bureau of Investigation; Fingerprinting; Forensic Science; Private Detectives; Robbery, Contemporary.

Further Readings

Baker, Thomas E. *Introductory Criminal Analysis: Crime Prevention and Intervention Strategies.* Upper Saddle River, NJ: Pearson Prentice Hall, 2005.
Emsley, Clive. *Police Detectives in History, 1750–1950.* Surrey, UK: Ashgate Publishing, 2006.
Kitaeff, Jack. *Forensic Psychology.* Upper Saddle River, NJ: Pearson Prentice Hall, 2011.
Rossmo, D. Kim. *Geographic Profiling.* Boca Raton, FL: CRC Press, 1999.
Swanson, Charles R., Neil Chameleon, Leonard Territo, and Robert Taylor. *Criminal Investigation,* 10th ed. New York: McGraw-Hill, 2010.

Deterrence, Theory of

The theory of deterrence attempts to answer one of the most fundamental questions concerning crime: Why do individuals commit criminal and/or deviant acts? Deterrence theory attempts to answer this question by examining the choices and subsequent actions of the offender. Deterrence theory has its roots in the historical evolution of crime and punishment.

Judicial systems within feudal states were ruthless in their approach to crime control. During the Middle Ages and into the late 1700s, judicial representatives often punished criminals in an extremely harsh manner with little concern for the circumstances surrounding the act. The goal of the punishment during this time period was to punish all criminals so brutally that the criminal and others witnessing the punishment would not commit similar acts. This approach to punishment was effective in terms of preventing the accused from committing further criminal acts because the offender was often killed or incapacitated. However, this approach to handling crime was not effective at preventing future crime by other individuals.

During the late 18th century, scholars began to recognize this shortcoming, and began to recognize the need for reform that would eliminate the long-standing injustices present in the justice system. These changes largely came through the writings of two classical criminologists—Cesare Beccaria and Jeremy Bentham.

Cesare Beccaria was a visionary scholar in that he recognized the torturous and biased way that justice was being administered during his time. Beccaria subsequently pioneered discourse that guides the justice system to this day. His seminal work, *On Crimes and Punishment*, was published in 1776 and has since been recognized as the founding doctrine for what scholars now label deterrence theory.

The ideas that Beccaria discussed in *On Crimes and Punishment* were simple, yet groundbreaking for his era. The general idea that Beccaria outlined in his work was that crime and deviance occur when the potential positive rewards for committing a certain act outweigh the potential negative consequences. Since Beccaria's time, the theory has advanced and evolved as societies have experienced social change, and it is now one of the most researched and cited theories in criminology.

The theory of deterrence has been widely used in the field of criminology to conduct research on various types of deviant acts. The deviant acts that have been examined in the past range from speeding to homicide. In addition to being used in academe, the theory of deterrence has gained popularity among politicians, criminal justice practitioners, and criminal justice policy makers.

Basic Tenet of Deterrence Theory

The modern conception of deterrence theory is grounded in ideas that are fundamental to classical criminology. Inherent in the ideology of classical criminology is the thought that humans are rational actors capable of exercising free will. Assuming that humans are rational actors, classical criminologists such as Cesare Beccaria and Jeremy Bentham posited that individual behavior is guided by a series of calculations that are actually a type of cost-benefit analysis.

The cost-benefit analysis is sometimes linked to the pleasure-pain principle. The calculations made by individual social actors are attributed to things such as individual experiences, knowledge of codified laws, and the degree to which one has a vested interest in societal mores, folkways, and laws. Scholars sometimes argue that the theory of deterrence can be described as a process wherein social actors calculate risks and rewards prior to choosing to perform certain acts.

Historically, criminologists have recognized the utility of a criminal justice system that promotes the positive control and prevention of crime through clear legal standards and unambiguous societal norms. A prerequisite for understanding deterrence theory is understanding of the ability to make rational and calculated decisions concerning personal behavior. Once this is achieved, scholars argue, deterrence theory gains predictability with reference to human behavior. Scholars posit that individuals will not commit crime once one attaches more negative attributes to the risk or consequences associated with a certain behavior than positive attributes. If the negative consequences do not outweigh the potential benefits, crime is more likely to occur. Bentham and Beccaria recognized these ideas and lobbied for their integration into the ideologies behind crime and punishment.

Specifically, Beccaria held that punishment should be only severe enough to deter and no harsher. Beccaria also held that punishment should occur within a short period of time after the offense. Lastly, Beccaria believed that the consequences associated with a given crime must be certain. The basic tenets of deterrence theory suggest that crime will not occur when punishment is "swift, severe, and certain." Under the classical criminology paradigm, punishment for any given offense must only be as severe, certain, and swift as is needed to prevent future offending.

Considering contemporary approaches to punishment, the idea that punishment should follow this ideology has brought about much debate. Some scholars argue that contemporary criminal justice policies have brought about laws that are too severe and ineffective. The most common argument that scholars pose following this belief concerns capital punishment. The central question concerning capital punishment is, "What is the purpose of the death penalty?" Popular answers to this question include responses such as "retribution," "incapacitation," and "deterrence." Debates among practitioners and academics often focus on the latter of these purposes.

Those arguing against capital punishment believe that the modern conception of deterrence is not aligned with the intent that Beccaria originally described in *On Crimes and Punishment*. These scholars hold that the death penalty is too severe and does not deter future offending. Under this conception of deterrence theory, those who commit a crime that is punishable by the death penalty are involved in a situation wherein they will take extreme measures to avoid punishment. This occurs because the punishment often goes unobserved by the general public and because crimes that are punishable by capital punishment are often "passion" crimes that are committed with little regard for the negative consequences.

Other debates surrounding deterrence theory are often centered on the importance and relevance of the three tenets of the theory. Scholars often ask, "Which of the three basic tenets play the most important role in deterring crime—severity, swiftness, or certainty?" Most scholars and criminal justice practitioners who debate this question take the position that certainty is the most important tenet of deterrence theory. Within the deterrence paradigm, certainty refers to the odds that one will be arrested, convicted, and punished for a given offense. Swiftness refers to the amount of time between the commission of an act and the application of punishment. Severity refers to the harshness or negative consequences associated with a given crime. When contemplating the importance of each one of these tenets, it is important to recognize that they are not mutually exclusive. And, no one tenet can be described as having more power to deter.

Scholars still posit that certainty is the most important when planning criminal justice policies, practices, and procedures. The reasoning behind this position is usually rooted in the other tenets of the theory. Certainty is often cited as being more effective because when the severity of a given punishment is extreme, the application of the respective punishment becomes less likely. Swiftness is the least often debated among the three tenets of deterrence theory, most likely because the contemporary criminal justice system does not expedite punishment enough to make it relevant to the deterrence argument.

Types of Deterrence

Deterrence theorists and criminal justice practitioners often reduce deterrence theory into two explicit types of deterrence—general and specific. Specific deterrence occurs when an individual receives some type of punishment for an offense. For example, an offender who is found guilty of a traffic violation may be charged a fine as punishment for the offense. The intent behind the punishment is to make the fine expensive enough that the offender will abstain from committing future traffic violations out of the fear of losing more money. The other type, general deterrence, is deterrence that is witnessed by other individuals when punishment is being given to offenders other than oneself.

Deterrence Theory Today and Tomorrow

Today, the policy and practice implications of deterrence theory continue to be relevant to scholars and practitioners, especially law enforcement agencies, prosecutors, and legislators. Deterrence theory continues to be one of the most discussed theories in academe and one of the most utilized theories among practitioners. The most popular studies of deterrence look at the effect of capital punishment on homicide rates.

Another emerging trend within the deterrence discourse is the examination of the relationship between the traditional conception of deterrence and informal deterrence. Researchers have displayed a growing interest in understanding how informal deterrence or informal social sanctions influence one toward or away from crime and deviance. Informal sanctions, in this context, can be described as the actions of one's family, friends, and significant others following a crime and the subsequent punishment. The results of such studies generally indicate that the informal sanctions that often follow formal sanctions strongly deter individuals from future offending. In light of this movement, researchers examining deterrence argue that looking at informal deterrence integrates other theories to the point that deterrence theory is no longer deterrence theory because it begins to expand beyond the law. Regardless of these arguments, deterrence theory has withstood the test of time and will continue to be relevant within criminology.

Michael J. Reed
Mississippi State University

See Also: Capital Punishment; Corrections; Crime in America, Causes; Crime Prevention; Criminology; Cruel and Unusual Punishment; Executions; History of Crime and Punishment in America: 1783–1850; Punishment Within Prison; Retributivism; Sentencing; Theories of Crime.

Further Readings
Baker, Thomas and Alex Piquero. "Assessing the Perceived Benefits—Criminal Offending Relationship." *Journal of Criminal Justice*, v.34 (2010).
Gerber, Rudolph and John Johnson. *The Top Ten Death Penalty Myths: The Politics of Crime Control*. Westport, CT: Praeger, 2007.
Grasmick, Harold and George Bryjak. "The Deterrent Effect of Perceived Severity of Punishment." *Social Forces*, v.59/2 (1980).
Jacobs, Bruce. "Deterrence and Deterrability." *Criminology*, v.48/2 (2010).
McConville, Sean. *The Use of Punishment*. Portland, OR: Willan Publishing, 2003.

Detroit, Michigan

The history of crime and justice in Detroit, Michigan, is consistent with that in other large industrial cities in the east and midwest. In the 19th century, Detroit struggled to establish order in a growing city. In the 20th century, a manufacturing boom and later decline contributed to problems with serious crime, while racial tensions complicated the relationship between the police and the city's population.

The city of Detroit, founded in 1701, faced relatively little disorder until it began to grow rapidly in the middle of the 19th century, attracting immigrants particularly from Germany and Ireland. Law and order became a bigger concern for Detroit's citizens in the 1850s and 1860s as crime became concentrated in the city's downtown business district. Burglaries, muggings, and public disorder—often associated with young, unmarried male workers—prompted business leaders and residents of respectable neighborhoods to demand a professional police force. In response, the state legislature created the Detroit Metropolitan Police force in 1865. By the 1870s, the police had largely brought disorder under control by concentrating patrols downtown and in the nearby disreputable districts, providing lodging for transients, and making arrests for offenses against public order such as drunkenness and disorderly conduct.

Detroit's police gradually shifted from their order maintenance role in the 19th century to presenting themselves as service providers and crime fighters in the 20th century. Some police commissioners

These moving vans needed a police and National Guard escort while transporting new black tenants' furniture into the Sojourner Truth Homes federal housing project in Detroit in 1942 after a violent riot by white neighbors trying to prevent them from moving into the project. The next year, a three-day riot broke out in which whites attacked African American neighborhoods and African Americans looted white-owned stores. The riot led to the deaths of 17 African Americans at the hands of the Detroit police.

such as James M. Couzens (1916–18) and James K. Watkins (1931–33) emphasized police efficiency and attempts to work with the broader community, even as other commissioners such as James W. Inches (1919–23) emphasized efforts to respond vigorously to crime by increasing the number of officers on street patrol. The sudden growth of the automobile industry and military production during World War I contributed to a sudden increase in population in the 1910s and a corresponding increase in the amount of crime. The number of police officers grew at the same pace as the population, but rank-and-file officers may not have fully embraced the stated ideals of their commissioners. Throughout the first two-thirds of the 20th century, the Detroit police remained comprised almost entirely of working-class white men with limited training, despite the opening of a training school in 1911.

The Great Migration and Beyond
With the Great Migration bringing African American migrants to cities in the urban north beginning in the 1910s, racial tensions became a central theme in the 20th-century history of criminal justice in cities such as Detroit. African Americans were attracted by the job opportunities created by the boom in the automobile and munitions industries, and their numbers increased from roughly 5,700 in 1910 to roughly 149,000 in 1940. The resulting racial conflicts were highlighted by the arrest and trial of Ossian Sweet in 1925.

After Sweet, an African American physician, moved into a home in a previously all-white neighborhood, a mob surrounded his house. Someone fired shots from the home into the crowd, killing one person, and police arrested Sweet and other defenders of the house. After one highly publicized trial ended in a mistrial, Sweet was eventually acquitted. In addition, 1920s investigations by both the National Association for the Advancement of Colored People (NAACP) and the Mayor's Committee on Race Relations revealed that police officers routinely brutalized African Americans.

Conflicts between African Americans and whites over jobs and housing escalated in the 1940s with renewed industrial growth and migration prompted by World War II. In June 1943, a series of brawls between African Americans and whites escalated into a riot lasting three days. African Americans looted white-owned stores, and whites attacked African American neighborhoods. The police tended to side with the white rioters, shooting 17 African Americans to death.

Racial tensions and police violence persisted in the post–World War II period. Detroit's industrial economy peaked and began to decline, even as the Great Migration continued. The African American population exceeded 660,000 in 1970, while the police force remained overwhelmingly white; the few African Americans who were hired met hostility from their fellow officers. Many examples of police abuse persisted in the 1950s and 1960s. One 1957 report by the NAACP cited more than 100 incidents in a seven-month period, the majority involving violence; in 1965, an elite black social organization complained to the mayor of hundreds of injuries to African Americans inflicted by police officers. In July 1967, a police raid on an illegal after-hours saloon prompted a violent backlash by African Americans, which rapidly became a major riot. Unlike the 1943 riot, the 1967 riot mostly involved African Americans revolting against the effects of discrimination and a deindustrializing economy. After five days of violence in which 43 people died (33 African Americans) and property destruction reached millions of dollars, federal troops quelled the violence. Relations between the police and the African American community continued to deteriorate with the 1971 formation of a special undercover police unit called Stop the Robberies, Enjoy Safe Streets (STRESS). In its first year, the STRESS unit made more than 1,400 arrests and killed 10 suspects, nine of whom were African American.

Since the 1970s, crime and justice have remained major issues in Detroit. The decline of the automobile industry has also continued to reduce job opportunities. In this context, Detroit has experienced consistently high crime rates. At times, it has had the highest homicide rate of any large city in the United States, earning it a reputation as the nation's murder capital. The Detroit police, however, have sought to improve relations with the community. Beginning with the 1973 election of Coleman Young, Detroit's first African American mayor, the police department became much more racially integrated. Young also abolished the STRESS unit. The police established community ministations in the 1980s, intended to help incorporate officers into neighborhoods and to help city residents feel safer. A Justice Department investigation beginning in 2000 revealed that police use of force remained a problem. The investigation resulted in a 2003 consent decree governing arrest, restraint of suspects, and detention. In addition, the number of Detroit police officers dropped by more than 25 percent between 2000 and 2007.

David B. Wolcott
Independent Scholar

See Also: 1921 to 1940 Primary Documents; 1961 to 1980 Primary Documents; African Americans; Michigan; Police Abuse; Race-Based Crime; Racism; Riots.

Further Readings
Boyle, Kevin. *Arc of Justice: A Saga of Race, Civil Rights, and Murder in the Jazz Age*. New York: Henry Holt, 2004.
Schneider, John C. *Detroit and the Problem of Order, 1830–1880*. Lincoln: University of Nebraska Press, 1980.
Thompson, Heather Ann. *Whose Detroit?: Politics, Labor, and Race in a Modern American City*. Ithaca, NY: Cornell University Press, 2001.

Devery, William

William S. Devery (1857–1919), nicknamed "Big Bill," "Big Fellow," and "Big Chief," was a controversial New York City police official and the first chief of police after the consolidation of New York City in 1898. He was born in New York City to impoverished Irish immigrants and raised in a West Side tenement district. Devery joined the police force in 1878 and was appointed roundsman in 1881, sergeant in 1883, captain in 1891, inspector in 1898, deputy chief of police in 1898, chief of police in 1898, and deputy police commissioner in 1901. Devery joined the Democratic Party as a young man and eventually allied himself to Tammany Hall. He was befriended by Tammany leader Richard Crocker and served as one of his chief assistants throughout his career.

From 1891 to 1893, Devery was a captain in the tenderloin district. He developed a reputation for tolerating prostitution, gambling, illegal saloons, and other elements of the underground economy. Devery privately claimed that "police graft" exceeded $3 million annually. In particular, he was charged with working in alliance with the "poolroom trust" headed by professional gambler Frank J. Farrell and headquartered on West 30th St. near Sixth Avenue and half a block from the West 30th St. police station. In 1893, Devery was transferred to the Lower East Side, just east of the Bowery. Devery's toleration of "vice" attracted extensive criticism from the Reverend Charles Parkhurst and Frank Moss, who instigated four charges against Devery in 1893; Devery, however, was acquitted.

Parkhurst, Moss, Anthony Comstock, Theodore Roosevelt, and Republican officials continued collecting evidence against Devery. In 1894, during the Lexow Committee investigation, Devery was charged with accepting a bribe. Police department officials tried Devery in absentia for extortion (he claimed he was ill) and dismissed him from the department. A year later, the New York Supreme Court overturned the dismissal.

In 1896, Devery was tried and acquitted of extortion. In 1901, Devery was tried and acquitted for neglect of duty and oppression. That same year, the Republican-controlled legislature eliminated the chief of police position by a legislative statute. But police commissioner Michael Murphy (with support from Mayor Robert VanWyck) appointed Devery deputy commissioner of police, and he remained the acting head of the force.

Devery was severely criticized for defending police brutality, first against agents representing the Society for the Prevention of Crime in 1893 and against African Americans in the tenderloin police riot of 1900. Devery also attempted to influence the national election of 1900 by ordering police officers to ignore orders from the state election bureau. New York governor and Republican vice presidential candidate Theodore Roosevelt intervened and ordered New York mayor Robert Van Wyck to rescind Devery's order.

Devery retired with an estimated wealth of $900,000, despite a total official income of $58,000 during his 24-year law enforcement career. Devery's toleration of underworld activities convinced critics such as *Gunton's Magazine* that he was "the culmination of official vice" and "the concentrated nastiness of political depravity."

But Devery was popular in the Irish and immigrant communities, in part because he practiced an informal, less professional form of policing. Many nights, Devery stood in front of an Eighth Avenue saloon known as the Pump, leaning on a fireplug and listening to complaints from the poor, pimps, policemen, widows, and anyone who felt aggrieved. As a Tammany politician, he intervened on behalf of many. Devery was noted for his inventive slang, witty one-liners, and beginning many public pronouncements with "Touchin' on and appertainin' to."

In 1902, Devery successfully ran for district leader in his Chelsea neighborhood. A year later, however, Tammany leaders Richard Croker and Charles Murphy considered Devery and "Deveryism" a liability and refused to support his mayoral campaign. Devery ran as an independent candidate and attracted a little more than 2,200 votes. In 1903, Devery and Frank J. Farrell purchased the Baltimore Orioles baseball team for $18,000. They promptly moved the club to New York and renamed the team the Highlanders, making the organization the first American League franchise in New York. In 1913, they became the Yankees. The team enjoyed little success, so in 1915, Devery and Farrell sold the team to Jacob Ruppert and Tillinghast Huston for $460,000. Devery also sold real estate in Manhattan and Far Rockaway and owned a large West End Avenue mansion in Manhattan. He died of apoplexy on June 20, 1919, in his home in Far Rockaway, New York.

Timothy J. Gilfoyle
Loyola University Chicago

See Also: Corruption, History of; New York; Police, History of; Reform, Police and Enforcement; Roosevelt, Theodore (Administration of).

Further Readings

Barker, Thomas and David L. Carter. *Police Deviance*, 3rd ed. Cincinnati, OH: Anderson Publishing, 1994.

Steffens, Lincoln. *The Autobiography of Lincoln Steffens*. New York: Harcourt, Brace & Co., 1931.

Still, Charles Edwin. *Styles in Crime*. Philadelphia: Lippincott, 1938.

Dewey, Thomas E.

Thomas E. Dewey (1902–71) was a federal and state prosecutor, district attorney, governor of New York, and the Republican presidential candidate in 1944 and 1948. Dewey is best known to criminal justicians for his war on organized crime in New York during the 1930s. After earning a law degree from Columbia Law School in 1925, Dewey worked as a prosecutor and then went into private practice. In the early 1930s, Dewey returned to public service as a special prosecutor, charged with investigating corruption and organized crime in New York.

THE BIG CHIEF'S FAIRY GODMOTHER
Mr. Devery tells "where he got it"

This 1902 cartoon titled "The Big Chief's Fairy Godmother" shows William Devery showered in coins by a fairy whose wings are made of playing cards and is captioned "Mr. Devery tells 'where he got it.'" Devery retired with an estimated $900,000.

In 1935, Dewey assembled a staff of over 100 to target organized crime and the political corruption related to such enterprises. Dewey went after prominent New York City gangster Arthur Flegenheimer, better known as "Dutch" Schultz, who had made millions with an illegal alcohol bootlegging enterprise during the 1920s and then continued with other criminal activities after Prohibition ended. Lacking direct evidence of Schultz's involvement in criminal enterprises such as extortion, numbers running, and union racketeering, Dewey instead charged Schultz with tax evasion for failing to report the proceeds of his criminal activities. Schultz's first trial, in 1935, resulted in a hung jury. He was acquitted in a second trial after spreading money around the small town in which the trial was held.

By 1935, New York crime gang bosses had formed a syndicate, which met to make and enforce rules designed to minimize violent warfare among the city's gangsters. Schultz proposed to the syndicate that Dewey be murdered in order to stop his investigations into organized crime. Agents from Murder Inc., a gangland hit squad, tailed Dewey and developed a plan to assassinate him. Before the plot could be carried out, the syndicate leaders decided to call it off because killing such a high profile lawman would increase surveillance of organized crime and potentially expose the entire syndicate to federal charges. The mob leaders decided that it would be better to undermine Dewey's cases by killing his witnesses instead. Schultz announced that he would have Dewey killed anyway, in defiance of the syndicate. The syndicate responded by having Schultz assassinated. In 1936, Dewey won a conviction against Gurrah Shapiro, a founder of Murder Inc. who was involved in garment district labor racketeering and protection rackets. Shapiro had been the only syndicate boss who agreed with Schultz about assassinating Dewey. Shapiro received a two-year prison sentence for violating federal antitrust laws.

Dewey also went after Louis "Lepke" Buchalter, a full partner in Shapiro's criminal enterprises. Lepke reportedly surrendered to federal authorities on the condition that they not turn him over to Dewey. Lepke received 30 years for narcotics trafficking and labor racketeering. He was later convicted of murder and became the highest-ranking organized crime boss ever executed for his crimes. Dewey then set his sights on Charles "Lucky" Luciano, another syndicate boss. Dewey won convictions on 90 counts related to Luciano's prostitution rackets. Luciano received a sentence of 30 to 50 years in prison. In 1937, Dewey was elected New York district attorney.

He won a conviction against Tammany Hall leader Jimmy Hines on corruption charges. Dewey ran for governor in 1938, but lost. He failed to win the Republican presidential nomination in 1940 but was elected governor of New York State in 1942. Dewey's third term as governor ended in 1955, after which Dewey returned to private practice. President Richard Nixon offered Dewey the position of chief justice of the U.S. Supreme Court in 1968. Dewey declined, and he died three years later.

Dewey received criticism for his relationships with mob figures. As governor, Dewey approved "Lucky" Luciano's transfer to a minimum-security prison and eventually approved Luciano's parole and deportation to Italy. Luciano would later claim that the mob had contributed to Dewey's campaign fund in exchange for his release. In the early 1950s, Dewey refused to testify before the U.S. Senate's Kefauver Commission—then investigating organized crime—about his actions related to Luciano's pardon. In the 1960s, Dewey became a major shareholder in a firm with Caribbean gambling interests, run by Meyer Lansky—another mob boss. Charges against Dewey's integrity notwithstanding, Dewey won numerous convictions against powerful mob figures between 1935 and 1937, thus establishing his place in history as one of the first significant organized crime fighters in the United States.

Thomas F. Brown
Virginia Wesleyan College

See Also: District Attorney; Luciano, "Lucky"; Organized Crime, History of; Schultz, "Dutch."

Further Readings
Smith, Richard Norton. *Thomas E. Dewey and His Times*. New York: Simon & Schuster, 1982.
Stolberg, Mary. *Fighting Organized Crime: Politics, Justice, and the Legacy of Thomas E. Dewey*. Evanston, IL: Northeastern University Press, 1995.